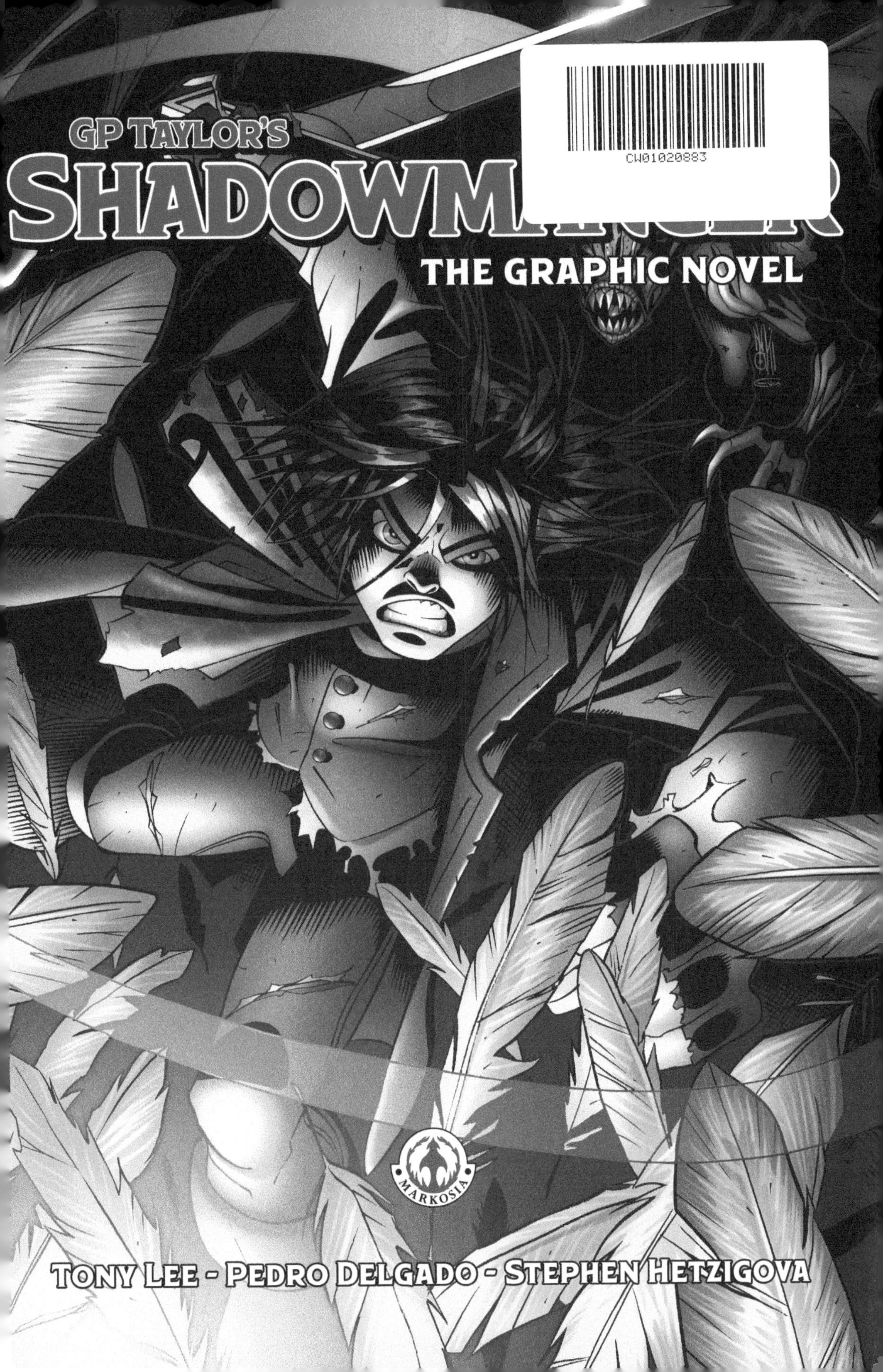

GP TAYLOR'S
SHADOWM
THE GRAPHIC NOVEL
MARKOSIA
TONY LEE - PEDRO DELGADO - STEPHEN HETZIGOVA

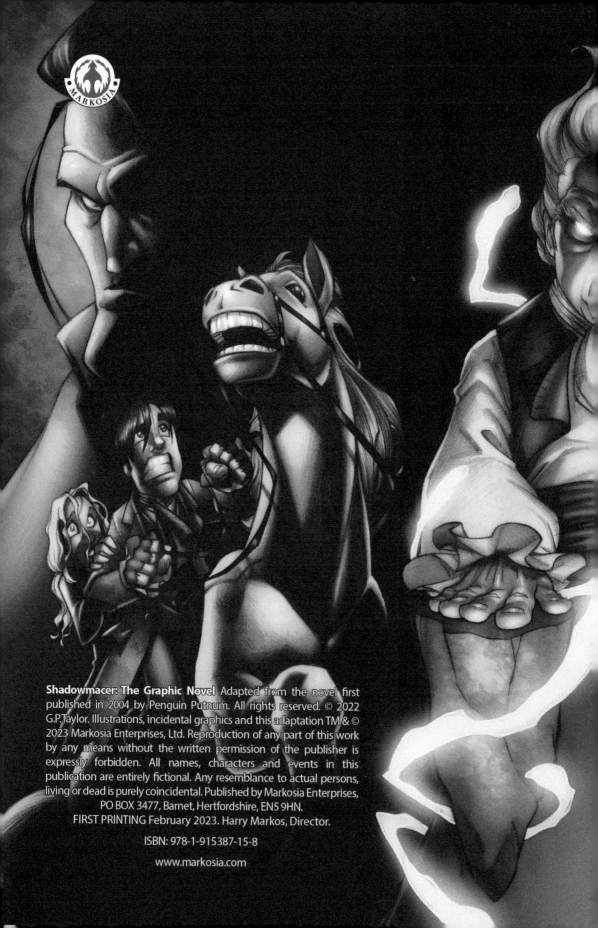

Shadowmacer: The Graphic Novel Adapted from the novel first published in 2004 by Penguin Putnum. All rights reserved. © 2022 G.P.Taylor. Illustrations, incidental graphics and this adaptation TM & © 2023 Markosia Enterprises, Ltd. Reproduction of any part of this work by any means without the written permission of the publisher is expressly forbidden. All names, characters and events in this publication are entirely fictional. Any resemblance to actual persons, living or dead is purely coincidental. Published by Markosia Enterprises, PO BOX 3477, Barnet, Hertfordshire, EN5 9HN. FIRST PRINTING February 2023. Harry Markos, Director.

ISBN: 978-1-915387-15-8

www.markosia.com

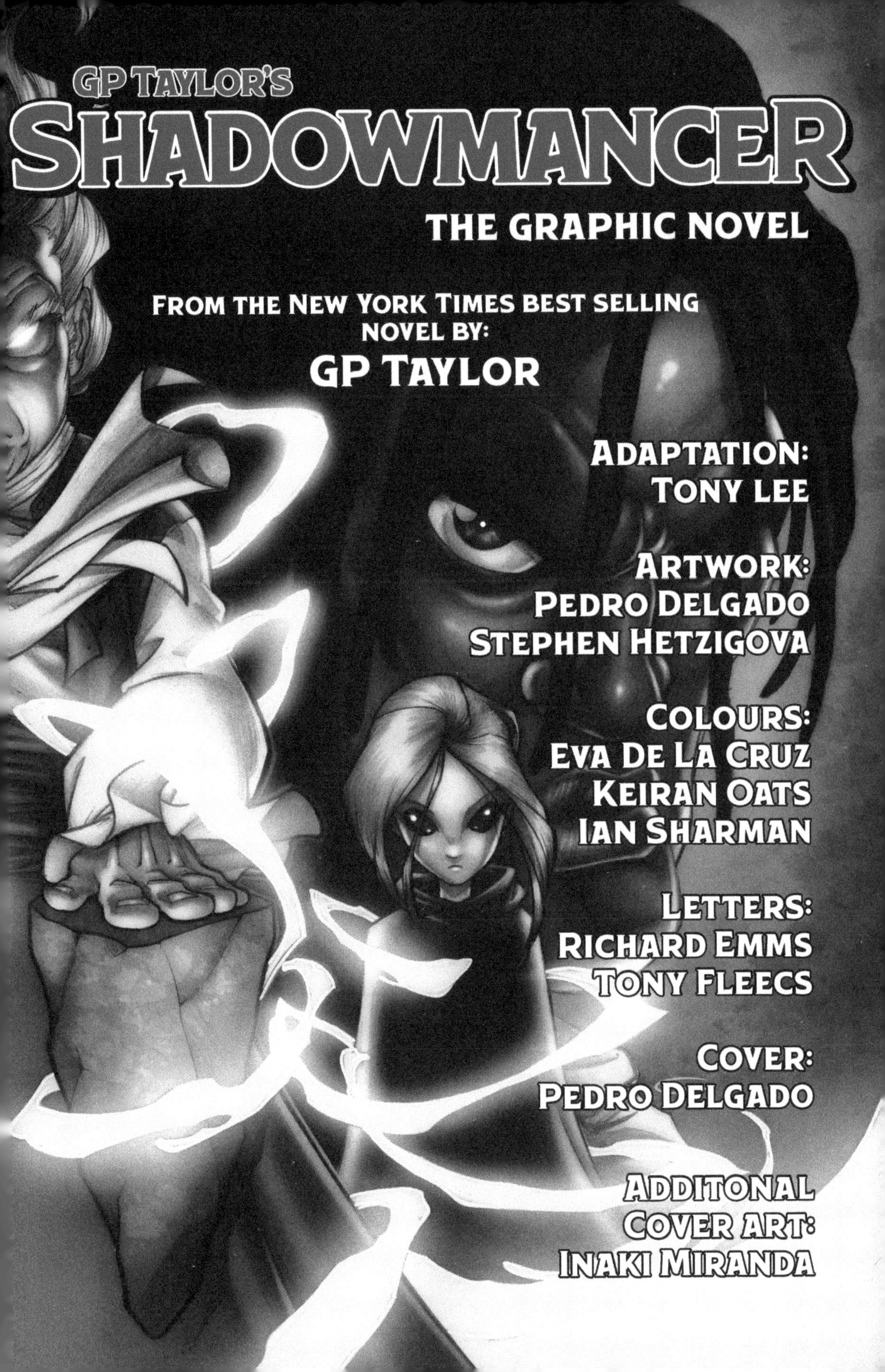

GP TAYLOR'S

SHADOWMANCER

THE GRAPHIC NOVEL

FROM THE NEW YORK TIMES BEST SELLING NOVEL BY:

GP TAYLOR

ADAPTATION:
TONY LEE

ARTWORK:
PEDRO DELGADO
STEPHEN HETZIGOVA

COLOURS:
EVA DE LA CRUZ
KEIRAN OATS
IAN SHARMAN

LETTERS:
RICHARD EMMS
TONY FLEECS

COVER:
PEDRO DELGADO

ADDITONAL COVER ART:
INAKI MIRANDA

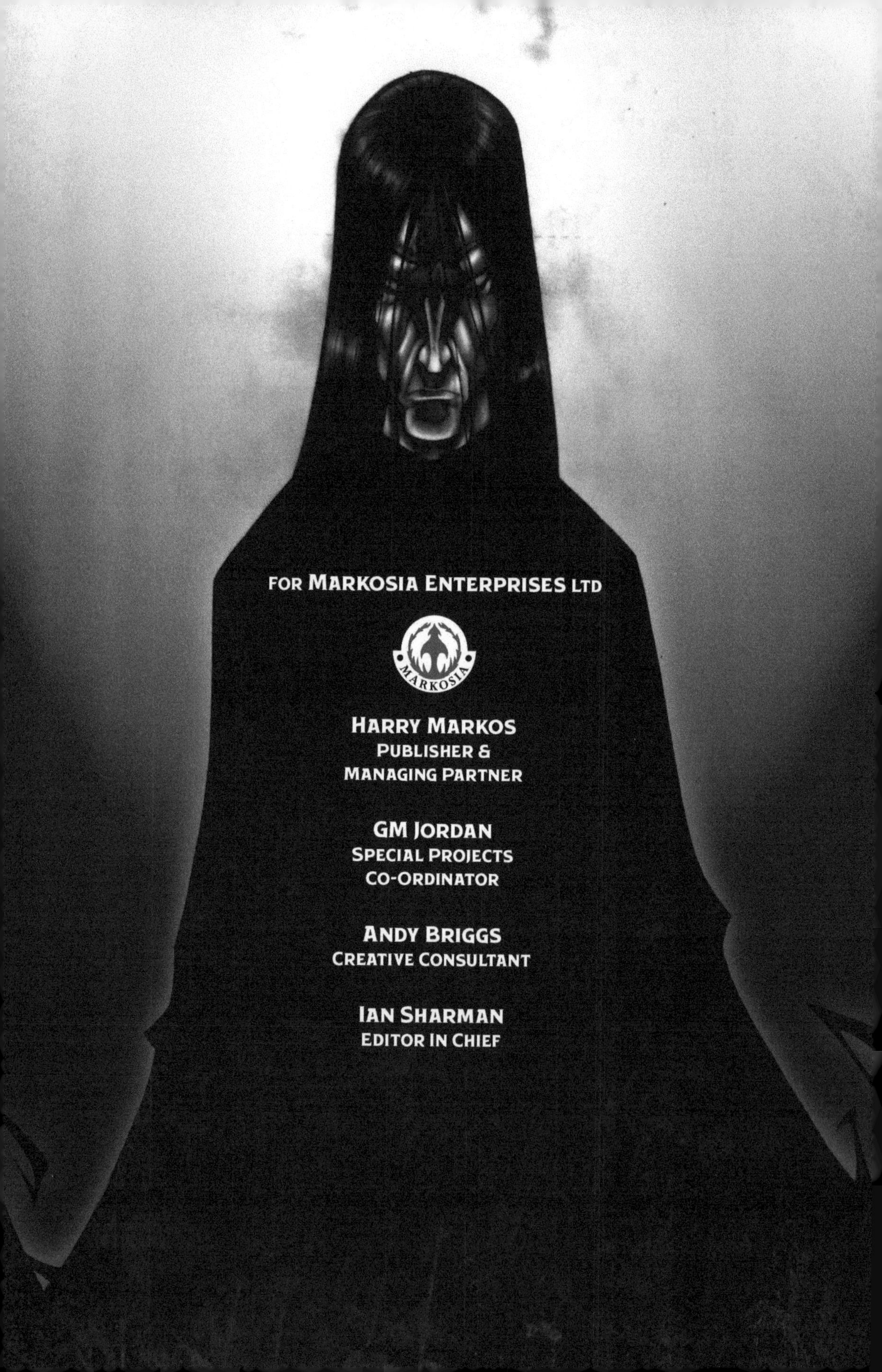

FOR MARKOSIA ENTERPRISES LTD

HARRY MARKOS
PUBLISHER &
MANAGING PARTNER

GM JORDAN
SPECIAL PROJECTS
CO-ORDINATOR

ANDY BRIGGS
CREATIVE CONSULTANT

IAN SHARMAN
EDITOR IN CHIEF

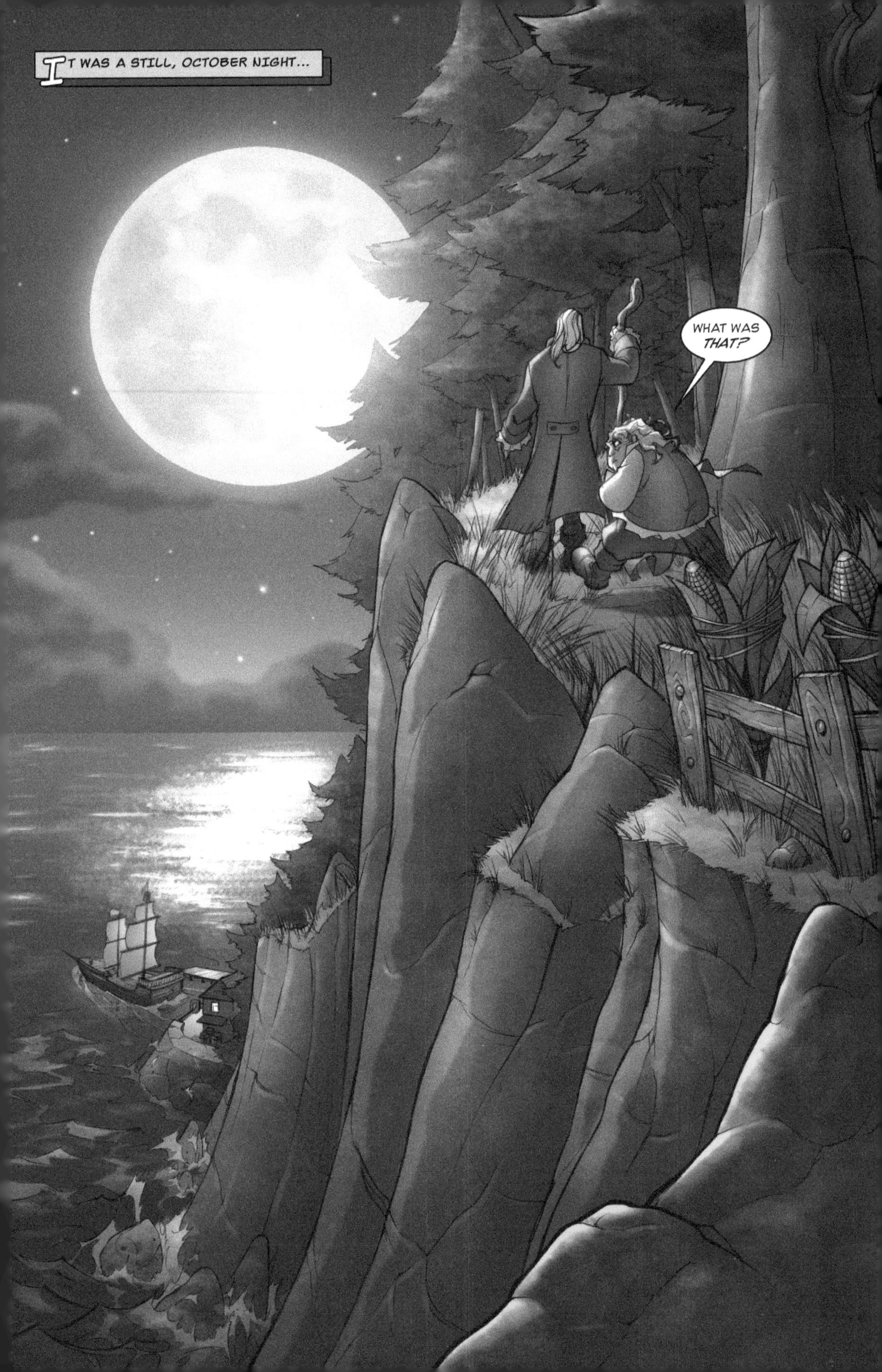
IT WAS A STILL, OCTOBER NIGHT...
WHAT WAS THAT?

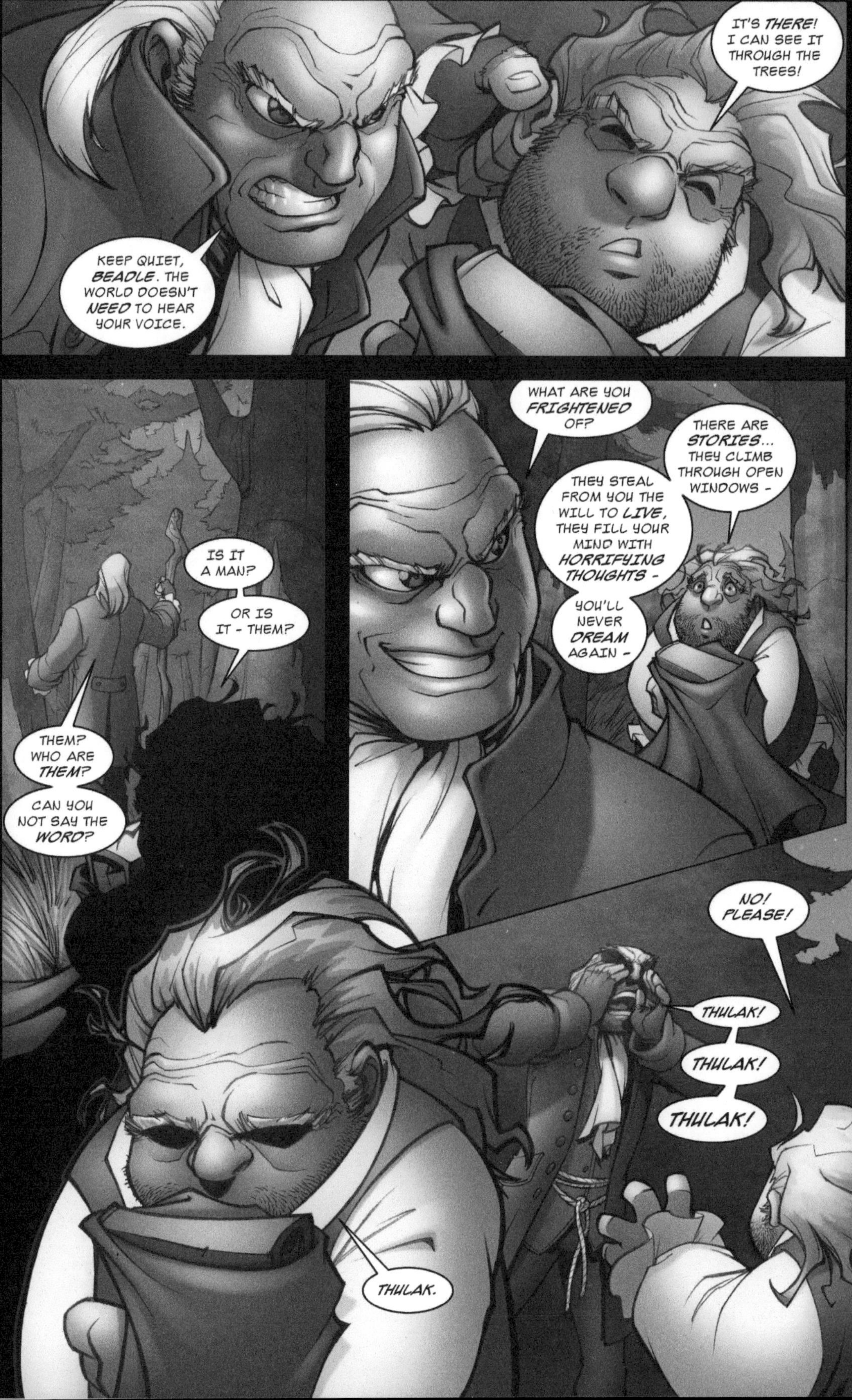
IT'S THERE! I CAN SEE IT THROUGH THE TREES!
KEEP QUIET, BEADLE. THE WORLD DOESN'T NEED TO HEAR YOUR VOICE.
IS IT A MAN?
OR IS IT - THEM?
THEM? WHO ARE THEM?
CAN YOU NOT SAY THE WORD?
WHAT ARE YOU FRIGHTENED OF?
THERE ARE STORIES... THEY CLIMB THROUGH OPEN WINDOWS -
THEY STEAL FROM YOU THE WILL TO LIVE, THEY FILL YOUR MIND WITH HORRIFYING THOUGHTS -
YOU'LL NEVER DREAM AGAIN -
NO! PLEASE!
THULAK!
THULAK!
THULAK!
THULAK.

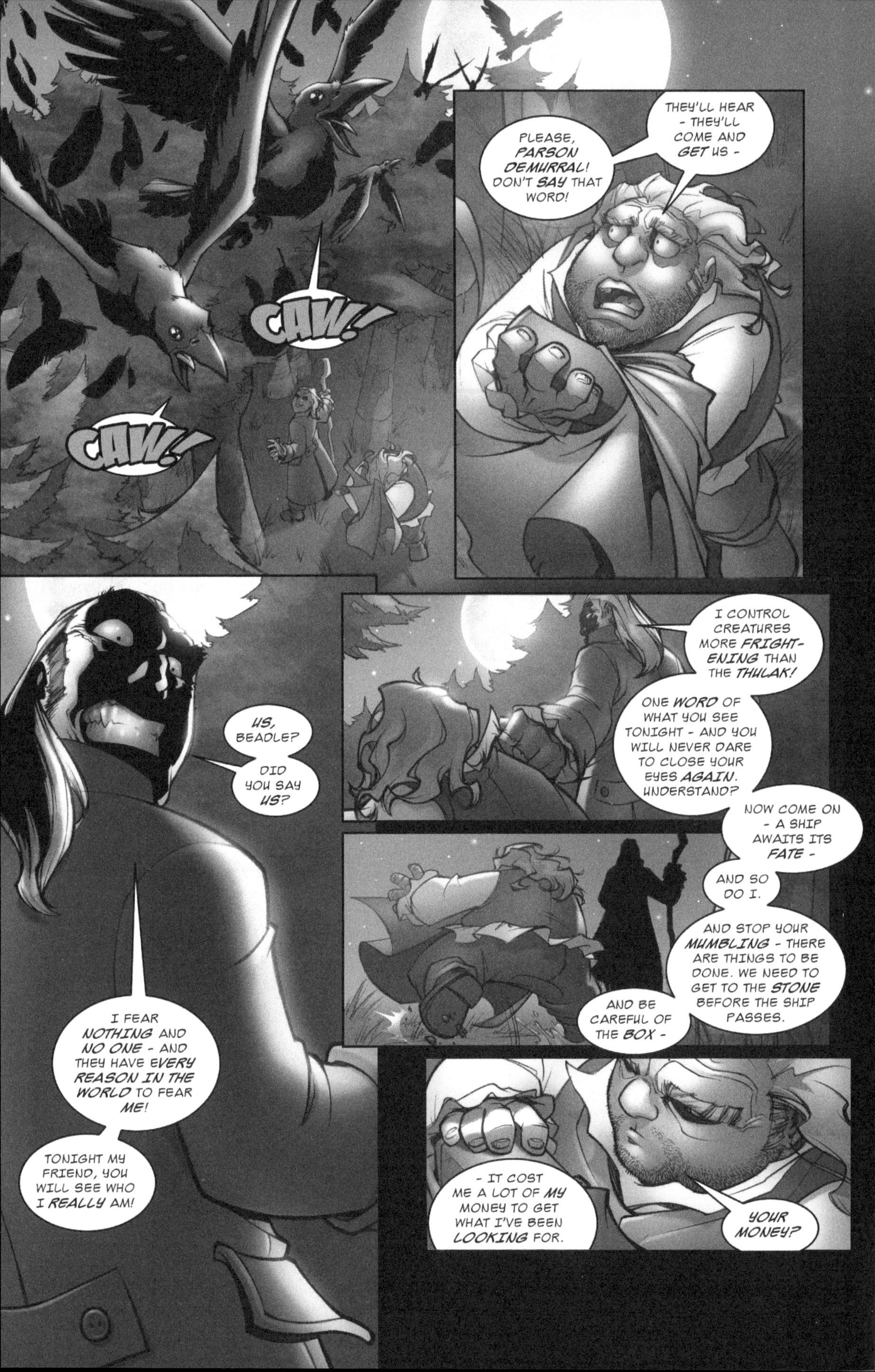
PLEASE, PARSON DEMURRAL! DON'T SAY THAT WORD!
THEY'LL HEAR - THEY'LL COME AND GET US -
CAW!
CAW!
US, BEADLE?
DID YOU SAY US?
I FEAR NOTHING AND NO ONE - AND THEY HAVE EVERY REASON IN THE WORLD TO FEAR ME!
TONIGHT MY FRIEND, YOU WILL SEE WHO I REALLY AM!
I CONTROL CREATURES MORE FRIGHT-ENING THAN THE THULAK!
ONE WORD OF WHAT YOU SEE TONIGHT - AND YOU WILL NEVER DARE TO CLOSE YOUR EYES AGAIN. UNDERSTAND?
NOW COME ON - A SHIP AWAITS ITS FATE -
AND SO DO I.
AND STOP YOUR MUMBLING - THERE ARE THINGS TO BE DONE. WE NEED TO GET TO THE STONE BEFORE THE SHIP PASSES.
AND BE CAREFUL OF THE BOX -
- IT COST ME A LOT OF MY MONEY TO GET WHAT I'VE BEEN LOOKING FOR.
YOUR MONEY?

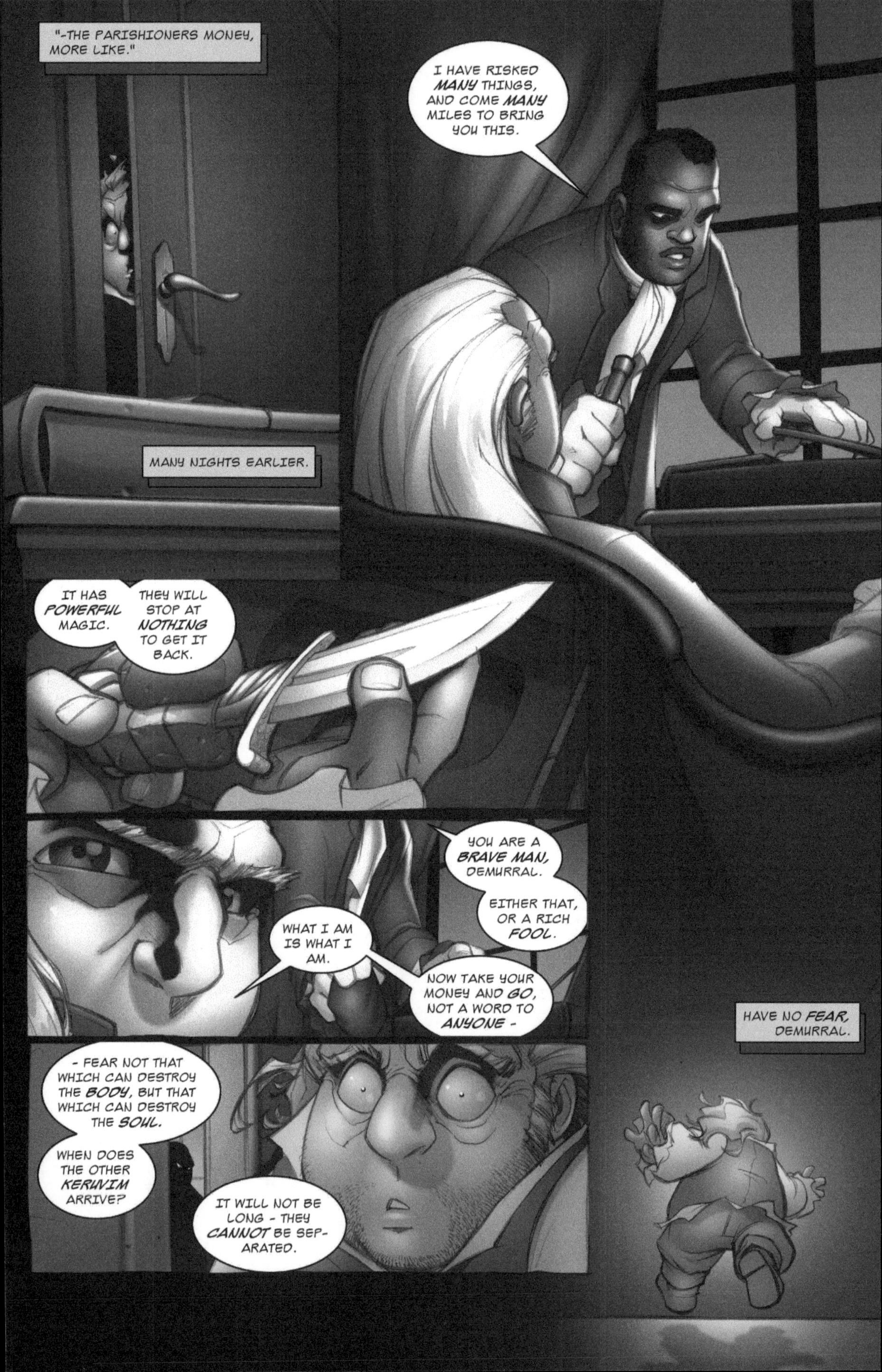
"-THE PARISHIONERS MONEY, MORE LIKE."
I HAVE RISKED *MANY* THINGS, AND COME *MANY* MILES TO BRING YOU THIS.
MANY NIGHTS EARLIER.
IT HAS *POWERFUL* MAGIC.
THEY WILL STOP AT *NOTHING* TO GET IT BACK.
YOU ARE A *BRAVE MAN,* DEMURRAL.
EITHER THAT, OR A RICH *FOOL*.
WHAT I AM IS WHAT I AM.
NOW TAKE YOUR MONEY AND *GO,* NOT A WORD TO *ANYONE* -
HAVE NO *FEAR,* DEMURRAL.
- FEAR NOT THAT WHICH CAN DESTROY THE *BODY*, BUT THAT WHICH CAN DESTROY THE *SOUL.*
WHEN DOES THE OTHER *KERUVIM* ARRIVE?
IT WILL NOT BE LONG - THEY *CANNOT* BE SEP- ARATED.

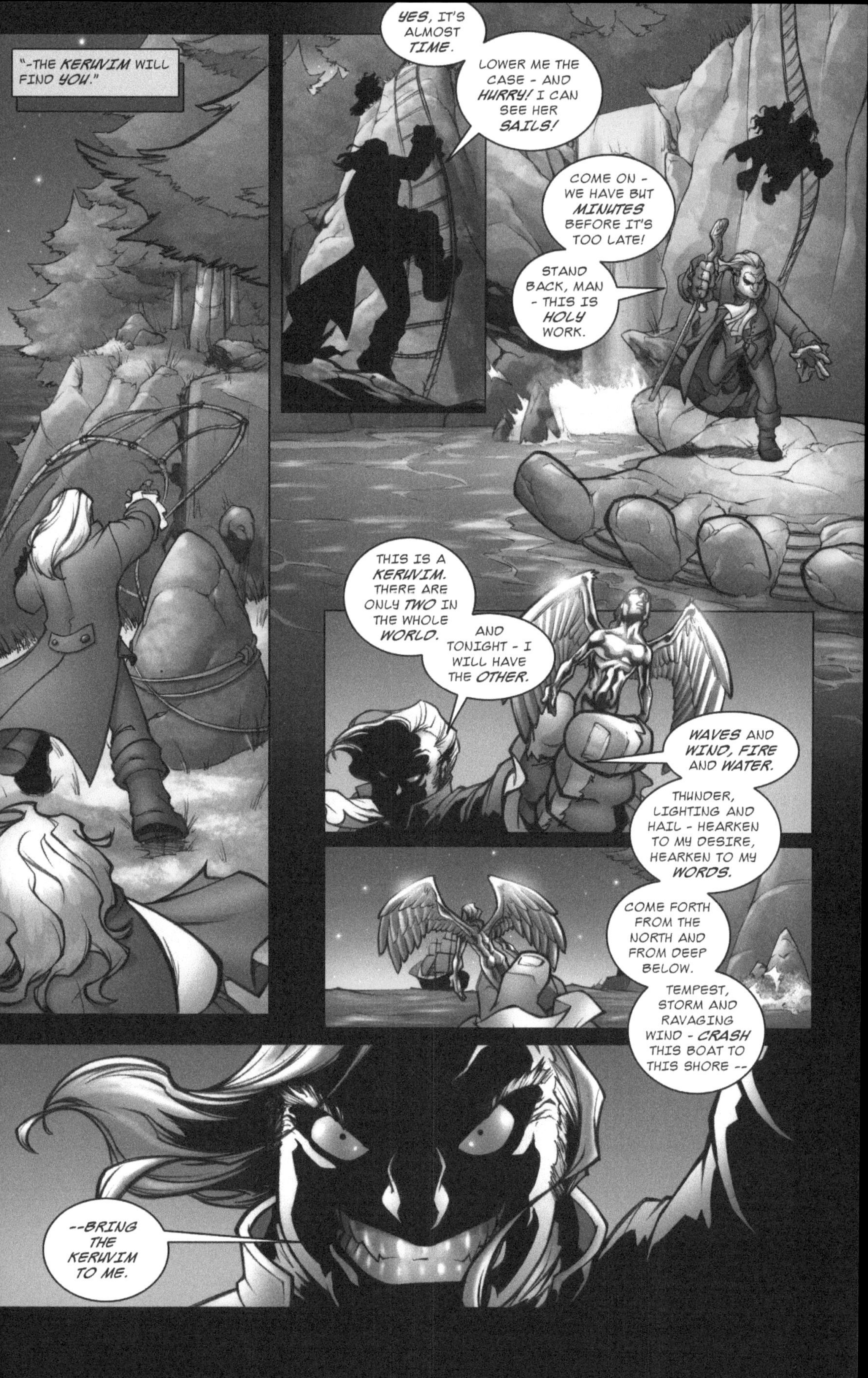

"-THE KERUVIM WILL FIND YOU."
YES, IT'S ALMOST TIME.
LOWER ME THE CASE - AND HURRY! I CAN SEE HER SAILS!
COME ON - WE HAVE BUT MINUTES BEFORE IT'S TOO LATE!
STAND BACK, MAN - THIS IS HOLY WORK.
THIS IS A KERUVIM. THERE ARE ONLY TWO IN THE WHOLE WORLD.
AND TONIGHT - I WILL HAVE THE OTHER.
WAVES AND WIND, FIRE AND WATER.
THUNDER, LIGHTING AND HAIL - HEARKEN TO MY DESIRE, HEARKEN TO MY WORDS.
COME FORTH FROM THE NORTH AND FROM DEEP BELOW.
TEMPEST, STORM AND RAVAGING WIND - CRASH THIS BOAT TO THIS SHORE --
--BRING THE KERUVIM TO ME.

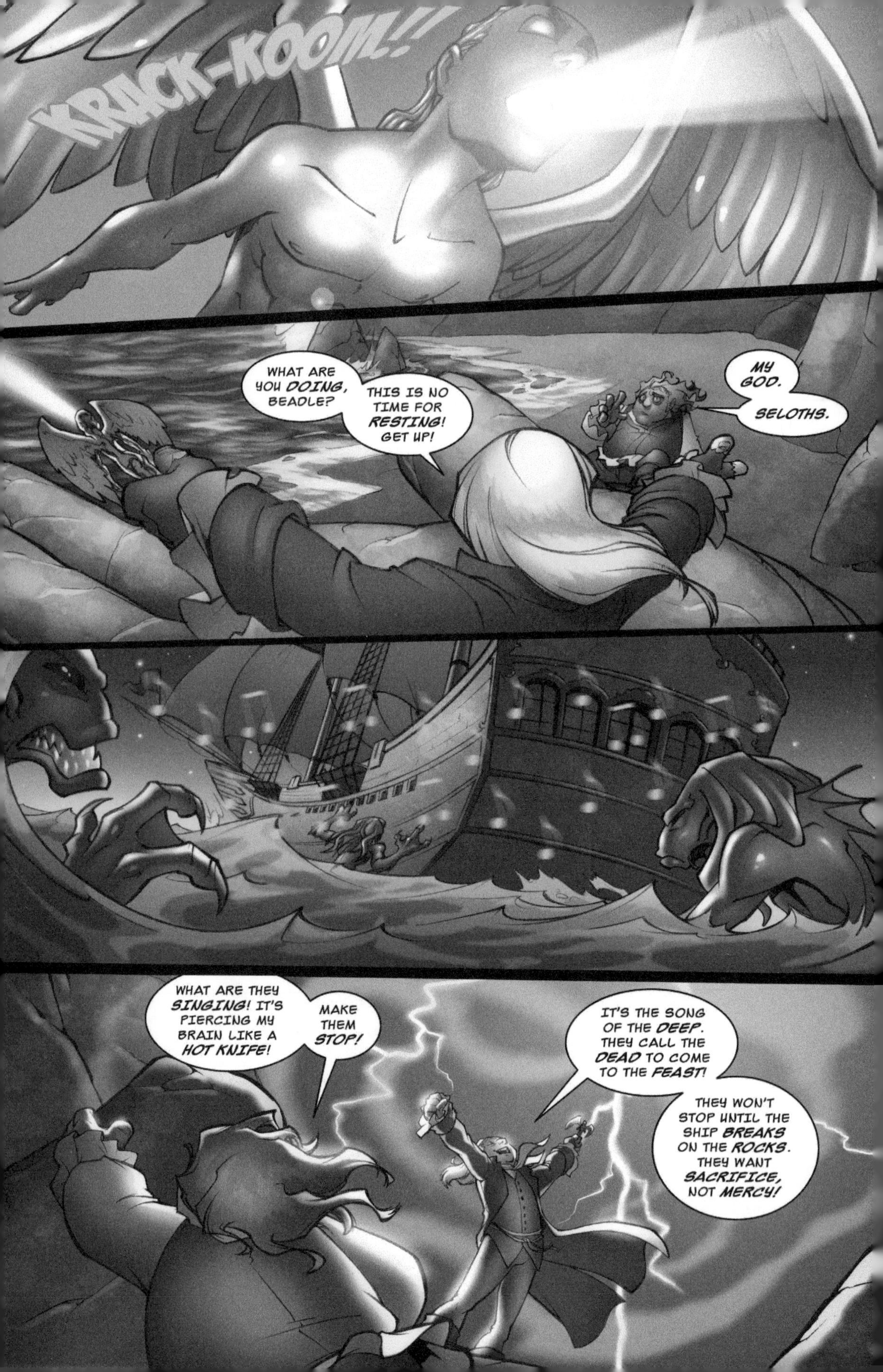
KRACK-KOOM!!
WHAT ARE YOU DOING, BEADLE?
THIS IS NO TIME FOR RESTING! GET UP!
MY GOD.
SELOTHS.
WHAT ARE THEY SINGING! IT'S PIERCING MY BRAIN LIKE A HOT KNIFE!
MAKE THEM STOP!
IT'S THE SONG OF THE DEEP. THEY CALL THE DEAD TO COME TO THE FEAST!
THEY WON'T STOP UNTIL THE SHIP BREAKS ON THE ROCKS. THEY WANT SACRIFICE, NOT MERCY!

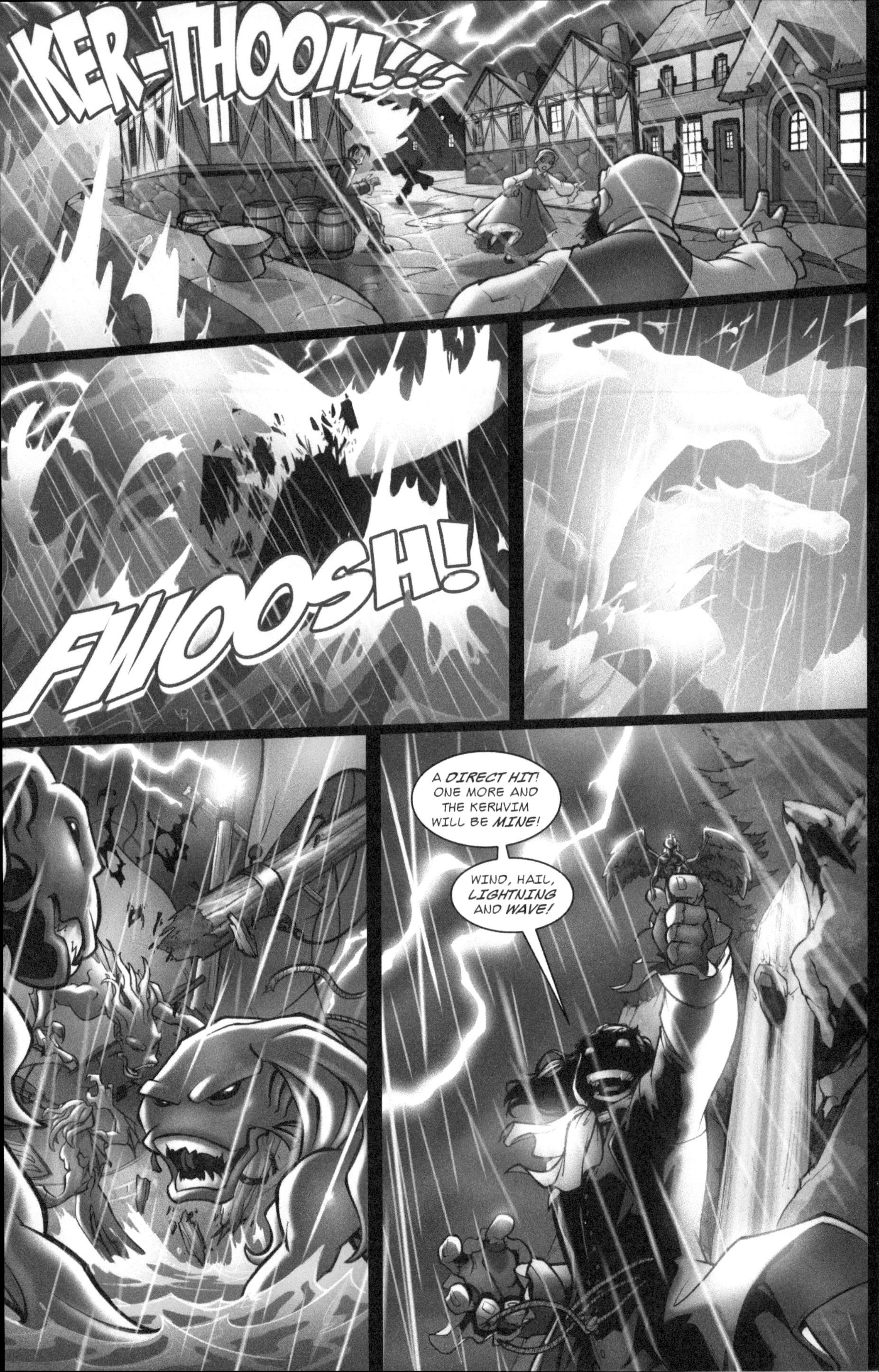
KER-THOOM!!!
FWOOSH!
A DIRECT HIT! ONE MORE AND THE KERUVIM WILL BE MINE!
WIND, HAIL, LIGHTNING AND WAVE!

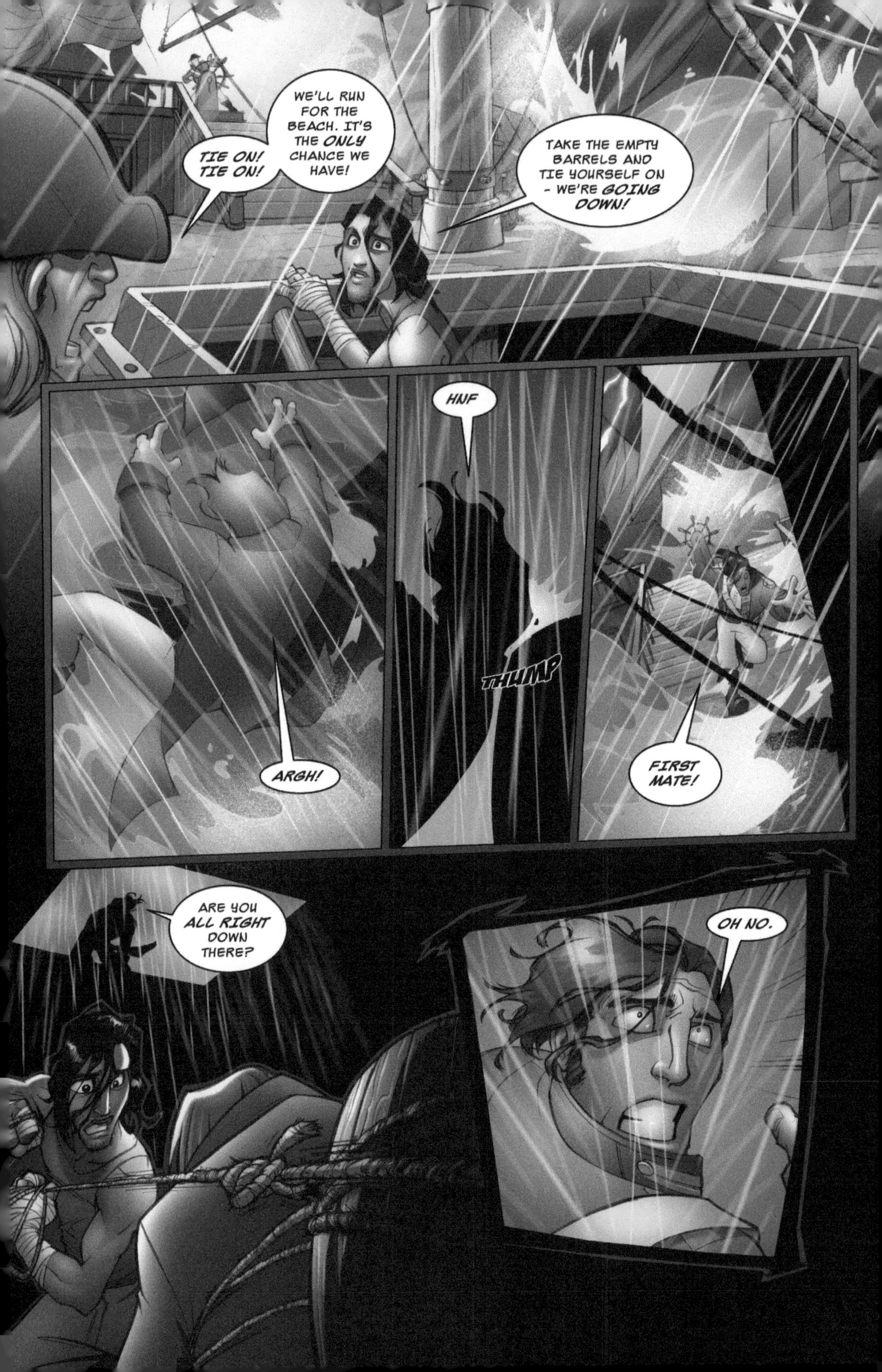

TIE ON! TIE ON!
WE'LL RUN FOR THE BEACH. IT'S THE ONLY CHANCE WE HAVE!
TAKE THE EMPTY BARRELS AND TIE YOURSELF ON - WE'RE GOING DOWN!
ARGH!
HNF
THUMP
FIRST MATE!
ARE YOU ALL RIGHT DOWN THERE?
OH NO.

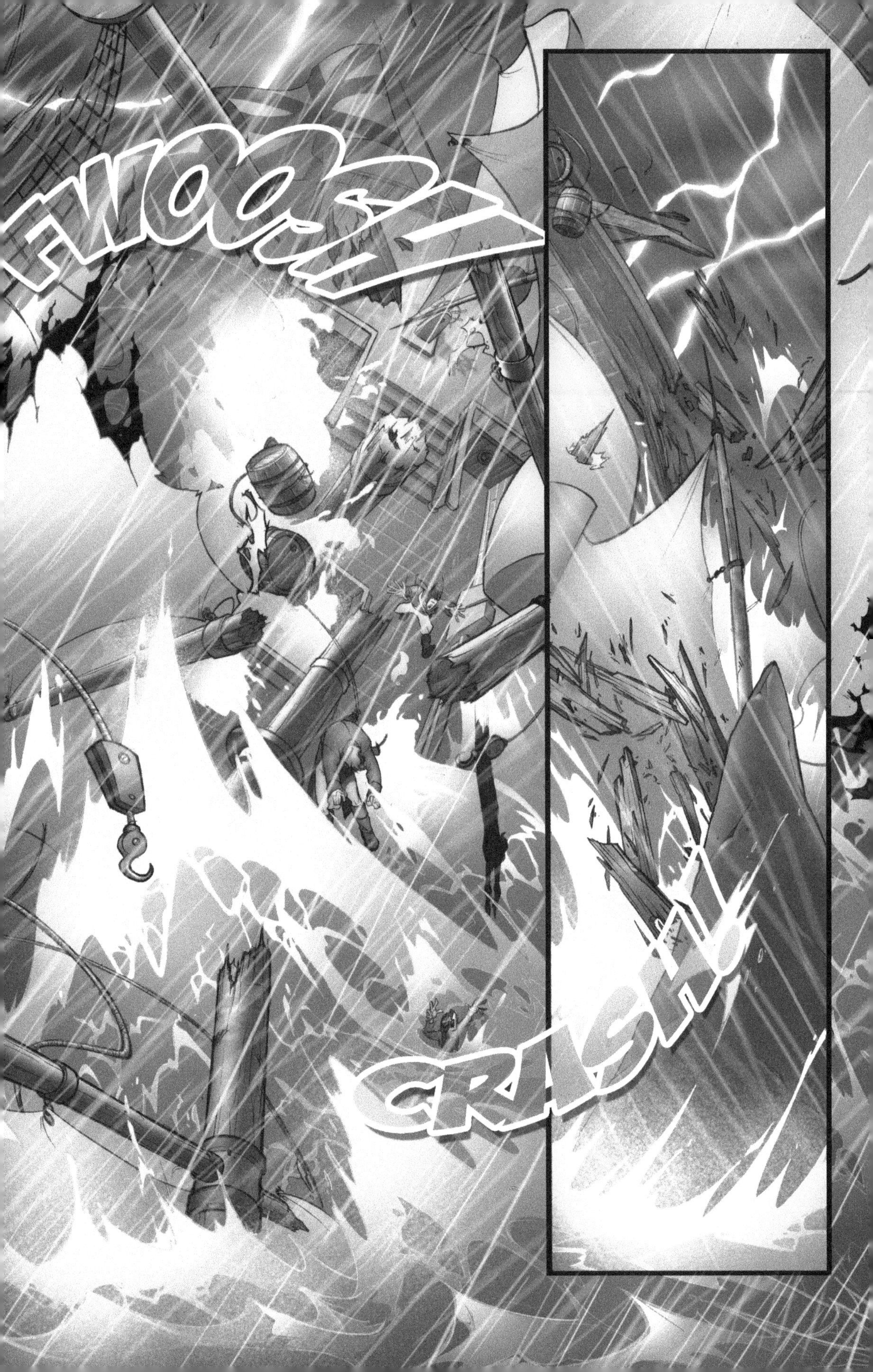
FWOOSH
CRASH!

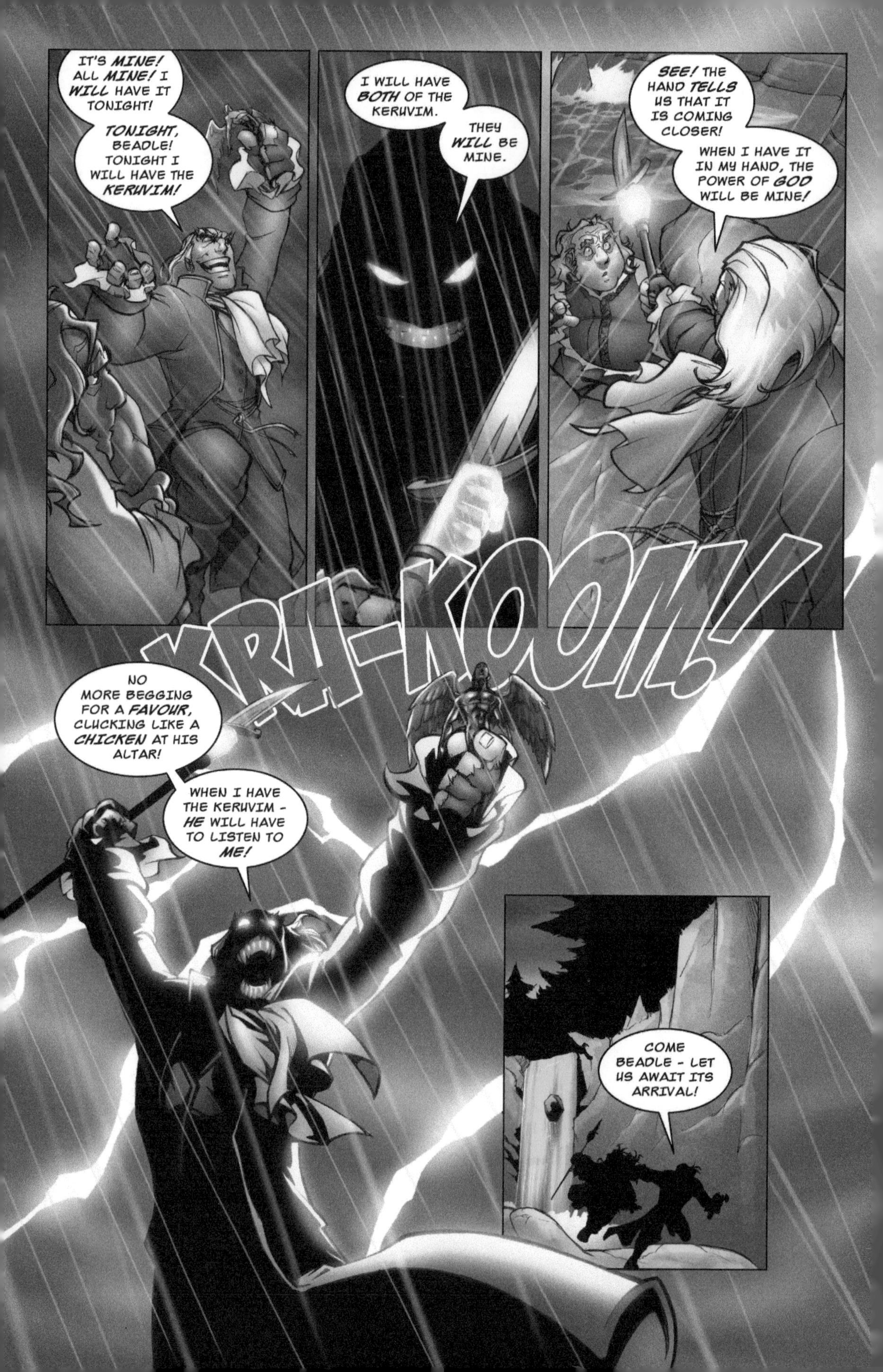
IT'S MINE! ALL MINE! I WILL HAVE IT TONIGHT!
TONIGHT, BEADLE! TONIGHT I WILL HAVE THE KERUVIM!
I WILL HAVE BOTH OF THE KERUVIM.
THEY WILL BE MINE.
SEE! THE HAND TELLS US THAT IT IS COMING CLOSER!
WHEN I HAVE IT IN MY HAND, THE POWER OF GOD WILL BE MINE!
KRA-KOOM!
NO MORE BEGGING FOR A FAVOUR, CLUCKING LIKE A CHICKEN AT HIS ALTAR!
WHEN I HAVE THE KERUVIM - HE WILL HAVE TO LISTEN TO ME!
COME BEADLE - LET US AWAIT ITS ARRIVAL!

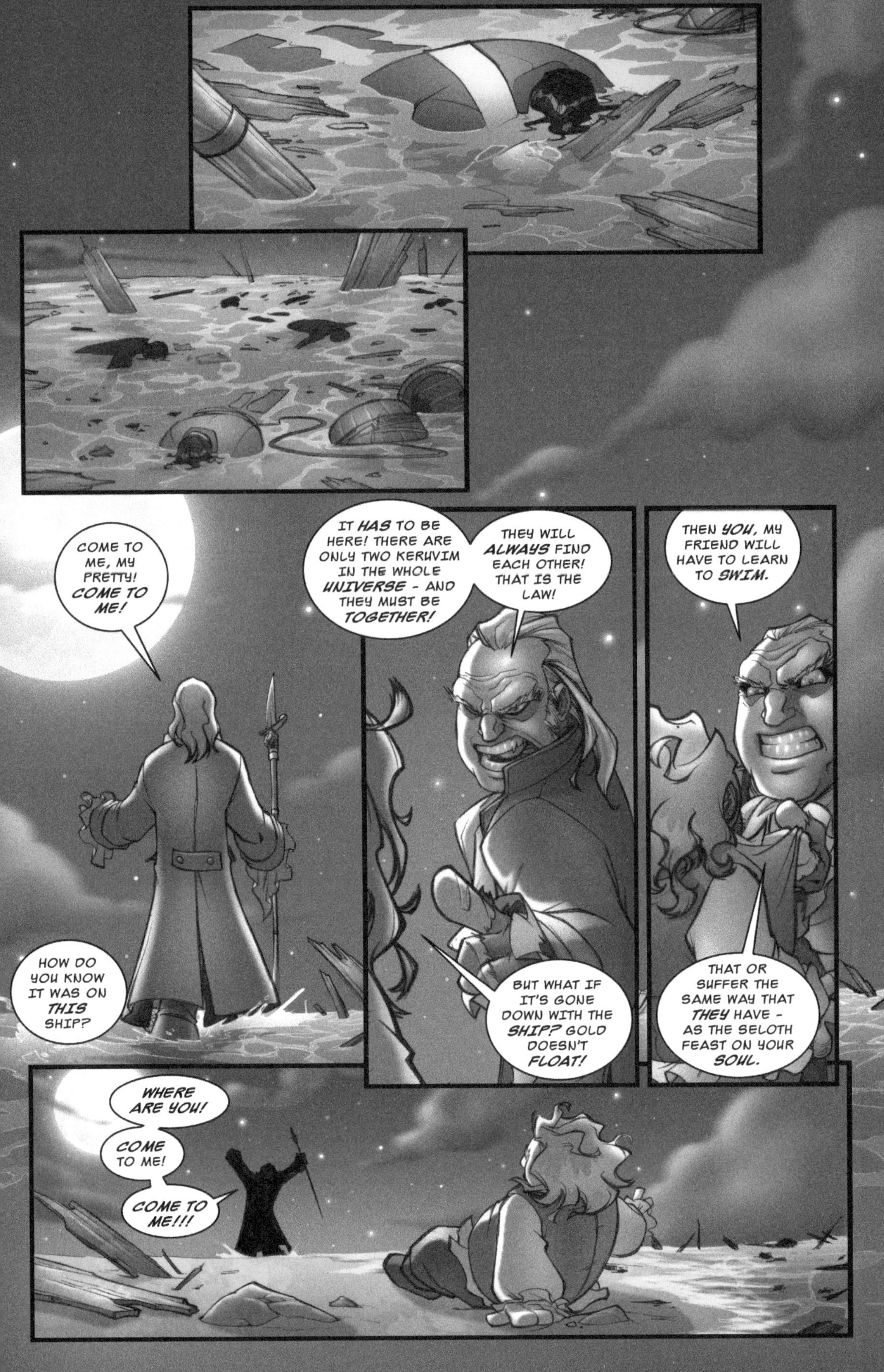

COME TO ME, MY PRETTY! COME TO ME!
HOW DO YOU KNOW IT WAS ON THIS SHIP?
IT HAS TO BE HERE! THERE ARE ONLY TWO KERUVIM IN THE WHOLE UNIVERSE - AND THEY MUST BE TOGETHER!
THEY WILL ALWAYS FIND EACH OTHER! THAT IS THE LAW!
BUT WHAT IF IT'S GONE DOWN WITH THE SHIP? GOLD DOESN'T FLOAT!
THEN YOU, MY FRIEND WILL HAVE TO LEARN TO SWIM.
THAT OR SUFFER THE SAME WAY THAT THEY HAVE - AS THE SELOTH FEAST ON YOUR SOUL.
WHERE ARE YOU!
COME TO ME!
COME TO ME!!!

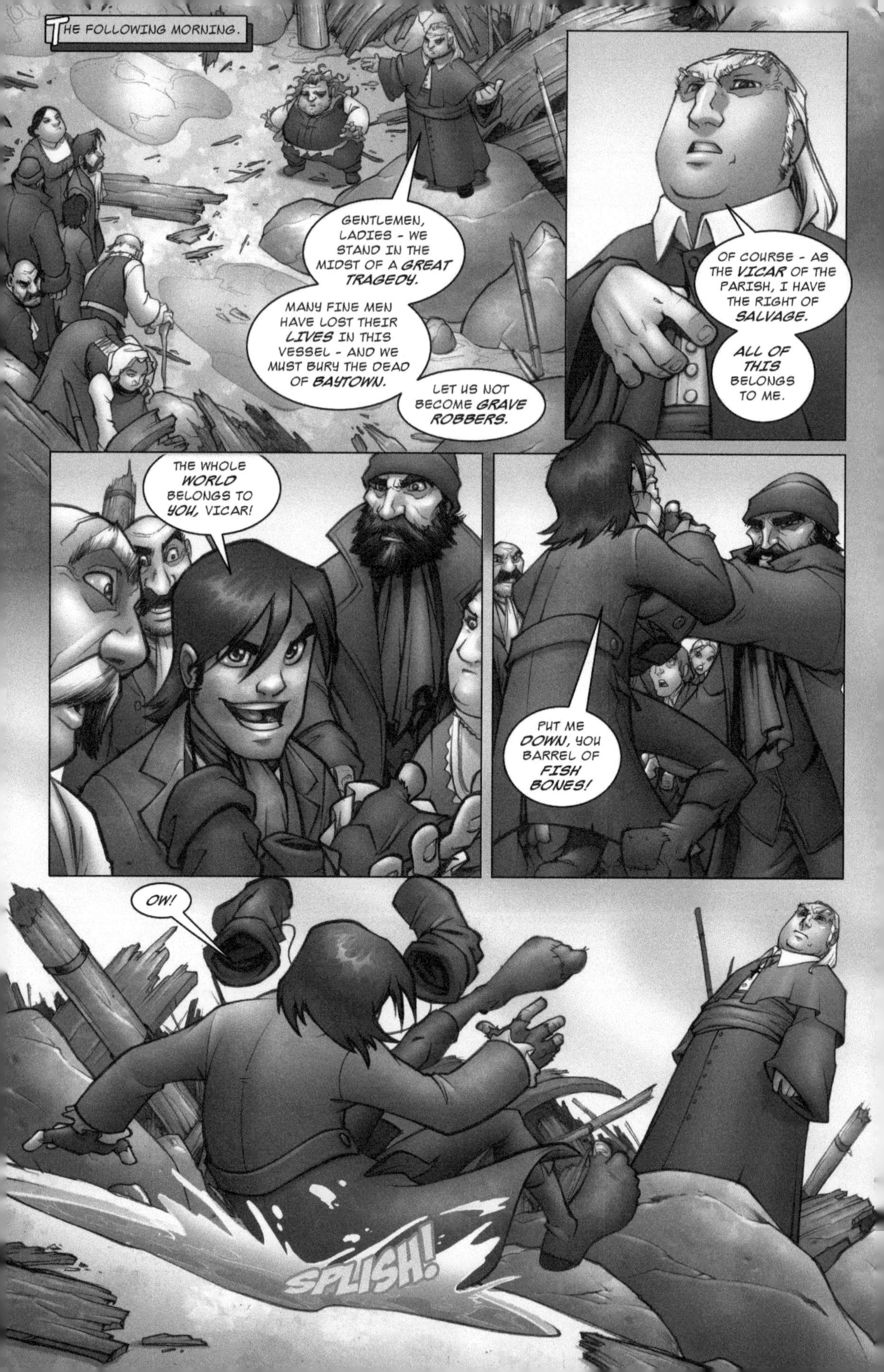
THE FOLLOWING MORNING.
GENTLEMEN, LADIES - WE STAND IN THE MIDST OF A GREAT TRAGEDY.
MANY FINE MEN HAVE LOST THEIR LIVES IN THIS VESSEL - AND WE MUST BURY THE DEAD OF BAYTOWN.
LET US NOT BECOME GRAVE ROBBERS.
OF COURSE - AS THE VICAR OF THE PARISH, I HAVE THE RIGHT OF SALVAGE.
ALL OF THIS BELONGS TO ME.
THE WHOLE WORLD BELONGS TO YOU, VICAR!
PUT ME DOWN, YOU BARREL OF FISH BONES!
OW!
SPLISH!

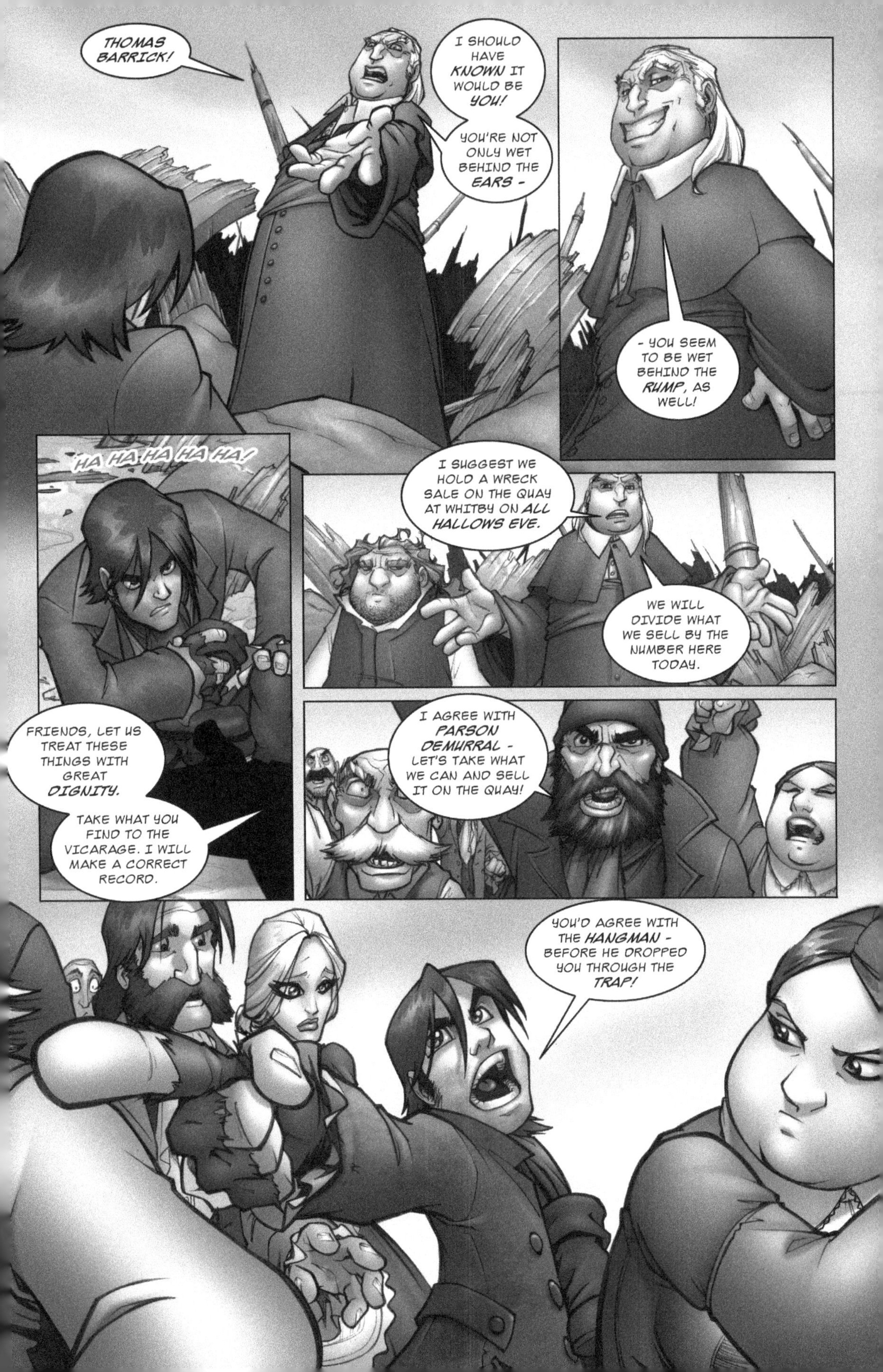
THOMAS BARRICK!
I SHOULD HAVE KNOWN IT WOULD BE YOU!
YOU'RE NOT ONLY WET BEHIND THE EARS -
- YOU SEEM TO BE WET BEHIND THE RUMP, AS WELL!
HA HA HA HA HA!
I SUGGEST WE HOLD A WRECK SALE ON THE QUAY AT WHITBY ON ALL HALLOWS EVE.
WE WILL DIVIDE WHAT WE SELL BY THE NUMBER HERE TODAY.
FRIENDS, LET US TREAT THESE THINGS WITH GREAT DIGNITY.
TAKE WHAT YOU FIND TO THE VICARAGE. I WILL MAKE A CORRECT RECORD.
I AGREE WITH PARSON DEMURRAL - LET'S TAKE WHAT WE CAN AND SELL IT ON THE QUAY!
YOU'D AGREE WITH THE HANGMAN - BEFORE HE DROPPED YOU THROUGH THE TRAP!

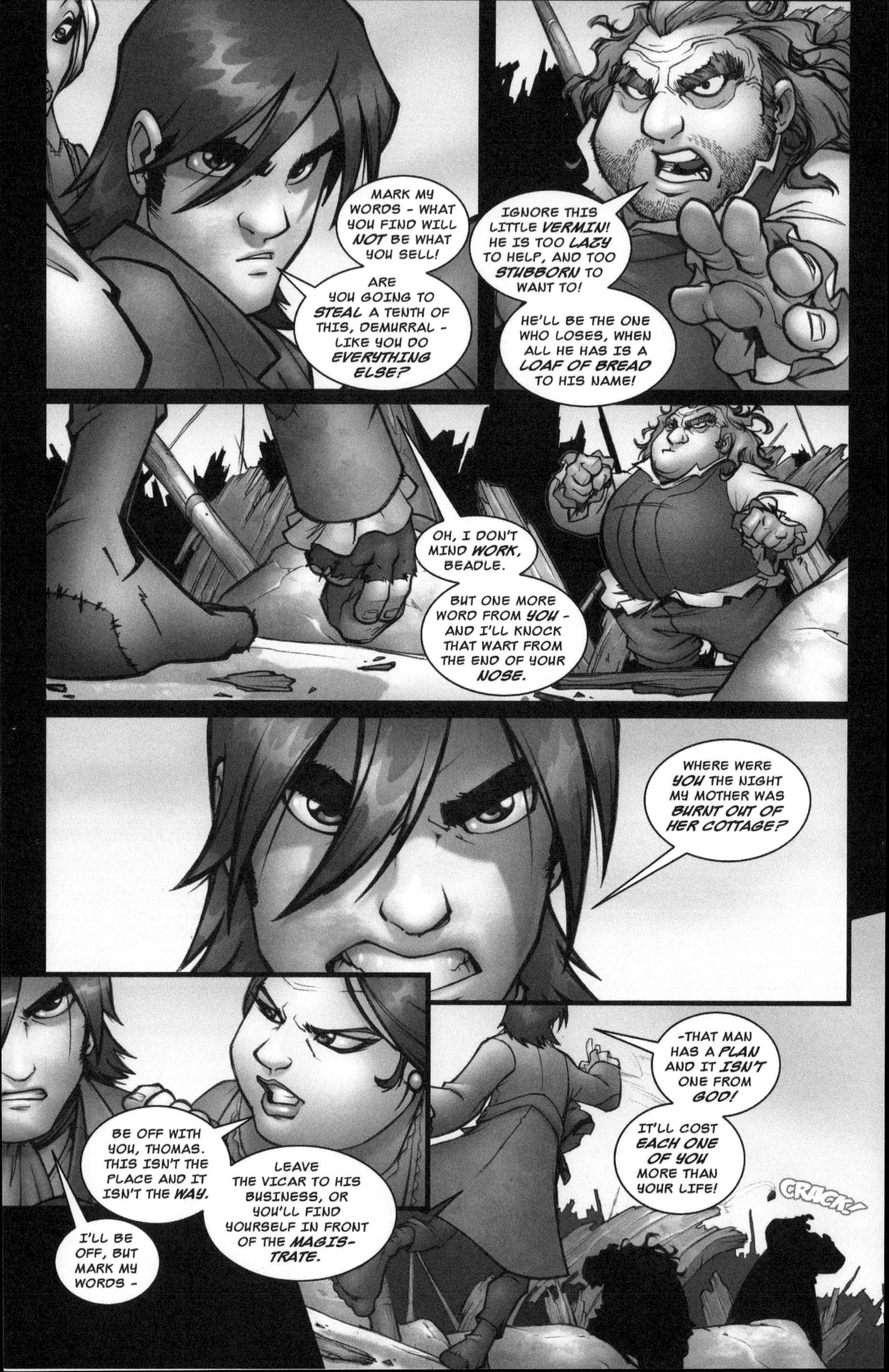
MARK MY WORDS - WHAT YOU FIND WILL NOT BE WHAT YOU SELL!
ARE YOU GOING TO STEAL A TENTH OF THIS, DEMURRAL - LIKE YOU DO EVERYTHING ELSE?
IGNORE THIS LITTLE VERMIN! HE IS TOO LAZY TO HELP, AND TOO STUBBORN TO WANT TO!
HE'LL BE THE ONE WHO LOSES, WHEN ALL HE HAS IS A LOAF OF BREAD TO HIS NAME!
OH, I DON'T MIND WORK, BEADLE.
BUT ONE MORE WORD FROM YOU - AND I'LL KNOCK THAT WART FROM THE END OF YOUR NOSE.
WHERE WERE YOU THE NIGHT MY MOTHER WAS BURNT OUT OF HER COTTAGE?
BE OFF WITH YOU, THOMAS. THIS ISN'T THE PLACE AND IT ISN'T THE WAY.
LEAVE THE VICAR TO HIS BUSINESS, OR YOU'LL FIND YOURSELF IN FRONT OF THE MAGIS-TRATE.
I'LL BE OFF, BUT MARK MY WORDS -
-THAT MAN HAS A PLAN AND IT ISN'T ONE FROM GOD!
IT'LL COST EACH ONE OF YOU MORE THAN YOUR LIFE!
CRACK!

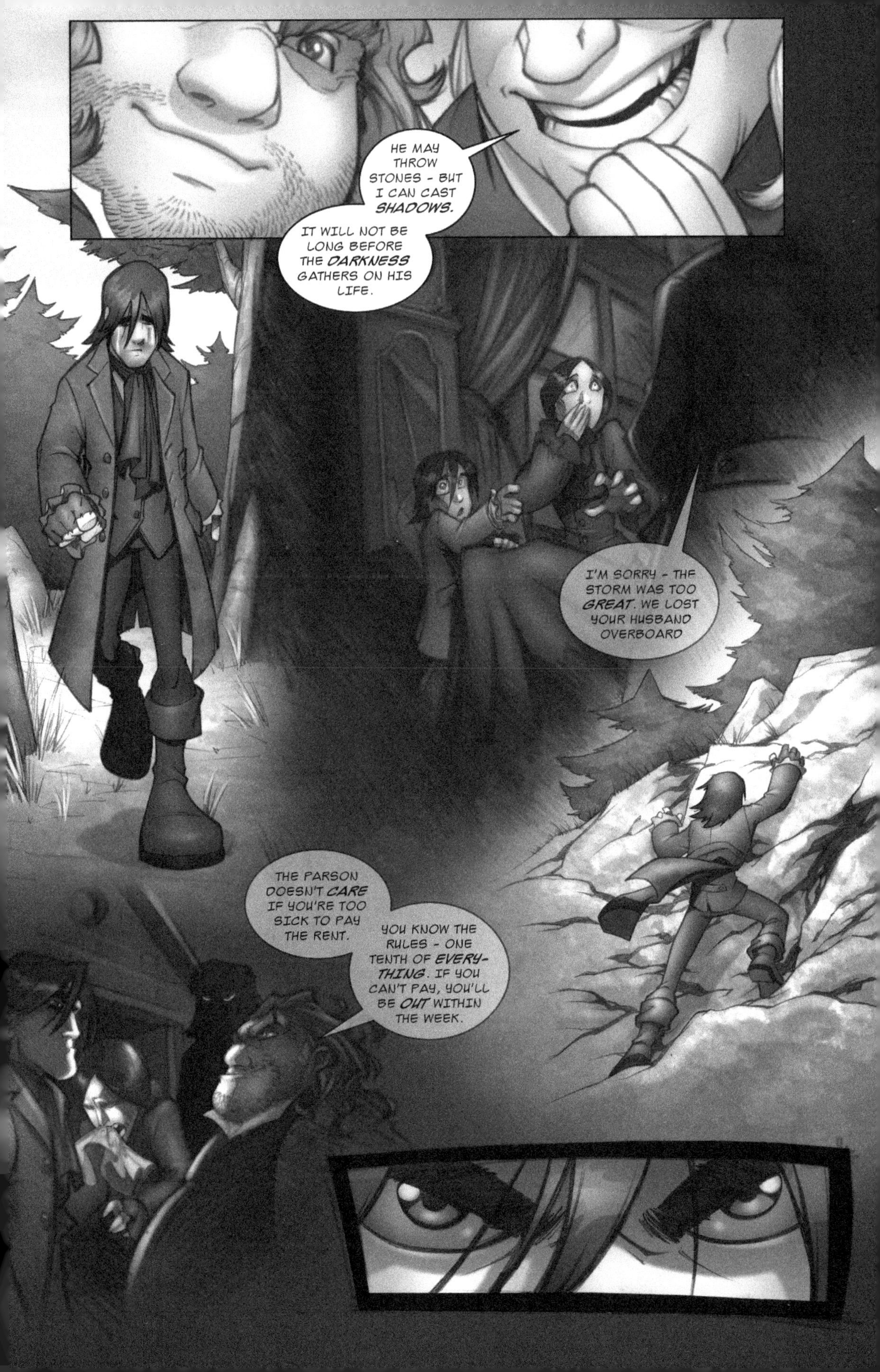
HE MAY THROW STONES - BUT I CAN CAST SHADOWS.
IT WILL NOT BE LONG BEFORE THE DARKNESS GATHERS ON HIS LIFE.
I'M SORRY - THE STORM WAS TOO GREAT. WE LOST YOUR HUSBAND OVERBOARD
THE PARSON DOESN'T CARE IF YOU'RE TOO SICK TO PAY THE RENT.
YOU KNOW THE RULES - ONE TENTH OF EVERYTHING. IF YOU CAN'T PAY, YOU'LL BE OUT WITHIN THE WEEK.

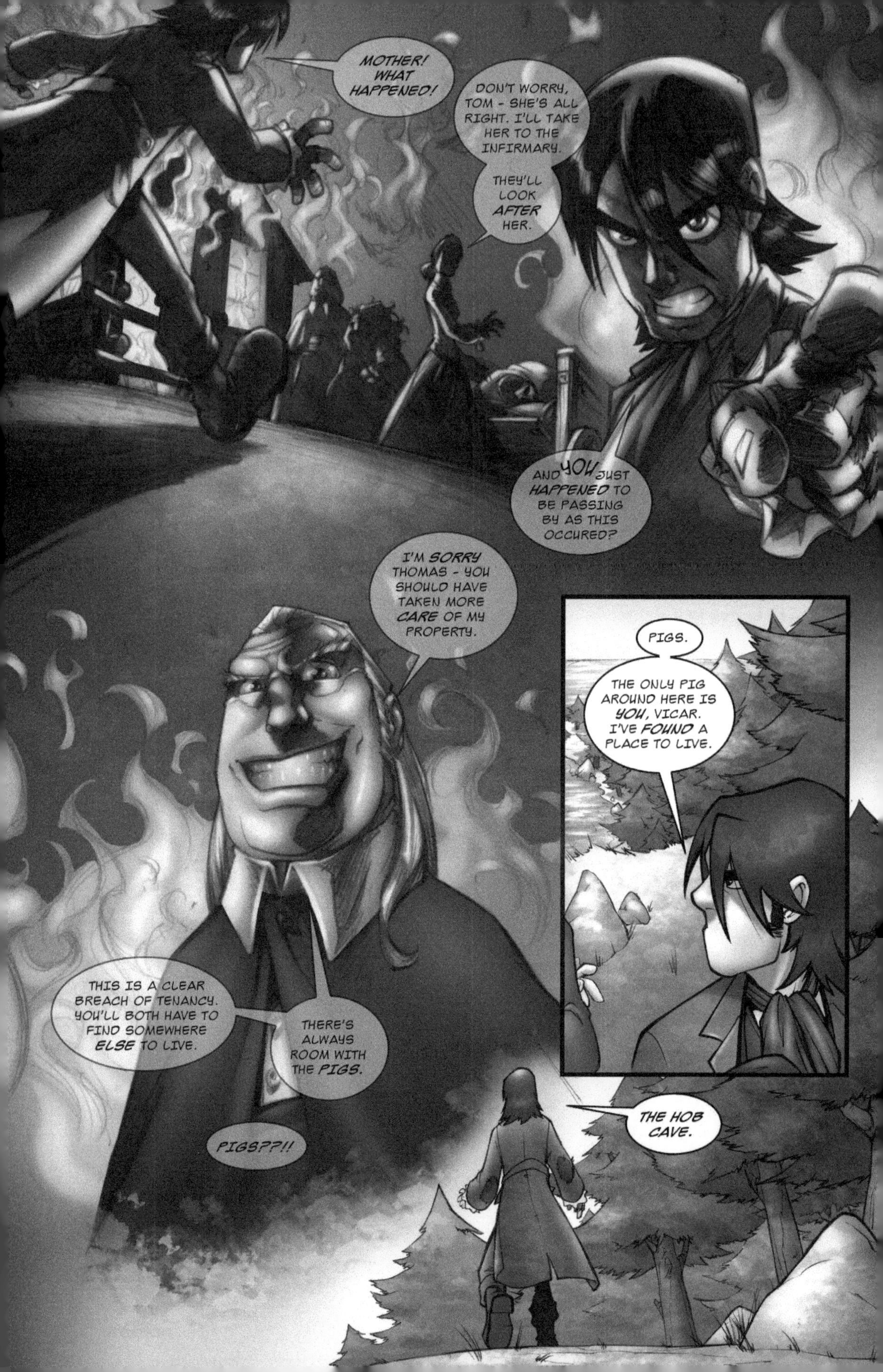
MOTHER! WHAT HAPPENED!
DON'T WORRY, TOM - SHE'S ALL RIGHT. I'LL TAKE HER TO THE INFIRMARY.
THEY'LL LOOK AFTER HER.
AND YOU JUST HAPPENED TO BE PASSING BY AS THIS OCCURED?
I'M SORRY THOMAS - YOU SHOULD HAVE TAKEN MORE CARE OF MY PROPERTY.
THIS IS A CLEAR BREACH OF TENANCY. YOU'LL BOTH HAVE TO FIND SOMEWHERE ELSE TO LIVE.
THERE'S ALWAYS ROOM WITH THE PIGS.
PIGS??!!
PIGS.
THE ONLY PIG AROUND HERE IS YOU, VICAR. I'VE FOUND A PLACE TO LIVE.
THE HOB CAVE.

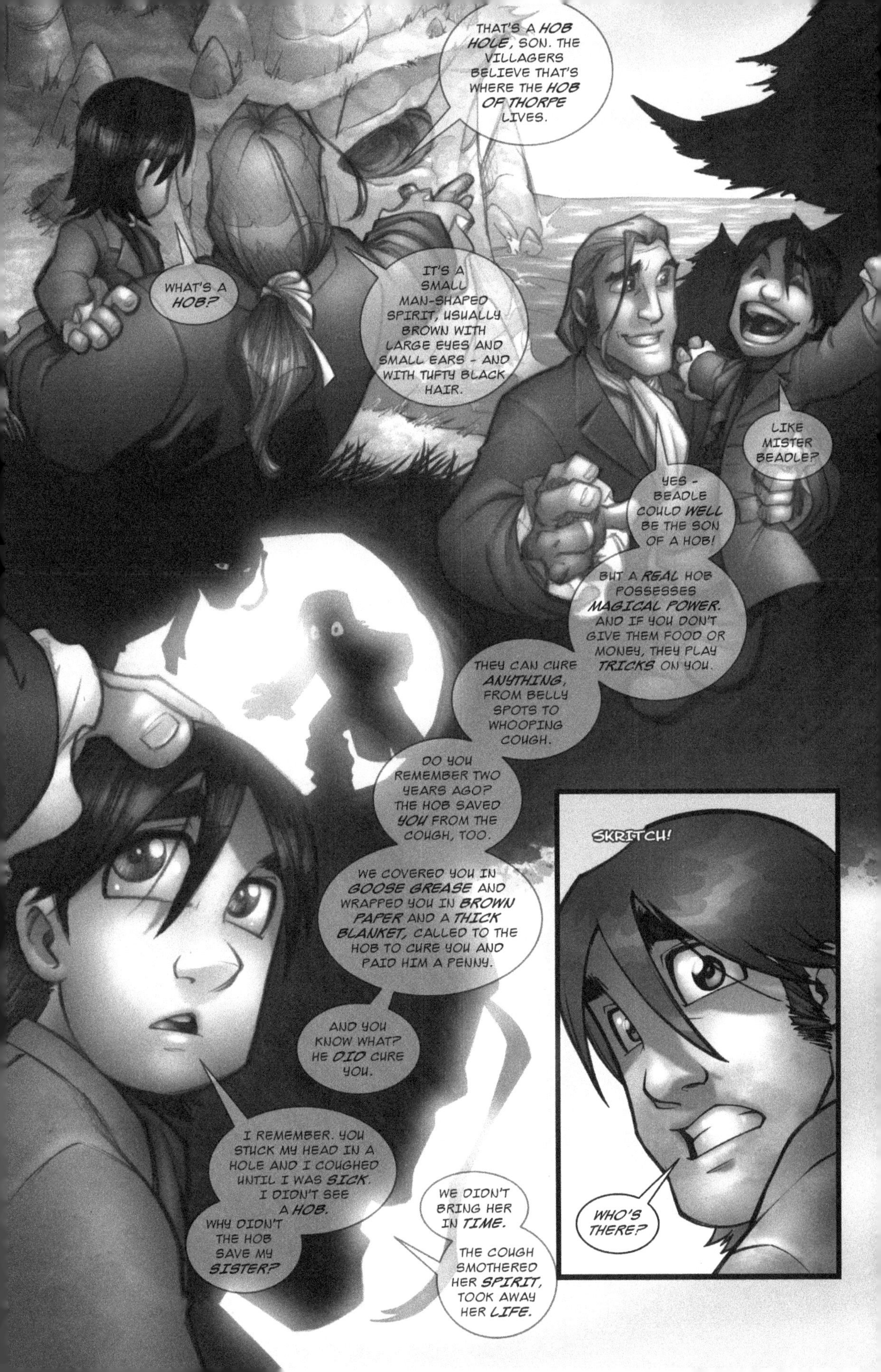
THAT'S A HOB HOLE, SON. THE VILLAGERS BELIEVE THAT'S WHERE THE HOB OF THORPE LIVES.
WHAT'S A HOB?
IT'S A SMALL MAN-SHAPED SPIRIT, USUALLY BROWN WITH LARGE EYES AND SMALL EARS - AND WITH TUFTY BLACK HAIR.
LIKE MISTER BEADLE?
YES - BEADLE COULD WELL BE THE SON OF A HOB!
BUT A REAL HOB POSSESSES MAGICAL POWER. AND IF YOU DON'T GIVE THEM FOOD OR MONEY, THEY PLAY TRICKS ON YOU.
THEY CAN CURE ANYTHING, FROM BELLY SPOTS TO WHOOPING COUGH.
DO YOU REMEMBER TWO YEARS AGO? THE HOB SAVED YOU FROM THE COUGH, TOO.
WE COVERED YOU IN GOOSE GREASE AND WRAPPED YOU IN BROWN PAPER AND A THICK BLANKET, CALLED TO THE HOB TO CURE YOU AND PAID HIM A PENNY.
AND YOU KNOW WHAT? HE DID CURE YOU.
I REMEMBER. YOU STUCK MY HEAD IN A HOLE AND I COUGHED UNTIL I WAS SICK. I DIDN'T SEE A HOB.
WHY DIDN'T THE HOB SAVE MY SISTER?
WE DIDN'T BRING HER IN TIME.
THE COUGH SMOTHERED HER SPIRIT, TOOK AWAY HER LIFE.
SKRITCH!
WHO'S THERE?

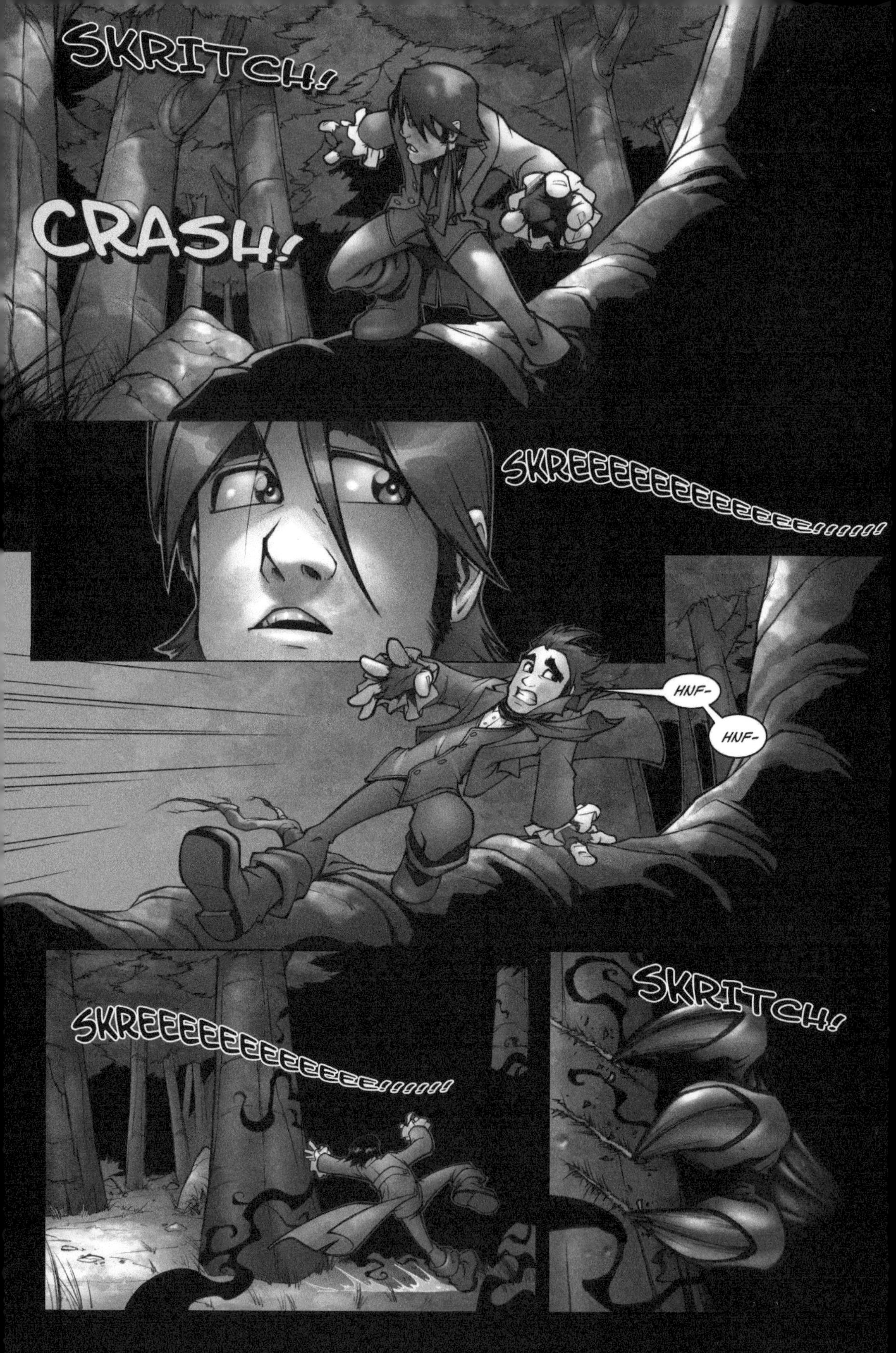
SKRITCH!
CRASH!
SKREEEEEEEEEEEEEE!!!!!!
HNF-
HNF-
SKREEEEEEEEEEEEEE!!!!!!
SKRITCH!

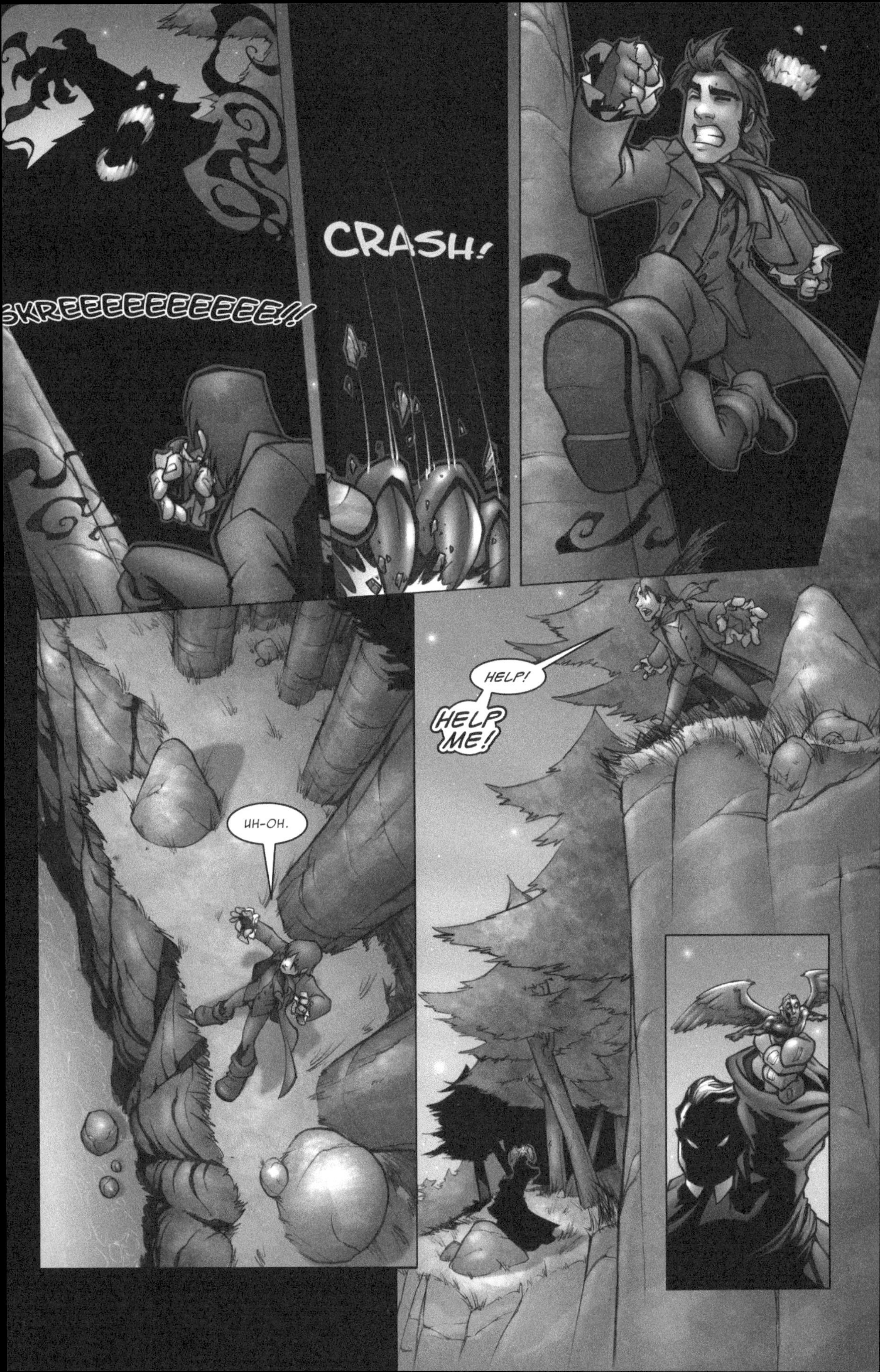
SKREEEEEEEEEEEE!!!
CRASH!
UH-OH.
HELP!
HELP ME!

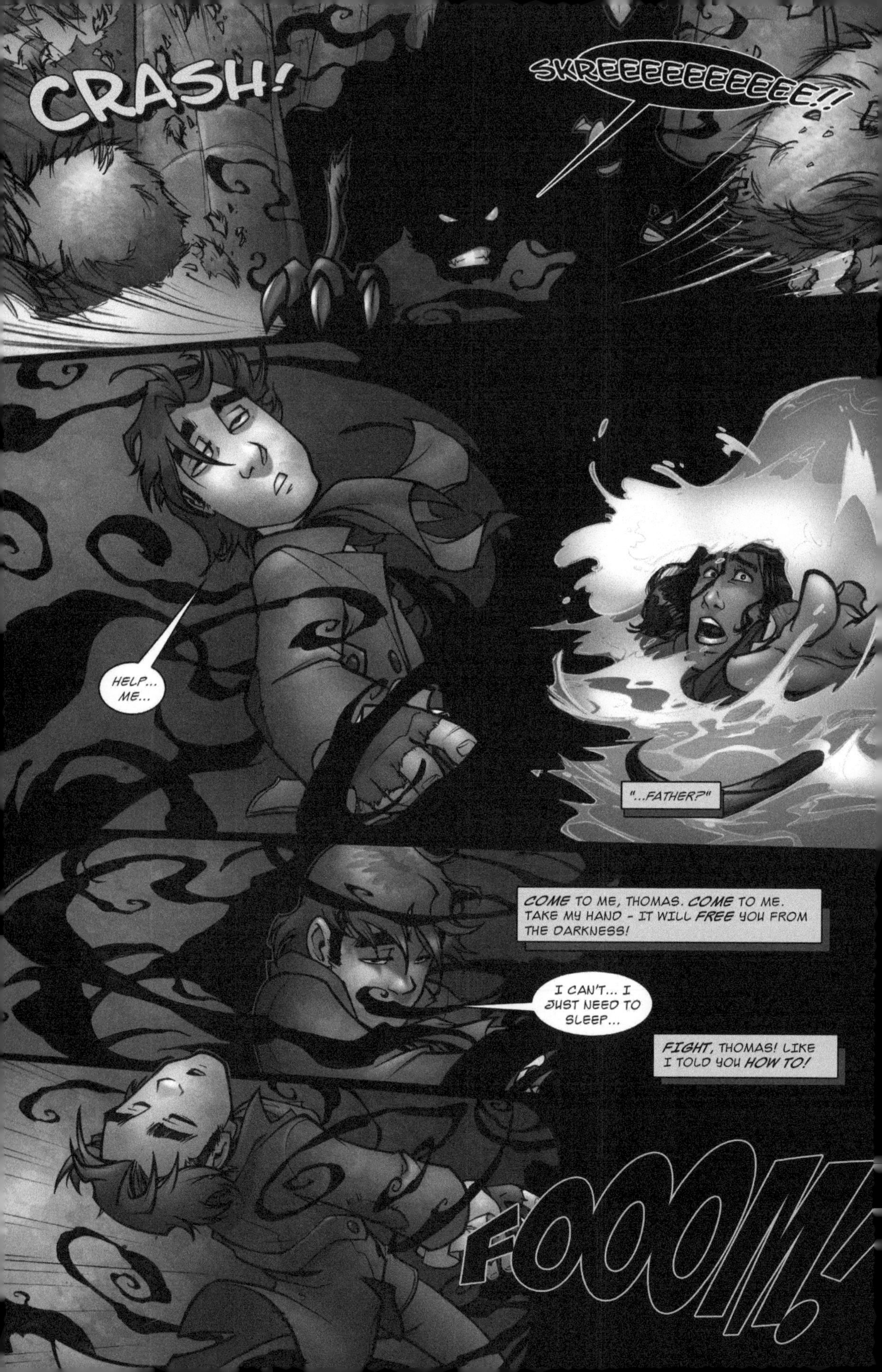
CRASH!
SKREEEEEEEEEEEE!!
HELP... ME...
"...FATHER?"
COME TO ME, THOMAS. COME TO ME. TAKE MY HAND – IT WILL FREE YOU FROM THE DARKNESS!
I CAN'T... I JUST NEED TO SLEEP...
FIGHT, THOMAS! LIKE I TOLD YOU HOW TO!
FOOOM!

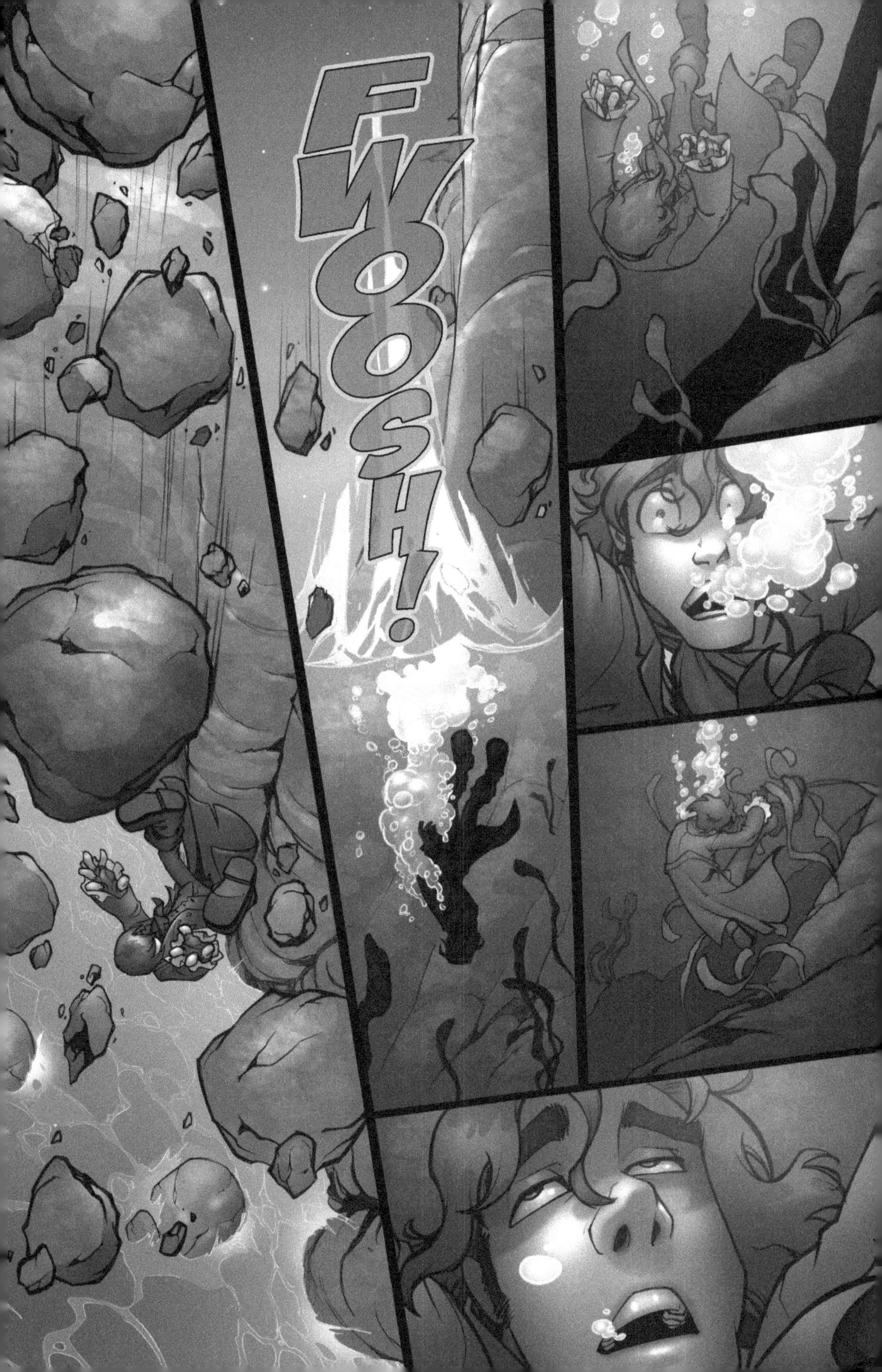
FWOOSH!

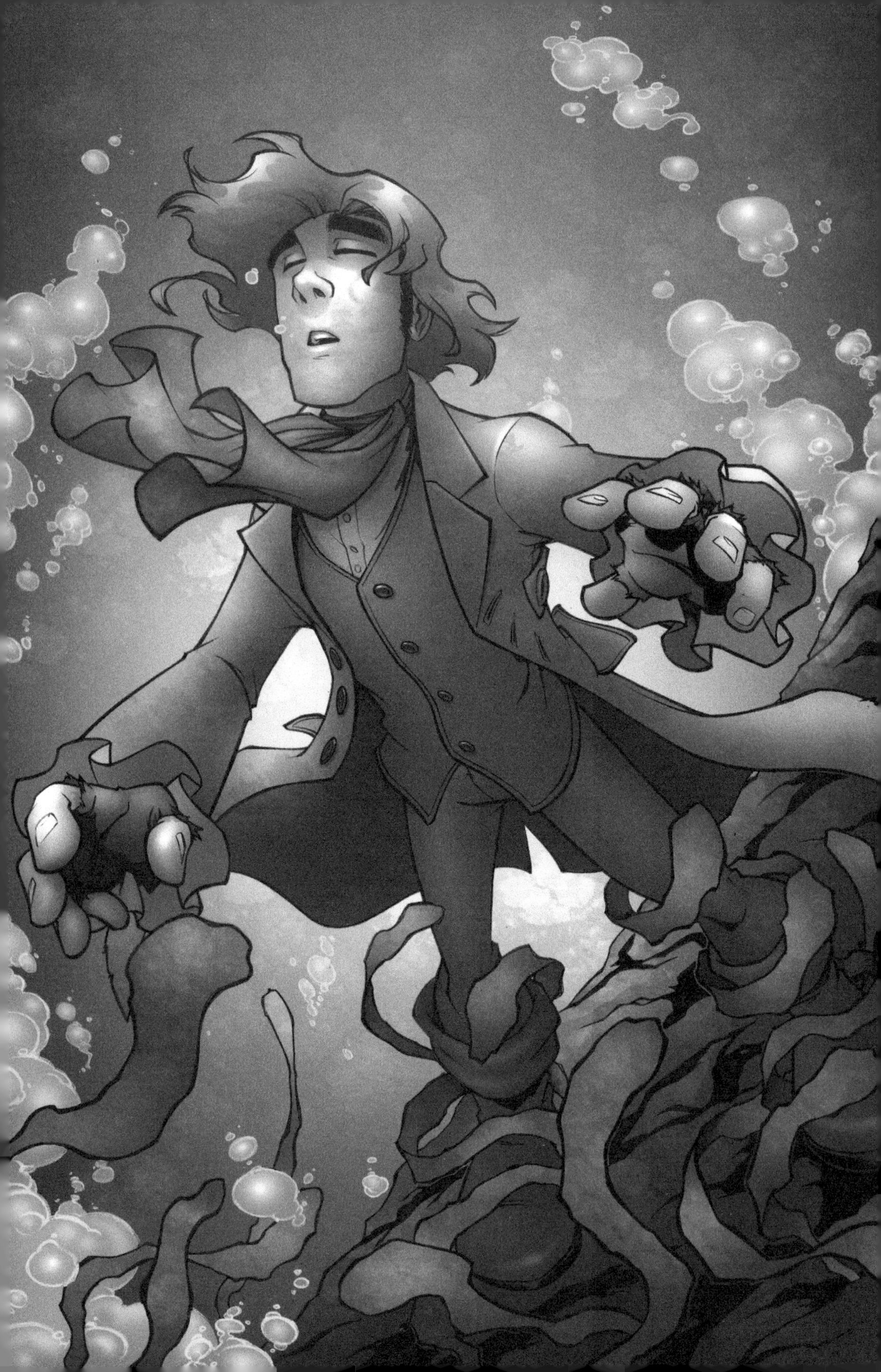

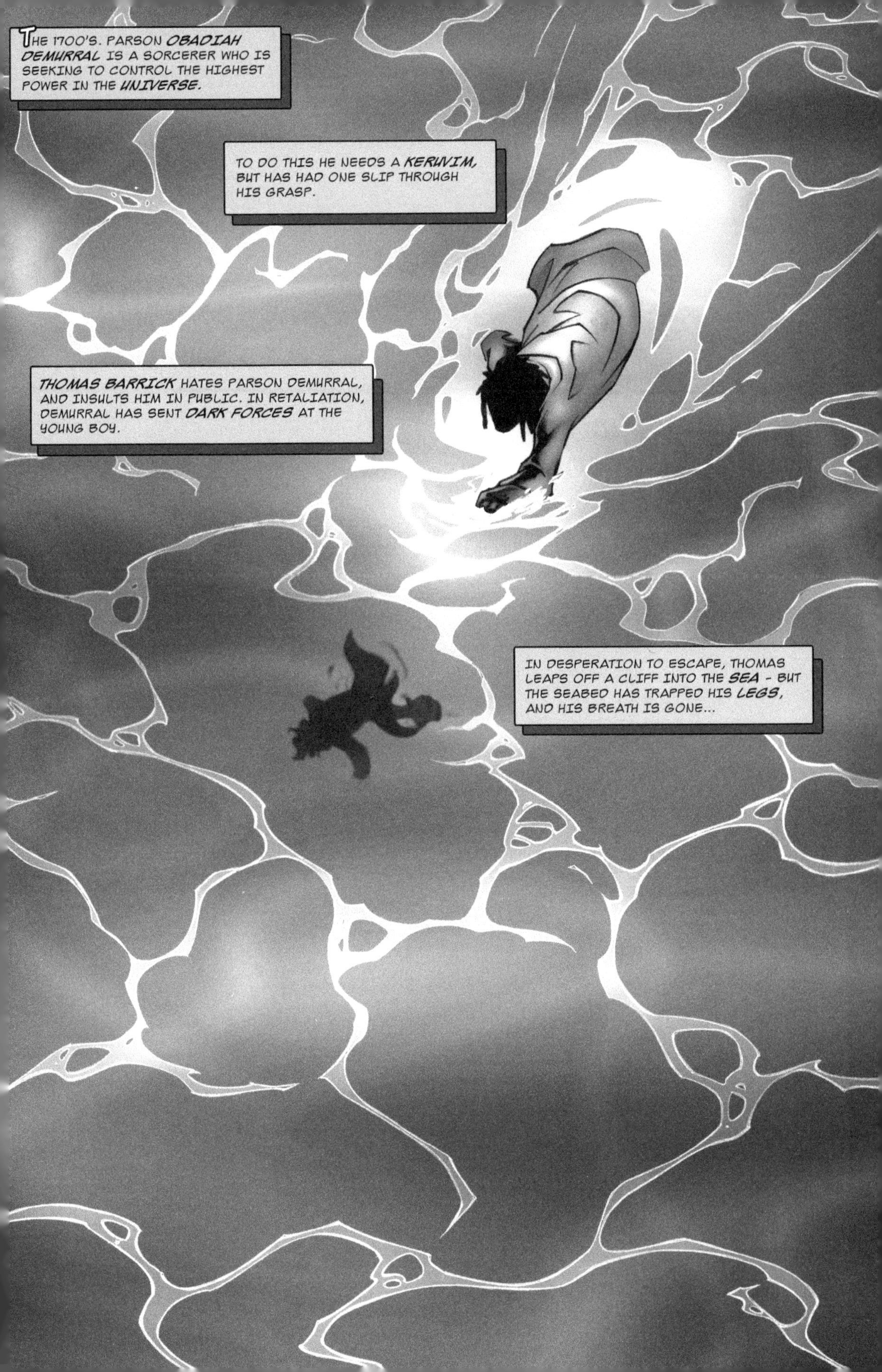
THE 1700'S. PARSON OBADIAH DEMURRAL IS A SORCERER WHO IS SEEKING TO CONTROL THE HIGHEST POWER IN THE UNIVERSE.
TO DO THIS HE NEEDS A KERUVIM, BUT HAS HAD ONE SLIP THROUGH HIS GRASP.
THOMAS BARRICK HATES PARSON DEMURRAL, AND INSULTS HIM IN PUBLIC. IN RETALIATION, DEMURRAL HAS SENT DARK FORCES AT THE YOUNG BOY.
IN DESPERATION TO ESCAPE, THOMAS LEAPS OFF A CLIFF INTO THE SEA - BUT THE SEABED HAS TRAPPED HIS LEGS, AND HIS BREATH IS GONE...

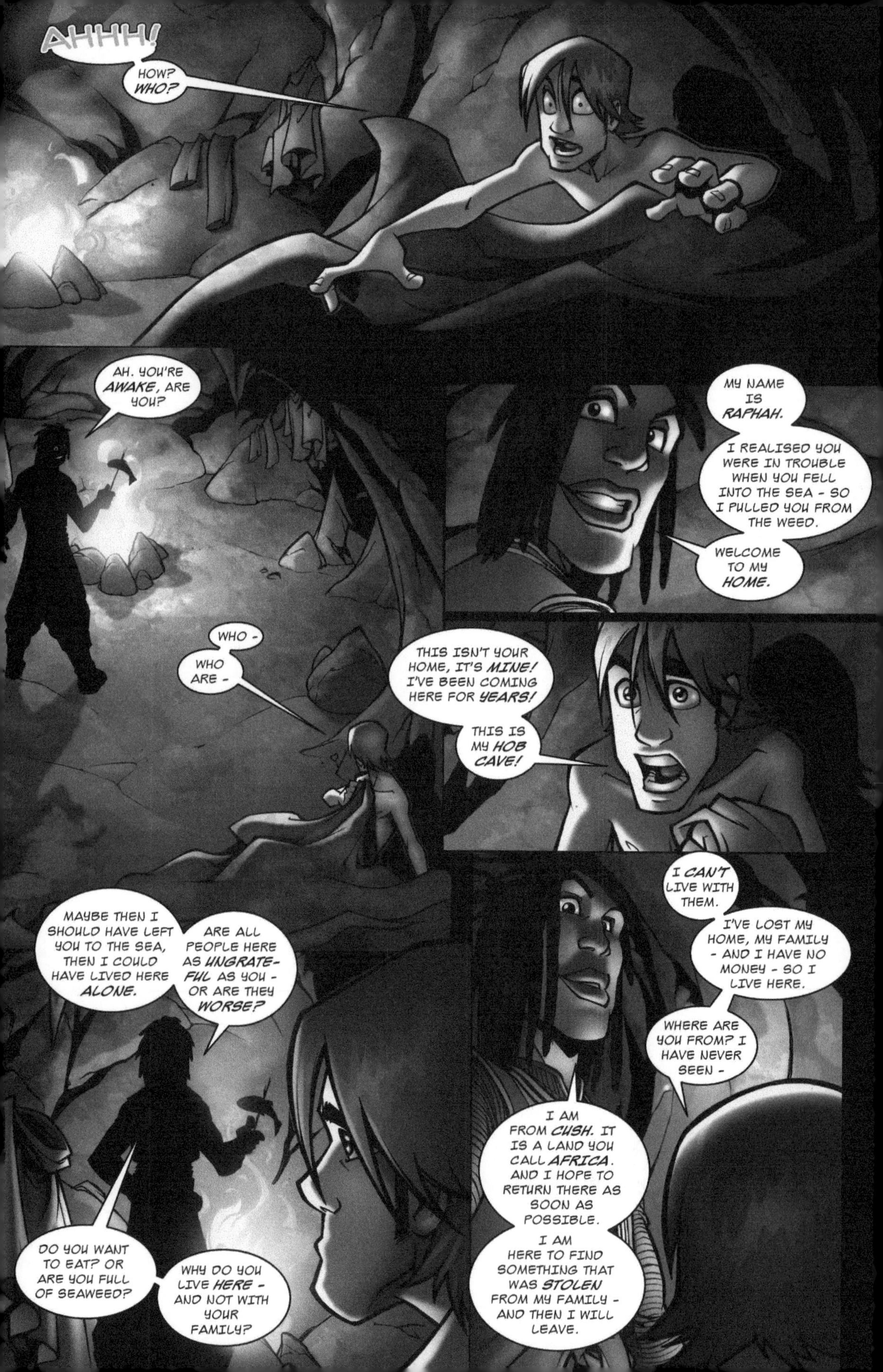
AHHH!
HOW? WHO?
AH. YOU'RE AWAKE, ARE YOU?
MY NAME IS RAPHAH.
I REALISED YOU WERE IN TROUBLE WHEN YOU FELL INTO THE SEA - SO I PULLED YOU FROM THE WEED.
WELCOME TO MY HOME.
WHO -
WHO ARE -
THIS ISN'T YOUR HOME, IT'S MINE! I'VE BEEN COMING HERE FOR YEARS!
THIS IS MY HOB CAVE!
MAYBE THEN I SHOULD HAVE LEFT YOU TO THE SEA, THEN I COULD HAVE LIVED HERE ALONE.
ARE ALL PEOPLE HERE AS UNGRATE-FUL AS YOU - OR ARE THEY WORSE?
DO YOU WANT TO EAT? OR ARE YOU FULL OF SEAWEED?
WHY DO YOU LIVE HERE - AND NOT WITH YOUR FAMILY?
I CAN'T LIVE WITH THEM.
I'VE LOST MY HOME, MY FAMILY - AND I HAVE NO MONEY - SO I LIVE HERE.
WHERE ARE YOU FROM? I HAVE NEVER SEEN -
I AM FROM CUSH. IT IS A LAND YOU CALL AFRICA. AND I HOPE TO RETURN THERE AS SOON AS POSSIBLE.
I AM HERE TO FIND SOMETHING THAT WAS STOLEN FROM MY FAMILY - AND THEN I WILL LEAVE.

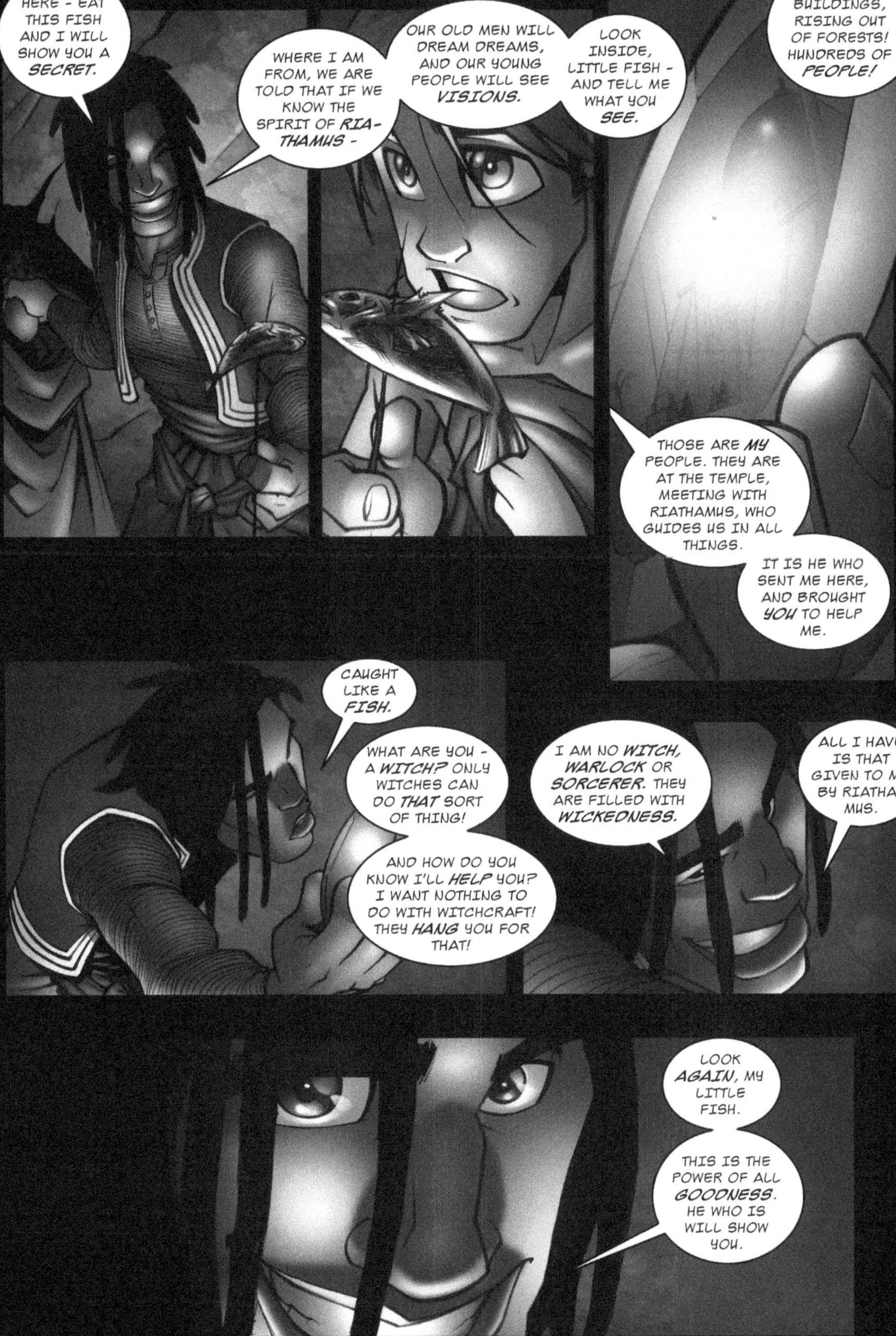
HERE - EAT THIS FISH AND I WILL SHOW YOU A SECRET.
WHERE I AM FROM, WE ARE TOLD THAT IF WE KNOW THE SPIRIT OF RIA-THAMUS -
OUR OLD MEN WILL DREAM DREAMS, AND OUR YOUNG PEOPLE WILL SEE VISIONS.
LOOK INSIDE, LITTLE FISH - AND TELL ME WHAT YOU SEE.
I CAN SEE BUILDINGS, RISING OUT OF FORESTS! HUNDREDS OF PEOPLE!
THOSE ARE MY PEOPLE. THEY ARE AT THE TEMPLE, MEETING WITH RIATHAMUS, WHO GUIDES US IN ALL THINGS.
IT IS HE WHO SENT ME HERE, AND BROUGHT YOU TO HELP ME.
CAUGHT LIKE A FISH.
WHAT ARE YOU - A WITCH? ONLY WITCHES CAN DO THAT SORT OF THING!
AND HOW DO YOU KNOW I'LL HELP YOU? I WANT NOTHING TO DO WITH WITCHCRAFT! THEY HANG YOU FOR THAT!
I AM NO WITCH, WARLOCK OR SORCERER. THEY ARE FILLED WITH WICKEDNESS.
ALL I HAVE IS THAT GIVEN TO ME BY RIATHA-MUS.
LOOK AGAIN, MY LITTLE FISH.
THIS IS THE POWER OF ALL GOODNESS. HE WHO IS WILL SHOW YOU.

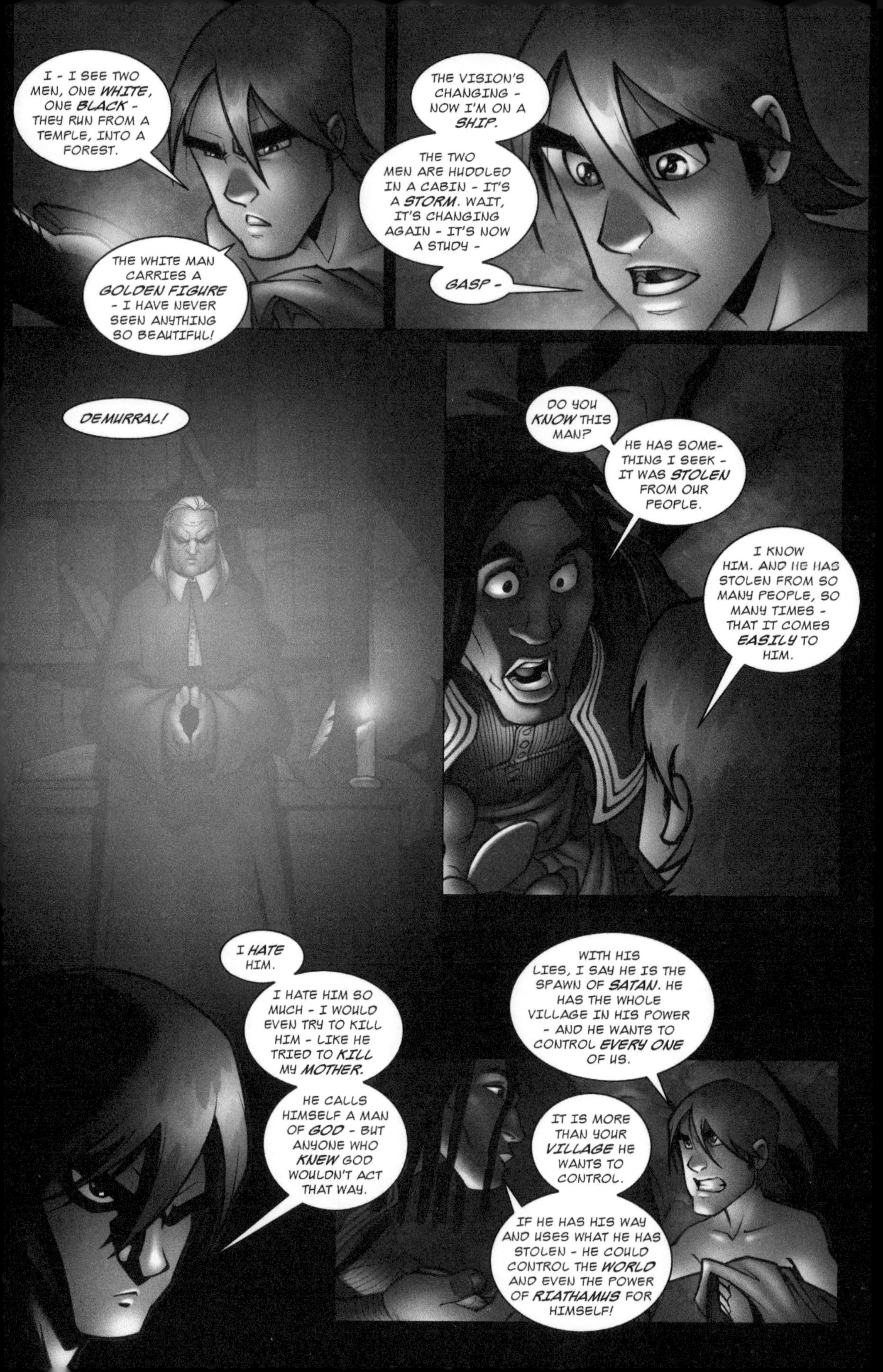

I - I SEE TWO MEN, ONE WHITE, ONE BLACK - THEY RUN FROM A TEMPLE, INTO A FOREST.
THE WHITE MAN CARRIES A GOLDEN FIGURE - I HAVE NEVER SEEN ANYTHING SO BEAUTIFUL!
THE VISION'S CHANGING - NOW I'M ON A SHIP.
THE TWO MEN ARE HUDDLED IN A CABIN - IT'S A STORM. WAIT, IT'S CHANGING AGAIN - IT'S NOW A STUDY -
GASP -
DEMURRAL!
DO YOU KNOW THIS MAN?
HE HAS SOMETHING I SEEK - IT WAS STOLEN FROM OUR PEOPLE.
I KNOW HIM. AND HE HAS STOLEN FROM SO MANY PEOPLE, SO MANY TIMES - THAT IT COMES EASILY TO HIM.
I HATE HIM.
I HATE HIM SO MUCH - I WOULD EVEN TRY TO KILL HIM - LIKE HE TRIED TO KILL MY MOTHER.
HE CALLS HIMSELF A MAN OF GOD - BUT ANYONE WHO KNEW GOD WOULDN'T ACT THAT WAY.
WITH HIS LIES, I SAY HE IS THE SPAWN OF SATAN. HE HAS THE WHOLE VILLAGE IN HIS POWER - AND HE WANTS TO CONTROL EVERY ONE OF US.
IT IS MORE THAN YOUR VILLAGE HE WANTS TO CONTROL.
IF HE HAS HIS WAY AND USES WHAT HE HAS STOLEN - HE COULD CONTROL THE WORLD AND EVEN THE POWER OF RIATHAMUS FOR HIMSELF!

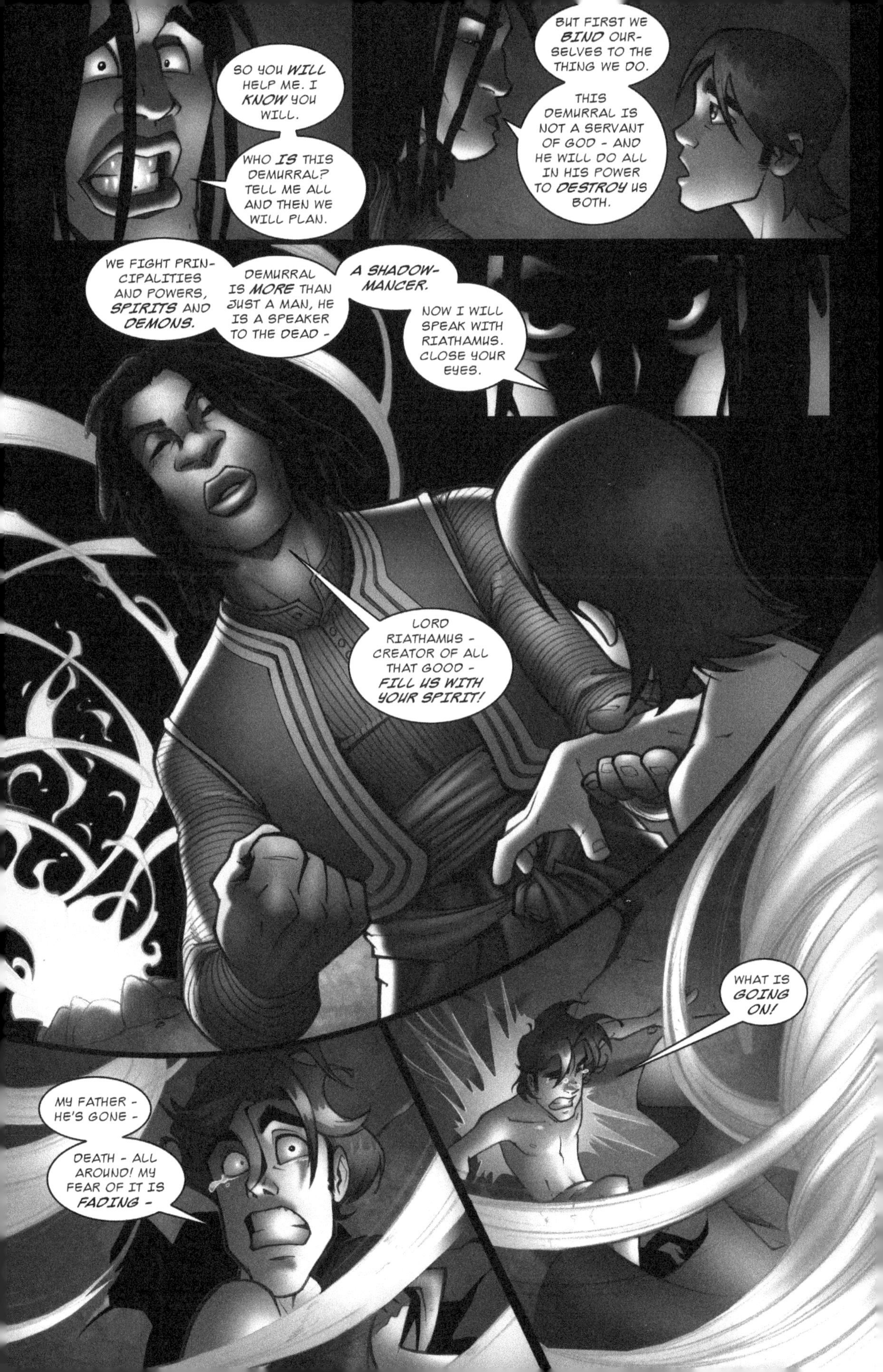
SO YOU WILL HELP ME. I KNOW YOU WILL.
WHO IS THIS DEMURRAL? TELL ME ALL AND THEN WE WILL PLAN.
BUT FIRST WE BIND OURSELVES TO THE THING WE DO.
THIS DEMURRAL IS NOT A SERVANT OF GOD - AND HE WILL DO ALL IN HIS POWER TO DESTROY US BOTH.
WE FIGHT PRINCIPALITIES AND POWERS, SPIRITS AND DEMONS.
DEMURRAL IS MORE THAN JUST A MAN, HE IS A SPEAKER TO THE DEAD -
A SHADOWMANCER.
NOW I WILL SPEAK WITH RIATHAMUS. CLOSE YOUR EYES.
LORD RIATHAMUS - CREATOR OF ALL THAT GOOD - FILL US WITH YOUR SPIRIT!
WHAT IS GOING ON!
MY FATHER - HE'S GONE -
DEATH - ALL AROUND! MY FEAR OF IT IS FADING -

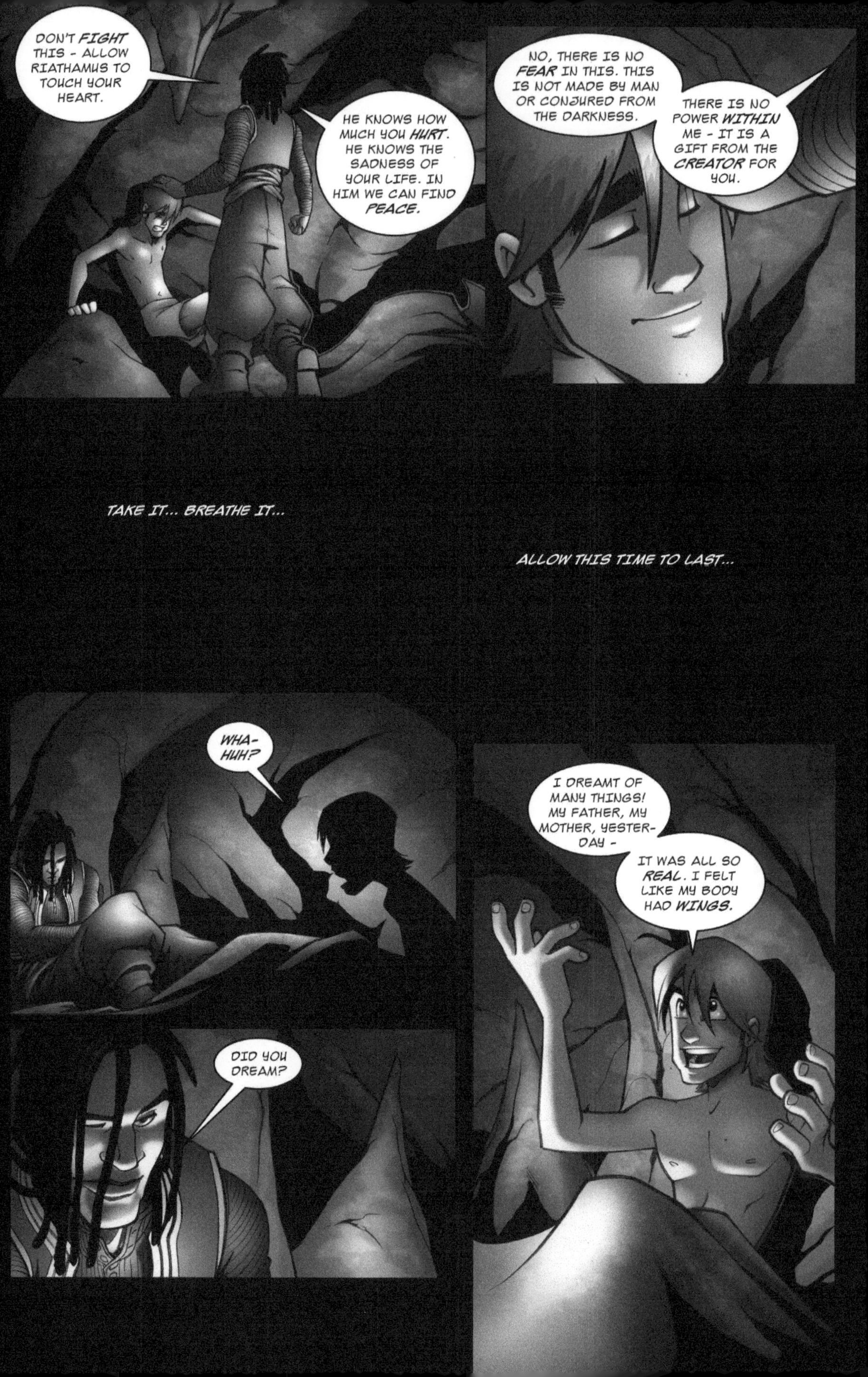
DON'T FIGHT THIS - ALLOW RIATHAMUS TO TOUCH YOUR HEART.
HE KNOWS HOW MUCH YOU HURT. HE KNOWS THE SADNESS OF YOUR LIFE. IN HIM WE CAN FIND PEACE.
NO, THERE IS NO FEAR IN THIS. THIS IS NOT MADE BY MAN OR CONJURED FROM THE DARKNESS.
THERE IS NO POWER WITHIN ME - IT IS A GIFT FROM THE CREATOR FOR YOU.
TAKE IT... BREATHE IT...
ALLOW THIS TIME TO LAST...
WHA-HUH?
DID YOU DREAM?
I DREAMT OF MANY THINGS! MY FATHER, MY MOTHER, YESTER-DAY -
IT WAS ALL SO REAL. I FELT LIKE MY BODY HAD WINGS.

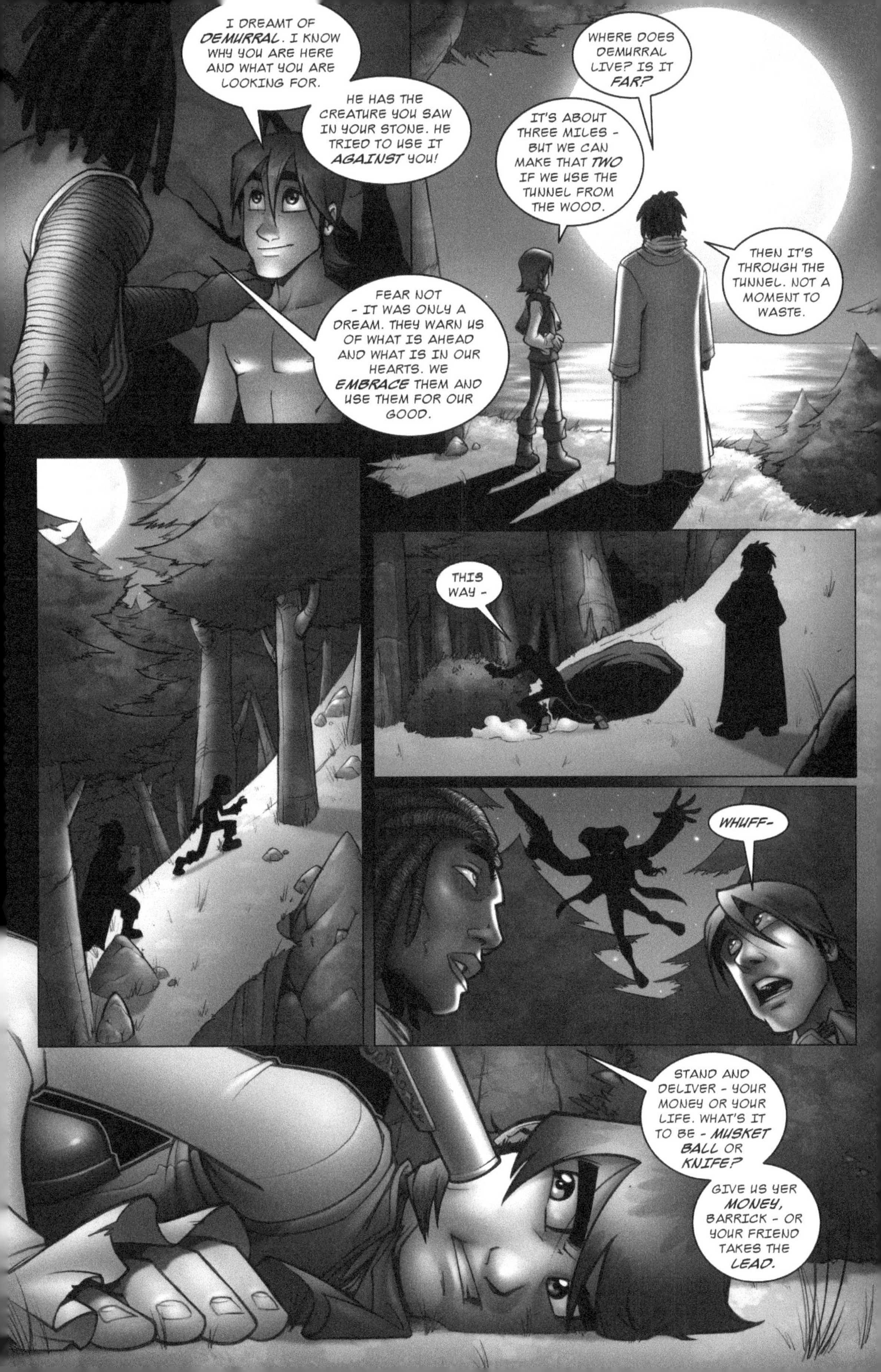

I DREAMT OF DEMURRAL. I KNOW WHY YOU ARE HERE AND WHAT YOU ARE LOOKING FOR.
HE HAS THE CREATURE YOU SAW IN YOUR STONE. HE TRIED TO USE IT AGAINST YOU!
FEAR NOT - IT WAS ONLY A DREAM. THEY WARN US OF WHAT IS AHEAD AND WHAT IS IN OUR HEARTS. WE EMBRACE THEM AND USE THEM FOR OUR GOOD.
WHERE DOES DEMURRAL LIVE? IS IT FAR?
IT'S ABOUT THREE MILES - BUT WE CAN MAKE THAT TWO IF WE USE THE TUNNEL FROM THE WOOD.
THEN IT'S THROUGH THE TUNNEL. NOT A MOMENT TO WASTE.
THIS WAY -
WHUFF-
STAND AND DELIVER - YOUR MONEY OR YOUR LIFE. WHAT'S IT TO BE - MUSKET BALL OR KNIFE?
GIVE US YER MONEY, BARRICK - OR YOUR FRIEND TAKES THE LEAD.

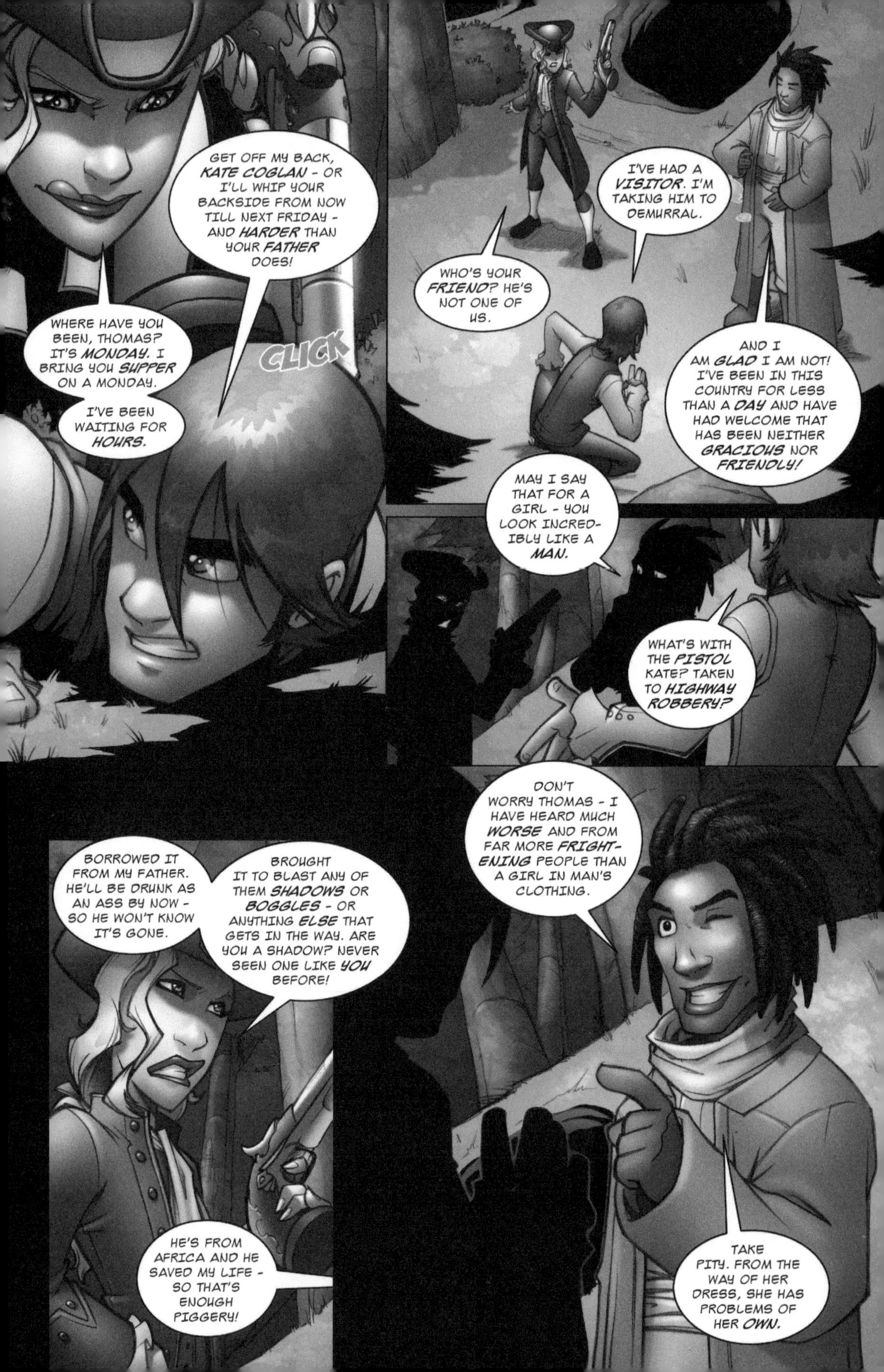
WHERE HAVE YOU BEEN, THOMAS? IT'S MONDAY. I BRING YOU SUPPER ON A MONDAY.
I'VE BEEN WAITING FOR HOURS.
CLICK
GET OFF MY BACK, KATE COGLAN - OR I'LL WHIP YOUR BACKSIDE FROM NOW TILL NEXT FRIDAY - AND HARDER THAN YOUR FATHER DOES!
WHO'S YOUR FRIEND? HE'S NOT ONE OF US.
I'VE HAD A VISITOR. I'M TAKING HIM TO DEMURRAL.
AND I AM GLAD I AM NOT! I'VE BEEN IN THIS COUNTRY FOR LESS THAN A DAY AND HAVE HAD WELCOME THAT HAS BEEN NEITHER GRACIOUS NOR FRIENDLY!
MAY I SAY THAT FOR A GIRL - YOU LOOK INCREDIBLY LIKE A MAN.
WHAT'S WITH THE PISTOL KATE? TAKEN TO HIGHWAY ROBBERY?
BORROWED IT FROM MY FATHER. HE'LL BE DRUNK AS AN ASS BY NOW - SO HE WON'T KNOW IT'S GONE.
BROUGHT IT TO BLAST ANY OF THEM SHADOWS OR BOGGLES - OR ANYTHING ELSE THAT GETS IN THE WAY. ARE YOU A SHADOW? NEVER SEEN ONE LIKE YOU BEFORE!
HE'S FROM AFRICA AND HE SAVED MY LIFE - SO THAT'S ENOUGH PIGGERY!
DON'T WORRY THOMAS - I HAVE HEARD MUCH WORSE AND FROM FAR MORE FRIGHTENING PEOPLE THAN A GIRL IN MAN'S CLOTHING.
TAKE PITY. FROM THE WAY OF HER DRESS, SHE HAS PROBLEMS OF HER OWN.

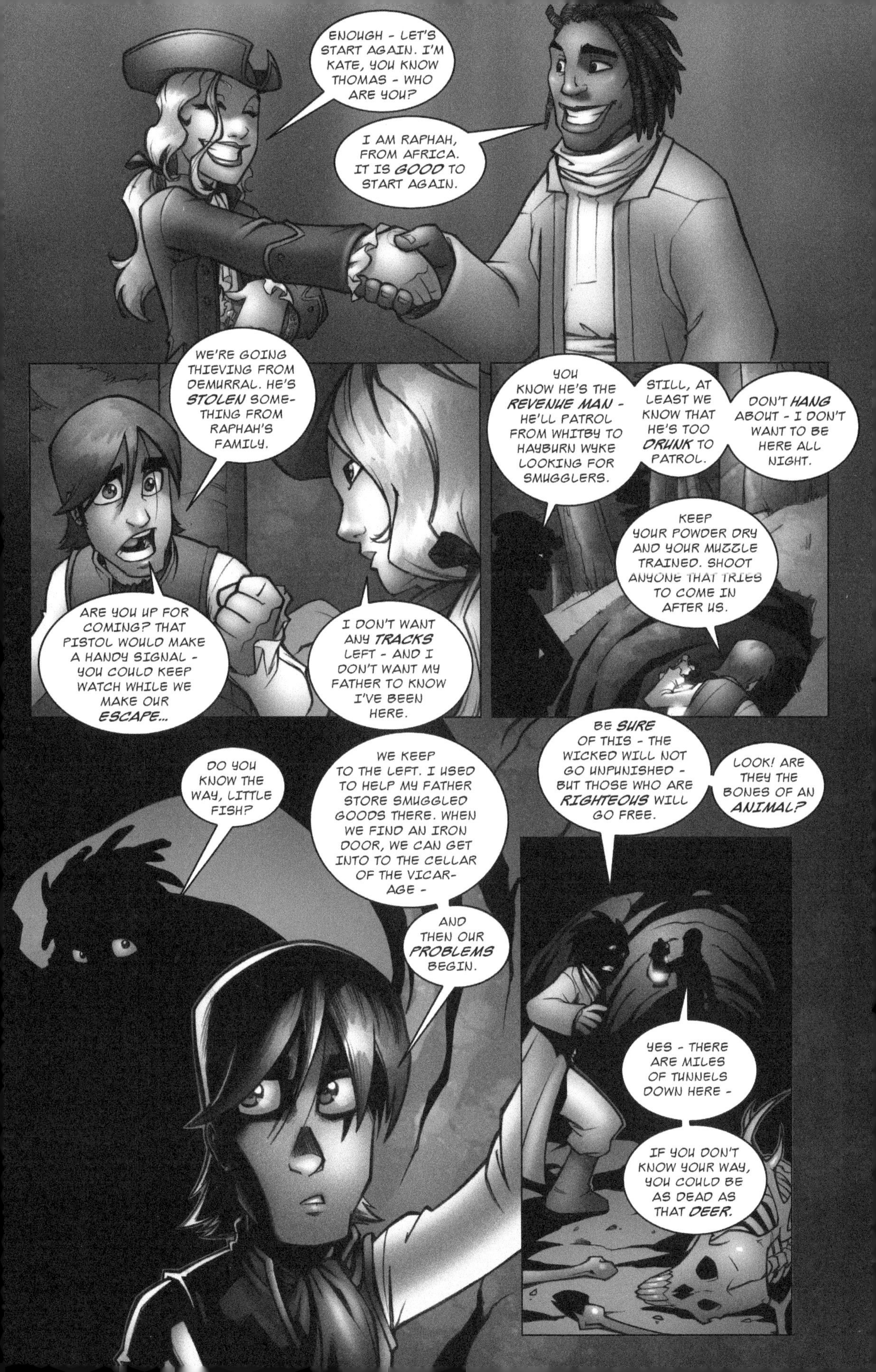
ENOUGH - LET'S START AGAIN. I'M KATE, YOU KNOW THOMAS - WHO ARE YOU?
I AM RAPHAH, FROM AFRICA. IT IS GOOD TO START AGAIN.
WE'RE GOING THIEVING FROM DEMURRAL. HE'S STOLEN SOMETHING FROM RAPHAH'S FAMILY.
ARE YOU UP FOR COMING? THAT PISTOL WOULD MAKE A HANDY SIGNAL - YOU COULD KEEP WATCH WHILE WE MAKE OUR ESCAPE...
I DON'T WANT ANY TRACKS LEFT - AND I DON'T WANT MY FATHER TO KNOW I'VE BEEN HERE.
YOU KNOW HE'S THE REVENUE MAN - HE'LL PATROL FROM WHITBY TO HAYBURN WYKE LOOKING FOR SMUGGLERS.
STILL, AT LEAST WE KNOW THAT HE'S TOO DRUNK TO PATROL.
DON'T HANG ABOUT - I DON'T WANT TO BE HERE ALL NIGHT.
KEEP YOUR POWDER DRY AND YOUR MUZZLE TRAINED. SHOOT ANYONE THAT TRIES TO COME IN AFTER US.
DO YOU KNOW THE WAY, LITTLE FISH?
WE KEEP TO THE LEFT. I USED TO HELP MY FATHER STORE SMUGGLED GOODS THERE. WHEN WE FIND AN IRON DOOR, WE CAN GET INTO TO THE CELLAR OF THE VICAR-AGE -
AND THEN OUR PROBLEMS BEGIN.
BE SURE OF THIS - THE WICKED WILL NOT GO UNPUNISHED - BUT THOSE WHO ARE RIGHTEOUS WILL GO FREE.
LOOK! ARE THEY THE BONES OF AN ANIMAL?
YES - THERE ARE MILES OF TUNNELS DOWN HERE -
IF YOU DON'T KNOW YOUR WAY, YOU COULD BE AS DEAD AS THAT DEER.

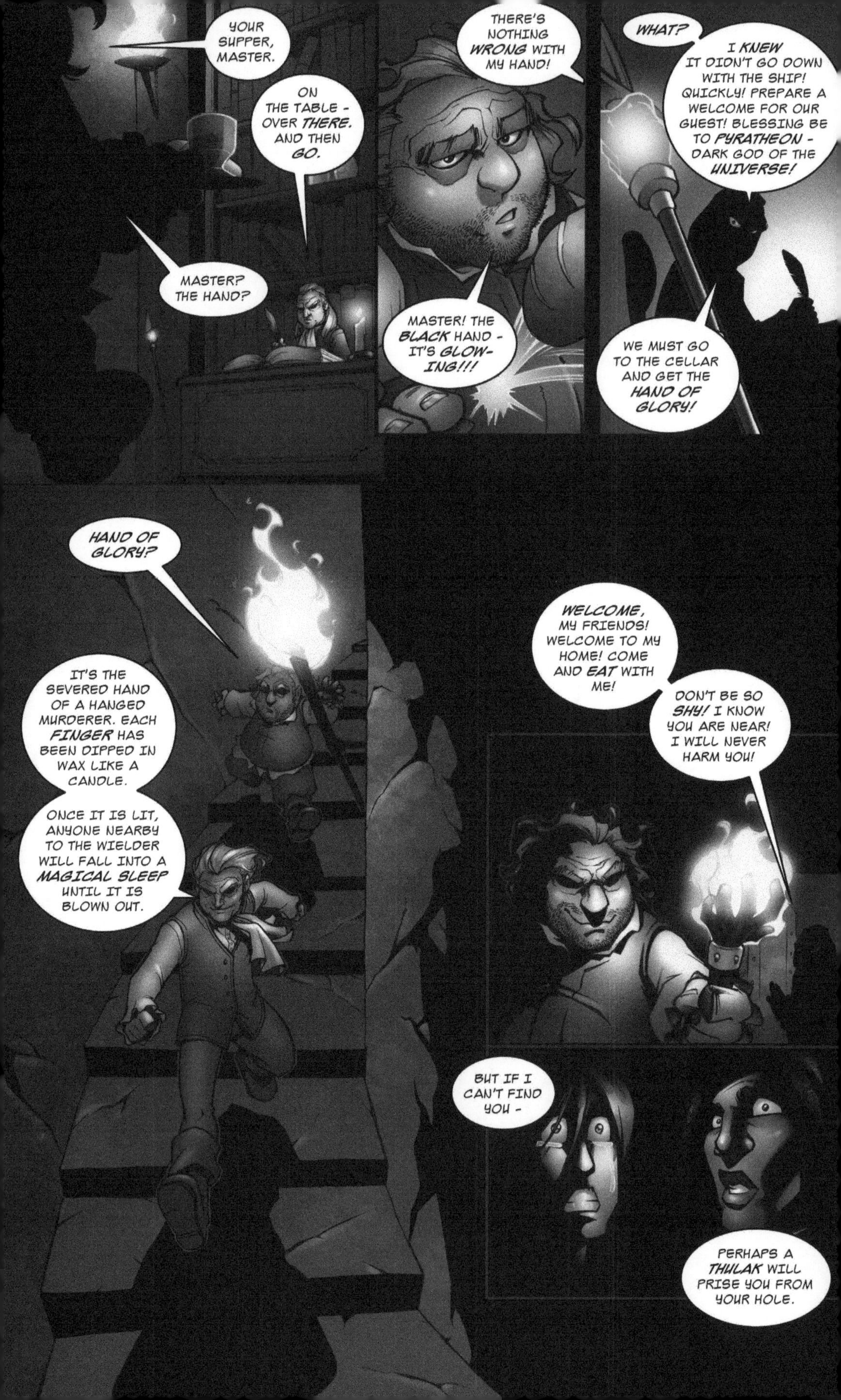
YOUR SUPPER, MASTER.
ON THE TABLE - OVER THERE. AND THEN GO.
MASTER? THE HAND?
THERE'S NOTHING WRONG WITH MY HAND!
MASTER! THE BLACK HAND - IT'S GLOWING!!!
WHAT?
I KNEW IT DIDN'T GO DOWN WITH THE SHIP! QUICKLY! PREPARE A WELCOME FOR OUR GUEST! BLESSING BE TO PYRATHEON - DARK GOD OF THE UNIVERSE!
WE MUST GO TO THE CELLAR AND GET THE HAND OF GLORY!
HAND OF GLORY?
IT'S THE SEVERED HAND OF A HANGED MURDERER. EACH FINGER HAS BEEN DIPPED IN WAX LIKE A CANDLE.
ONCE IT IS LIT, ANYONE NEARBY TO THE WIELDER WILL FALL INTO A MAGICAL SLEEP UNTIL IT IS BLOWN OUT.
WELCOME, MY FRIENDS! WELCOME TO MY HOME! COME AND EAT WITH ME!
DON'T BE SO SHY! I KNOW YOU ARE NEAR! I WILL NEVER HARM YOU!
BUT IF I CAN'T FIND YOU -
PERHAPS A THULAK WILL PRISE YOU FROM YOUR HOLE.

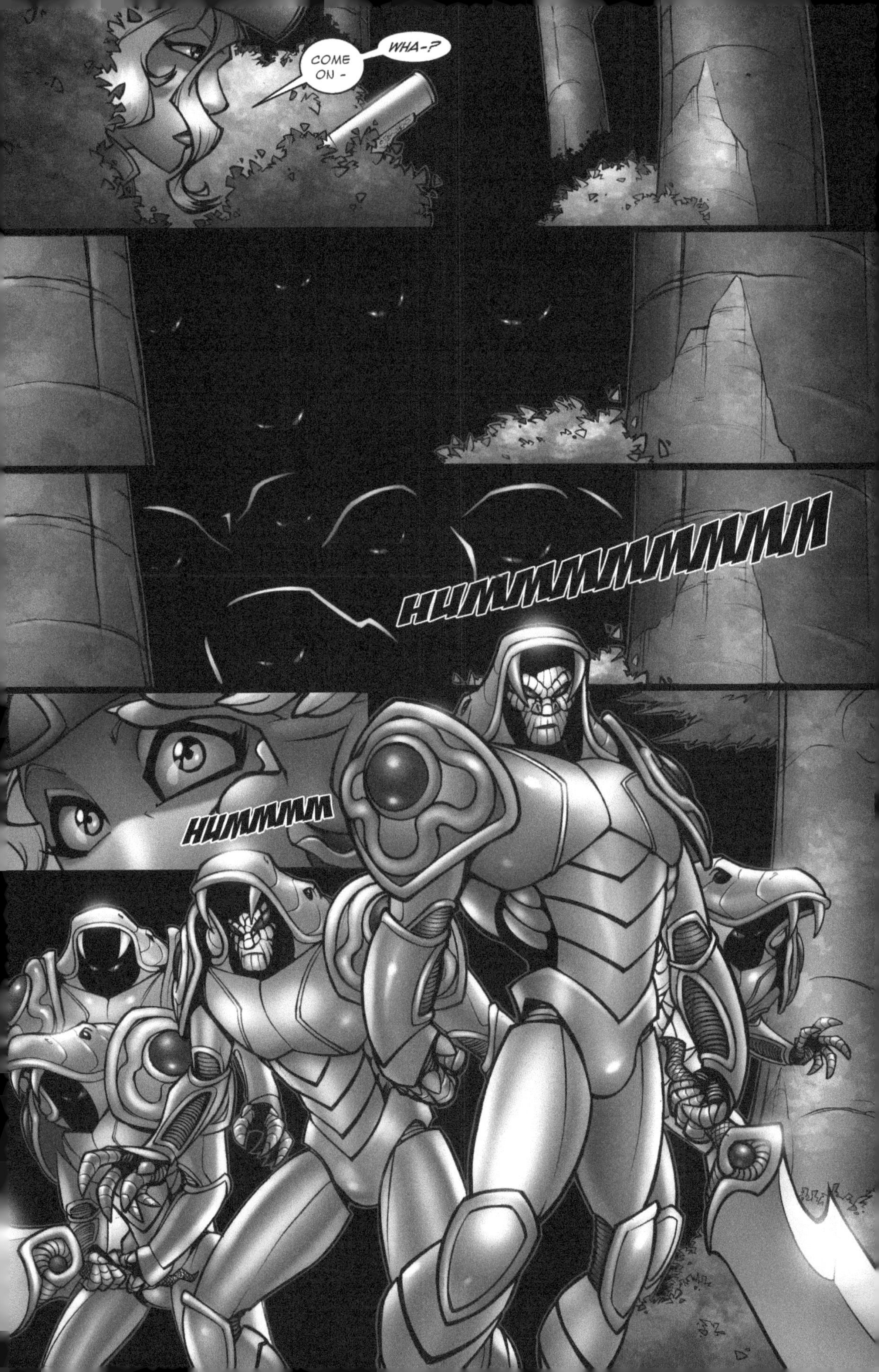
COME ON -
WHA-?
HUMMMMMMMMMMM
HUMMMM

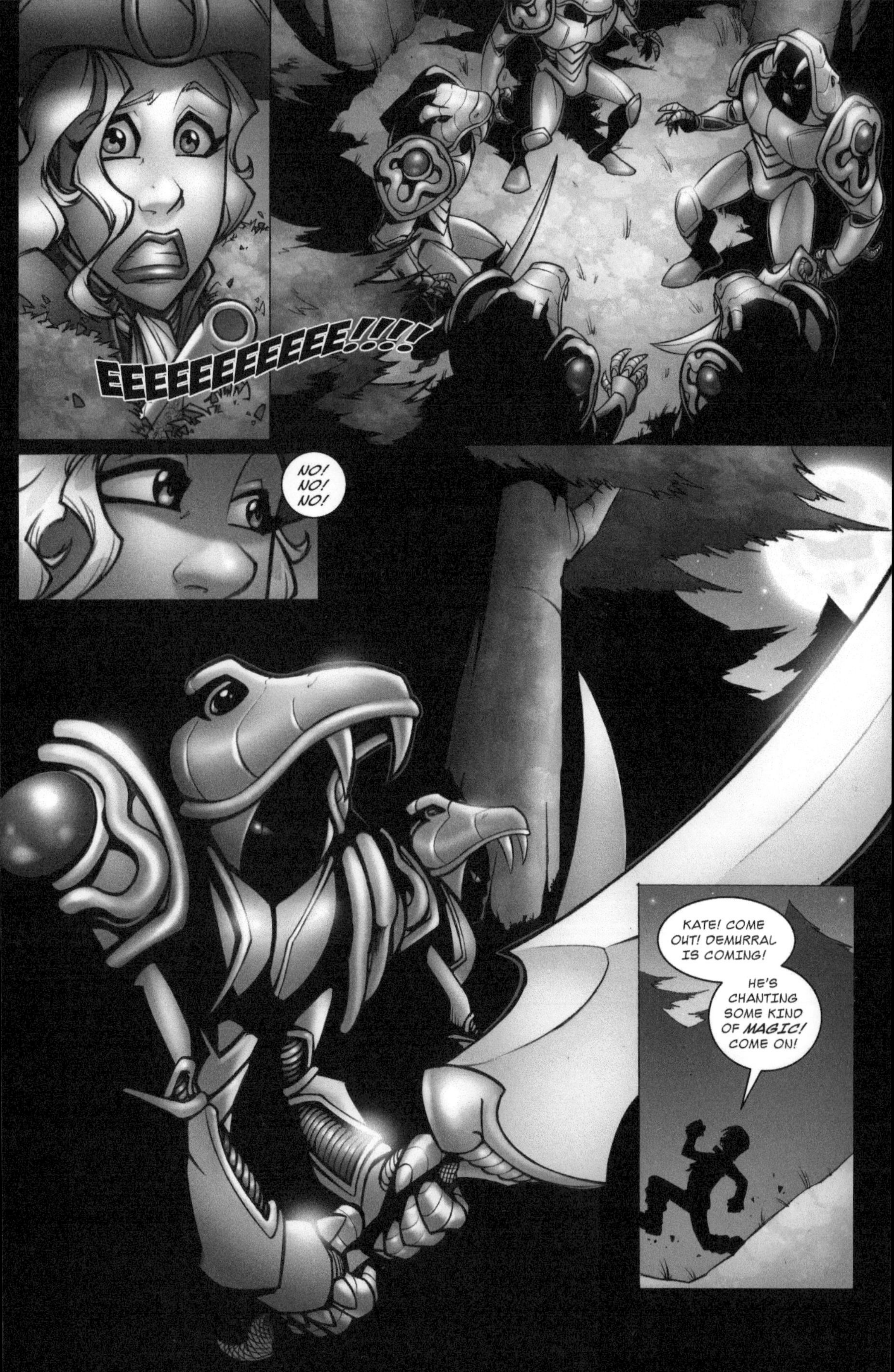
EEEEEEEEEEE!!!!!
NO! NO! NO!
KATE! COME OUT! DEMURRAL IS COMING!
HE'S CHANTING SOME KIND OF MAGIC! COME ON!

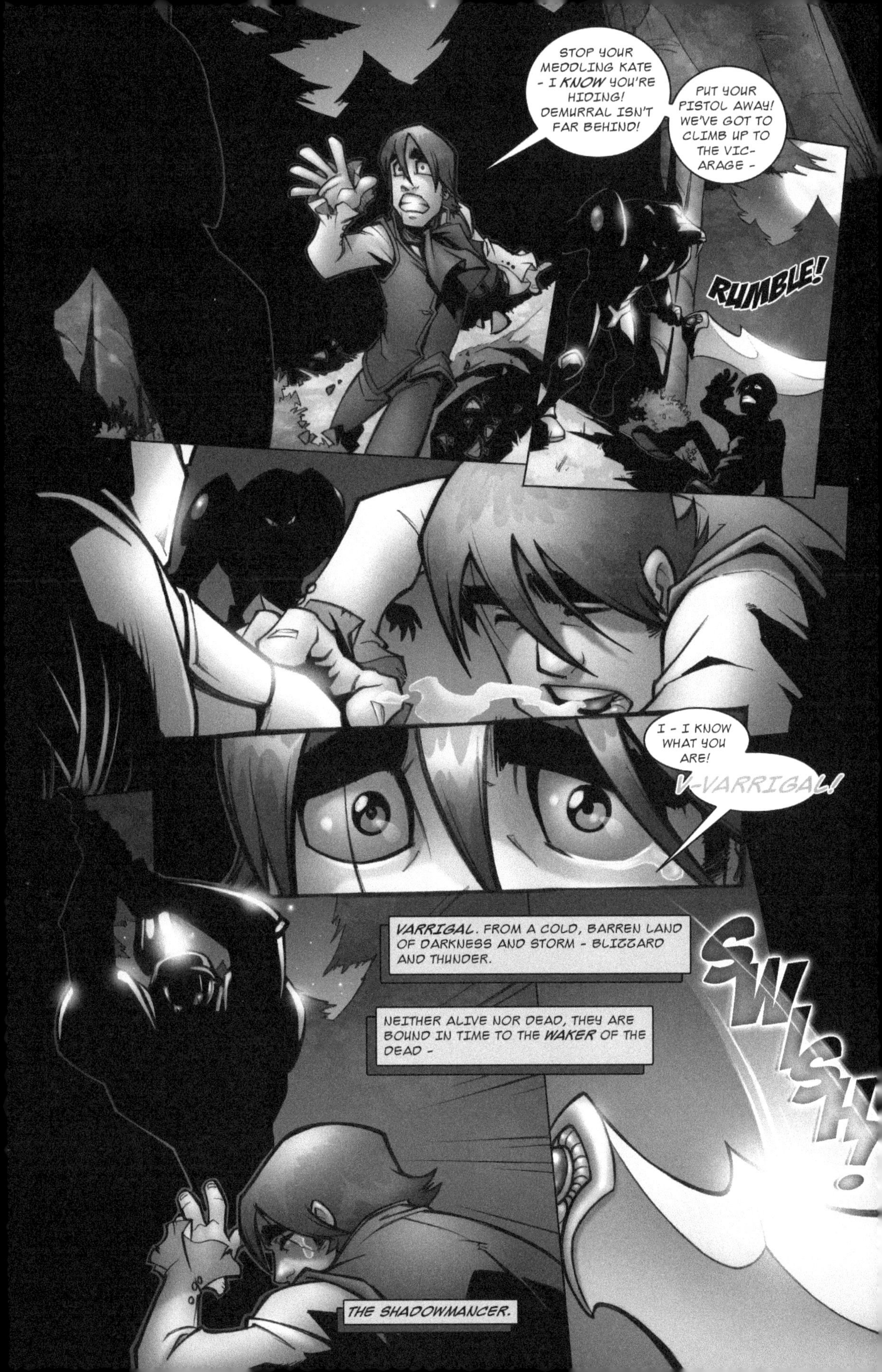
STOP YOUR MEDDLING KATE - I KNOW YOU'RE HIDING! DEMURRAL ISN'T FAR BEHIND!
PUT YOUR PISTOL AWAY! WE'VE GOT TO CLIMB UP TO THE VIC-ARAGE -
RUMBLE!
I - I KNOW WHAT YOU ARE! V-VARRIGAL!
VARRIGAL. FROM A COLD, BARREN LAND OF DARKNESS AND STORM - BLIZZARD AND THUNDER.
SWISH!
NEITHER ALIVE NOR DEAD, THEY ARE BOUND IN TIME TO THE WAKER OF THE DEAD -
THE SHADOWMANCER.

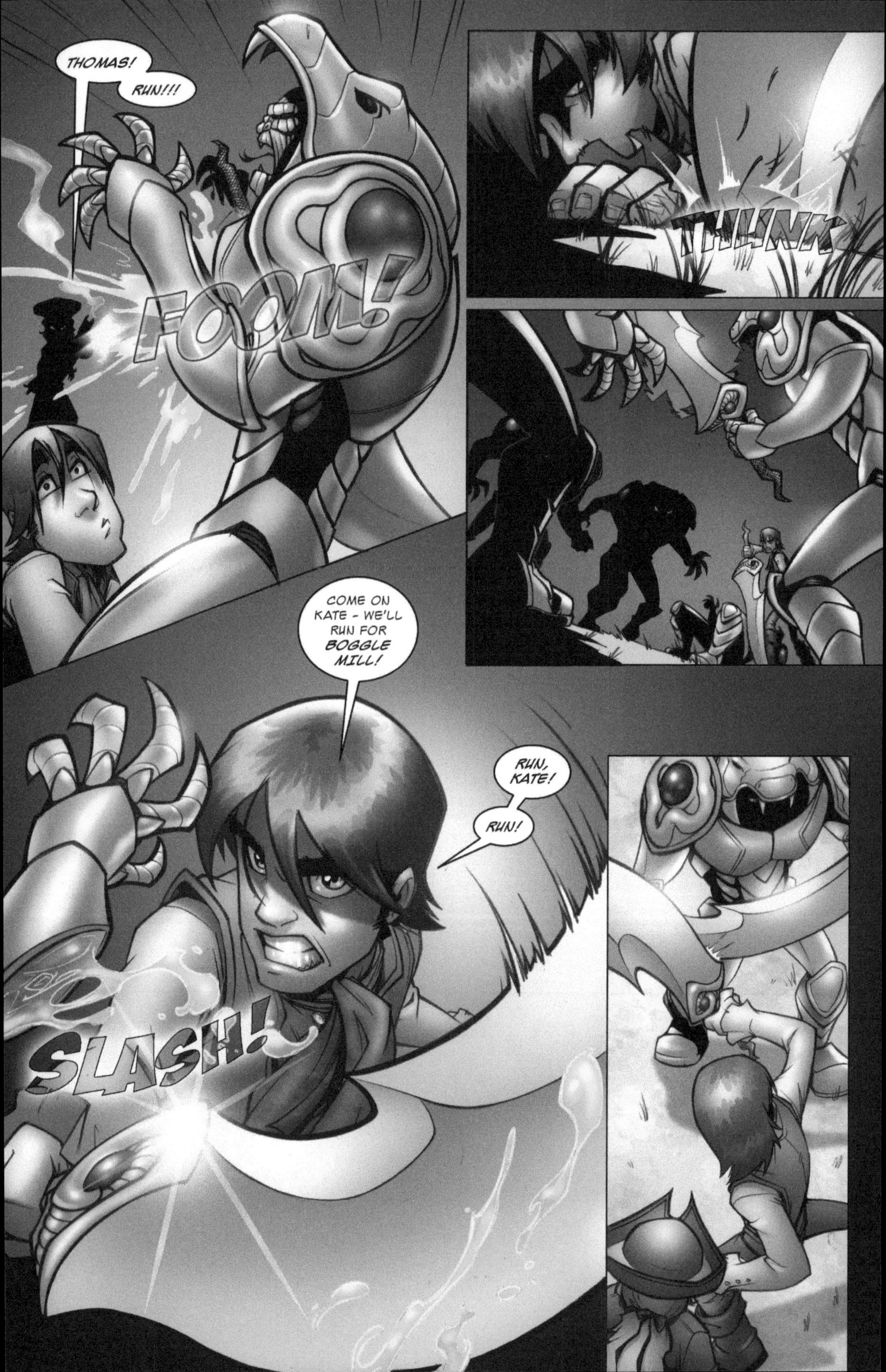
THOMAS!
RUN!!!
FOOM!
THUNK
COME ON KATE - WE'LL RUN FOR BOGGLE MILL!
RUN, KATE!
RUN!
SLASH!

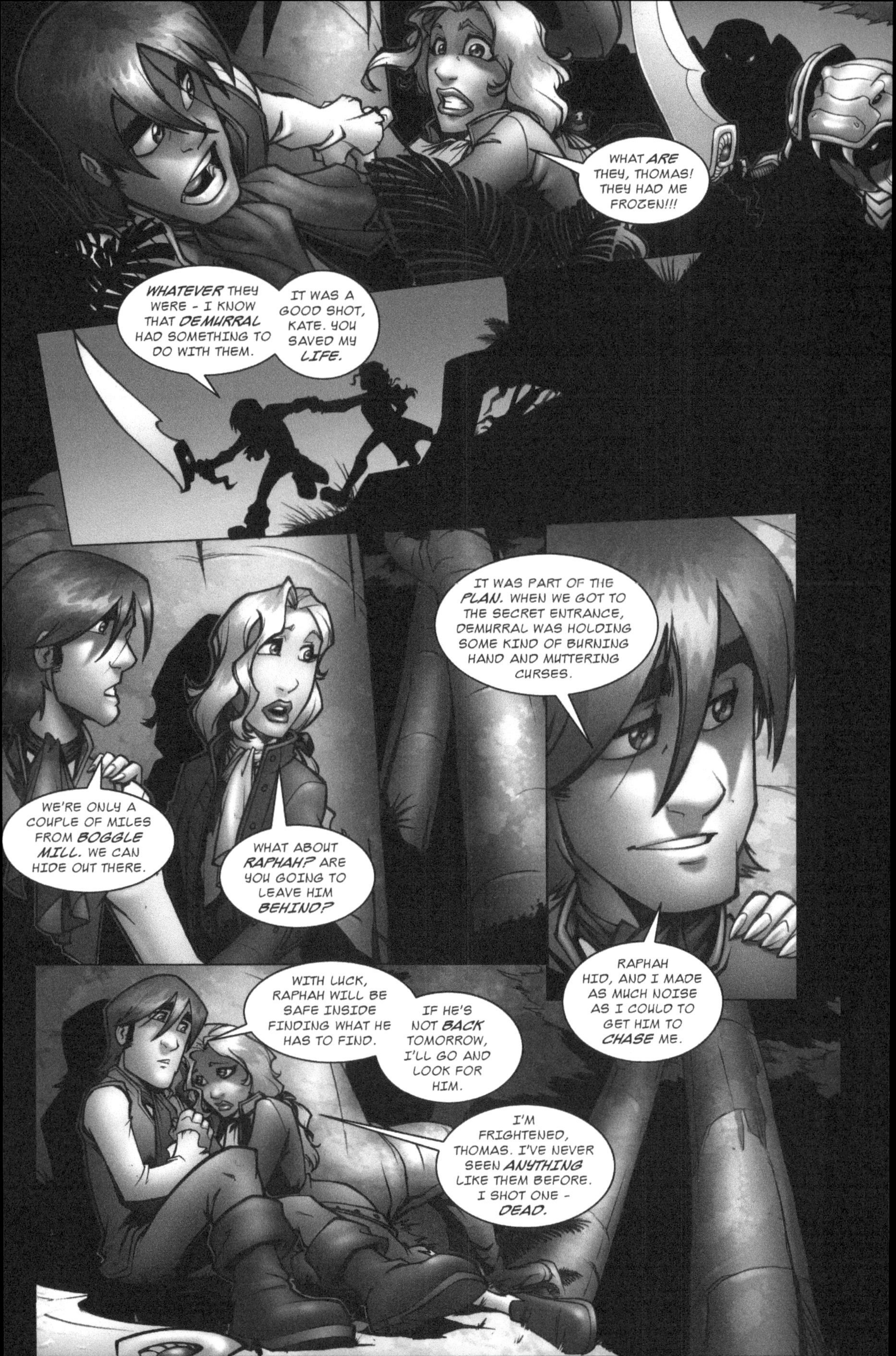
WHAT ARE THEY, THOMAS! THEY HAD ME FROZEN!!!
WHATEVER THEY WERE - I KNOW THAT DEMURRAL HAD SOMETHING TO DO WITH THEM.
IT WAS A GOOD SHOT, KATE. YOU SAVED MY LIFE.
WE'RE ONLY A COUPLE OF MILES FROM BOGGLE MILL. WE CAN HIDE OUT THERE.
WHAT ABOUT RAPHAH? ARE YOU GOING TO LEAVE HIM BEHIND?
IT WAS PART OF THE PLAN. WHEN WE GOT TO THE SECRET ENTRANCE, DEMURRAL WAS HOLDING SOME KIND OF BURNING HAND AND MUTTERING CURSES.
RAPHAH HID, AND I MADE AS MUCH NOISE AS I COULD TO GET HIM TO CHASE ME.
WITH LUCK, RAPHAH WILL BE SAFE INSIDE FINDING WHAT HE HAS TO FIND.
IF HE'S NOT BACK TOMORROW, I'LL GO AND LOOK FOR HIM.
I'M FRIGHTENED, THOMAS. I'VE NEVER SEEN ANYTHING LIKE THEM BEFORE. I SHOT ONE - DEAD.

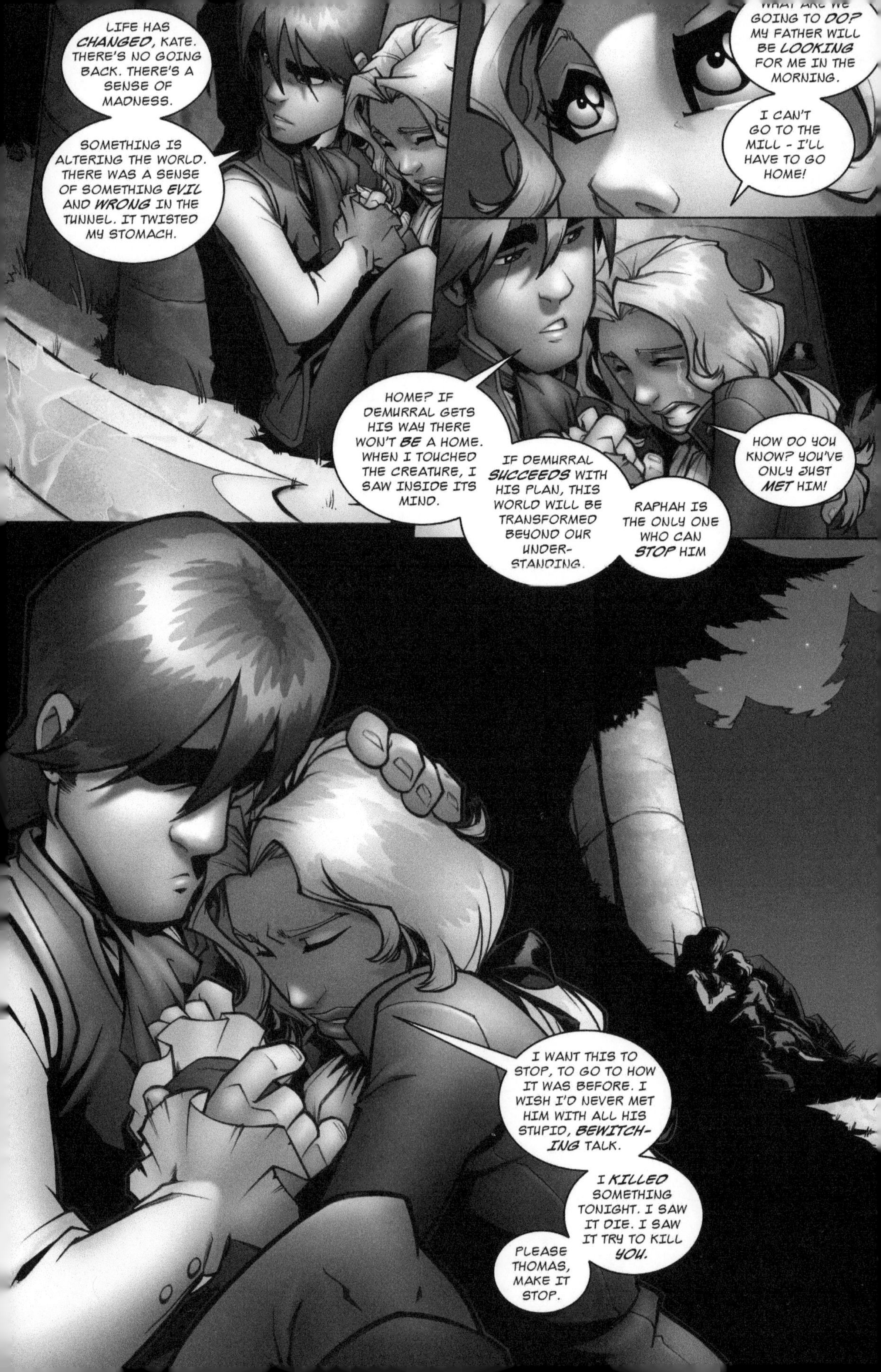
LIFE HAS CHANGED, KATE. THERE'S NO GOING BACK. THERE'S A SENSE OF MADNESS.
SOMETHING IS ALTERING THE WORLD. THERE WAS A SENSE OF SOMETHING EVIL AND WRONG IN THE TUNNEL. IT TWISTED MY STOMACH.
GOING TO DO? MY FATHER WILL BE LOOKING FOR ME IN THE MORNING.
I CAN'T GO TO THE MILL - I'LL HAVE TO GO HOME!
HOME? IF DEMURRAL GETS HIS WAY THERE WON'T BE A HOME. WHEN I TOUCHED THE CREATURE, I SAW INSIDE ITS MIND.
IF DEMURRAL SUCCEEDS WITH HIS PLAN, THIS WORLD WILL BE TRANSFORMED BEYOND OUR UNDER-STANDING.
HOW DO YOU KNOW? YOU'VE ONLY JUST MET HIM!
RAPHAH IS THE ONLY ONE WHO CAN STOP HIM
I WANT THIS TO STOP, TO GO TO HOW IT WAS BEFORE. I WISH I'D NEVER MET HIM WITH ALL HIS STUPID, BEWITCH-ING TALK.
I KILLED SOMETHING TONIGHT. I SAW IT DIE. I SAW IT TRY TO KILL YOU.
PLEASE THOMAS, MAKE IT STOP.

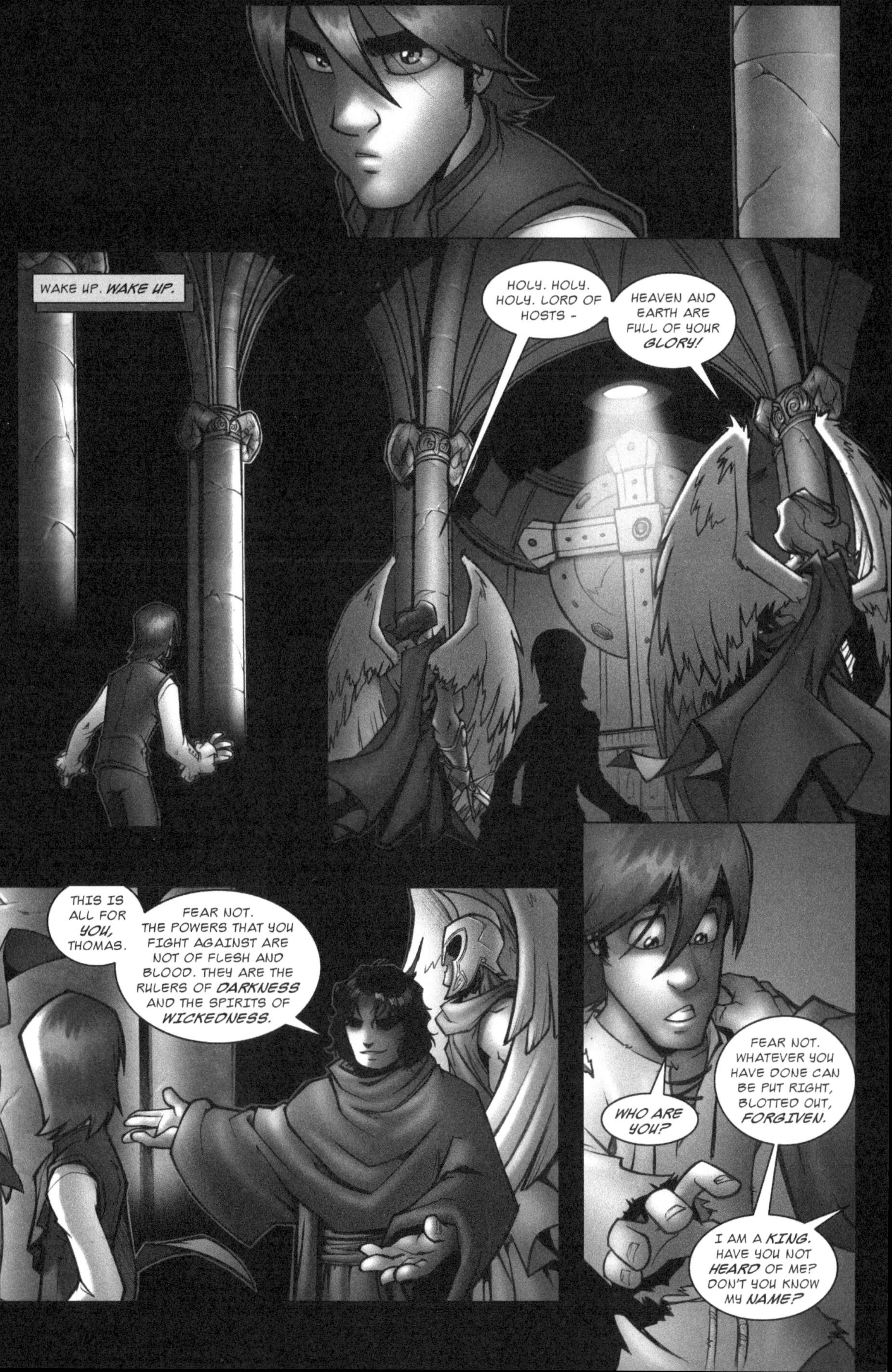
WAKE UP. WAKE UP.
HOLY. HOLY. HOLY. LORD OF HOSTS -
HEAVEN AND EARTH ARE FULL OF YOUR GLORY!
THIS IS ALL FOR YOU, THOMAS.
FEAR NOT. THE POWERS THAT YOU FIGHT AGAINST ARE NOT OF FLESH AND BLOOD. THEY ARE THE RULERS OF DARKNESS AND THE SPIRITS OF WICKEDNESS.
WHO ARE YOU?
FEAR NOT. WHATEVER YOU HAVE DONE CAN BE PUT RIGHT, BLOTTED OUT, FORGIVEN.
I AM A KING. HAVE YOU NOT HEARD OF ME? DON'T YOU KNOW MY NAME?

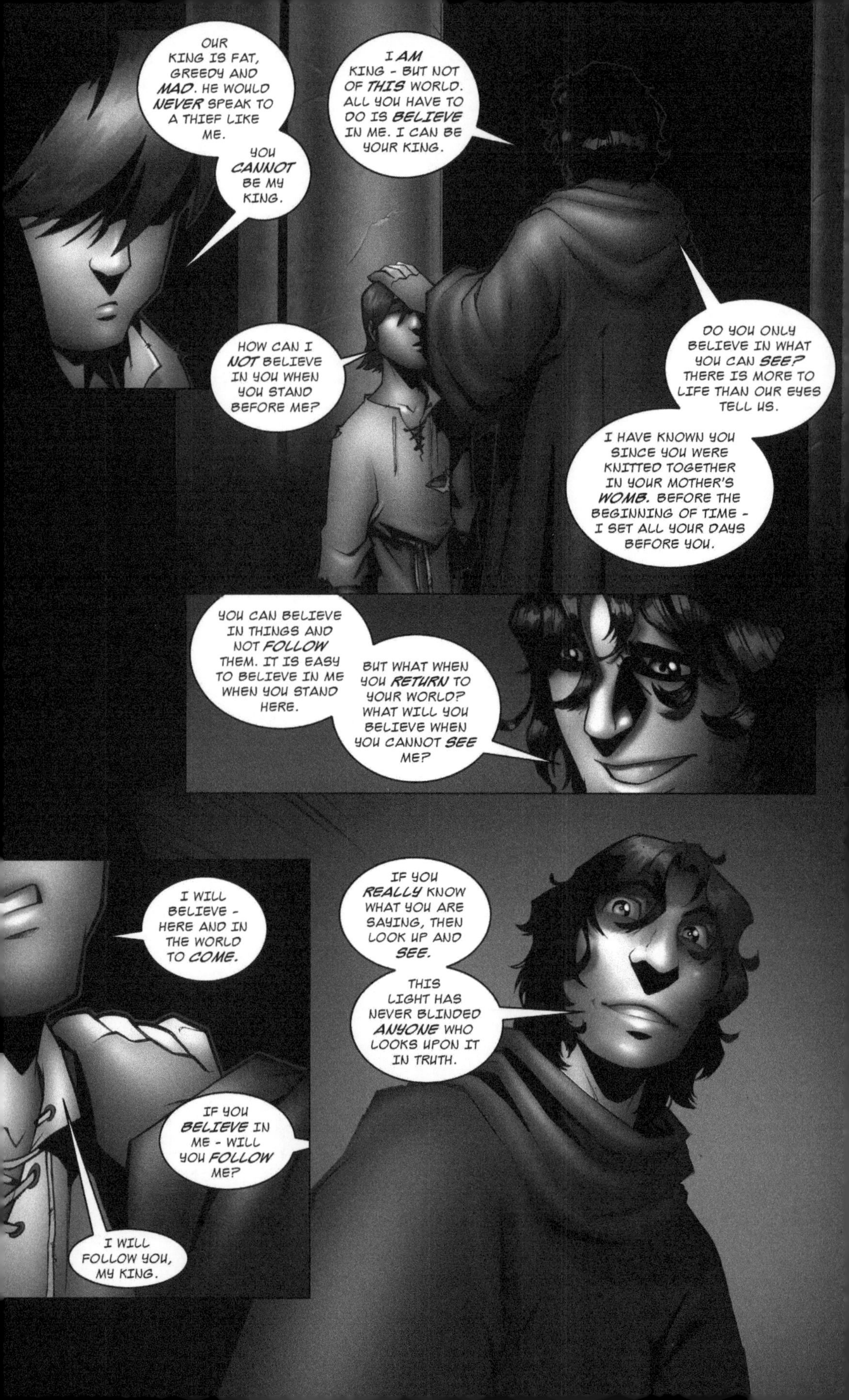
OUR KING IS FAT, GREEDY AND MAD. HE WOULD NEVER SPEAK TO A THIEF LIKE ME.
YOU CANNOT BE MY KING.
I AM KING - BUT NOT OF THIS WORLD. ALL YOU HAVE TO DO IS BELIEVE IN ME. I CAN BE YOUR KING.
HOW CAN I NOT BELIEVE IN YOU WHEN YOU STAND BEFORE ME?
DO YOU ONLY BELIEVE IN WHAT YOU CAN SEE? THERE IS MORE TO LIFE THAN OUR EYES TELL US.
I HAVE KNOWN YOU SINCE YOU WERE KNITTED TOGETHER IN YOUR MOTHER'S WOMB. BEFORE THE BEGINNING OF TIME - I SET ALL YOUR DAYS BEFORE YOU.
YOU CAN BELIEVE IN THINGS AND NOT FOLLOW THEM. IT IS EASY TO BELIEVE IN ME WHEN YOU STAND HERE.
BUT WHAT WHEN YOU RETURN TO YOUR WORLD? WHAT WILL YOU BELIEVE WHEN YOU CANNOT SEE ME?
I WILL BELIEVE - HERE AND IN THE WORLD TO COME.
IF YOU REALLY KNOW WHAT YOU ARE SAYING, THEN LOOK UP AND SEE.
THIS LIGHT HAS NEVER BLINDED ANYONE WHO LOOKS UPON IT IN TRUTH.
IF YOU BELIEVE IN ME - WILL YOU FOLLOW ME?
I WILL FOLLOW YOU, MY KING.

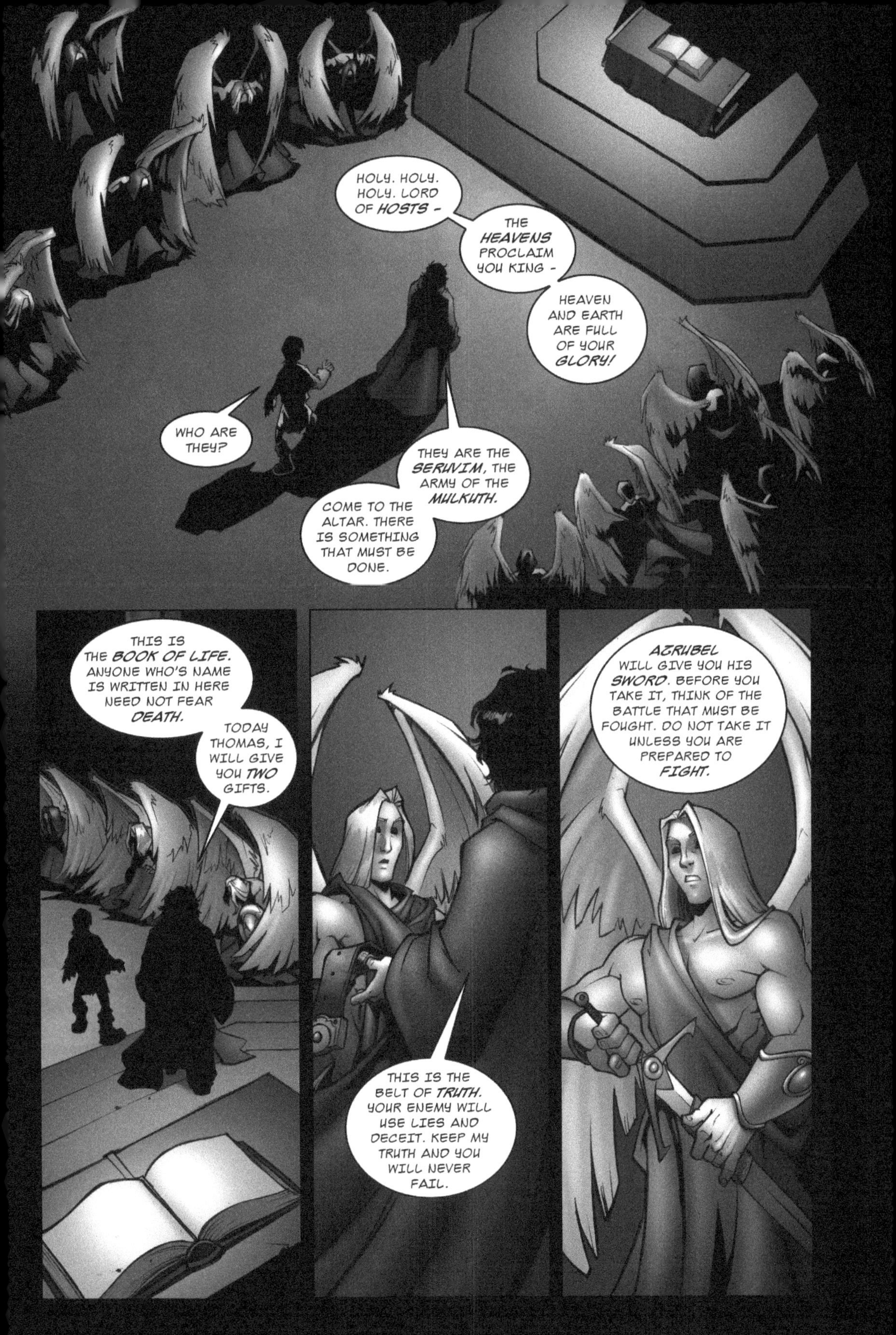
HOLY. HOLY. HOLY. LORD OF HOSTS -
THE HEAVENS PROCLAIM YOU KING -
HEAVEN AND EARTH ARE FULL OF YOUR GLORY!
WHO ARE THEY?
THEY ARE THE SERUVIM, THE ARMY OF THE MULKUTH.
COME TO THE ALTAR. THERE IS SOMETHING THAT MUST BE DONE.
THIS IS THE BOOK OF LIFE. ANYONE WHO'S NAME IS WRITTEN IN HERE NEED NOT FEAR DEATH.
TODAY THOMAS, I WILL GIVE YOU TWO GIFTS.
THIS IS THE BELT OF TRUTH. YOUR ENEMY WILL USE LIES AND DECEIT. KEEP MY TRUTH AND YOU WILL NEVER FAIL.
AZRUBEL WILL GIVE YOU HIS SWORD. BEFORE YOU TAKE IT, THINK OF THE BATTLE THAT MUST BE FOUGHT. DO NOT TAKE IT UNLESS YOU ARE PREPARED TO FIGHT.

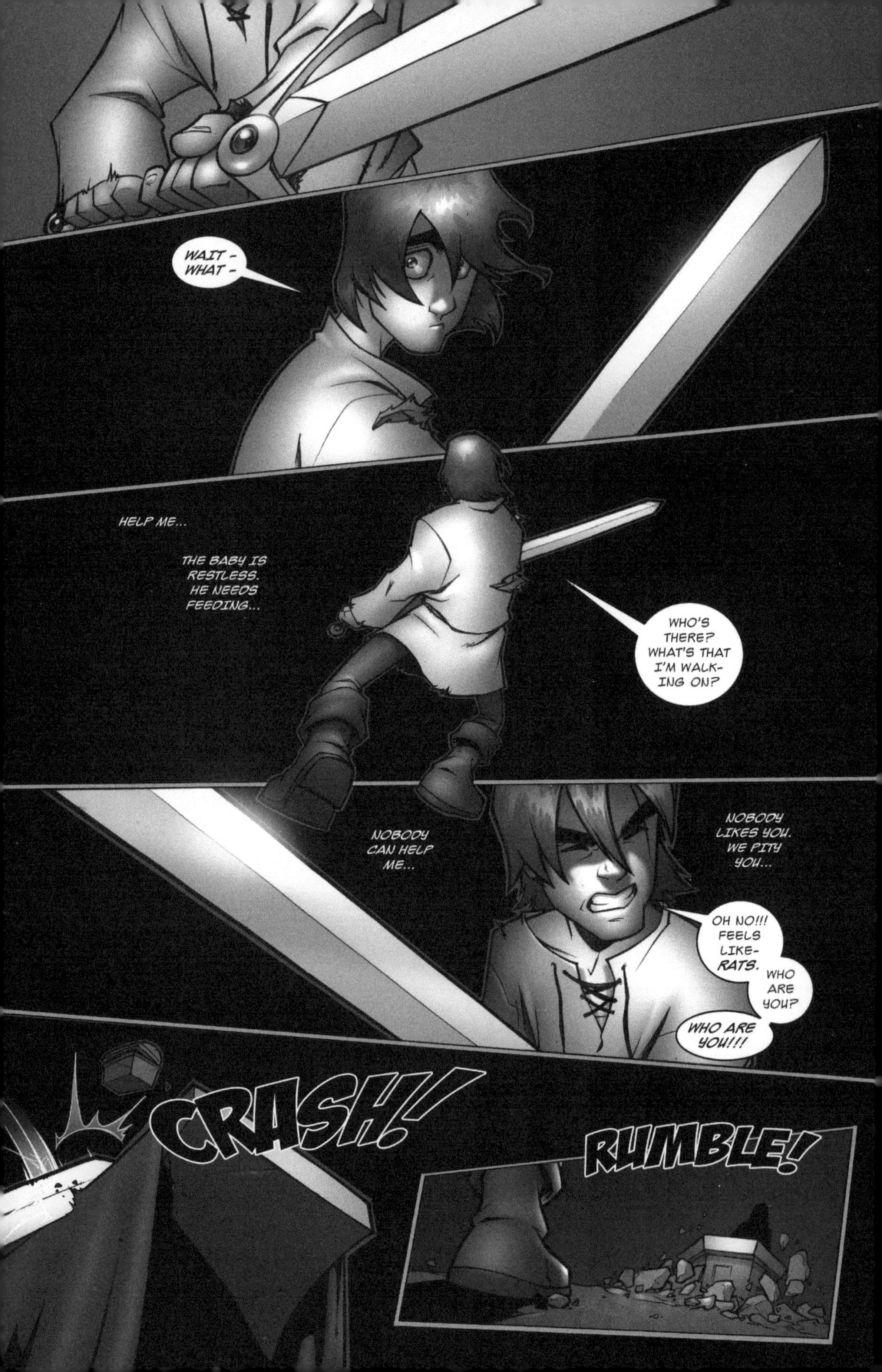
WAIT - WHAT -
HELP ME...
THE BABY IS RESTLESS. HE NEEDS FEEDING...
WHO'S THERE? WHAT'S THAT I'M WALKING ON?
NOBODY CAN HELP ME...
NOBODY LIKES YOU. WE PITY YOU...
OH NO!!! FEELS LIKE- RATS.
WHO ARE YOU?
WHO ARE YOU!!!
CRASH!
RUMBLE!

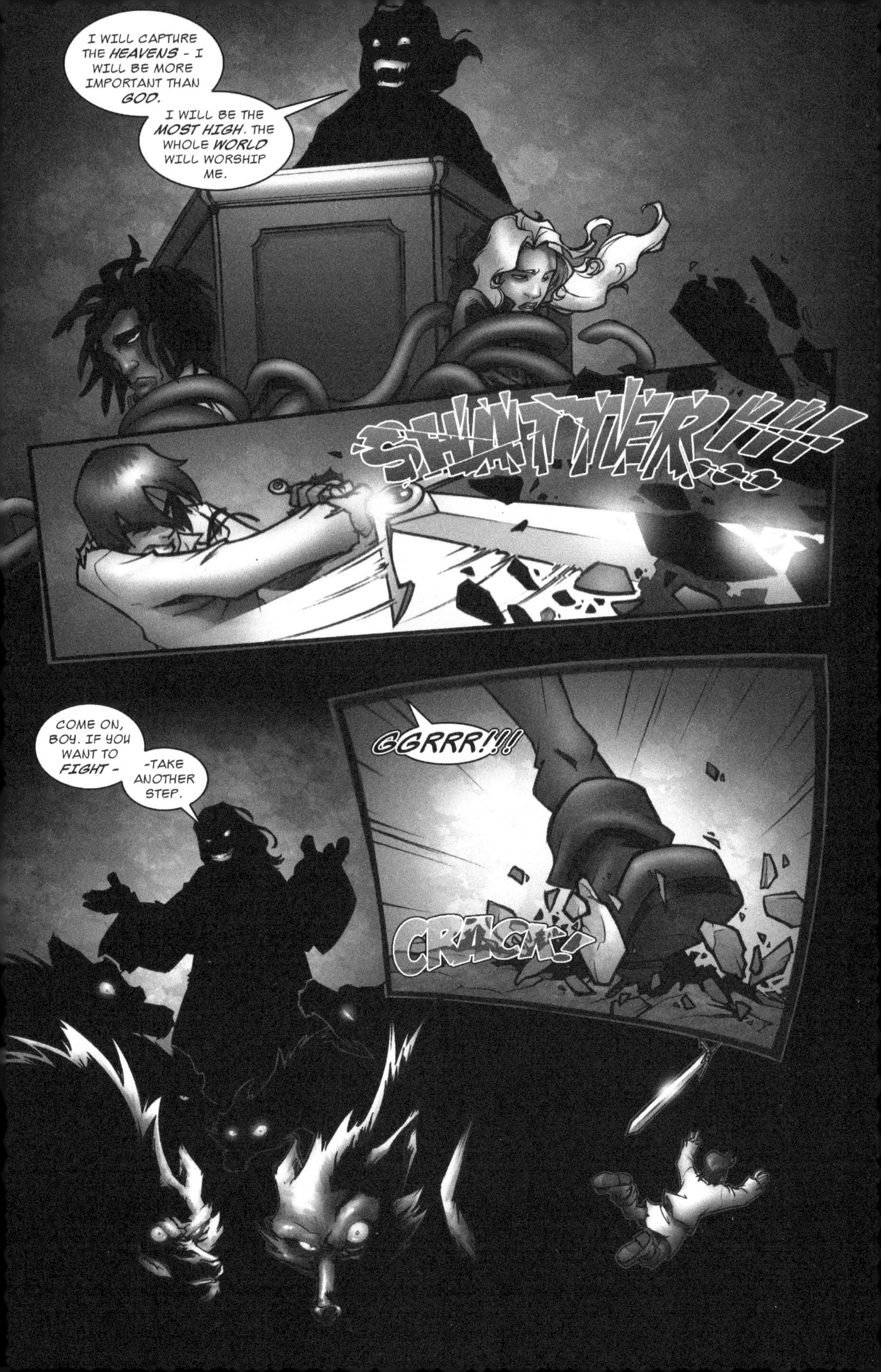
I WILL CAPTURE THE HEAVENS - I WILL BE MORE IMPORTANT THAN GOD.
I WILL BE THE MOST HIGH. THE WHOLE WORLD WILL WORSHIP ME.
SHATTER!!!!
GGRRR!!!
CRACK!
COME ON, BOY. IF YOU WANT TO FIGHT -
-TAKE ANOTHER STEP.

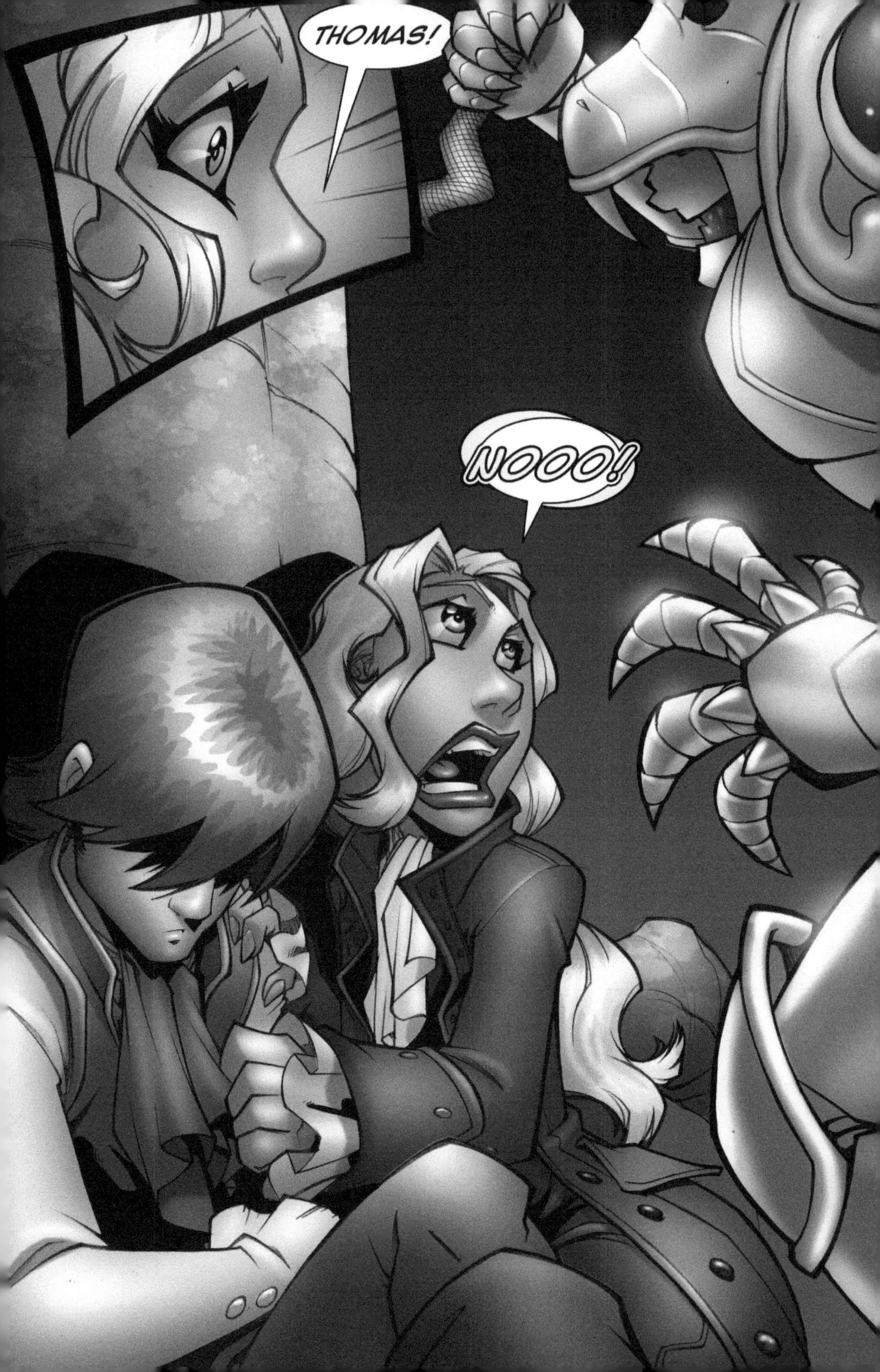
THOMAS!
NOOO!

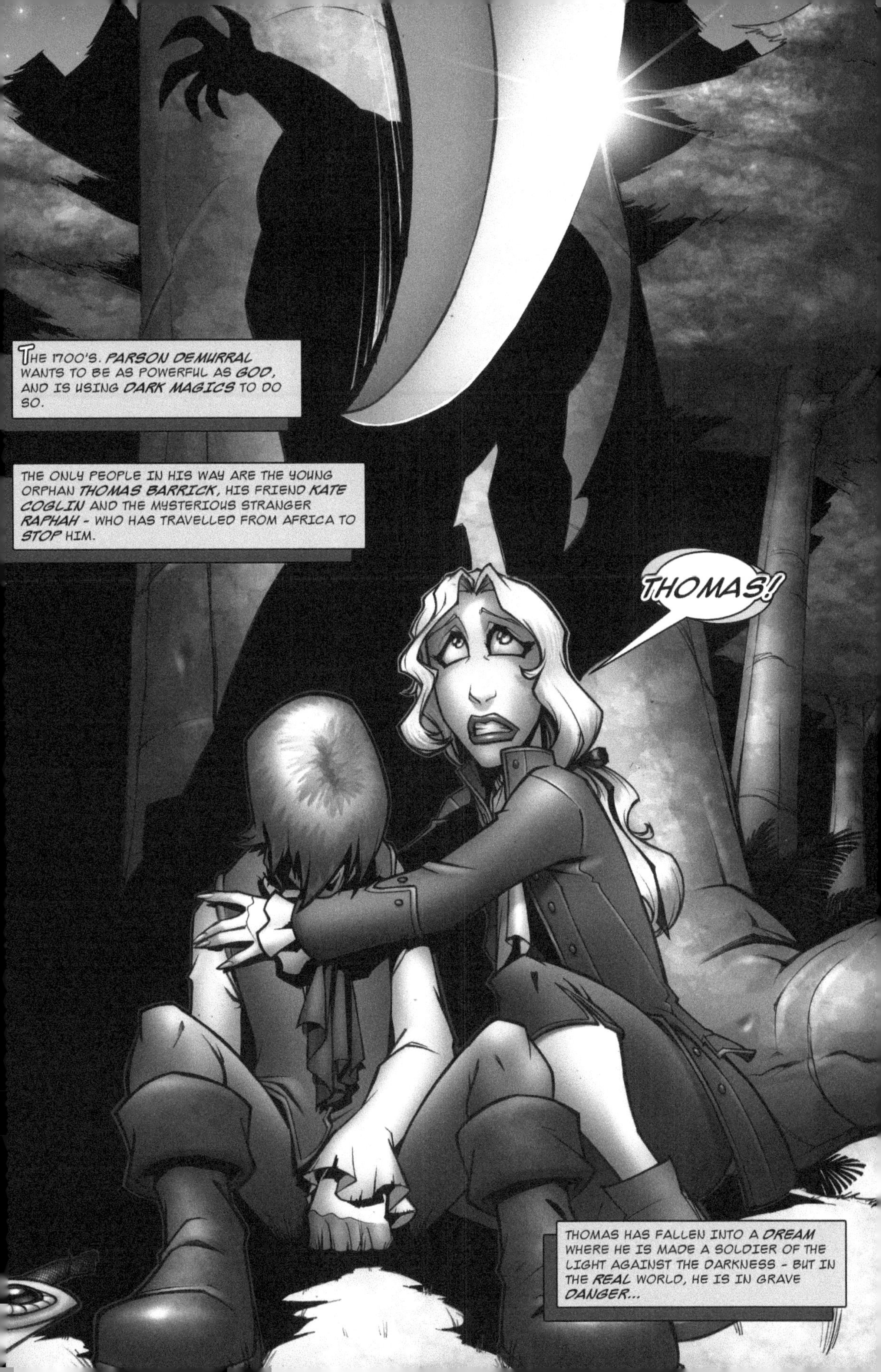
THE 1700'S. PARSON DEMURRAL WANTS TO BE AS POWERFUL AS GOD, AND IS USING DARK MAGICS TO DO SO.
THE ONLY PEOPLE IN HIS WAY ARE THE YOUNG ORPHAN THOMAS BARRICK, HIS FRIEND KATE COGLIN AND THE MYSTERIOUS STRANGER RAPHAH - WHO HAS TRAVELLED FROM AFRICA TO STOP HIM.
THOMAS!
THOMAS HAS FALLEN INTO A DREAM WHERE HE IS MADE A SOLDIER OF THE LIGHT AGAINST THE DARKNESS - BUT IN THE REAL WORLD, HE IS IN GRAVE DANGER...

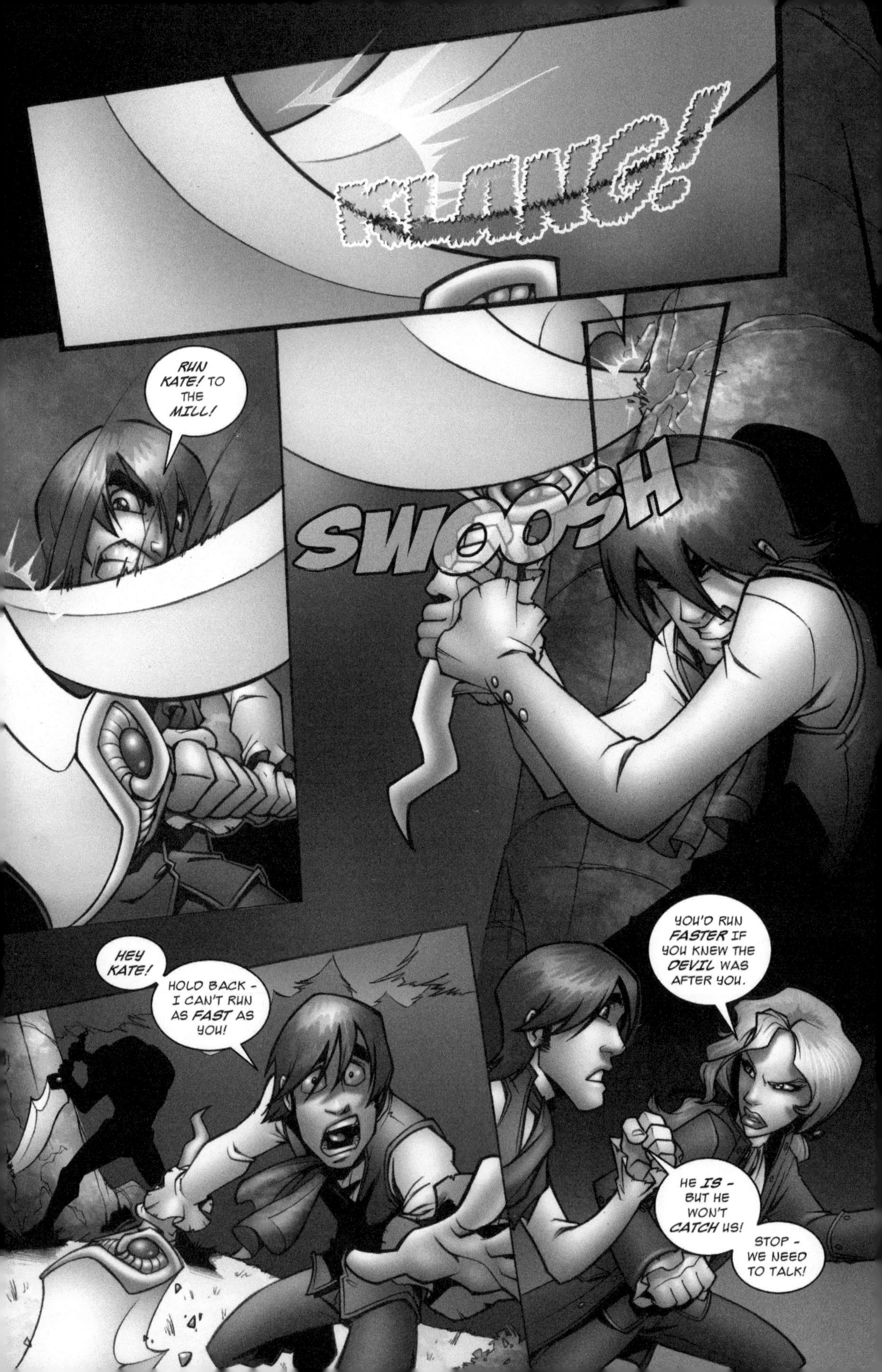
KLANG!
RUN KATE! TO THE MILL!
SWOOSH
HEY KATE!
HOLD BACK - I CAN'T RUN AS FAST AS YOU!
YOU'D RUN FASTER IF YOU KNEW THE DEVIL WAS AFTER YOU.
HE IS - BUT HE WON'T CATCH US!
STOP - WE NEED TO TALK!

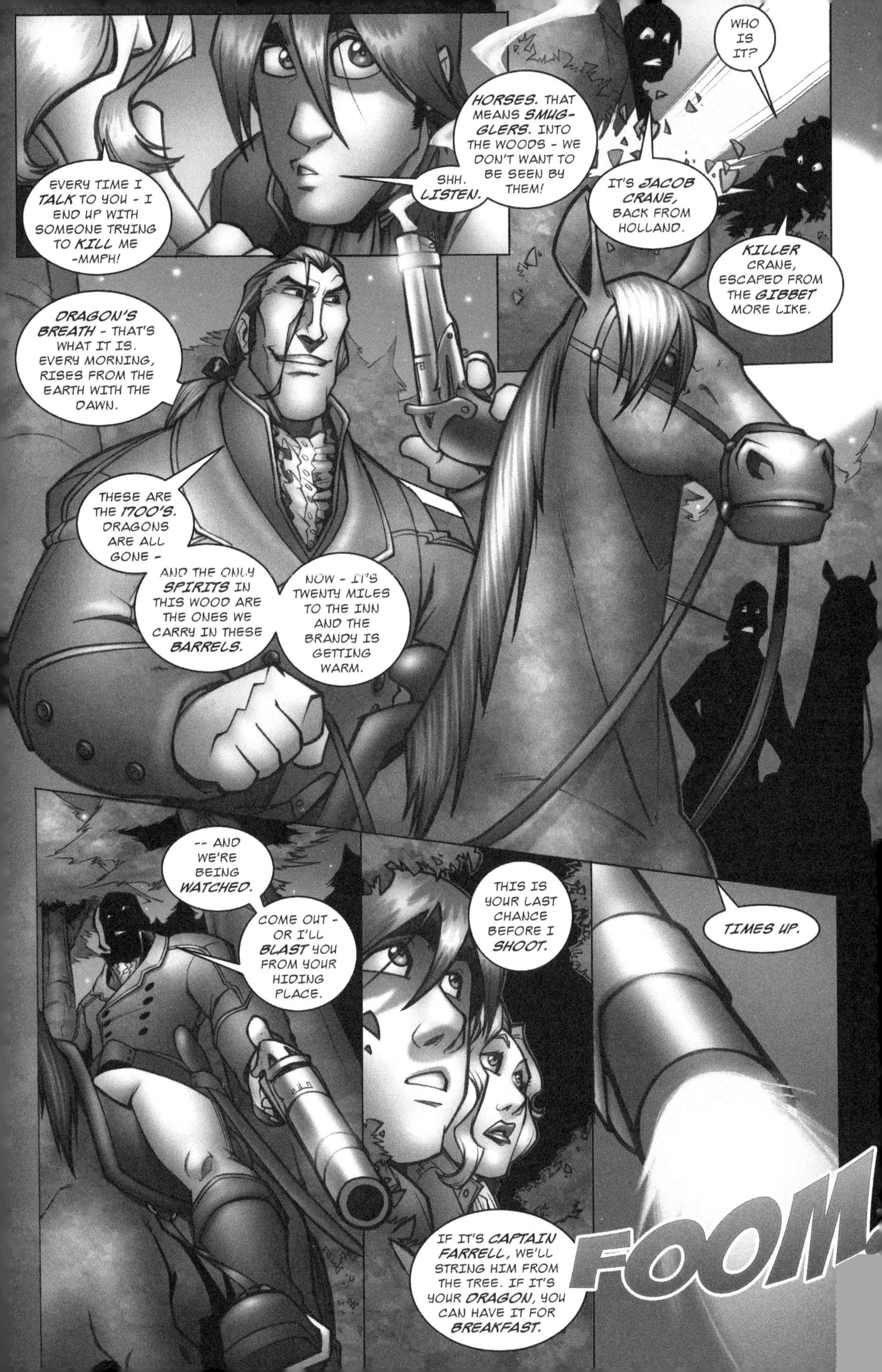
EVERY TIME I TALK TO YOU - I END UP WITH SOMEONE TRYING TO KILL ME -MMPH!
SHH. LISTEN.
HORSES. THAT MEANS SMUGGLERS. INTO THE WOODS - WE DON'T WANT TO BE SEEN BY THEM!
WHO IS IT?
IT'S JACOB CRANE, BACK FROM HOLLAND.
KILLER CRANE, ESCAPED FROM THE GIBBET MORE LIKE.
DRAGON'S BREATH - THAT'S WHAT IT IS. EVERY MORNING, RISES FROM THE EARTH WITH THE DAWN.
THESE ARE THE 1700'S. DRAGONS ARE ALL GONE -
AND THE ONLY SPIRITS IN THIS WOOD ARE THE ONES WE CARRY IN THESE BARRELS.
NOW - IT'S TWENTY MILES TO THE INN AND THE BRANDY IS GETTING WARM.
-- AND WE'RE BEING WATCHED.
COME OUT - OR I'LL BLAST YOU FROM YOUR HIDING PLACE.
THIS IS YOUR LAST CHANCE BEFORE I SHOOT.
TIMES UP.
IF IT'S CAPTAIN FARRELL, WE'LL STRING HIM FROM THE TREE. IF IT'S YOUR DRAGON, YOU CAN HAVE IT FOR BREAKFAST.
FOOM!

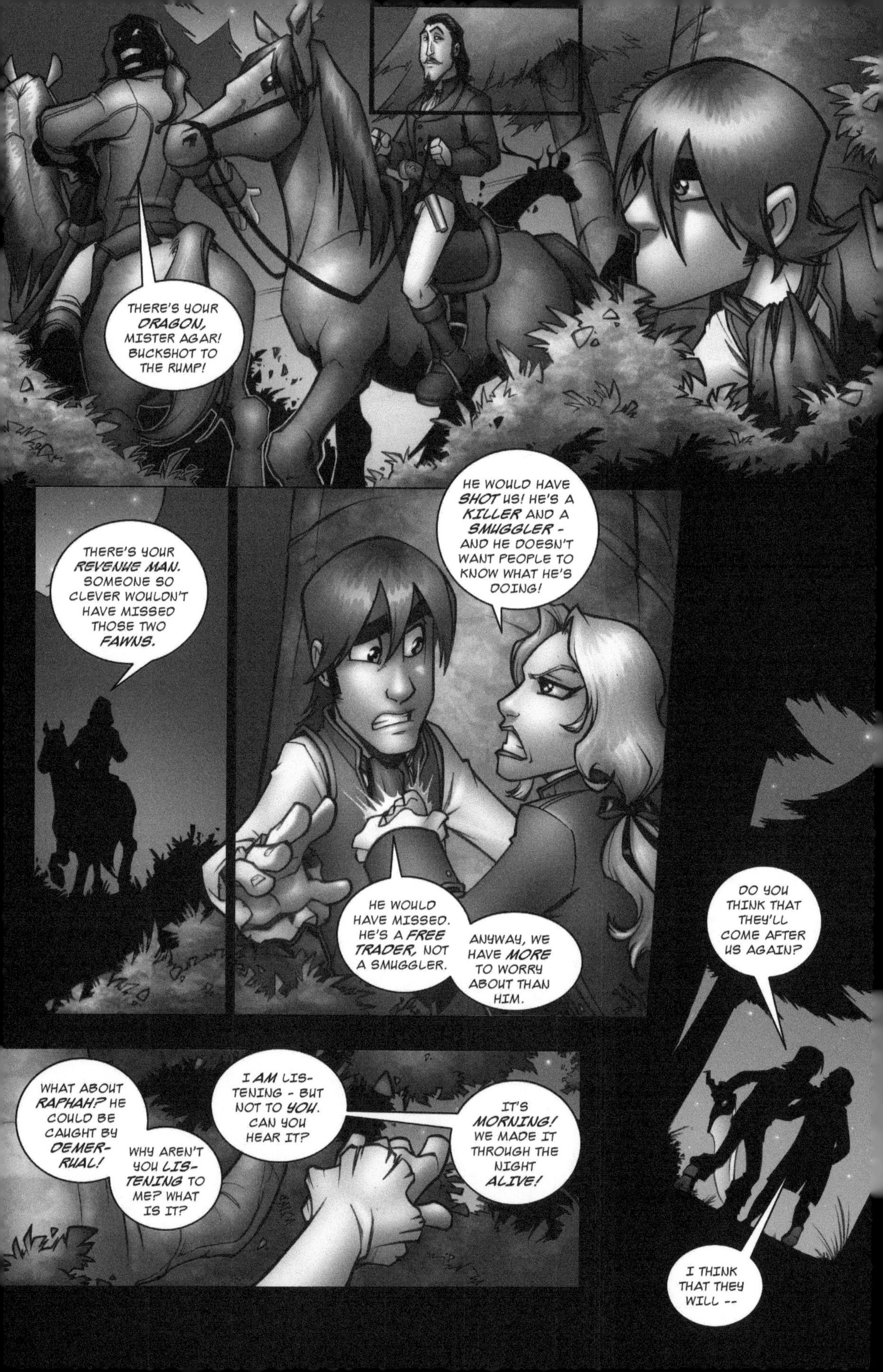
THERE'S YOUR DRAGON, MISTER AGAR! BUCKSHOT TO THE RUMP!
THERE'S YOUR REVENUE MAN. SOMEONE SO CLEVER WOULDN'T HAVE MISSED THOSE TWO FAWNS.
HE WOULD HAVE SHOT US! HE'S A KILLER AND A SMUGGLER - AND HE DOESN'T WANT PEOPLE TO KNOW WHAT HE'S DOING!
HE WOULD HAVE MISSED. HE'S A FREE TRADER, NOT A SMUGGLER.
ANYWAY, WE HAVE MORE TO WORRY ABOUT THAN HIM.
DO YOU THINK THAT THEY'LL COME AFTER US AGAIN?
I THINK THAT THEY WILL --
WHAT ABOUT RAPHAH? HE COULD BE CAUGHT BY DEMER-RUAL!
WHY AREN'T YOU LIS-TENING TO ME? WHAT IS IT?
I AM LIS-TENING - BUT NOT TO YOU. CAN YOU HEAR IT?
IT'S MORNING! WE MADE IT THROUGH THE NIGHT ALIVE!

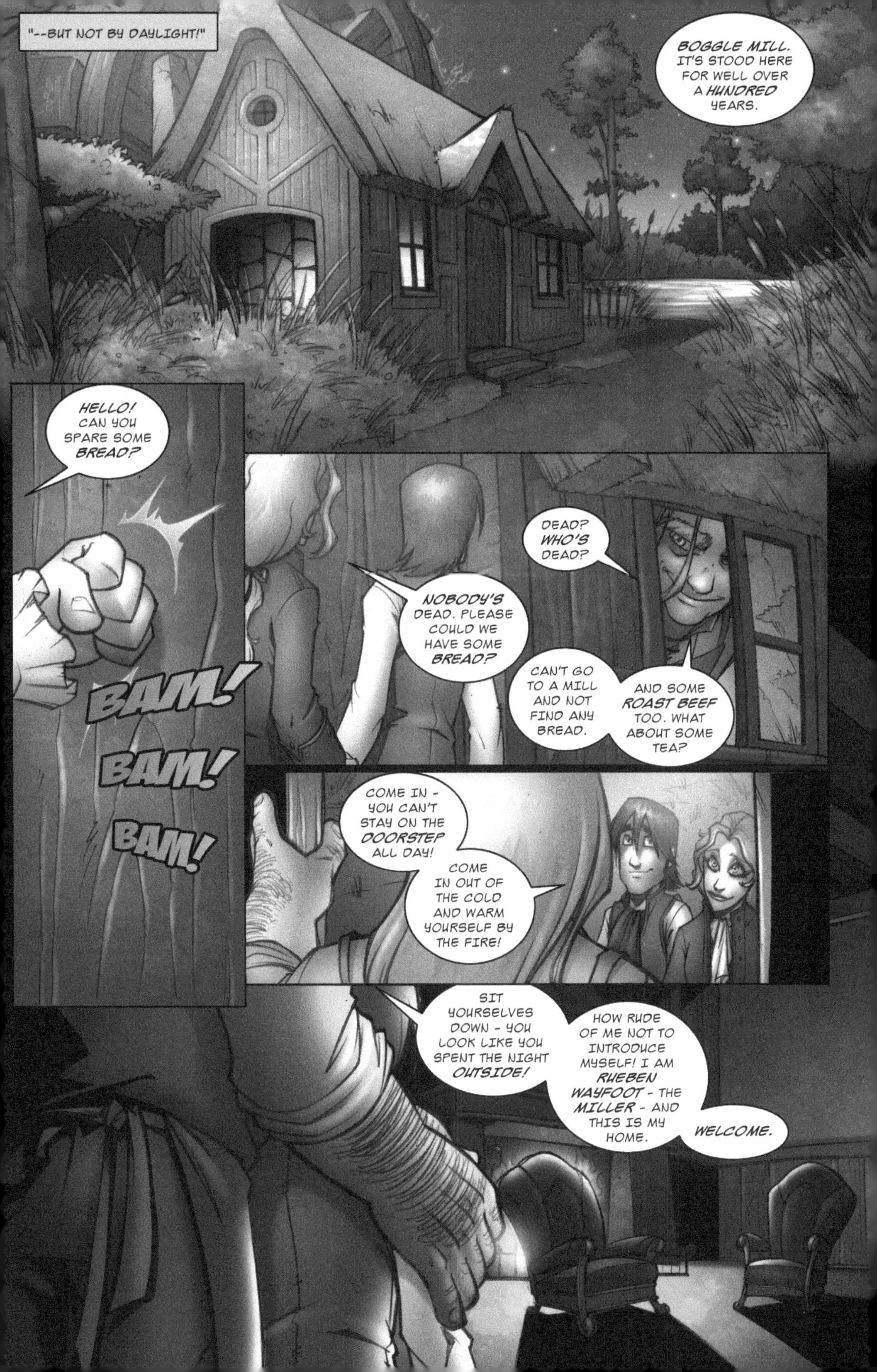
"--BUT NOT BY DAYLIGHT!"
BOGGLE MILL. IT'S STOOD HERE FOR WELL OVER A HUNDRED YEARS.
HELLO! CAN YOU SPARE SOME BREAD?
BAM!
BAM!
BAM!
DEAD? WHO'S DEAD?
NOBODY'S DEAD. PLEASE COULD WE HAVE SOME BREAD?
CAN'T GO TO A MILL AND NOT FIND ANY BREAD.
AND SOME ROAST BEEF TOO. WHAT ABOUT SOME TEA?
COME IN - YOU CAN'T STAY ON THE DOORSTEP ALL DAY!
COME IN OUT OF THE COLD AND WARM YOURSELF BY THE FIRE!
SIT YOURSELVES DOWN - YOU LOOK LIKE YOU SPENT THE NIGHT OUTSIDE!
HOW RUDE OF ME NOT TO INTRODUCE MYSELF! I AM RUEBEN WAYFOOT - THE MILLER - AND THIS IS MY HOME.
WELCOME.

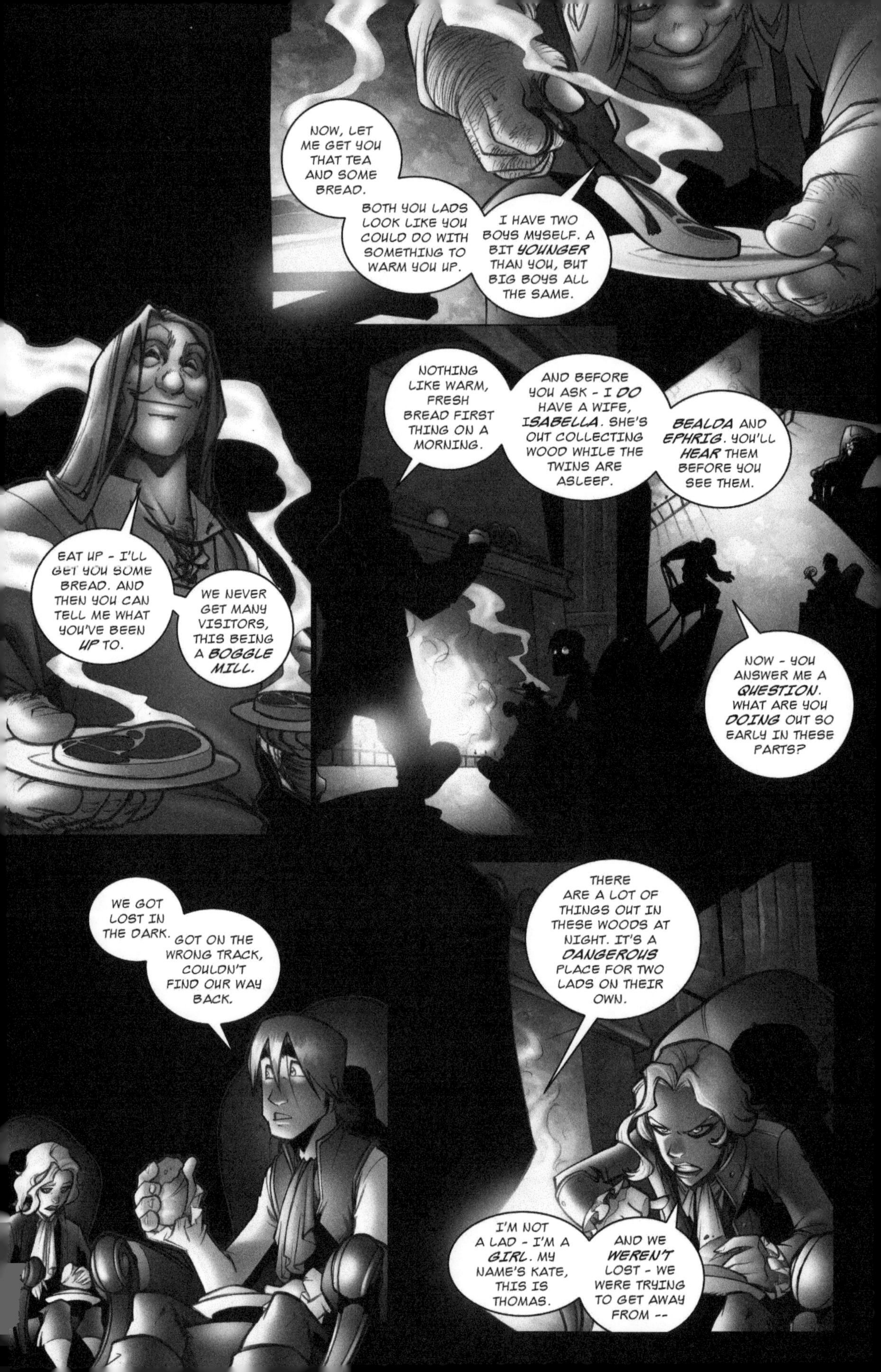
NOW, LET ME GET YOU THAT TEA AND SOME BREAD.
BOTH YOU LADS LOOK LIKE YOU COULD DO WITH SOMETHING TO WARM YOU UP.
I HAVE TWO BOYS MYSELF. A BIT *YOUNGER* THAN YOU, BUT BIG BOYS ALL THE SAME.
EAT UP - I'LL GET YOU SOME BREAD. AND THEN YOU CAN TELL ME WHAT YOU'VE BEEN *UP* TO.
WE NEVER GET MANY VISITORS, THIS BEING A *BOGGLE MILL.*
NOTHING LIKE WARM, FRESH BREAD FIRST THING ON A MORNING.
AND BEFORE YOU ASK - I *DO* HAVE A WIFE, *ISABELLA*. SHE'S OUT COLLECTING WOOD WHILE THE TWINS ARE ASLEEP.
BEALDA AND *EPHRIG*. YOU'LL *HEAR* THEM BEFORE YOU SEE THEM.
NOW - YOU ANSWER ME A *QUESTION*. WHAT ARE YOU *DOING* OUT SO EARLY IN THESE PARTS?
WE GOT LOST IN THE DARK.
GOT ON THE WRONG TRACK, COULDN'T FIND OUR WAY BACK.
THERE ARE A LOT OF THINGS OUT IN THESE WOODS AT NIGHT. IT'S A *DANGEROUS* PLACE FOR TWO LADS ON THEIR OWN.
I'M NOT A LAD - I'M A *GIRL*. MY NAME'S KATE, THIS IS THOMAS.
AND WE *WEREN'T* LOST - WE WERE TRYING TO GET AWAY FROM --

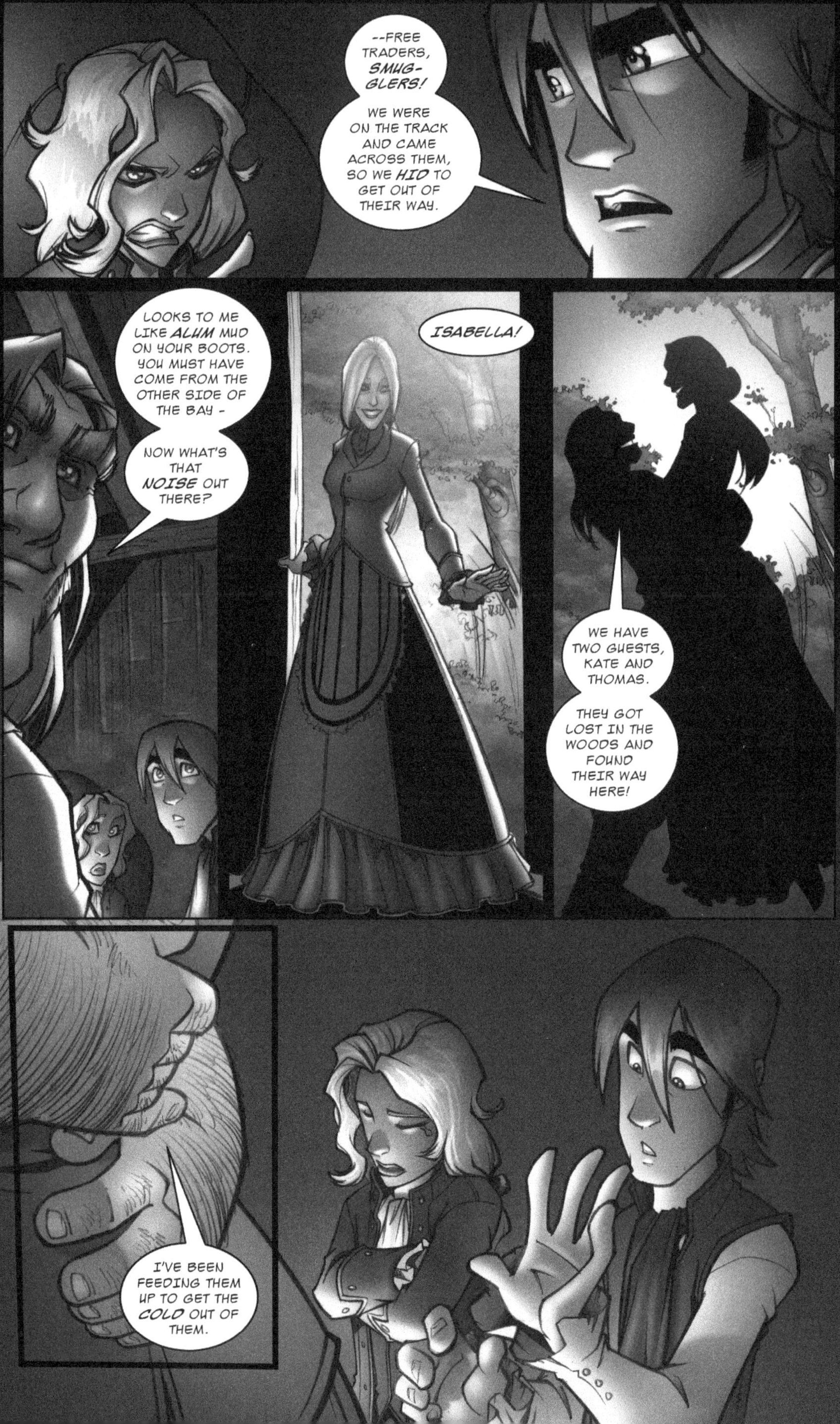
--FREE TRADERS, SMUGGLERS!
WE WERE ON THE TRACK AND CAME ACROSS THEM, SO WE HID TO GET OUT OF THEIR WAY.
LOOKS TO ME LIKE ALUM MUD ON YOUR BOOTS. YOU MUST HAVE COME FROM THE OTHER SIDE OF THE BAY -
NOW WHAT'S THAT NOISE OUT THERE?
ISABELLA!
WE HAVE TWO GUESTS, KATE AND THOMAS.
THEY GOT LOST IN THE WOODS AND FOUND THEIR WAY HERE!
I'VE BEEN FEEDING THEM UP TO GET THE COLD OUT OF THEM.

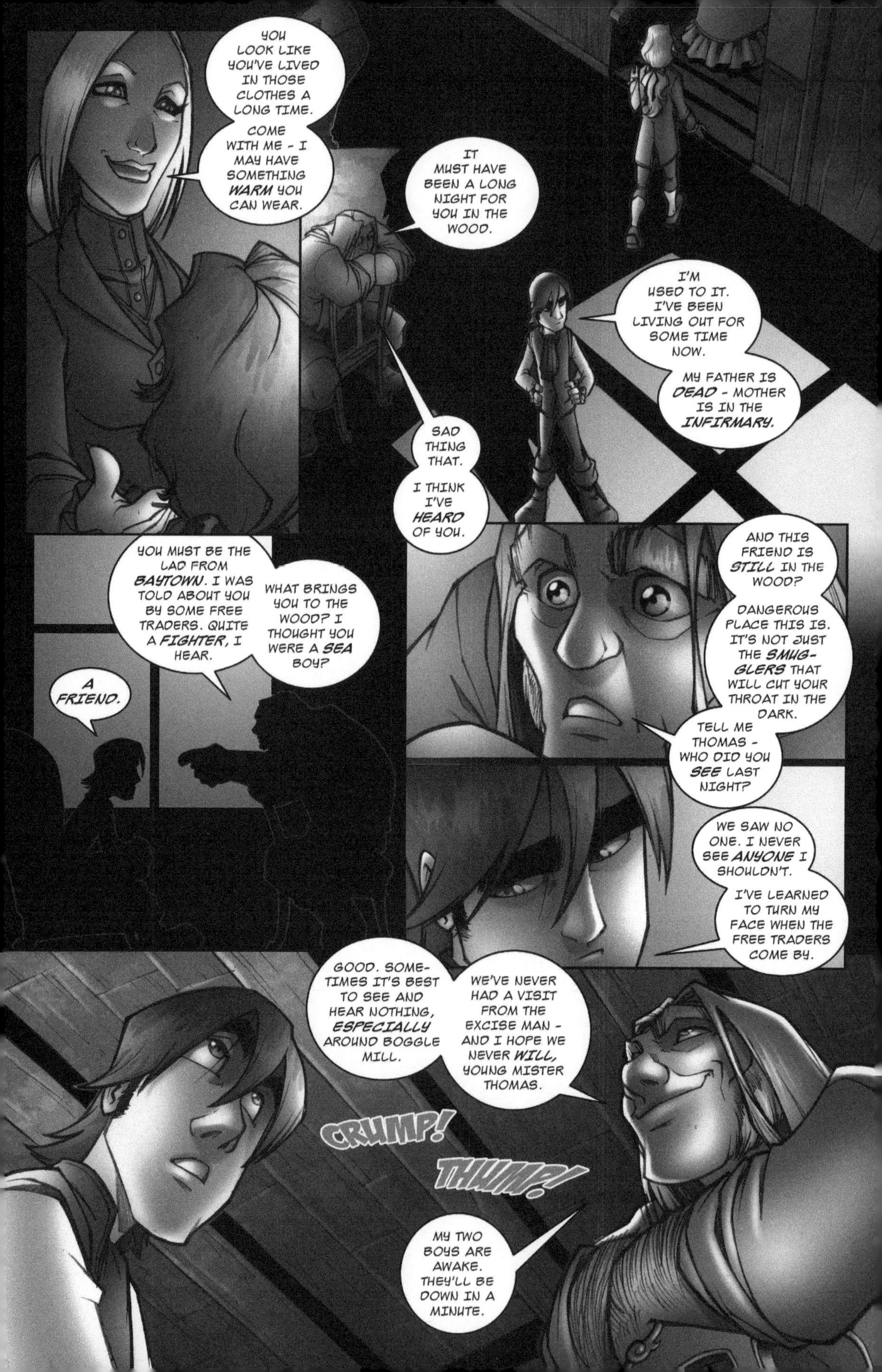

YOU LOOK LIKE YOU'VE LIVED IN THOSE CLOTHES A LONG TIME.
COME WITH ME - I MAY HAVE SOMETHING WARM YOU CAN WEAR.
IT MUST HAVE BEEN A LONG NIGHT FOR YOU IN THE WOOD.
I'M USED TO IT. I'VE BEEN LIVING OUT FOR SOME TIME NOW.
MY FATHER IS DEAD - MOTHER IS IN THE INFIRMARY.
SAD THING THAT.
I THINK I'VE HEARD OF YOU.
YOU MUST BE THE LAD FROM BAYTOWN. I WAS TOLD ABOUT YOU BY SOME FREE TRADERS. QUITE A FIGHTER, I HEAR.
WHAT BRINGS YOU TO THE WOOD? I THOUGHT YOU WERE A SEA BOY?
A FRIEND.
AND THIS FRIEND IS STILL IN THE WOOD?
DANGEROUS PLACE THIS IS. IT'S NOT JUST THE SMUG-GLERS THAT WILL CUT YOUR THROAT IN THE DARK.
TELL ME THOMAS - WHO DID YOU SEE LAST NIGHT?
WE SAW NO ONE. I NEVER SEE ANYONE I SHOULDN'T.
I'VE LEARNED TO TURN MY FACE WHEN THE FREE TRADERS COME BY.
GOOD. SOME-TIMES IT'S BEST TO SEE AND HEAR NOTHING, ESPECIALLY AROUND BOGGLE MILL.
WE'VE NEVER HAD A VISIT FROM THE EXCISE MAN - AND I HOPE WE NEVER WILL, YOUNG MISTER THOMAS.
CRUMP!
THUMP!
MY TWO BOYS ARE AWAKE. THEY'LL BE DOWN IN A MINUTE.

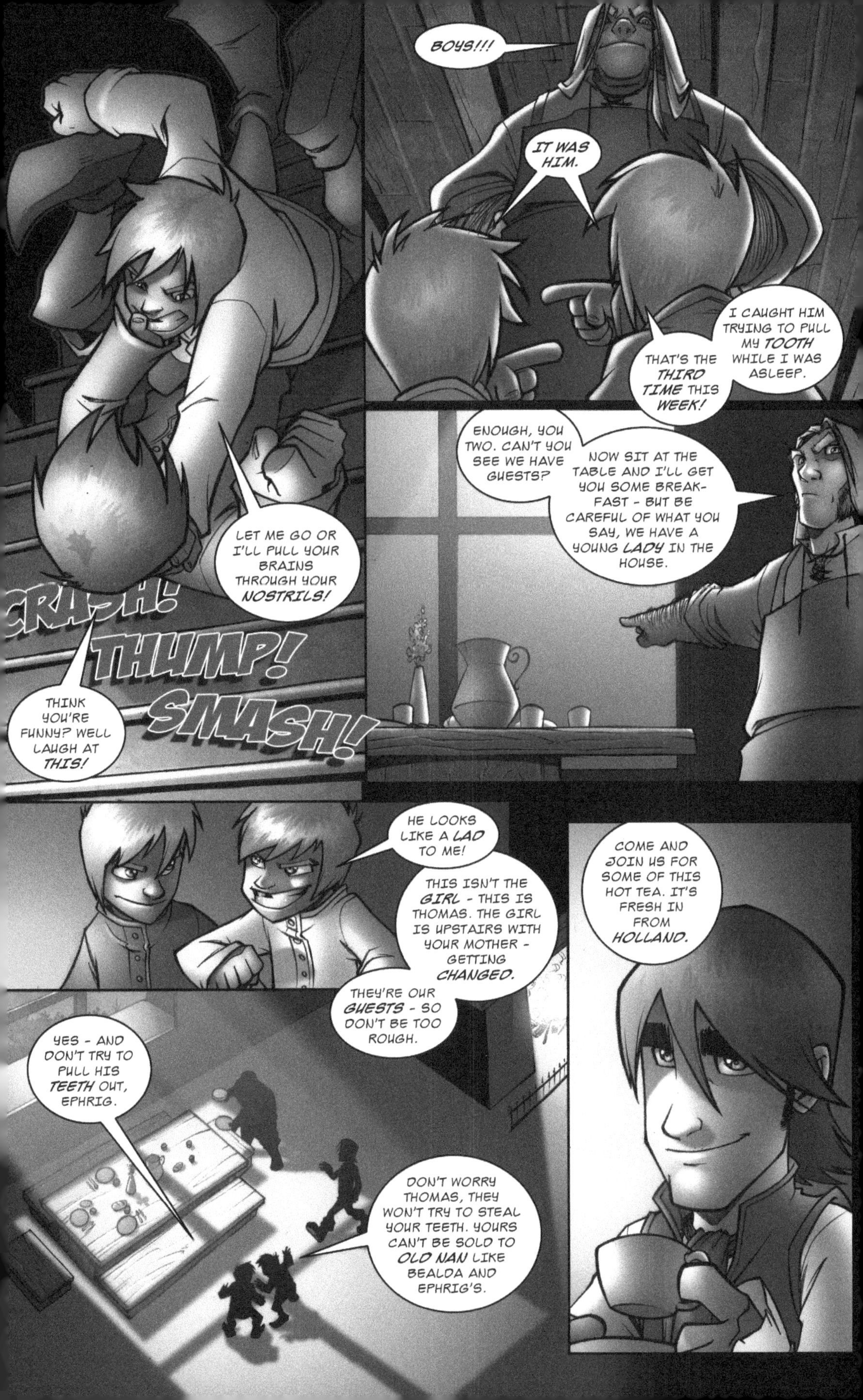
BOYS!!!
IT WAS HIM.
I CAUGHT HIM TRYING TO PULL MY TOOTH WHILE I WAS ASLEEP.
THAT'S THE THIRD TIME THIS WEEK!
LET ME GO OR I'LL PULL YOUR BRAINS THROUGH YOUR NOSTRILS!
CRASH!
THINK YOU'RE FUNNY? WELL LAUGH AT THIS!
THUMP!
SMASH!
ENOUGH, YOU TWO. CAN'T YOU SEE WE HAVE GUESTS?
NOW SIT AT THE TABLE AND I'LL GET YOU SOME BREAK-FAST - BUT BE CAREFUL OF WHAT YOU SAY, WE HAVE A YOUNG LADY IN THE HOUSE.
HE LOOKS LIKE A LAD TO ME!
THIS ISN'T THE GIRL - THIS IS THOMAS. THE GIRL IS UPSTAIRS WITH YOUR MOTHER - GETTING CHANGED.
THEY'RE OUR GUESTS - SO DON'T BE TOO ROUGH.
YES - AND DON'T TRY TO PULL HIS TEETH OUT, EPHRIG.
DON'T WORRY THOMAS, THEY WON'T TRY TO STEAL YOUR TEETH. YOURS CAN'T BE SOLD TO OLD NAN LIKE BEALDA AND EPHRIG'S.
COME AND JOIN US FOR SOME OF THIS HOT TEA. IT'S FRESH IN FROM HOLLAND.

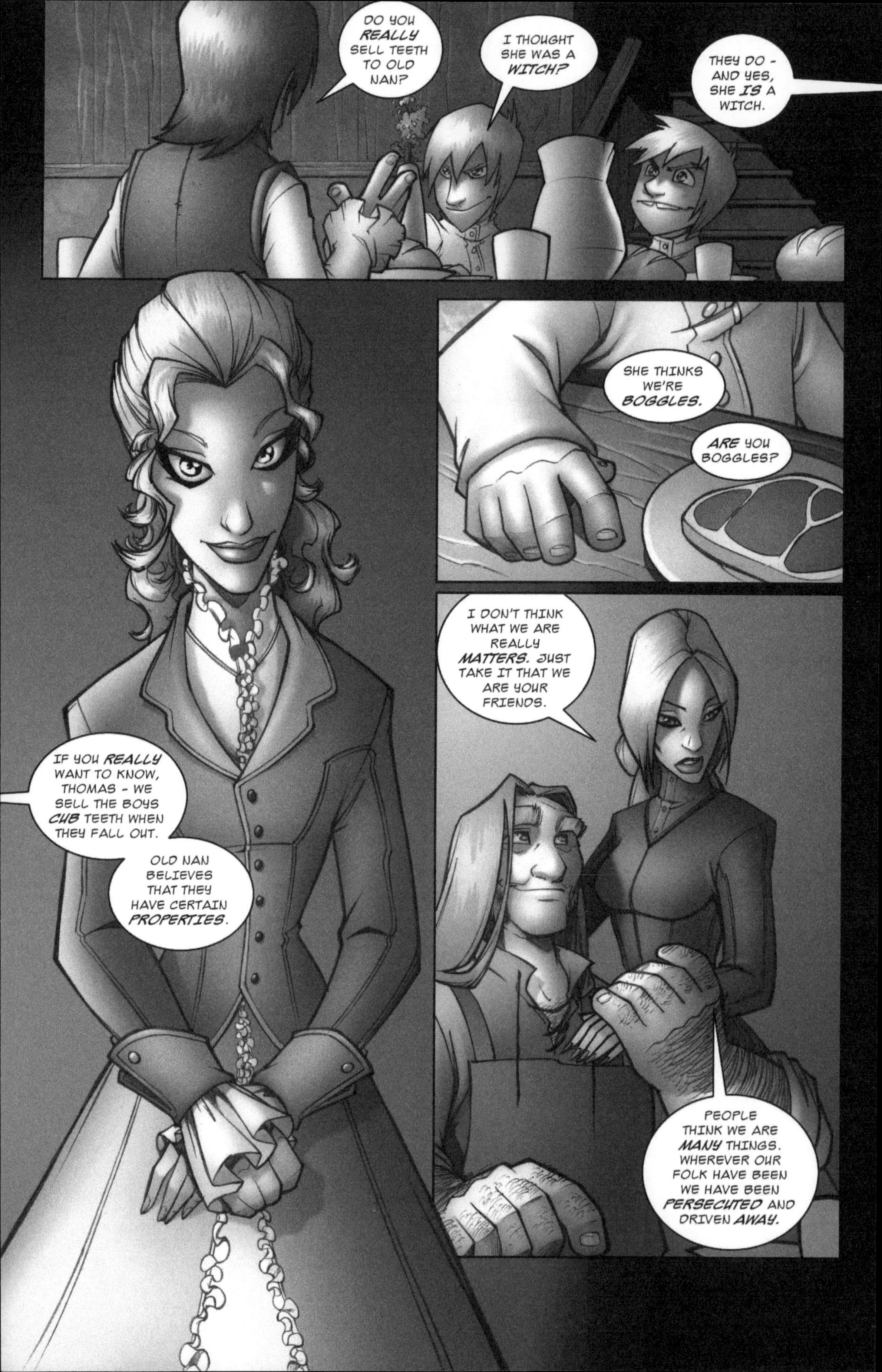
DO YOU REALLY SELL TEETH TO OLD NAN?
I THOUGHT SHE WAS A WITCH?
THEY DO - AND YES, SHE IS A WITCH.
SHE THINKS WE'RE BOGGLES.
ARE YOU BOGGLES?
IF YOU REALLY WANT TO KNOW, THOMAS - WE SELL THE BOYS CUB TEETH WHEN THEY FALL OUT.
OLD NAN BELIEVES THAT THEY HAVE CERTAIN PROPERTIES.
I DON'T THINK WHAT WE ARE REALLY MATTERS. JUST TAKE IT THAT WE ARE YOUR FRIENDS.
PEOPLE THINK WE ARE MANY THINGS. WHEREVER OUR FOLK HAVE BEEN WE HAVE BEEN PERSECUTED AND DRIVEN AWAY.

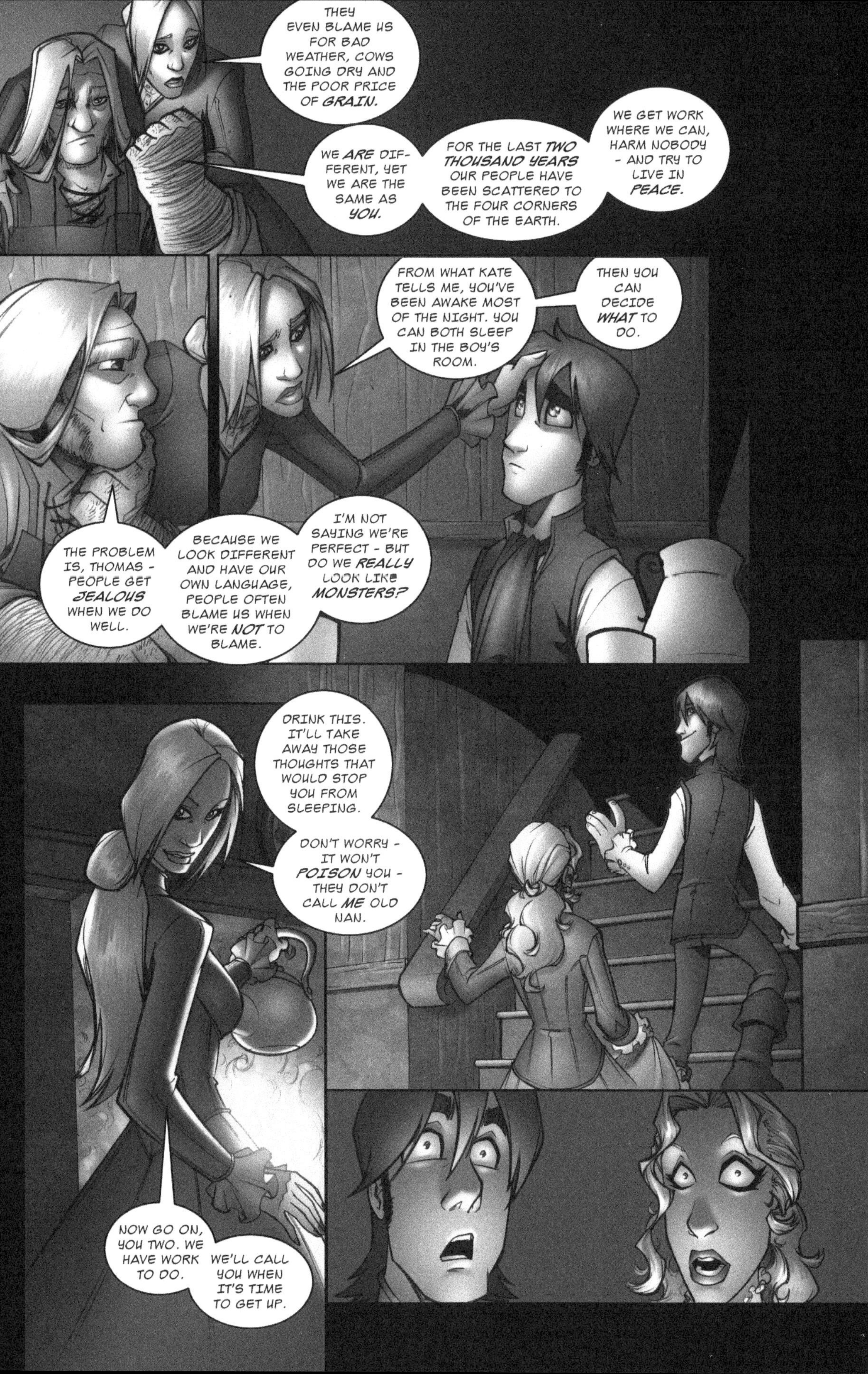
THEY EVEN BLAME US FOR BAD WEATHER, COWS GOING DRY AND THE POOR PRICE OF GRAIN.
WE ARE DIF-FERENT, YET WE ARE THE SAME AS YOU.
FOR THE LAST TWO THOUSAND YEARS OUR PEOPLE HAVE BEEN SCATTERED TO THE FOUR CORNERS OF THE EARTH.
WE GET WORK WHERE WE CAN, HARM NOBODY - AND TRY TO LIVE IN PEACE.
THE PROBLEM IS, THOMAS - PEOPLE GET JEALOUS WHEN WE DO WELL.
BECAUSE WE LOOK DIFFERENT AND HAVE OUR OWN LANGUAGE, PEOPLE OFTEN BLAME US WHEN WE'RE NOT TO BLAME.
I'M NOT SAYING WE'RE PERFECT - BUT DO WE REALLY LOOK LIKE MONSTERS?
FROM WHAT KATE TELLS ME, YOU'VE BEEN AWAKE MOST OF THE NIGHT. YOU CAN BOTH SLEEP IN THE BOY'S ROOM.
THEN YOU CAN DECIDE WHAT TO DO.
DRINK THIS. IT'LL TAKE AWAY THOSE THOUGHTS THAT WOULD STOP YOU FROM SLEEPING.
DON'T WORRY - IT WON'T POISON YOU - THEY DON'T CALL ME OLD NAN.
NOW GO ON, YOU TWO. WE HAVE WORK TO DO.
WE'LL CALL YOU WHEN IT'S TIME TO GET UP.

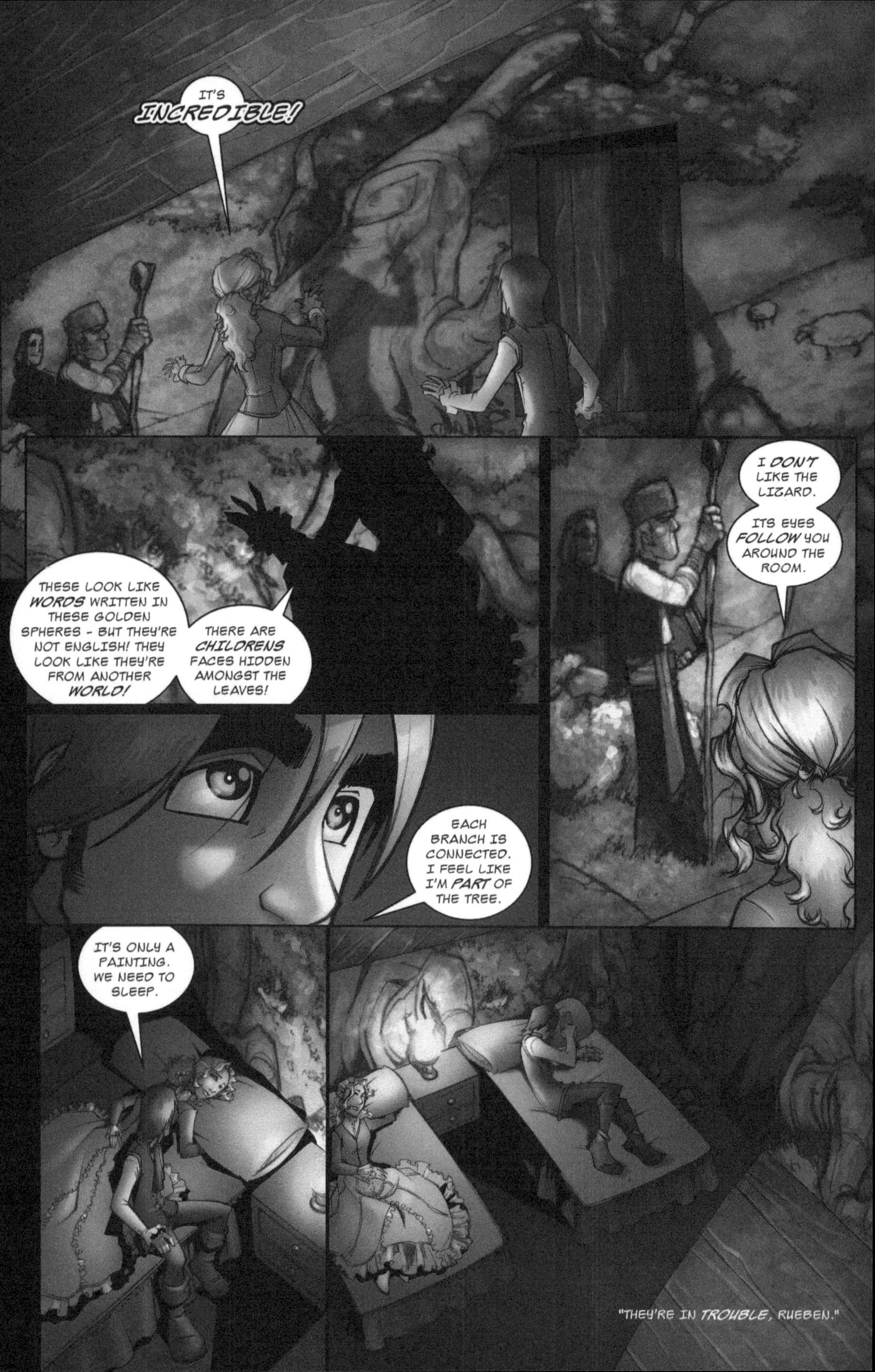
IT'S INCREDIBLE!
THESE LOOK LIKE WORDS WRITTEN IN THESE GOLDEN SPHERES - BUT THEY'RE NOT ENGLISH! THEY LOOK LIKE THEY'RE FROM ANOTHER WORLD!
THERE ARE CHILDRENS FACES HIDDEN AMONGST THE LEAVES!
I DON'T LIKE THE LIZARD.
ITS EYES FOLLOW YOU AROUND THE ROOM.
EACH BRANCH IS CONNECTED. I FEEL LIKE I'M PART OF THE TREE.
IT'S ONLY A PAINTING. WE NEED TO SLEEP.
"THEY'RE IN TROUBLE, RUEBEN."

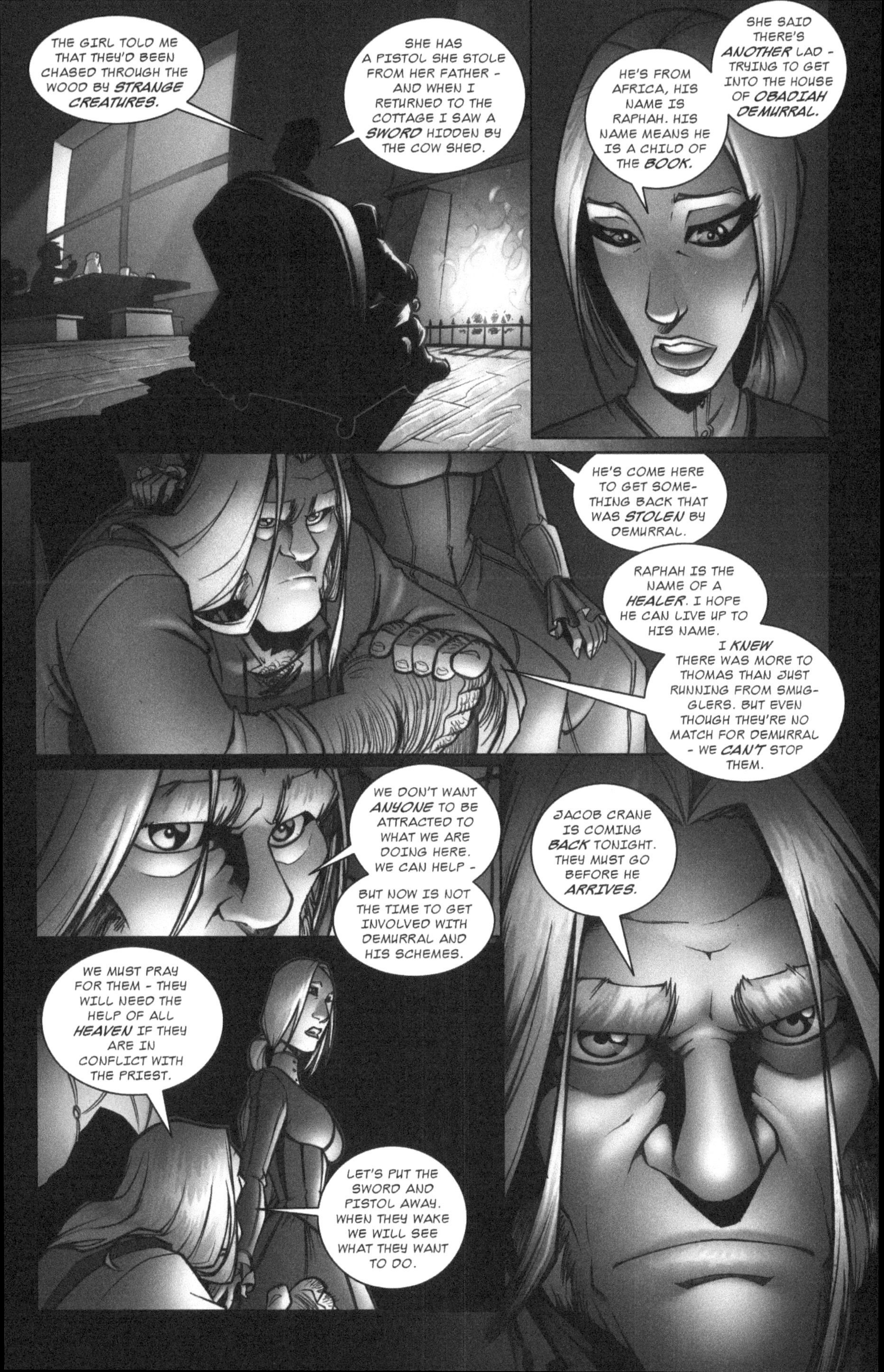
THE GIRL TOLD ME THAT THEY'D BEEN CHASED THROUGH THE WOOD BY STRANGE CREATURES.
SHE HAS A PISTOL SHE STOLE FROM HER FATHER - AND WHEN I RETURNED TO THE COTTAGE I SAW A SWORD HIDDEN BY THE COW SHED.
SHE SAID THERE'S ANOTHER LAD - TRYING TO GET INTO THE HOUSE OF OBADIAH DEMURRAL.
HE'S FROM AFRICA, HIS NAME IS RAPHAH. HIS NAME MEANS HE IS A CHILD OF THE BOOK.
HE'S COME HERE TO GET SOME-THING BACK THAT WAS STOLEN BY DEMURRAL.
RAPHAH IS THE NAME OF A HEALER. I HOPE HE CAN LIVE UP TO HIS NAME.
I KNEW THERE WAS MORE TO THOMAS THAN JUST RUNNING FROM SMUG-GLERS. BUT EVEN THOUGH THEY'RE NO MATCH FOR DEMURRAL - WE CAN'T STOP THEM.
WE DON'T WANT ANYONE TO BE ATTRACTED TO WHAT WE ARE DOING HERE. WE CAN HELP -
BUT NOW IS NOT THE TIME TO GET INVOLVED WITH DEMURRAL AND HIS SCHEMES.
JACOB CRANE IS COMING BACK TONIGHT. THEY MUST GO BEFORE HE ARRIVES.
WE MUST PRAY FOR THEM - THEY WILL NEED THE HELP OF ALL HEAVEN IF THEY ARE IN CONFLICT WITH THE PRIEST.
LET'S PUT THE SWORD AND PISTOL AWAY. WHEN THEY WAKE WE WILL SEE WHAT THEY WANT TO DO.

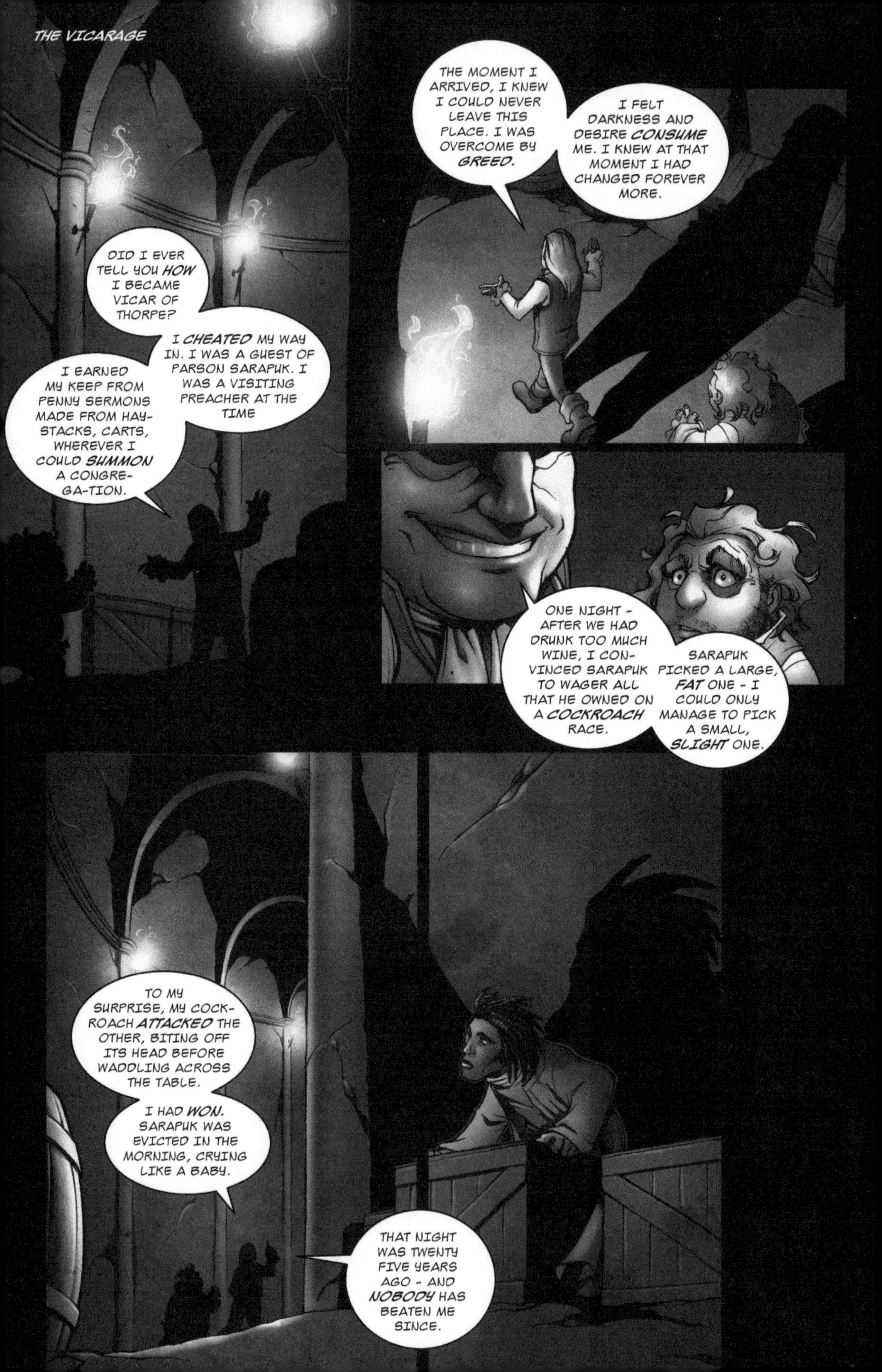
DID I EVER TELL YOU HOW I BECAME VICAR OF THORPE?
I CHEATED MY WAY IN. I WAS A GUEST OF PARSON SARAPUK. I WAS A VISITING PREACHER AT THE TIME
I EARNED MY KEEP FROM PENNY SERMONS MADE FROM HAY-STACKS, CARTS, WHEREVER I COULD SUMMON A CONGRE-GA-TION.
THE MOMENT I ARRIVED, I KNEW I COULD NEVER LEAVE THIS PLACE. I WAS OVERCOME BY GREED.
I FELT DARKNESS AND DESIRE CONSUME ME. I KNEW AT THAT MOMENT I HAD CHANGED FOREVER MORE.
ONE NIGHT - AFTER WE HAD DRUNK TOO MUCH WINE, I CON-VINCED SARAPUK TO WAGER ALL THAT HE OWNED ON A COCKROACH RACE.
SARAPUK PICKED A LARGE, FAT ONE - I COULD ONLY MANAGE TO PICK A SMALL, SLIGHT ONE.
TO MY SURPRISE, MY COCK-ROACH ATTACKED THE OTHER, BITING OFF ITS HEAD BEFORE WADDLING ACROSS THE TABLE.
I HAD WON. SARAPUK WAS EVICTED IN THE MORNING, CRYING LIKE A BABY.
THAT NIGHT WAS TWENTY FIVE YEARS AGO - AND NOBODY HAS BEATEN ME SINCE.

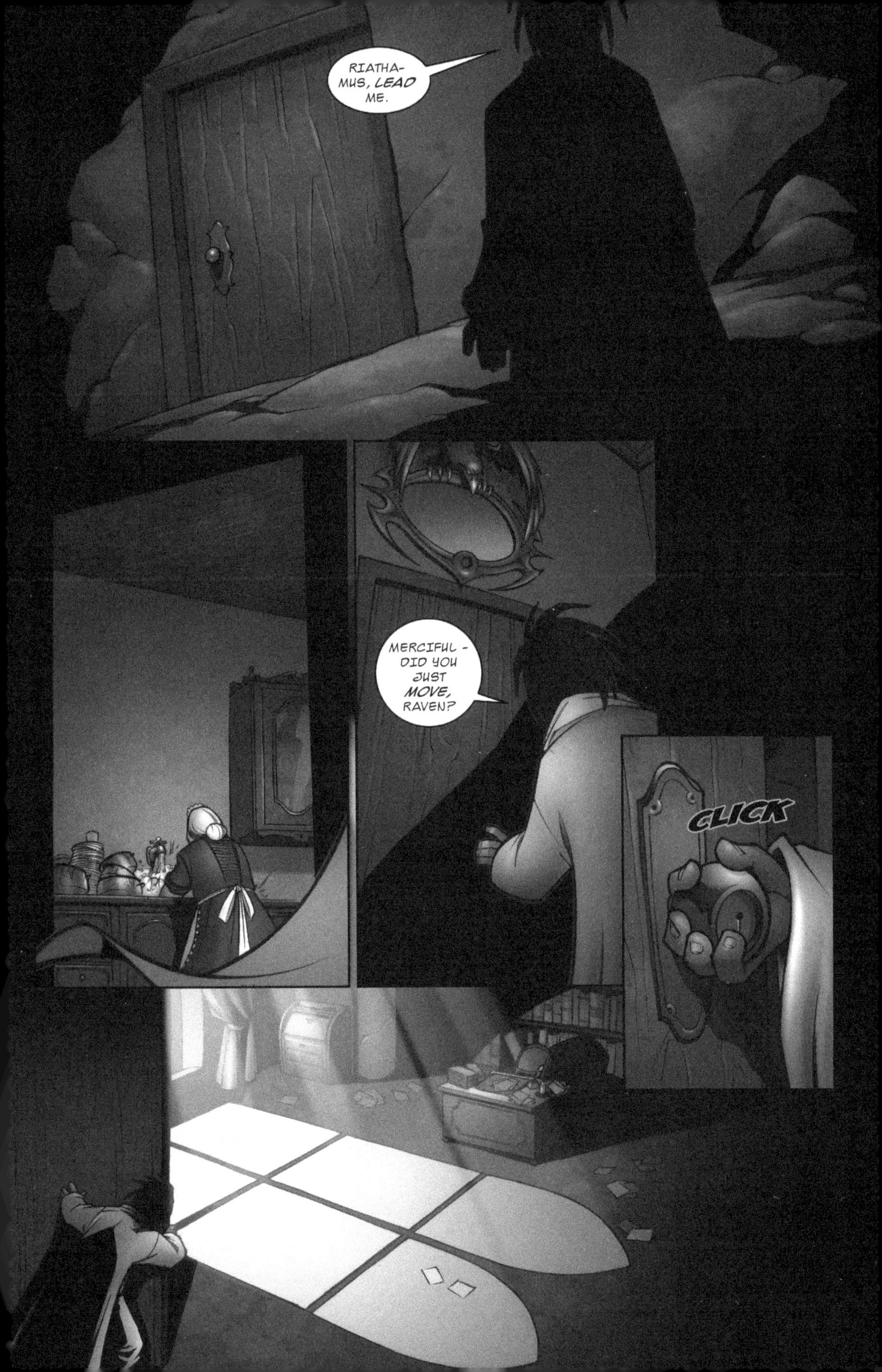
RIATHA-
MUS, LEAD
ME.
MERCIFUL -
DID YOU
JUST
MOVE,
RAVEN?
CLICK

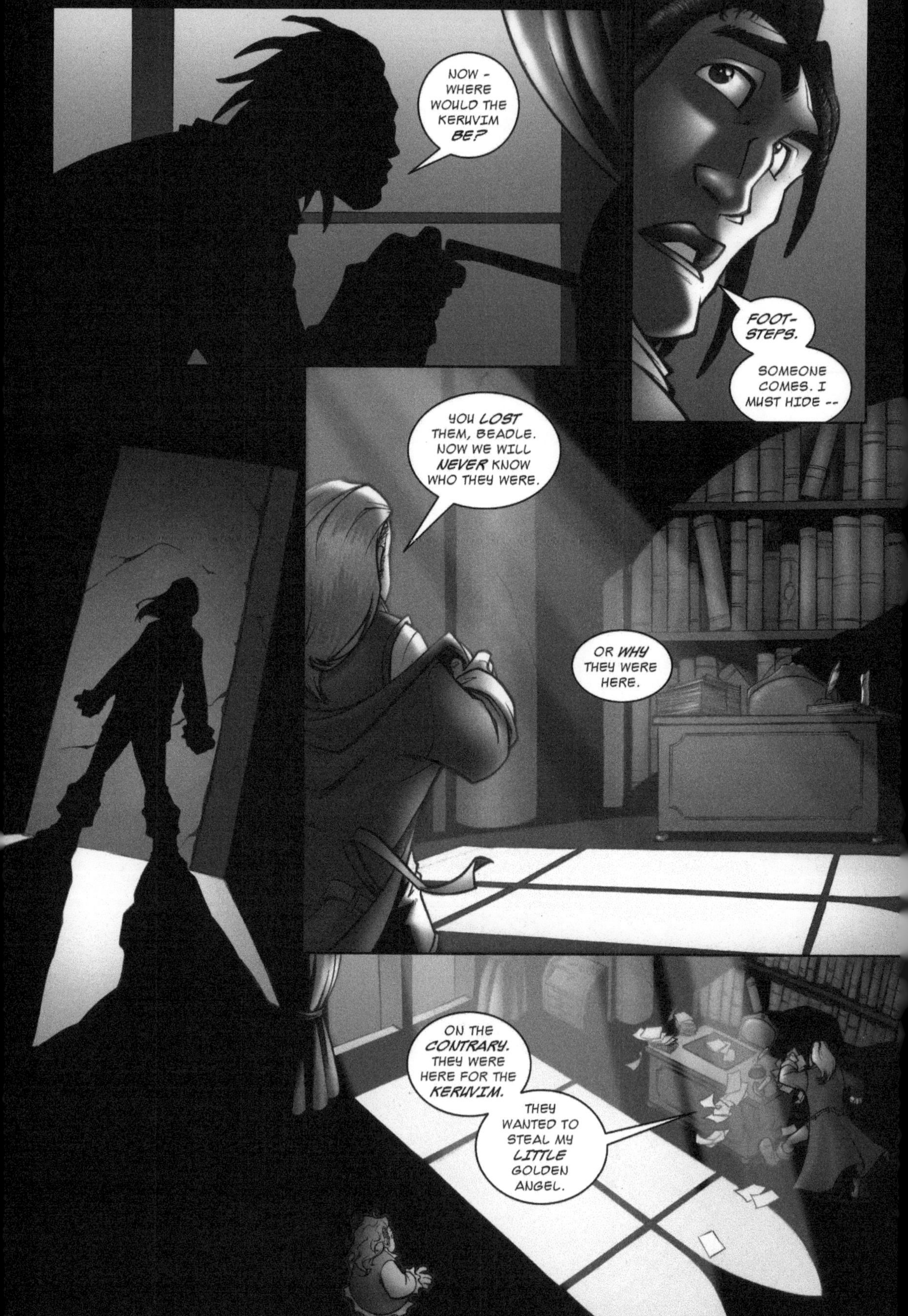
NOW - WHERE WOULD THE KERUVIM BE?
FOOT-STEPS.
SOMEONE COMES. I MUST HIDE --
YOU LOST THEM, BEADLE. NOW WE WILL NEVER KNOW WHO THEY WERE.
OR WHY THEY WERE HERE.
ON THE CONTRARY. THEY WERE HERE FOR THE KERUVIM.
THEY WANTED TO STEAL MY LITTLE GOLDEN ANGEL.

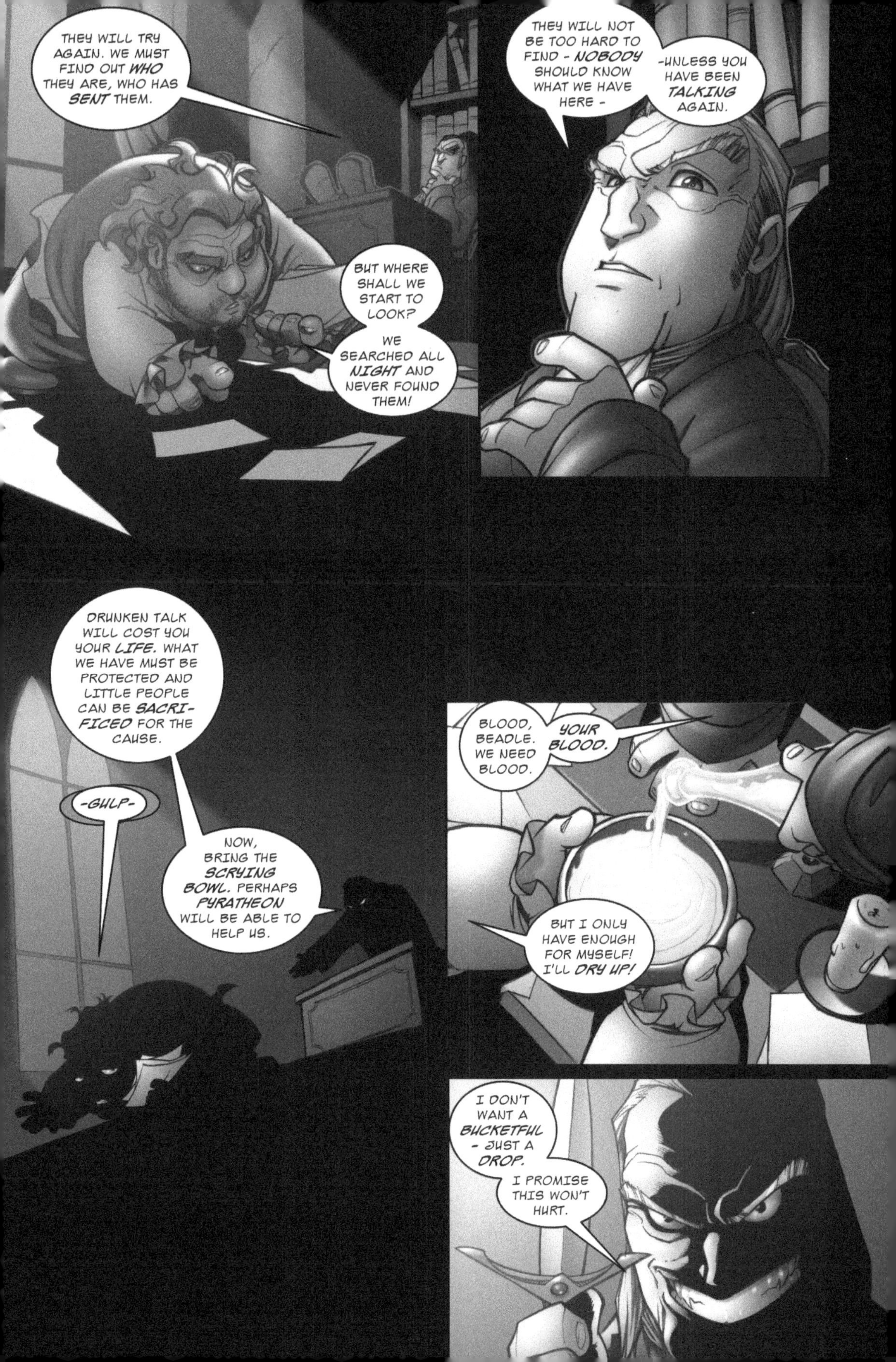
THEY WILL TRY AGAIN. WE MUST FIND OUT WHO THEY ARE, WHO HAS SENT THEM.
BUT WHERE SHALL WE START TO LOOK?
WE SEARCHED ALL NIGHT AND NEVER FOUND THEM!
THEY WILL NOT BE TOO HARD TO FIND - NOBODY SHOULD KNOW WHAT WE HAVE HERE -
-UNLESS YOU HAVE BEEN TALKING AGAIN.
DRUNKEN TALK WILL COST YOU YOUR LIFE. WHAT WE HAVE MUST BE PROTECTED AND LITTLE PEOPLE CAN BE SACRI-FICED FOR THE CAUSE.
-GULP-
NOW, BRING THE SCRYING BOWL. PERHAPS PYRATHEON WILL BE ABLE TO HELP US.
BLOOD, BEADLE. WE NEED BLOOD.
YOUR BLOOD.
BUT I ONLY HAVE ENOUGH FOR MYSELF! I'LL DRY UP!
I DON'T WANT A BUCKETFUL - JUST A DROP.
I PROMISE THIS WON'T HURT.

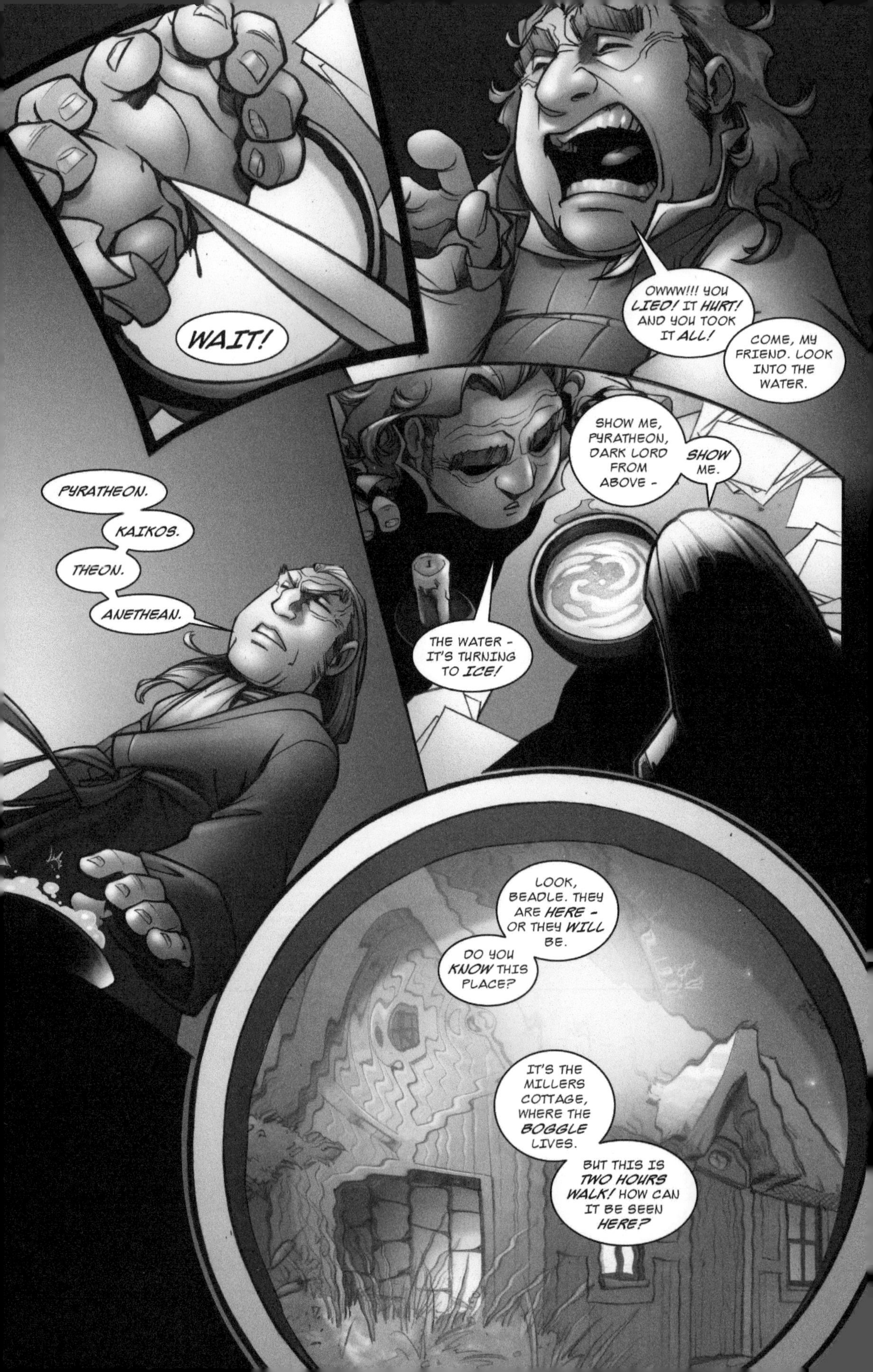
WAIT!
OWWW!!! YOU LIED! IT HURT! AND YOU TOOK IT ALL!
COME, MY FRIEND. LOOK INTO THE WATER.
SHOW ME, PYRATHEON, DARK LORD FROM ABOVE -
SHOW ME.
PYRATHEON.
KAIKOS.
THEON.
ANETHEAN.
THE WATER - IT'S TURNING TO ICE!
LOOK, BEADLE. THEY ARE HERE - OR THEY WILL BE.
DO YOU KNOW THIS PLACE?
IT'S THE MILLERS COTTAGE, WHERE THE BOGGLE LIVES.
BUT THIS IS TWO HOURS WALK! HOW CAN IT BE SEEN HERE?

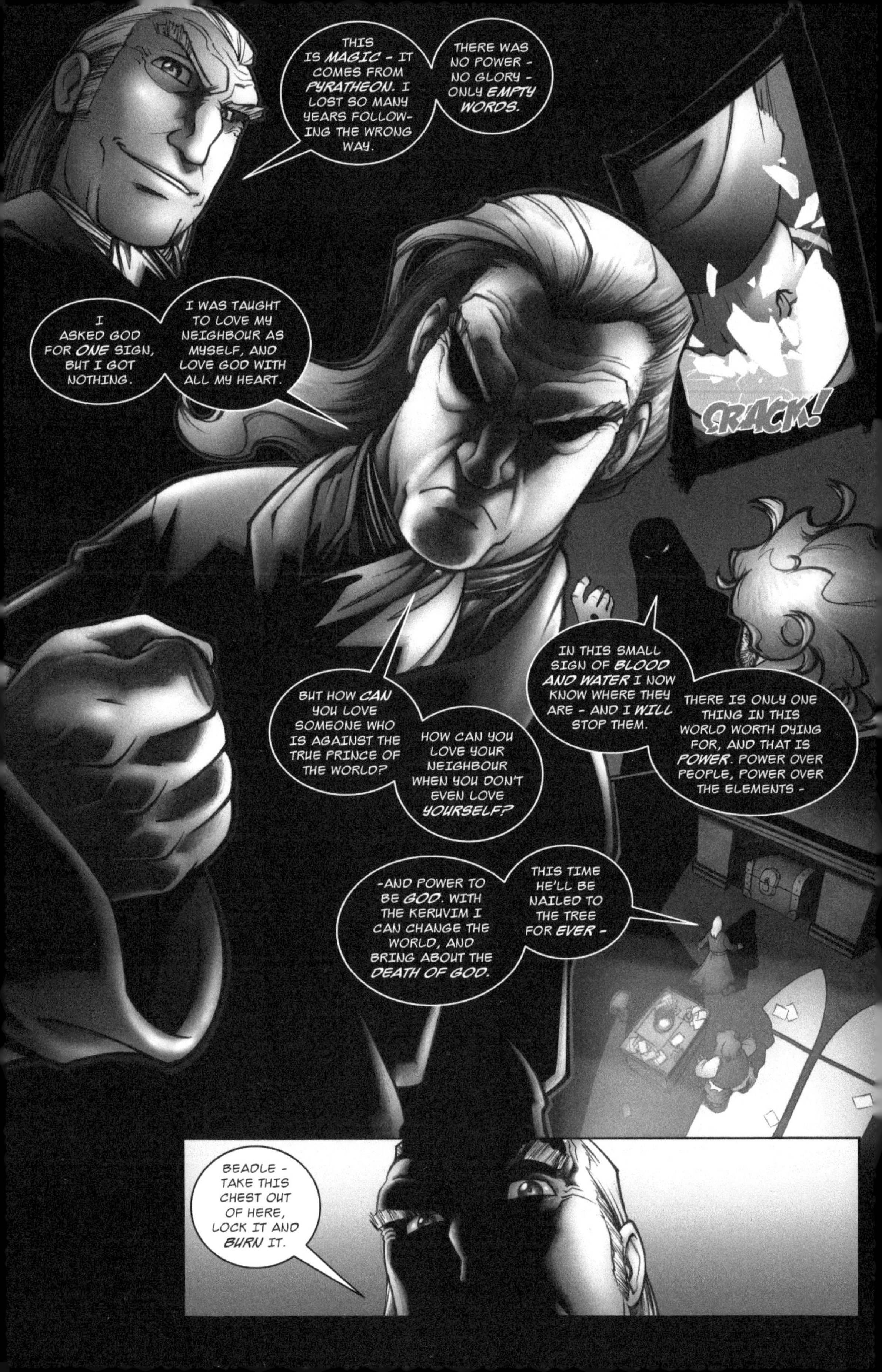
THIS IS MAGIC - IT COMES FROM PYRATHEON. I LOST SO MANY YEARS FOLLOWING THE WRONG WAY.
THERE WAS NO POWER - NO GLORY - ONLY EMPTY WORDS.
I ASKED GOD FOR ONE SIGN, BUT I GOT NOTHING.
I WAS TAUGHT TO LOVE MY NEIGHBOUR AS MYSELF, AND LOVE GOD WITH ALL MY HEART.
CRACK!
BUT HOW CAN YOU LOVE SOMEONE WHO IS AGAINST THE TRUE PRINCE OF THE WORLD?
HOW CAN YOU LOVE YOUR NEIGHBOUR WHEN YOU DON'T EVEN LOVE YOURSELF?
IN THIS SMALL SIGN OF BLOOD AND WATER I NOW KNOW WHERE THEY ARE - AND I WILL STOP THEM.
THERE IS ONLY ONE THING IN THIS WORLD WORTH DYING FOR, AND THAT IS POWER. POWER OVER PEOPLE, POWER OVER THE ELEMENTS -
-AND POWER TO BE GOD. WITH THE KERUVIM I CAN CHANGE THE WORLD, AND BRING ABOUT THE DEATH OF GOD.
THIS TIME HE'LL BE NAILED TO THE TREE FOR EVER -
BEADLE - TAKE THIS CHEST OUT OF HERE, LOCK IT AND BURN IT.

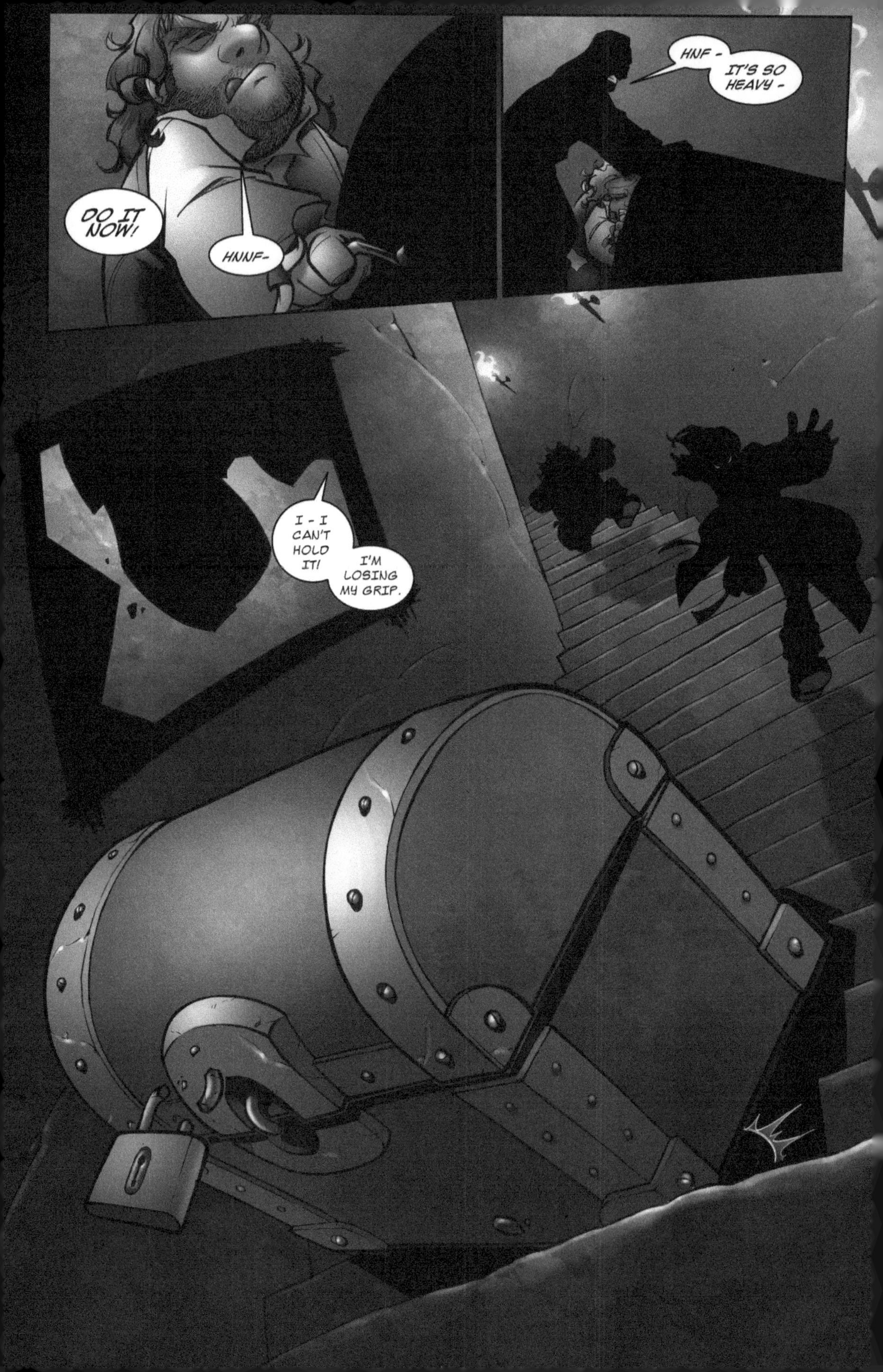
DO IT NOW!
HNNF-
HNF -
IT'S SO HEAVY -
I - I CAN'T HOLD IT!
I'M LOSING MY GRIP.

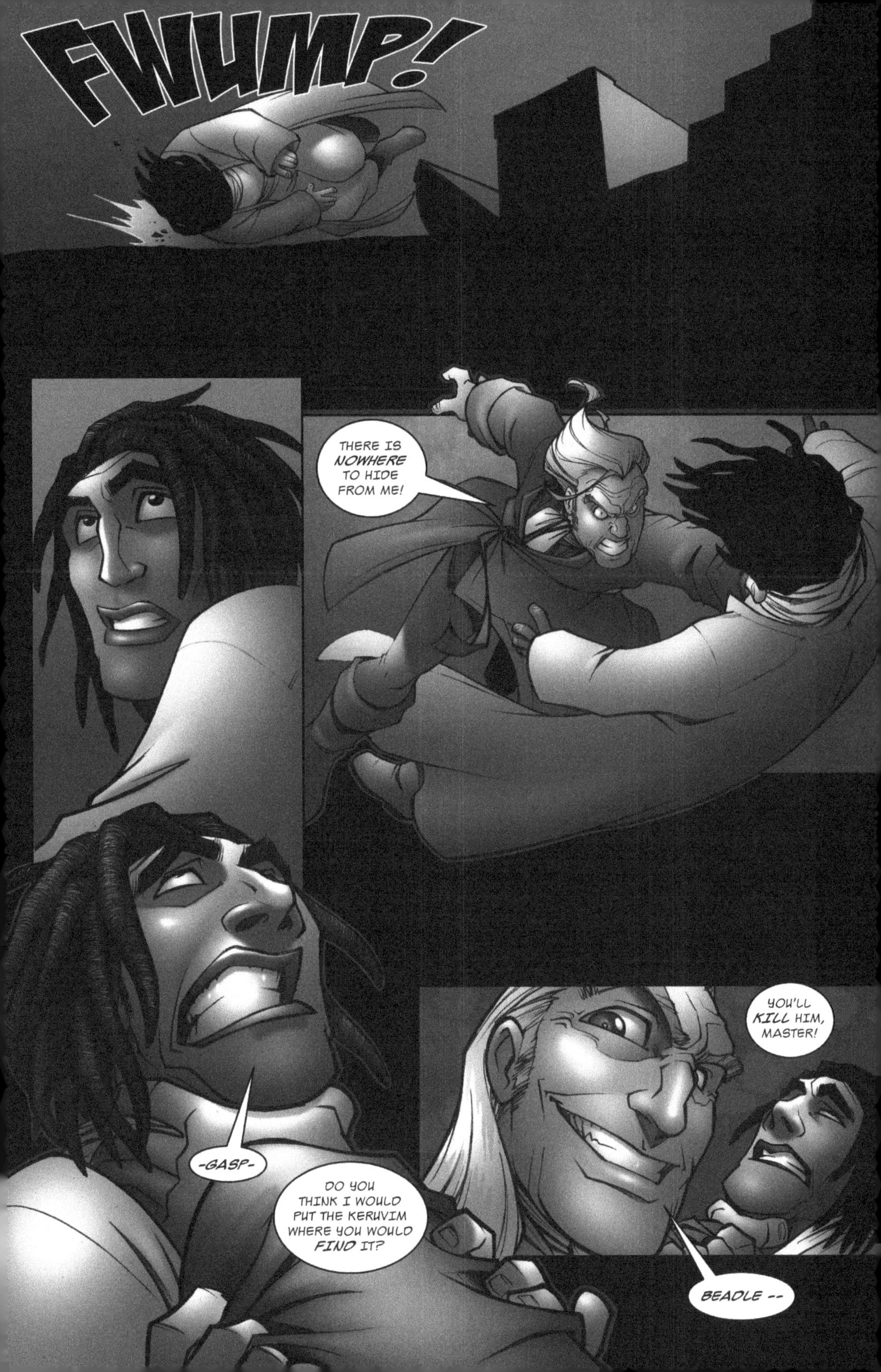
FWUMP!
THERE IS NOWHERE TO HIDE FROM ME!
-GASP-
DO YOU THINK I WOULD PUT THE KERUVIM WHERE YOU WOULD FIND IT?
YOU'LL KILL HIM, MASTER!
BEADLE --

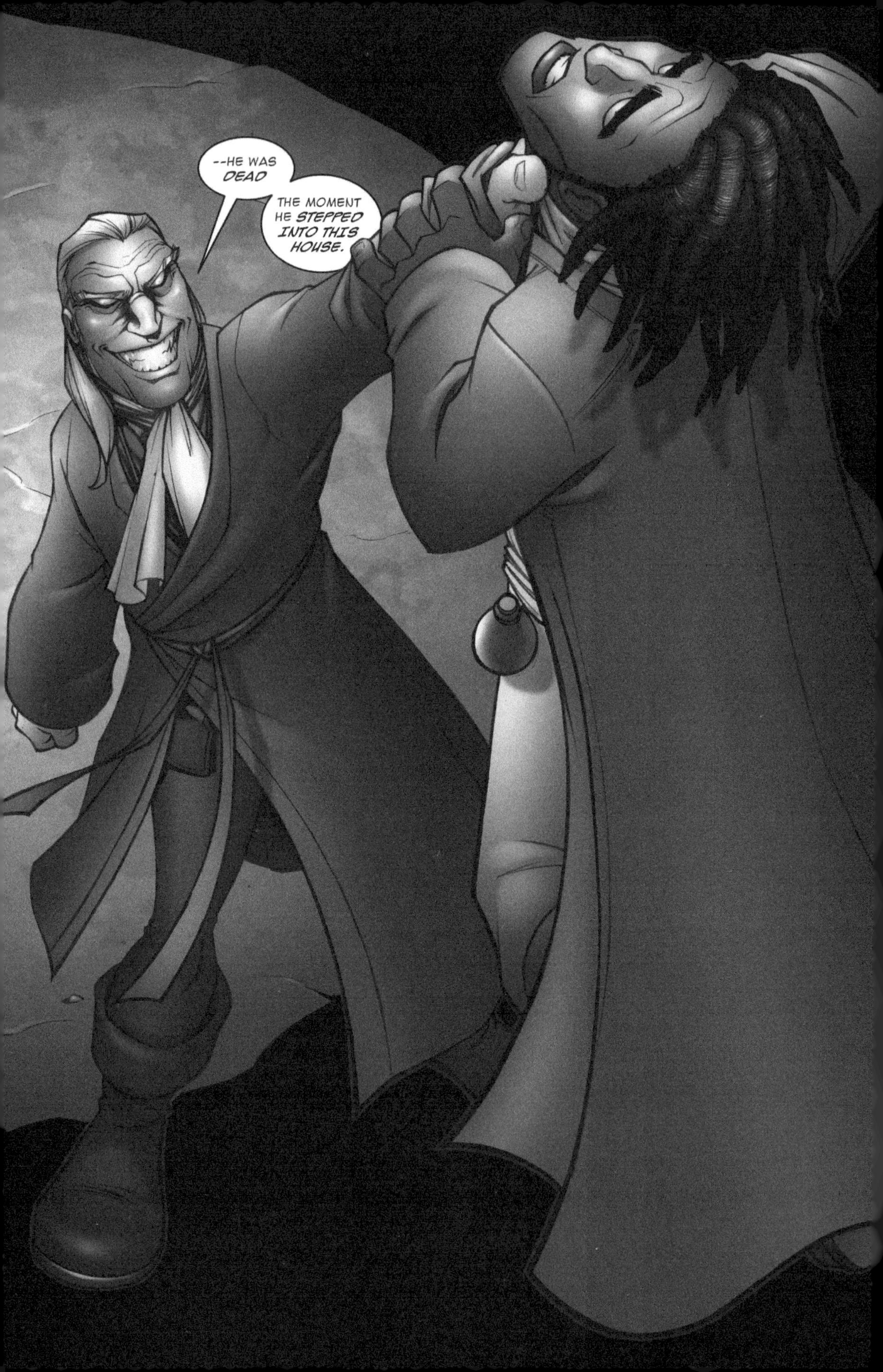
--HE WAS DEAD
THE MOMENT HE STEPPED INTO THIS HOUSE.

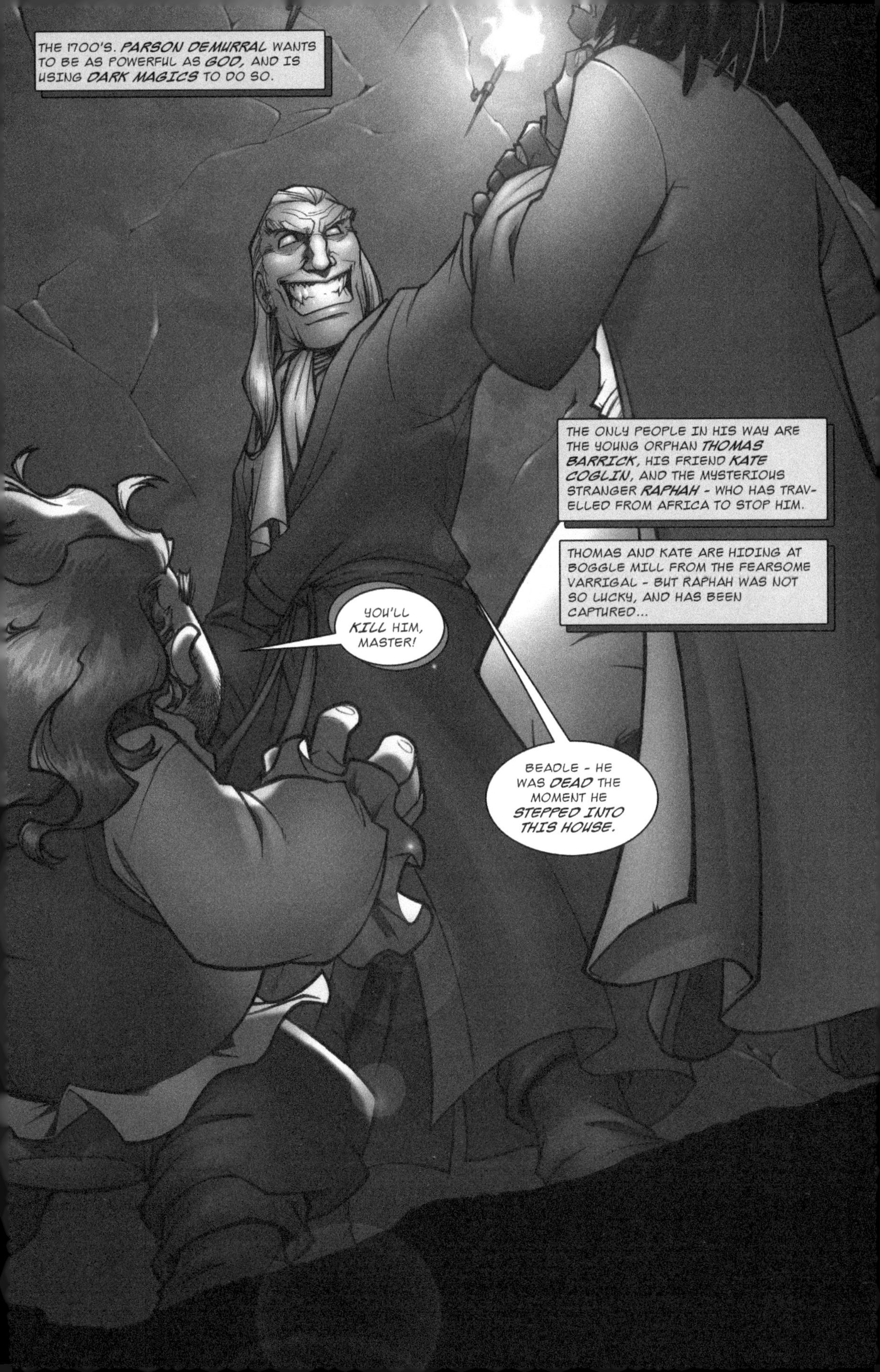
THE 1700'S. PARSON DEMURRAL WANTS TO BE AS POWERFUL AS GOD, AND IS USING DARK MAGICS TO DO SO.
THE ONLY PEOPLE IN HIS WAY ARE THE YOUNG ORPHAN THOMAS BARRICK, HIS FRIEND KATE COGLIN, AND THE MYSTERIOUS STRANGER RAPHAH - WHO HAS TRAVELLED FROM AFRICA TO STOP HIM.
THOMAS AND KATE ARE HIDING AT BOGGLE MILL FROM THE FEARSOME VARRIGAL - BUT RAPHAH WAS NOT SO LUCKY, AND HAS BEEN CAPTURED...
YOU'LL KILL HIM, MASTER!
BEADLE - HE WAS DEAD THE MOMENT HE STEPPED INTO THIS HOUSE.

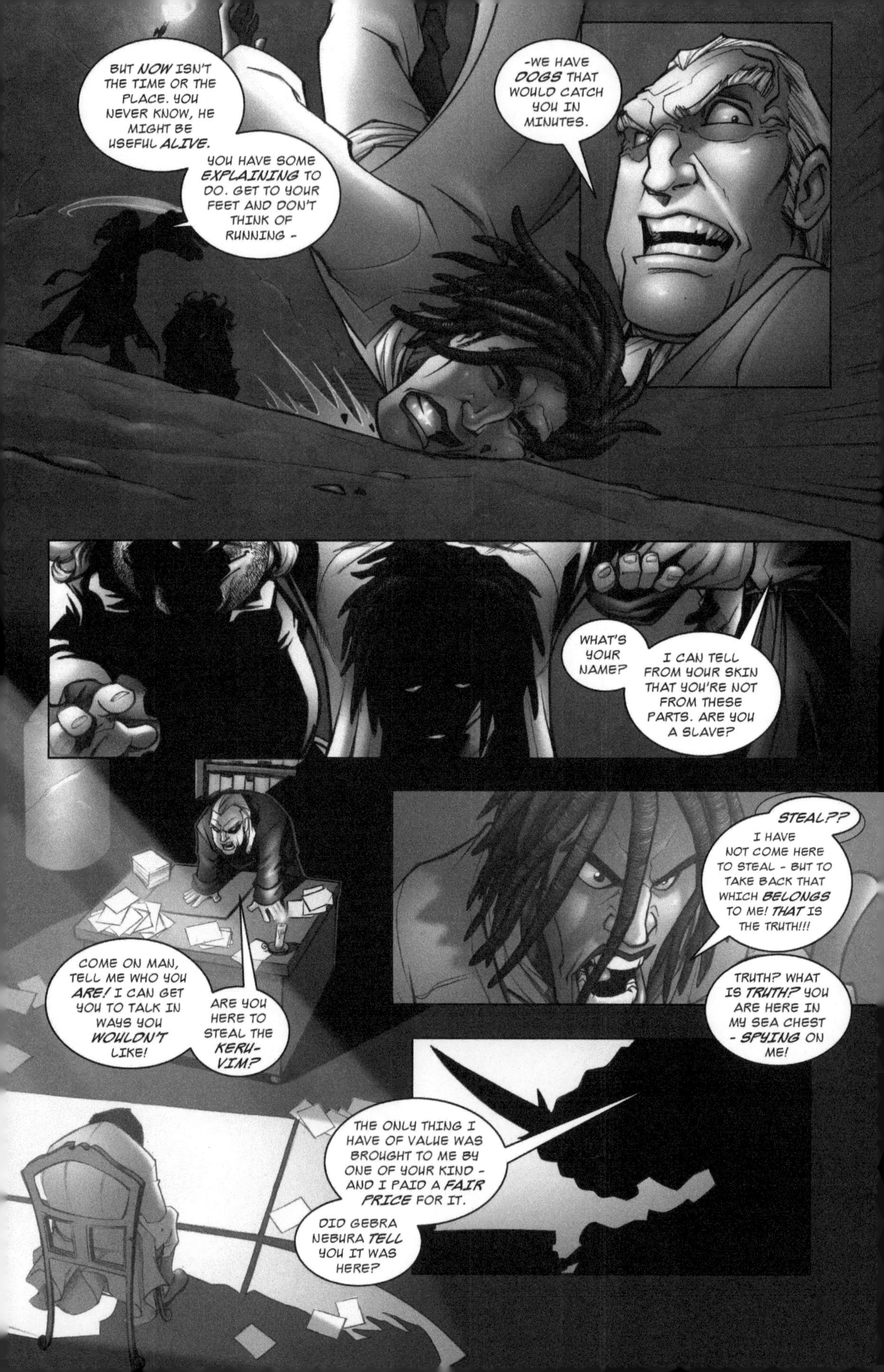
BUT NOW ISN'T THE TIME OR THE PLACE. YOU NEVER KNOW, HE MIGHT BE USEFUL ALIVE.
YOU HAVE SOME EXPLAINING TO DO. GET TO YOUR FEET AND DON'T THINK OF RUNNING -
-WE HAVE DOGS THAT WOULD CATCH YOU IN MINUTES.
WHAT'S YOUR NAME?
I CAN TELL FROM YOUR SKIN THAT YOU'RE NOT FROM THESE PARTS. ARE YOU A SLAVE?
COME ON MAN, TELL ME WHO YOU ARE! I CAN GET YOU TO TALK IN WAYS YOU WOULDN'T LIKE!
ARE YOU HERE TO STEAL THE KERU-VIM?
STEAL??
I HAVE NOT COME HERE TO STEAL - BUT TO TAKE BACK THAT WHICH BELONGS TO ME! THAT IS THE TRUTH!!!
TRUTH? WHAT IS TRUTH? YOU ARE HERE IN MY SEA CHEST - SPYING ON ME!
THE ONLY THING I HAVE OF VALUE WAS BROUGHT TO ME BY ONE OF YOUR KIND - AND I PAID A FAIR PRICE FOR IT.
DID GEBRA NEBURA TELL YOU IT WAS HERE?

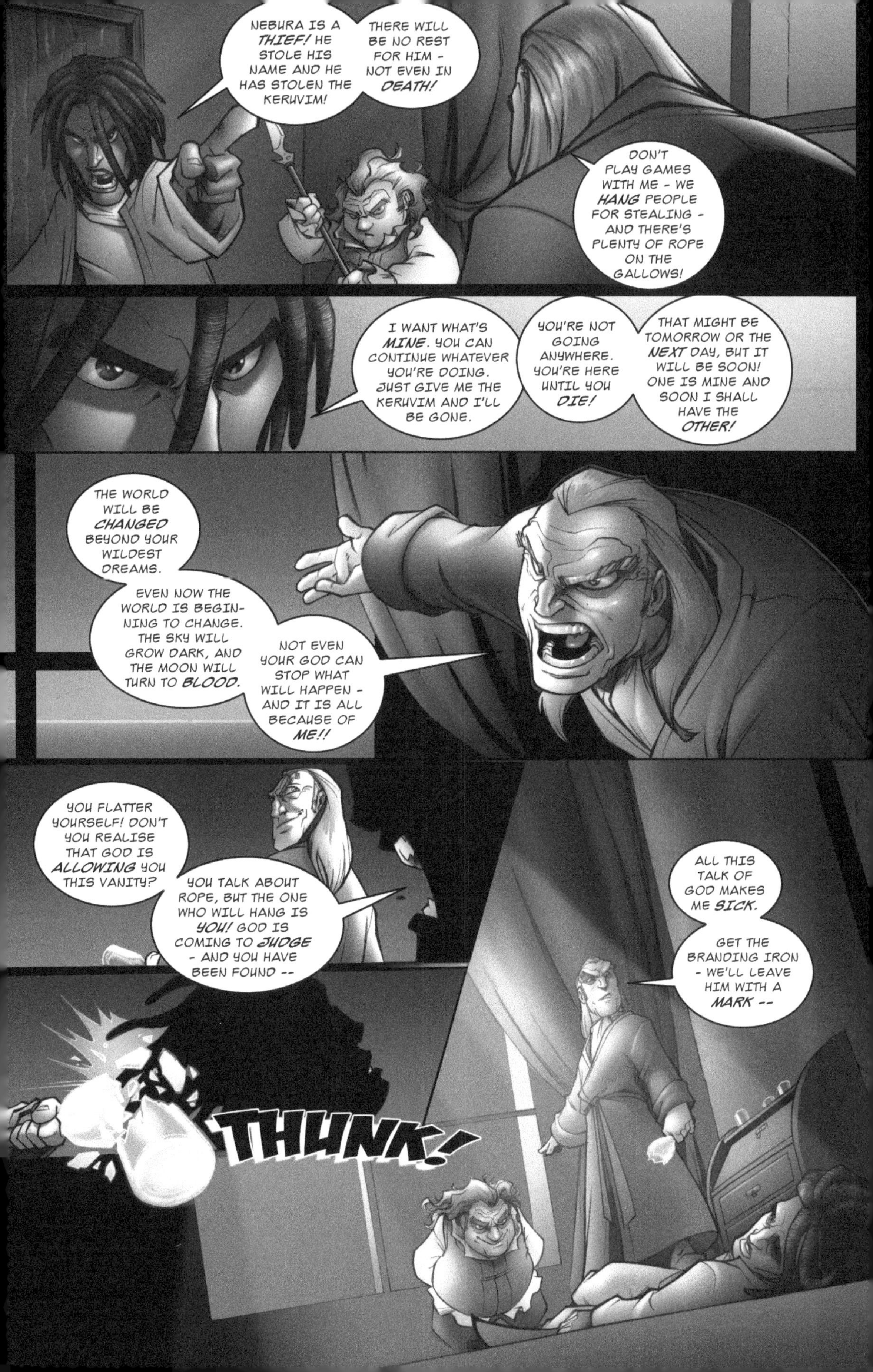
NEBURA IS A THIEF! HE STOLE HIS NAME AND HE HAS STOLEN THE KERUVIM!
THERE WILL BE NO REST FOR HIM - NOT EVEN IN DEATH!
DON'T PLAY GAMES WITH ME - WE HANG PEOPLE FOR STEALING - AND THERE'S PLENTY OF ROPE ON THE GALLOWS!
I WANT WHAT'S MINE. YOU CAN CONTINUE WHATEVER YOU'RE DOING. JUST GIVE ME THE KERUVIM AND I'LL BE GONE.
YOU'RE NOT GOING ANYWHERE. YOU'RE HERE UNTIL YOU DIE!
THAT MIGHT BE TOMORROW OR THE NEXT DAY, BUT IT WILL BE SOON! ONE IS MINE AND SOON I SHALL HAVE THE OTHER!
THE WORLD WILL BE CHANGED BEYOND YOUR WILDEST DREAMS.
EVEN NOW THE WORLD IS BEGINNING TO CHANGE. THE SKY WILL GROW DARK, AND THE MOON WILL TURN TO BLOOD.
NOT EVEN YOUR GOD CAN STOP WHAT WILL HAPPEN - AND IT IS ALL BECAUSE OF ME!!
YOU FLATTER YOURSELF! DON'T YOU REALISE THAT GOD IS ALLOWING YOU THIS VANITY?
YOU TALK ABOUT ROPE, BUT THE ONE WHO WILL HANG IS YOU! GOD IS COMING TO JUDGE - AND YOU HAVE BEEN FOUND --
ALL THIS TALK OF GOD MAKES ME SICK.
GET THE BRANDING IRON - WE'LL LEAVE HIM WITH A MARK --
THUNK!

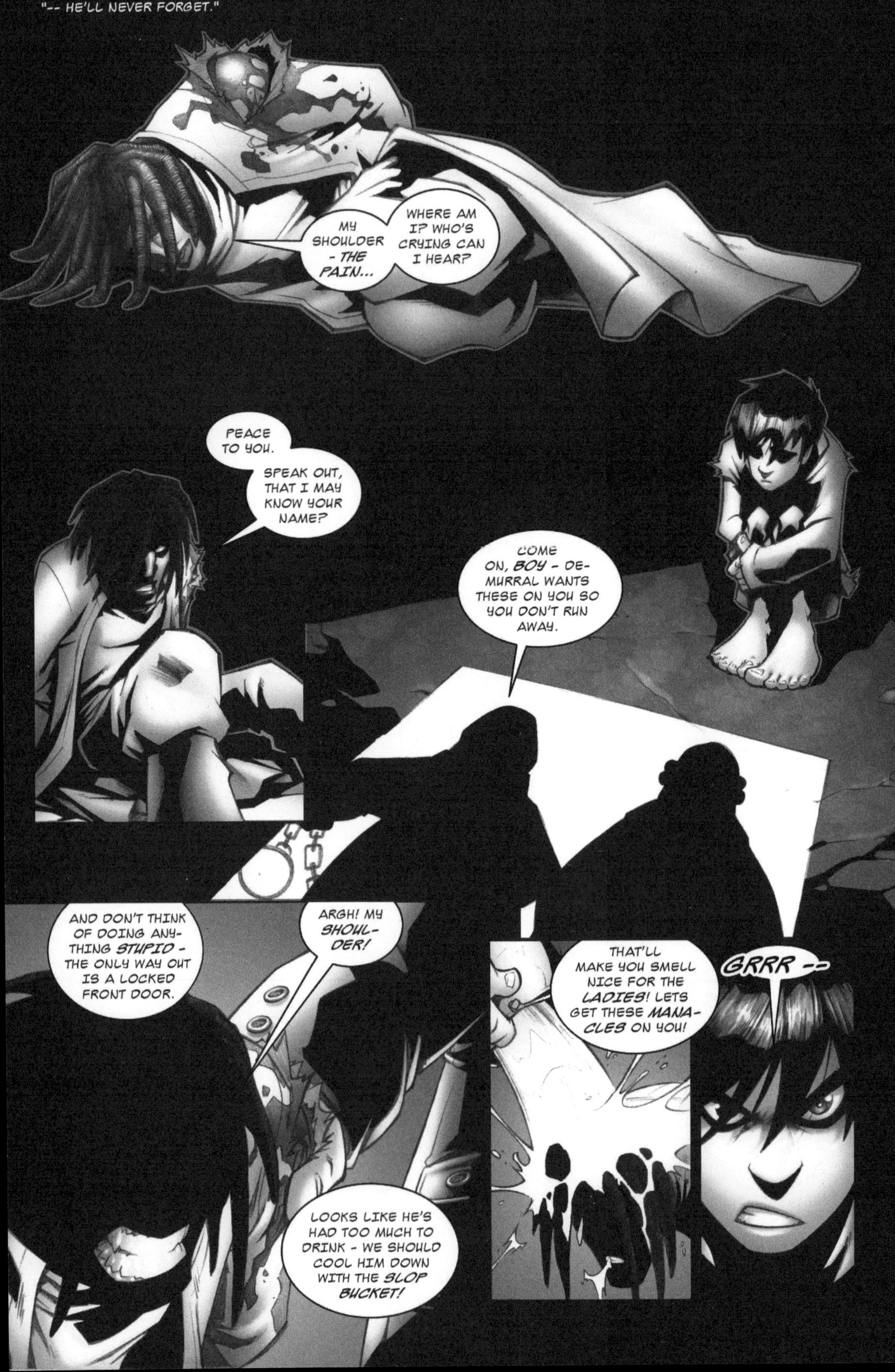
"-- HE'LL NEVER FORGET."
MY SHOULDER - THE PAIN...
WHERE AM I? WHO'S CRYING CAN I HEAR?
PEACE TO YOU.
SPEAK OUT, THAT I MAY KNOW YOUR NAME?
COME ON, BOY - DEMURRAL WANTS THESE ON YOU SO YOU DON'T RUN AWAY.
AND DON'T THINK OF DOING ANYTHING STUPID - THE ONLY WAY OUT IS A LOCKED FRONT DOOR.
ARGH! MY SHOULDER!
LOOKS LIKE HE'S HAD TOO MUCH TO DRINK - WE SHOULD COOL HIM DOWN WITH THE SLOP BUCKET!
THAT'LL MAKE YOU SMELL NICE FOR THE LADIES! LETS GET THESE MANACLES ON YOU!
GRRR --

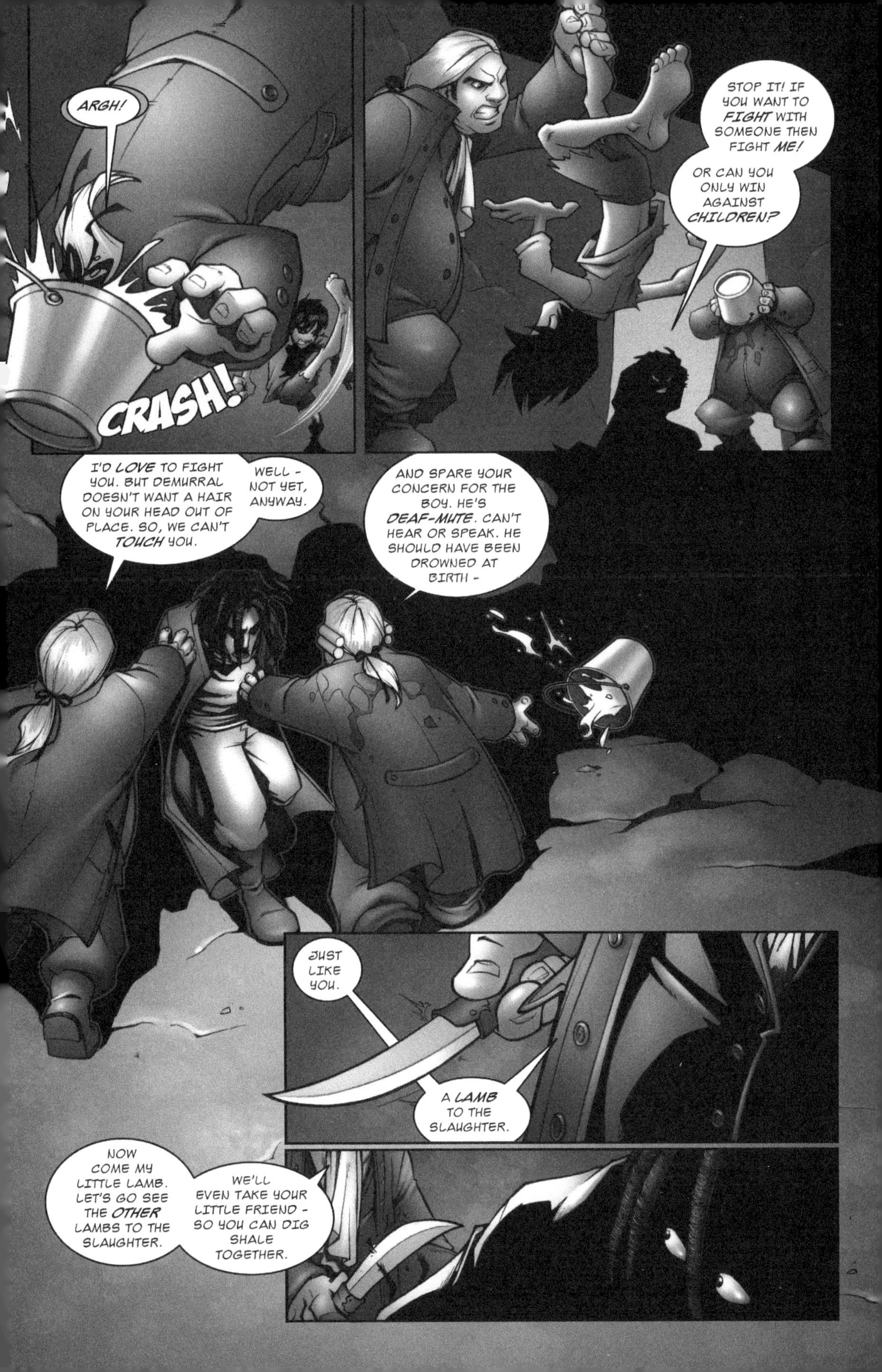
ARGH!
CRASH!
STOP IT! IF YOU WANT TO FIGHT WITH SOMEONE THEN FIGHT ME!
OR CAN YOU ONLY WIN AGAINST CHILDREN?
I'D LOVE TO FIGHT YOU. BUT DEMURRAL DOESN'T WANT A HAIR ON YOUR HEAD OUT OF PLACE. SO, WE CAN'T TOUCH YOU.
WELL - NOT YET, ANYWAY.
AND SPARE YOUR CONCERN FOR THE BOY. HE'S DEAF-MUTE. CAN'T HEAR OR SPEAK. HE SHOULD HAVE BEEN DROWNED AT BIRTH -
JUST LIKE YOU.
A LAMB TO THE SLAUGHTER.
NOW COME MY LITTLE LAMB. LET'S GO SEE THE OTHER LAMBS TO THE SLAUGHTER.
WE'LL EVEN TAKE YOUR LITTLE FRIEND - SO YOU CAN DIG SHALE TOGETHER.

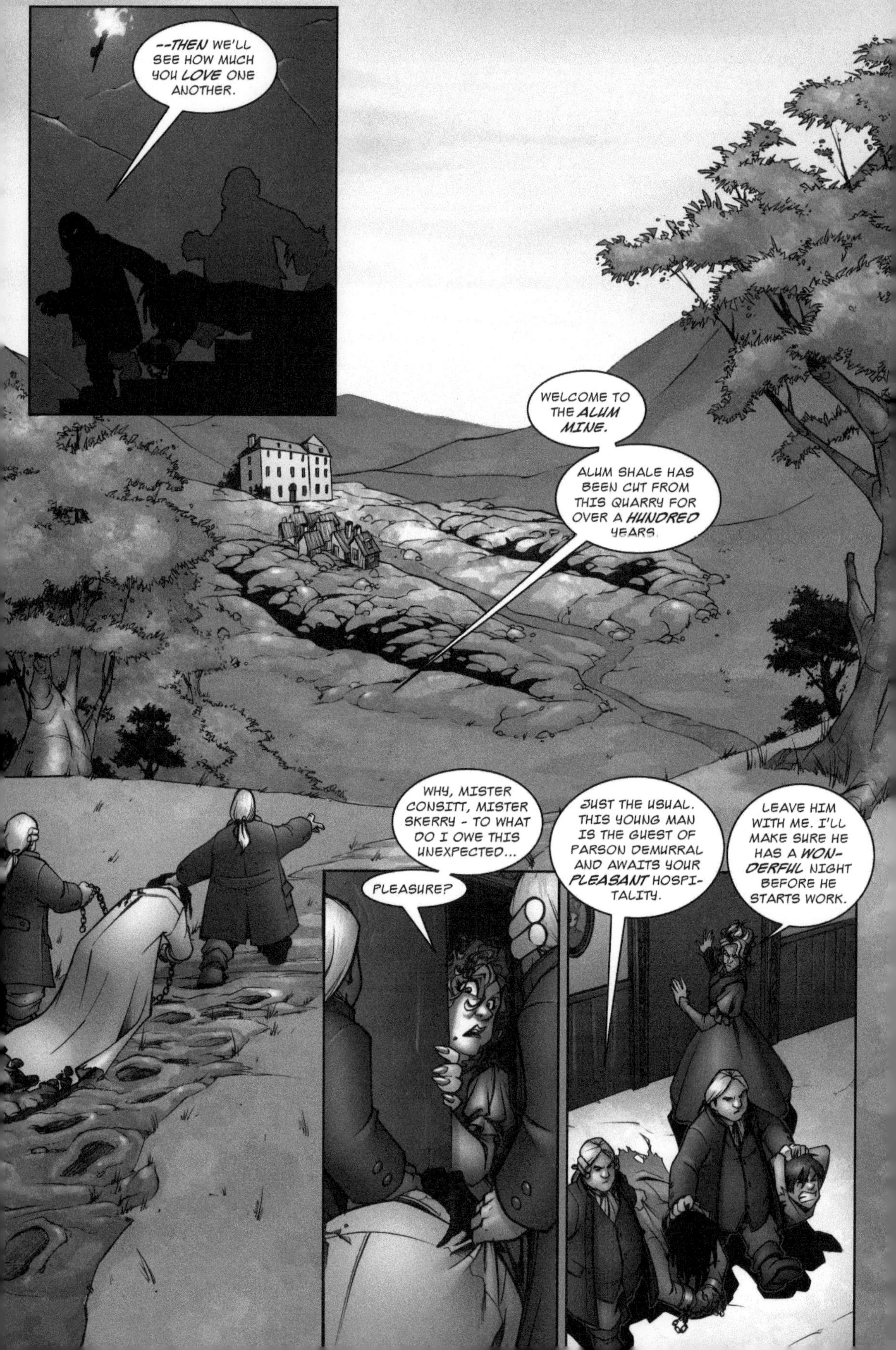
--THEN WE'LL SEE HOW MUCH YOU LOVE ONE ANOTHER.
WELCOME TO THE ALUM MINE.
ALUM SHALE HAS BEEN CUT FROM THIS QUARRY FOR OVER A HUNDRED YEARS.
WHY, MISTER CONSITT, MISTER SKERRY - TO WHAT DO I OWE THIS UNEXPECTED...
PLEASURE?
JUST THE USUAL. THIS YOUNG MAN IS THE GUEST OF PARSON DEMURRAL AND AWAITS YOUR PLEASANT HOSPI-TALITY.
LEAVE HIM WITH ME. I'LL MAKE SURE HE HAS A WON-DERFUL NIGHT BEFORE HE STARTS WORK.

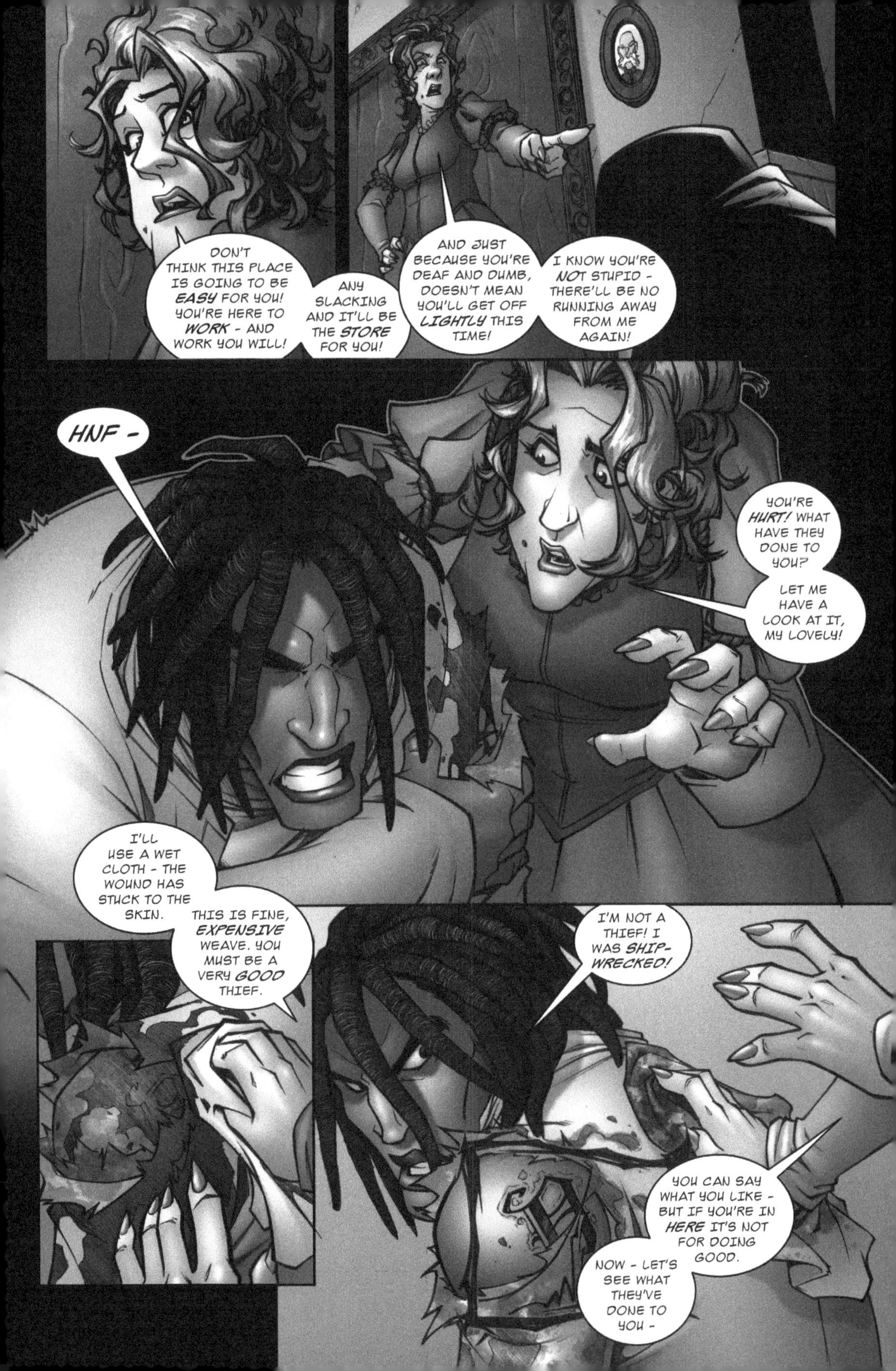
DON'T THINK THIS PLACE IS GOING TO BE EASY FOR YOU! YOU'RE HERE TO WORK - AND WORK YOU WILL!
ANY SLACKING AND IT'LL BE THE STORE FOR YOU!
AND JUST BECAUSE YOU'RE DEAF AND DUMB, DOESN'T MEAN YOU'LL GET OFF LIGHTLY THIS TIME!
I KNOW YOU'RE NOT STUPID - THERE'LL BE NO RUNNING AWAY FROM ME AGAIN!
HNF -
YOU'RE HURT! WHAT HAVE THEY DONE TO YOU?
LET ME HAVE A LOOK AT IT, MY LOVELY!
I'LL USE A WET CLOTH - THE WOUND HAS STUCK TO THE SKIN.
THIS IS FINE, EXPENSIVE WEAVE. YOU MUST BE A VERY GOOD THIEF.
I'M NOT A THIEF! I WAS SHIP-WRECKED!
YOU CAN SAY WHAT YOU LIKE - BUT IF YOU'RE IN HERE IT'S NOT FOR DOING GOOD.
NOW - LET'S SEE WHAT THEY'VE DONE TO YOU -

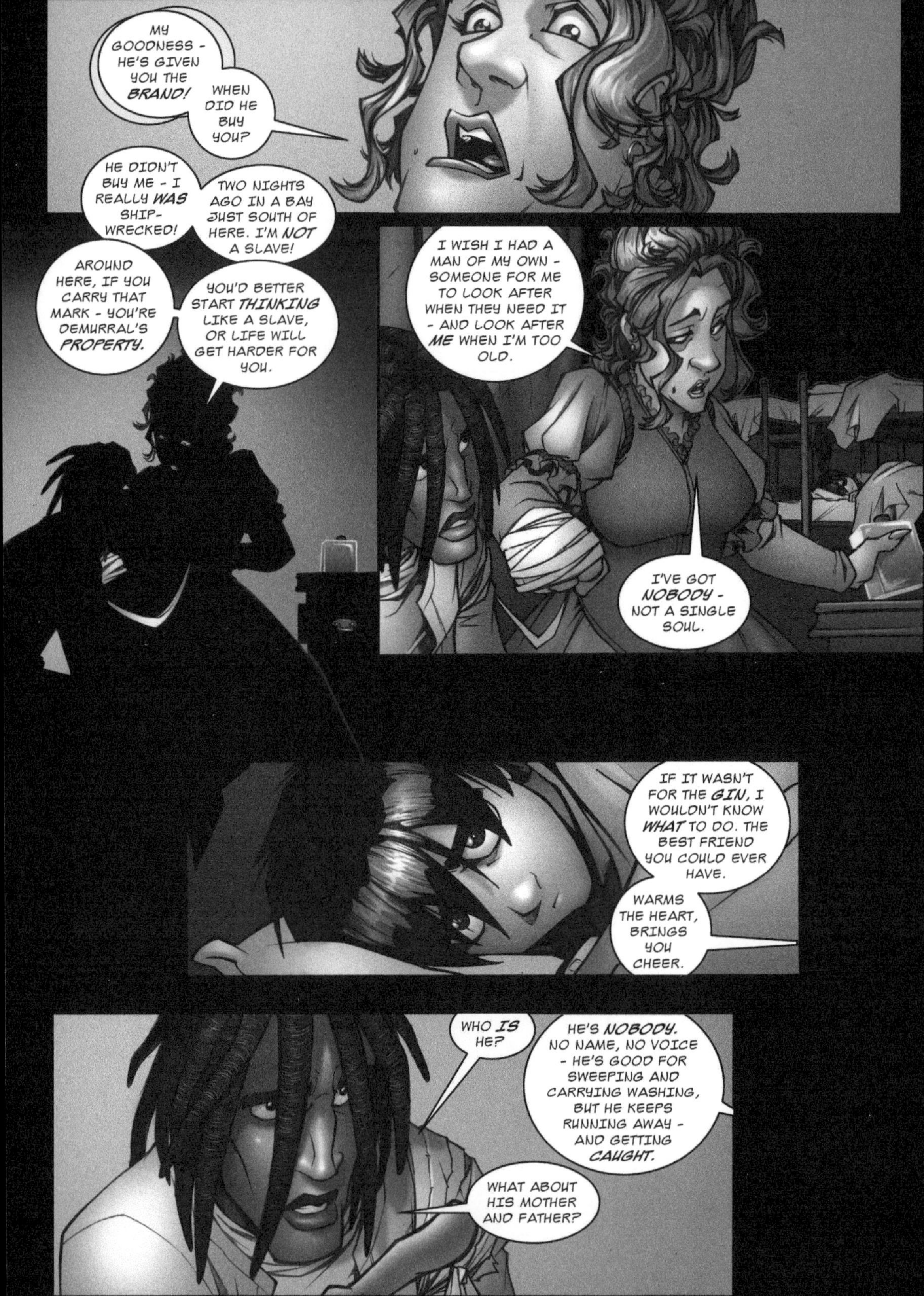
MY GOODNESS - HE'S GIVEN YOU THE BRAND!
WHEN DID HE BUY YOU?
HE DIDN'T BUY ME - I REALLY WAS SHIP-WRECKED!
TWO NIGHTS AGO IN A BAY JUST SOUTH OF HERE. I'M NOT A SLAVE!
AROUND HERE, IF YOU CARRY THAT MARK - YOU'RE DEMURRAL'S PROPERTY.
YOU'D BETTER START THINKING LIKE A SLAVE, OR LIFE WILL GET HARDER FOR YOU.
I WISH I HAD A MAN OF MY OWN - SOMEONE FOR ME TO LOOK AFTER WHEN THEY NEED IT - AND LOOK AFTER ME WHEN I'M TOO OLD.
I'VE GOT NOBODY - NOT A SINGLE SOUL.
IF IT WASN'T FOR THE GIN, I WOULDN'T KNOW WHAT TO DO. THE BEST FRIEND YOU COULD EVER HAVE.
WARMS THE HEART, BRINGS YOU CHEER.
WHO IS HE?
HE'S NOBODY. NO NAME, NO VOICE - HE'S GOOD FOR SWEEPING AND CARRYING WASHING, BUT HE KEEPS RUNNING AWAY - AND GETTING CAUGHT.
WHAT ABOUT HIS MOTHER AND FATHER?

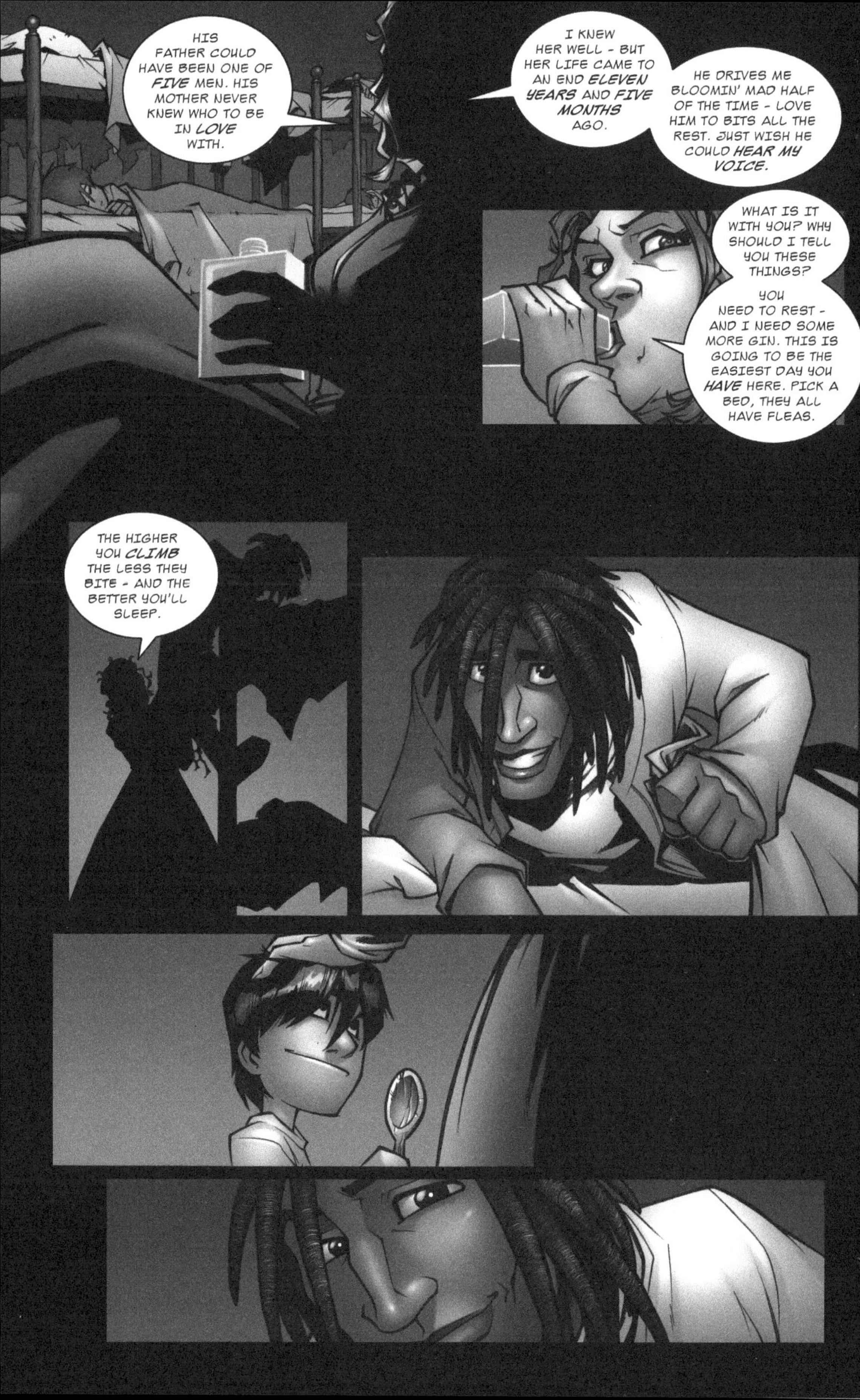
HIS FATHER COULD HAVE BEEN ONE OF FIVE MEN. HIS MOTHER NEVER KNEW WHO TO BE IN LOVE WITH.
I KNEW HER WELL - BUT HER LIFE CAME TO AN END ELEVEN YEARS AND FIVE MONTHS AGO.
HE DRIVES ME BLOOMIN' MAD HALF OF THE TIME - LOVE HIM TO BITS ALL THE REST. JUST WISH HE COULD HEAR MY VOICE.
WHAT IS IT WITH YOU? WHY SHOULD I TELL YOU THESE THINGS?
YOU NEED TO REST - AND I NEED SOME MORE GIN. THIS IS GOING TO BE THE EASIEST DAY YOU HAVE HERE. PICK A BED, THEY ALL HAVE FLEAS.
THE HIGHER YOU CLIMB THE LESS THEY BITE - AND THE BETTER YOU'LL SLEEP.

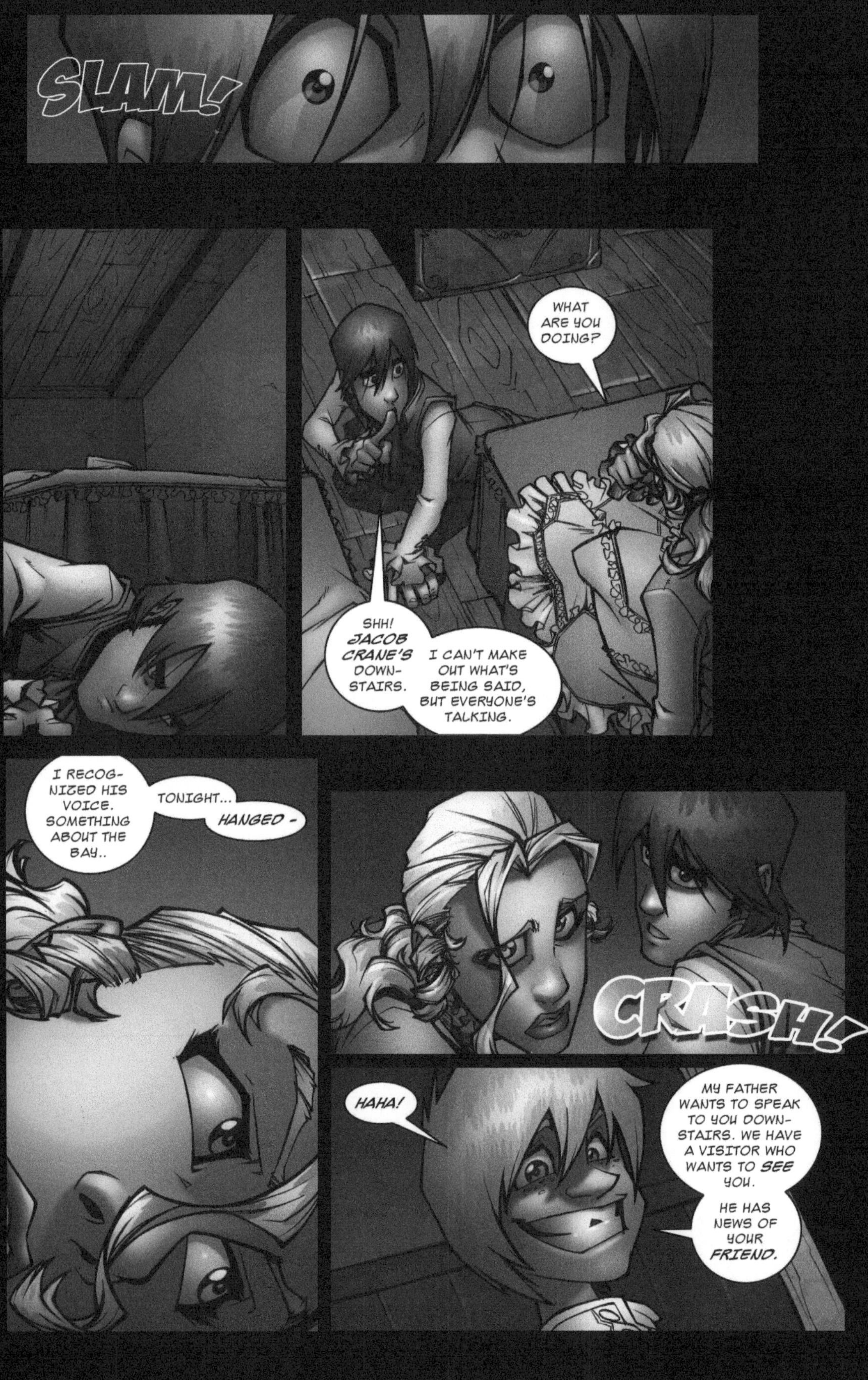
SLAM!
WHAT ARE YOU DOING?
SHH! JACOB CRANE'S DOWN-STAIRS.
I CAN'T MAKE OUT WHAT'S BEING SAID, BUT EVERYONE'S TALKING.
I RECOG-NIZED HIS VOICE. SOMETHING ABOUT THE BAY..
TONIGHT...
HANGED -
CRASH!
HAHA!
MY FATHER WANTS TO SPEAK TO YOU DOWN-STAIRS. WE HAVE A VISITOR WHO WANTS TO SEE YOU.
HE HAS NEWS OF YOUR FRIEND.

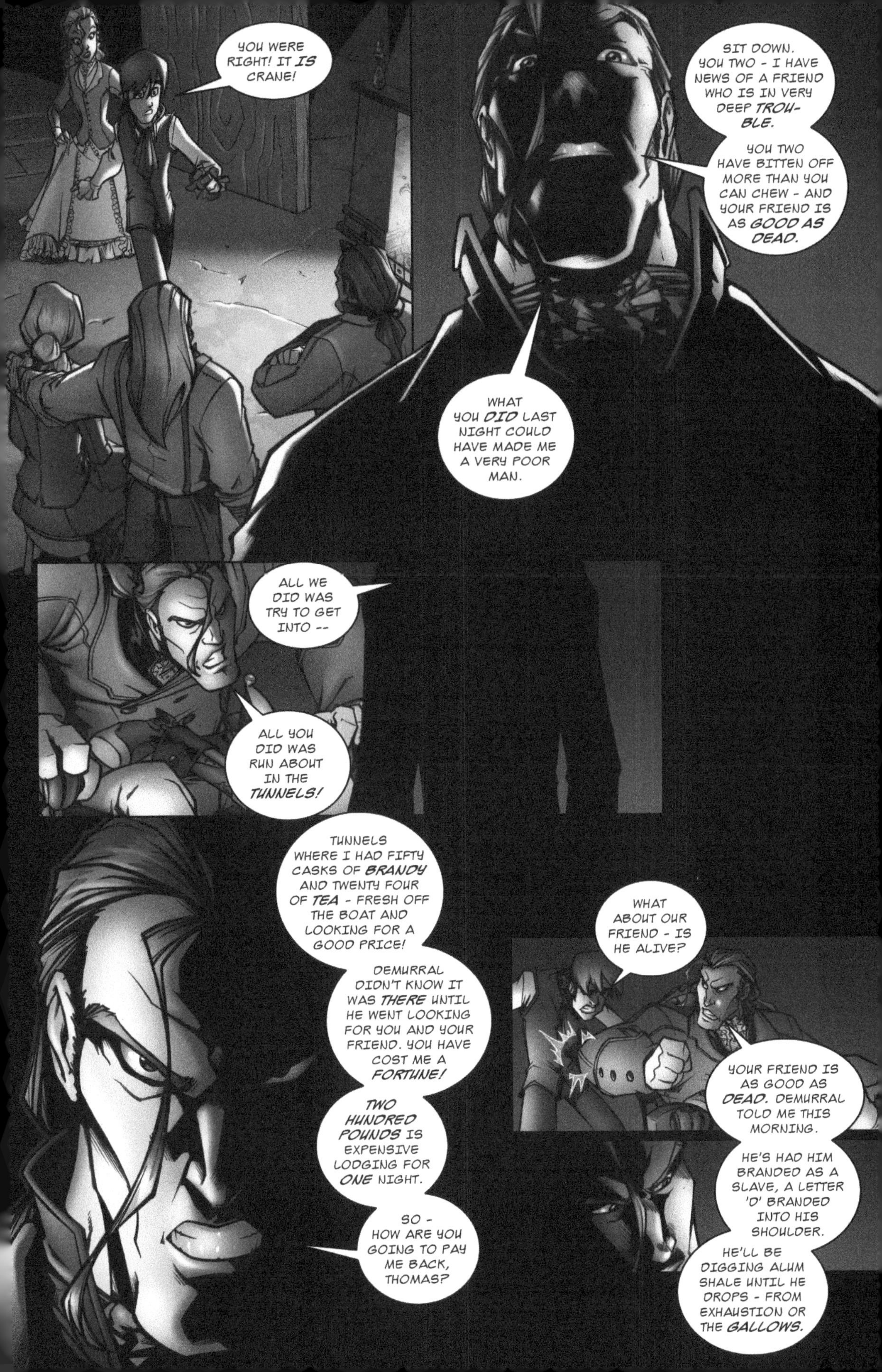
YOU WERE RIGHT! IT IS CRANE!
SIT DOWN. YOU TWO - I HAVE NEWS OF A FRIEND WHO IS IN VERY DEEP TROUBLE.
YOU TWO HAVE BITTEN OFF MORE THAN YOU CAN CHEW - AND YOUR FRIEND IS AS GOOD AS DEAD.
WHAT YOU DID LAST NIGHT COULD HAVE MADE ME A VERY POOR MAN.
ALL WE DID WAS TRY TO GET INTO --
ALL YOU DID WAS RUN ABOUT IN THE TUNNELS!
TUNNELS WHERE I HAD FIFTY CASKS OF BRANDY AND TWENTY FOUR OF TEA - FRESH OFF THE BOAT AND LOOKING FOR A GOOD PRICE!
DEMURRAL DIDN'T KNOW IT WAS THERE UNTIL HE WENT LOOKING FOR YOU AND YOUR FRIEND. YOU HAVE COST ME A FORTUNE!
TWO HUNDRED POUNDS IS EXPENSIVE LODGING FOR ONE NIGHT.
SO - HOW ARE YOU GOING TO PAY ME BACK, THOMAS?
WHAT ABOUT OUR FRIEND - IS HE ALIVE?
YOUR FRIEND IS AS GOOD AS DEAD. DEMURRAL TOLD ME THIS MORNING.
HE'S HAD HIM BRANDED AS A SLAVE, A LETTER 'D' BRANDED INTO HIS SHOULDER.
HE'LL BE DIGGING ALUM SHALE UNTIL HE DROPS - FROM EXHAUSTION OR THE GALLOWS.

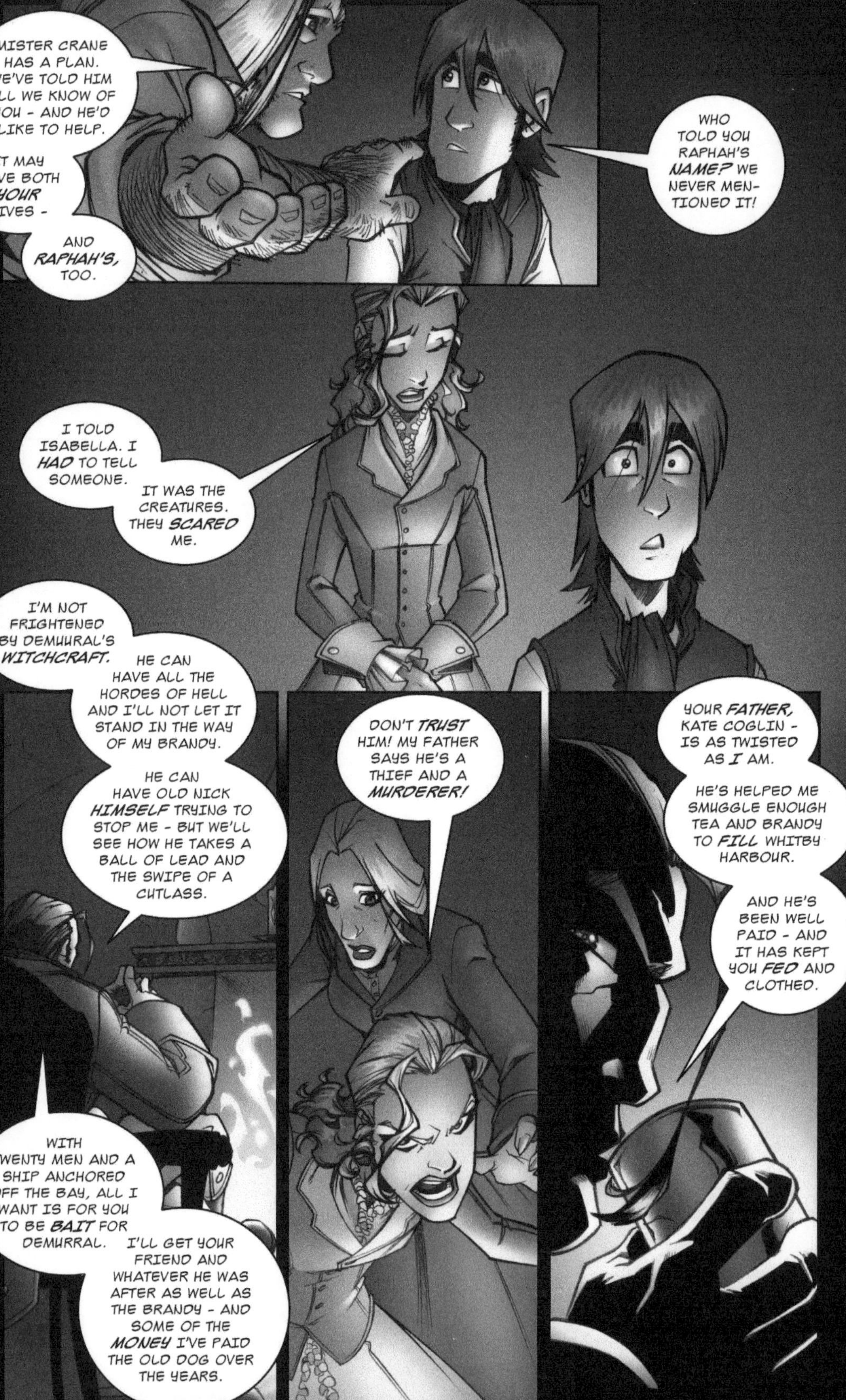
MISTER CRANE HAS A PLAN. WE'VE TOLD HIM ALL WE KNOW OF YOU - AND HE'D LIKE TO HELP.
IT MAY SAVE BOTH YOUR LIVES -
AND RAPHAH'S, TOO.
WHO TOLD YOU RAPHAH'S NAME? WE NEVER MEN-TIONED IT!
I TOLD ISABELLA. I HAD TO TELL SOMEONE.
IT WAS THE CREATURES. THEY SCARED ME.
I'M NOT FRIGHTENED BY DEMURRAL'S WITCHCRAFT.
HE CAN HAVE ALL THE HORDES OF HELL AND I'LL NOT LET IT STAND IN THE WAY OF MY BRANDY.
HE CAN HAVE OLD NICK HIMSELF TRYING TO STOP ME - BUT WE'LL SEE HOW HE TAKES A BALL OF LEAD AND THE SWIPE OF A CUTLASS.
WITH TWENTY MEN AND A SHIP ANCHORED OFF THE BAY, ALL I WANT IS FOR YOU TO BE BAIT FOR DEMURRAL.
I'LL GET YOUR FRIEND AND WHATEVER HE WAS AFTER AS WELL AS THE BRANDY - AND SOME OF THE MONEY I'VE PAID THE OLD DOG OVER THE YEARS.
DON'T TRUST HIM! MY FATHER SAYS HE'S A THIEF AND A MURDERER!
YOUR FATHER, KATE COGLIN - IS AS TWISTED AS I AM.
HE'S HELPED ME SMUGGLE ENOUGH TEA AND BRANDY TO FILL WHITBY HARBOUR.
AND HE'S BEEN WELL PAID - AND IT HAS KEPT YOU FED AND CLOTHED.

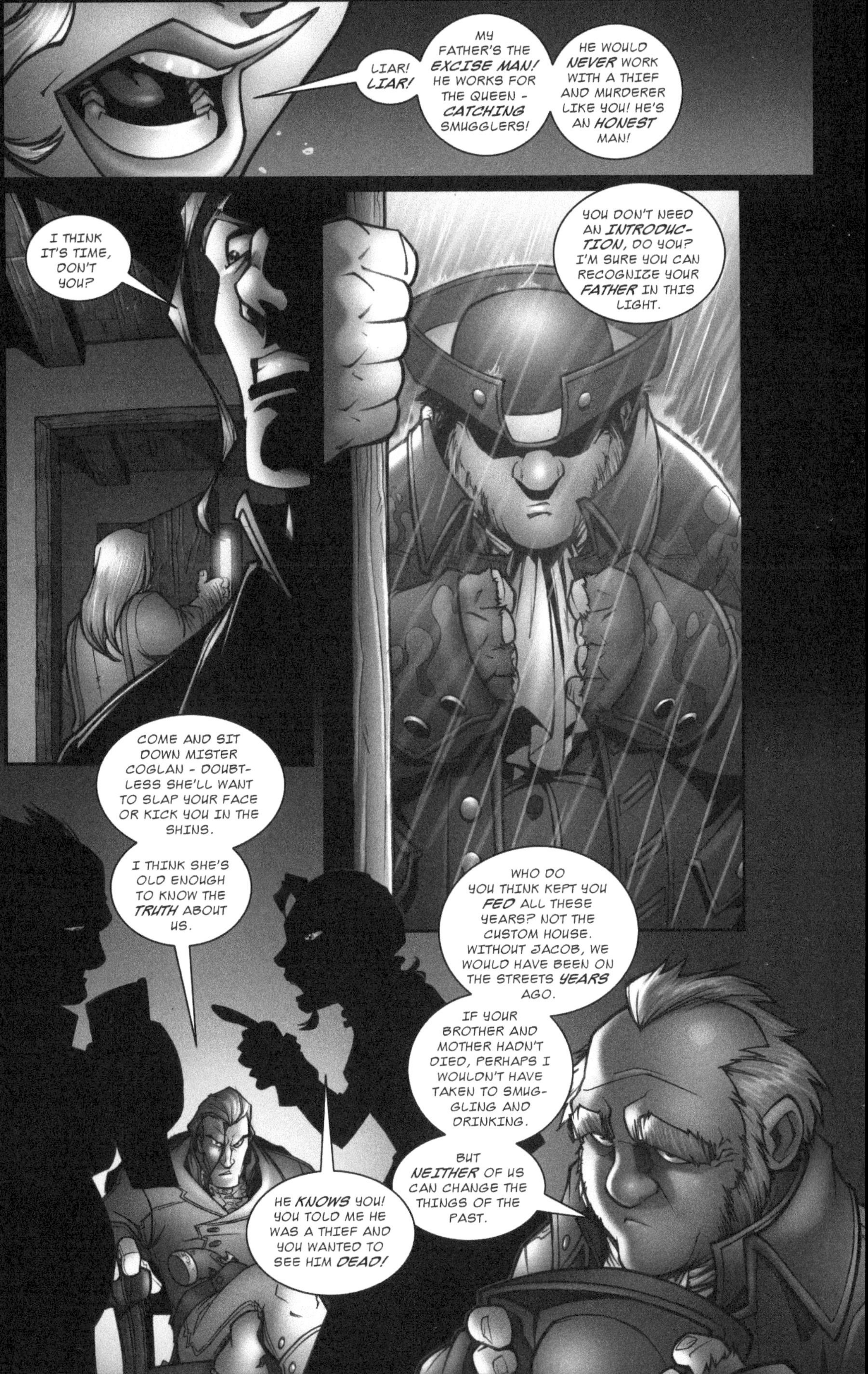
LIAR! LIAR!
MY FATHER'S THE EXCISE MAN! HE WORKS FOR THE QUEEN - CATCHING SMUGGLERS!
HE WOULD NEVER WORK WITH A THIEF AND MURDERER LIKE YOU! HE'S AN HONEST MAN!
I THINK IT'S TIME, DON'T YOU?
YOU DON'T NEED AN INTRODUCTION, DO YOU? I'M SURE YOU CAN RECOGNIZE YOUR FATHER IN THIS LIGHT.
COME AND SIT DOWN MISTER COGLAN - DOUBTLESS SHE'LL WANT TO SLAP YOUR FACE OR KICK YOU IN THE SHINS.
I THINK SHE'S OLD ENOUGH TO KNOW THE TRUTH ABOUT US.
HE KNOWS YOU! YOU TOLD ME HE WAS A THIEF AND YOU WANTED TO SEE HIM DEAD!
WHO DO YOU THINK KEPT YOU FED ALL THESE YEARS? NOT THE CUSTOM HOUSE. WITHOUT JACOB, WE WOULD HAVE BEEN ON THE STREETS YEARS AGO.
IF YOUR BROTHER AND MOTHER HADN'T DIED, PERHAPS I WOULDN'T HAVE TAKEN TO SMUGGLING AND DRINKING.
BUT NEITHER OF US CAN CHANGE THE THINGS OF THE PAST.

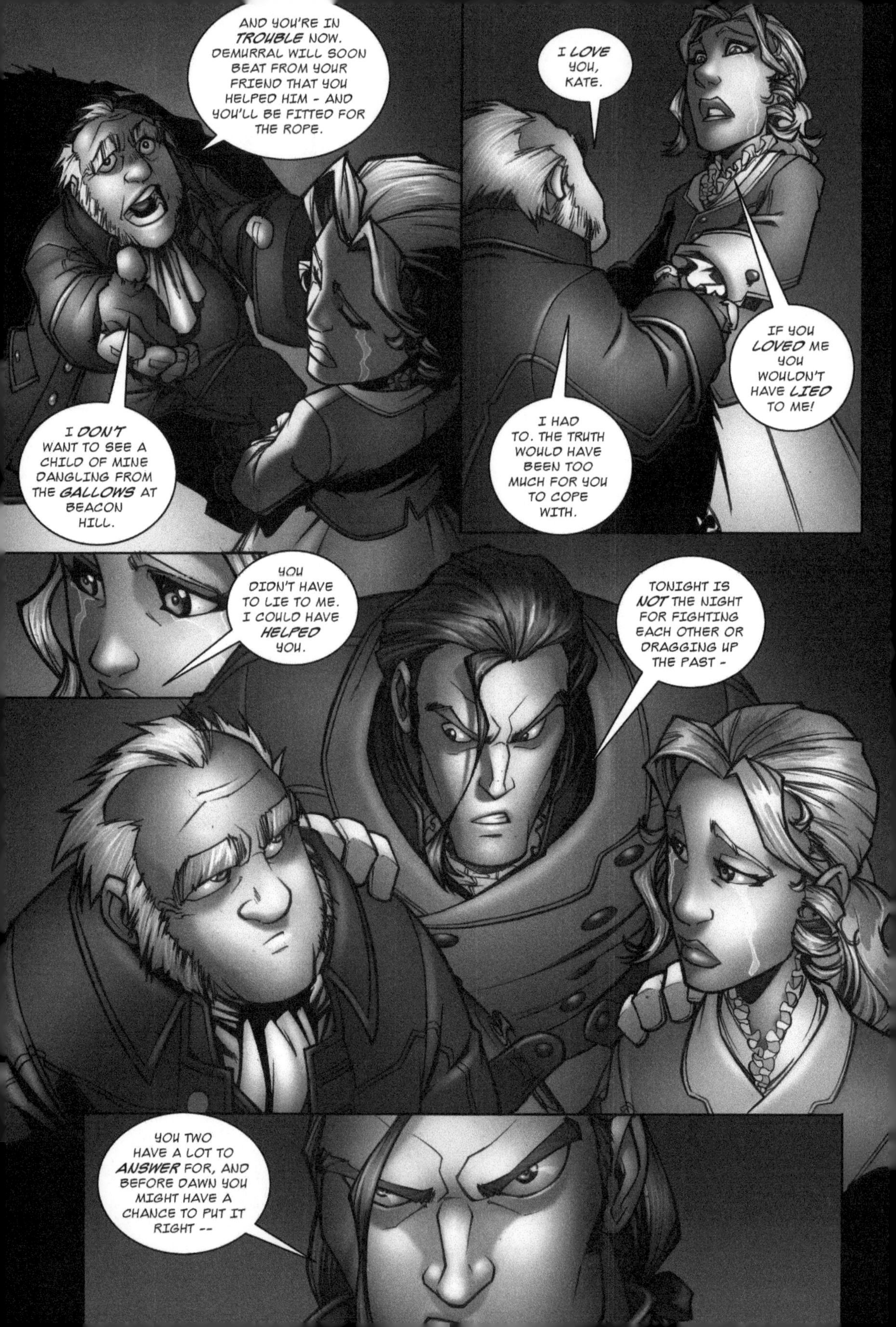
AND YOU'RE IN TROUBLE NOW. DEMURRAL WILL SOON BEAT FROM YOUR FRIEND THAT YOU HELPED HIM - AND YOU'LL BE FITTED FOR THE ROPE.
I DON'T WANT TO SEE A CHILD OF MINE DANGLING FROM THE GALLOWS AT BEACON HILL.
I LOVE YOU, KATE.
IF YOU LOVED ME YOU WOULDN'T HAVE LIED TO ME!
I HAD TO. THE TRUTH WOULD HAVE BEEN TOO MUCH FOR YOU TO COPE WITH.
YOU DIDN'T HAVE TO LIE TO ME. I COULD HAVE HELPED YOU.
TONIGHT IS NOT THE NIGHT FOR FIGHTING EACH OTHER OR DRAGGING UP THE PAST -
YOU TWO HAVE A LOT TO ANSWER FOR, AND BEFORE DAWN YOU MIGHT HAVE A CHANCE TO PUT IT RIGHT --

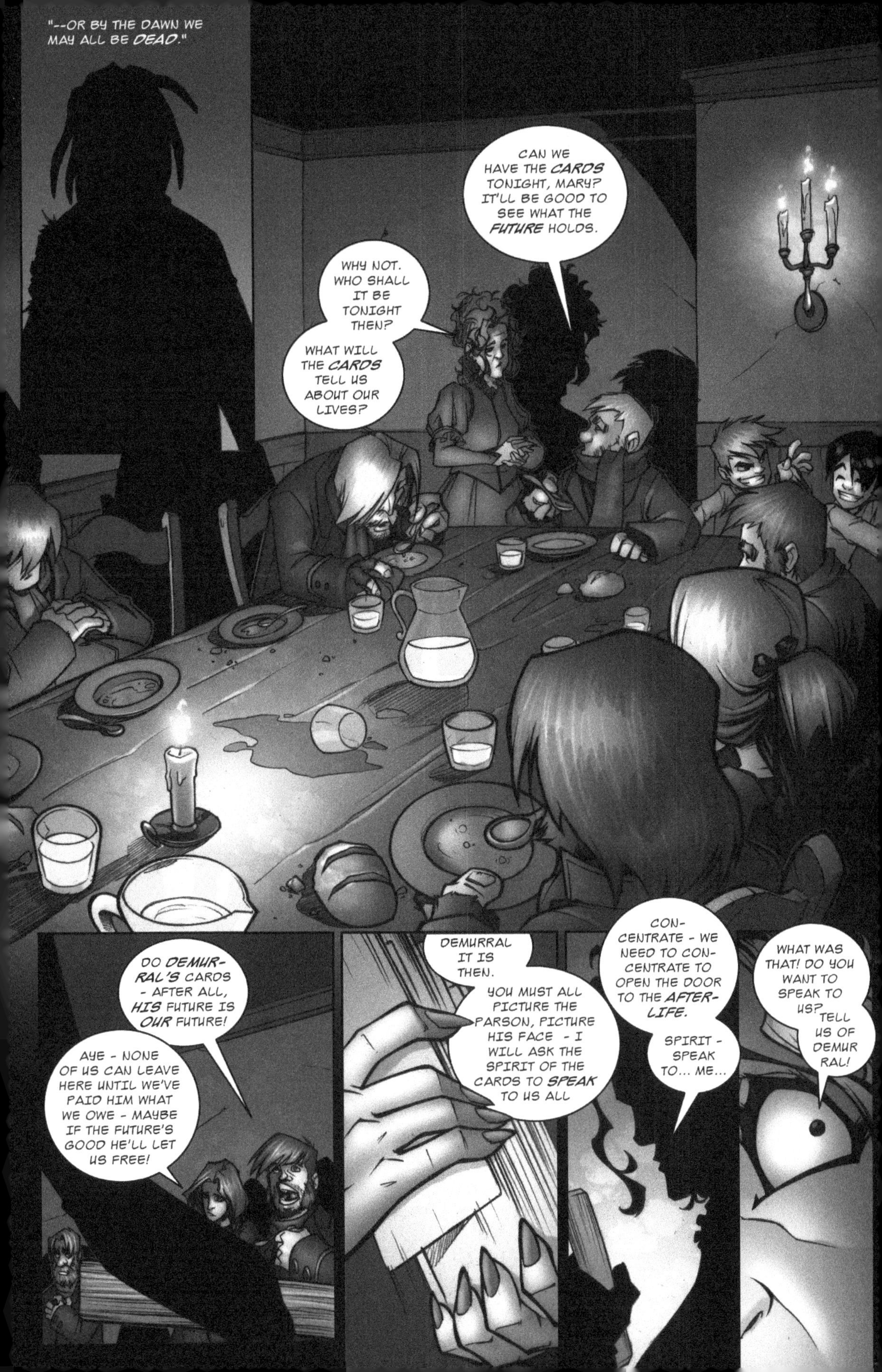
"--OR BY THE DAWN WE MAY ALL BE DEAD."
CAN WE HAVE THE CARDS TONIGHT, MARY? IT'LL BE GOOD TO SEE WHAT THE FUTURE HOLDS.
WHY NOT. WHO SHALL IT BE TONIGHT THEN?
WHAT WILL THE CARDS TELL US ABOUT OUR LIVES?
DO DEMUR-RAL'S CARDS - AFTER ALL, HIS FUTURE IS OUR FUTURE!
AYE - NONE OF US CAN LEAVE HERE UNTIL WE'VE PAID HIM WHAT WE OWE - MAYBE IF THE FUTURE'S GOOD HE'LL LET US FREE!
DEMURRAL IT IS THEN.
YOU MUST ALL PICTURE THE PARSON, PICTURE HIS FACE - I WILL ASK THE SPIRIT OF THE CARDS TO SPEAK TO US ALL
CON-CENTRATE - WE NEED TO CON-CENTRATE TO OPEN THE DOOR TO THE AFTER-LIFE.
SPIRIT - SPEAK TO... ME...
WHAT WAS THAT! DO YOU WANT TO SPEAK TO US?
TELL US OF DEMUR RAL!

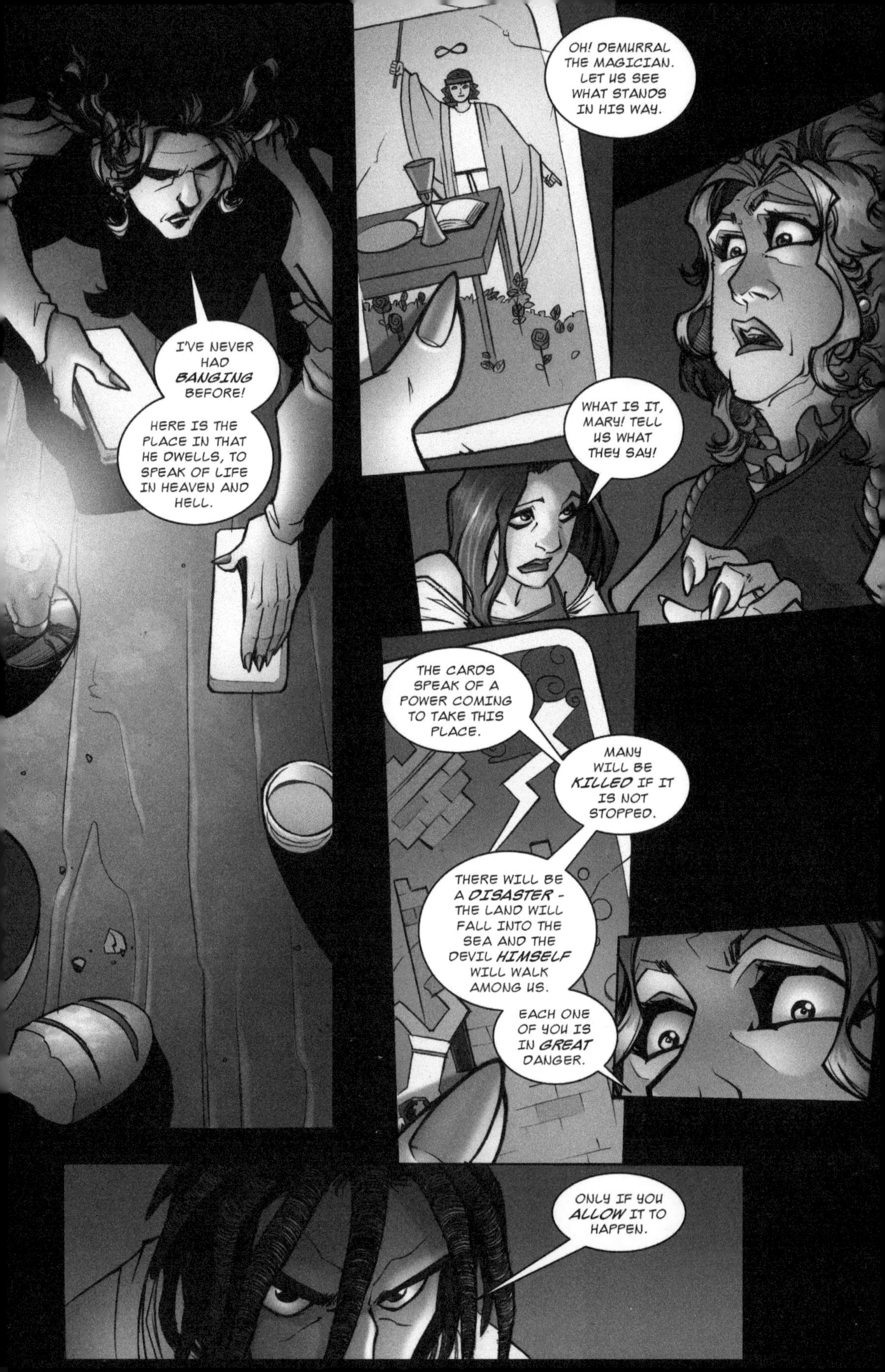
I'VE NEVER HAD BANGING BEFORE!
HERE IS THE PLACE IN THAT HE DWELLS, TO SPEAK OF LIFE IN HEAVEN AND HELL.
OH! DEMURRAL THE MAGICIAN. LET US SEE WHAT STANDS IN HIS WAY.
WHAT IS IT, MARY! TELL US WHAT THEY SAY!
THE CARDS SPEAK OF A POWER COMING TO TAKE THIS PLACE.
MANY WILL BE KILLED IF IT IS NOT STOPPED.
THERE WILL BE A DISASTER - THE LAND WILL FALL INTO THE SEA AND THE DEVIL HIMSELF WILL WALK AMONG US.
EACH ONE OF YOU IS IN GREAT DANGER.
ONLY IF YOU ALLOW IT TO HAPPEN.

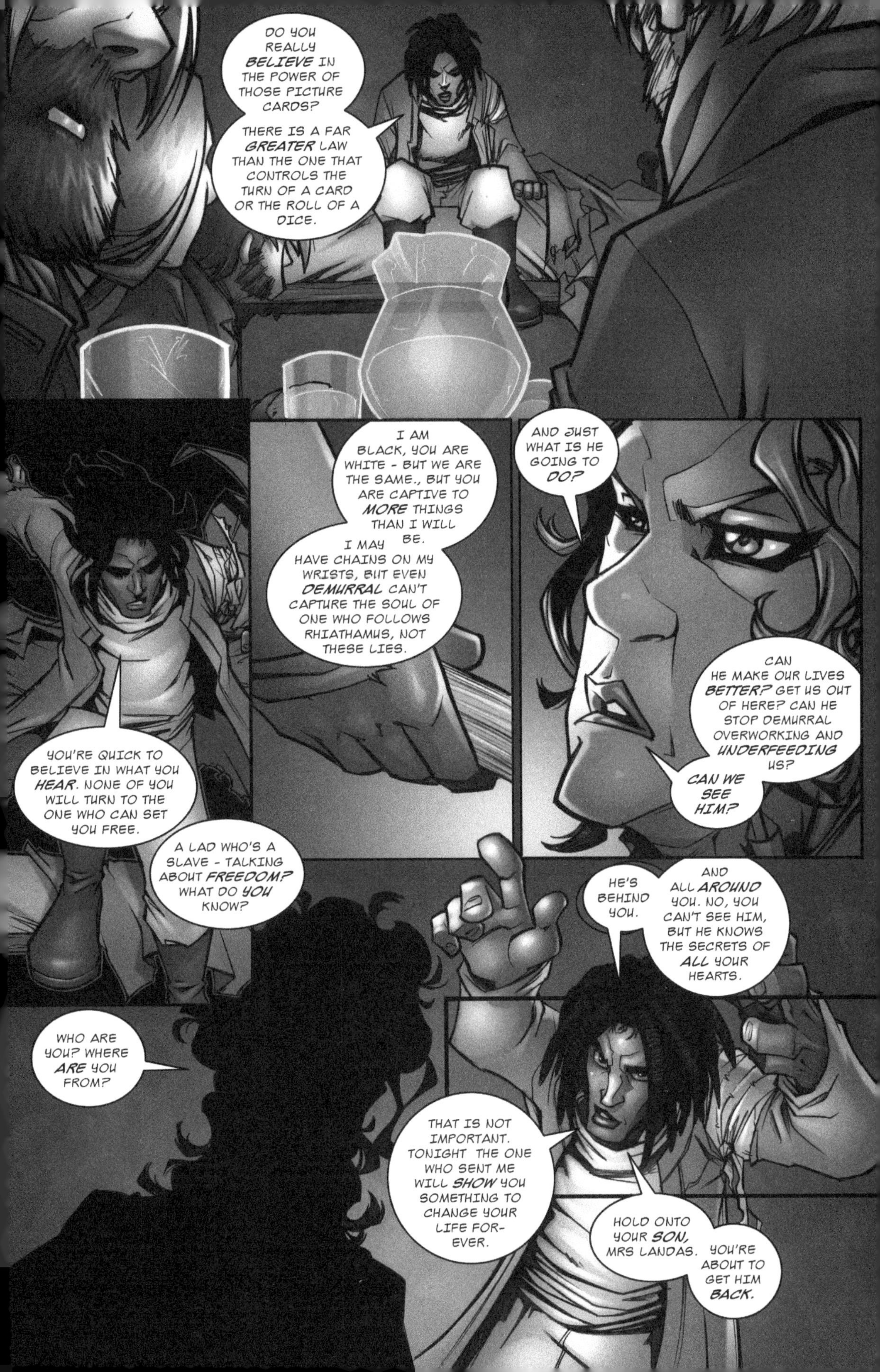
DO YOU REALLY BELIEVE IN THE POWER OF THOSE PICTURE CARDS?
THERE IS A FAR GREATER LAW THAN THE ONE THAT CONTROLS THE TURN OF A CARD OR THE ROLL OF A DICE.
I AM BLACK, YOU ARE WHITE - BUT WE ARE THE SAME., BUT YOU ARE CAPTIVE TO MORE THINGS THAN I WILL BE.
I MAY HAVE CHAINS ON MY WRISTS, BUT EVEN DEMURRAL CAN'T CAPTURE THE SOUL OF ONE WHO FOLLOWS RHIATHAMUS, NOT THESE LIES.
AND JUST WHAT IS HE GOING TO DO?
CAN HE MAKE OUR LIVES BETTER? GET US OUT OF HERE? CAN HE STOP DEMURRAL OVERWORKING AND UNDERFEEDING US?
CAN WE SEE HIM?
YOU'RE QUICK TO BELIEVE IN WHAT YOU HEAR. NONE OF YOU WILL TURN TO THE ONE WHO CAN SET YOU FREE.
A LAD WHO'S A SLAVE - TALKING ABOUT FREEDOM? WHAT DO YOU KNOW?
HE'S BEHIND YOU.
AND ALL AROUND YOU. NO, YOU CAN'T SEE HIM, BUT HE KNOWS THE SECRETS OF ALL YOUR HEARTS.
WHO ARE YOU? WHERE ARE YOU FROM?
THAT IS NOT IMPORTANT. TONIGHT THE ONE WHO SENT ME WILL SHOW YOU SOMETHING TO CHANGE YOUR LIFE FOR-EVER.
HOLD ONTO YOUR SON, MRS LANDAS.
YOU'RE ABOUT TO GET HIM BACK.

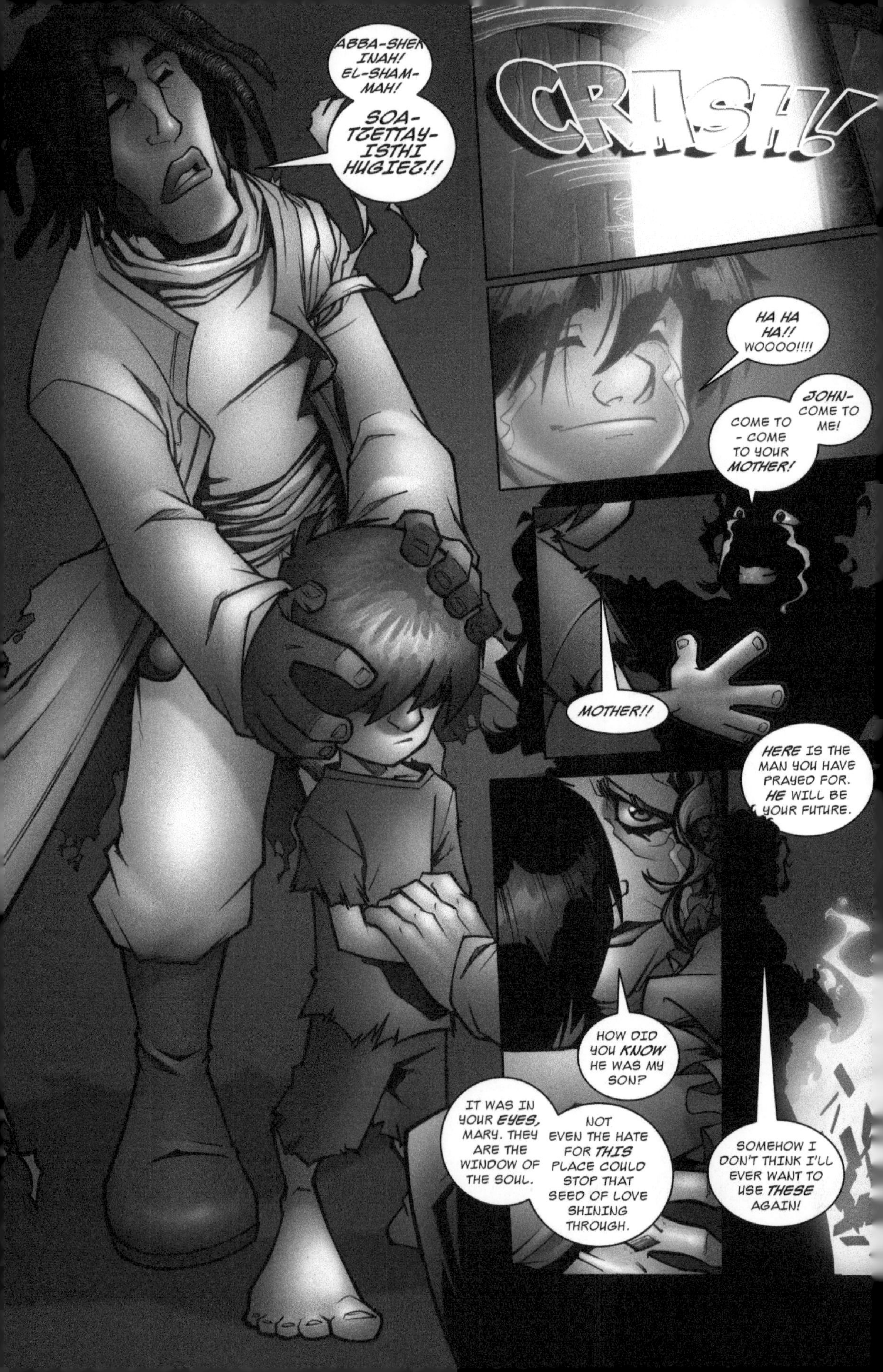
ABBA-SHEK INAH! EL-SHAM-MAH!
SOA-TZETTAY-ISTHI HUGIEZ!!
CRASH!
HA HA HA!! WOOOO!!!!
JOHN- COME TO ME!
COME TO - COME TO YOUR MOTHER!
MOTHER!!
HERE IS THE MAN YOU HAVE PRAYED FOR. HE WILL BE YOUR FUTURE.
HOW DID YOU KNOW HE WAS MY SON?
IT WAS IN YOUR EYES, MARY. THEY ARE THE WINDOW OF THE SOUL.
NOT EVEN THE HATE FOR THIS PLACE COULD STOP THAT SEED OF LOVE SHINING THROUGH.
SOMEHOW I DON'T THINK I'LL EVER WANT TO USE THESE AGAIN!

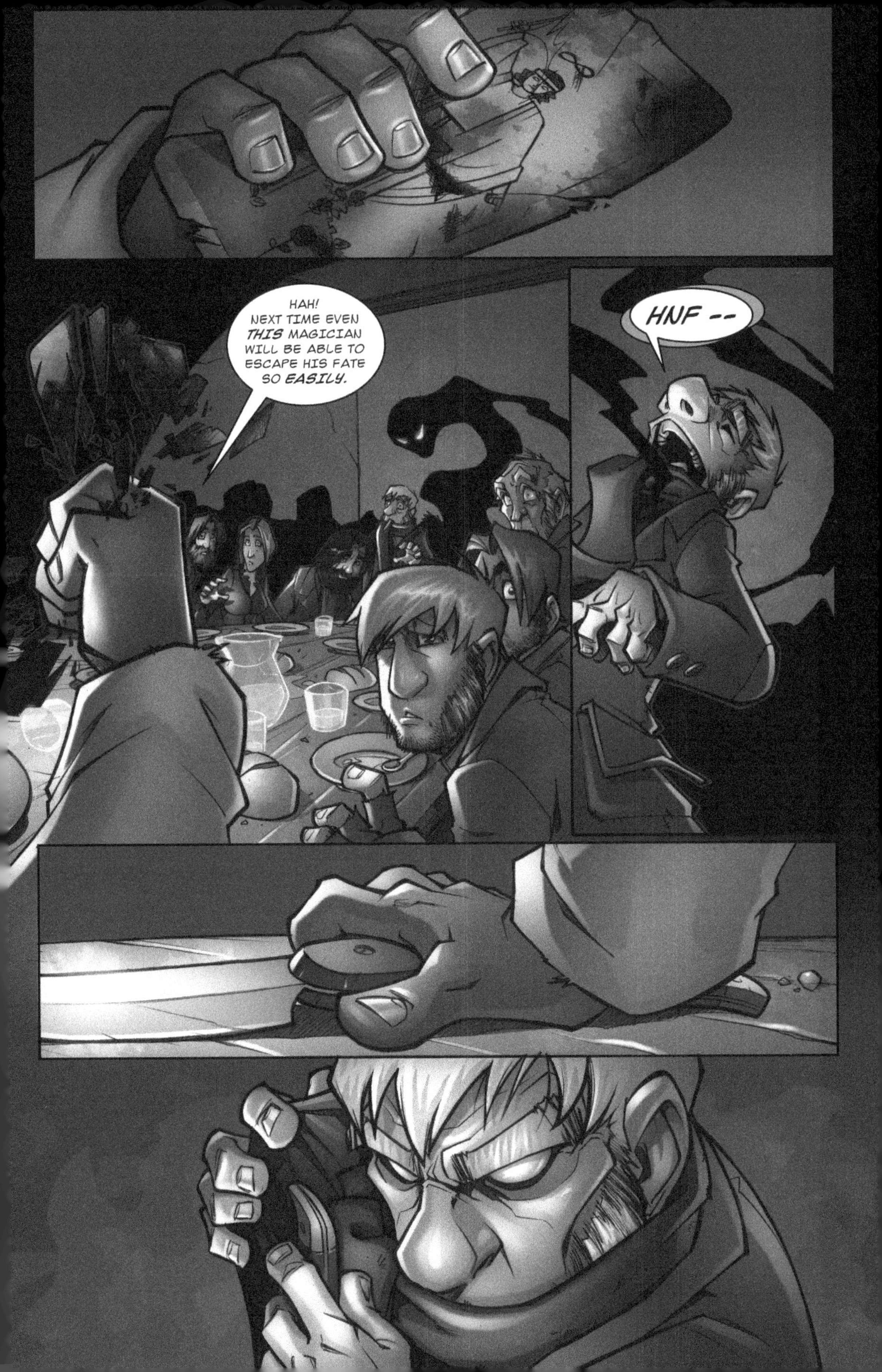
HAH!
NEXT TIME EVEN THIS MAGICIAN WILL BE ABLE TO ESCAPE HIS FATE SO EASILY.
HNF --

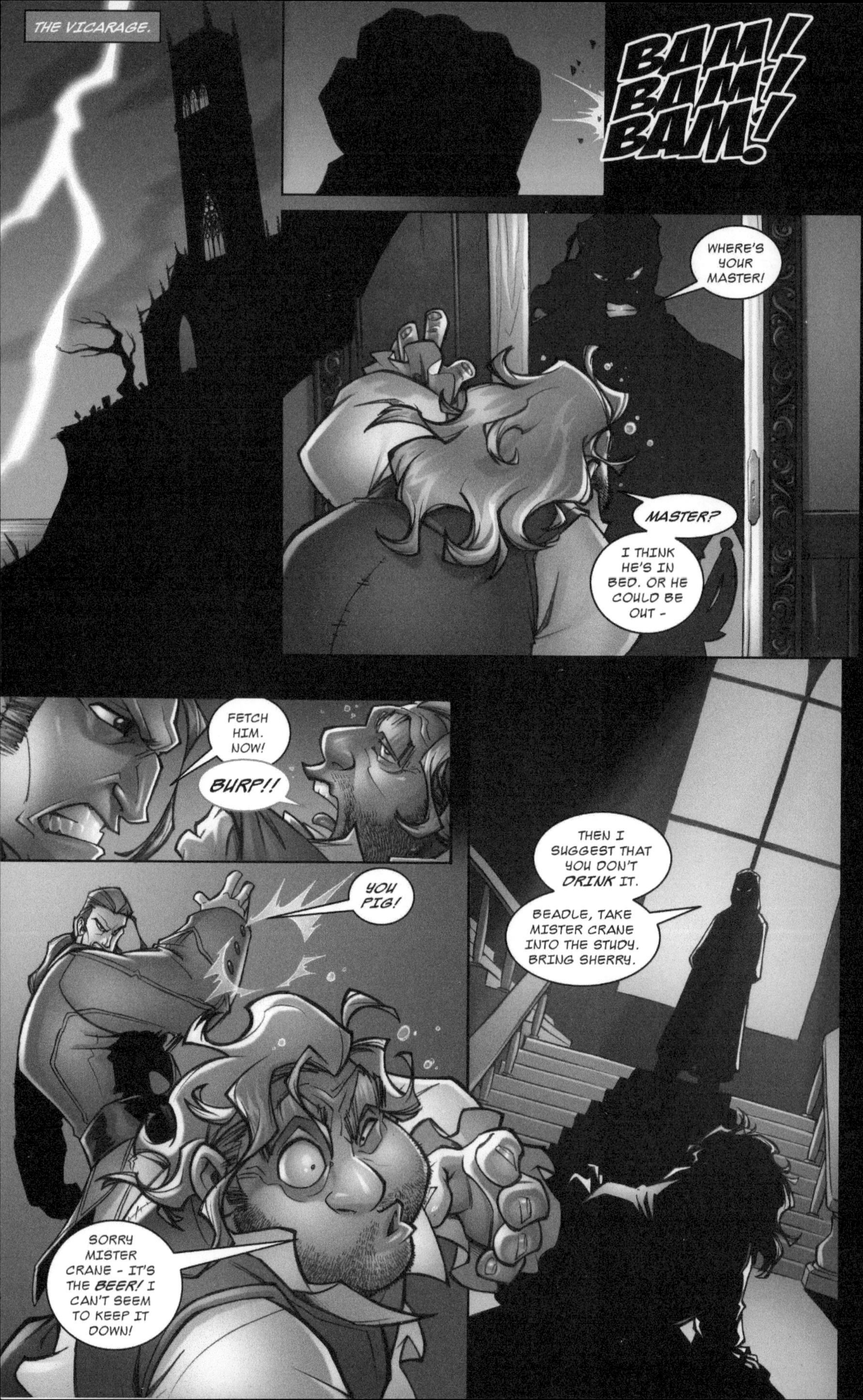
THE VICARAGE.
BAM! BAM! BAM!
WHERE'S YOUR MASTER!
MASTER?
I THINK HE'S IN BED. OR HE COULD BE OUT -
FETCH HIM. NOW!
BURP!!
YOU PIG!
SORRY MISTER CRANE - IT'S THE BEER! I CAN'T SEEM TO KEEP IT DOWN!
THEN I SUGGEST THAT YOU DON'T DRINK IT.
BEADLE, TAKE MISTER CRANE INTO THE STUDY. BRING SHERRY.

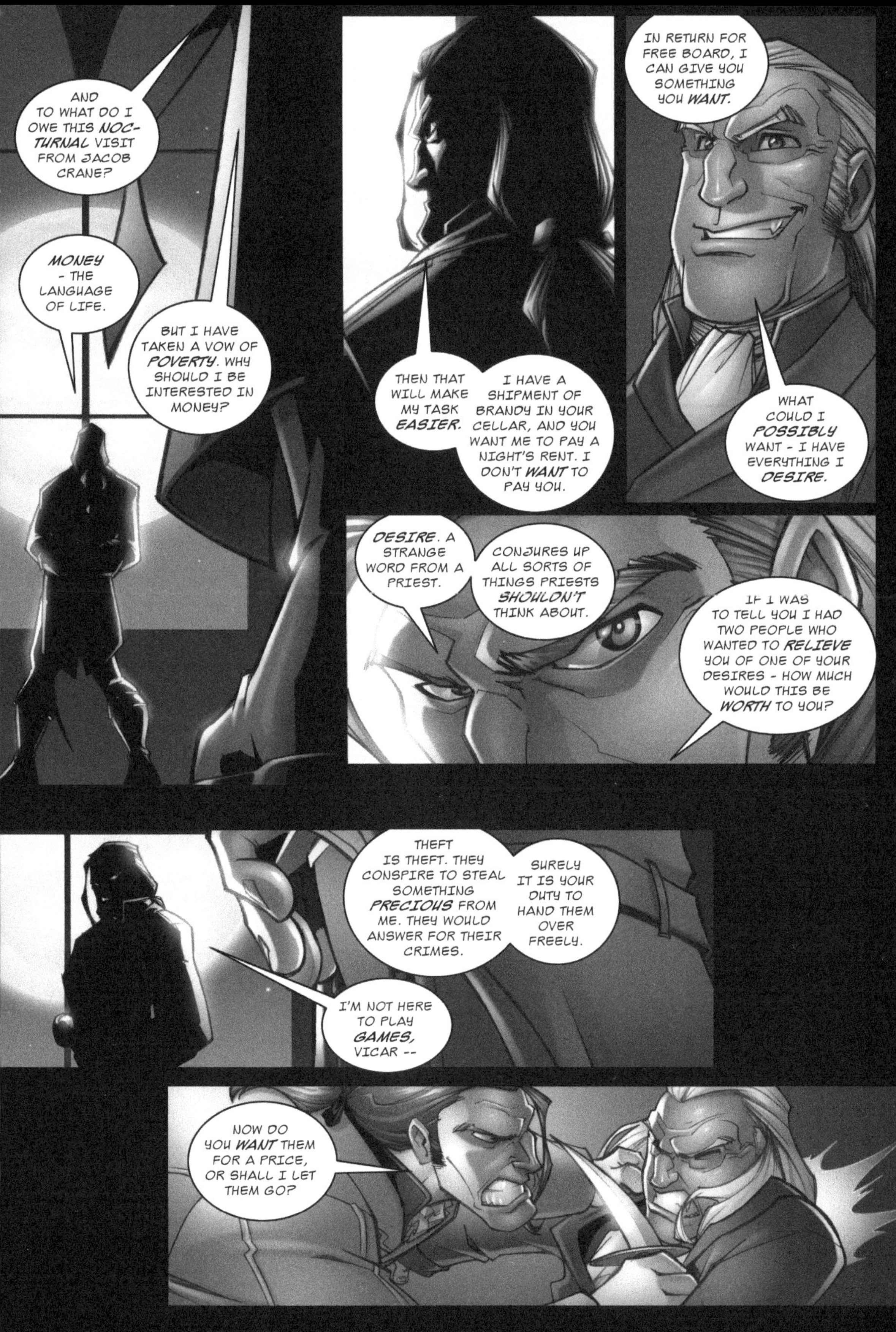
AND TO WHAT DO I OWE THIS NOC-TURNAL VISIT FROM JACOB CRANE?
MONEY - THE LANGUAGE OF LIFE.
BUT I HAVE TAKEN A VOW OF POVERTY. WHY SHOULD I BE INTERESTED IN MONEY?
THEN THAT WILL MAKE MY TASK EASIER.
I HAVE A SHIPMENT OF BRANDY IN YOUR CELLAR, AND YOU WANT ME TO PAY A NIGHT'S RENT. I DON'T WANT TO PAY YOU.
IN RETURN FOR FREE BOARD, I CAN GIVE YOU SOMETHING YOU WANT.
WHAT COULD I POSSIBLY WANT - I HAVE EVERYTHING I DESIRE.
DESIRE. A STRANGE WORD FROM A PRIEST.
CONJURES UP ALL SORTS OF THINGS PRIESTS SHOULDN'T THINK ABOUT.
IF I WAS TO TELL YOU I HAD TWO PEOPLE WHO WANTED TO RELIEVE YOU OF ONE OF YOUR DESIRES - HOW MUCH WOULD THIS BE WORTH TO YOU?
THEFT IS THEFT. THEY CONSPIRE TO STEAL SOMETHING PRECIOUS FROM ME. THEY WOULD ANSWER FOR THEIR CRIMES.
SURELY IT IS YOUR DUTY TO HAND THEM OVER FREELY.
I'M NOT HERE TO PLAY GAMES, VICAR --
NOW DO YOU WANT THEM FOR A PRICE, OR SHALL I LET THEM GO?

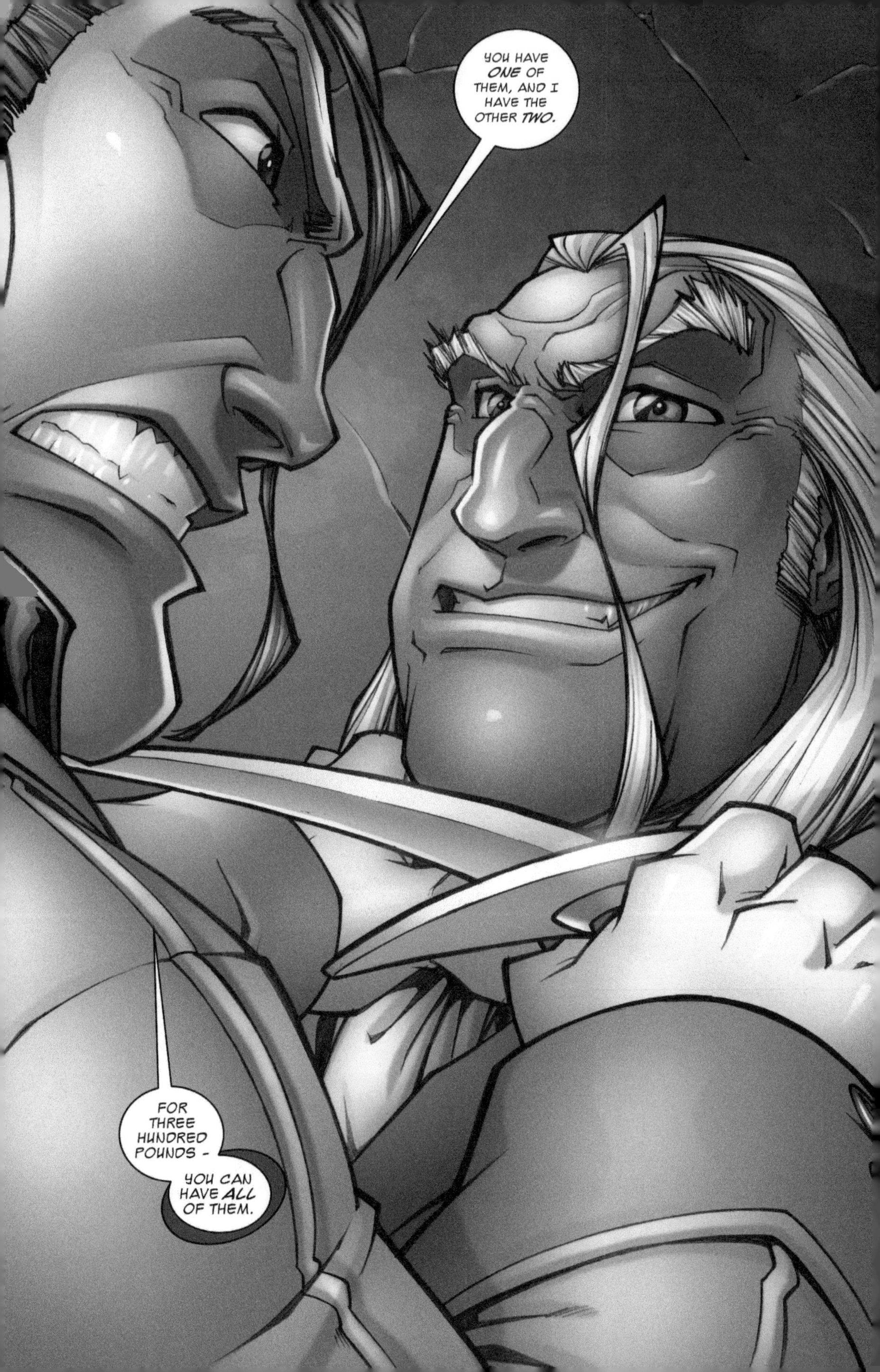
YOU HAVE ONE OF THEM, AND I HAVE THE OTHER TWO.
FOR THREE HUNDRED POUNDS -
YOU CAN HAVE ALL OF THEM.

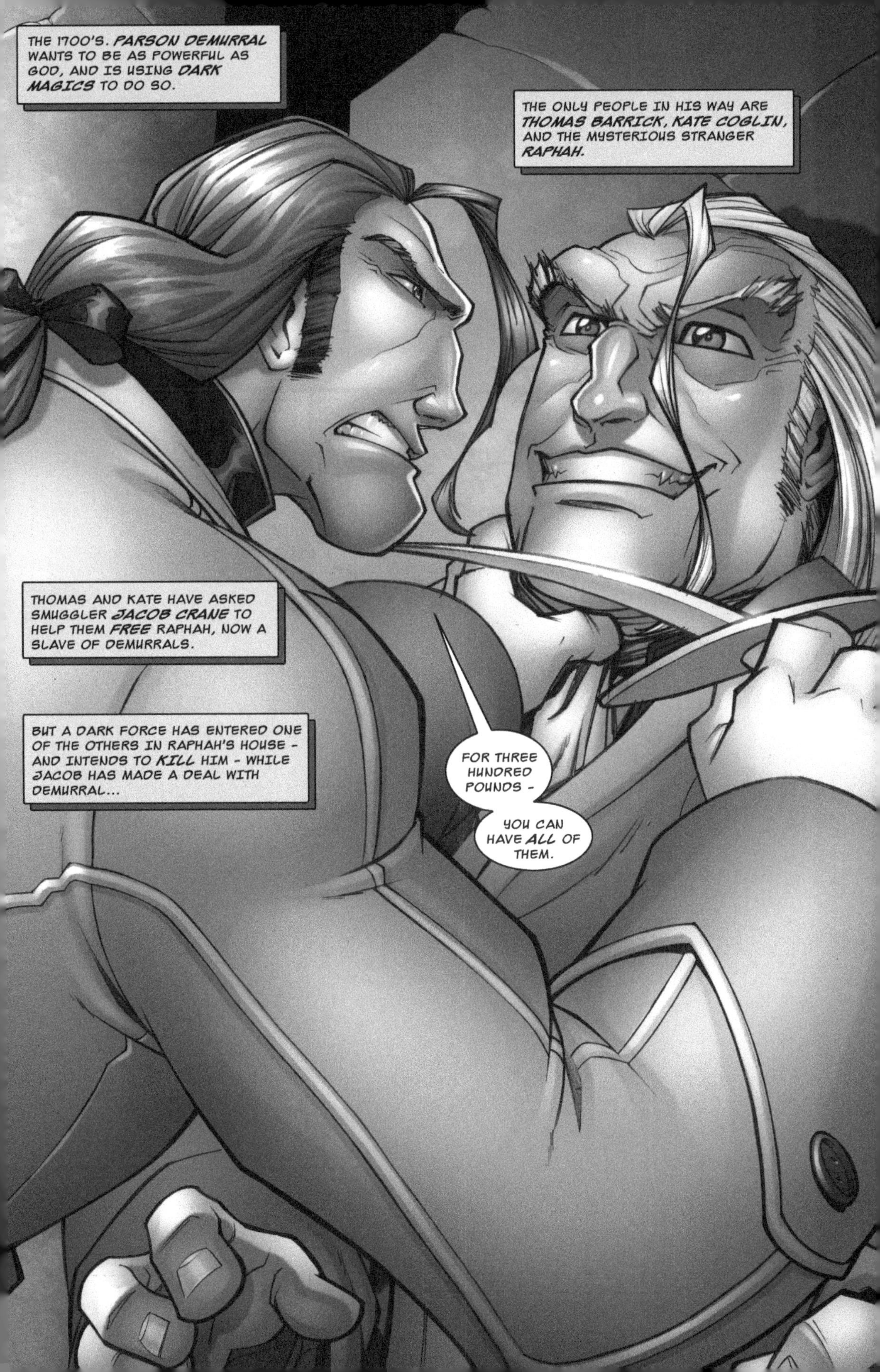
THE 1700'S. PARSON DEMURRAL WANTS TO BE AS POWERFUL AS GOD, AND IS USING DARK MAGICS TO DO SO.
THE ONLY PEOPLE IN HIS WAY ARE THOMAS BARRICK, KATE COGLIN, AND THE MYSTERIOUS STRANGER RAPHAH.
THOMAS AND KATE HAVE ASKED SMUGGLER JACOB CRANE TO HELP THEM FREE RAPHAH, NOW A SLAVE OF DEMURRALS.
BUT A DARK FORCE HAS ENTERED ONE OF THE OTHERS IN RAPHAH'S HOUSE - AND INTENDS TO KILL HIM - WHILE JACOB HAS MADE A DEAL WITH DEMURRAL...
FOR THREE HUNDRED POUNDS -
YOU CAN HAVE ALL OF THEM.

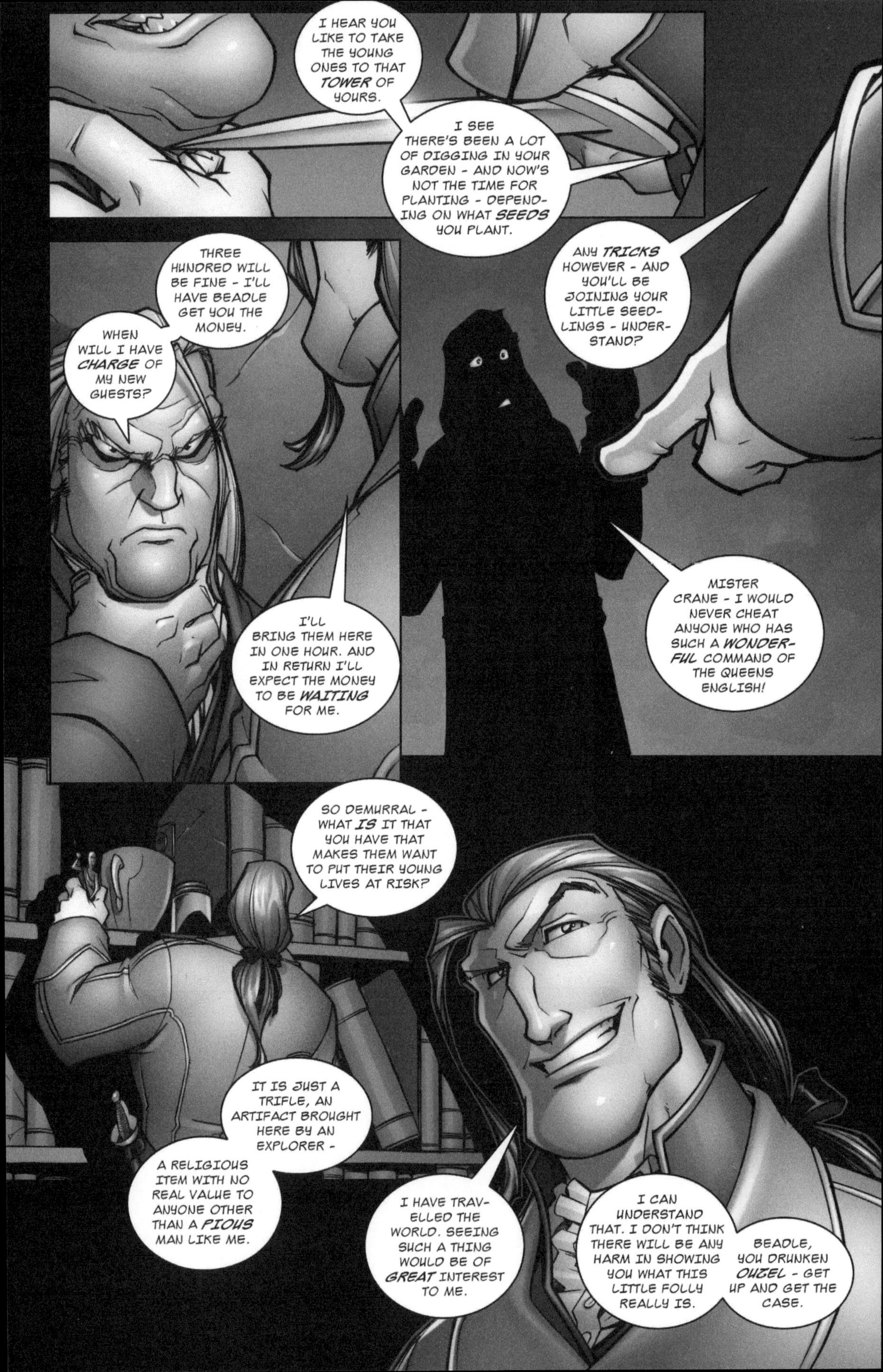
I HEAR YOU LIKE TO TAKE THE YOUNG ONES TO THAT TOWER OF YOURS.
I SEE THERE'S BEEN A LOT OF DIGGING IN YOUR GARDEN - AND NOW'S NOT THE TIME FOR PLANTING - DEPENDING ON WHAT SEEDS YOU PLANT.
ANY TRICKS HOWEVER - AND YOU'LL BE JOINING YOUR LITTLE SEEDLINGS - UNDERSTAND?
THREE HUNDRED WILL BE FINE - I'LL HAVE BEADLE GET YOU THE MONEY.
WHEN WILL I HAVE CHARGE OF MY NEW GUESTS?
I'LL BRING THEM HERE IN ONE HOUR. AND IN RETURN I'LL EXPECT THE MONEY TO BE WAITING FOR ME.
MISTER CRANE - I WOULD NEVER CHEAT ANYONE WHO HAS SUCH A WONDERFUL COMMAND OF THE QUEENS ENGLISH!
SO DEMURRAL - WHAT IS IT THAT YOU HAVE THAT MAKES THEM WANT TO PUT THEIR YOUNG LIVES AT RISK?
IT IS JUST A TRIFLE, AN ARTIFACT BROUGHT HERE BY AN EXPLORER -
A RELIGIOUS ITEM WITH NO REAL VALUE TO ANYONE OTHER THAN A PIOUS MAN LIKE ME.
I HAVE TRAVELLED THE WORLD. SEEING SUCH A THING WOULD BE OF GREAT INTEREST TO ME.
I CAN UNDERSTAND THAT. I DON'T THINK THERE WILL BE ANY HARM IN SHOWING YOU WHAT THIS LITTLE FOLLY REALLY IS.
BEADLE, YOU DRUNKEN OUZEL - GET UP AND GET THE CASE.

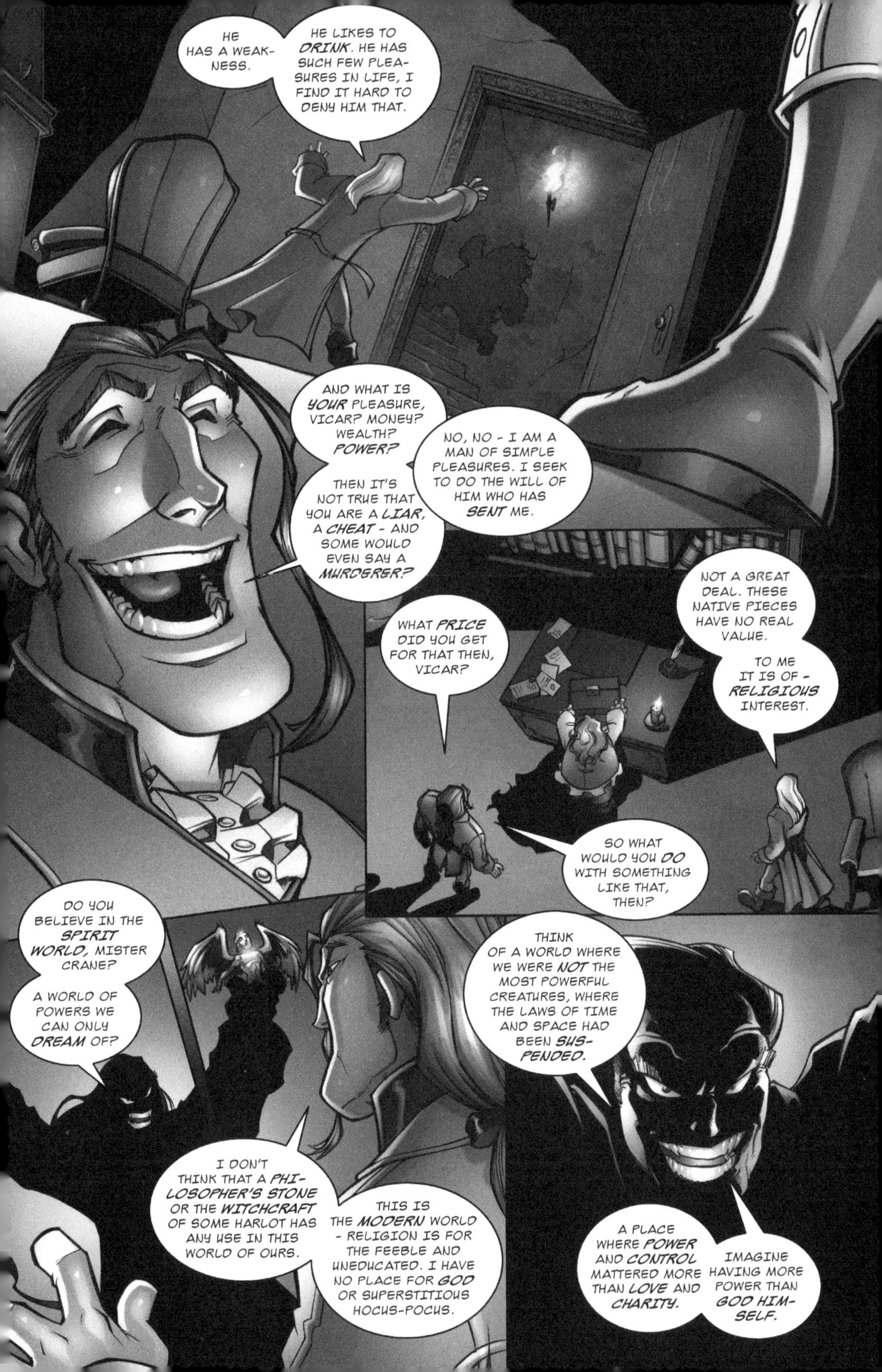

HE HAS A WEAKNESS.
HE LIKES TO DRINK. HE HAS SUCH FEW PLEASURES IN LIFE, I FIND IT HARD TO DENY HIM THAT.
AND WHAT IS YOUR PLEASURE, VICAR? MONEY? WEALTH? POWER?
NO, NO - I AM A MAN OF SIMPLE PLEASURES. I SEEK TO DO THE WILL OF HIM WHO HAS SENT ME.
THEN IT'S NOT TRUE THAT YOU ARE A LIAR, A CHEAT - AND SOME WOULD EVEN SAY A MURDERER?
WHAT PRICE DID YOU GET FOR THAT THEN, VICAR?
NOT A GREAT DEAL. THESE NATIVE PIECES HAVE NO REAL VALUE.
TO ME IT IS OF - RELIGIOUS INTEREST.
SO WHAT WOULD YOU DO WITH SOMETHING LIKE THAT, THEN?
DO YOU BELIEVE IN THE SPIRIT WORLD, MISTER CRANE?
A WORLD OF POWERS WE CAN ONLY DREAM OF?
I DON'T THINK THAT A PHILOSOPHER'S STONE OR THE WITCHCRAFT OF SOME HARLOT HAS ANY USE IN THIS WORLD OF OURS.
THIS IS THE MODERN WORLD - RELIGION IS FOR THE FEEBLE AND UNEDUCATED. I HAVE NO PLACE FOR GOD OR SUPERSTITIOUS HOCUS-POCUS.
THINK OF A WORLD WHERE WE WERE NOT THE MOST POWERFUL CREATURES, WHERE THE LAWS OF TIME AND SPACE HAD BEEN SUSPENDED.
A PLACE WHERE POWER AND CONTROL MATTERED MORE THAN LOVE AND CHARITY.
IMAGINE HAVING MORE POWER THAN GOD HIMSELF.

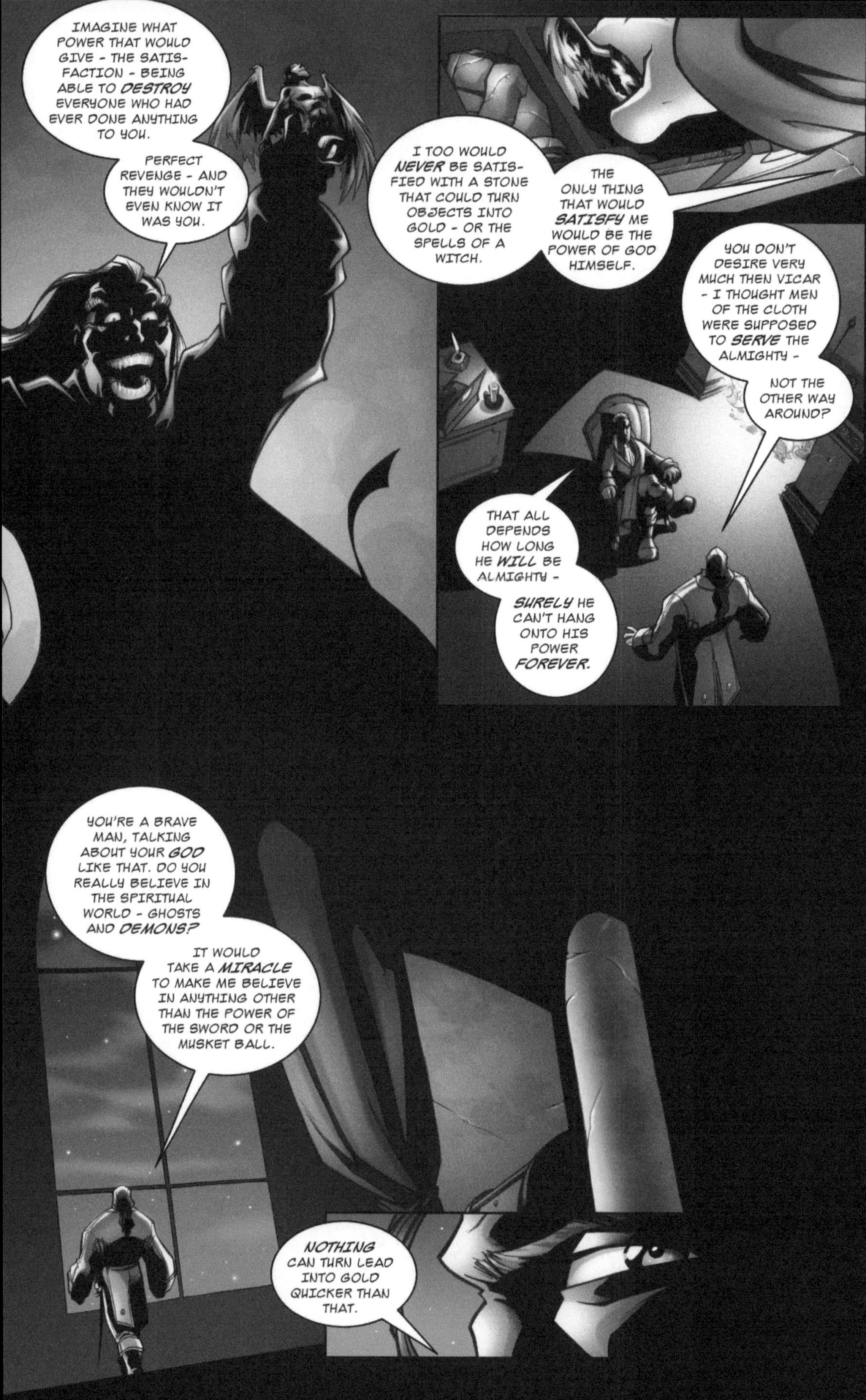
IMAGINE WHAT POWER THAT WOULD GIVE - THE SATIS-FACTION - BEING ABLE TO DESTROY EVERYONE WHO HAD EVER DONE ANYTHING TO YOU.
PERFECT REVENGE - AND THEY WOULDN'T EVEN KNOW IT WAS YOU.
I TOO WOULD NEVER BE SATIS-FIED WITH A STONE THAT COULD TURN OBJECTS INTO GOLD - OR THE SPELLS OF A WITCH.
THE ONLY THING THAT WOULD SATISFY ME WOULD BE THE POWER OF GOD HIMSELF.
YOU DON'T DESIRE VERY MUCH THEN VICAR - I THOUGHT MEN OF THE CLOTH WERE SUPPOSED TO SERVE THE ALMIGHTY -
NOT THE OTHER WAY AROUND?
THAT ALL DEPENDS HOW LONG HE WILL BE ALMIGHTY -
SURELY HE CAN'T HANG ONTO HIS POWER FOREVER.
YOU'RE A BRAVE MAN, TALKING ABOUT YOUR GOD LIKE THAT. DO YOU REALLY BELIEVE IN THE SPIRITUAL WORLD - GHOSTS AND DEMONS?
IT WOULD TAKE A MIRACLE TO MAKE ME BELIEVE IN ANYTHING OTHER THAN THE POWER OF THE SWORD OR THE MUSKET BALL.
NOTHING CAN TURN LEAD INTO GOLD QUICKER THAN THAT.

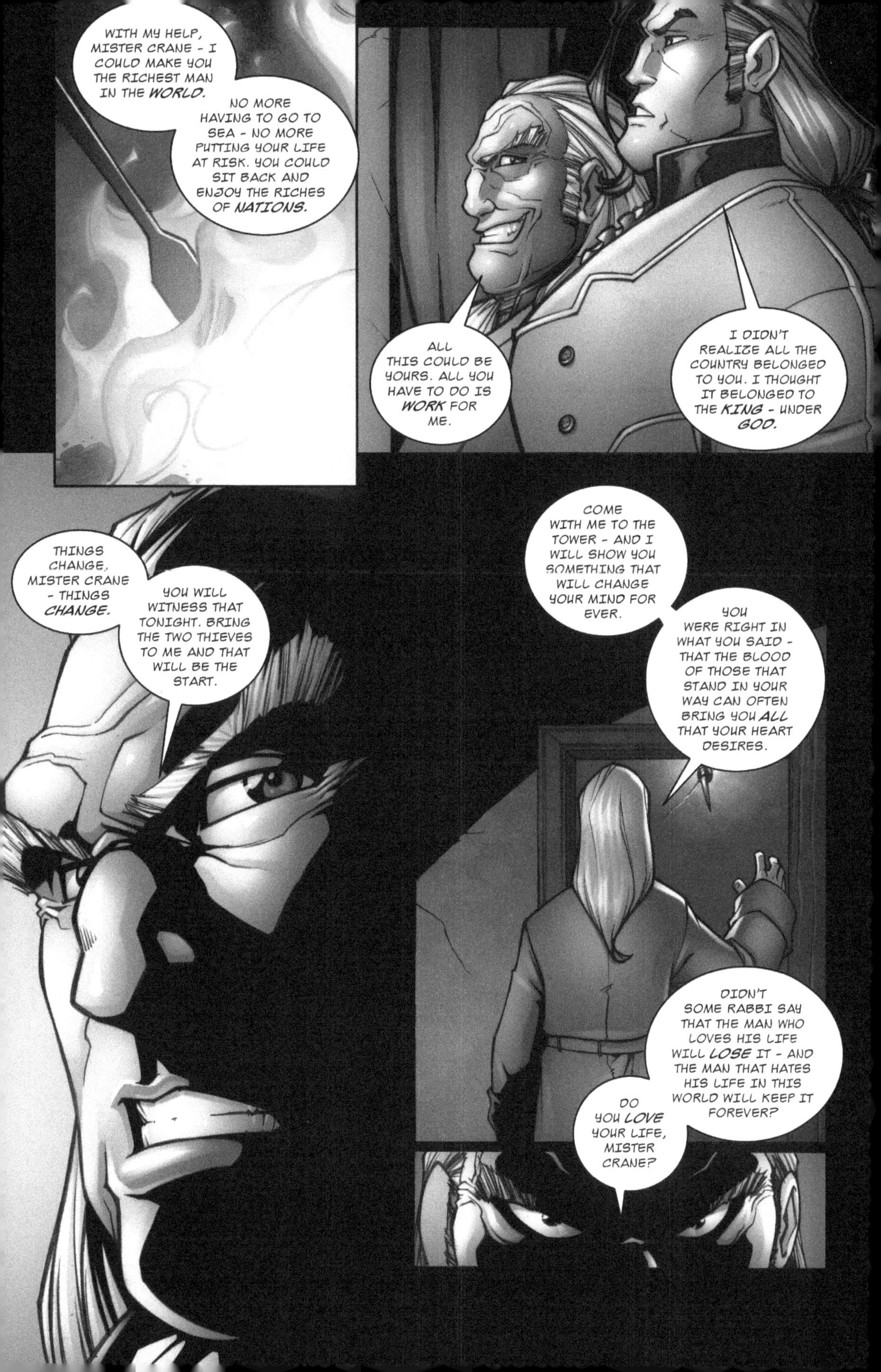
WITH MY HELP, MISTER CRANE - I COULD MAKE YOU THE RICHEST MAN IN THE *WORLD.*
NO MORE HAVING TO GO TO SEA - NO MORE PUTTING YOUR LIFE AT RISK. YOU COULD SIT BACK AND ENJOY THE RICHES OF *NATIONS.*
ALL THIS COULD BE YOURS. ALL YOU HAVE TO DO IS *WORK* FOR ME.
I DIDN'T REALIZE ALL THE COUNTRY BELONGED TO YOU. I THOUGHT IT BELONGED TO THE *KING* - UNDER *GOD.*
THINGS CHANGE, MISTER CRANE - THINGS *CHANGE.*
YOU WILL WITNESS THAT TONIGHT. BRING THE TWO THIEVES TO ME AND THAT WILL BE THE START.
COME WITH ME TO THE TOWER - AND I WILL SHOW YOU SOMETHING THAT WILL CHANGE YOUR MIND FOR EVER.
YOU WERE RIGHT IN WHAT YOU SAID - THAT THE BLOOD OF THOSE THAT STAND IN YOUR WAY CAN OFTEN BRING YOU *ALL* THAT YOUR HEART DESIRES.
DIDN'T SOME RABBI SAY THAT THE MAN WHO LOVES HIS LIFE WILL *LOSE* IT - AND THE MAN THAT HATES HIS LIFE IN THIS WORLD WILL KEEP IT FOREVER?
DO YOU *LOVE* YOUR LIFE, MISTER CRANE?

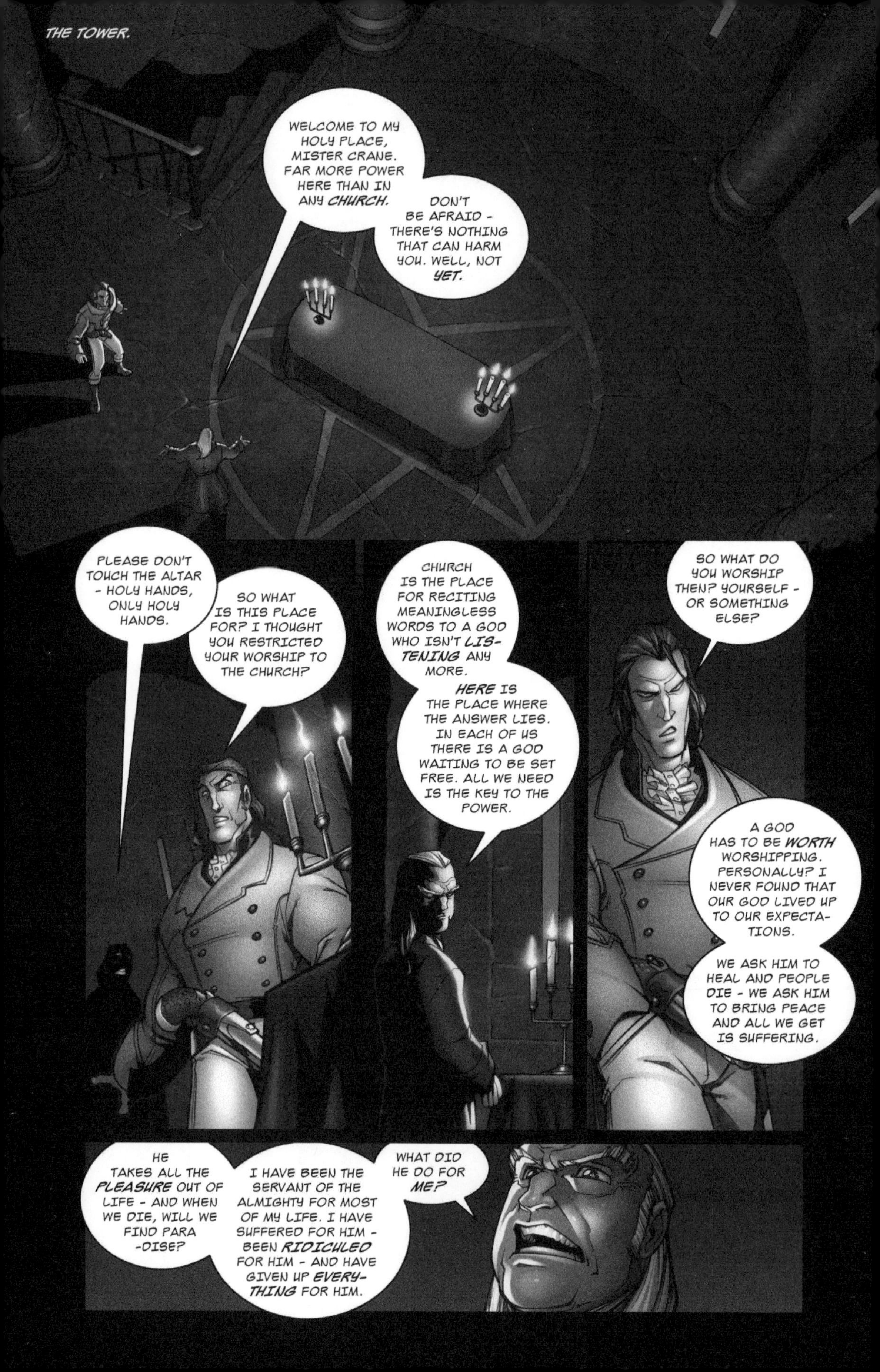
THE TOWER.
WELCOME TO MY HOLY PLACE, MISTER CRANE. FAR MORE POWER HERE THAN IN ANY CHURCH.
DON'T BE AFRAID - THERE'S NOTHING THAT CAN HARM YOU. WELL, NOT YET.
PLEASE DON'T TOUCH THE ALTAR - HOLY HANDS, ONLY HOLY HANDS.
SO WHAT IS THIS PLACE FOR? I THOUGHT YOU RESTRICTED YOUR WORSHIP TO THE CHURCH?
CHURCH IS THE PLACE FOR RECITING MEANINGLESS WORDS TO A GOD WHO ISN'T LISTENING ANY MORE.
HERE IS THE PLACE WHERE THE ANSWER LIES. IN EACH OF US THERE IS A GOD WAITING TO BE SET FREE. ALL WE NEED IS THE KEY TO THE POWER.
SO WHAT DO YOU WORSHIP THEN? YOURSELF - OR SOMETHING ELSE?
A GOD HAS TO BE WORTH WORSHIPPING. PERSONALLY? I NEVER FOUND THAT OUR GOD LIVED UP TO OUR EXPECTATIONS.
WE ASK HIM TO HEAL AND PEOPLE DIE - WE ASK HIM TO BRING PEACE AND ALL WE GET IS SUFFERING.
HE TAKES ALL THE PLEASURE OUT OF LIFE - AND WHEN WE DIE, WILL WE FIND PARA-DISE?
I HAVE BEEN THE SERVANT OF THE ALMIGHTY FOR MOST OF MY LIFE. I HAVE SUFFERED FOR HIM - BEEN RIDICULED FOR HIM - AND HAVE GIVEN UP EVERYTHING FOR HIM.
WHAT DID HE DO FOR ME?

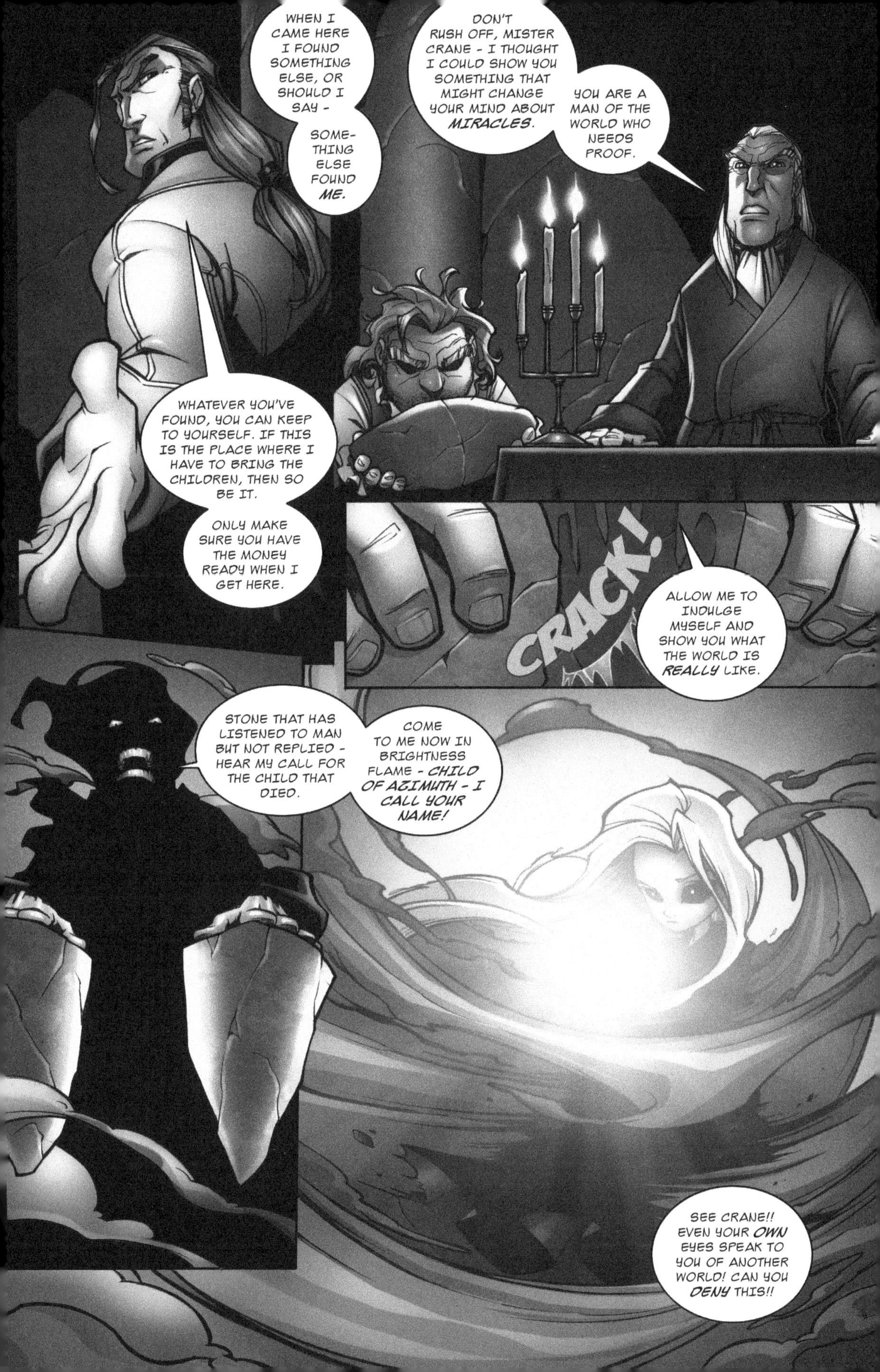
WHEN I CAME HERE I FOUND SOMETHING ELSE, OR SHOULD I SAY -
SOME-THING ELSE FOUND ME.
DON'T RUSH OFF, MISTER CRANE - I THOUGHT I COULD SHOW YOU SOMETHING THAT MIGHT CHANGE YOUR MIND ABOUT MIRACLES.
YOU ARE A MAN OF THE WORLD WHO NEEDS PROOF.
WHATEVER YOU'VE FOUND, YOU CAN KEEP TO YOURSELF. IF THIS IS THE PLACE WHERE I HAVE TO BRING THE CHILDREN, THEN SO BE IT.
ONLY MAKE SURE YOU HAVE THE MONEY READY WHEN I GET HERE.
CRACK!
ALLOW ME TO INDULGE MYSELF AND SHOW YOU WHAT THE WORLD IS REALLY LIKE.
STONE THAT HAS LISTENED TO MAN BUT NOT REPLIED - HEAR MY CALL FOR THE CHILD THAT DIED.
COME TO ME NOW IN BRIGHTNESS FLAME - CHILD OF AZIMUTH - I CALL YOUR NAME!
SEE CRANE!! EVEN YOUR OWN EYES SPEAK TO YOU OF ANOTHER WORLD! CAN YOU DENY THIS!!

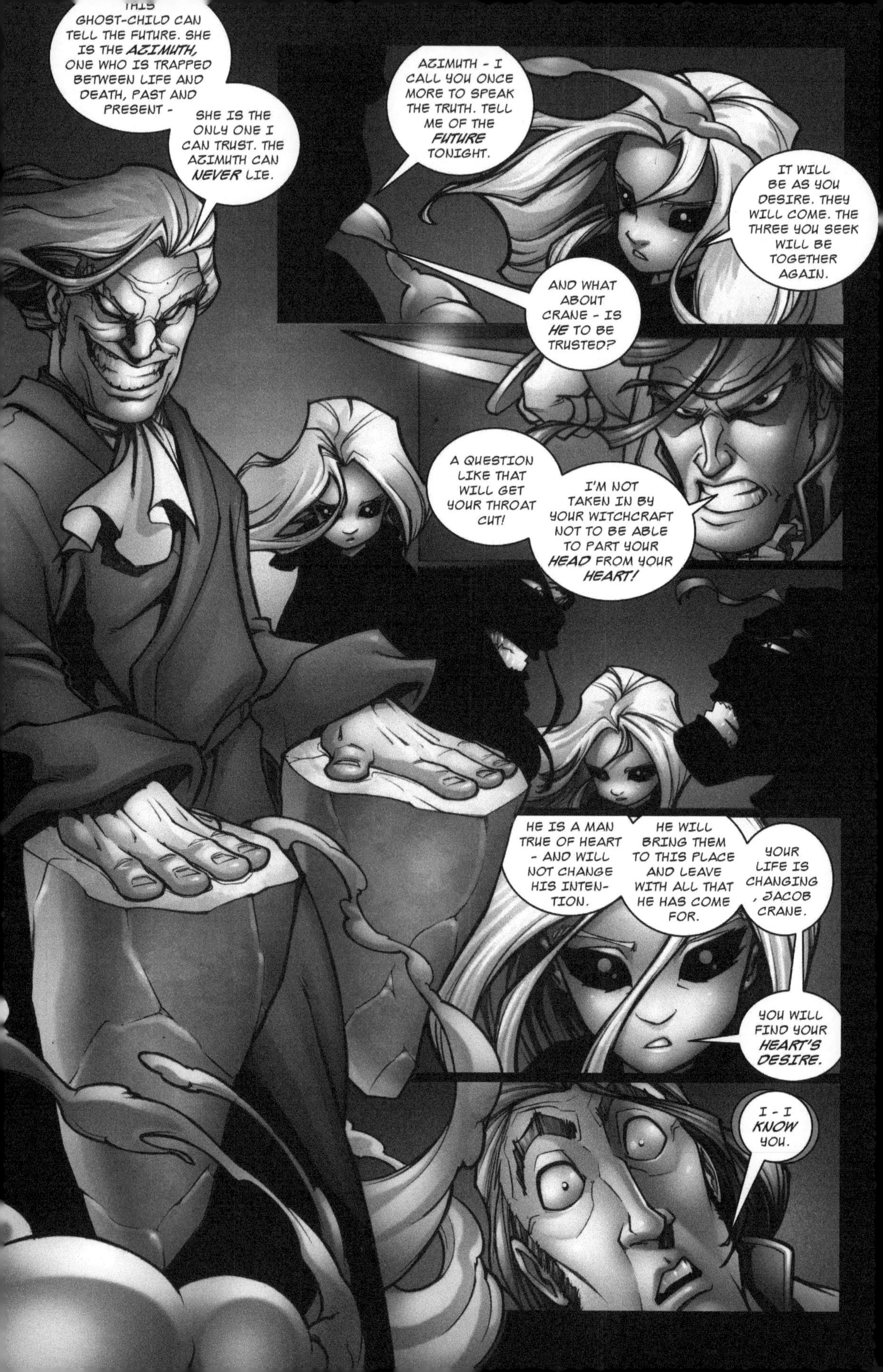
THIS GHOST-CHILD CAN TELL THE FUTURE. SHE IS THE AZIMUTH, ONE WHO IS TRAPPED BETWEEN LIFE AND DEATH, PAST AND PRESENT -
SHE IS THE ONLY ONE I CAN TRUST. THE AZIMUTH CAN NEVER LIE.
AZIMUTH - I CALL YOU ONCE MORE TO SPEAK THE TRUTH. TELL ME OF THE FUTURE TONIGHT.
IT WILL BE AS YOU DESIRE. THEY WILL COME. THE THREE YOU SEEK WILL BE TOGETHER AGAIN.
AND WHAT ABOUT CRANE - IS HE TO BE TRUSTED?
A QUESTION LIKE THAT WILL GET YOUR THROAT CUT!
I'M NOT TAKEN IN BY YOUR WITCHCRAFT NOT TO BE ABLE TO PART YOUR HEAD FROM YOUR HEART!
HE IS A MAN TRUE OF HEART - AND WILL NOT CHANGE HIS INTEN-TION.
HE WILL BRING THEM TO THIS PLACE AND LEAVE WITH ALL THAT HE HAS COME FOR.
YOUR LIFE IS CHANGING, JACOB CRANE.
YOU WILL FIND YOUR HEART'S DESIRE.
I - I KNOW YOU.

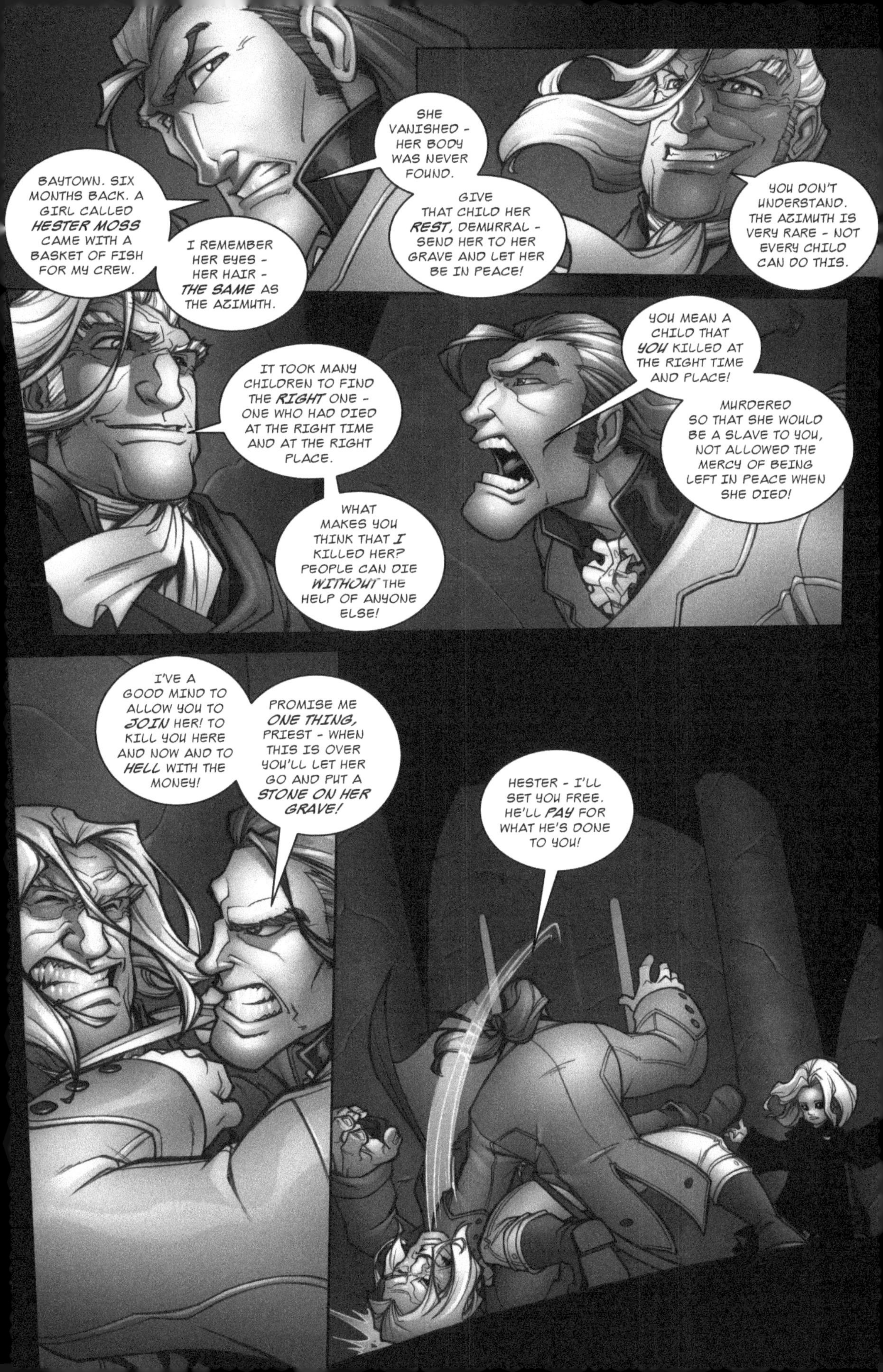
BAYTOWN. SIX MONTHS BACK. A GIRL CALLED HESTER MOSS CAME WITH A BASKET OF FISH FOR MY CREW.
I REMEMBER HER EYES - HER HAIR - THE SAME AS THE AZIMUTH.
SHE VANISHED - HER BODY WAS NEVER FOUND.
GIVE THAT CHILD HER REST, DEMURRAL - SEND HER TO HER GRAVE AND LET HER BE IN PEACE!
YOU DON'T UNDERSTAND. THE AZIMUTH IS VERY RARE - NOT EVERY CHILD CAN DO THIS.
IT TOOK MANY CHILDREN TO FIND THE RIGHT ONE - ONE WHO HAD DIED AT THE RIGHT TIME AND AT THE RIGHT PLACE.
WHAT MAKES YOU THINK THAT I KILLED HER? PEOPLE CAN DIE WITHOUT THE HELP OF ANYONE ELSE!
YOU MEAN A CHILD THAT YOU KILLED AT THE RIGHT TIME AND PLACE!
MURDERED SO THAT SHE WOULD BE A SLAVE TO YOU, NOT ALLOWED THE MERCY OF BEING LEFT IN PEACE WHEN SHE DIED!
I'VE A GOOD MIND TO ALLOW YOU TO JOIN HER! TO KILL YOU HERE AND NOW AND TO HELL WITH THE MONEY!
PROMISE ME ONE THING, PRIEST - WHEN THIS IS OVER YOU'LL LET HER GO AND PUT A STONE ON HER GRAVE!
HESTER - I'LL SET YOU FREE. HE'LL PAY FOR WHAT HE'S DONE TO YOU!

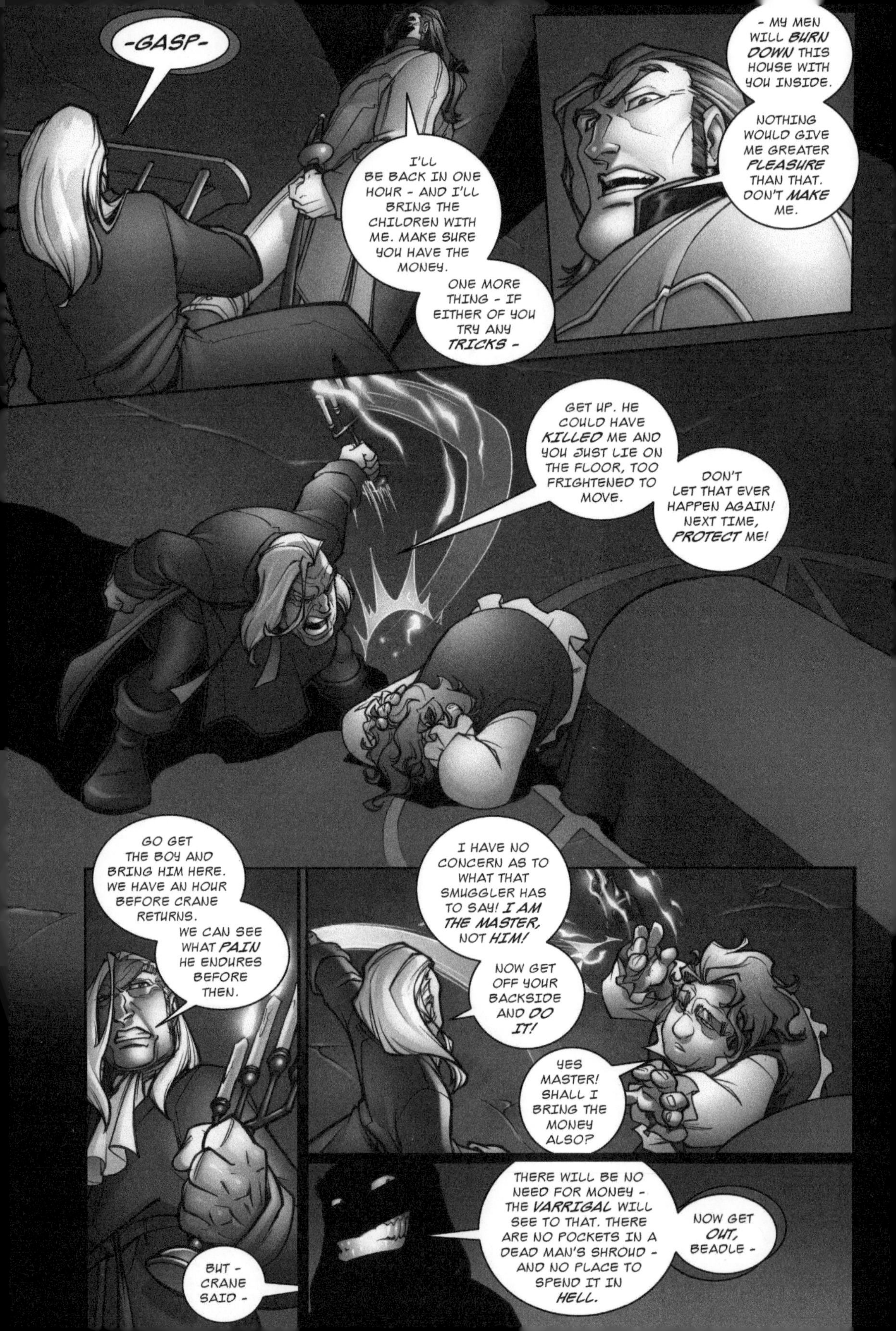
-GASP-
I'LL BE BACK IN ONE HOUR - AND I'LL BRING THE CHILDREN WITH ME. MAKE SURE YOU HAVE THE MONEY.
ONE MORE THING - IF EITHER OF YOU TRY ANY TRICKS -
- MY MEN WILL BURN DOWN THIS HOUSE WITH YOU INSIDE.
NOTHING WOULD GIVE ME GREATER PLEASURE THAN THAT. DON'T MAKE ME.
GET UP. HE COULD HAVE KILLED ME AND YOU JUST LIE ON THE FLOOR, TOO FRIGHTENED TO MOVE.
DON'T LET THAT EVER HAPPEN AGAIN! NEXT TIME, PROTECT ME!
GO GET THE BOY AND BRING HIM HERE. WE HAVE AN HOUR BEFORE CRANE RETURNS.
WE CAN SEE WHAT PAIN HE ENDURES BEFORE THEN.
BUT - CRANE SAID -
I HAVE NO CONCERN AS TO WHAT THAT SMUGGLER HAS TO SAY! I AM THE MASTER, NOT HIM!
NOW GET OFF YOUR BACKSIDE AND DO IT!
YES MASTER! SHALL I BRING THE MONEY ALSO?
THERE WILL BE NO NEED FOR MONEY - THE VARRIGAL WILL SEE TO THAT. THERE ARE NO POCKETS IN A DEAD MAN'S SHROUD - AND NO PLACE TO SPEND IT IN HELL.
NOW GET OUT, BEADLE -

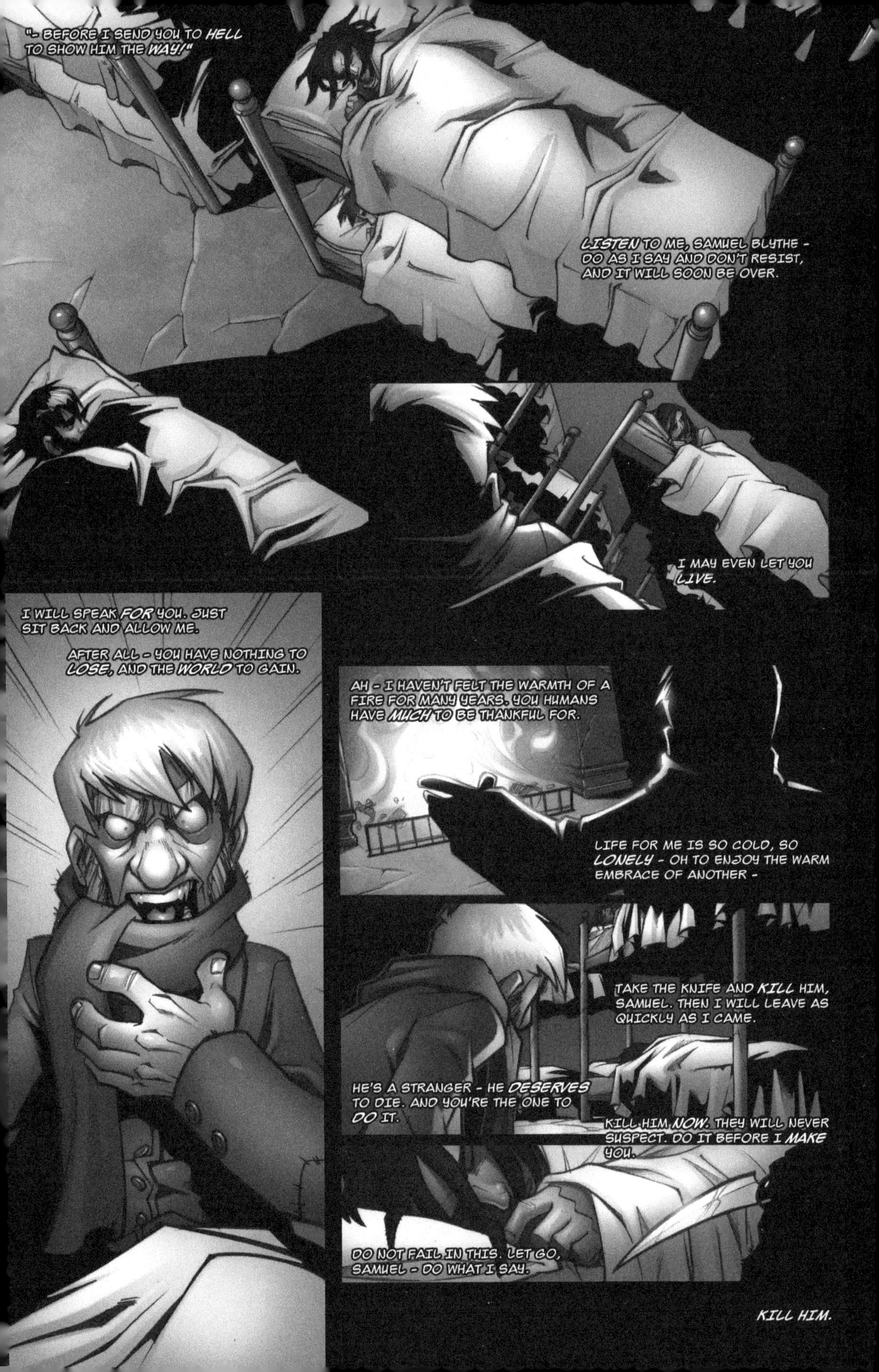
"- BEFORE I SEND YOU TO HELL TO SHOW HIM THE WAY!"
LISTEN TO ME, SAMUEL BLYTHE - DO AS I SAY AND DON'T RESIST, AND IT WILL SOON BE OVER.
I MAY EVEN LET YOU LIVE.
I WILL SPEAK FOR YOU. JUST SIT BACK AND ALLOW ME.
AFTER ALL - YOU HAVE NOTHING TO LOSE, AND THE WORLD TO GAIN.
AH - I HAVEN'T FELT THE WARMTH OF A FIRE FOR MANY YEARS. YOU HUMANS HAVE MUCH TO BE THANKFUL FOR.
LIFE FOR ME IS SO COLD, SO LONELY - OH TO ENJOY THE WARM EMBRACE OF ANOTHER -
TAKE THE KNIFE AND KILL HIM, SAMUEL. THEN I WILL LEAVE AS QUICKLY AS I CAME.
HE'S A STRANGER - HE DESERVES TO DIE. AND YOU'RE THE ONE TO DO IT.
KILL HIM NOW. THEY WILL NEVER SUSPECT. DO IT BEFORE I MAKE YOU.
DO NOT FAIL IN THIS. LET GO, SAMUEL - DO WHAT I SAY.
KILL HIM.

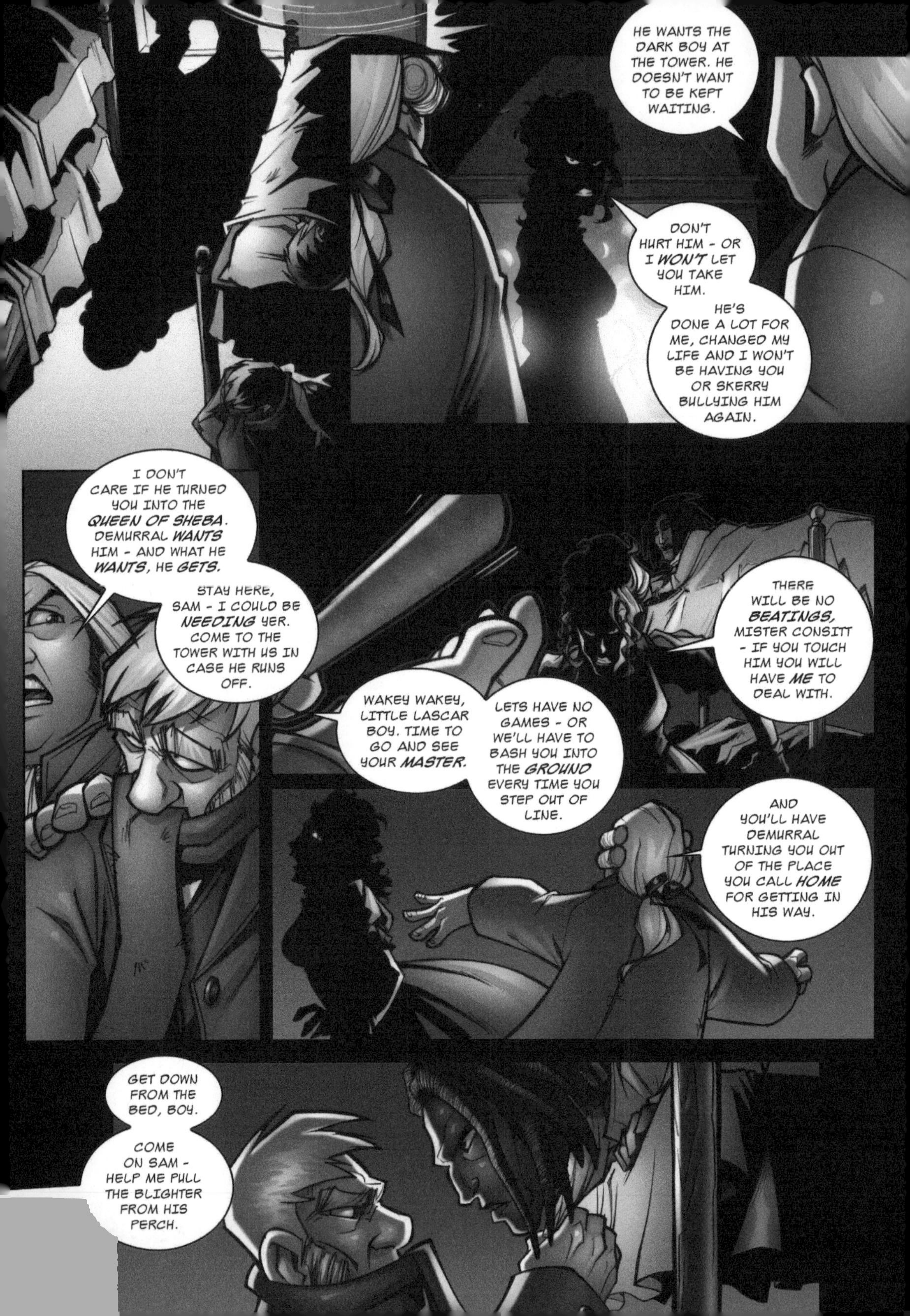

HE WANTS THE DARK BOY AT THE TOWER. HE DOESN'T WANT TO BE KEPT WAITING.
DON'T HURT HIM - OR I *WON'T* LET YOU TAKE HIM.
HE'S DONE A LOT FOR ME, CHANGED MY LIFE AND I WON'T BE HAVING YOU OR SKERRY BULLYING HIM AGAIN.
I DON'T CARE IF HE TURNED YOU INTO THE *QUEEN OF SHEBA*. DEMURRAL *WANTS* HIM - AND WHAT HE *WANTS*, HE *GETS.*
STAY HERE, SAM - I COULD BE *NEEDING* YER. COME TO THE TOWER WITH US IN CASE HE RUNS OFF.
WAKEY WAKEY, LITTLE LASCAR BOY. TIME TO GO AND SEE YOUR *MASTER.*
LETS HAVE NO GAMES - OR WE'LL HAVE TO BASH YOU INTO THE *GROUND* EVERY TIME YOU STEP OUT OF LINE.
THERE WILL BE NO *BEATINGS,* MISTER CONSITT - IF YOU TOUCH HIM YOU WILL HAVE *ME* TO DEAL WITH.
AND YOU'LL HAVE DEMURRAL TURNING YOU OUT OF THE PLACE YOU CALL *HOME* FOR GETTING IN HIS WAY.
GET DOWN FROM THE BED, BOY.
COME ON SAM - HELP ME PULL THE BLIGHTER FROM HIS PERCH.

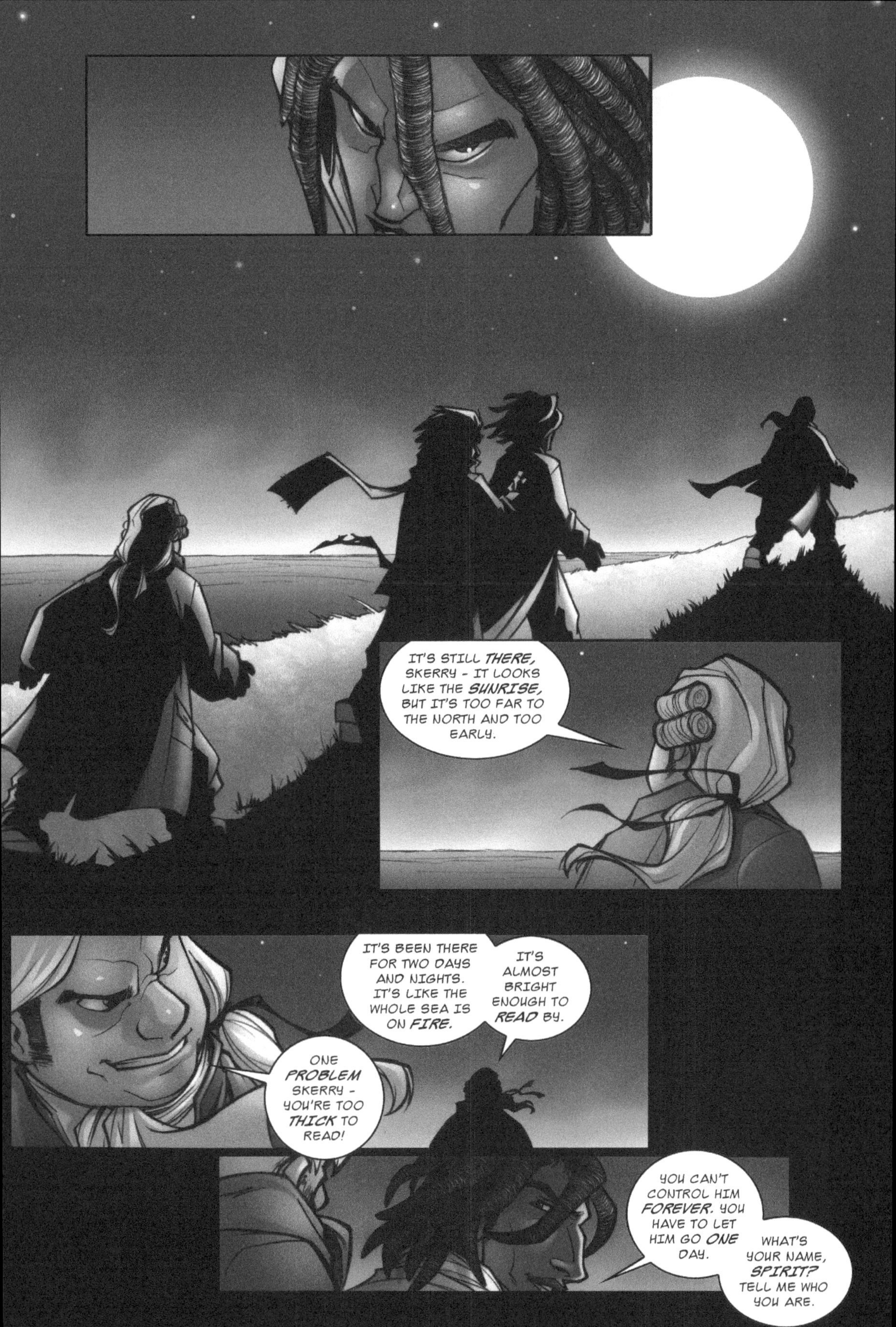
IT'S STILL *THERE,* SKERRY - IT LOOKS LIKE THE *SUNRISE,* BUT IT'S TOO FAR TO THE NORTH AND TOO EARLY.
IT'S BEEN THERE FOR TWO DAYS AND NIGHTS. IT'S LIKE THE WHOLE SEA IS ON *FIRE.*
IT'S ALMOST BRIGHT ENOUGH TO *READ* BY.
ONE *PROBLEM* SKERRY - YOU'RE TOO *THICK* TO READ!
YOU CAN'T CONTROL HIM *FOREVER.* YOU HAVE TO LET HIM GO *ONE* DAY.
WHAT'S YOUR NAME, *SPIRIT?* TELL ME WHO YOU ARE.

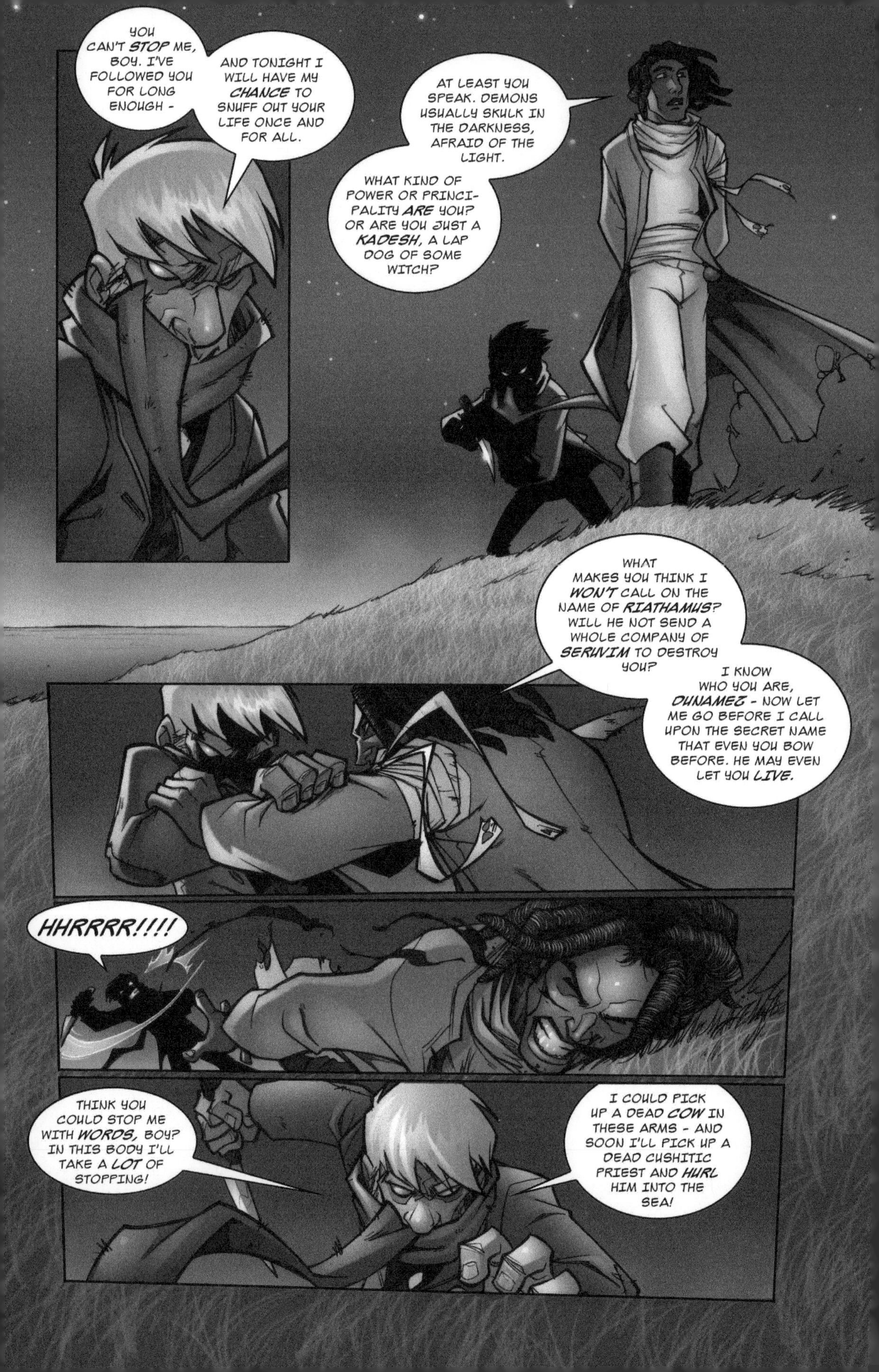
YOU CAN'T STOP ME, BOY. I'VE FOLLOWED YOU FOR LONG ENOUGH -
AND TONIGHT I WILL HAVE MY CHANCE TO SNUFF OUT YOUR LIFE ONCE AND FOR ALL.
AT LEAST YOU SPEAK. DEMONS USUALLY SKULK IN THE DARKNESS, AFRAID OF THE LIGHT.
WHAT KIND OF POWER OR PRINCIPALITY ARE YOU? OR ARE YOU JUST A KADESH, A LAP DOG OF SOME WITCH?
WHAT MAKES YOU THINK I WON'T CALL ON THE NAME OF RIATHAMUS? WILL HE NOT SEND A WHOLE COMPANY OF SERUVIM TO DESTROY YOU?
I KNOW WHO YOU ARE, DUNAMEZ - NOW LET ME GO BEFORE I CALL UPON THE SECRET NAME THAT EVEN YOU BOW BEFORE. HE MAY EVEN LET YOU LIVE.
HHRRRR!!!!
THINK YOU COULD STOP ME WITH WORDS, BOY? IN THIS BODY I'LL TAKE A LOT OF STOPPING!
I COULD PICK UP A DEAD COW IN THESE ARMS - AND SOON I'LL PICK UP A DEAD CUSHITIC PRIEST AND HURL HIM INTO THE SEA!

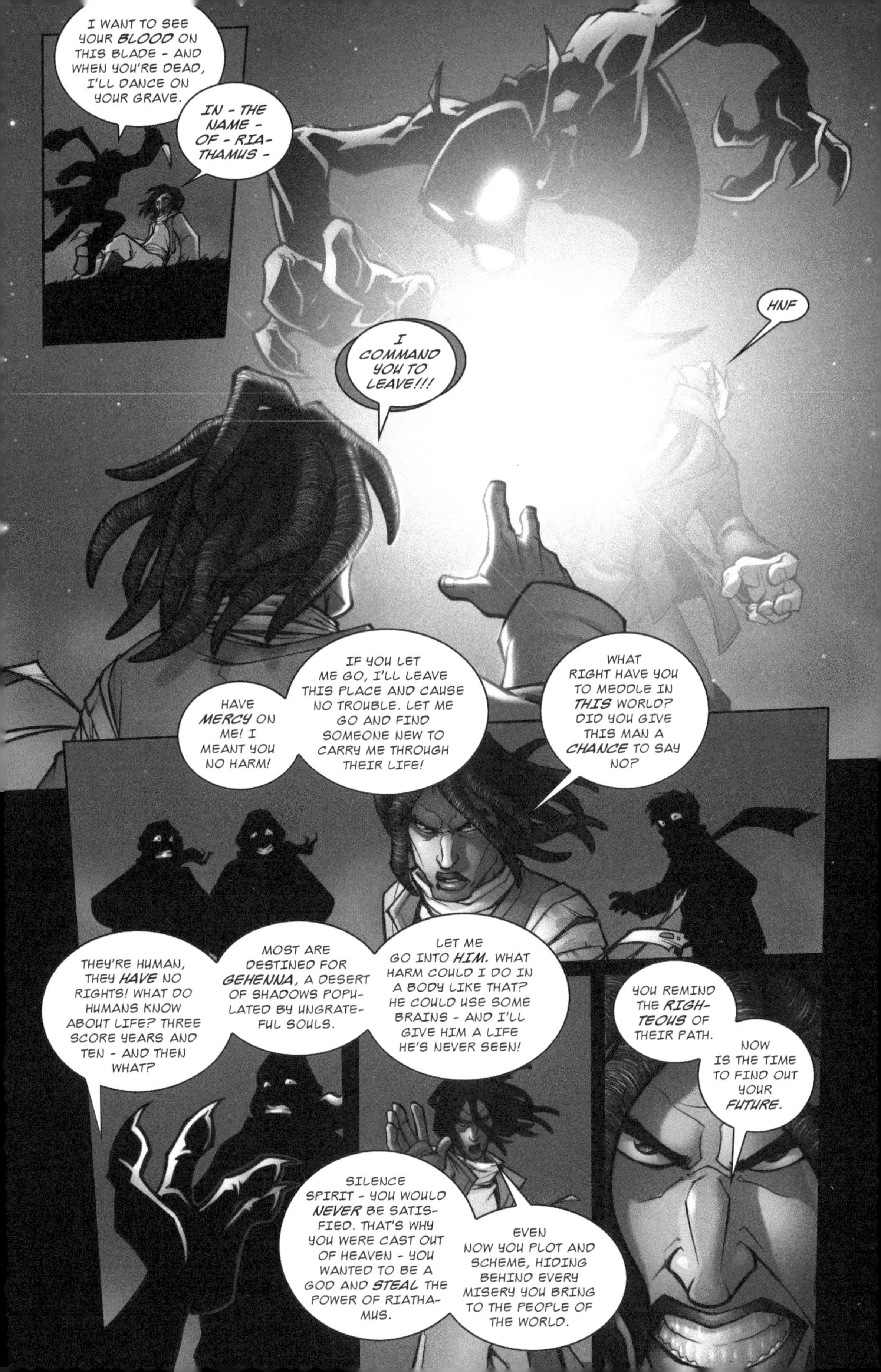
I WANT TO SEE YOUR BLOOD ON THIS BLADE - AND WHEN YOU'RE DEAD, I'LL DANCE ON YOUR GRAVE.
IN - THE NAME - OF - RIATHAMUS -
I COMMAND YOU TO LEAVE!!!
HNF
HAVE MERCY ON ME! I MEANT YOU NO HARM!
IF YOU LET ME GO, I'LL LEAVE THIS PLACE AND CAUSE NO TROUBLE. LET ME GO AND FIND SOMEONE NEW TO CARRY ME THROUGH THEIR LIFE!
WHAT RIGHT HAVE YOU TO MEDDLE IN THIS WORLD? DID YOU GIVE THIS MAN A CHANCE TO SAY NO?
THEY'RE HUMAN, THEY HAVE NO RIGHTS! WHAT DO HUMANS KNOW ABOUT LIFE? THREE SCORE YEARS AND TEN - AND THEN WHAT?
MOST ARE DESTINED FOR GEHENNA, A DESERT OF SHADOWS POPULATED BY UNGRATEFUL SOULS.
LET ME GO INTO HIM. WHAT HARM COULD I DO IN A BODY LIKE THAT? HE COULD USE SOME BRAINS - AND I'LL GIVE HIM A LIFE HE'S NEVER SEEN!
YOU REMIND THE RIGHTEOUS OF THEIR PATH.
NOW IS THE TIME TO FIND OUT YOUR FUTURE.
SILENCE SPIRIT - YOU WOULD NEVER BE SATISFIED. THAT'S WHY YOU WERE CAST OUT OF HEAVEN - YOU WANTED TO BE A GOD AND STEAL THE POWER OF RIATHAMUS.
EVEN NOW YOU PLOT AND SCHEME, HIDING BEHIND EVERY MISERY YOU BRING TO THE PEOPLE OF THE WORLD.

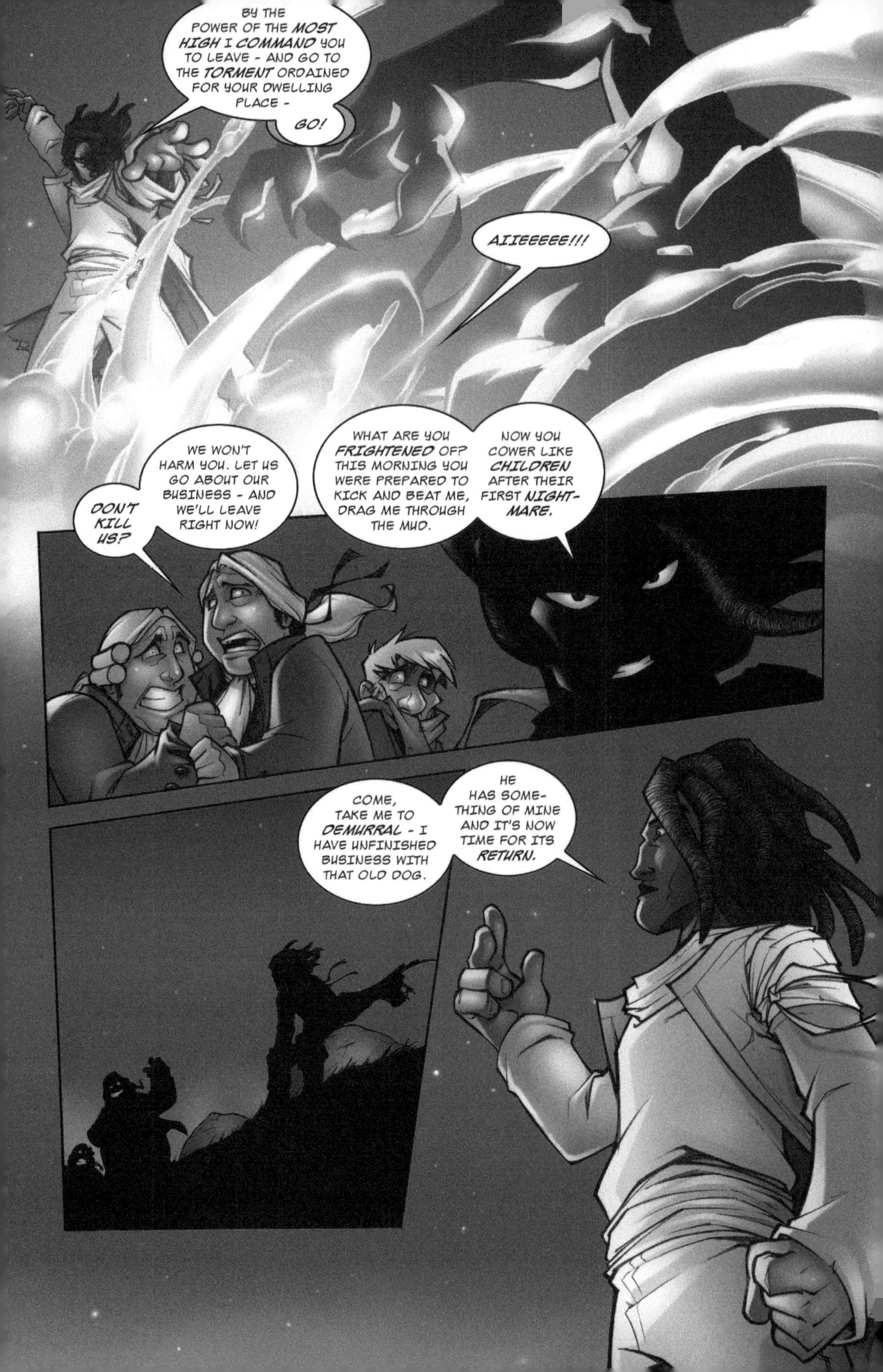
BY THE POWER OF THE MOST HIGH I COMMAND YOU TO LEAVE - AND GO TO THE TORMENT ORDAINED FOR YOUR DWELLING PLACE -
GO!
AIIEEEEE!!!
DON'T KILL US?
WE WON'T HARM YOU. LET US GO ABOUT OUR BUSINESS - AND WE'LL LEAVE RIGHT NOW!
WHAT ARE YOU FRIGHTENED OF? THIS MORNING YOU WERE PREPARED TO KICK AND BEAT ME, DRAG ME THROUGH THE MUD.
NOW YOU COWER LIKE CHILDREN AFTER THEIR FIRST NIGHT-MARE.
COME, TAKE ME TO DEMURRAL - I HAVE UNFINISHED BUSINESS WITH THAT OLD DOG.
HE HAS SOME-THING OF MINE AND IT'S NOW TIME FOR ITS RETURN.

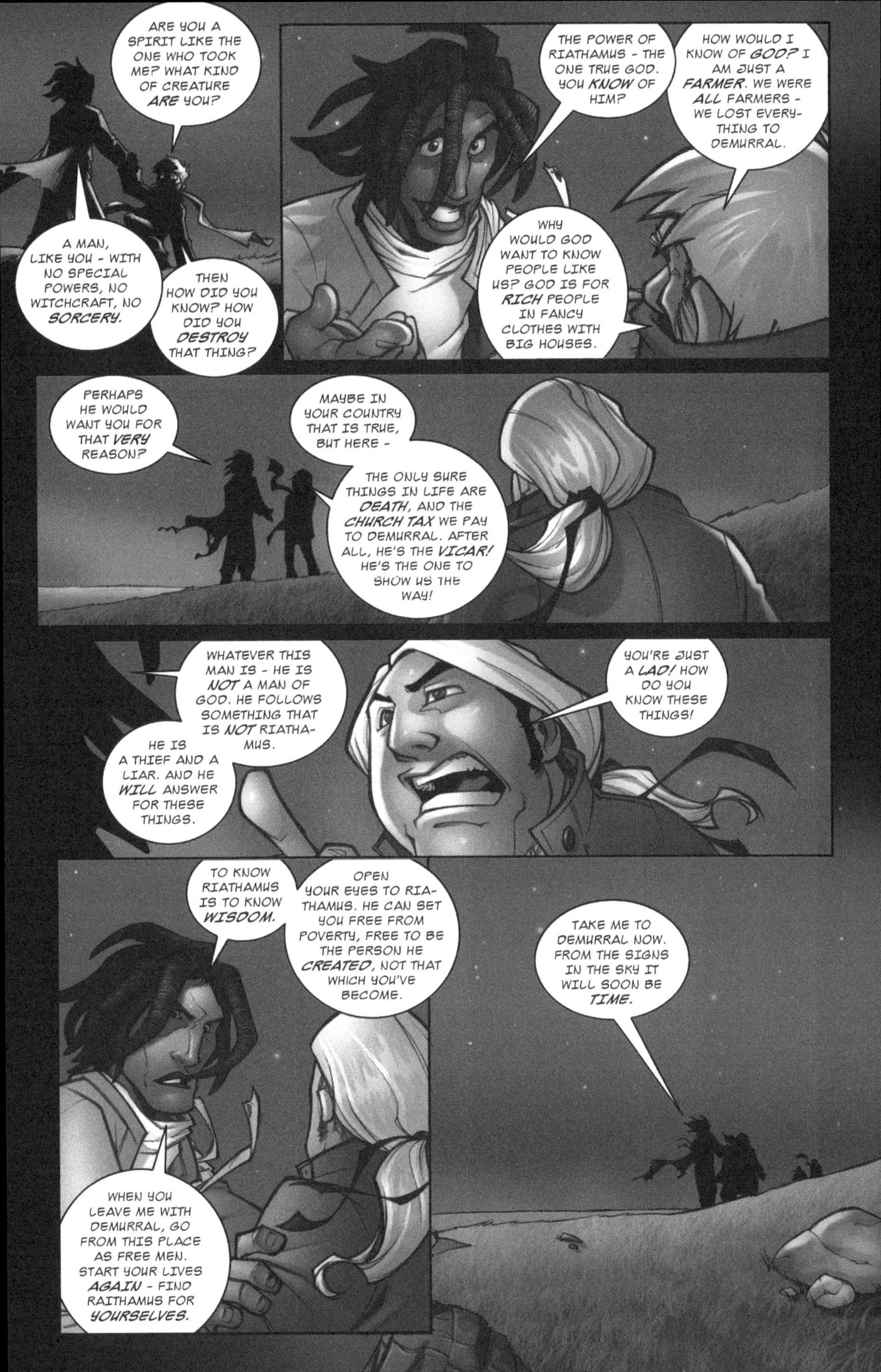
ARE YOU A SPIRIT LIKE THE ONE WHO TOOK ME? WHAT KIND OF CREATURE ARE YOU?
A MAN, LIKE YOU - WITH NO SPECIAL POWERS, NO WITCHCRAFT, NO SORCERY.
THEN HOW DID YOU KNOW? HOW DID YOU DESTROY THAT THING?
THE POWER OF RIATHAMUS - THE ONE TRUE GOD. YOU KNOW OF HIM?
HOW WOULD I KNOW OF GOD? I AM JUST A FARMER. WE WERE ALL FARMERS - WE LOST EVERYTHING TO DEMURRAL.
WHY WOULD GOD WANT TO KNOW PEOPLE LIKE US? GOD IS FOR RICH PEOPLE IN FANCY CLOTHES WITH BIG HOUSES.
PERHAPS HE WOULD WANT YOU FOR THAT VERY REASON?
MAYBE IN YOUR COUNTRY THAT IS TRUE, BUT HERE -
THE ONLY SURE THINGS IN LIFE ARE DEATH, AND THE CHURCH TAX WE PAY TO DEMURRAL. AFTER ALL, HE'S THE VICAR! HE'S THE ONE TO SHOW US THE WAY!
WHATEVER THIS MAN IS - HE IS NOT A MAN OF GOD. HE FOLLOWS SOMETHING THAT IS NOT RIATHAMUS.
HE IS A THIEF AND A LIAR. AND HE WILL ANSWER FOR THESE THINGS.
YOU'RE JUST A LAD! HOW DO YOU KNOW THESE THINGS!
TO KNOW RIATHAMUS IS TO KNOW WISDOM.
OPEN YOUR EYES TO RIATHAMUS. HE CAN SET YOU FREE FROM POVERTY, FREE TO BE THE PERSON HE CREATED, NOT THAT WHICH YOU'VE BECOME.
WHEN YOU LEAVE ME WITH DEMURRAL, GO FROM THIS PLACE AS FREE MEN. START YOUR LIVES AGAIN - FIND RAITHAMUS FOR YOURSELVES.
TAKE ME TO DEMURRAL NOW. FROM THE SIGNS IN THE SKY IT WILL SOON BE TIME.

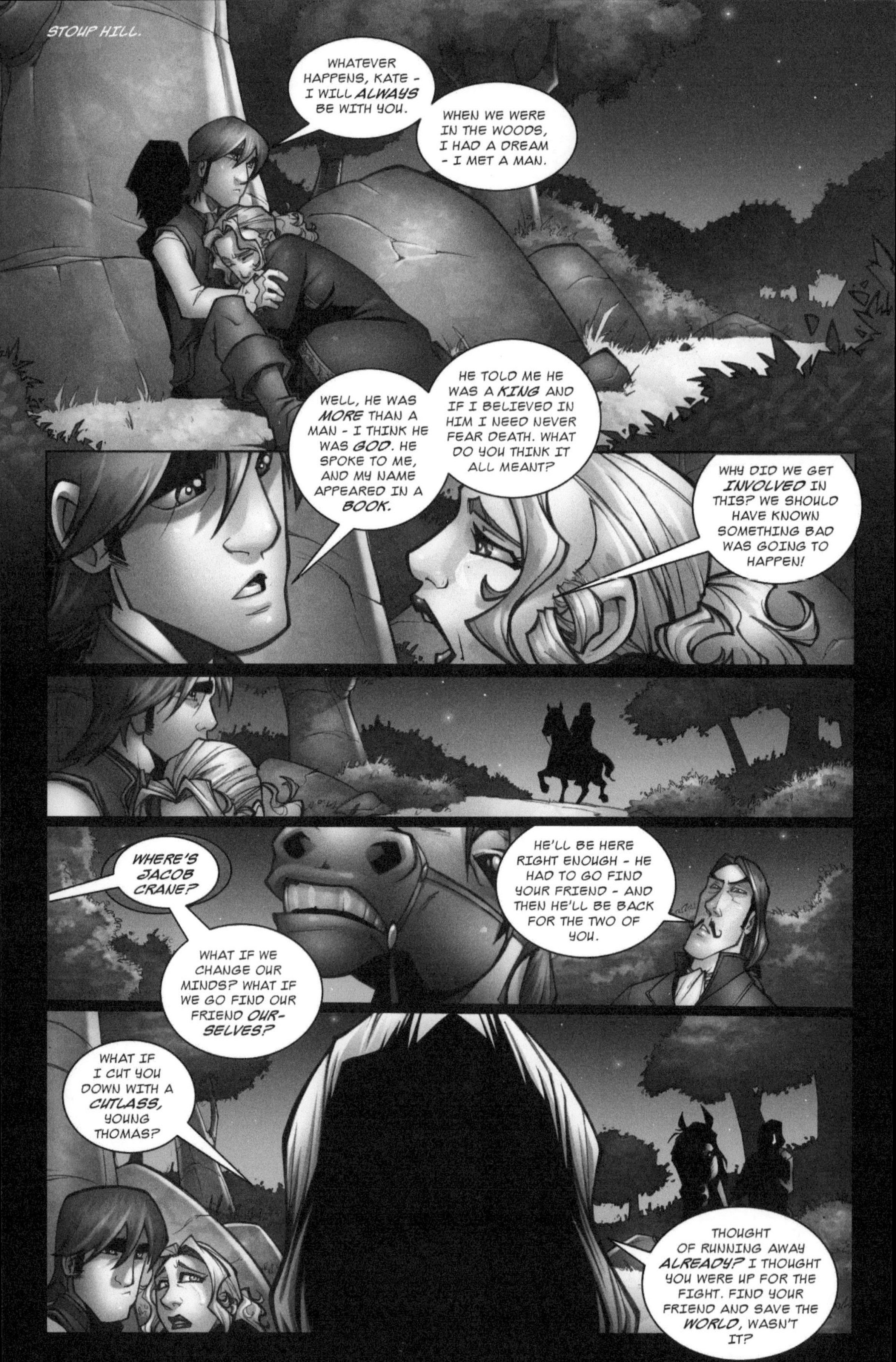
STOUP HILL.
WHATEVER HAPPENS, KATE - I WILL ALWAYS BE WITH YOU.
WHEN WE WERE IN THE WOODS, I HAD A DREAM - I MET A MAN.
WELL, HE WAS MORE THAN A MAN - I THINK HE WAS GOD. HE SPOKE TO ME, AND MY NAME APPEARED IN A BOOK.
HE TOLD ME HE WAS A KING AND IF I BELIEVED IN HIM I NEED NEVER FEAR DEATH. WHAT DO YOU THINK IT ALL MEANT?
WHY DID WE GET INVOLVED IN THIS? WE SHOULD HAVE KNOWN SOMETHING BAD WAS GOING TO HAPPEN!
WHERE'S JACOB CRANE?
HE'LL BE HERE RIGHT ENOUGH - HE HAD TO GO FIND YOUR FRIEND - AND THEN HE'LL BE BACK FOR THE TWO OF YOU.
WHAT IF WE CHANGE OUR MINDS? WHAT IF WE GO FIND OUR FRIEND OURSELVES?
WHAT IF I CUT YOU DOWN WITH A CUTLASS, YOUNG THOMAS?
THOUGHT OF RUNNING AWAY ALREADY? I THOUGHT YOU WERE UP FOR THE FIGHT. FIND YOUR FRIEND AND SAVE THE WORLD, WASN'T IT?

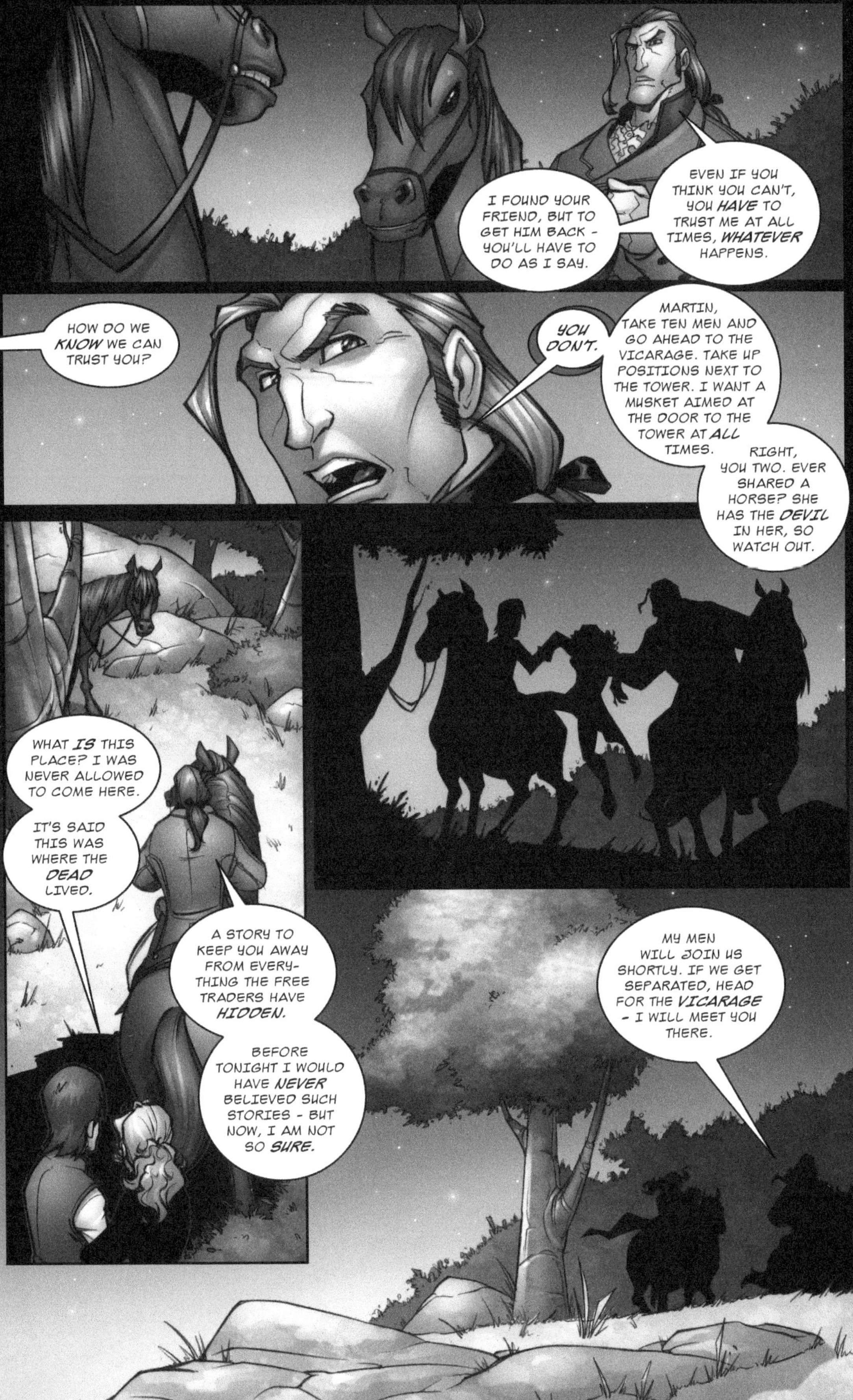
I FOUND YOUR FRIEND, BUT TO GET HIM BACK - YOU'LL HAVE TO DO AS I SAY.
EVEN IF YOU THINK YOU CAN'T, YOU HAVE TO TRUST ME AT ALL TIMES, WHATEVER HAPPENS.
HOW DO WE KNOW WE CAN TRUST YOU?
YOU DON'T.
MARTIN, TAKE TEN MEN AND GO AHEAD TO THE VICARAGE. TAKE UP POSITIONS NEXT TO THE TOWER. I WANT A MUSKET AIMED AT THE DOOR TO THE TOWER AT ALL TIMES.
RIGHT, YOU TWO. EVER SHARED A HORSE? SHE HAS THE DEVIL IN HER, SO WATCH OUT.
WHAT IS THIS PLACE? I WAS NEVER ALLOWED TO COME HERE.
IT'S SAID THIS WAS WHERE THE DEAD LIVED.
A STORY TO KEEP YOU AWAY FROM EVERY-THING THE FREE TRADERS HAVE HIDDEN.
BEFORE TONIGHT I WOULD HAVE NEVER BELIEVED SUCH STORIES - BUT NOW, I AM NOT SO SURE.
MY MEN WILL JOIN US SHORTLY. IF WE GET SEPARATED, HEAD FOR THE VICARAGE - I WILL MEET YOU THERE.

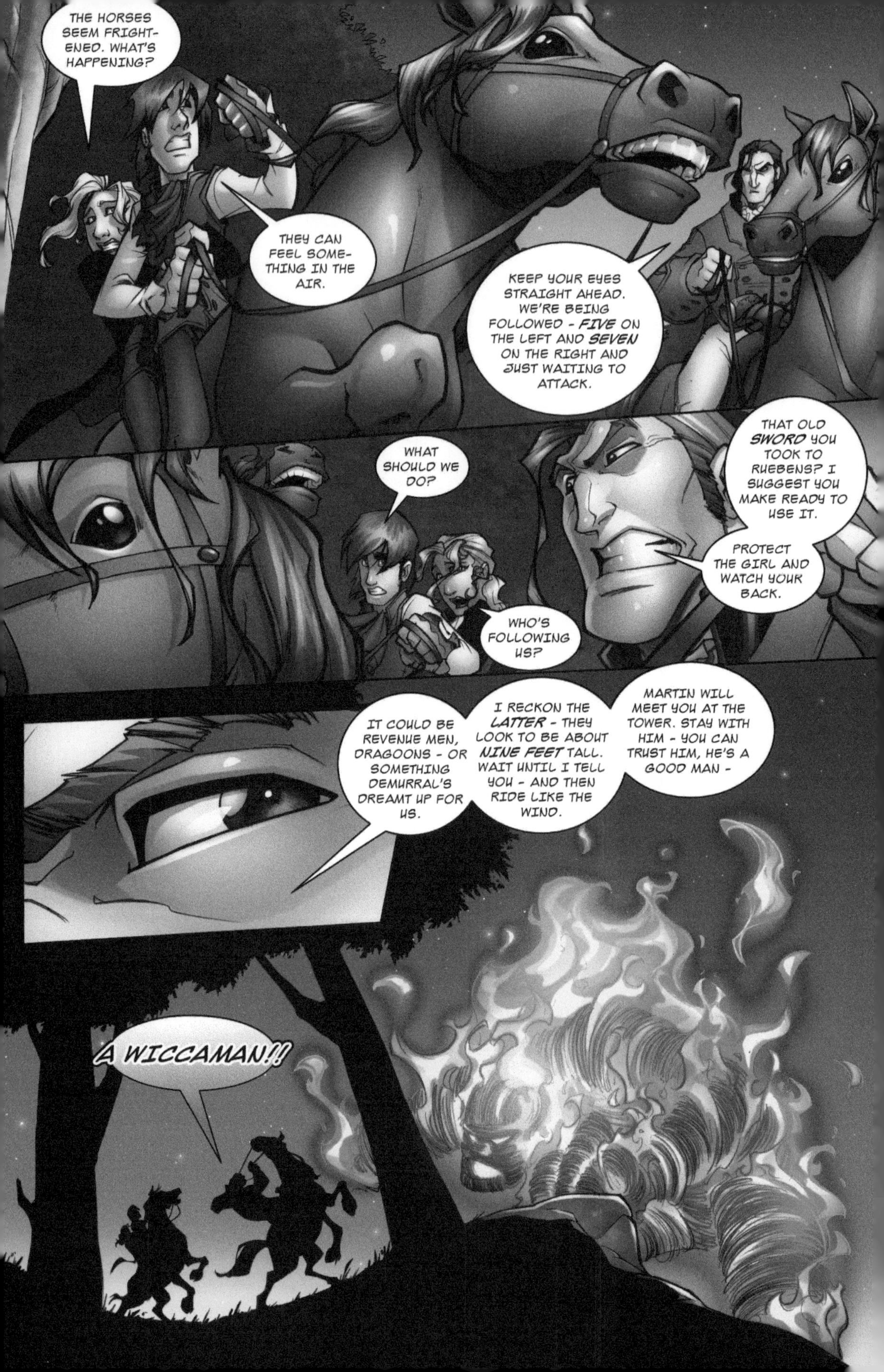
THE HORSES SEEM FRIGHT-ENED. WHAT'S HAPPENING?
THEY CAN FEEL SOME-THING IN THE AIR.
KEEP YOUR EYES STRAIGHT AHEAD. WE'RE BEING FOLLOWED - FIVE ON THE LEFT AND SEVEN ON THE RIGHT AND JUST WAITING TO ATTACK.
WHAT SHOULD WE DO?
THAT OLD SWORD YOU TOOK TO RUEBENS? I SUGGEST YOU MAKE READY TO USE IT.
PROTECT THE GIRL AND WATCH YOUR BACK.
WHO'S FOLLOWING US?
IT COULD BE REVENUE MEN, DRAGOONS - OR SOMETHING DEMURRAL'S DREAMT UP FOR US.
I RECKON THE LATTER - THEY LOOK TO BE ABOUT NINE FEET TALL. WAIT UNTIL I TELL YOU - AND THEN RIDE LIKE THE WIND.
MARTIN WILL MEET YOU AT THE TOWER. STAY WITH HIM - YOU CAN TRUST HIM, HE'S A GOOD MAN -
A WICCAMAN!!

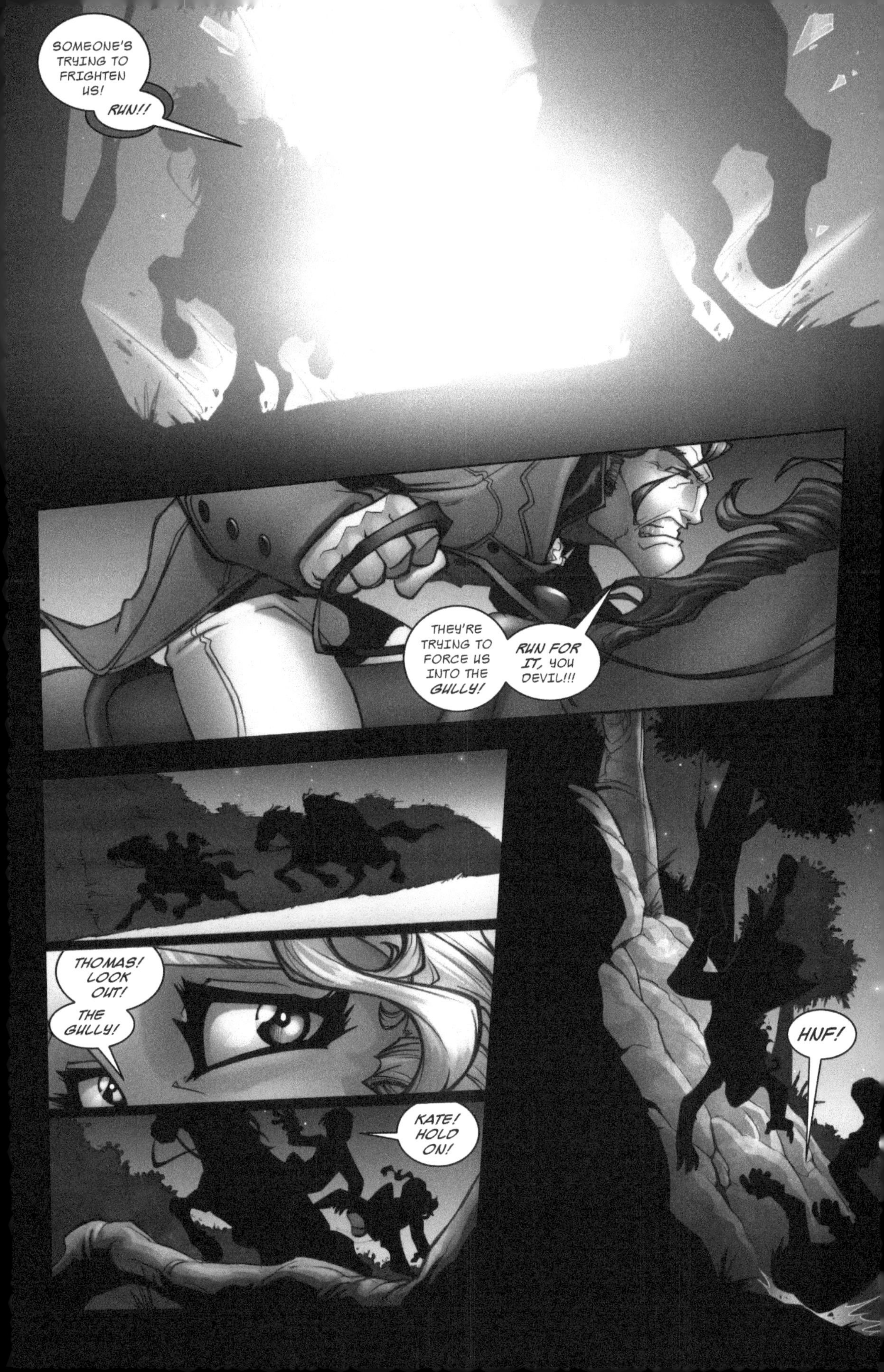
SOMEONE'S TRYING TO FRIGHTEN US!
RUN!!
THEY'RE TRYING TO FORCE US INTO THE GULLY!
RUN FOR IT, YOU DEVIL!!!
THOMAS! LOOK OUT!
THE GULLY!
KATE! HOLD ON!
HNF!

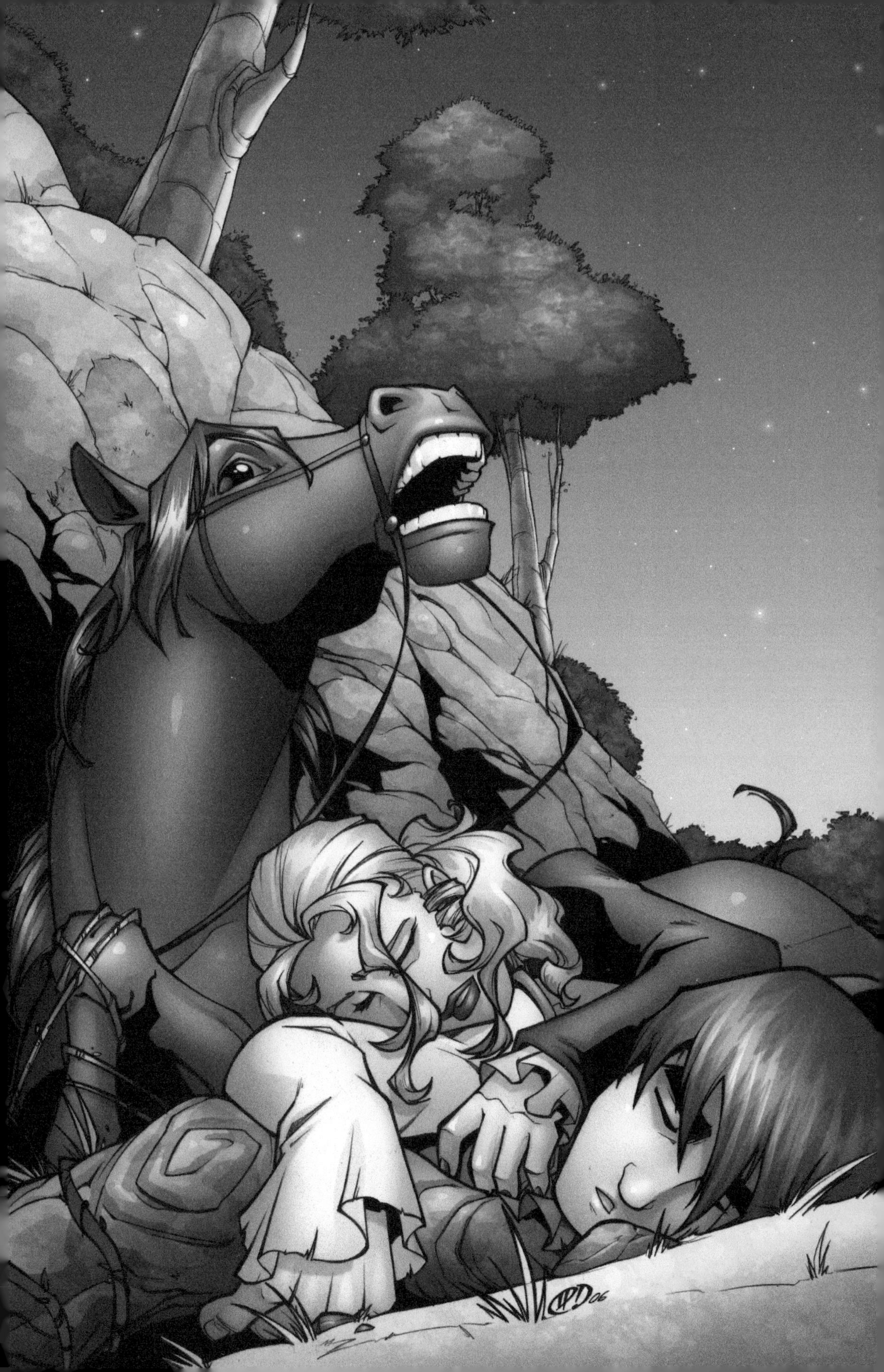

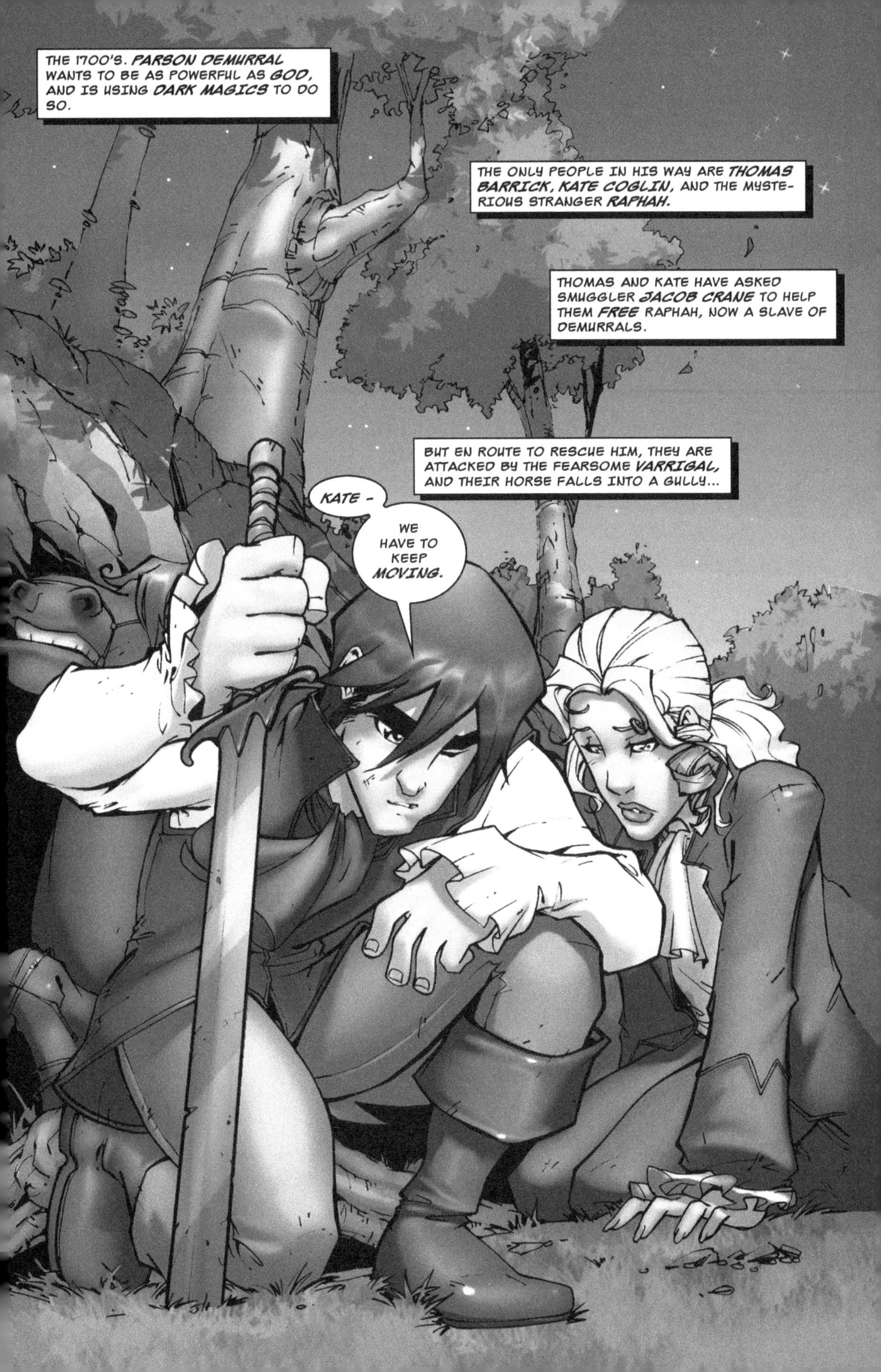
THE 1700'S. PARSON DEMURRAL WANTS TO BE AS POWERFUL AS GOD, AND IS USING DARK MAGICS TO DO SO.
THE ONLY PEOPLE IN HIS WAY ARE THOMAS BARRICK, KATE COGLIN, AND THE MYSTERIOUS STRANGER RAPHAH.
THOMAS AND KATE HAVE ASKED SMUGGLER JACOB CRANE TO HELP THEM FREE RAPHAH, NOW A SLAVE OF DEMURRALS.
BUT EN ROUTE TO RESCUE HIM, THEY ARE ATTACKED BY THE FEARSOME VARRIGAL, AND THEIR HORSE FALLS INTO A GULLY...
KATE -
WE HAVE TO KEEP MOVING.

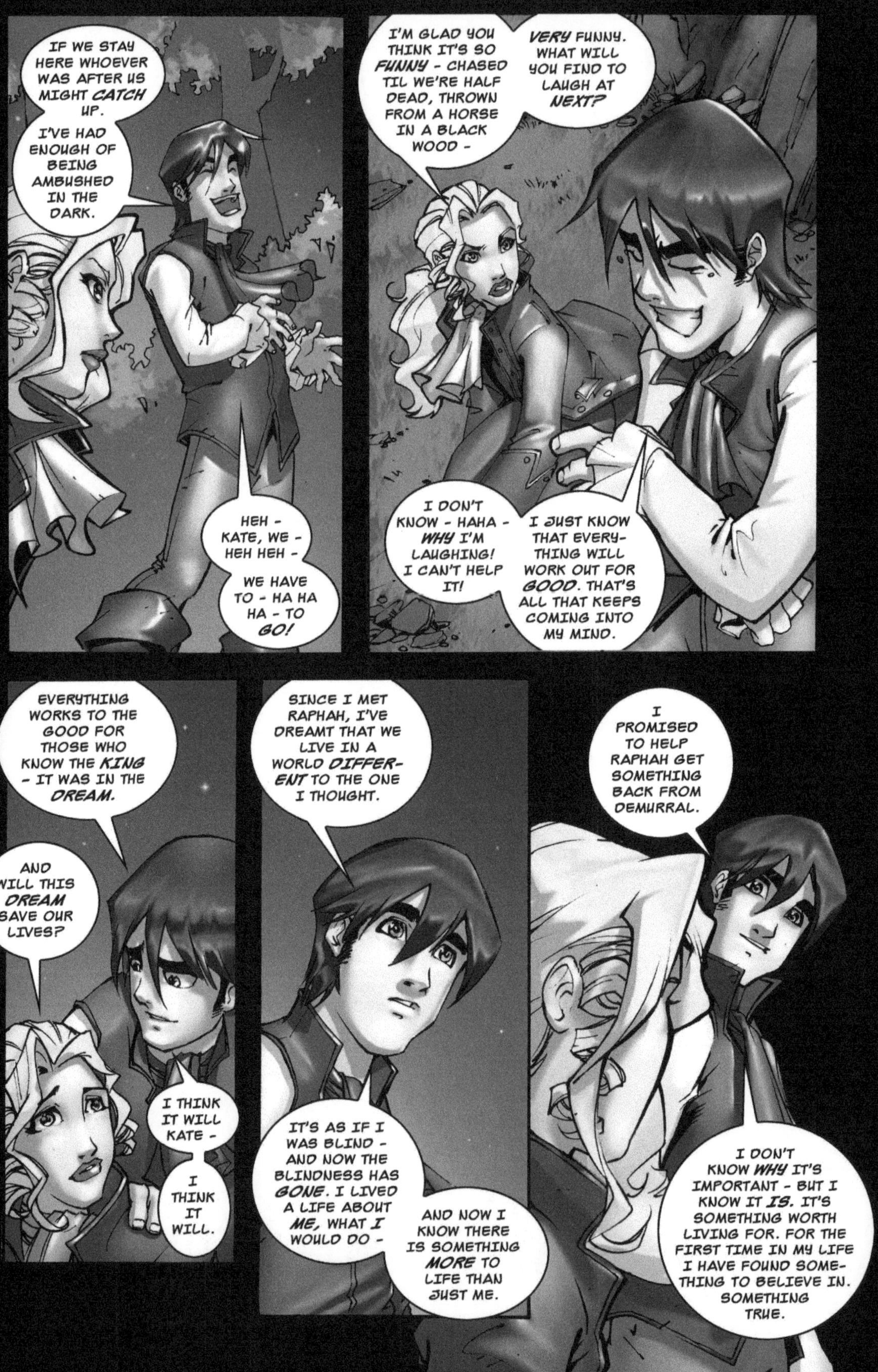
IF WE STAY HERE WHOEVER WAS AFTER US MIGHT CATCH UP.
I'VE HAD ENOUGH OF BEING AMBUSHED IN THE DARK.
HEH - KATE, WE - HEH HEH -
WE HAVE TO - HA HA HA - TO GO!
I'M GLAD YOU THINK IT'S SO FUNNY - CHASED TIL WE'RE HALF DEAD, THROWN FROM A HORSE IN A BLACK WOOD -
VERY FUNNY. WHAT WILL YOU FIND TO LAUGH AT NEXT?
I DON'T KNOW - HAHA - WHY I'M LAUGHING! I CAN'T HELP IT!
I JUST KNOW THAT EVERYTHING WILL WORK OUT FOR GOOD. THAT'S ALL THAT KEEPS COMING INTO MY MIND.
EVERYTHING WORKS TO THE GOOD FOR THOSE WHO KNOW THE KING - IT WAS IN THE DREAM.
AND WILL THIS DREAM SAVE OUR LIVES?
I THINK IT WILL KATE -
I THINK IT WILL.
SINCE I MET RAPHAH, I'VE DREAMT THAT WE LIVE IN A WORLD DIFFERENT TO THE ONE I THOUGHT.
IT'S AS IF I WAS BLIND - AND NOW THE BLINDNESS HAS GONE. I LIVED A LIFE ABOUT ME, WHAT I WOULD DO -
AND NOW I KNOW THERE IS SOMETHING MORE TO LIFE THAN JUST ME.
I PROMISED TO HELP RAPHAH GET SOMETHING BACK FROM DEMURRAL.
I DON'T KNOW WHY IT'S IMPORTANT - BUT I KNOW IT IS. IT'S SOMETHING WORTH LIVING FOR. FOR THE FIRST TIME IN MY LIFE I HAVE FOUND SOMETHING TO BELIEVE IN. SOMETHING TRUE.

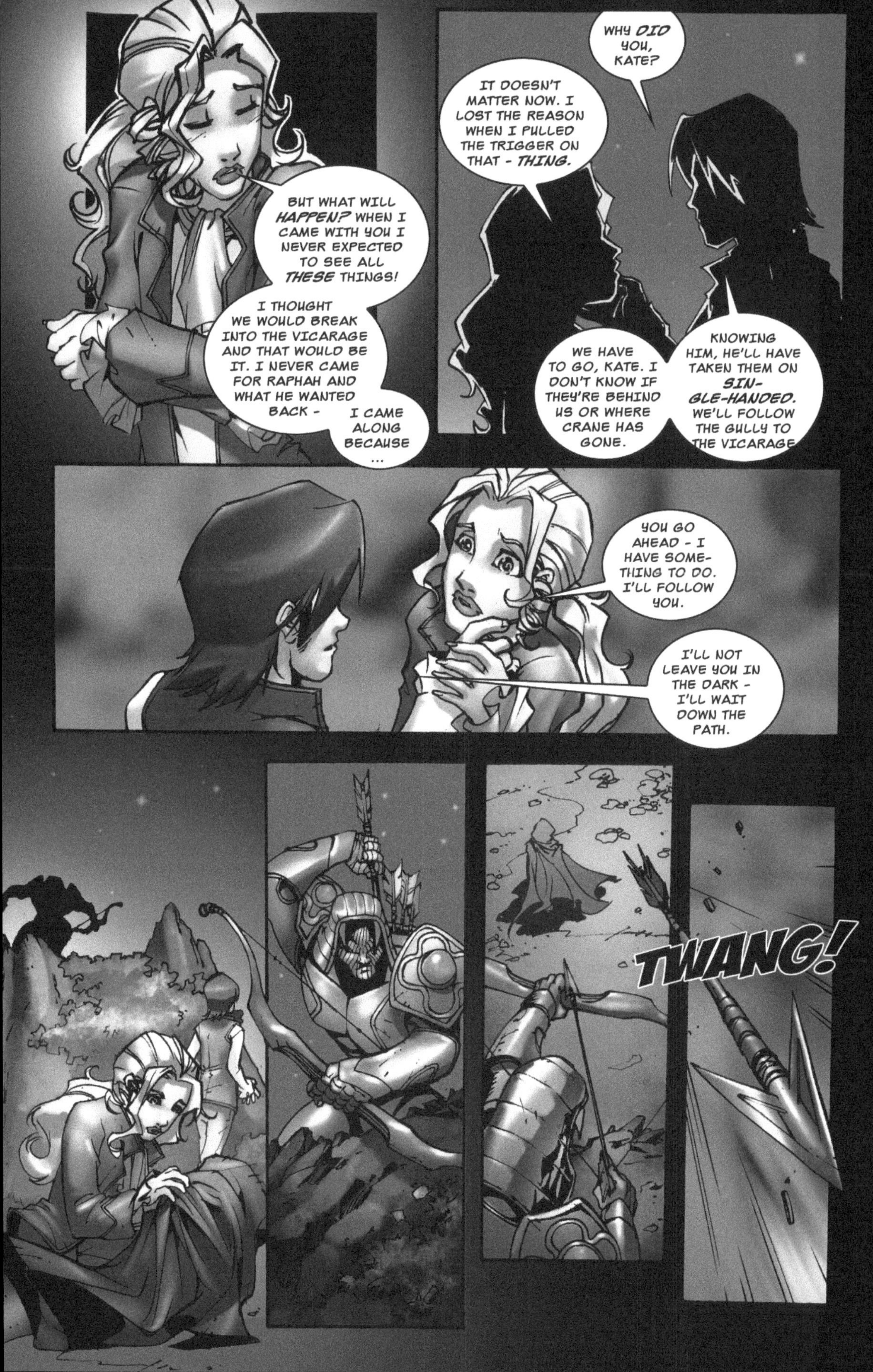
BUT WHAT WILL HAPPEN? WHEN I CAME WITH YOU I NEVER EXPECTED TO SEE ALL THESE THINGS!
I THOUGHT WE WOULD BREAK INTO THE VICARAGE AND THAT WOULD BE IT. I NEVER CAME FOR RAPHAH AND WHAT HE WANTED BACK -
I CAME ALONG BECAUSE ...
WHY DID YOU, KATE?
IT DOESN'T MATTER NOW. I LOST THE REASON WHEN I PULLED THE TRIGGER ON THAT - THING.
WE HAVE TO GO, KATE. I DON'T KNOW IF THEY'RE BEHIND US OR WHERE CRANE HAS GONE.
KNOWING HIM, HE'LL HAVE TAKEN THEM ON SIN-GLE-HANDED. WE'LL FOLLOW THE GULLY TO THE VICARAGE
YOU GO AHEAD - I HAVE SOME-THING TO DO. I'LL FOLLOW YOU.
I'LL NOT LEAVE YOU IN THE DARK - I'LL WAIT DOWN THE PATH.
TWANG!

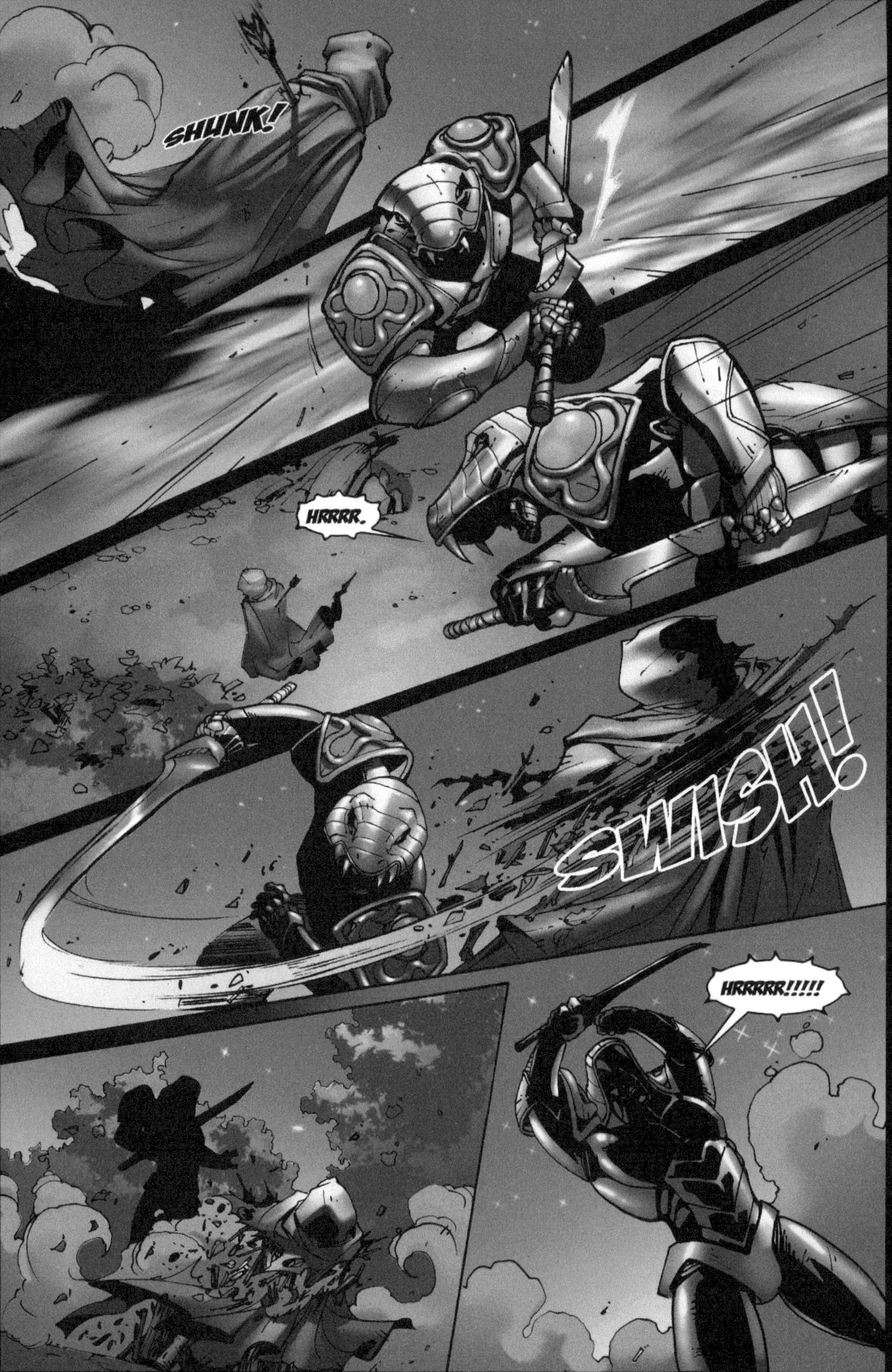
SHUNK!
HRRRR.
SWISH!
HRRRRR!!!!!

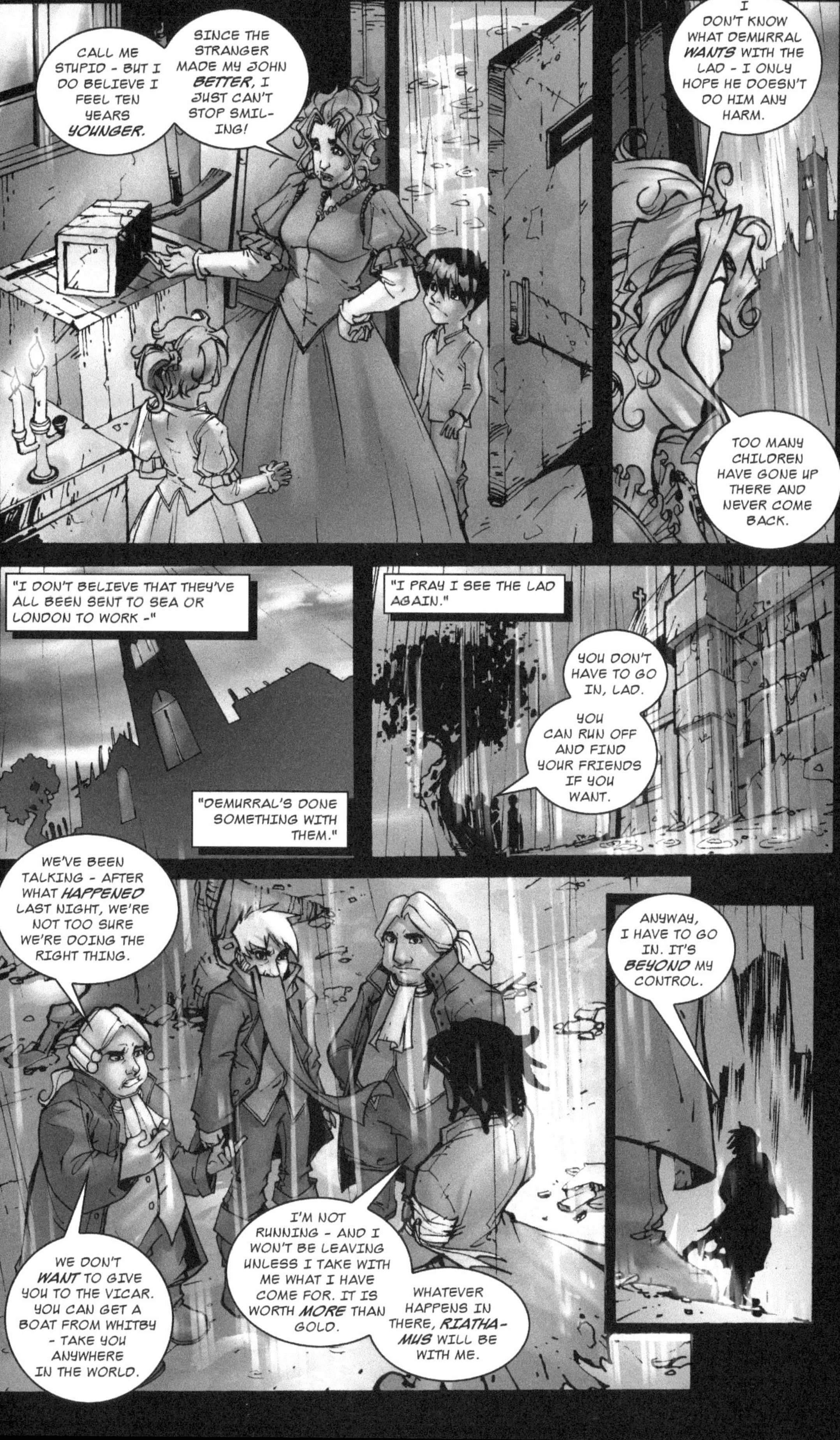
CALL ME STUPID - BUT I DO BELIEVE I FEEL TEN YEARS *YOUNGER.*
SINCE THE STRANGER MADE MY JOHN *BETTER*, I JUST CAN'T STOP SMIL- ING!
I DON'T KNOW WHAT DEMURRAL *WANTS* WITH THE LAD - I ONLY HOPE HE DOESN'T DO HIM ANY HARM.
TOO MANY CHILDREN HAVE GONE UP THERE AND NEVER COME BACK.
"I DON'T BELIEVE THAT THEY'VE ALL BEEN SENT TO SEA OR LONDON TO WORK -"
"DEMURRAL'S DONE SOMETHING WITH THEM."
"I PRAY I SEE THE LAD AGAIN."
YOU DON'T HAVE TO GO IN, LAD.
YOU CAN RUN OFF AND FIND YOUR FRIENDS IF YOU WANT.
WE'VE BEEN TALKING - AFTER WHAT *HAPPENED* LAST NIGHT, WE'RE NOT TOO SURE WE'RE DOING THE RIGHT THING.
WE DON'T *WANT* TO GIVE YOU TO THE VICAR. YOU CAN GET A BOAT FROM WHITBY - TAKE YOU ANYWHERE IN THE WORLD.
I'M NOT RUNNING - AND I WON'T BE LEAVING UNLESS I TAKE WITH ME WHAT I HAVE COME FOR. IT IS WORTH *MORE* THAN GOLD.
WHATEVER HAPPENS IN THERE, *RIATHA- MUS* WILL BE WITH ME.
ANYWAY, I HAVE TO GO IN. IT'S *BEYOND* MY CONTROL.

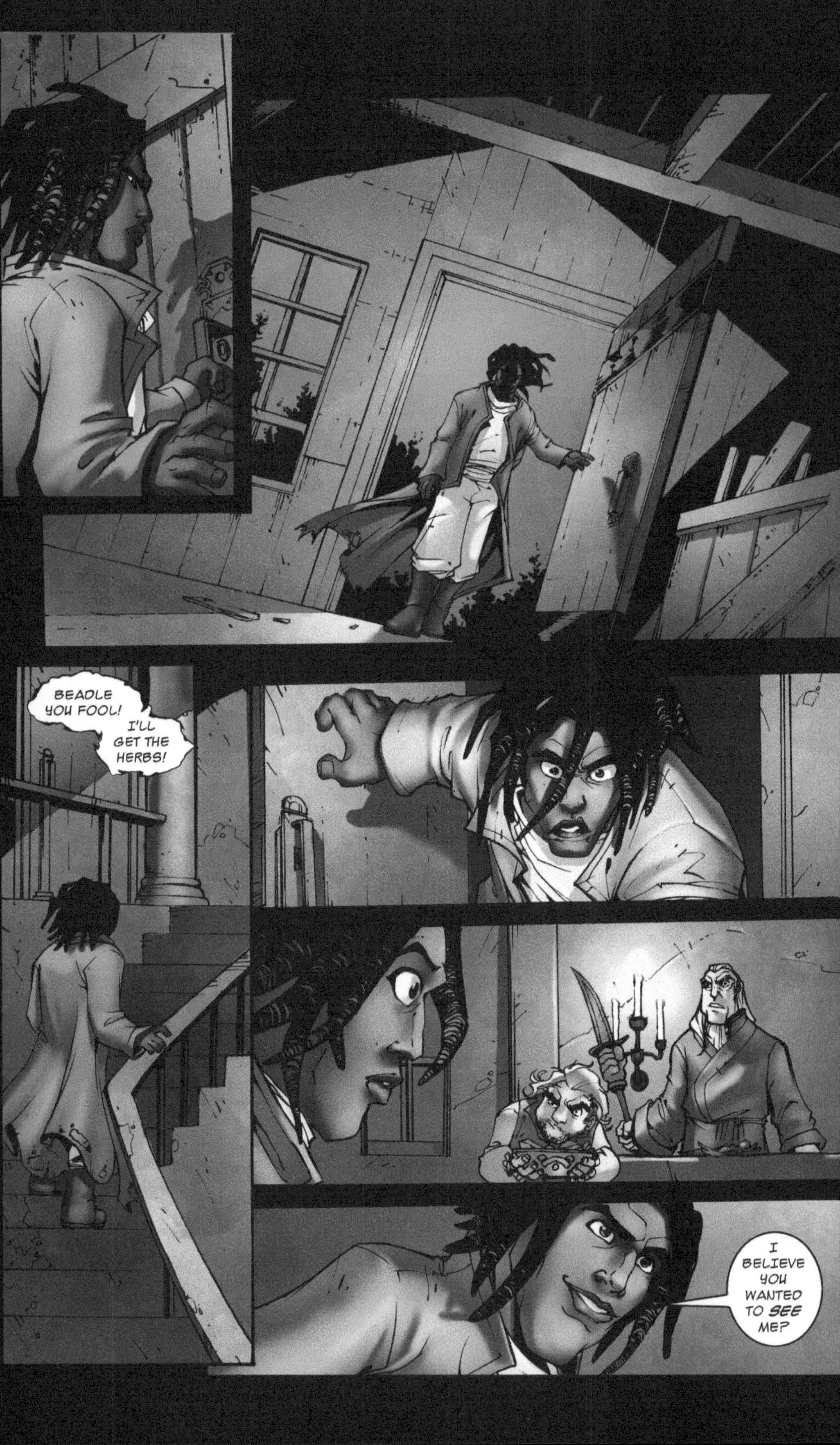
BEADLE YOU FOOL!
I'LL GET THE HERBS!
I BELIEVE YOU WANTED TO SEE ME?

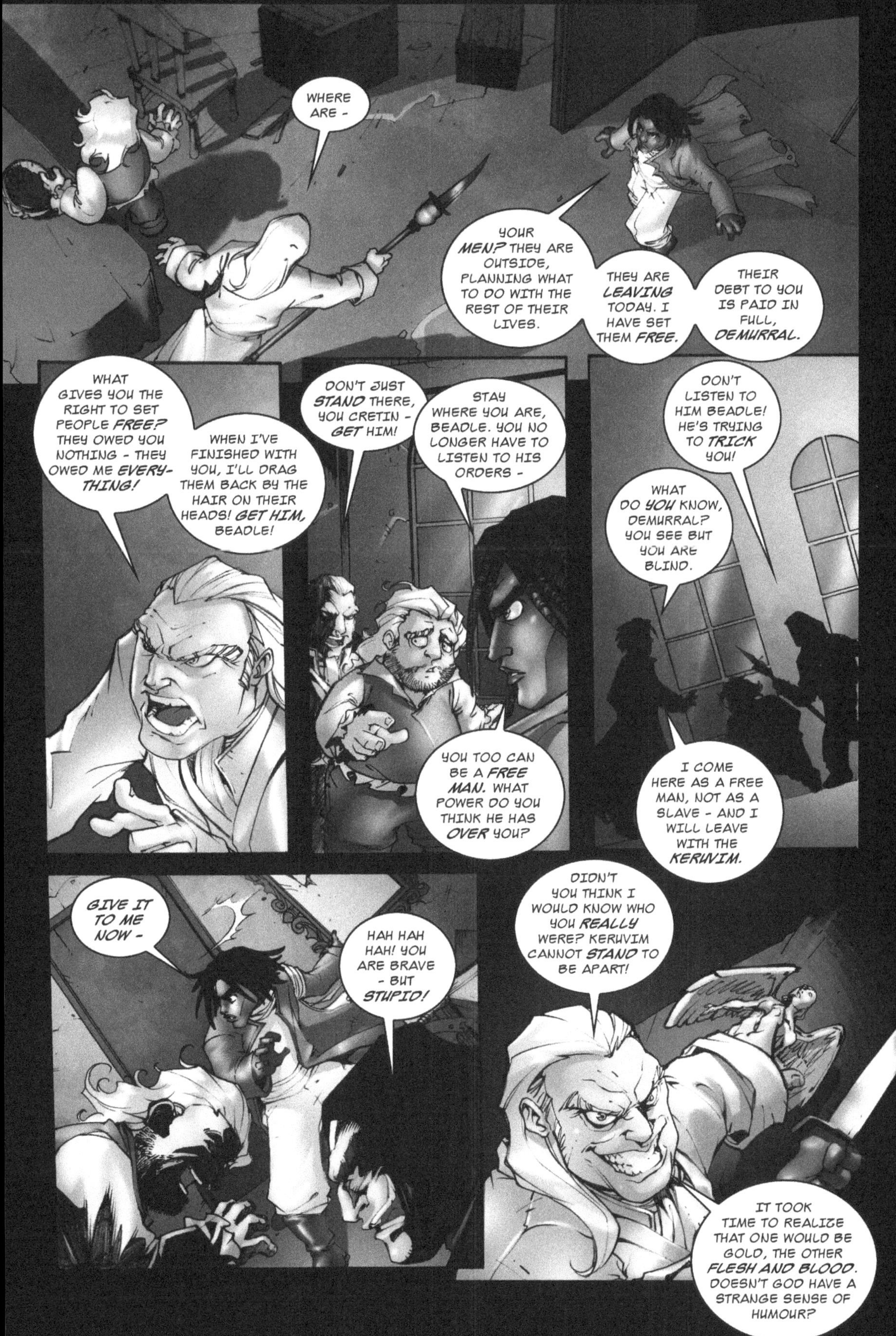
WHERE ARE -
YOUR MEN? THEY ARE OUTSIDE, PLANNING WHAT TO DO WITH THE REST OF THEIR LIVES.
THEY ARE LEAVING TODAY. I HAVE SET THEM FREE.
THEIR DEBT TO YOU IS PAID IN FULL, DEMURRAL.
WHAT GIVES YOU THE RIGHT TO SET PEOPLE FREE? THEY OWED YOU NOTHING - THEY OWED ME EVERY-THING!
WHEN I'VE FINISHED WITH YOU, I'LL DRAG THEM BACK BY THE HAIR ON THEIR HEADS! GET HIM, BEADLE!
DON'T JUST STAND THERE, YOU CRETIN - GET HIM!
STAY WHERE YOU ARE, BEADLE. YOU NO LONGER HAVE TO LISTEN TO HIS ORDERS -
YOU TOO CAN BE A FREE MAN. WHAT POWER DO YOU THINK HE HAS OVER YOU?
DON'T LISTEN TO HIM BEADLE! HE'S TRYING TO TRICK YOU!
WHAT DO YOU KNOW, DEMURRAL? YOU SEE BUT YOU ARE BLIND.
I COME HERE AS A FREE MAN, NOT AS A SLAVE - AND I WILL LEAVE WITH THE KERUVIM.
GIVE IT TO ME NOW -
HAH HAH HAH! YOU ARE BRAVE - BUT STUPID!
DIDN'T YOU THINK I WOULD KNOW WHO YOU REALLY WERE? KERUVIM CANNOT STAND TO BE APART!
IT TOOK TIME TO REALIZE THAT ONE WOULD BE GOLD, THE OTHER FLESH AND BLOOD. DOESN'T GOD HAVE A STRANGE SENSE OF HUMOUR?

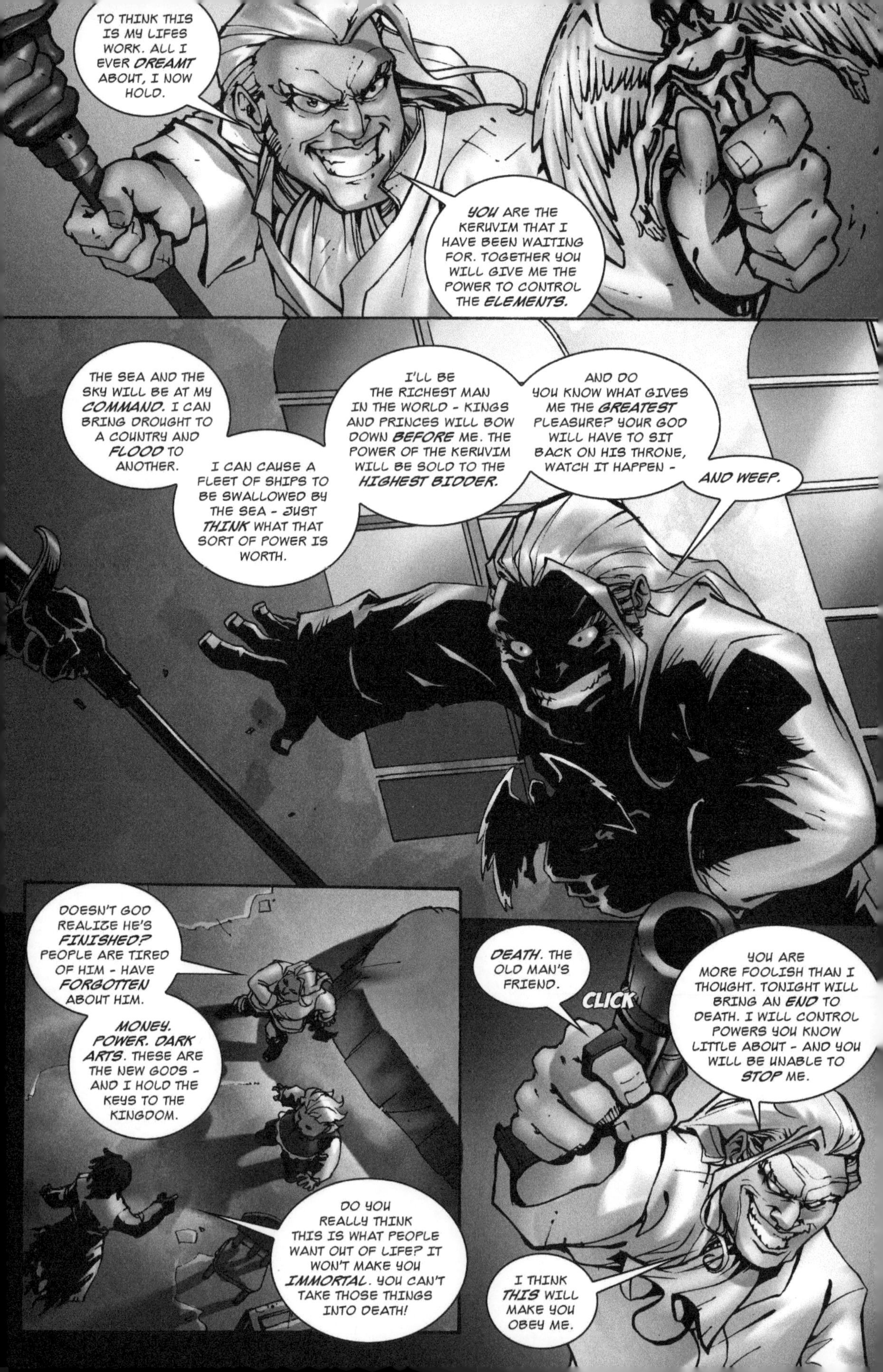
TO THINK THIS IS MY LIFES WORK. ALL I EVER DREAMT ABOUT, I NOW HOLD.
YOU ARE THE KERUVIM THAT I HAVE BEEN WAITING FOR. TOGETHER YOU WILL GIVE ME THE POWER TO CONTROL THE ELEMENTS.
THE SEA AND THE SKY WILL BE AT MY COMMAND. I CAN BRING DROUGHT TO A COUNTRY AND FLOOD TO ANOTHER.
I CAN CAUSE A FLEET OF SHIPS TO BE SWALLOWED BY THE SEA - JUST THINK WHAT THAT SORT OF POWER IS WORTH.
I'LL BE THE RICHEST MAN IN THE WORLD - KINGS AND PRINCES WILL BOW DOWN BEFORE ME. THE POWER OF THE KERUVIM WILL BE SOLD TO THE HIGHEST BIDDER.
AND DO YOU KNOW WHAT GIVES ME THE GREATEST PLEASURE? YOUR GOD WILL HAVE TO SIT BACK ON HIS THRONE, WATCH IT HAPPEN -
AND WEEP.
DOESN'T GOD REALIZE HE'S FINISHED? PEOPLE ARE TIRED OF HIM - HAVE FORGOTTEN ABOUT HIM.
MONEY. POWER. DARK ARTS. THESE ARE THE NEW GODS - AND I HOLD THE KEYS TO THE KINGDOM.
DO YOU REALLY THINK THIS IS WHAT PEOPLE WANT OUT OF LIFE? IT WON'T MAKE YOU IMMORTAL. YOU CAN'T TAKE THOSE THINGS INTO DEATH!
DEATH. THE OLD MAN'S FRIEND.
CLICK
YOU ARE MORE FOOLISH THAN I THOUGHT. TONIGHT WILL BRING AN END TO DEATH. I WILL CONTROL POWERS YOU KNOW LITTLE ABOUT - AND YOU WILL BE UNABLE TO STOP ME.
I THINK THIS WILL MAKE YOU OBEY ME.

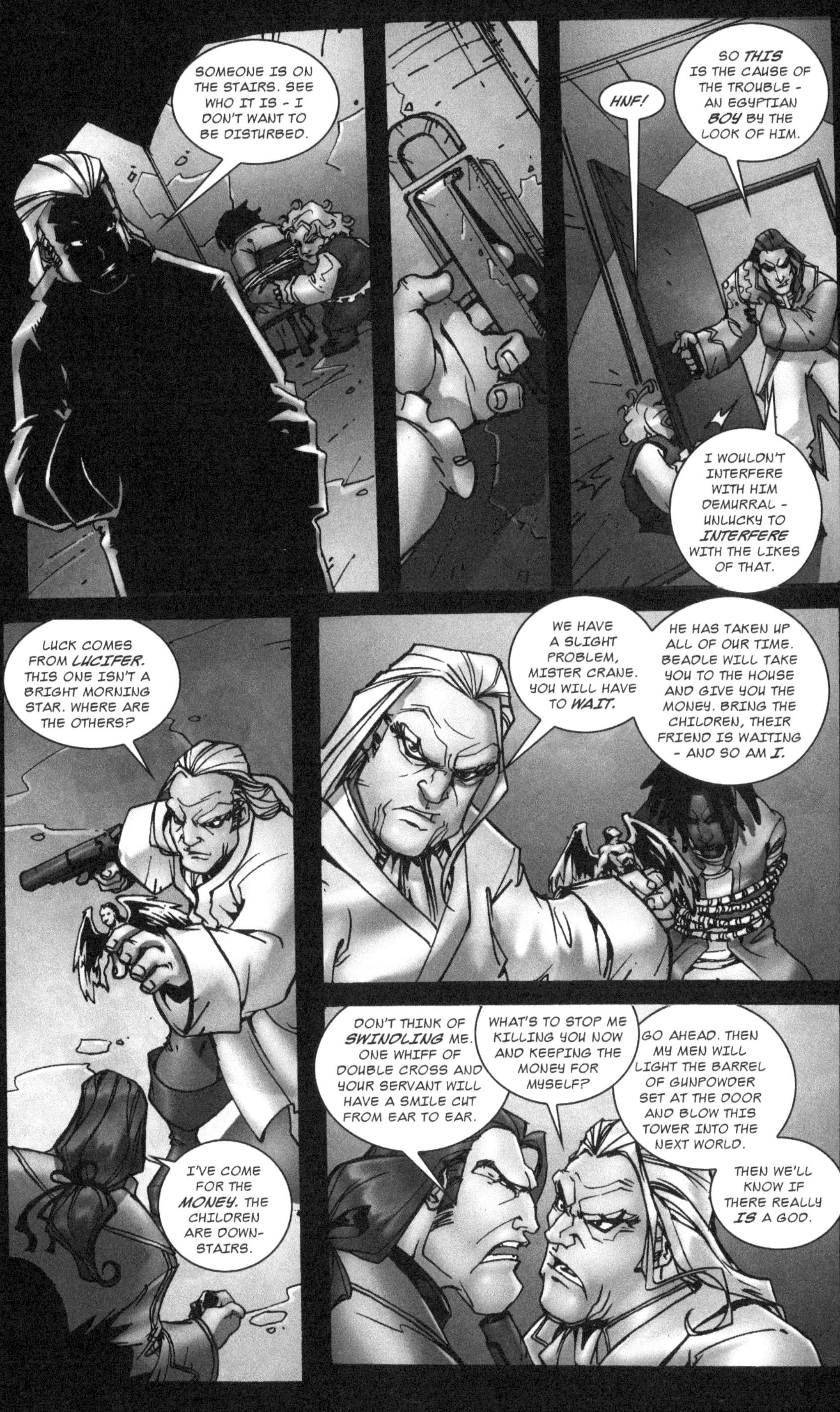
SOMEONE IS ON THE STAIRS. SEE WHO IT IS - I DON'T WANT TO BE DISTURBED.
HNF!
SO THIS IS THE CAUSE OF THE TROUBLE - AN EGYPTIAN BOY BY THE LOOK OF HIM.
I WOULDN'T INTERFERE WITH HIM DEMURRAL - UNLUCKY TO INTERFERE WITH THE LIKES OF THAT.
LUCK COMES FROM LUCIFER. THIS ONE ISN'T A BRIGHT MORNING STAR. WHERE ARE THE OTHERS?
I'VE COME FOR THE MONEY. THE CHILDREN ARE DOWN-STAIRS.
WE HAVE A SLIGHT PROBLEM, MISTER CRANE. YOU WILL HAVE TO WAIT.
HE HAS TAKEN UP ALL OF OUR TIME. BEADLE WILL TAKE YOU TO THE HOUSE AND GIVE YOU THE MONEY. BRING THE CHILDREN, THEIR FRIEND IS WAITING - AND SO AM I.
DON'T THINK OF SWINDLING ME. ONE WHIFF OF DOUBLE CROSS AND YOUR SERVANT WILL HAVE A SMILE CUT FROM EAR TO EAR.
WHAT'S TO STOP ME KILLING YOU NOW AND KEEPING THE MONEY FOR MYSELF?
GO AHEAD. THEN MY MEN WILL LIGHT THE BARREL OF GUNPOWDER SET AT THE DOOR AND BLOW THIS TOWER INTO THE NEXT WORLD.
THEN WE'LL KNOW IF THERE REALLY IS A GOD.

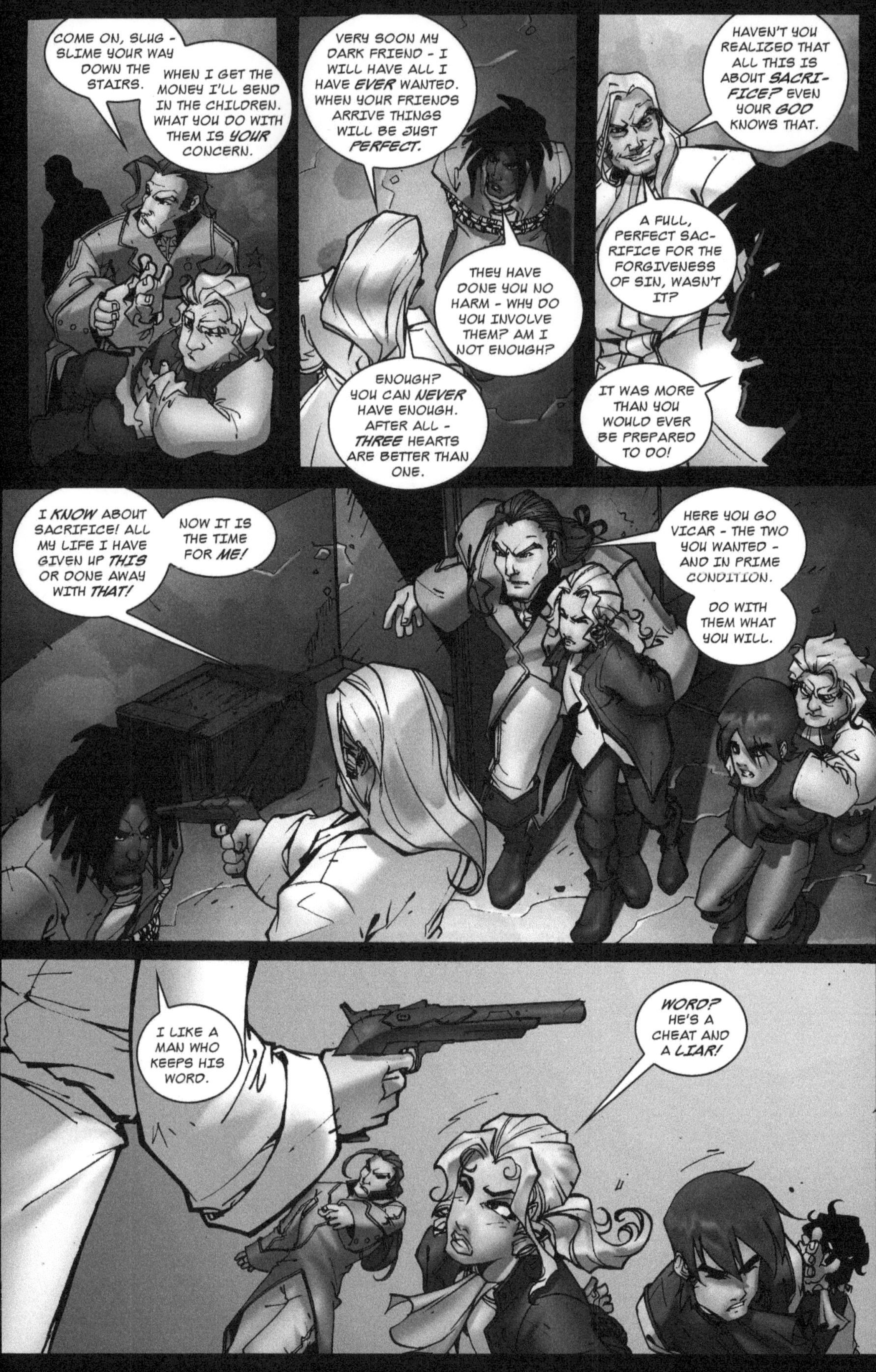
COME ON, SLUG - SLIME YOUR WAY DOWN THE STAIRS.
WHEN I GET THE MONEY I'LL SEND IN THE CHILDREN. WHAT YOU DO WITH THEM IS YOUR CONCERN.
VERY SOON MY DARK FRIEND - I WILL HAVE ALL I HAVE EVER WANTED. WHEN YOUR FRIENDS ARRIVE THINGS WILL BE JUST PERFECT.
THEY HAVE DONE YOU NO HARM - WHY DO YOU INVOLVE THEM? AM I NOT ENOUGH?
ENOUGH? YOU CAN NEVER HAVE ENOUGH. AFTER ALL - THREE HEARTS ARE BETTER THAN ONE.
HAVEN'T YOU REALIZED THAT ALL THIS IS ABOUT SACRI-FICE? EVEN YOUR GOD KNOWS THAT.
A FULL, PERFECT SAC-RIFICE FOR THE FORGIVENESS OF SIN, WASN'T IT?
IT WAS MORE THAN YOU WOULD EVER BE PREPARED TO DO!
I KNOW ABOUT SACRIFICE! ALL MY LIFE I HAVE GIVEN UP THIS OR DONE AWAY WITH THAT!
NOW IT IS THE TIME FOR ME!
HERE YOU GO VICAR - THE TWO YOU WANTED - AND IN PRIME CONDITION.
DO WITH THEM WHAT YOU WILL.
I LIKE A MAN WHO KEEPS HIS WORD.
WORD? HE'S A CHEAT AND A LIAR!

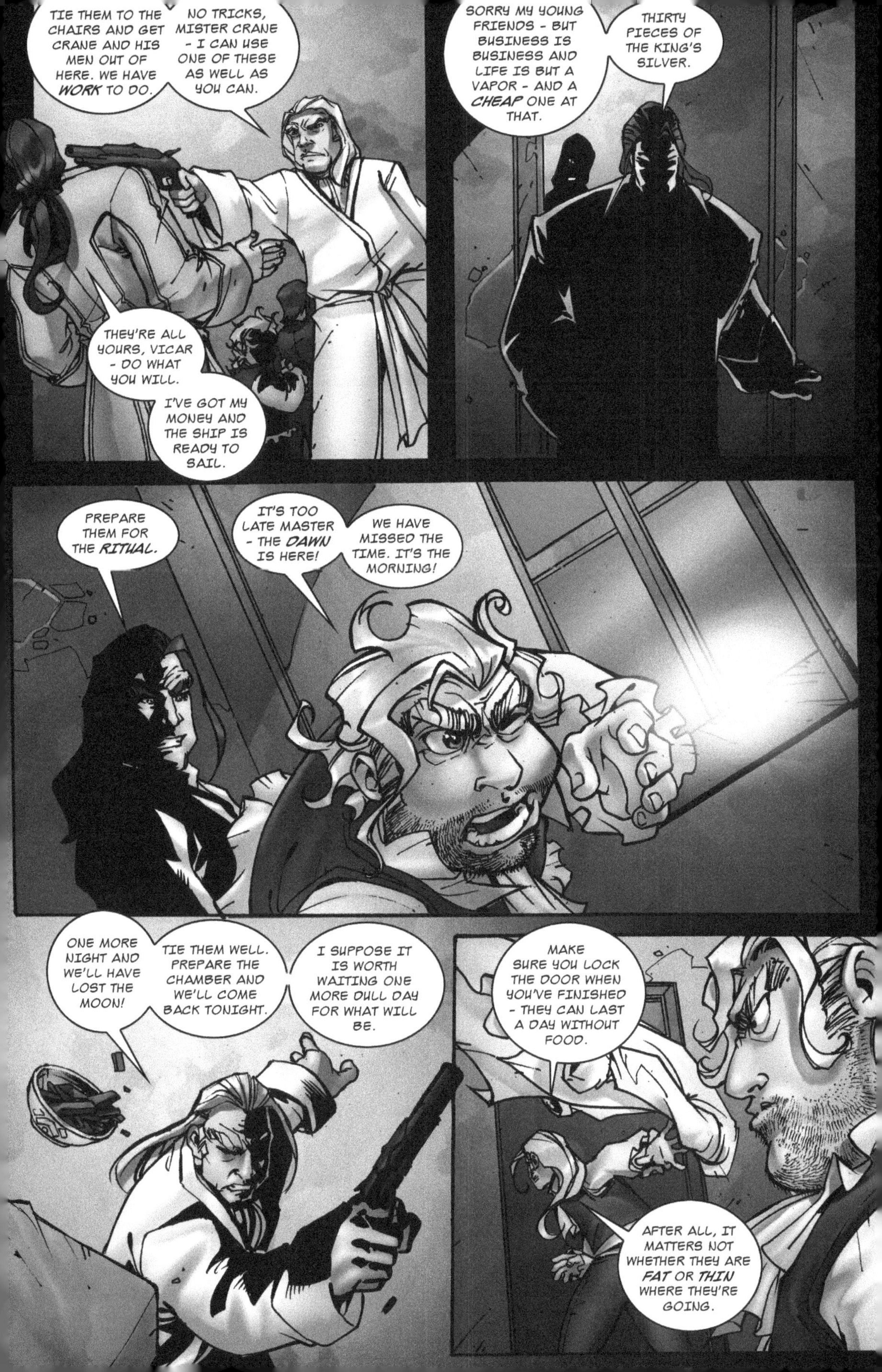

TIE THEM TO THE CHAIRS AND GET CRANE AND HIS MEN OUT OF HERE. WE HAVE WORK TO DO.
NO TRICKS, MISTER CRANE - I CAN USE ONE OF THESE AS WELL AS YOU CAN.
THEY'RE ALL YOURS, VICAR - DO WHAT YOU WILL.
I'VE GOT MY MONEY AND THE SHIP IS READY TO SAIL.
SORRY MY YOUNG FRIENDS - BUT BUSINESS IS BUSINESS AND LIFE IS BUT A VAPOR - AND A CHEAP ONE AT THAT.
THIRTY PIECES OF THE KING'S SILVER.
PREPARE THEM FOR THE RITUAL.
IT'S TOO LATE MASTER - THE DAWN IS HERE!
WE HAVE MISSED THE TIME. IT'S THE MORNING!
ONE MORE NIGHT AND WE'LL HAVE LOST THE MOON!
TIE THEM WELL. PREPARE THE CHAMBER AND WE'LL COME BACK TONIGHT.
I SUPPOSE IT IS WORTH WAITING ONE MORE DULL DAY FOR WHAT WILL BE.
MAKE SURE YOU LOCK THE DOOR WHEN YOU'VE FINISHED - THEY CAN LAST A DAY WITHOUT FOOD.
AFTER ALL, IT MATTERS NOT WHETHER THEY ARE FAT OR THIN WHERE THEY'RE GOING.

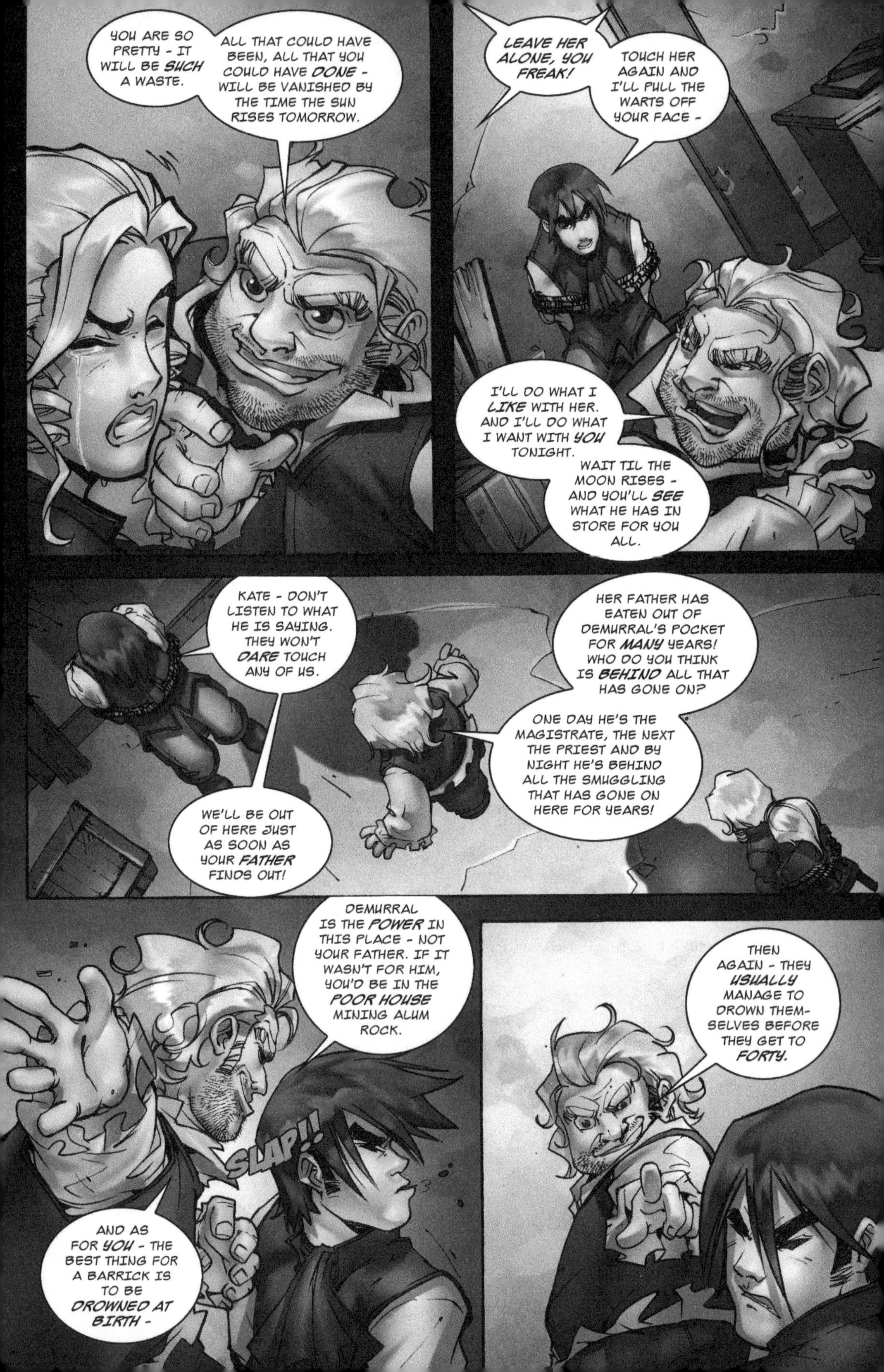

YOU ARE SO PRETTY - IT WILL BE SUCH A WASTE.
ALL THAT COULD HAVE BEEN, ALL THAT YOU COULD HAVE DONE - WILL BE VANISHED BY THE TIME THE SUN RISES TOMORROW.
LEAVE HER ALONE, YOU FREAK!
TOUCH HER AGAIN AND I'LL PULL THE WARTS OFF YOUR FACE -
I'LL DO WHAT I LIKE WITH HER. AND I'LL DO WHAT I WANT WITH YOU TONIGHT.
WAIT TIL THE MOON RISES - AND YOU'LL SEE WHAT HE HAS IN STORE FOR YOU ALL.
KATE - DON'T LISTEN TO WHAT HE IS SAYING. THEY WON'T DARE TOUCH ANY OF US.
WE'LL BE OUT OF HERE JUST AS SOON AS YOUR FATHER FINDS OUT!
HER FATHER HAS EATEN OUT OF DEMURRAL'S POCKET FOR MANY YEARS! WHO DO YOU THINK IS BEHIND ALL THAT HAS GONE ON?
ONE DAY HE'S THE MAGISTRATE, THE NEXT THE PRIEST AND BY NIGHT HE'S BEHIND ALL THE SMUGGLING THAT HAS GONE ON HERE FOR YEARS!
DEMURRAL IS THE POWER IN THIS PLACE - NOT YOUR FATHER. IF IT WASN'T FOR HIM, YOU'D BE IN THE POOR HOUSE MINING ALUM ROCK.
SLAP!!
AND AS FOR YOU - THE BEST THING FOR A BARRICK IS TO BE DROWNED AT BIRTH -
THEN AGAIN - THEY USUALLY MANAGE TO DROWN THEM-SELVES BEFORE THEY GET TO FORTY.

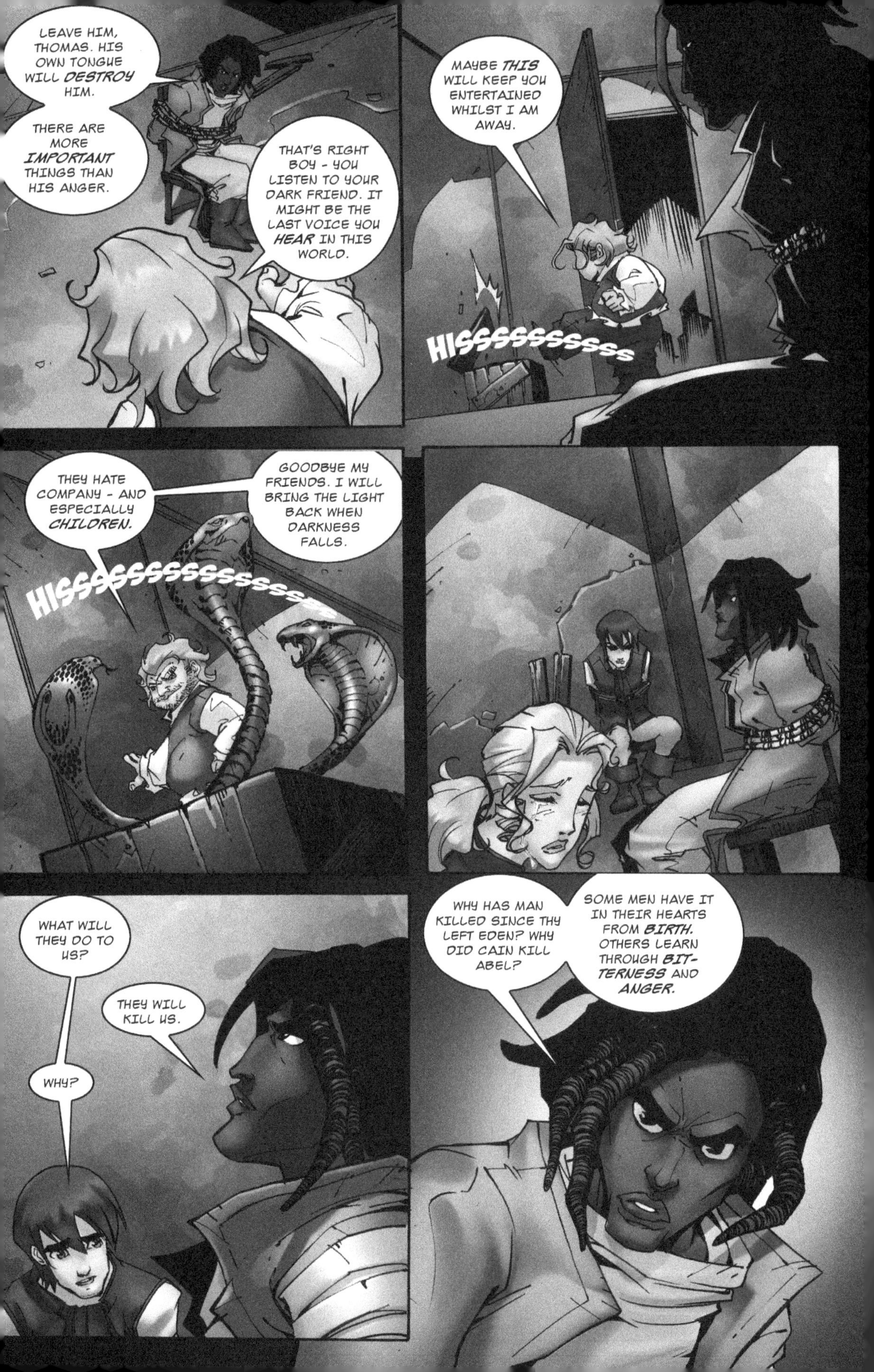
LEAVE HIM, THOMAS. HIS OWN TONGUE WILL DESTROY HIM.
THERE ARE MORE IMPORTANT THINGS THAN HIS ANGER.
THAT'S RIGHT BOY - YOU LISTEN TO YOUR DARK FRIEND. IT MIGHT BE THE LAST VOICE YOU HEAR IN THIS WORLD.
MAYBE THIS WILL KEEP YOU ENTERTAINED WHILST I AM AWAY.
HISSSSSSSSSSS
THEY HATE COMPANY - AND ESPECIALLY CHILDREN.
GOODBYE MY FRIENDS. I WILL BRING THE LIGHT BACK WHEN DARKNESS FALLS.
HISSSSSSSSSSSSSSSSS
WHAT WILL THEY DO TO US?
THEY WILL KILL US.
WHY?
WHY HAS MAN KILLED SINCE THY LEFT EDEN? WHY DID CAIN KILL ABEL?
SOME MEN HAVE IT IN THEIR HEARTS FROM BIRTH. OTHERS LEARN THROUGH BITTERNESS AND ANGER.

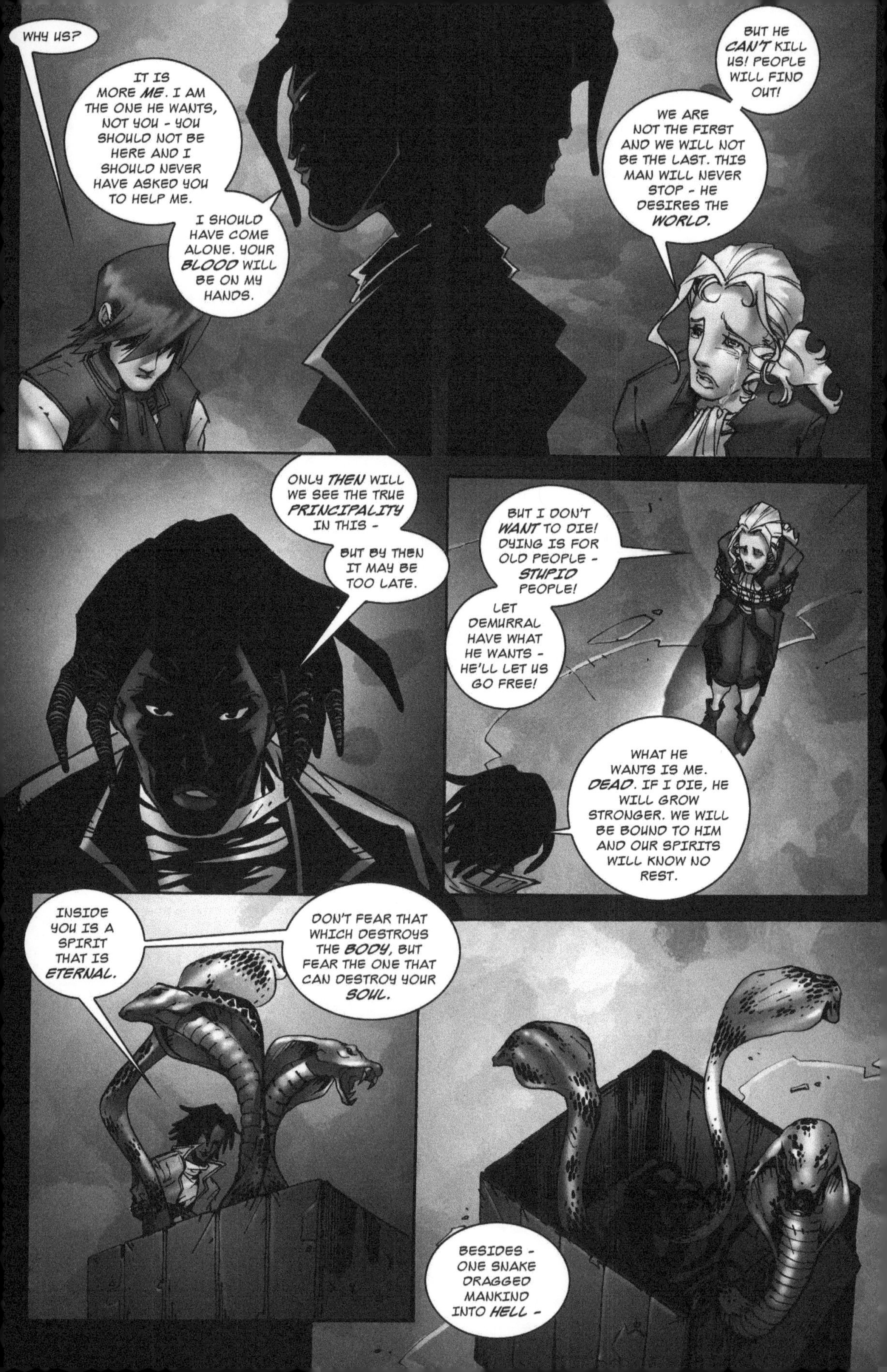
WHY US?
IT IS MORE ME. I AM THE ONE HE WANTS, NOT YOU - YOU SHOULD NOT BE HERE AND I SHOULD NEVER HAVE ASKED YOU TO HELP ME.
I SHOULD HAVE COME ALONE. YOUR BLOOD WILL BE ON MY HANDS.
BUT HE CAN'T KILL US! PEOPLE WILL FIND OUT!
WE ARE NOT THE FIRST AND WE WILL NOT BE THE LAST. THIS MAN WILL NEVER STOP - HE DESIRES THE WORLD.
ONLY THEN WILL WE SEE THE TRUE PRINCIPALITY IN THIS -
BUT BY THEN IT MAY BE TOO LATE.
BUT I DON'T WANT TO DIE! DYING IS FOR OLD PEOPLE - STUPID PEOPLE!
LET DEMURRAL HAVE WHAT HE WANTS - HE'LL LET US GO FREE!
WHAT HE WANTS IS ME. DEAD. IF I DIE, HE WILL GROW STRONGER. WE WILL BE BOUND TO HIM AND OUR SPIRITS WILL KNOW NO REST.
INSIDE YOU IS A SPIRIT THAT IS ETERNAL.
DON'T FEAR THAT WHICH DESTROYS THE BODY, BUT FEAR THE ONE THAT CAN DESTROY YOUR SOUL.
BESIDES - ONE SNAKE DRAGGED MANKIND INTO HELL -

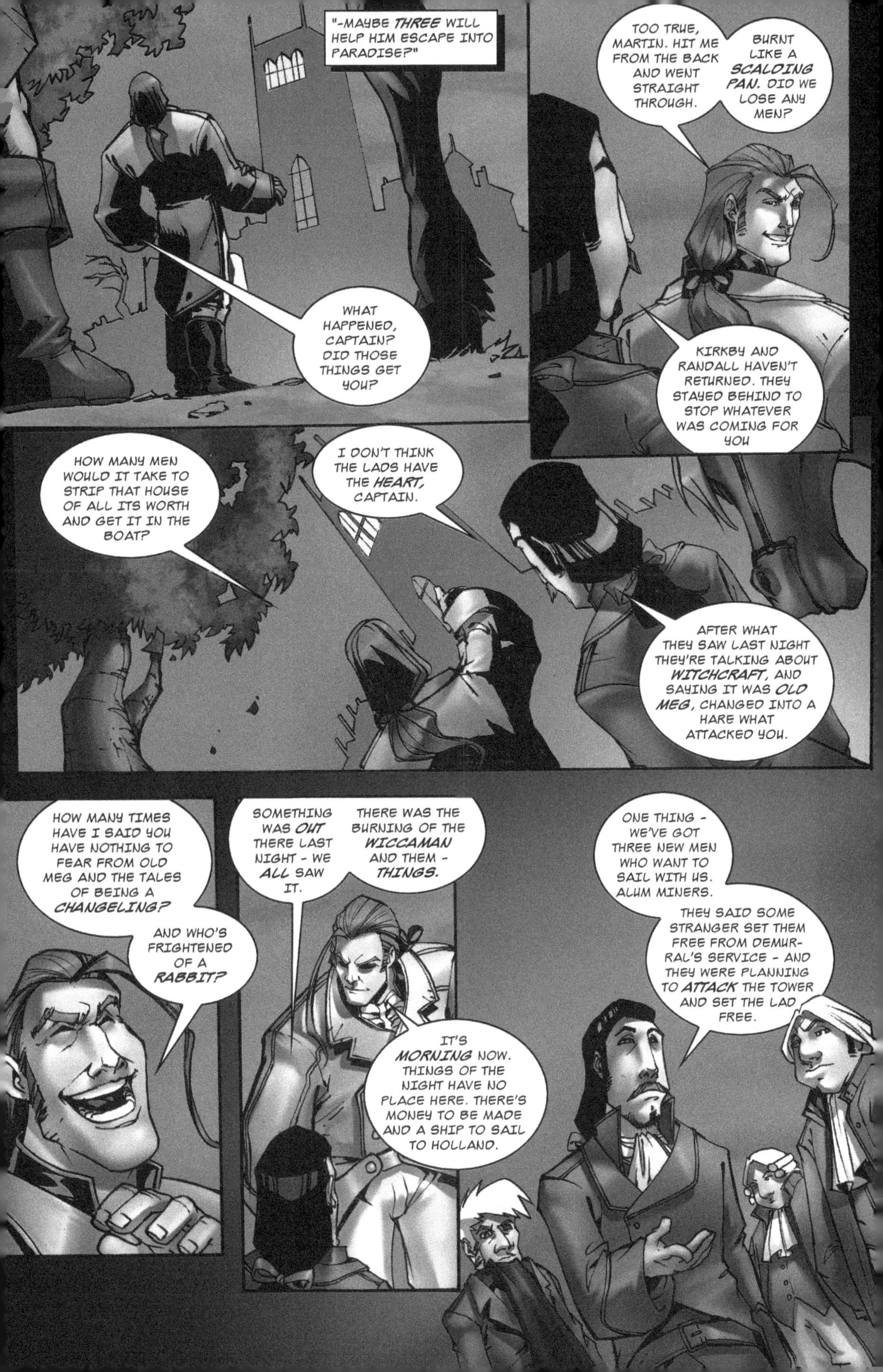
"-MAYBE THREE WILL HELP HIM ESCAPE INTO PARADISE?"
WHAT HAPPENED, CAPTAIN? DID THOSE THINGS GET YOU?
TOO TRUE, MARTIN. HIT ME FROM THE BACK AND WENT STRAIGHT THROUGH.
BURNT LIKE A SCALDING PAN. DID WE LOSE ANY MEN?
KIRKBY AND RANDALL HAVEN'T RETURNED. THEY STAYED BEHIND TO STOP WHATEVER WAS COMING FOR YOU
HOW MANY MEN WOULD IT TAKE TO STRIP THAT HOUSE OF ALL ITS WORTH AND GET IT IN THE BOAT?
I DON'T THINK THE LADS HAVE THE HEART, CAPTAIN.
AFTER WHAT THEY SAW LAST NIGHT THEY'RE TALKING ABOUT WITCHCRAFT, AND SAYING IT WAS OLD MEG, CHANGED INTO A HARE WHAT ATTACKED YOU.
HOW MANY TIMES HAVE I SAID YOU HAVE NOTHING TO FEAR FROM OLD MEG AND THE TALES OF BEING A CHANGELING?
AND WHO'S FRIGHTENED OF A RABBIT?
SOMETHING WAS OUT THERE LAST NIGHT - WE ALL SAW IT.
THERE WAS THE BURNING OF THE WICCAMAN AND THEM - THINGS.
IT'S MORNING NOW. THINGS OF THE NIGHT HAVE NO PLACE HERE. THERE'S MONEY TO BE MADE AND A SHIP TO SAIL TO HOLLAND.
ONE THING - WE'VE GOT THREE NEW MEN WHO WANT TO SAIL WITH US. ALUM MINERS.
THEY SAID SOME STRANGER SET THEM FREE FROM DEMUR-RAL'S SERVICE - AND THEY WERE PLANNING TO ATTACK THE TOWER AND SET THE LAD FREE.

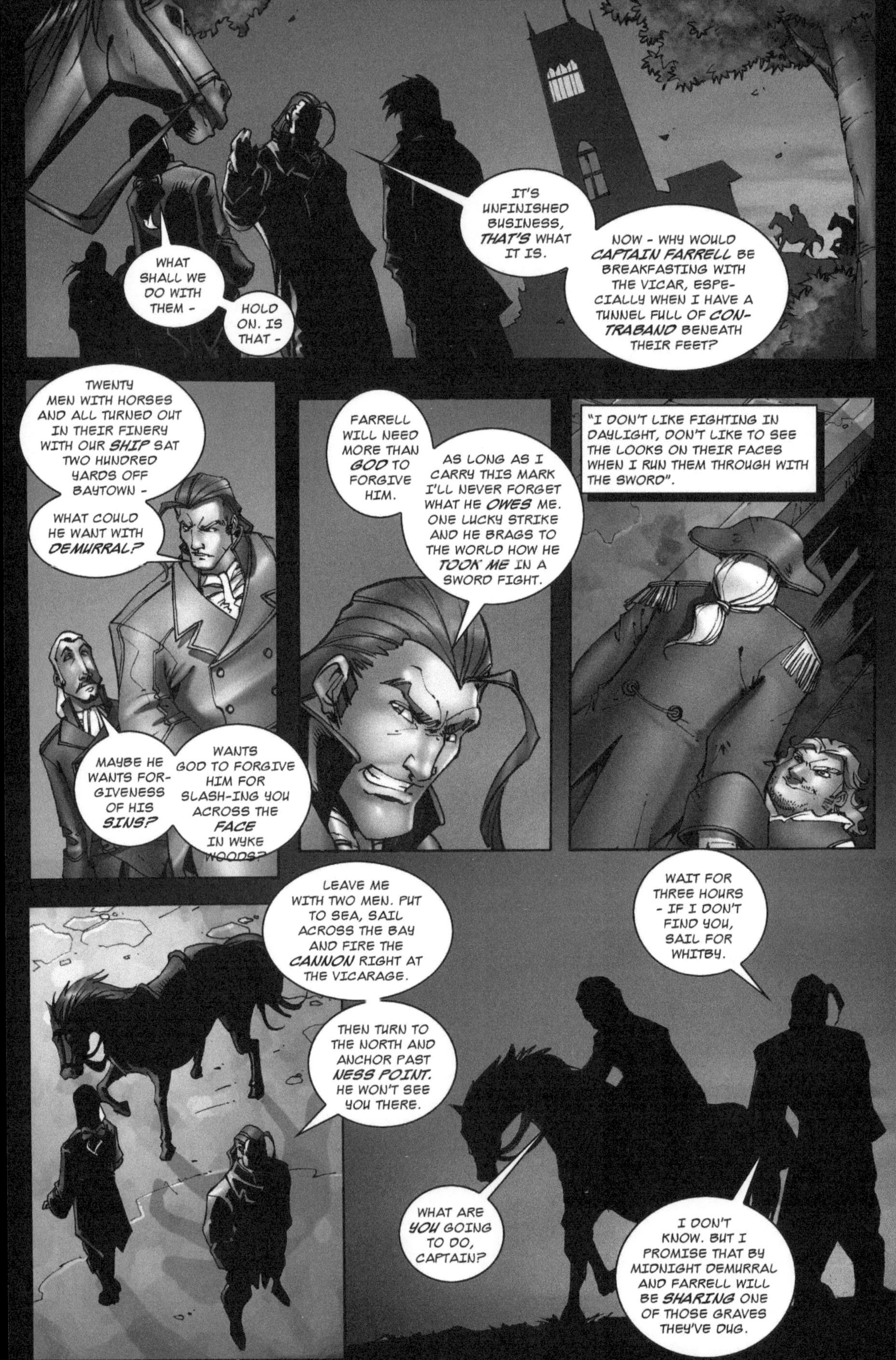
WHAT SHALL WE DO WITH THEM -
HOLD ON. IS THAT -
IT'S UNFINISHED BUSINESS, THAT'S WHAT IT IS.
NOW - WHY WOULD CAPTAIN FARRELL BE BREAKFASTING WITH THE VICAR, ESPE- CIALLY WHEN I HAVE A TUNNEL FULL OF CON- TRABAND BENEATH THEIR FEET?
TWENTY MEN WITH HORSES AND ALL TURNED OUT IN THEIR FINERY WITH OUR SHIP SAT TWO HUNDRED YARDS OFF BAYTOWN -
WHAT COULD HE WANT WITH DEMURRAL?
MAYBE HE WANTS FOR- GIVENESS OF HIS SINS?
WANTS GOD TO FORGIVE HIM FOR SLASH-ING YOU ACROSS THE FACE IN WYKE WOODS?
FARRELL WILL NEED MORE THAN GOD TO FORGIVE HIM.
AS LONG AS I CARRY THIS MARK I'LL NEVER FORGET WHAT HE OWES ME. ONE LUCKY STRIKE AND HE BRAGS TO THE WORLD HOW HE TOOK ME IN A SWORD FIGHT.
"I DON'T LIKE FIGHTING IN DAYLIGHT, DON'T LIKE TO SEE THE LOOKS ON THEIR FACES WHEN I RUN THEM THROUGH WITH THE SWORD".
LEAVE ME WITH TWO MEN. PUT TO SEA, SAIL ACROSS THE BAY AND FIRE THE CANNON RIGHT AT THE VICARAGE.
THEN TURN TO THE NORTH AND ANCHOR PAST NESS POINT. HE WON'T SEE YOU THERE.
WAIT FOR THREE HOURS - IF I DON'T FIND YOU, SAIL FOR WHITBY.
WHAT ARE YOU GOING TO DO, CAPTAIN?
I DON'T KNOW. BUT I PROMISE THAT BY MIDNIGHT DEMURRAL AND FARRELL WILL BE SHARING ONE OF THOSE GRAVES THEY'VE DUG.

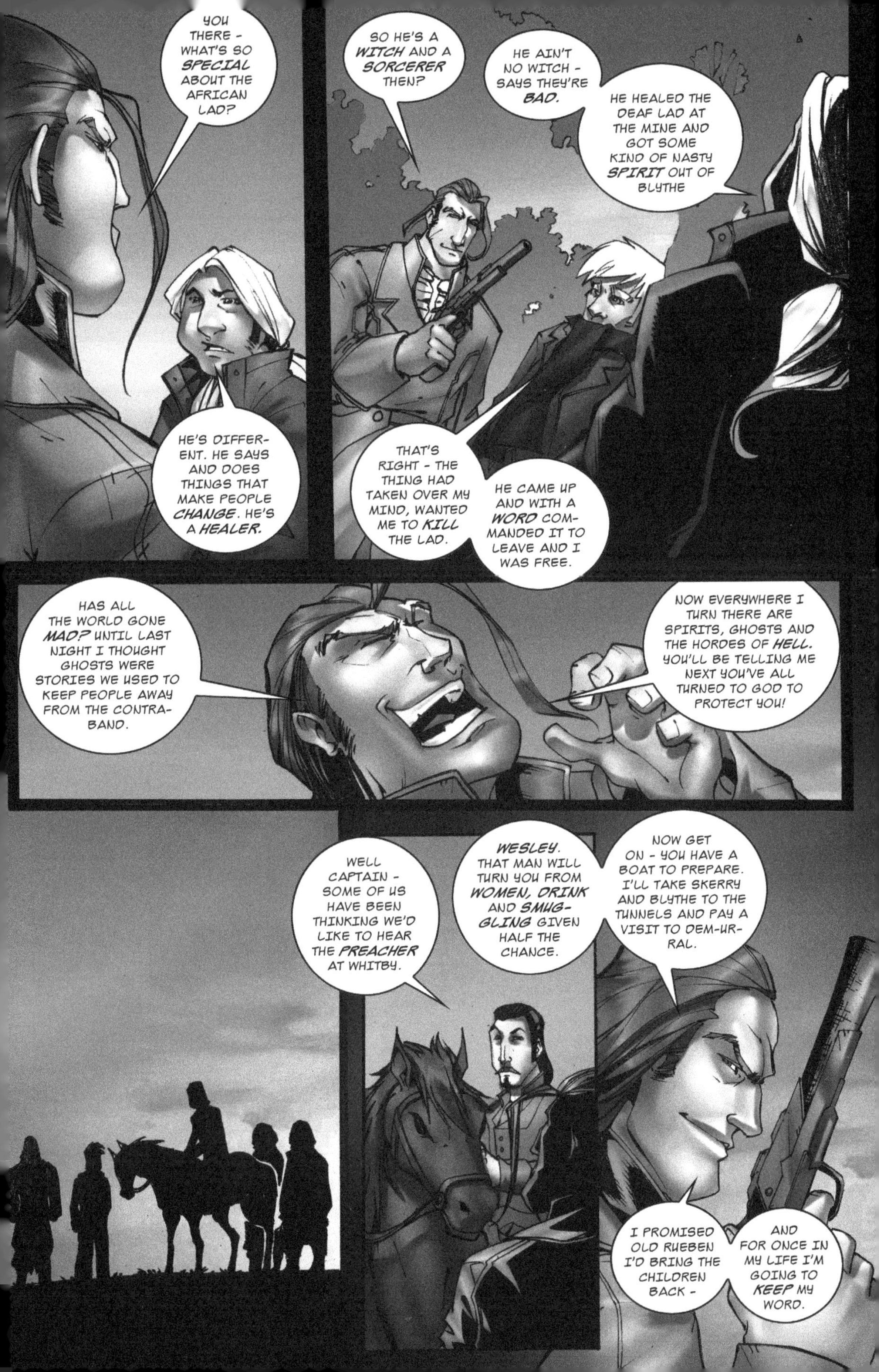
YOU THERE - WHAT'S SO SPECIAL ABOUT THE AFRICAN LAD?
HE'S DIFFERENT. HE SAYS AND DOES THINGS THAT MAKE PEOPLE CHANGE. HE'S A HEALER.
SO HE'S A WITCH AND A SORCERER THEN?
HE AIN'T NO WITCH - SAYS THEY'RE BAD.
HE HEALED THE DEAF LAD AT THE MINE AND GOT SOME KIND OF NASTY SPIRIT OUT OF BLYTHE
THAT'S RIGHT - THE THING HAD TAKEN OVER MY MIND, WANTED ME TO KILL THE LAD.
HE CAME UP AND WITH A WORD COMMANDED IT TO LEAVE AND I WAS FREE.
HAS ALL THE WORLD GONE MAD? UNTIL LAST NIGHT I THOUGHT GHOSTS WERE STORIES WE USED TO KEEP PEOPLE AWAY FROM THE CONTRABAND.
NOW EVERYWHERE I TURN THERE ARE SPIRITS, GHOSTS AND THE HORDES OF HELL. YOU'LL BE TELLING ME NEXT YOU'VE ALL TURNED TO GOD TO PROTECT YOU!
WELL CAPTAIN - SOME OF US HAVE BEEN THINKING WE'D LIKE TO HEAR THE PREACHER AT WHITBY.
WESLEY. THAT MAN WILL TURN YOU FROM WOMEN, DRINK AND SMUGGLING GIVEN HALF THE CHANCE.
NOW GET ON - YOU HAVE A BOAT TO PREPARE. I'LL TAKE SKERRY AND BLYTHE TO THE TUNNELS AND PAY A VISIT TO DEM-UR-RAL.
I PROMISED OLD RUEBEN I'D BRING THE CHILDREN BACK -
AND FOR ONCE IN MY LIFE I'M GOING TO KEEP MY WORD.

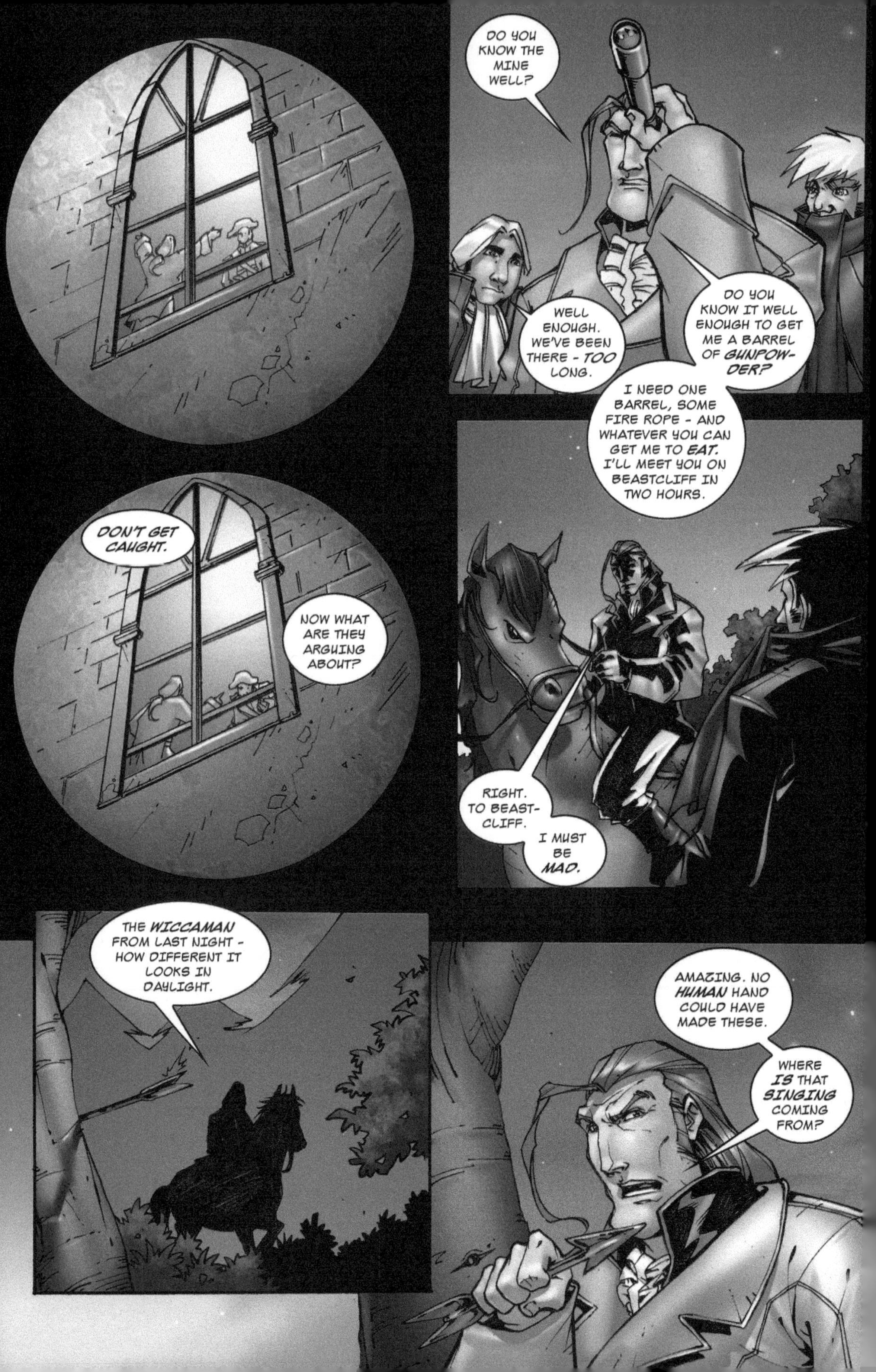
DO YOU KNOW THE MINE WELL?
WELL ENOUGH. WE'VE BEEN THERE - TOO LONG.
DO YOU KNOW IT WELL ENOUGH TO GET ME A BARREL OF GUNPOWDER?
I NEED ONE BARREL, SOME FIRE ROPE - AND WHATEVER YOU CAN GET ME TO EAT. I'LL MEET YOU ON BEASTCLIFF IN TWO HOURS.
DON'T GET CAUGHT.
NOW WHAT ARE THEY ARGUING ABOUT?
RIGHT. TO BEAST-CLIFF.
I MUST BE MAD.
THE WICCAMAN FROM LAST NIGHT - HOW DIFFERENT IT LOOKS IN DAYLIGHT.
AMAZING. NO HUMAN HAND COULD HAVE MADE THESE.
WHERE IS THAT SINGING COMING FROM?

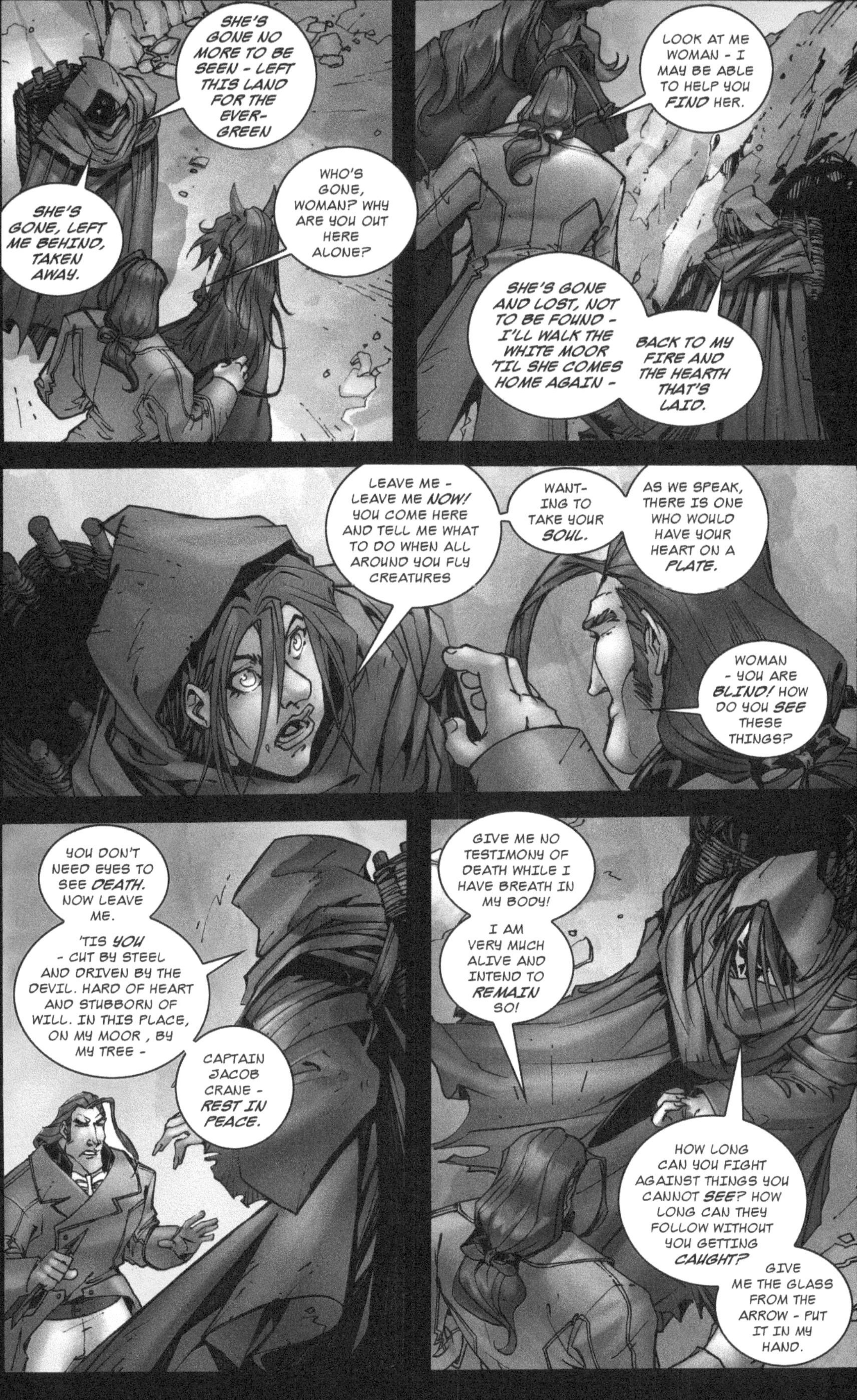
SHE'S GONE NO MORE TO BE SEEN - LEFT THIS LAND FOR THE EVER-GREEN
SHE'S GONE, LEFT ME BEHIND, TAKEN AWAY.
WHO'S GONE, WOMAN? WHY ARE YOU OUT HERE ALONE?
LOOK AT ME WOMAN - I MAY BE ABLE TO HELP YOU FIND HER.
SHE'S GONE AND LOST, NOT TO BE FOUND - I'LL WALK THE WHITE MOOR 'TIL SHE COMES HOME AGAIN -
BACK TO MY FIRE AND THE HEARTH THAT'S LAID.
LEAVE ME - LEAVE ME NOW! YOU COME HERE AND TELL ME WHAT TO DO WHEN ALL AROUND YOU FLY CREATURES
WANT-ING TO TAKE YOUR SOUL.
AS WE SPEAK, THERE IS ONE WHO WOULD HAVE YOUR HEART ON A PLATE.
WOMAN - YOU ARE BLIND! HOW DO YOU SEE THESE THINGS?
YOU DON'T NEED EYES TO SEE DEATH. NOW LEAVE ME.
'TIS YOU - CUT BY STEEL AND DRIVEN BY THE DEVIL. HARD OF HEART AND STUBBORN OF WILL. IN THIS PLACE, ON MY MOOR , BY MY TREE -
CAPTAIN JACOB CRANE - REST IN PEACE.
GIVE ME NO TESTIMONY OF DEATH WHILE I HAVE BREATH IN MY BODY!
I AM VERY MUCH ALIVE AND INTEND TO REMAIN SO!
HOW LONG CAN YOU FIGHT AGAINST THINGS YOU CANNOT SEE? HOW LONG CAN THEY FOLLOW WITHOUT YOU GETTING CAUGHT?
GIVE ME THE GLASS FROM THE ARROW - PUT IT IN MY HAND.

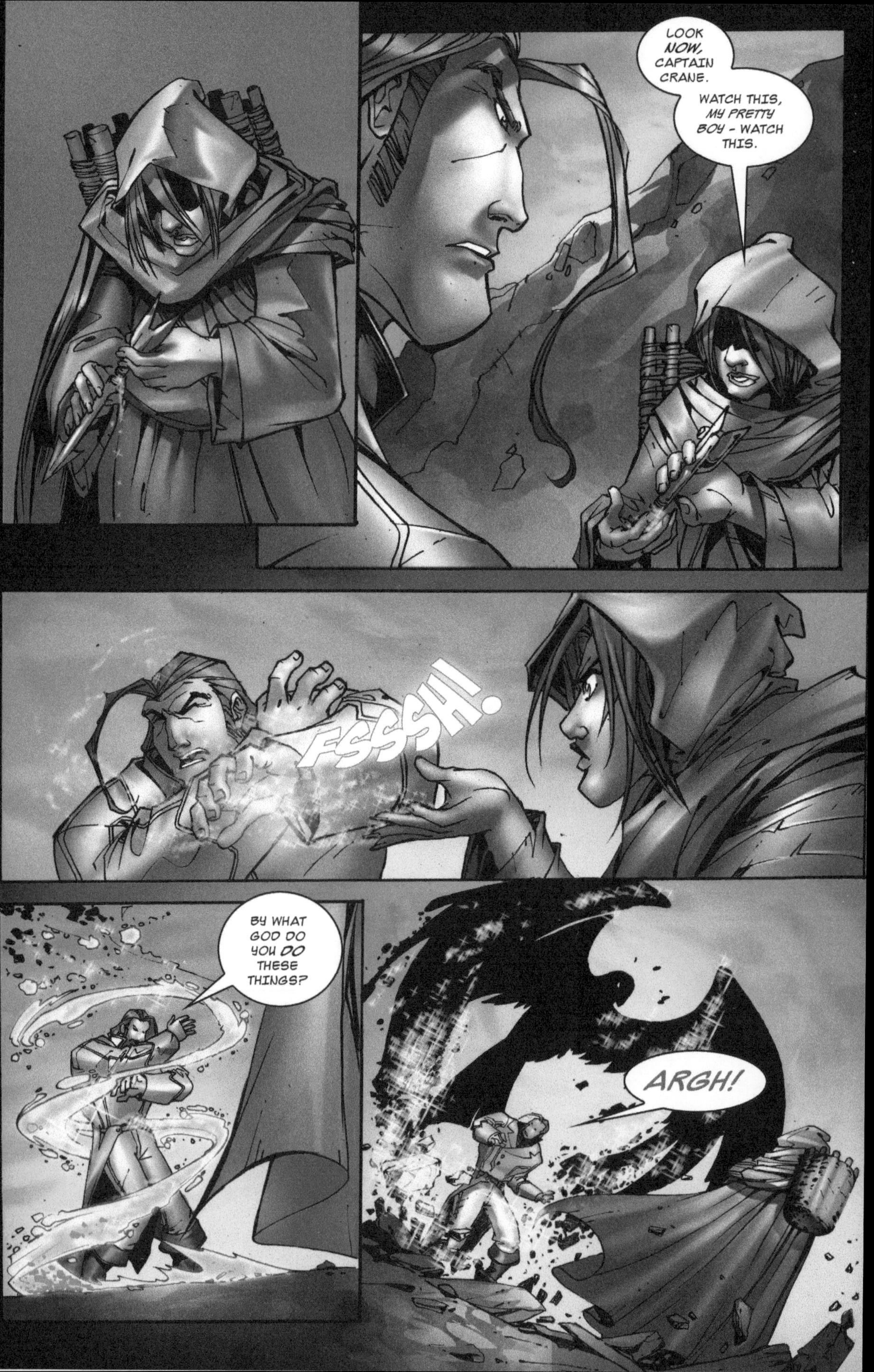
LOOK NOW, CAPTAIN CRANE.
WATCH THIS, MY PRETTY BOY - WATCH THIS.
FSSSH!
BY WHAT GOD DO YOU DO THESE THINGS?
ARGH!

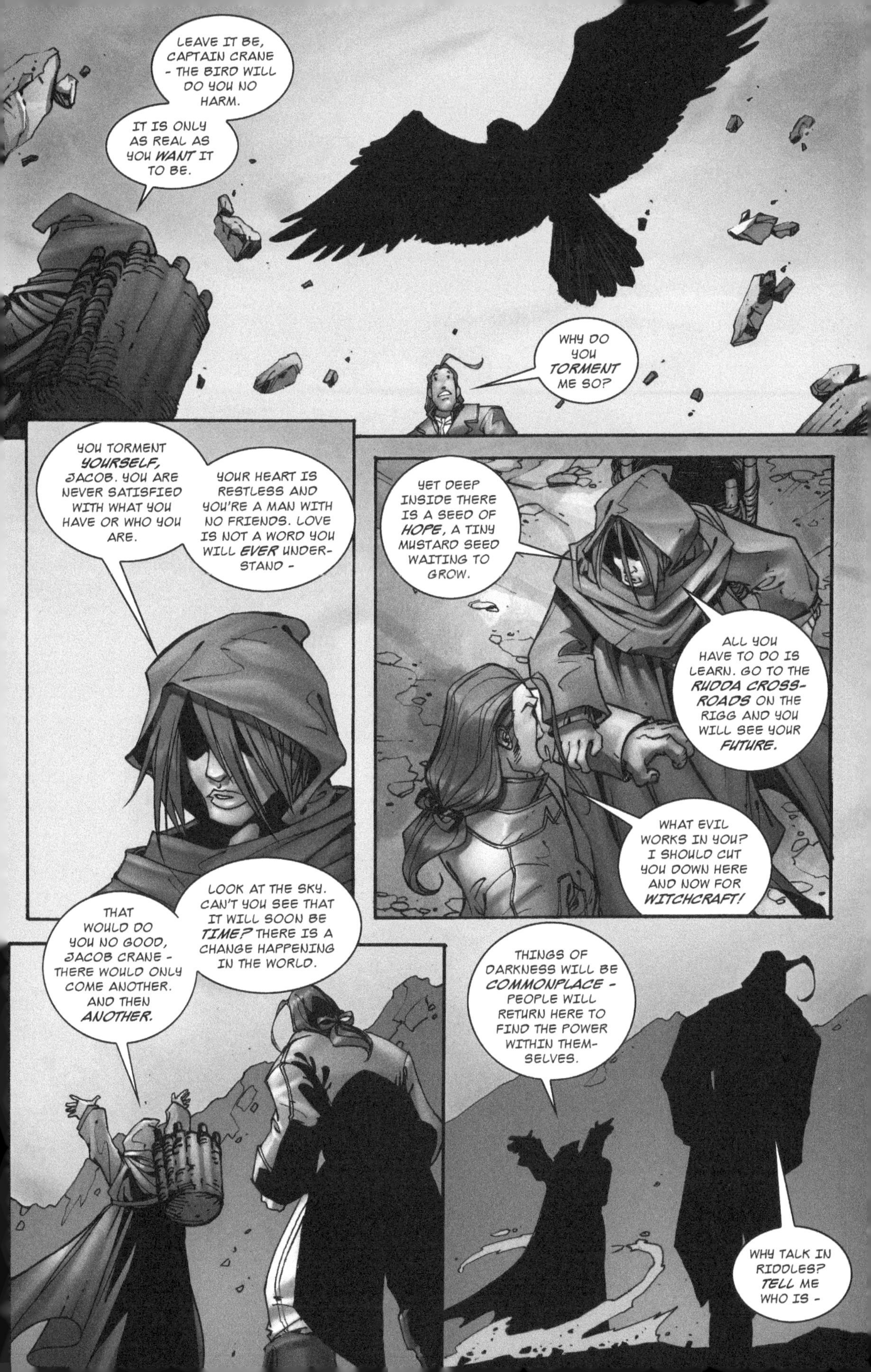
LEAVE IT BE, CAPTAIN CRANE - THE BIRD WILL DO YOU NO HARM.
IT IS ONLY AS REAL AS YOU WANT IT TO BE.
WHY DO YOU TORMENT ME SO?
YOU TORMENT YOURSELF, JACOB. YOU ARE NEVER SATISFIED WITH WHAT YOU HAVE OR WHO YOU ARE.
YOUR HEART IS RESTLESS AND YOU'RE A MAN WITH NO FRIENDS. LOVE IS NOT A WORD YOU WILL EVER UNDERSTAND -
YET DEEP INSIDE THERE IS A SEED OF HOPE, A TINY MUSTARD SEED WAITING TO GROW.
ALL YOU HAVE TO DO IS LEARN. GO TO THE RUDDA CROSS-ROADS ON THE RIGG AND YOU WILL SEE YOUR FUTURE.
WHAT EVIL WORKS IN YOU? I SHOULD CUT YOU DOWN HERE AND NOW FOR WITCHCRAFT!
THAT WOULD DO YOU NO GOOD, JACOB CRANE - THERE WOULD ONLY COME ANOTHER. AND THEN ANOTHER.
LOOK AT THE SKY. CAN'T YOU SEE THAT IT WILL SOON BE TIME? THERE IS A CHANGE HAPPENING IN THE WORLD.
THINGS OF DARKNESS WILL BE COMMONPLACE - PEOPLE WILL RETURN HERE TO FIND THE POWER WITHIN THEM-SELVES.
WHY TALK IN RIDDLES? TELL ME WHO IS -

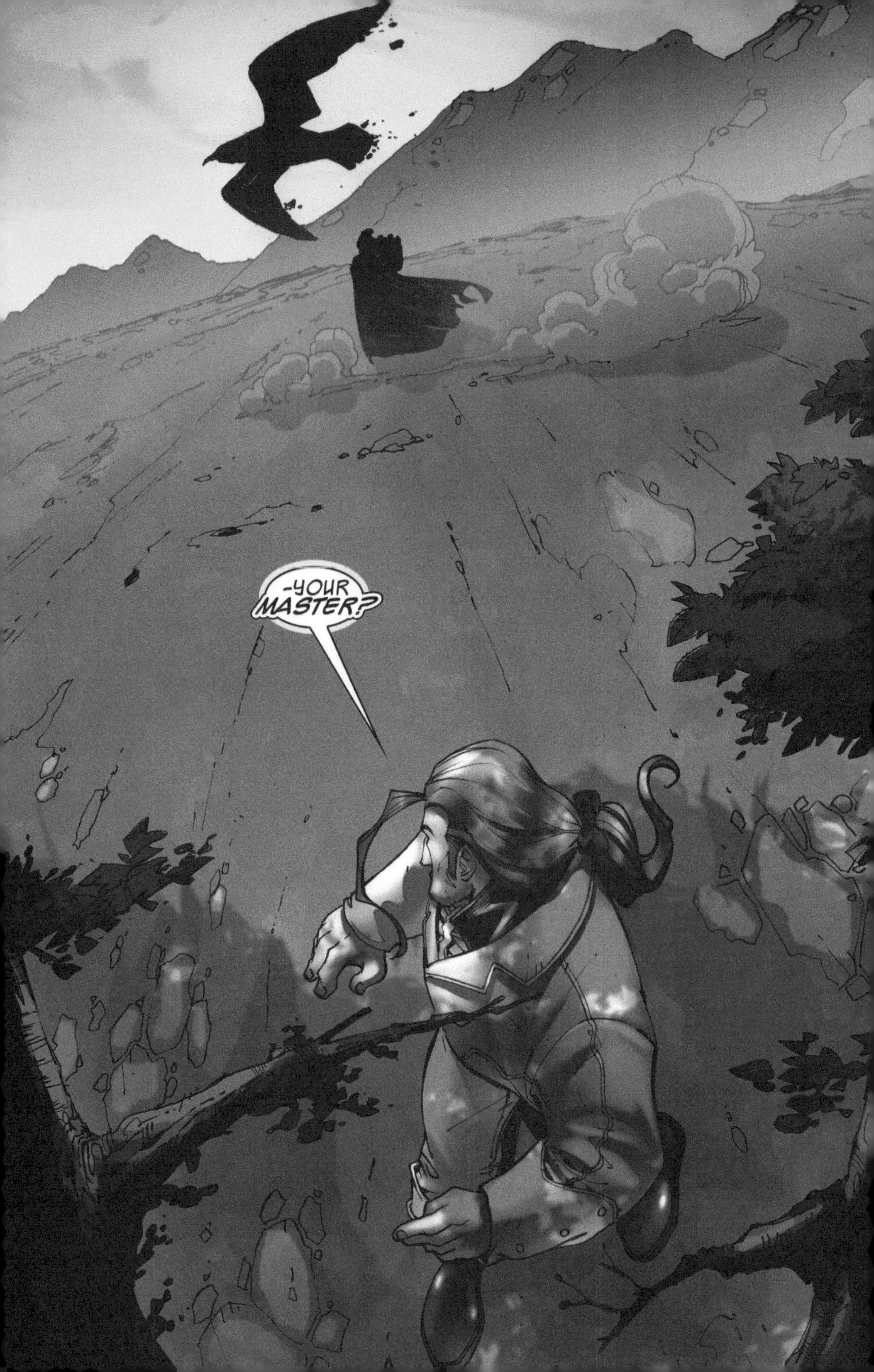
-YOUR MASTER?

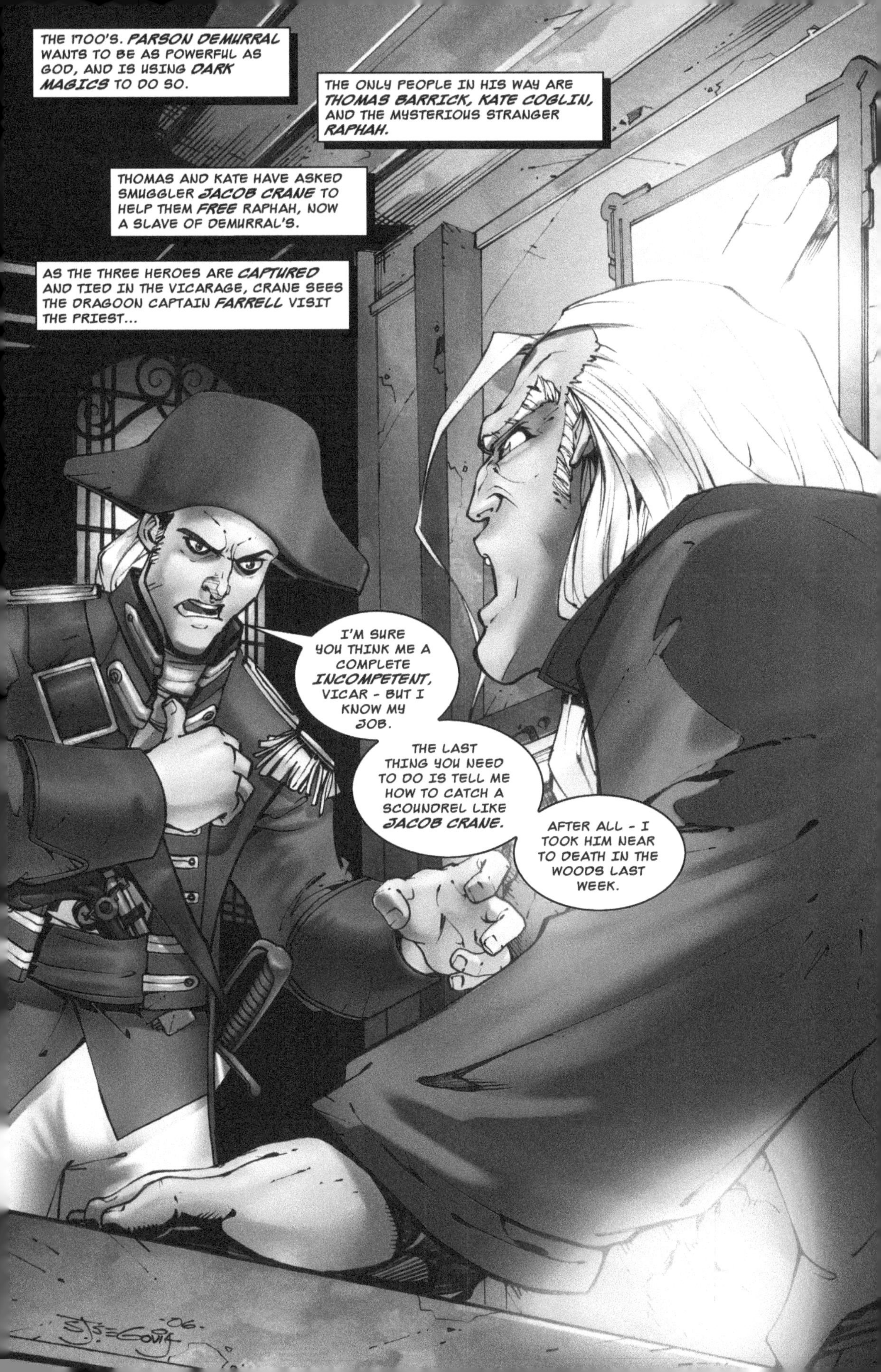
THE 1700'S. PARSON DEMURRAL WANTS TO BE AS POWERFUL AS GOD, AND IS USING DARK MAGICS TO DO SO.
THE ONLY PEOPLE IN HIS WAY ARE THOMAS BARRICK, KATE COGLIN, AND THE MYSTERIOUS STRANGER RAPHAH.
THOMAS AND KATE HAVE ASKED SMUGGLER JACOB CRANE TO HELP THEM FREE RAPHAH, NOW A SLAVE OF DEMURRAL'S.
AS THE THREE HEROES ARE CAPTURED AND TIED IN THE VICARAGE, CRANE SEES THE DRAGOON CAPTAIN FARRELL VISIT THE PRIEST...
I'M SURE YOU THINK ME A COMPLETE INCOMPETENT, VICAR - BUT I KNOW MY JOB.
THE LAST THING YOU NEED TO DO IS TELL ME HOW TO CATCH A SCOUNDREL LIKE JACOB CRANE.
AFTER ALL - I TOOK HIM NEAR TO DEATH IN THE WOODS LAST WEEK.

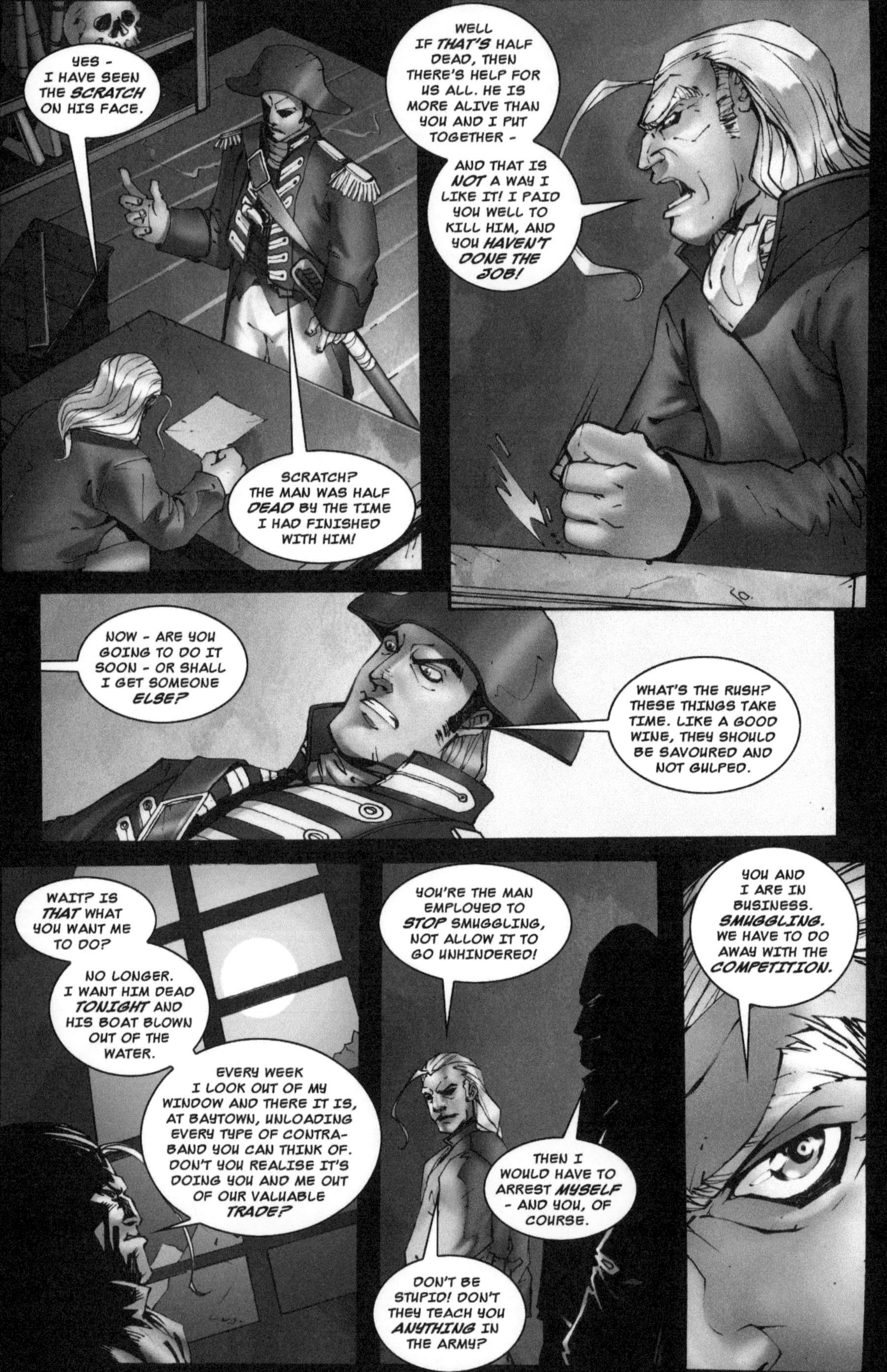
YES - I HAVE SEEN THE *SCRATCH* ON HIS FACE.
SCRATCH? THE MAN WAS HALF *DEAD* BY THE TIME I HAD FINISHED WITH HIM!
WELL IF *THAT'S* HALF DEAD, THEN THERE'S HELP FOR US ALL. HE IS MORE ALIVE THAN YOU AND I PUT TOGETHER -
AND THAT IS *NOT* A WAY I LIKE IT! I PAID YOU WELL TO KILL HIM, AND YOU *HAVEN'T DONE THE JOB!*
NOW - ARE YOU GOING TO DO IT SOON - OR SHALL I GET SOMEONE *ELSE?*
WHAT'S THE RUSH? THESE THINGS TAKE TIME. LIKE A GOOD WINE, THEY SHOULD BE SAVOURED AND NOT GULPED.
WAIT? IS *THAT* WHAT YOU WANT ME TO DO?
NO LONGER. I WANT HIM DEAD *TONIGHT* AND HIS BOAT BLOWN OUT OF THE WATER.
EVERY WEEK I LOOK OUT OF MY WINDOW AND THERE IT IS, AT BAYTOWN, UNLOADING EVERY TYPE OF CONTRA-BAND YOU CAN THINK OF. DON'T YOU REALISE IT'S DOING YOU AND ME OUT OF OUR VALUABLE *TRADE?*
YOU'RE THE MAN EMPLOYED TO *STOP* SMUGGLING, NOT ALLOW IT TO GO UNHINDERED!
THEN I WOULD HAVE TO ARREST *MYSELF* - AND YOU, OF COURSE.
DON'T BE STUPID! DON'T THEY TEACH YOU *ANYTHING* IN THE ARMY?
YOU AND I ARE IN BUSINESS. *SMUGGLING.* WE HAVE TO DO AWAY WITH THE *COMPETITION.*

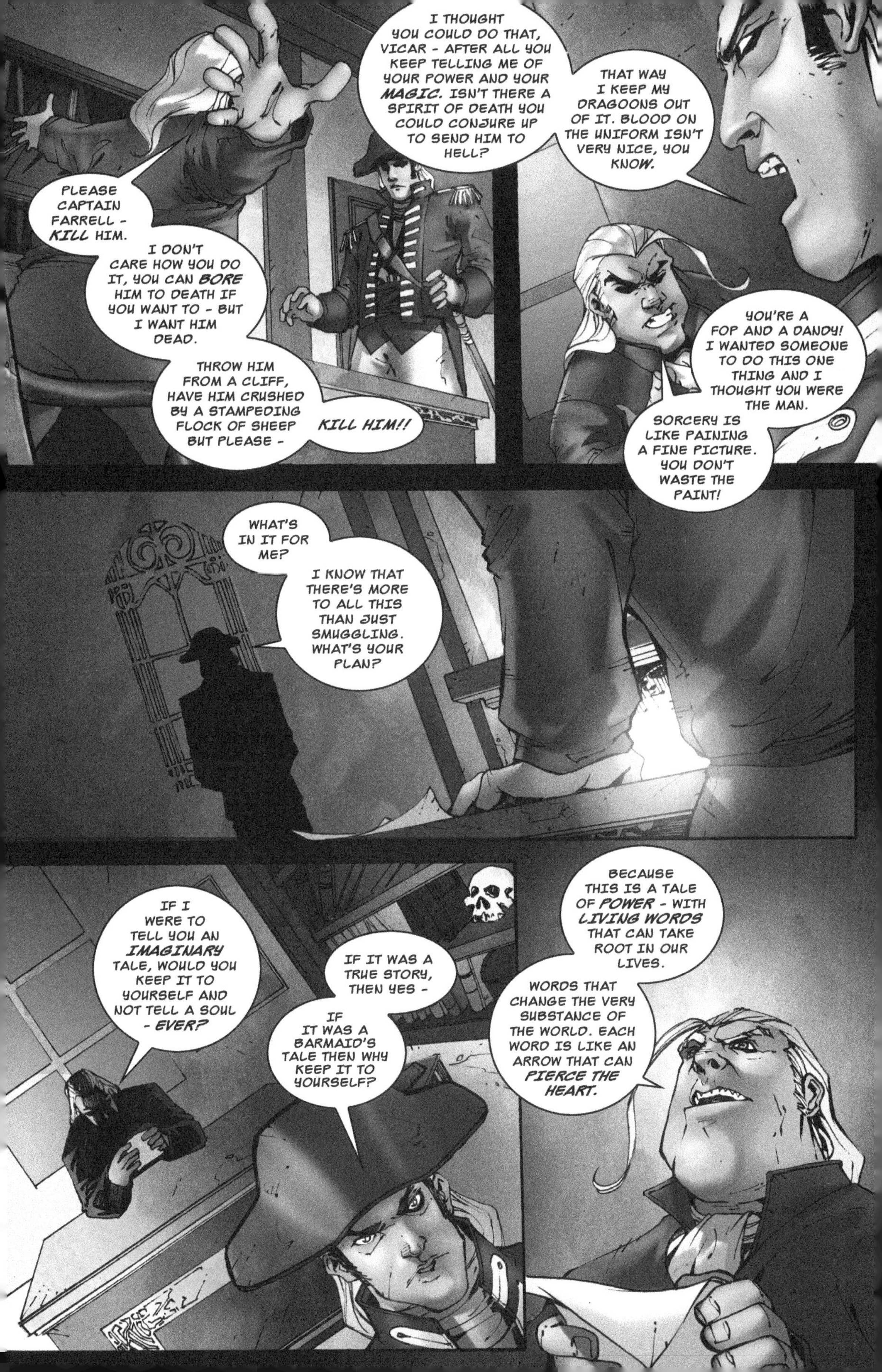
PLEASE CAPTAIN FARRELL - KILL HIM.
I DON'T CARE HOW YOU DO IT, YOU CAN BORE HIM TO DEATH IF YOU WANT TO - BUT I WANT HIM DEAD.
THROW HIM FROM A CLIFF, HAVE HIM CRUSHED BY A STAMPEDING FLOCK OF SHEEP BUT PLEASE -
KILL HIM!!
I THOUGHT YOU COULD DO THAT, VICAR - AFTER ALL YOU KEEP TELLING ME OF YOUR POWER AND YOUR MAGIC. ISN'T THERE A SPIRIT OF DEATH YOU COULD CONJURE UP TO SEND HIM TO HELL?
THAT WAY I KEEP MY DRAGOONS OUT OF IT. BLOOD ON THE UNIFORM ISN'T VERY NICE, YOU KNOW.
YOU'RE A FOP AND A DANDY! I WANTED SOMEONE TO DO THIS ONE THING AND I THOUGHT YOU WERE THE MAN.
SORCERY IS LIKE PAINING A FINE PICTURE. YOU DON'T WASTE THE PAINT!
WHAT'S IN IT FOR ME?
I KNOW THAT THERE'S MORE TO ALL THIS THAN JUST SMUGGLING. WHAT'S YOUR PLAN?
IF I WERE TO TELL YOU AN IMAGINARY TALE, WOULD YOU KEEP IT TO YOURSELF AND NOT TELL A SOUL - EVER?
IF IT WAS A TRUE STORY, THEN YES -
IF IT WAS A BARMAID'S TALE THEN WHY KEEP IT TO YOURSELF?
BECAUSE THIS IS A TALE OF POWER - WITH LIVING WORDS THAT CAN TAKE ROOT IN OUR LIVES.
WORDS THAT CHANGE THE VERY SUBSTANCE OF THE WORLD. EACH WORD IS LIKE AN ARROW THAT CAN PIERCE THE HEART.

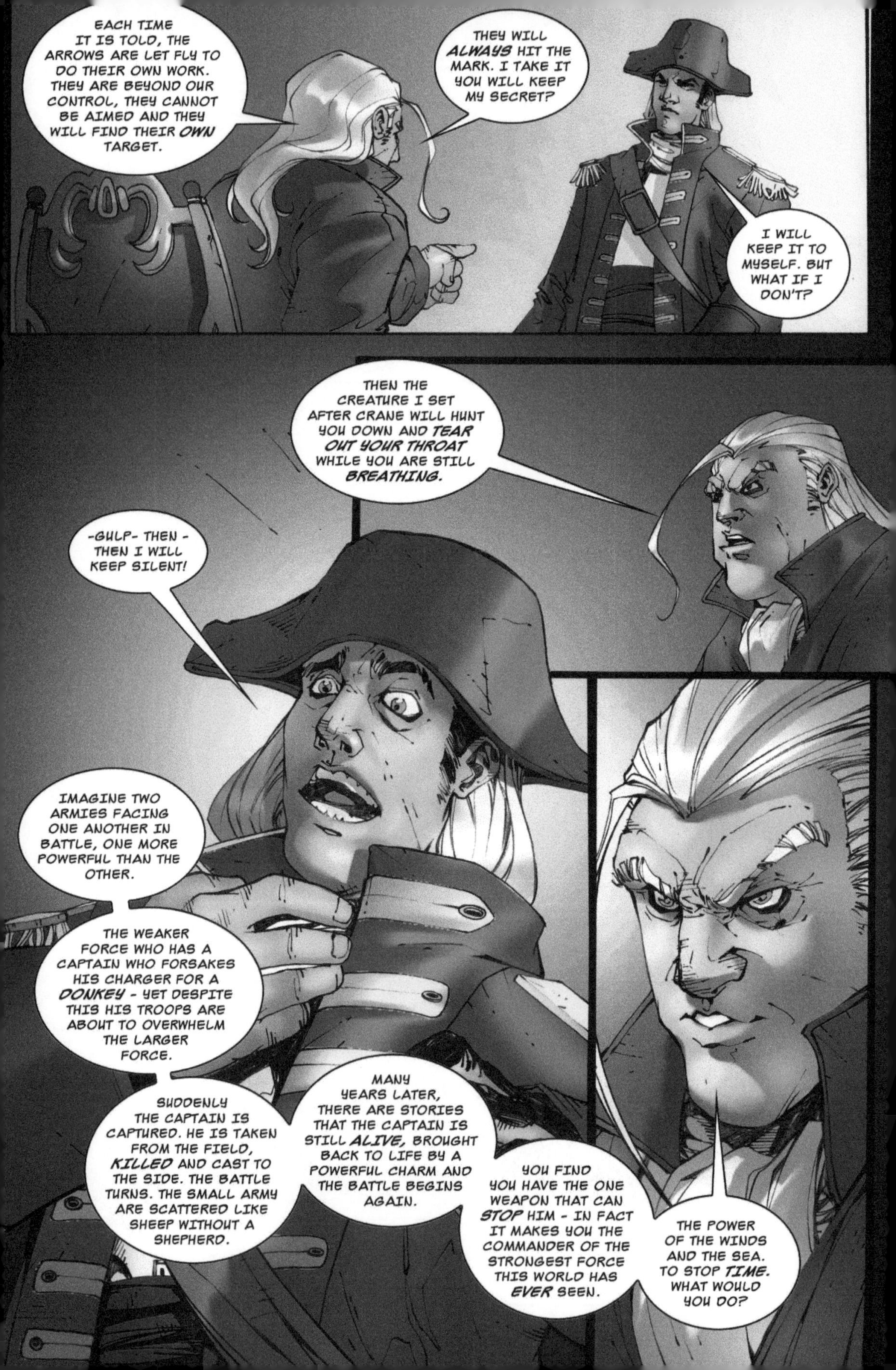

EACH TIME IT IS TOLD, THE ARROWS ARE LET FLY TO DO THEIR OWN WORK. THEY ARE BEYOND OUR CONTROL, THEY CANNOT BE AIMED AND THEY WILL FIND THEIR *OWN* TARGET.
THEY WILL *ALWAYS* HIT THE MARK. I TAKE IT YOU WILL KEEP MY SECRET?
I WILL KEEP IT TO MYSELF. BUT WHAT IF I DON'T?
THEN THE CREATURE I SET AFTER CRANE WILL HUNT YOU DOWN AND *TEAR OUT YOUR THROAT* WHILE YOU ARE STILL *BREATHING.*
-GULP- THEN - THEN I WILL KEEP SILENT!
IMAGINE TWO ARMIES FACING ONE ANOTHER IN BATTLE, ONE MORE POWERFUL THAN THE OTHER.
THE WEAKER FORCE WHO HAS A CAPTAIN WHO FORSAKES HIS CHARGER FOR A *DONKEY* - YET DESPITE THIS HIS TROOPS ARE ABOUT TO OVERWHELM THE LARGER FORCE.
SUDDENLY THE CAPTAIN IS CAPTURED. HE IS TAKEN FROM THE FIELD, *KILLED* AND CAST TO THE SIDE. THE BATTLE TURNS. THE SMALL ARMY ARE SCATTERED LIKE SHEEP WITHOUT A SHEPHERD.
MANY YEARS LATER, THERE ARE STORIES THAT THE CAPTAIN IS STILL *ALIVE,* BROUGHT BACK TO LIFE BY A POWERFUL CHARM AND THE BATTLE BEGINS AGAIN.
YOU FIND YOU HAVE THE ONE WEAPON THAT CAN *STOP* HIM - IN FACT IT MAKES YOU THE COMMANDER OF THE STRONGEST FORCE THIS WORLD HAS *EVER* SEEN.
THE POWER OF THE WINDS AND THE SEA. TO STOP *TIME.* WHAT WOULD YOU DO?

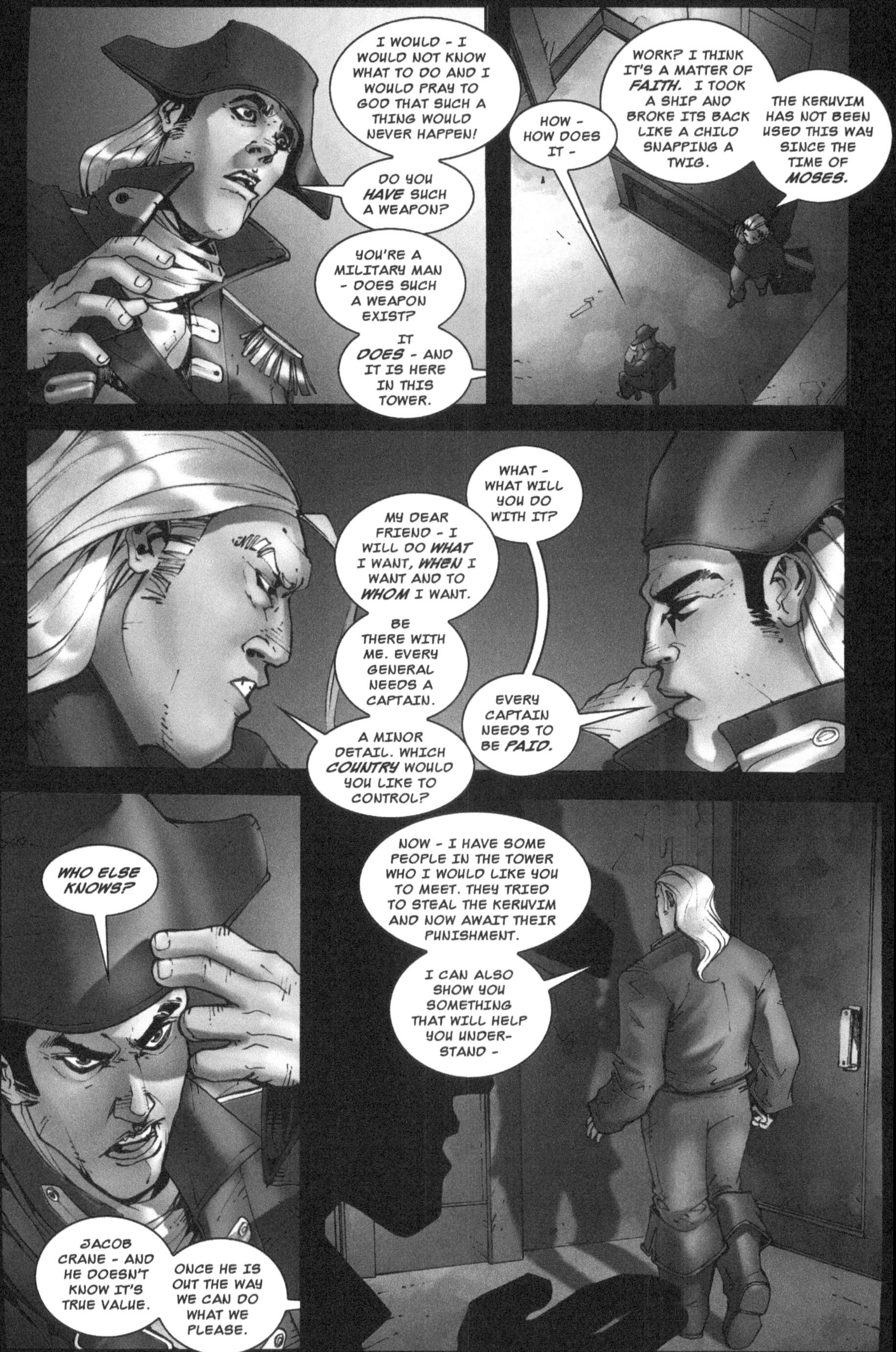
I WOULD - I WOULD NOT KNOW WHAT TO DO AND I WOULD PRAY TO GOD THAT SUCH A THING WOULD NEVER HAPPEN!
DO YOU HAVE SUCH A WEAPON?
YOU'RE A MILITARY MAN - DOES SUCH A WEAPON EXIST?
IT DOES - AND IT IS HERE IN THIS TOWER.
HOW - HOW DOES IT -
WORK? I THINK IT'S A MATTER OF FAITH. I TOOK A SHIP AND BROKE ITS BACK LIKE A CHILD SNAPPING A TWIG.
THE KERUVIM HAS NOT BEEN USED THIS WAY SINCE THE TIME OF MOSES.
WHAT - WHAT WILL YOU DO WITH IT?
MY DEAR FRIEND - I WILL DO WHAT I WANT, WHEN I WANT AND TO WHOM I WANT.
BE THERE WITH ME. EVERY GENERAL NEEDS A CAPTAIN.
EVERY CAPTAIN NEEDS TO BE PAID.
A MINOR DETAIL. WHICH COUNTRY WOULD YOU LIKE TO CONTROL?
WHO ELSE KNOWS?
JACOB CRANE - AND HE DOESN'T KNOW IT'S TRUE VALUE.
ONCE HE IS OUT THE WAY WE CAN DO WHAT WE PLEASE.
NOW - I HAVE SOME PEOPLE IN THE TOWER WHO I WOULD LIKE YOU TO MEET. THEY TRIED TO STEAL THE KERUVIM AND NOW AWAIT THEIR PUNISHMENT.
I CAN ALSO SHOW YOU SOMETHING THAT WILL HELP YOU UNDER-STAND -

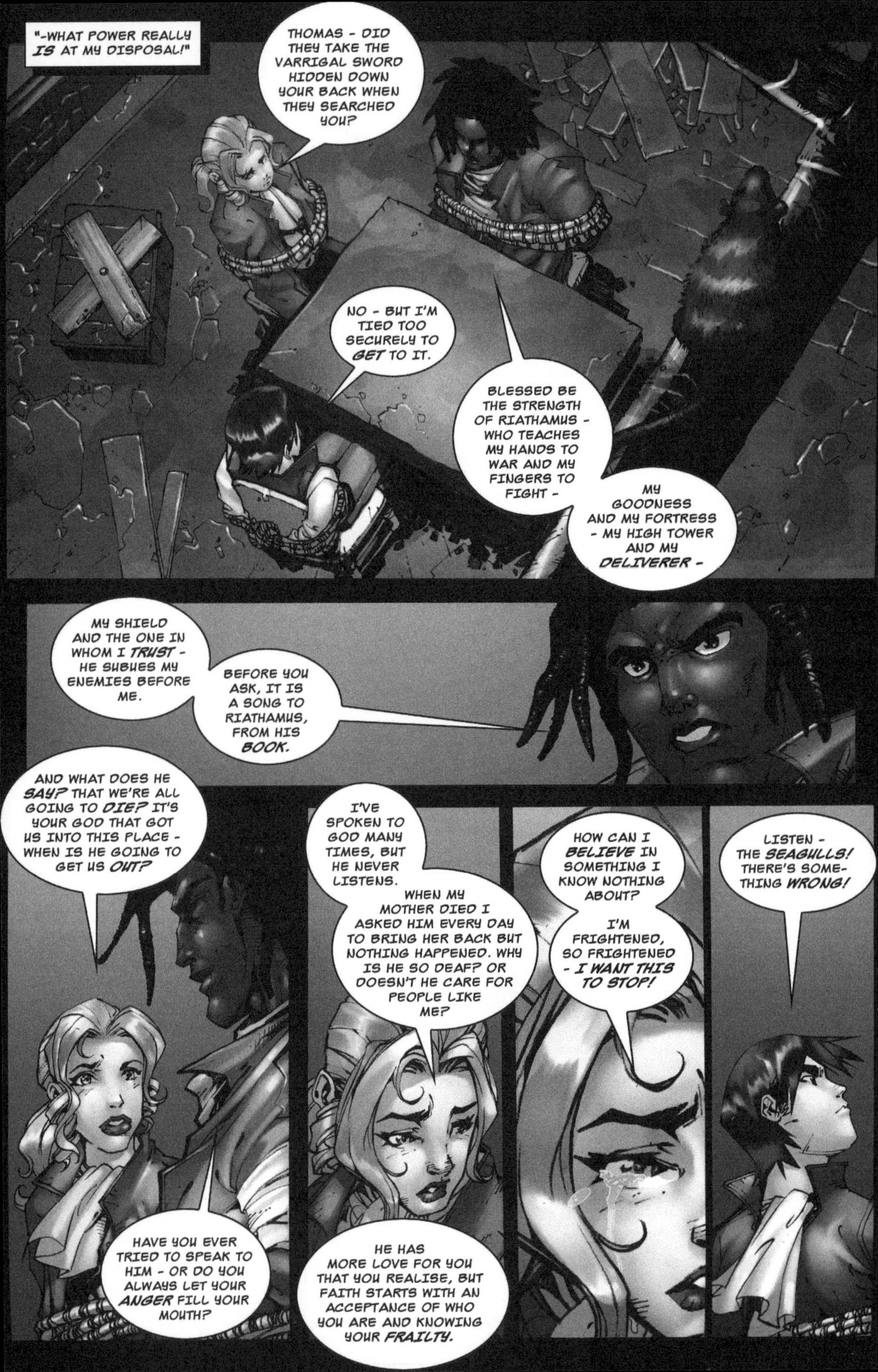
"-WHAT POWER REALLY *IS* AT MY DISPOSAL!"
THOMAS - DID THEY TAKE THE VARRIGAL SWORD HIDDEN DOWN YOUR BACK WHEN THEY SEARCHED YOU?
NO - BUT I'M TIED TOO SECURELY TO *GET* TO IT.
BLESSED BE THE STRENGTH OF RIATHAMUS - WHO TEACHES MY HANDS TO WAR AND MY FINGERS TO FIGHT -
MY GOODNESS AND MY FORTRESS - MY HIGH TOWER AND MY *DELIVERER* -
MY SHIELD AND THE ONE IN WHOM I *TRUST* - HE SUBUES MY ENEMIES BEFORE ME.
BEFORE YOU ASK, IT IS A SONG TO RIATHAMUS, FROM HIS *BOOK.*
AND WHAT DOES HE *SAY?* THAT WE'RE ALL GOING TO *DIE?* IT'S YOUR GOD THAT GOT US INTO THIS PLACE - WHEN IS HE GOING TO GET US *OUT?*
HAVE YOU EVER TRIED TO SPEAK TO HIM - OR DO YOU ALWAYS LET YOUR *ANGER* FILL YOUR MOUTH?
I'VE SPOKEN TO GOD MANY TIMES, BUT HE NEVER LISTENS.
WHEN MY MOTHER DIED I ASKED HIM EVERY DAY TO BRING HER BACK BUT NOTHING HAPPENED. WHY IS HE SO DEAF? OR DOESN'T HE CARE FOR PEOPLE LIKE ME?
HE HAS MORE LOVE FOR YOU THAT YOU REALISE, BUT FAITH STARTS WITH AN ACCEPTANCE OF WHO YOU ARE AND KNOWING YOUR *FRAILTY.*
HOW CAN I *BELIEVE* IN SOMETHING I KNOW NOTHING ABOUT?
I'M FRIGHTENED, SO FRIGHTENED - *I WANT THIS TO STOP!*
LISTEN - THE *SEAGULLS!* THERE'S SOME-THING *WRONG!*

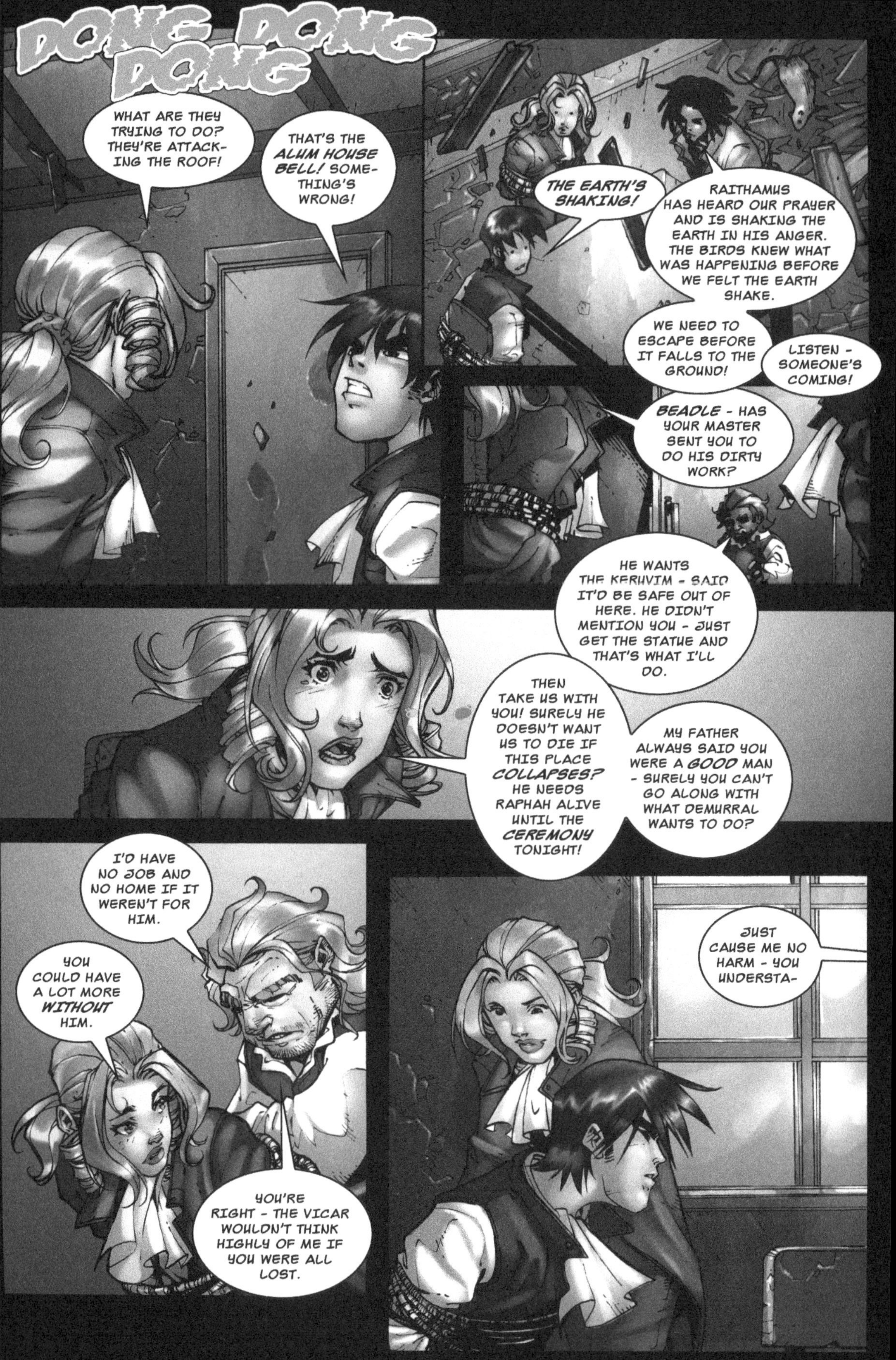
DONG DONG DONG
WHAT ARE THEY TRYING TO DO? THEY'RE ATTACKING THE ROOF!
THAT'S THE ALUM HOUSE BELL! SOMETHING'S WRONG!
THE EARTH'S SHAKING!
RAITHAMUS HAS HEARD OUR PRAYER AND IS SHAKING THE EARTH IN HIS ANGER. THE BIRDS KNEW WHAT WAS HAPPENING BEFORE WE FELT THE EARTH SHAKE.
WE NEED TO ESCAPE BEFORE IT FALLS TO THE GROUND!
LISTEN - SOMEONE'S COMING!
BEADLE - HAS YOUR MASTER SENT YOU TO DO HIS DIRTY WORK?
HE WANTS THE KERUVIM - SAID IT'D BE SAFE OUT OF HERE. HE DIDN'T MENTION YOU - JUST GET THE STATUE AND THAT'S WHAT I'LL DO.
THEN TAKE US WITH YOU! SURELY HE DOESN'T WANT US TO DIE IF THIS PLACE COLLAPSES? HE NEEDS RAPHAH ALIVE UNTIL THE CEREMONY TONIGHT!
MY FATHER ALWAYS SAID YOU WERE A GOOD MAN - SURELY YOU CAN'T GO ALONG WITH WHAT DEMURRAL WANTS TO DO?
I'D HAVE NO JOB AND NO HOME IF IT WEREN'T FOR HIM.
YOU COULD HAVE A LOT MORE WITHOUT HIM.
YOU'RE RIGHT - THE VICAR WOULDN'T THINK HIGHLY OF ME IF YOU WERE ALL LOST.
JUST CAUSE ME NO HARM - YOU UNDERSTA-

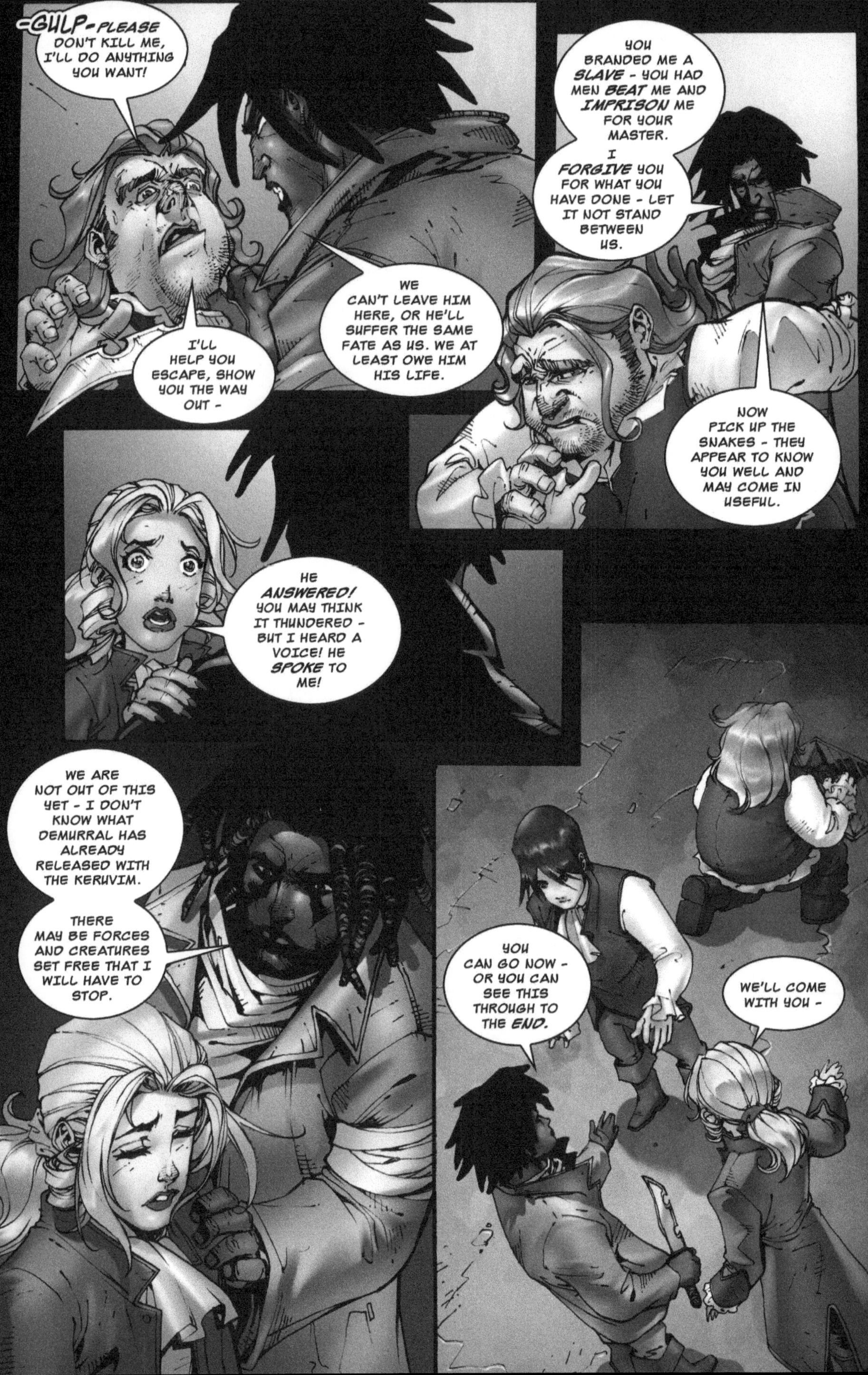
-GULP- PLEASE DON'T KILL ME, I'LL DO ANYTHING YOU WANT!
I'LL HELP YOU ESCAPE, SHOW YOU THE WAY OUT -
WE CAN'T LEAVE HIM HERE, OR HE'LL SUFFER THE SAME FATE AS US. WE AT LEAST OWE HIM HIS LIFE.
YOU BRANDED ME A SLAVE - YOU HAD MEN BEAT ME AND IMPRISON ME FOR YOUR MASTER.
I FORGIVE YOU FOR WHAT YOU HAVE DONE - LET IT NOT STAND BETWEEN US.
NOW PICK UP THE SNAKES - THEY APPEAR TO KNOW YOU WELL AND MAY COME IN USEFUL.
HE ANSWERED! YOU MAY THINK IT THUNDERED - BUT I HEARD A VOICE! HE SPOKE TO ME!
WE ARE NOT OUT OF THIS YET - I DON'T KNOW WHAT DEMURRAL HAS ALREADY RELEASED WITH THE KERUVIM.
THERE MAY BE FORCES AND CREATURES SET FREE THAT I WILL HAVE TO STOP.
YOU CAN GO NOW - OR YOU CAN SEE THIS THROUGH TO THE END.
WE'LL COME WITH YOU -

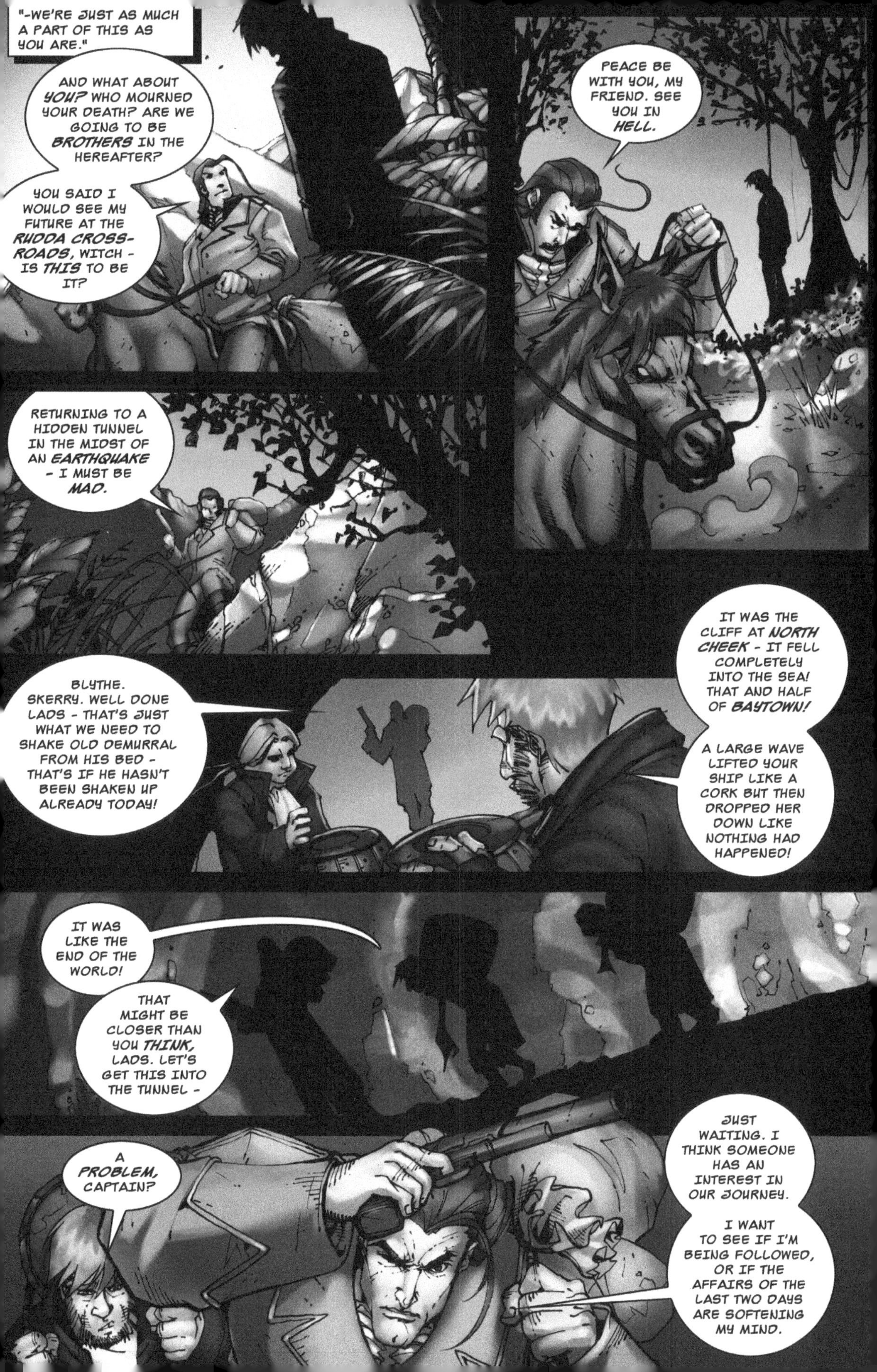
"-WE'RE JUST AS MUCH A PART OF THIS AS YOU ARE."
AND WHAT ABOUT *YOU?* WHO MOURNED YOUR DEATH? ARE WE GOING TO BE *BROTHERS* IN THE HEREAFTER?
YOU SAID I WOULD SEE MY FUTURE AT THE *RUDDA CROSS-ROADS*, WITCH - IS *THIS* TO BE IT?
PEACE BE WITH YOU, MY FRIEND. SEE YOU IN *HELL.*
RETURNING TO A HIDDEN TUNNEL IN THE MIDST OF AN *EARTHQUAKE* - I MUST BE *MAD.*
BLYTHE. SKERRY. WELL DONE LADS - THAT'S JUST WHAT WE NEED TO SHAKE OLD DEMURRAL FROM HIS BED - THAT'S IF HE HASN'T BEEN SHAKEN UP ALREADY TODAY!
IT WAS THE CLIFF AT *NORTH CHEEK* - IT FELL COMPLETELY INTO THE SEA! THAT AND HALF OF *BAYTOWN!*
A LARGE WAVE LIFTED YOUR SHIP LIKE A CORK BUT THEN DROPPED HER DOWN LIKE NOTHING HAD HAPPENED!
IT WAS LIKE THE END OF THE WORLD!
THAT MIGHT BE CLOSER THAN YOU *THINK,* LADS. LET'S GET THIS INTO THE TUNNEL -
A *PROBLEM,* CAPTAIN?
JUST WAITING. I THINK SOMEONE HAS AN INTEREST IN OUR JOURNEY.
I WANT TO SEE IF I'M BEING FOLLOWED, OR IF THE AFFAIRS OF THE LAST TWO DAYS ARE SOFTENING MY MIND.

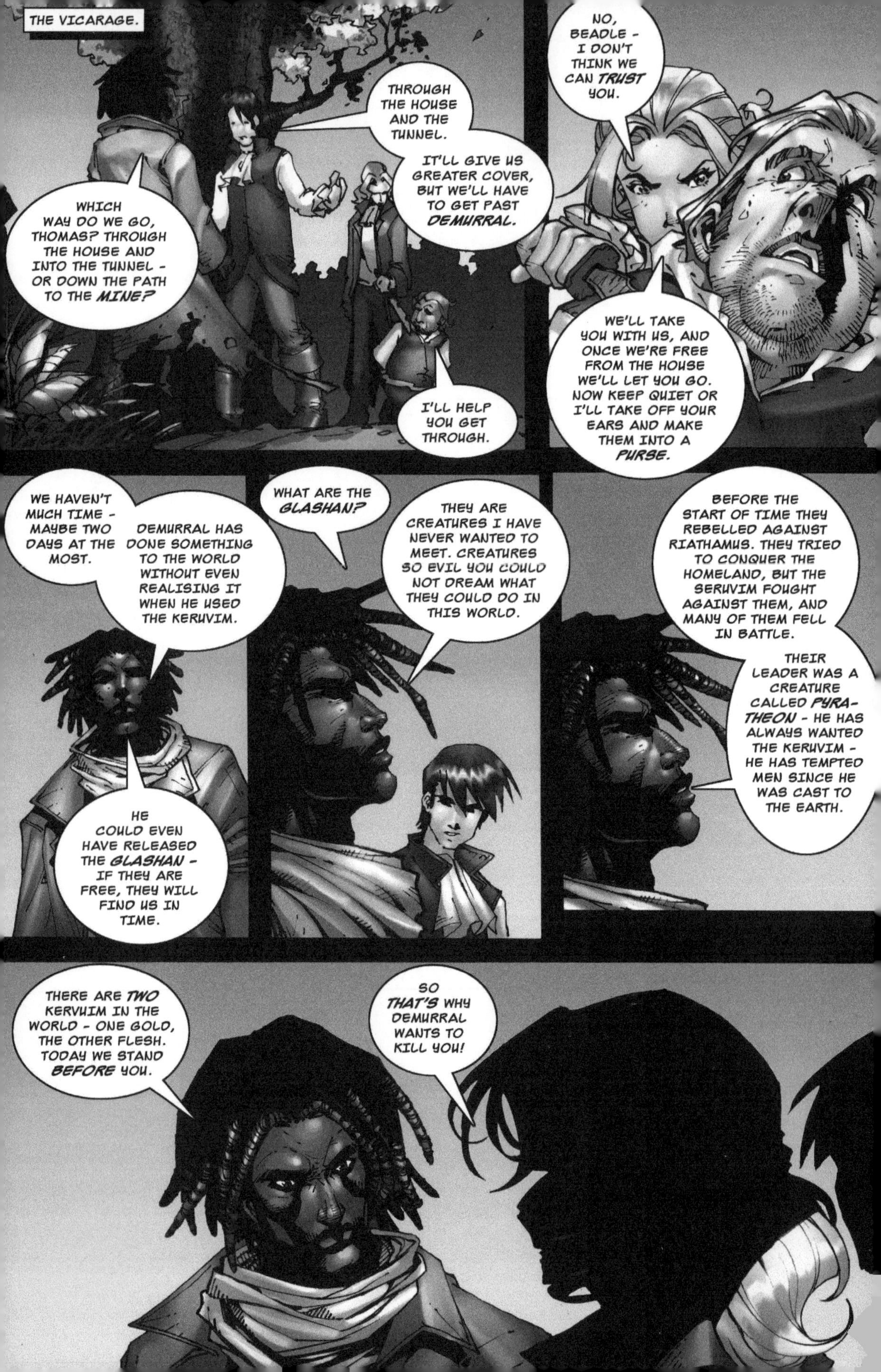
THE VICARAGE.
WHICH WAY DO WE GO, THOMAS? THROUGH THE HOUSE AND INTO THE TUNNEL - OR DOWN THE PATH TO THE MINE?
THROUGH THE HOUSE AND THE TUNNEL.
IT'LL GIVE US GREATER COVER, BUT WE'LL HAVE TO GET PAST DEMURRAL.
I'LL HELP YOU GET THROUGH.
NO, BEADLE - I DON'T THINK WE CAN TRUST YOU.
WE'LL TAKE YOU WITH US, AND ONCE WE'RE FREE FROM THE HOUSE WE'LL LET YOU GO. NOW KEEP QUIET OR I'LL TAKE OFF YOUR EARS AND MAKE THEM INTO A PURSE.
WE HAVEN'T MUCH TIME - MAYBE TWO DAYS AT THE MOST.
DEMURRAL HAS DONE SOMETHING TO THE WORLD WITHOUT EVEN REALISING IT WHEN HE USED THE KERUVIM.
HE COULD EVEN HAVE RELEASED THE GLASHAN - IF THEY ARE FREE, THEY WILL FIND US IN TIME.
WHAT ARE THE GLASHAN?
THEY ARE CREATURES I HAVE NEVER WANTED TO MEET. CREATURES SO EVIL YOU COULD NOT DREAM WHAT THEY COULD DO IN THIS WORLD.
BEFORE THE START OF TIME THEY REBELLED AGAINST RIATHAMUS. THEY TRIED TO CONQUER THE HOMELAND, BUT THE SERUVIM FOUGHT AGAINST THEM, AND MANY OF THEM FELL IN BATTLE.
THEIR LEADER WAS A CREATURE CALLED PYRA-THEON - HE HAS ALWAYS WANTED THE KERUVIM - HE HAS TEMPTED MEN SINCE HE WAS CAST TO THE EARTH.
THERE ARE TWO KERVUIM IN THE WORLD - ONE GOLD, THE OTHER FLESH. TODAY WE STAND BEFORE YOU.
SO THAT'S WHY DEMURRAL WANTS TO KILL YOU!

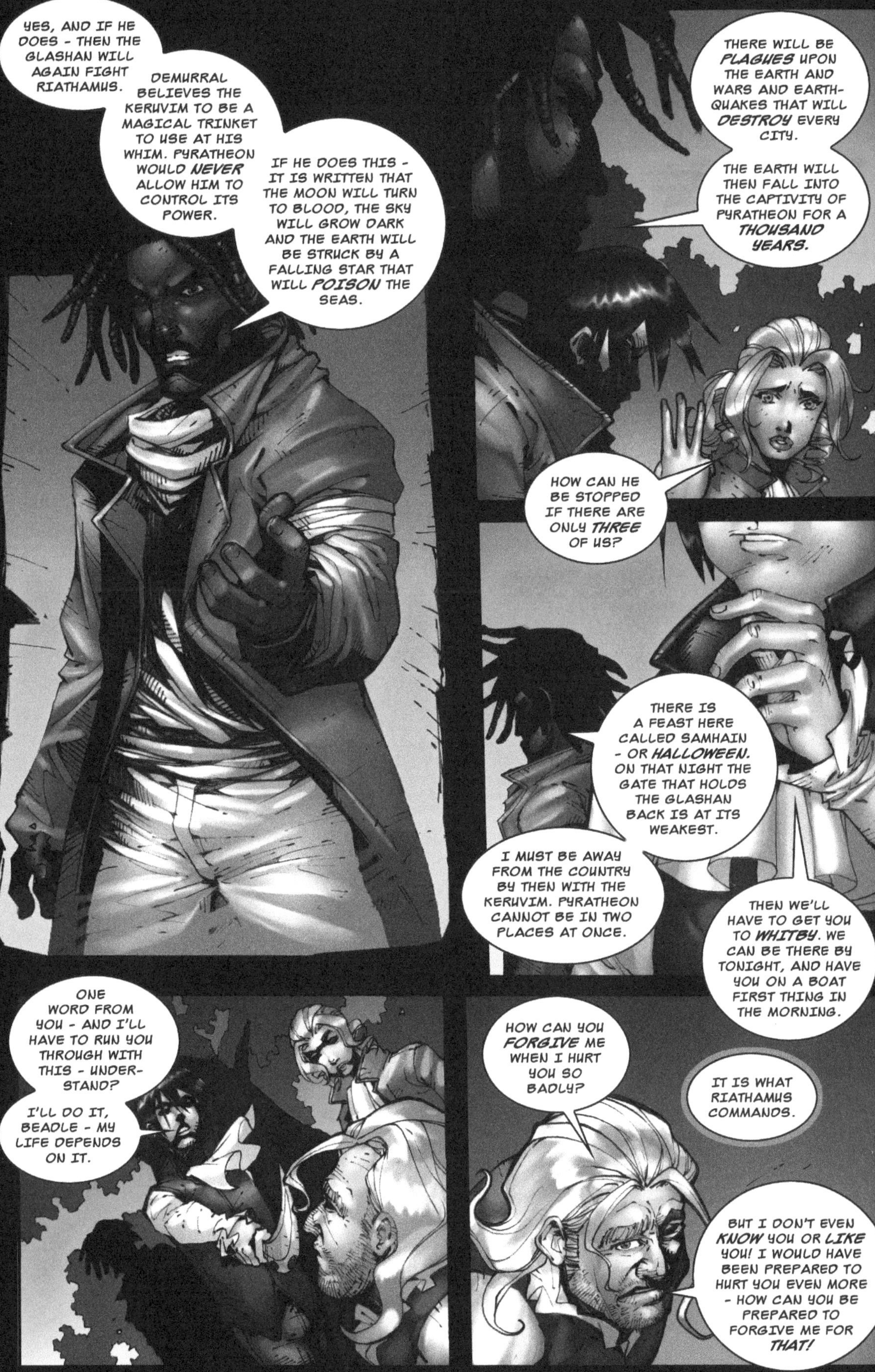
YES, AND IF HE DOES - THEN THE GLASHAN WILL AGAIN FIGHT RIATHAMUS.
DEMURRAL BELIEVES THE KERUVIM TO BE A MAGICAL TRINKET TO USE AT HIS WHIM. PYRATHEON WOULD NEVER ALLOW HIM TO CONTROL ITS POWER.
IF HE DOES THIS - IT IS WRITTEN THAT THE MOON WILL TURN TO BLOOD, THE SKY WILL GROW DARK AND THE EARTH WILL BE STRUCK BY A FALLING STAR THAT WILL POISON THE SEAS.
THERE WILL BE PLAGUES UPON THE EARTH AND WARS AND EARTH-QUAKES THAT WILL DESTROY EVERY CITY.
THE EARTH WILL THEN FALL INTO THE CAPTIVITY OF PYRATHEON FOR A THOUSAND YEARS.
HOW CAN HE BE STOPPED IF THERE ARE ONLY THREE OF US?
THERE IS A FEAST HERE CALLED SAMHAIN - OR HALLOWEEN. ON THAT NIGHT THE GATE THAT HOLDS THE GLASHAN BACK IS AT ITS WEAKEST.
I MUST BE AWAY FROM THE COUNTRY BY THEN WITH THE KERUVIM. PYRATHEON CANNOT BE IN TWO PLACES AT ONCE.
THEN WE'LL HAVE TO GET YOU TO WHITBY. WE CAN BE THERE BY TONIGHT, AND HAVE YOU ON A BOAT FIRST THING IN THE MORNING.
ONE WORD FROM YOU - AND I'LL HAVE TO RUN YOU THROUGH WITH THIS - UNDER-STAND?
I'LL DO IT, BEADLE - MY LIFE DEPENDS ON IT.
HOW CAN YOU FORGIVE ME WHEN I HURT YOU SO BADLY?
IT IS WHAT RIATHAMUS COMMANDS.
BUT I DON'T EVEN KNOW YOU OR LIKE YOU! I WOULD HAVE BEEN PREPARED TO HURT YOU EVEN MORE - HOW CAN YOU BE PREPARED TO FORGIVE ME FOR THAT!

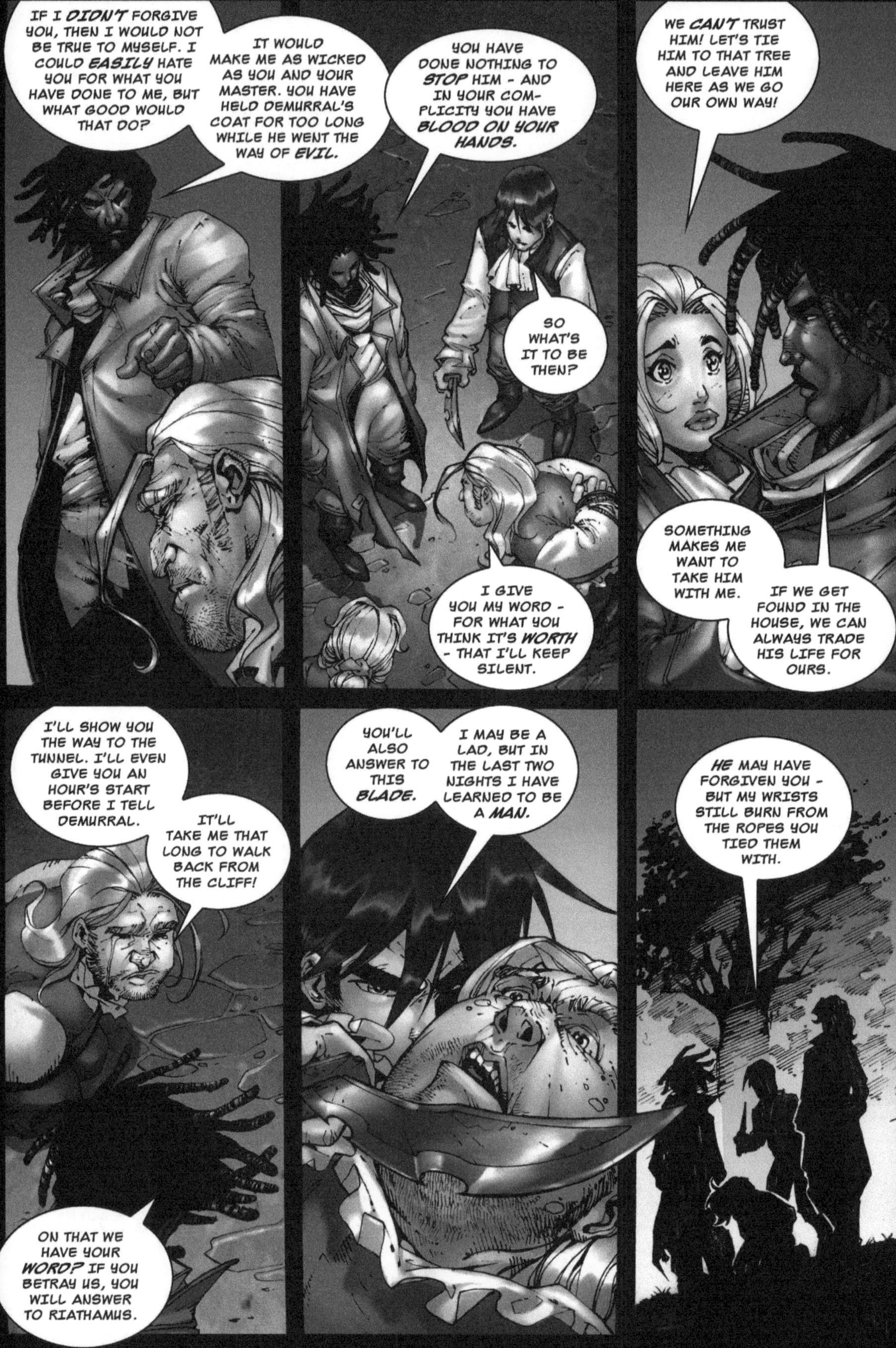
IF I DIDN'T FORGIVE YOU, THEN I WOULD NOT BE TRUE TO MYSELF. I COULD EASILY HATE YOU FOR WHAT YOU HAVE DONE TO ME, BUT WHAT GOOD WOULD THAT DO?
IT WOULD MAKE ME AS WICKED AS YOU AND YOUR MASTER. YOU HAVE HELD DEMURRAL'S COAT FOR TOO LONG WHILE HE WENT THE WAY OF EVIL.
YOU HAVE DONE NOTHING TO STOP HIM - AND IN YOUR COMPLICITY YOU HAVE BLOOD ON YOUR HANDS.
SO WHAT'S IT TO BE THEN?
I GIVE YOU MY WORD - FOR WHAT YOU THINK IT'S WORTH - THAT I'LL KEEP SILENT.
WE CAN'T TRUST HIM! LET'S TIE HIM TO THAT TREE AND LEAVE HIM HERE AS WE GO OUR OWN WAY!
SOMETHING MAKES ME WANT TO TAKE HIM WITH ME.
IF WE GET FOUND IN THE HOUSE, WE CAN ALWAYS TRADE HIS LIFE FOR OURS.
I'LL SHOW YOU THE WAY TO THE TUNNEL. I'LL EVEN GIVE YOU AN HOUR'S START BEFORE I TELL DEMURRAL.
IT'LL TAKE ME THAT LONG TO WALK BACK FROM THE CLIFF!
ON THAT WE HAVE YOUR WORD? IF YOU BETRAY US, YOU WILL ANSWER TO RIATHAMUS.
YOU'LL ALSO ANSWER TO THIS BLADE.
I MAY BE A LAD, BUT IN THE LAST TWO NIGHTS I HAVE LEARNED TO BE A MAN.
HE MAY HAVE FORGIVEN YOU - BUT MY WRISTS STILL BURN FROM THE ROPES YOU TIED THEM WITH.

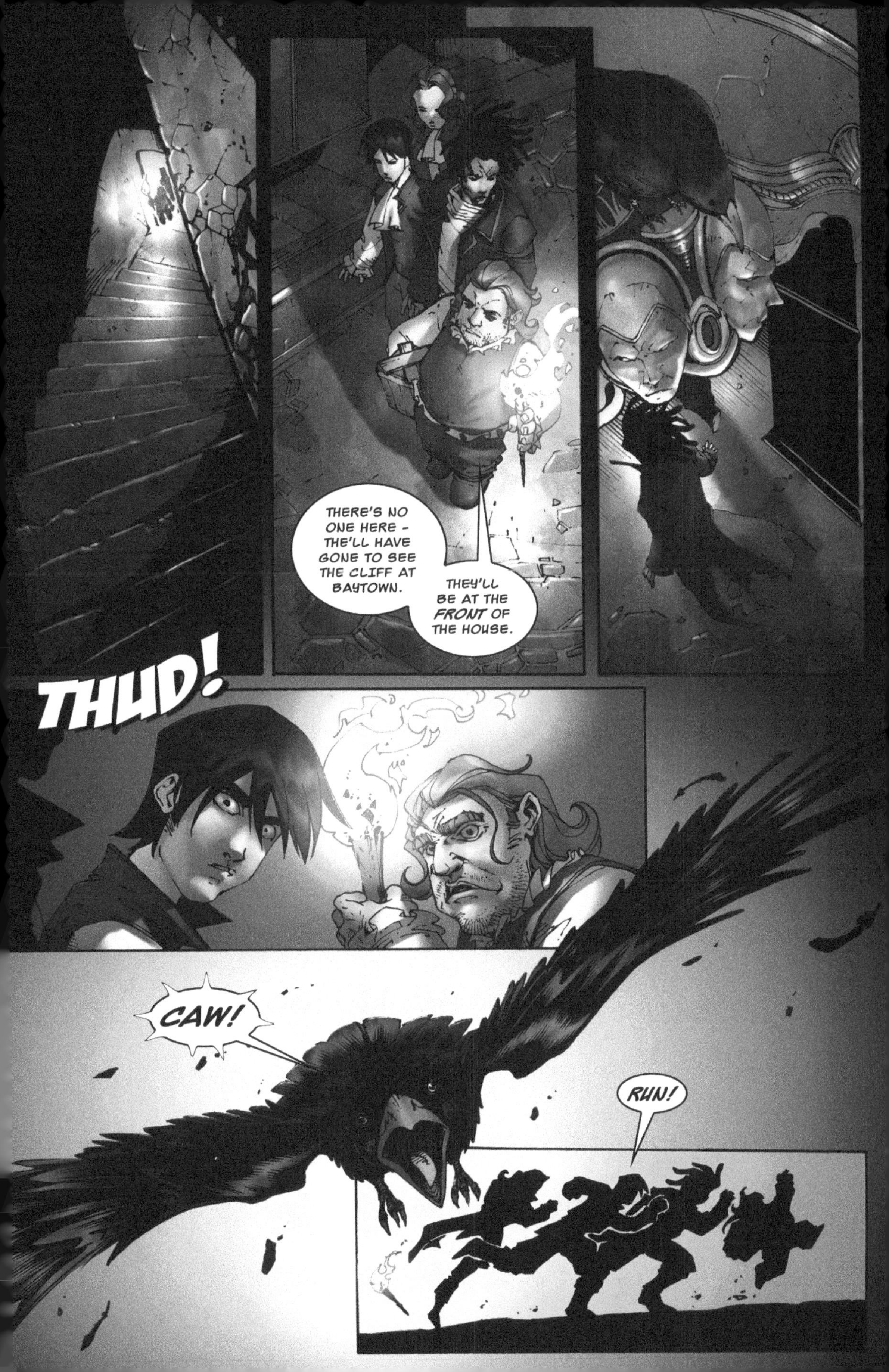
THERE'S NO ONE HERE - THE'LL HAVE GONE TO SEE THE CLIFF AT BAYTOWN.
THEY'LL BE AT THE *FRONT* OF THE HOUSE.
THUD!
CAW!
RUN!

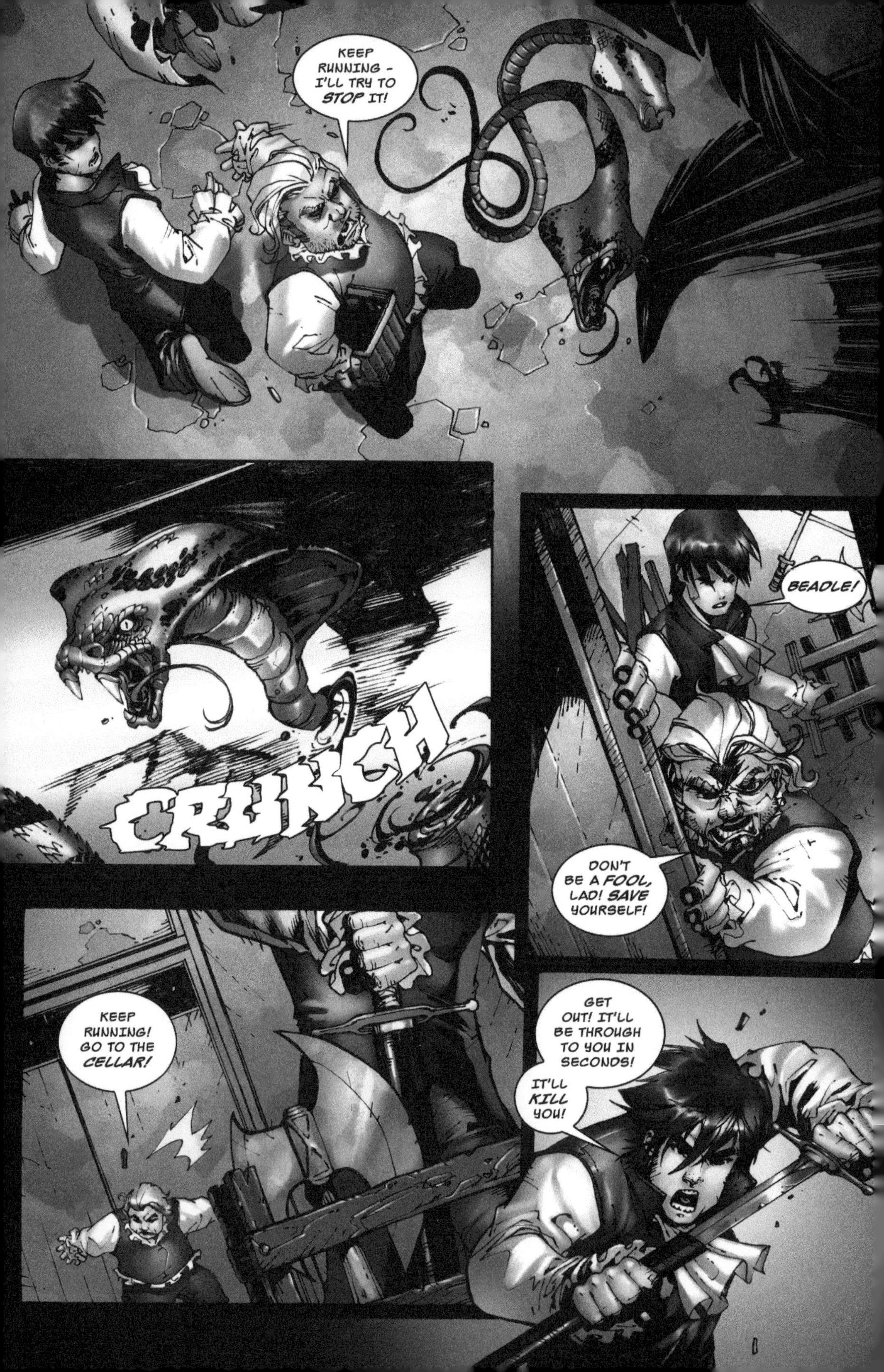
KEEP RUNNING - I'LL TRY TO STOP IT!
CRUNCH
BEADLE!
DON'T BE A FOOL, LAD! SAVE YOURSELF!
KEEP RUNNING! GO TO THE CELLAR!
GET OUT! IT'LL BE THROUGH TO YOU IN SECONDS!
IT'LL KILL YOU!

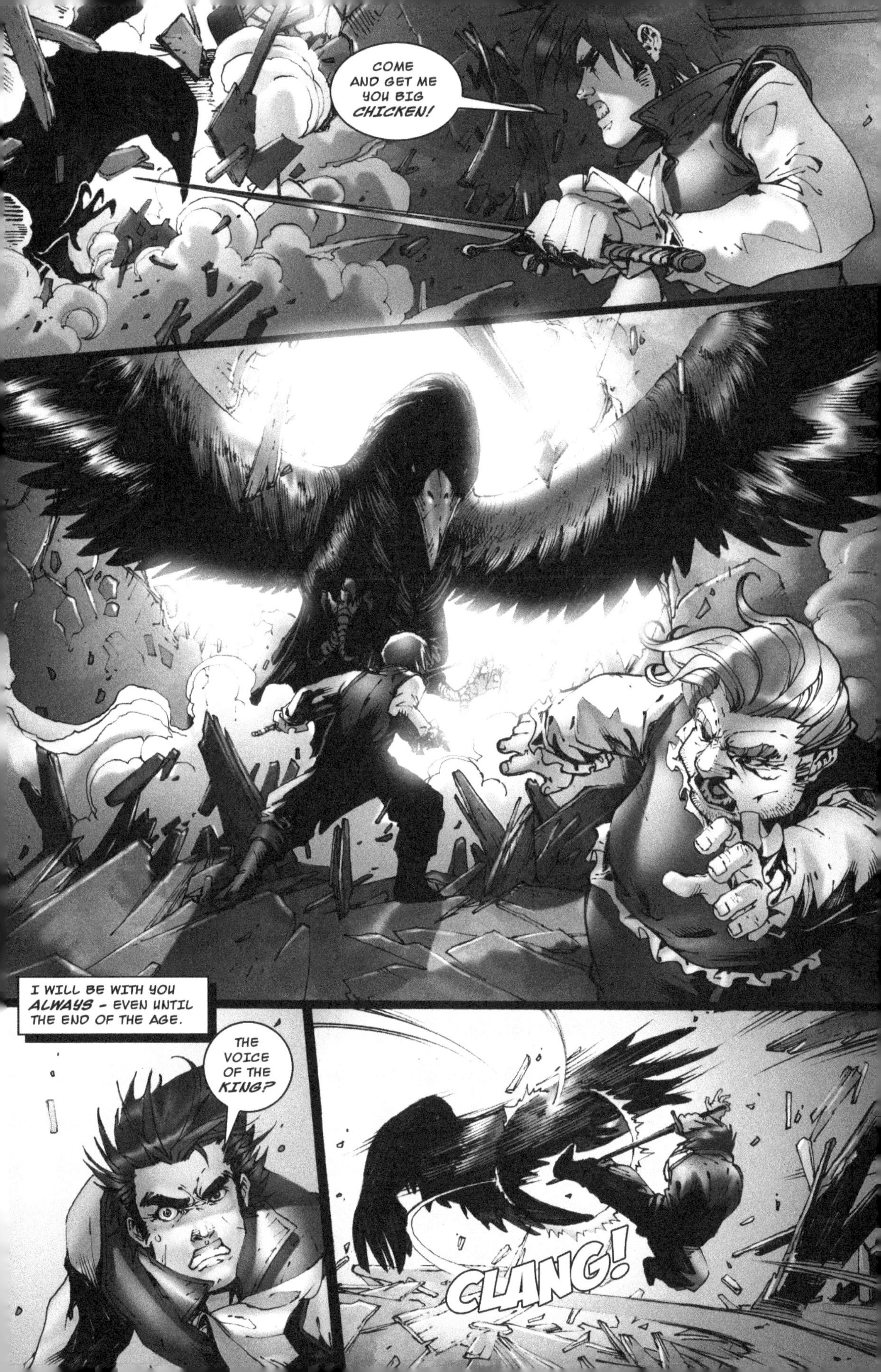
COME AND GET ME YOU BIG CHICKEN!
I WILL BE WITH YOU ALWAYS - EVEN UNTIL THE END OF THE AGE.
THE VOICE OF THE KING?
CLANG!

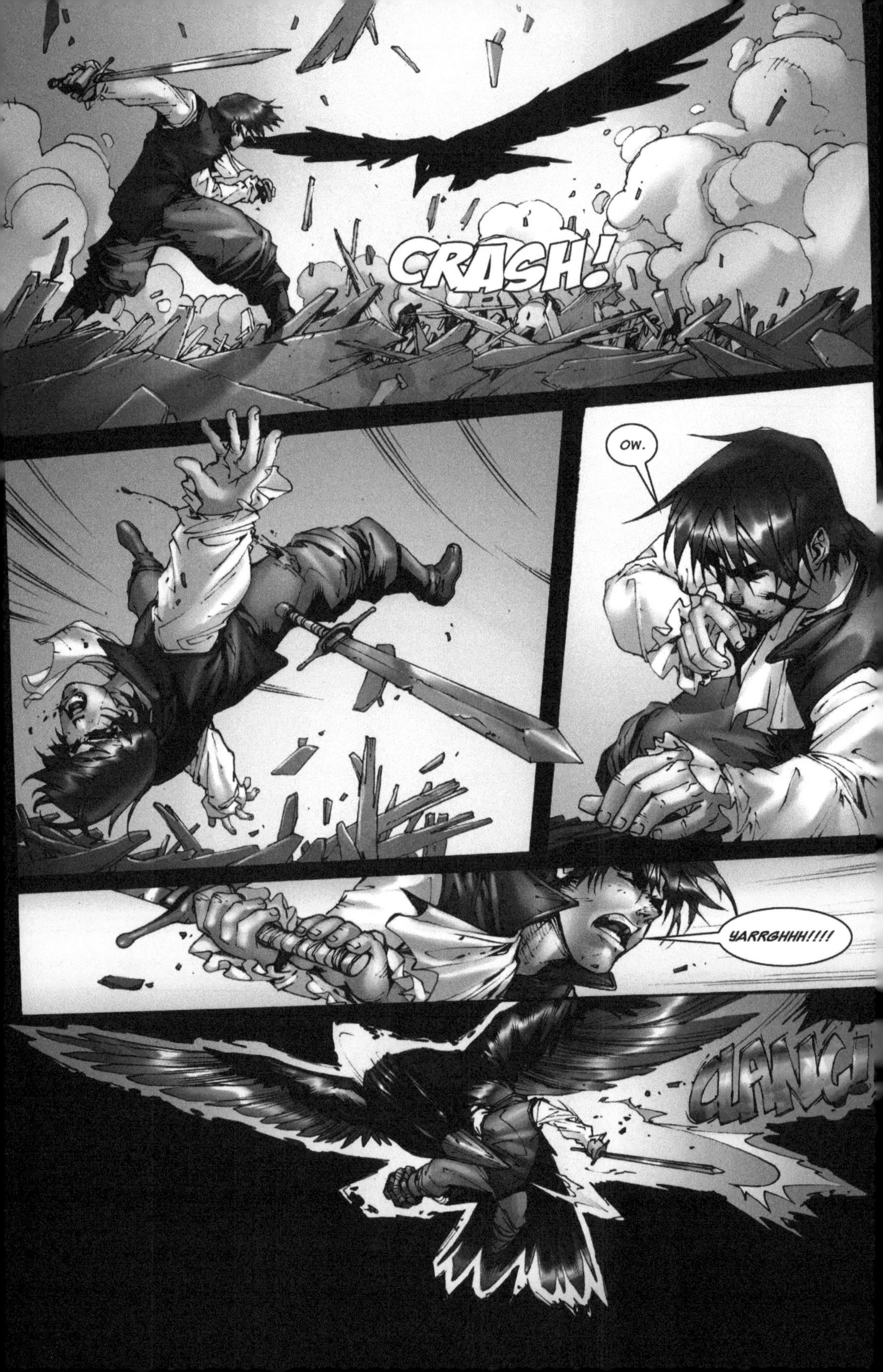
CRASH!
OW.
YARRGHHH!!!!
CLANG!

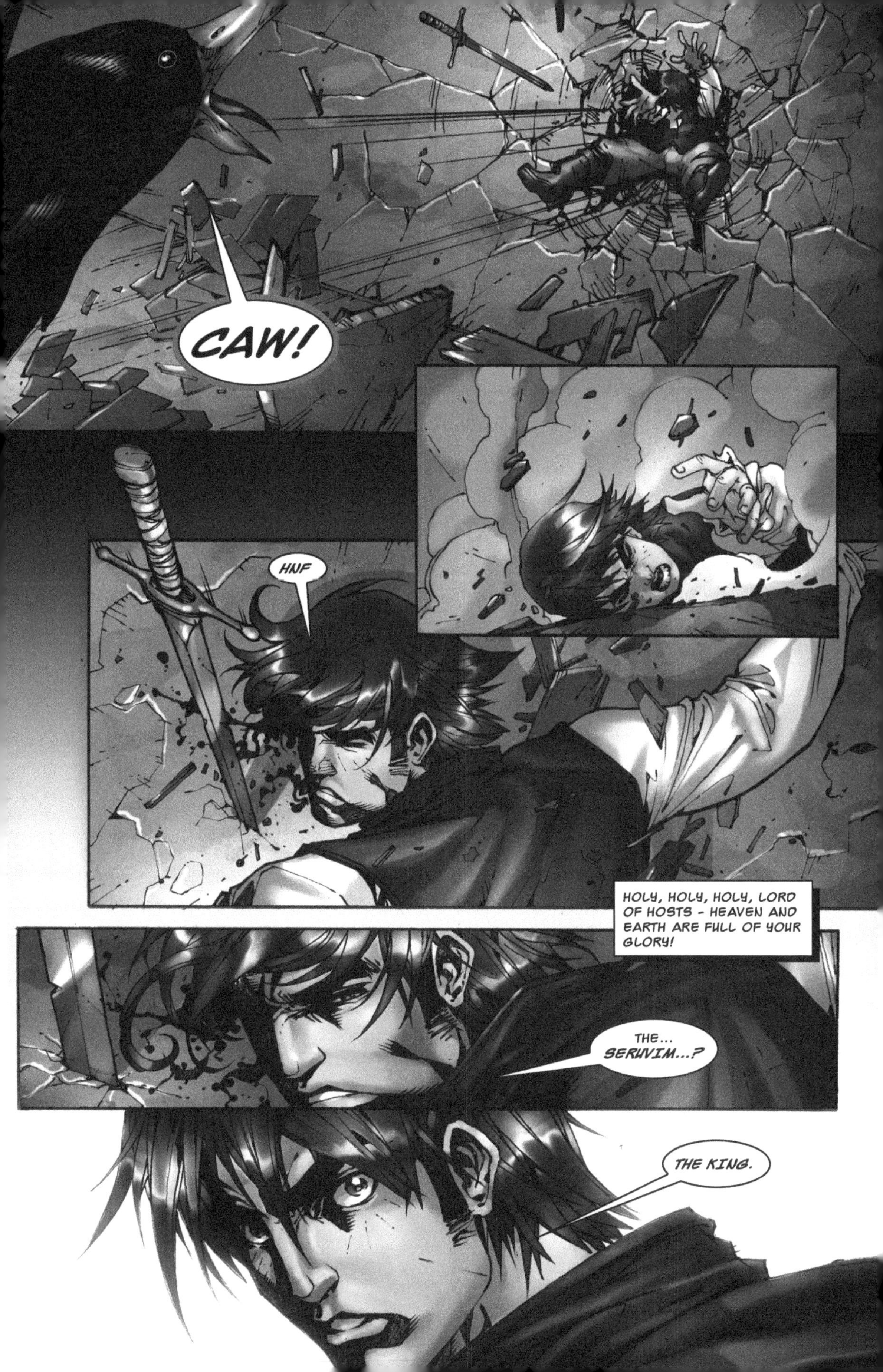
CAW!
HNF
HOLY, HOLY, HOLY, LORD OF HOSTS - HEAVEN AND EARTH ARE FULL OF YOUR GLORY!
THE... SERUVIM...?
THE KING.

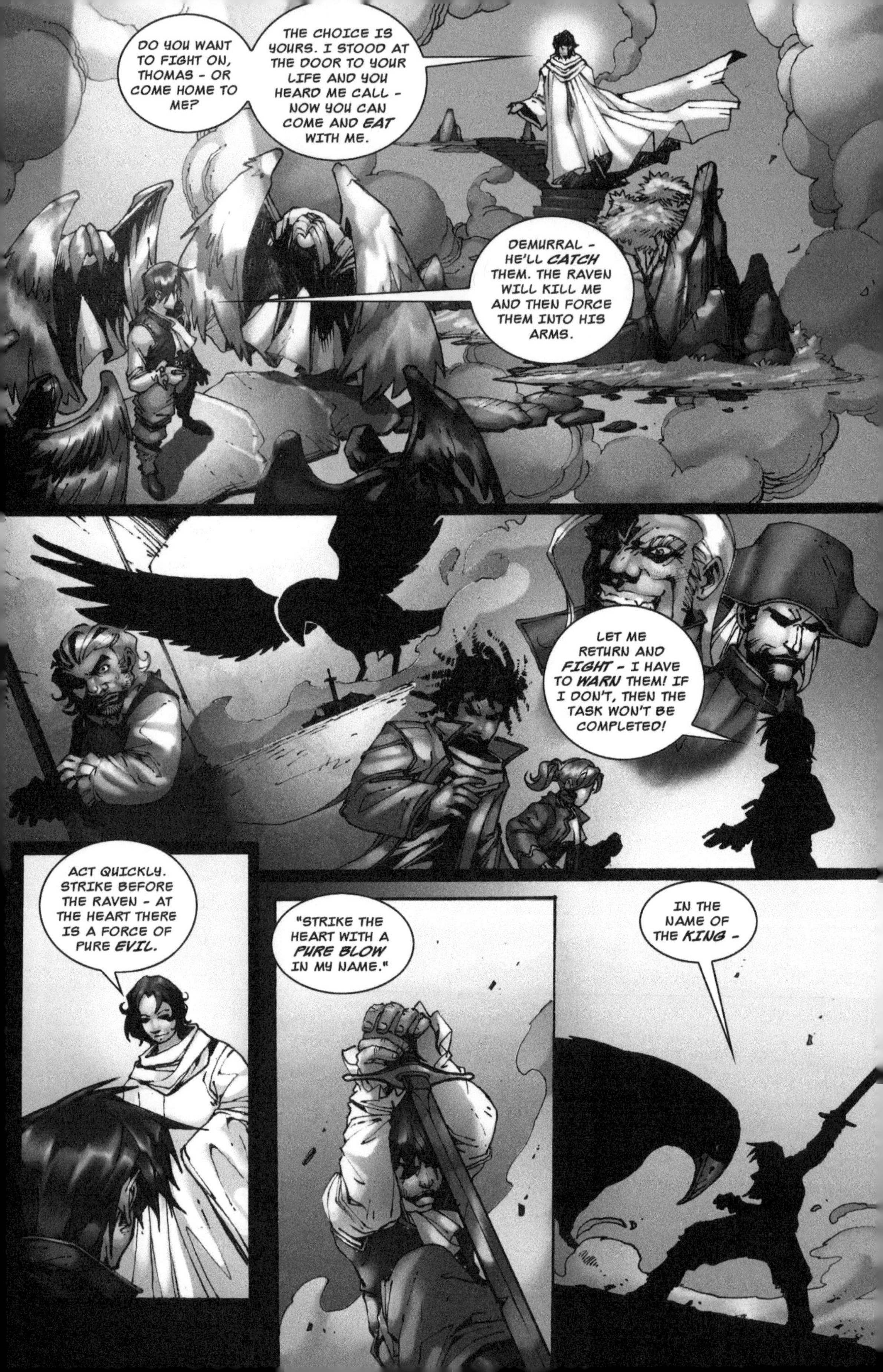
DO YOU WANT TO FIGHT ON, THOMAS - OR COME HOME TO ME?
THE CHOICE IS YOURS. I STOOD AT THE DOOR TO YOUR LIFE AND YOU HEARD ME CALL - NOW YOU CAN COME AND EAT WITH ME.
DEMURRAL - HE'LL CATCH THEM. THE RAVEN WILL KILL ME AND THEN FORCE THEM INTO HIS ARMS.
LET ME RETURN AND FIGHT - I HAVE TO WARN THEM! IF I DON'T, THEN THE TASK WON'T BE COMPLETED!
ACT QUICKLY. STRIKE BEFORE THE RAVEN - AT THE HEART THERE IS A FORCE OF PURE EVIL.
"STRIKE THE HEART WITH A PURE BLOW IN MY NAME."
IN THE NAME OF THE KING -

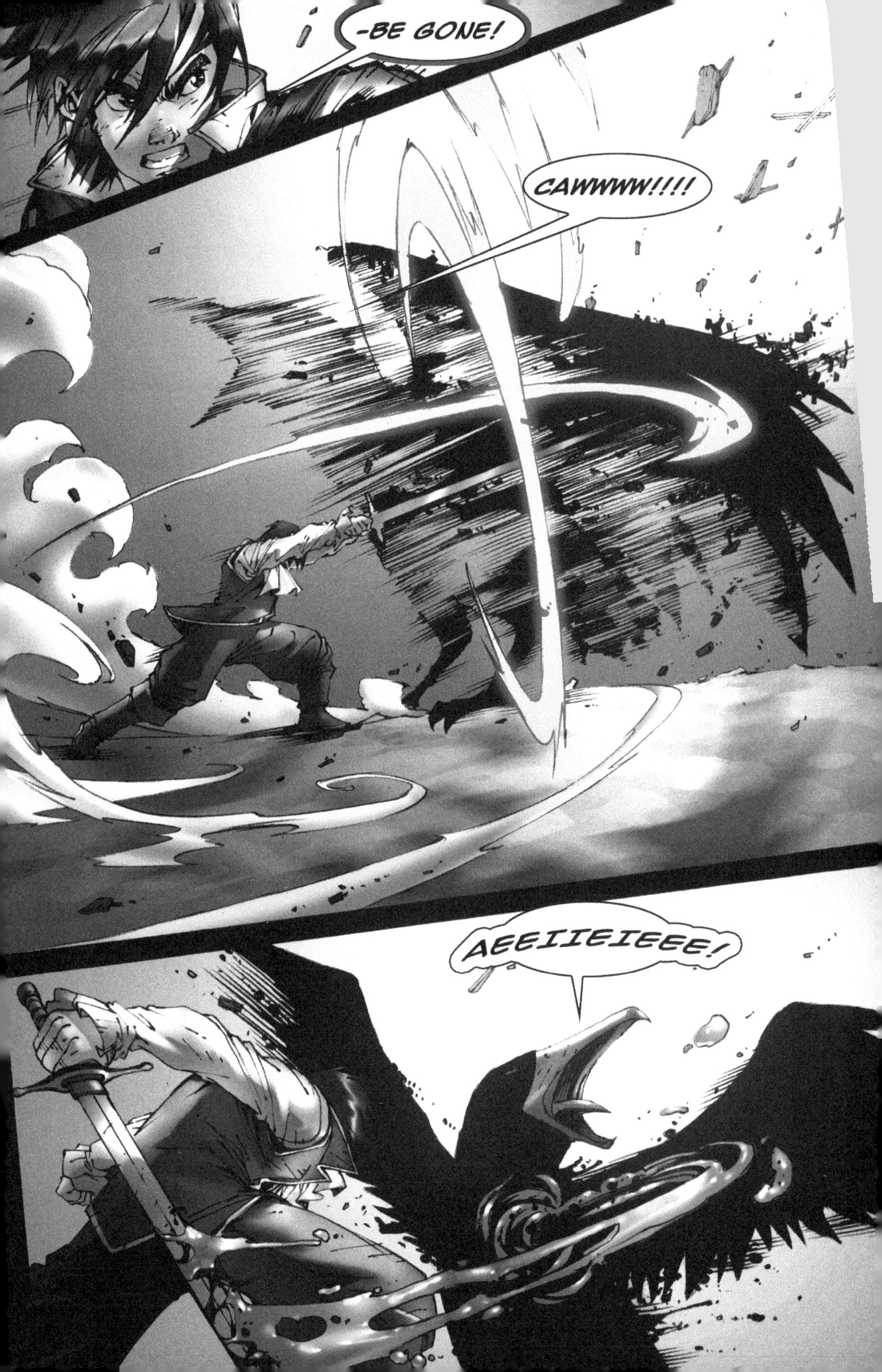
-BE GONE!
CAWWWW!!!!
AEEIIEIEEE!

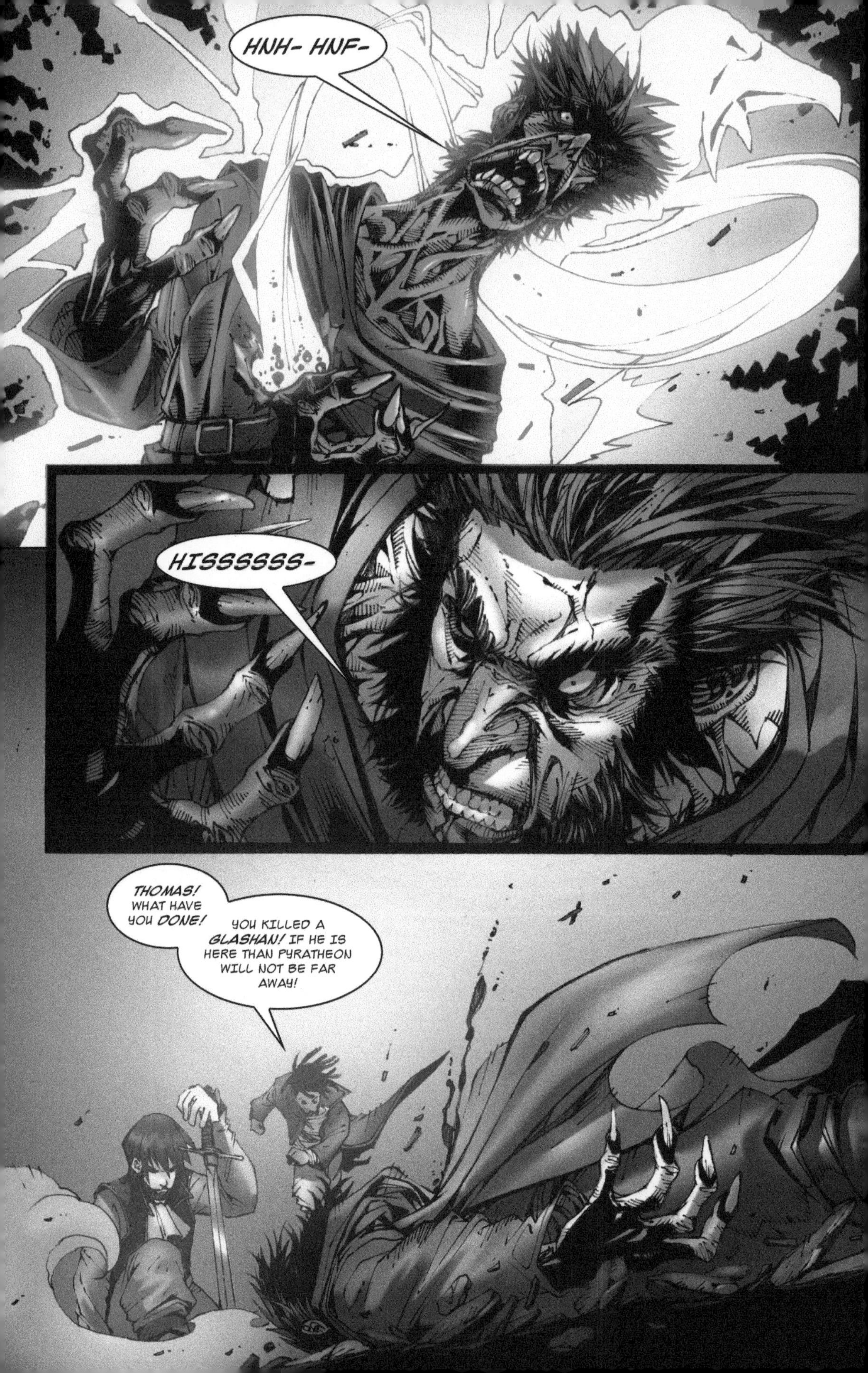
HNH- HNF-
HISSSSSS-
THOMAS! WHAT HAVE YOU DONE!
YOU KILLED A GLASHAN! IF HE IS HERE THAN PYRATHEON WILL NOT BE FAR AWAY!

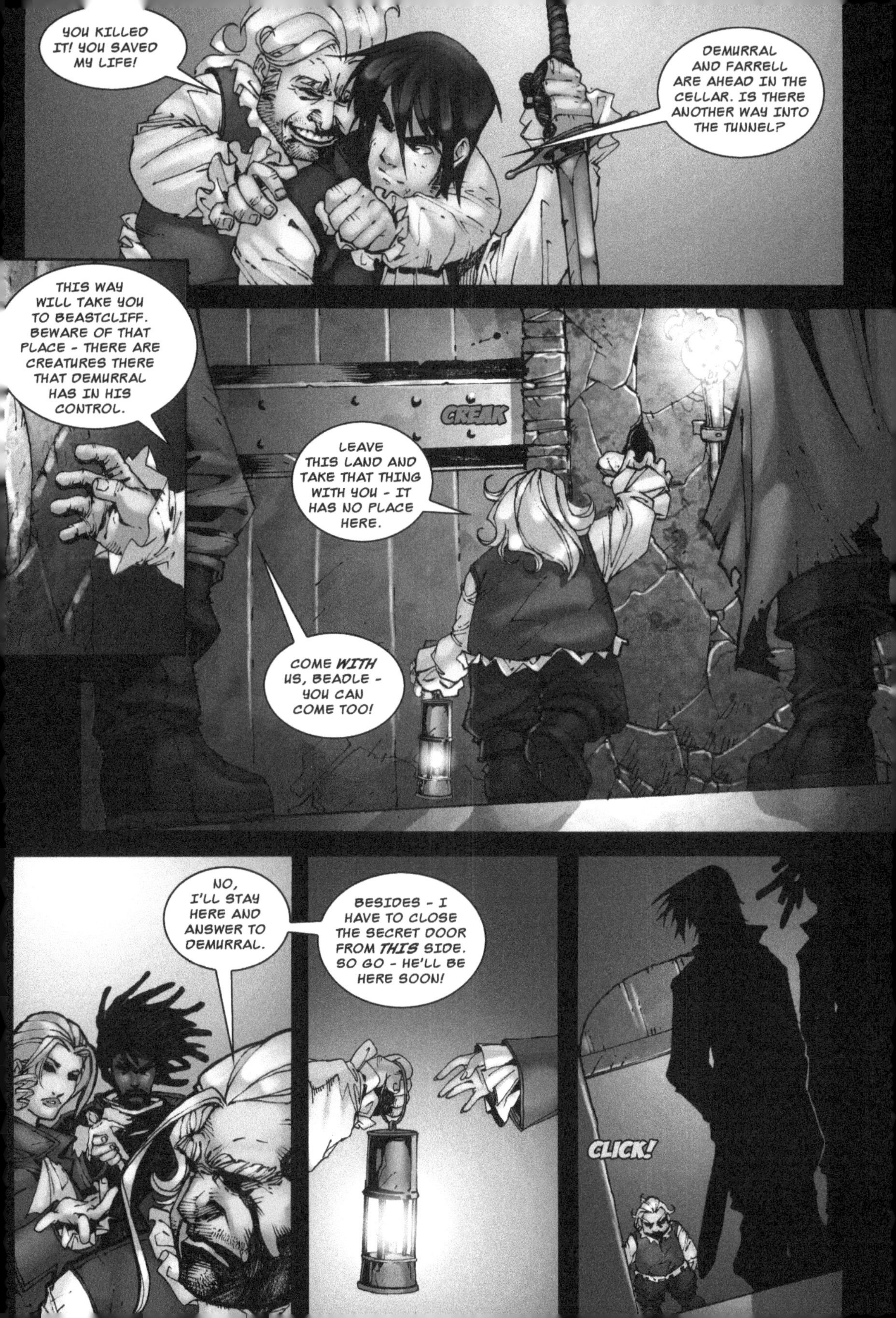
YOU KILLED IT! YOU SAVED MY LIFE!
DEMURRAL AND FARRELL ARE AHEAD IN THE CELLAR. IS THERE ANOTHER WAY INTO THE TUNNEL?
THIS WAY WILL TAKE YOU TO BEASTCLIFF. BEWARE OF THAT PLACE - THERE ARE CREATURES THERE THAT DEMURRAL HAS IN HIS CONTROL.
CREAK
LEAVE THIS LAND AND TAKE THAT THING WITH YOU - IT HAS NO PLACE HERE.
COME WITH US, BEADLE - YOU CAN COME TOO!
NO, I'LL STAY HERE AND ANSWER TO DEMURRAL.
BESIDES - I HAVE TO CLOSE THE SECRET DOOR FROM THIS SIDE. SO GO - HE'LL BE HERE SOON!
CLICK!

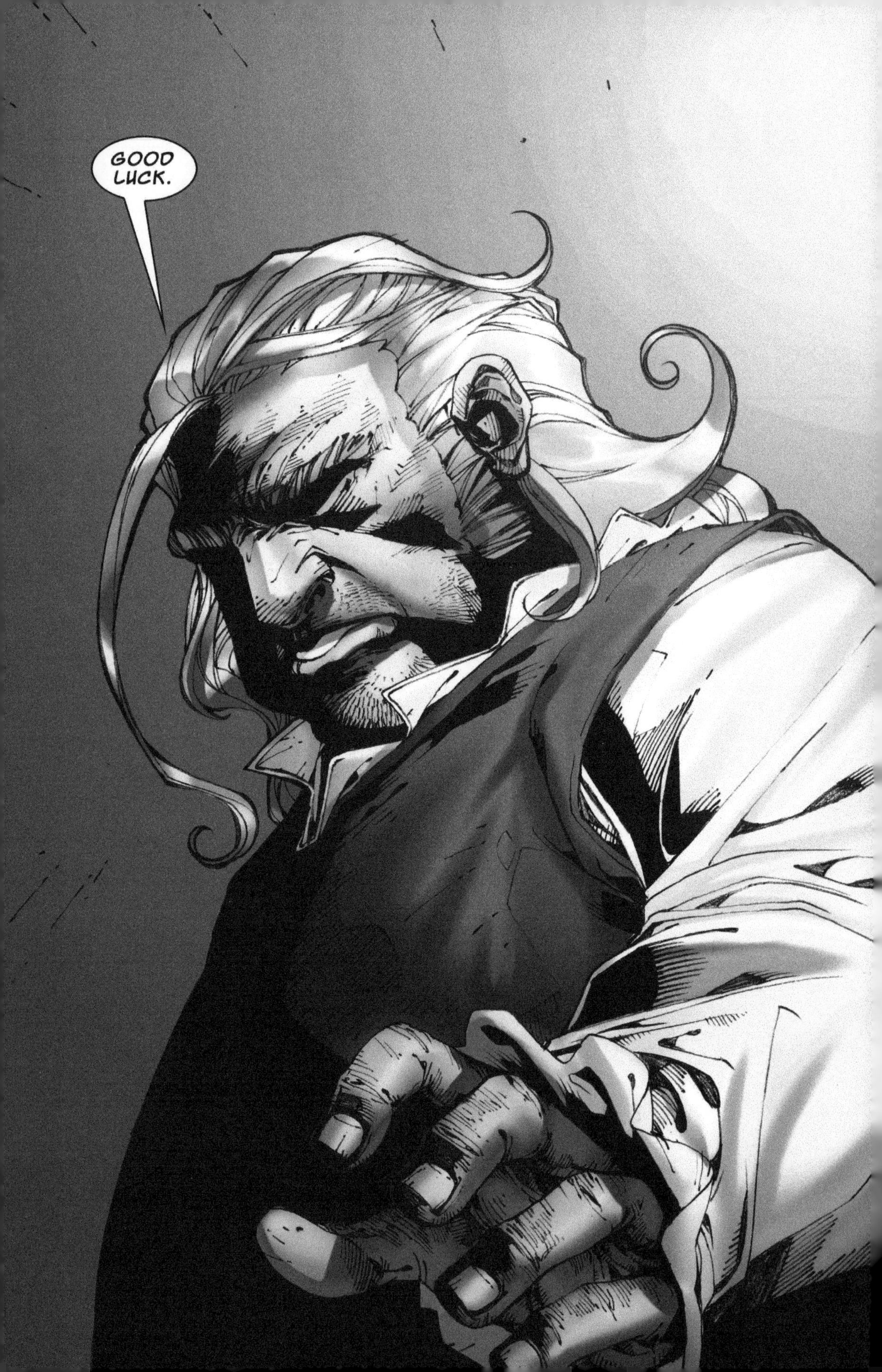
GOOD LUCK.

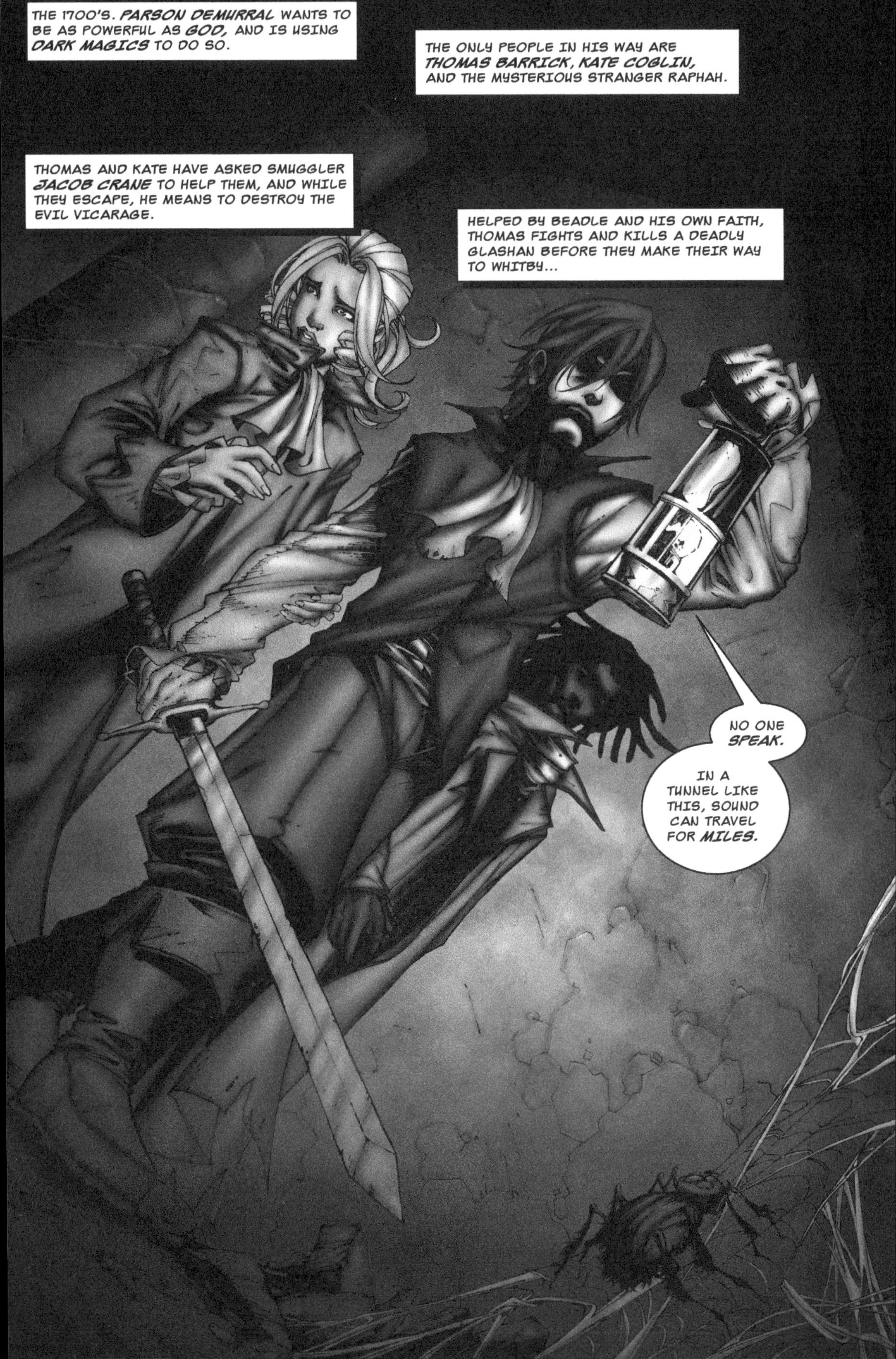
THE 1700'S. PARSON DEMURRAL WANTS TO BE AS POWERFUL AS GOD, AND IS USING DARK MAGICS TO DO SO.
THE ONLY PEOPLE IN HIS WAY ARE THOMAS BARRICK, KATE COGLIN, AND THE MYSTERIOUS STRANGER RAPHAH.
THOMAS AND KATE HAVE ASKED SMUGGLER JACOB CRANE TO HELP THEM, AND WHILE THEY ESCAPE, HE MEANS TO DESTROY THE EVIL VICARAGE.
HELPED BY BEADLE AND HIS OWN FAITH, THOMAS FIGHTS AND KILLS A DEADLY GLASHAN BEFORE THEY MAKE THEIR WAY TO WHITBY...
NO ONE SPEAK.
IN A TUNNEL LIKE THIS, SOUND CAN TRAVEL FOR MILES.

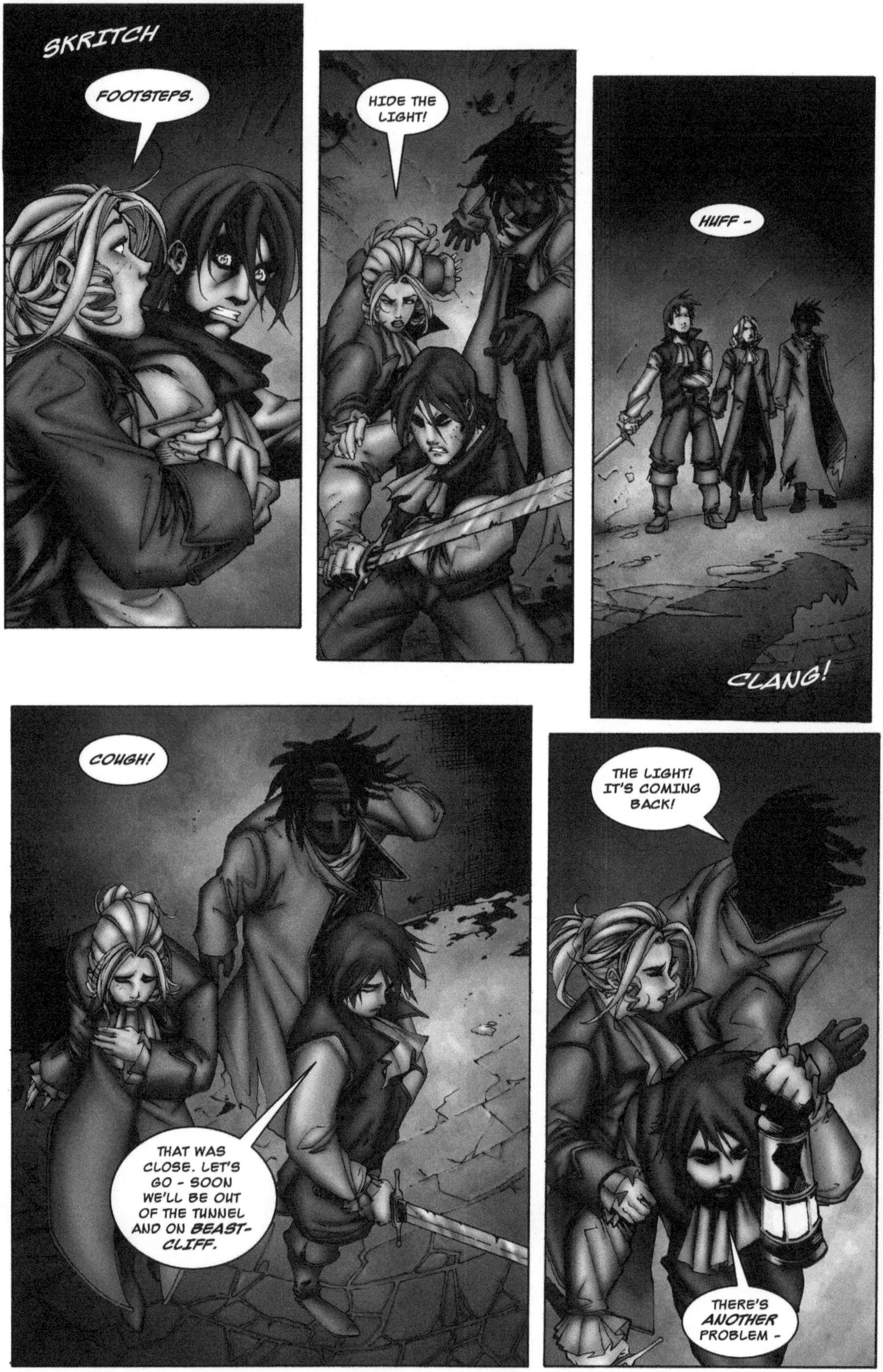
SKRITCH
FOOTSTEPS.
HIDE THE LIGHT!
HUFF -
CLANG!
COUGH!
THAT WAS CLOSE. LET'S GO - SOON WE'LL BE OUT OF THE TUNNEL AND ON BEAST-CLIFF.
THE LIGHT! IT'S COMING BACK!
THERE'S ANOTHER PROBLEM -

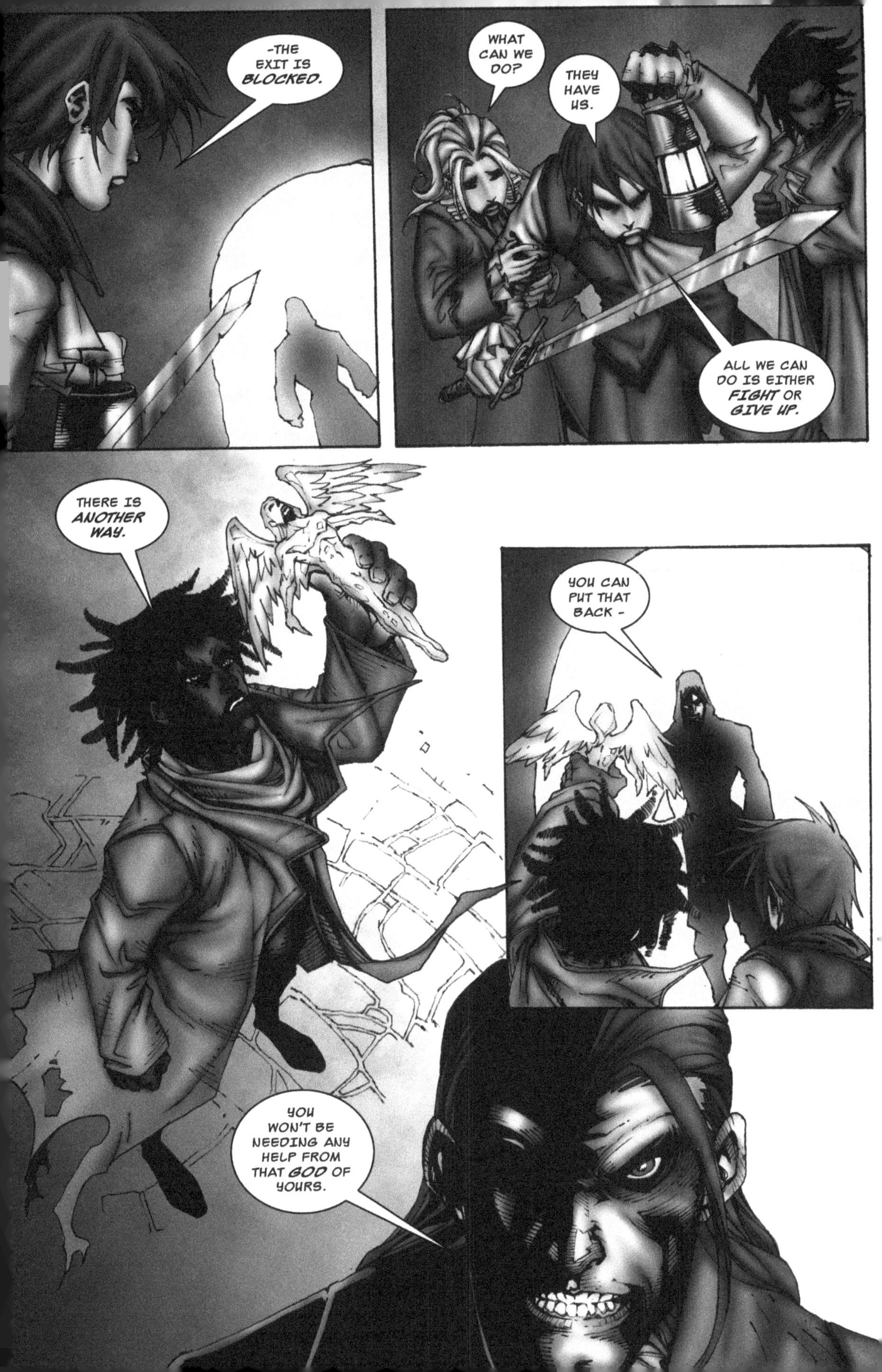
-THE EXIT IS BLOCKED.
WHAT CAN WE DO?
THEY HAVE US.
ALL WE CAN DO IS EITHER FIGHT OR GIVE UP.
THERE IS ANOTHER WAY.
YOU CAN PUT THAT BACK -
YOU WON'T BE NEEDING ANY HELP FROM THAT GOD OF YOURS.

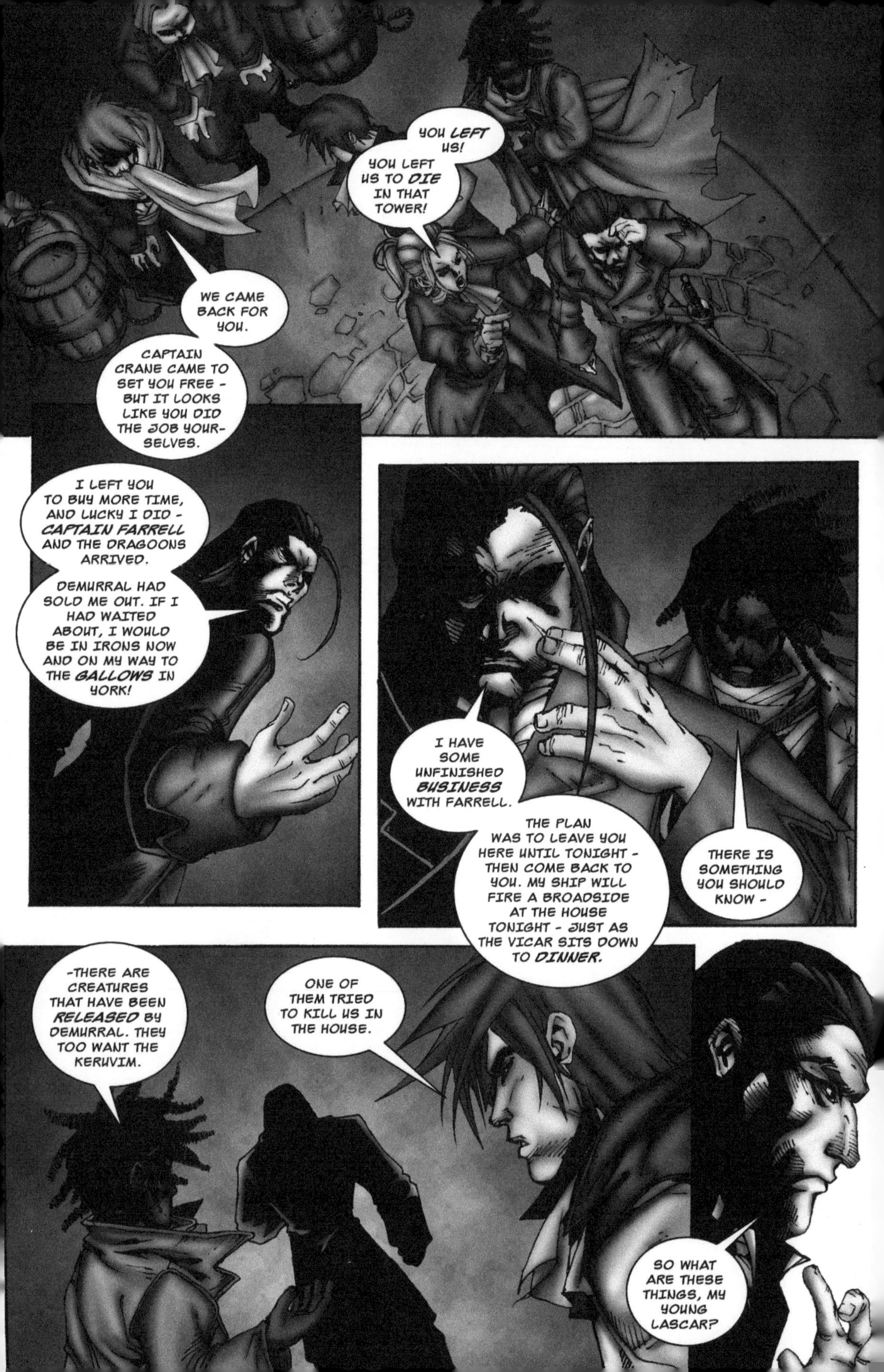
YOU LEFT US!
YOU LEFT US TO DIE IN THAT TOWER!
WE CAME BACK FOR YOU.
CAPTAIN CRANE CAME TO SET YOU FREE - BUT IT LOOKS LIKE YOU DID THE JOB YOURSELVES.
I LEFT YOU TO BUY MORE TIME, AND LUCKY I DID - CAPTAIN FARRELL AND THE DRAGOONS ARRIVED.
DEMURRAL HAD SOLD ME OUT. IF I HAD WAITED ABOUT, I WOULD BE IN IRONS NOW AND ON MY WAY TO THE GALLOWS IN YORK!
I HAVE SOME UNFINISHED BUSINESS WITH FARRELL.
THE PLAN WAS TO LEAVE YOU HERE UNTIL TONIGHT - THEN COME BACK TO YOU. MY SHIP WILL FIRE A BROADSIDE AT THE HOUSE TONIGHT - JUST AS THE VICAR SITS DOWN TO DINNER.
THERE IS SOMETHING YOU SHOULD KNOW -
-THERE ARE CREATURES THAT HAVE BEEN RELEASED BY DEMURRAL. THEY TOO WANT THE KERUVIM.
ONE OF THEM TRIED TO KILL US IN THE HOUSE.
SO WHAT ARE THESE THINGS, MY YOUNG LASCAR?

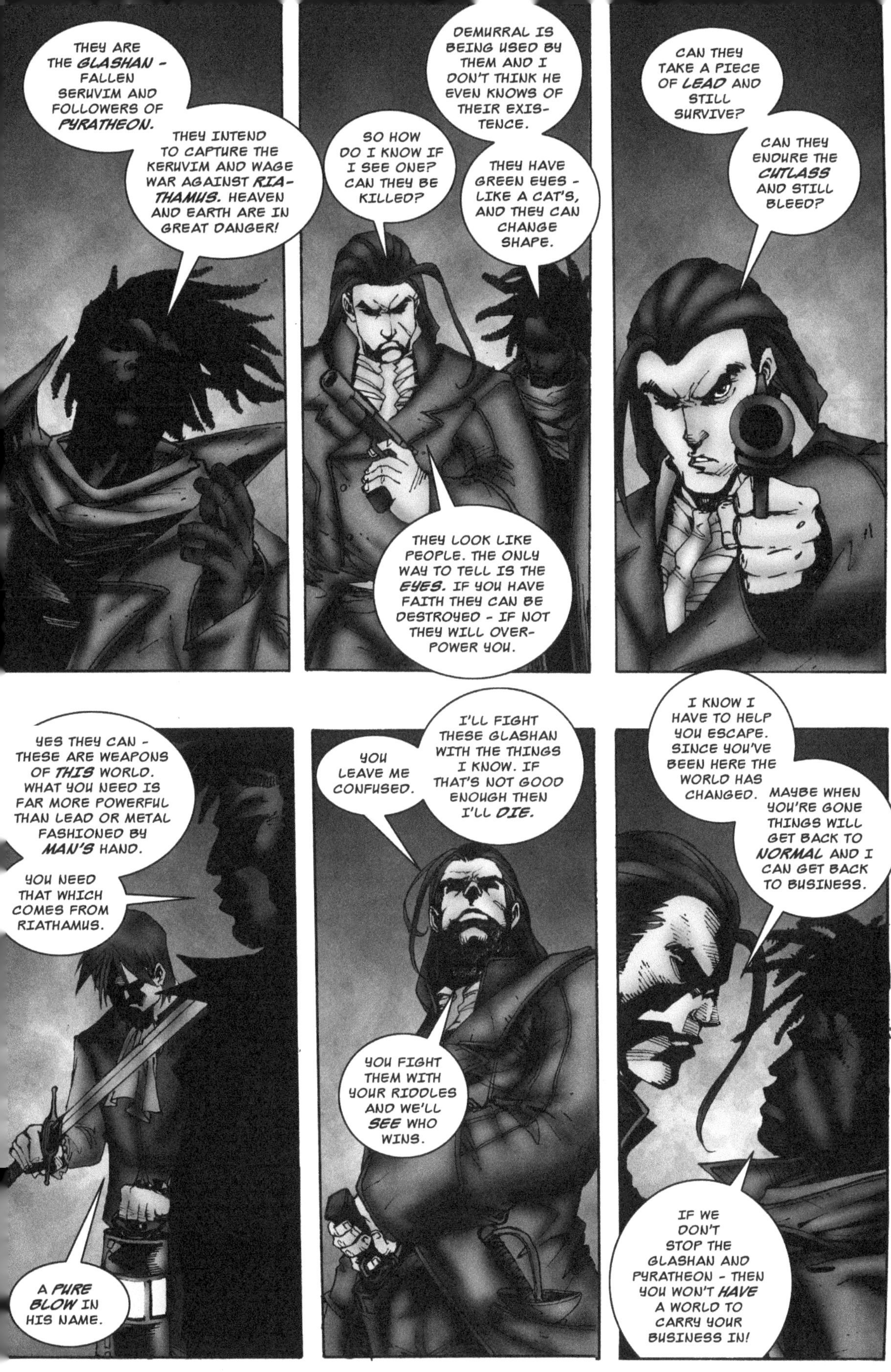

THEY ARE THE GLASHAN - FALLEN SERUVIM AND FOLLOWERS OF PYRATHEON.
THEY INTEND TO CAPTURE THE KERUVIM AND WAGE WAR AGAINST RIATHAMUS. HEAVEN AND EARTH ARE IN GREAT DANGER!
SO HOW DO I KNOW IF I SEE ONE? CAN THEY BE KILLED?
DEMURRAL IS BEING USED BY THEM AND I DON'T THINK HE EVEN KNOWS OF THEIR EXISTENCE.
THEY HAVE GREEN EYES - LIKE A CAT'S, AND THEY CAN CHANGE SHAPE.
THEY LOOK LIKE PEOPLE. THE ONLY WAY TO TELL IS THE EYES. IF YOU HAVE FAITH THEY CAN BE DESTROYED - IF NOT THEY WILL OVERPOWER YOU.
CAN THEY TAKE A PIECE OF LEAD AND STILL SURVIVE?
CAN THEY ENDURE THE CUTLASS AND STILL BLEED?
YES THEY CAN - THESE ARE WEAPONS OF THIS WORLD. WHAT YOU NEED IS FAR MORE POWERFUL THAN LEAD OR METAL FASHIONED BY MAN'S HAND.
YOU NEED THAT WHICH COMES FROM RIATHAMUS.
A PURE BLOW IN HIS NAME.
YOU LEAVE ME CONFUSED.
I'LL FIGHT THESE GLASHAN WITH THE THINGS I KNOW. IF THAT'S NOT GOOD ENOUGH THEN I'LL DIE.
YOU FIGHT THEM WITH YOUR RIDDLES AND WE'LL SEE WHO WINS.
I KNOW I HAVE TO HELP YOU ESCAPE. SINCE YOU'VE BEEN HERE THE WORLD HAS CHANGED.
MAYBE WHEN YOU'RE GONE THINGS WILL GET BACK TO NORMAL AND I CAN GET BACK TO BUSINESS.
IF WE DON'T STOP THE GLASHAN AND PYRATHEON - THEN YOU WON'T HAVE A WORLD TO CARRY YOUR BUSINESS IN!

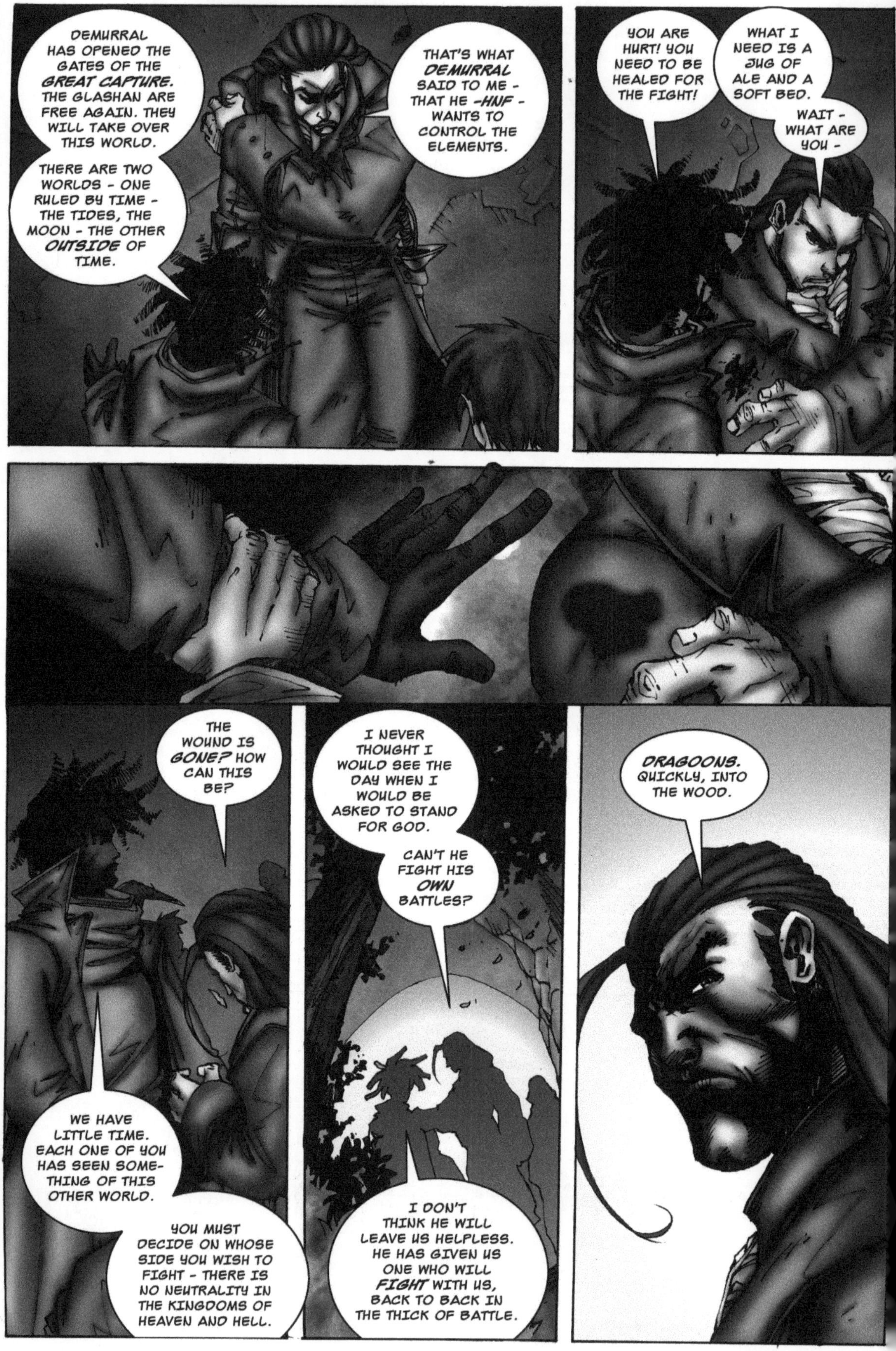
DEMURRAL HAS OPENED THE GATES OF THE GREAT CAPTURE. THE GLASHAN ARE FREE AGAIN. THEY WILL TAKE OVER THIS WORLD.
THERE ARE TWO WORLDS - ONE RULED BY TIME - THE TIDES, THE MOON - THE OTHER OUTSIDE OF TIME.
THAT'S WHAT DEMURRAL SAID TO ME - THAT HE -HNF - WANTS TO CONTROL THE ELEMENTS.
YOU ARE HURT! YOU NEED TO BE HEALED FOR THE FIGHT!
WHAT I NEED IS A JUG OF ALE AND A SOFT BED.
WAIT - WHAT ARE YOU -
THE WOUND IS GONE? HOW CAN THIS BE?
WE HAVE LITTLE TIME. EACH ONE OF YOU HAS SEEN SOMETHING OF THIS OTHER WORLD.
YOU MUST DECIDE ON WHOSE SIDE YOU WISH TO FIGHT - THERE IS NO NEUTRALITY IN THE KINGDOMS OF HEAVEN AND HELL.
I NEVER THOUGHT I WOULD SEE THE DAY WHEN I WOULD BE ASKED TO STAND FOR GOD.
CAN'T HE FIGHT HIS OWN BATTLES?
I DON'T THINK HE WILL LEAVE US HELPLESS. HE HAS GIVEN US ONE WHO WILL FIGHT WITH US, BACK TO BACK IN THE THICK OF BATTLE.
DRAGOONS. QUICKLY, INTO THE WOOD.

THIS IS THE PLACE OF THE *VARRIGAL*! THEY MIGHT BE HERE AGAIN!

WHATEVER THEY ARE, THEY CAN'T STOP US - WE HAVE THREE PISTOLS, A BARREL OF POWDER AND TWO SWORDS -

- THAT'S ENOUGH FOR *TWENTY* DRAGOONS.

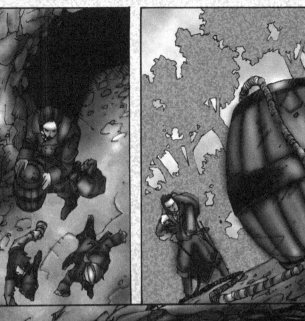

DRAW YOUR PISTOLS. THEY MAY BE ANYWHERE DOWN HERE.

FARRELL.

HISSS

WHAT THE -

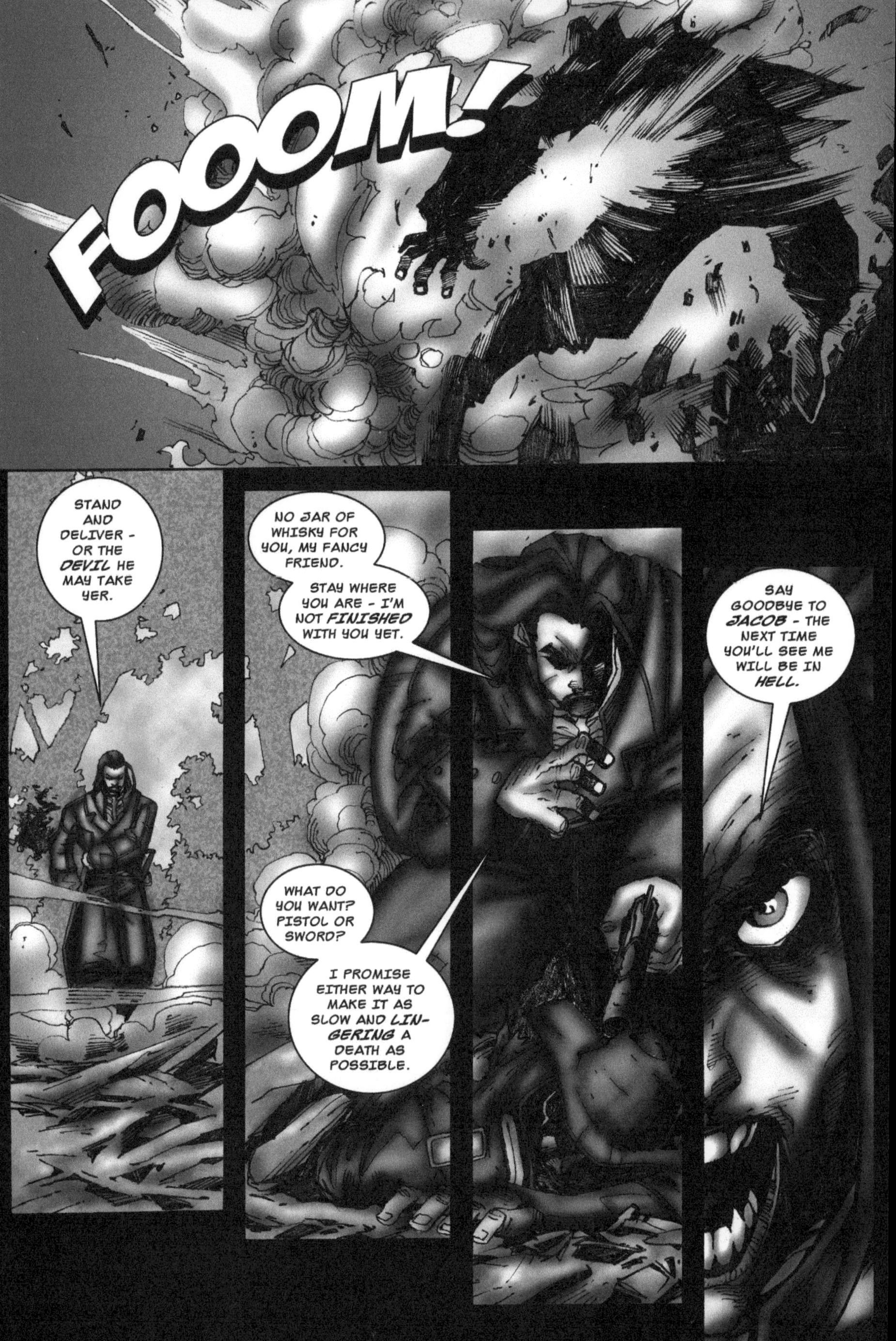
FOOOM!
STAND AND DELIVER - OR THE DEVIL HE MAY TAKE YER.
NO JAR OF WHISKY FOR YOU, MY FANCY FRIEND.
STAY WHERE YOU ARE - I'M NOT FINISHED WITH YOU YET.
WHAT DO YOU WANT? PISTOL OR SWORD?
I PROMISE EITHER WAY TO MAKE IT AS SLOW AND LIN-GERING A DEATH AS POSSIBLE.
SAY GOODBYE TO JACOB - THE NEXT TIME YOU'LL SEE ME WILL BE IN HELL.

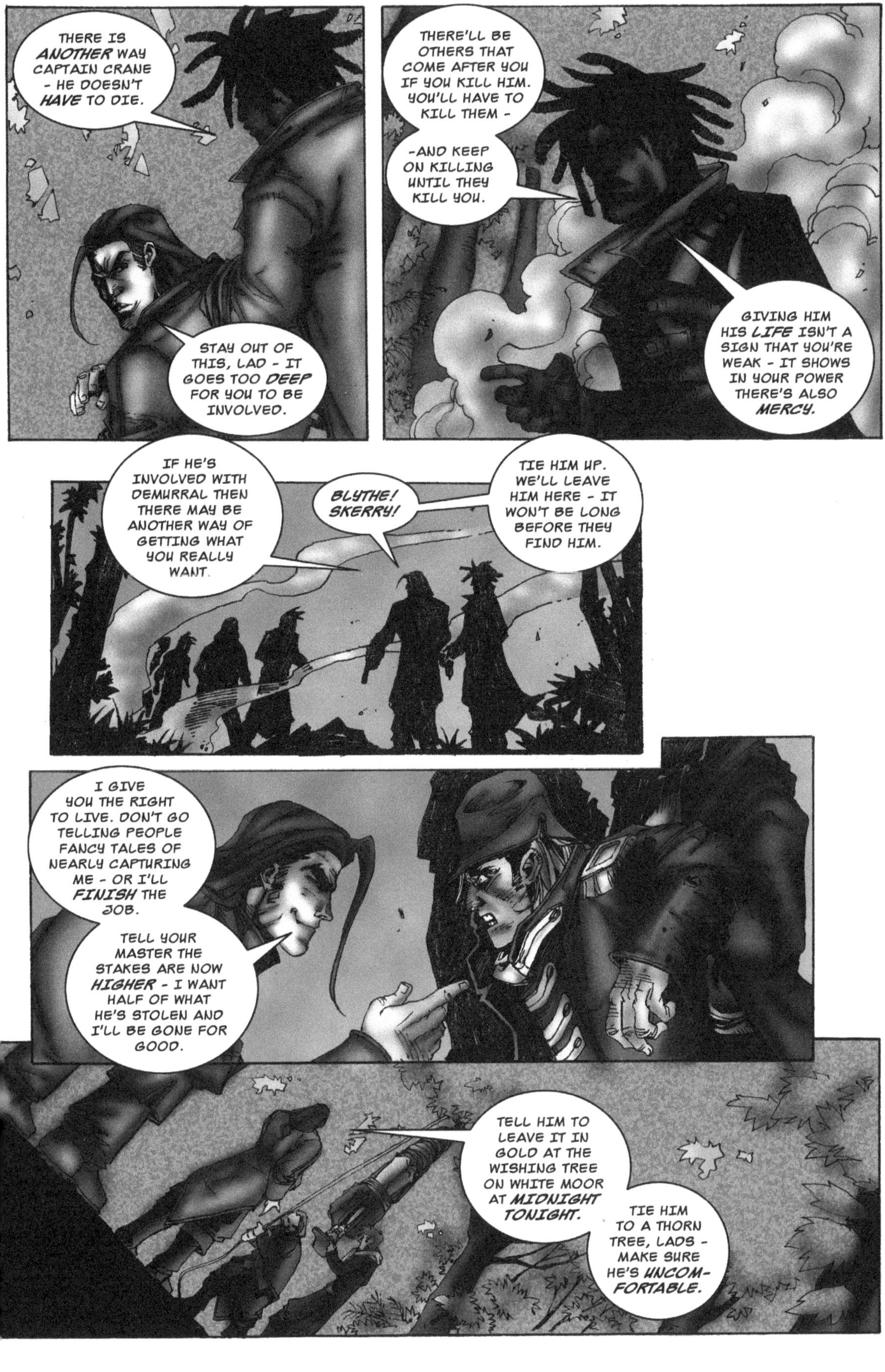
THERE IS ANOTHER WAY CAPTAIN CRANE - HE DOESN'T HAVE TO DIE.
STAY OUT OF THIS, LAD - IT GOES TOO DEEP FOR YOU TO BE INVOLVED.
THERE'LL BE OTHERS THAT COME AFTER YOU IF YOU KILL HIM. YOU'LL HAVE TO KILL THEM -
-AND KEEP ON KILLING UNTIL THEY KILL YOU.
GIVING HIM HIS LIFE ISN'T A SIGN THAT YOU'RE WEAK - IT SHOWS IN YOUR POWER THERE'S ALSO MERCY.
IF HE'S INVOLVED WITH DEMURRAL THEN THERE MAY BE ANOTHER WAY OF GETTING WHAT YOU REALLY WANT.
BLYTHE! SKERRY!
TIE HIM UP. WE'LL LEAVE HIM HERE - IT WON'T BE LONG BEFORE THEY FIND HIM.
I GIVE YOU THE RIGHT TO LIVE. DON'T GO TELLING PEOPLE FANCY TALES OF NEARLY CAPTURING ME - OR I'LL FINISH THE JOB.
TELL YOUR MASTER THE STAKES ARE NOW HIGHER - I WANT HALF OF WHAT HE'S STOLEN AND I'LL BE GONE FOR GOOD.
TELL HIM TO LEAVE IT IN GOLD AT THE WISHING TREE ON WHITE MOOR AT MIDNIGHT TONIGHT.
TIE HIM TO A THORN TREE, LADS - MAKE SURE HE'S UNCOMFORTABLE.

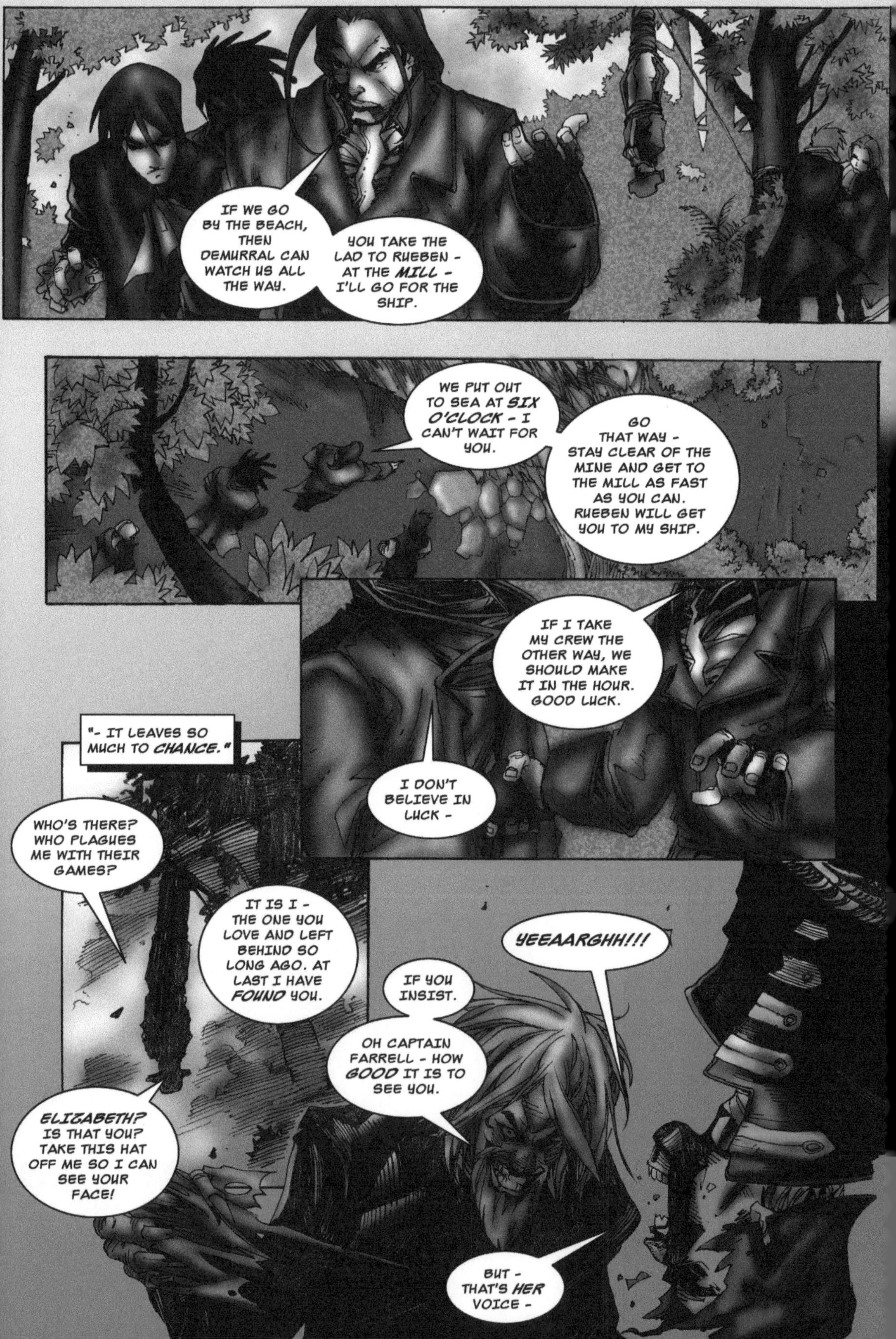
IF WE GO BY THE BEACH, THEN DEMURRAL CAN WATCH US ALL THE WAY.
YOU TAKE THE LAD TO RUEBEN - AT THE MILL - I'LL GO FOR THE SHIP.
WE PUT OUT TO SEA AT SIX O'CLOCK - I CAN'T WAIT FOR YOU.
GO THAT WAY - STAY CLEAR OF THE MINE AND GET TO THE MILL AS FAST AS YOU CAN. RUEBEN WILL GET YOU TO MY SHIP.
IF I TAKE MY CREW THE OTHER WAY, WE SHOULD MAKE IT IN THE HOUR. GOOD LUCK.
I DON'T BELIEVE IN LUCK -
"- IT LEAVES SO MUCH TO CHANCE."
WHO'S THERE? WHO PLAGUES ME WITH THEIR GAMES?
IT IS I - THE ONE YOU LOVE AND LEFT BEHIND SO LONG AGO. AT LAST I HAVE FOUND YOU.
ELIZABETH? IS THAT YOU? TAKE THIS HAT OFF ME SO I CAN SEE YOUR FACE!
IF YOU INSIST.
OH CAPTAIN FARRELL - HOW GOOD IT IS TO SEE YOU.
YEEAARGHH!!!
BUT - THAT'S HER VOICE -

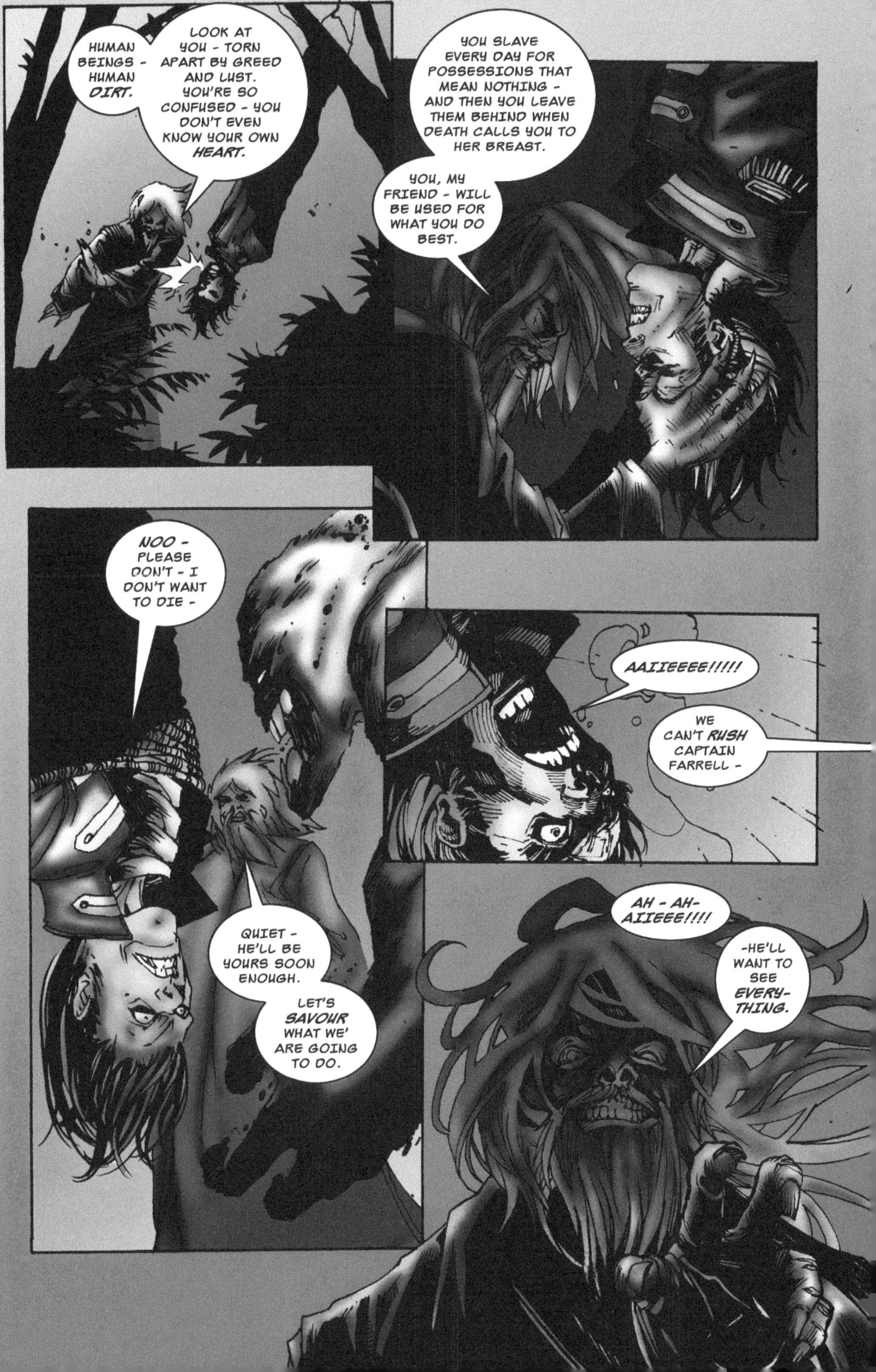
HUMAN BEINGS - HUMAN DIRT.
LOOK AT YOU - TORN APART BY GREED AND LUST. YOU'RE SO CONFUSED - YOU DON'T EVEN KNOW YOUR OWN HEART.
YOU SLAVE EVERY DAY FOR POSSESSIONS THAT MEAN NOTHING - AND THEN YOU LEAVE THEM BEHIND WHEN DEATH CALLS YOU TO HER BREAST.
YOU, MY FRIEND - WILL BE USED FOR WHAT YOU DO BEST.
NOO - PLEASE DON'T - I DON'T WANT TO DIE -
QUIET - HE'LL BE YOURS SOON ENOUGH.
LET'S SAVOUR WHAT WE' ARE GOING TO DO.
AAIIEEEE!!!!!
WE CAN'T RUSH CAPTAIN FARRELL -
AH - AH- AIIEEE!!!!
-HE'LL WANT TO SEE EVERY-THING.

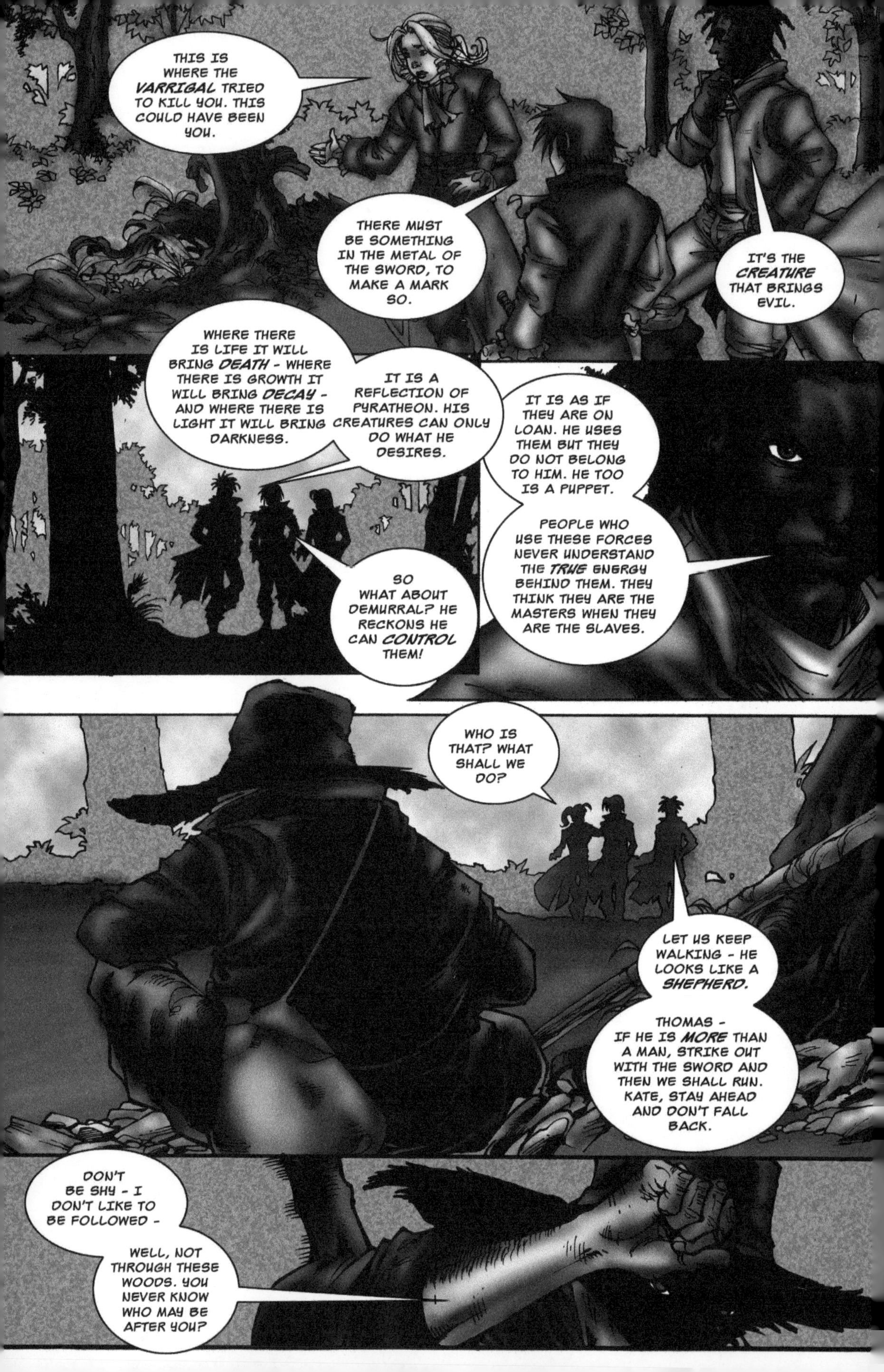
THIS IS WHERE THE VARRIGAL TRIED TO KILL YOU. THIS COULD HAVE BEEN YOU.
THERE MUST BE SOMETHING IN THE METAL OF THE SWORD, TO MAKE A MARK SO.
IT'S THE CREATURE THAT BRINGS EVIL.
WHERE THERE IS LIFE IT WILL BRING DEATH - WHERE THERE IS GROWTH IT WILL BRING DECAY - AND WHERE THERE IS LIGHT IT WILL BRING DARKNESS.
IT IS A REFLECTION OF PYRATHEON. HIS CREATURES CAN ONLY DO WHAT HE DESIRES.
SO WHAT ABOUT DEMURRAL? HE RECKONS HE CAN CONTROL THEM!
IT IS AS IF THEY ARE ON LOAN. HE USES THEM BUT THEY DO NOT BELONG TO HIM. HE TOO IS A PUPPET.
PEOPLE WHO USE THESE FORCES NEVER UNDERSTAND THE TRUE ENERGY BEHIND THEM. THEY THINK THEY ARE THE MASTERS WHEN THEY ARE THE SLAVES.
WHO IS THAT? WHAT SHALL WE DO?
LET US KEEP WALKING - HE LOOKS LIKE A SHEPHERD.
THOMAS - IF HE IS MORE THAN A MAN, STRIKE OUT WITH THE SWORD AND THEN WE SHALL RUN. KATE, STAY AHEAD AND DON'T FALL BACK.
DON'T BE SHY - I DON'T LIKE TO BE FOLLOWED -
WELL, NOT THROUGH THESE WOODS. YOU NEVER KNOW WHO MAY BE AFTER YOU?

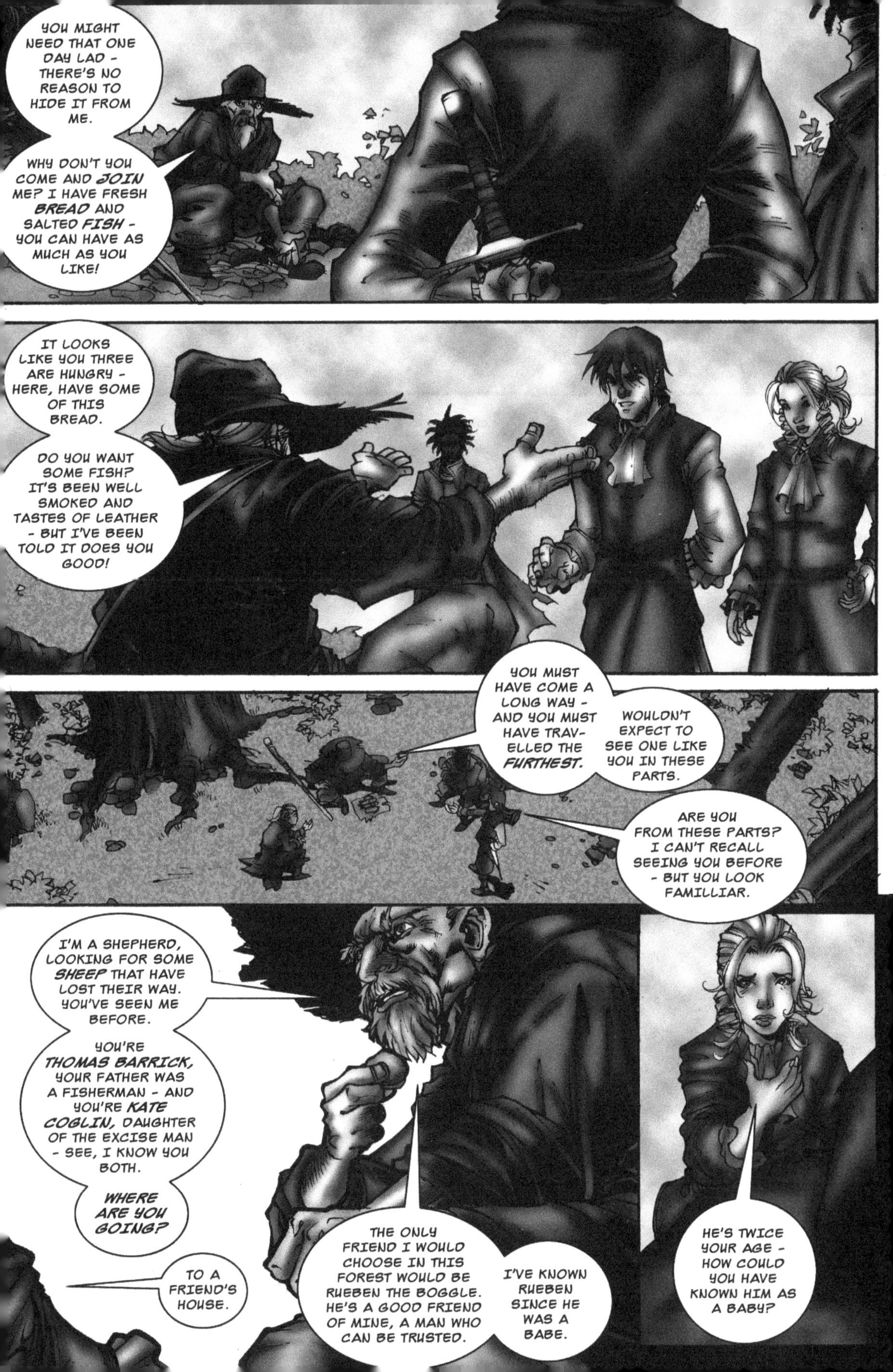
YOU MIGHT NEED THAT ONE DAY LAD - THERE'S NO REASON TO HIDE IT FROM ME.
WHY DON'T YOU COME AND JOIN ME? I HAVE FRESH BREAD AND SALTED FISH - YOU CAN HAVE AS MUCH AS YOU LIKE!
IT LOOKS LIKE YOU THREE ARE HUNGRY - HERE, HAVE SOME OF THIS BREAD.
DO YOU WANT SOME FISH? IT'S BEEN WELL SMOKED AND TASTES OF LEATHER - BUT I'VE BEEN TOLD IT DOES YOU GOOD!
YOU MUST HAVE COME A LONG WAY - AND YOU MUST HAVE TRAV-ELLED THE FURTHEST.
WOULDN'T EXPECT TO SEE ONE LIKE YOU IN THESE PARTS.
ARE YOU FROM THESE PARTS? I CAN'T RECALL SEEING YOU BEFORE - BUT YOU LOOK FAMILLIAR.
I'M A SHEPHERD, LOOKING FOR SOME SHEEP THAT HAVE LOST THEIR WAY. YOU'VE SEEN ME BEFORE.
YOU'RE THOMAS BARRICK, YOUR FATHER WAS A FISHERMAN - AND YOU'RE KATE COGLIN, DAUGHTER OF THE EXCISE MAN - SEE, I KNOW YOU BOTH.
WHERE ARE YOU GOING?
TO A FRIEND'S HOUSE.
THE ONLY FRIEND I WOULD CHOOSE IN THIS FOREST WOULD BE RUEBEN THE BOGGLE. HE'S A GOOD FRIEND OF MINE, A MAN WHO CAN BE TRUSTED.
I'VE KNOWN RUEBEN SINCE HE WAS A BABE.
HE'S TWICE YOUR AGE - HOW COULD YOU HAVE KNOWN HIM AS A BABY?

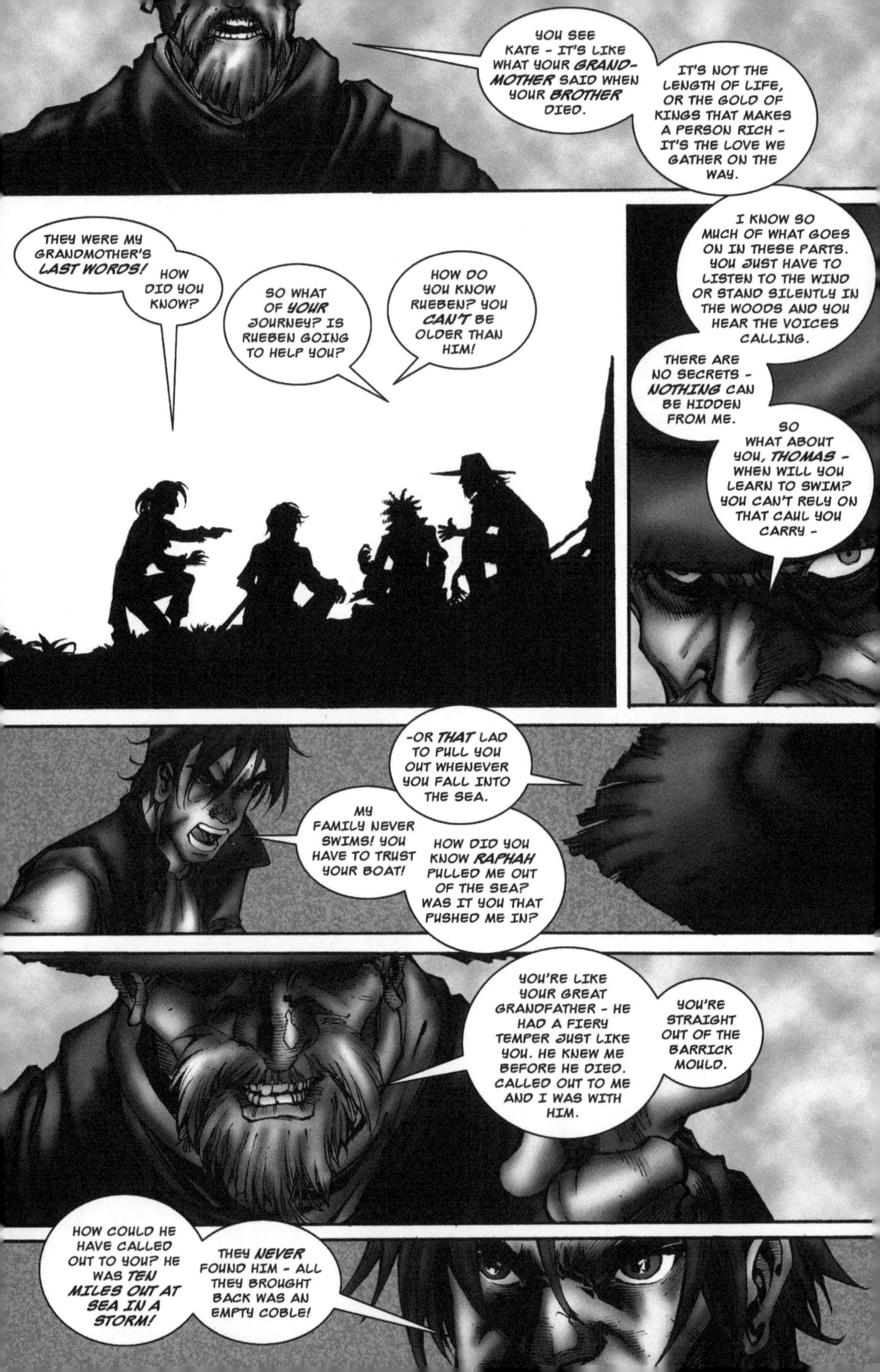
YOU SEE KATE - IT'S LIKE WHAT YOUR GRANDMOTHER SAID WHEN YOUR BROTHER DIED.
IT'S NOT THE LENGTH OF LIFE, OR THE GOLD OF KINGS THAT MAKES A PERSON RICH - IT'S THE LOVE WE GATHER ON THE WAY.
THEY WERE MY GRANDMOTHER'S LAST WORDS!
HOW DID YOU KNOW?
SO WHAT OF YOUR JOURNEY? IS RUEBEN GOING TO HELP YOU?
HOW DO YOU KNOW RUEBEN? YOU CAN'T BE OLDER THAN HIM!
I KNOW SO MUCH OF WHAT GOES ON IN THESE PARTS. YOU JUST HAVE TO LISTEN TO THE WIND OR STAND SILENTLY IN THE WOODS AND YOU HEAR THE VOICES CALLING.
THERE ARE NO SECRETS - NOTHING CAN BE HIDDEN FROM ME.
SO WHAT ABOUT YOU, THOMAS - WHEN WILL YOU LEARN TO SWIM? YOU CAN'T RELY ON THAT CAUL YOU CARRY -
-OR THAT LAD TO PULL YOU OUT WHENEVER YOU FALL INTO THE SEA.
MY FAMILY NEVER SWIMS! YOU HAVE TO TRUST YOUR BOAT!
HOW DID YOU KNOW RAPHAH PULLED ME OUT OF THE SEA? WAS IT YOU THAT PUSHED ME IN?
YOU'RE LIKE YOUR GREAT GRANDFATHER - HE HAD A FIERY TEMPER JUST LIKE YOU. HE KNEW ME BEFORE HE DIED. CALLED OUT TO ME AND I WAS WITH HIM.
YOU'RE STRAIGHT OUT OF THE BARRICK MOULD.
HOW COULD HE HAVE CALLED OUT TO YOU? HE WAS TEN MILES OUT AT SEA IN A STORM!
THEY NEVER FOUND HIM - ALL THEY BROUGHT BACK WAS AN EMPTY COBLE!

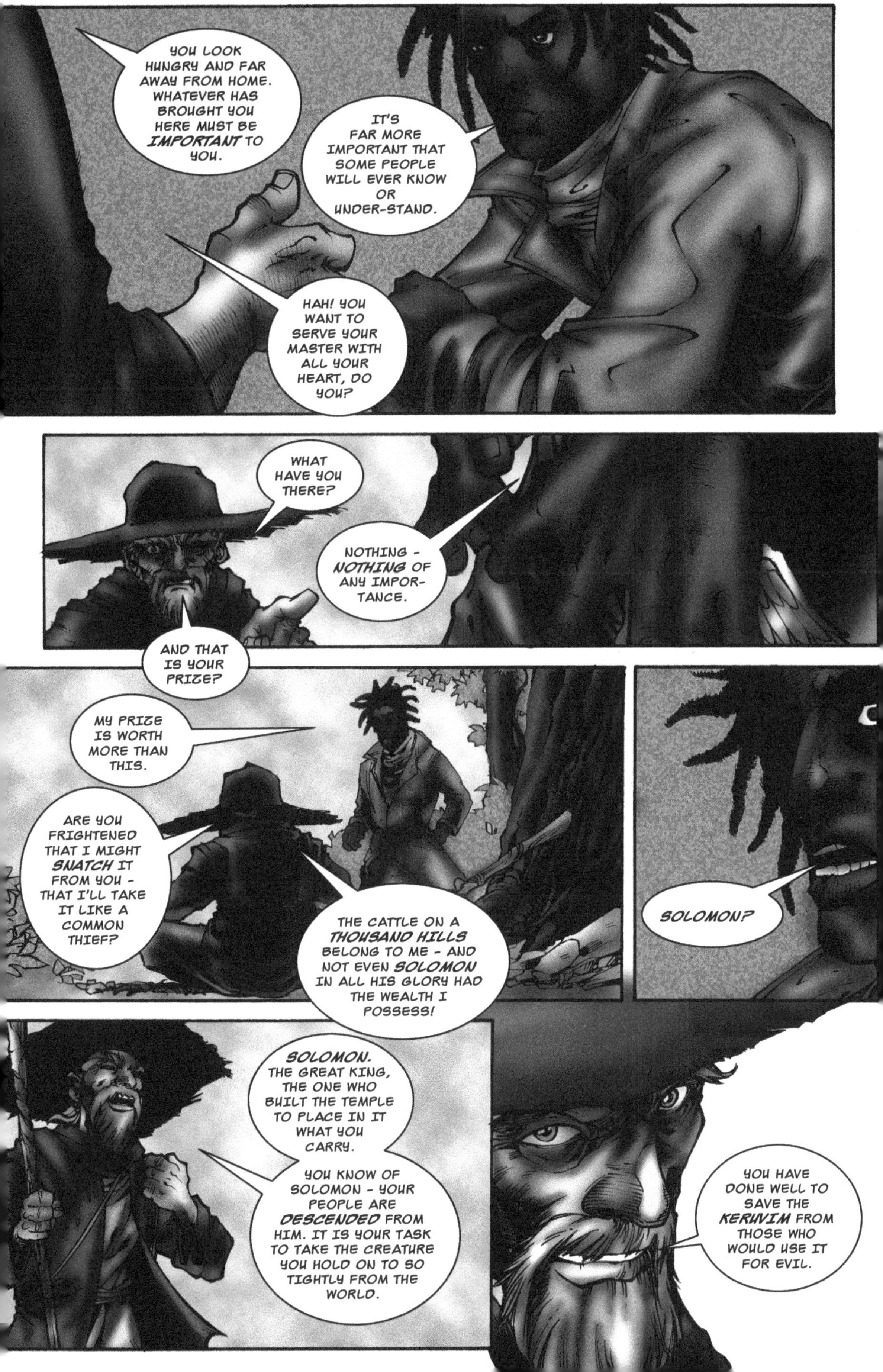
YOU LOOK HUNGRY AND FAR AWAY FROM HOME. WHATEVER HAS BROUGHT YOU HERE MUST BE *IMPORTANT* TO YOU.
IT'S FAR MORE IMPORTANT THAT SOME PEOPLE WILL EVER KNOW OR UNDER-STAND.
HAH! YOU WANT TO SERVE YOUR MASTER WITH ALL YOUR HEART, DO YOU?
WHAT HAVE YOU THERE?
NOTHING - *NOTHING* OF ANY IMPOR-TANCE.
AND THAT IS YOUR PRIZE?
MY PRIZE IS WORTH MORE THAN THIS.
ARE YOU FRIGHTENED THAT I MIGHT *SNATCH* IT FROM YOU - THAT I'LL TAKE IT LIKE A COMMON THIEF?
THE CATTLE ON A *THOUSAND HILLS* BELONG TO ME - AND NOT EVEN *SOLOMON* IN ALL HIS GLORY HAD THE WEALTH I POSSESS!
SOLOMON?
SOLOMON. THE GREAT KING, THE ONE WHO BUILT THE TEMPLE TO PLACE IN IT WHAT YOU CARRY.
YOU KNOW OF SOLOMON - YOUR PEOPLE ARE *DESCENDED* FROM HIM. IT IS YOUR TASK TO TAKE THE CREATURE YOU HOLD ON TO SO TIGHTLY FROM THE WORLD.
YOU HAVE DONE WELL TO SAVE THE *KERUVIM* FROM THOSE WHO WOULD USE IT FOR EVIL.

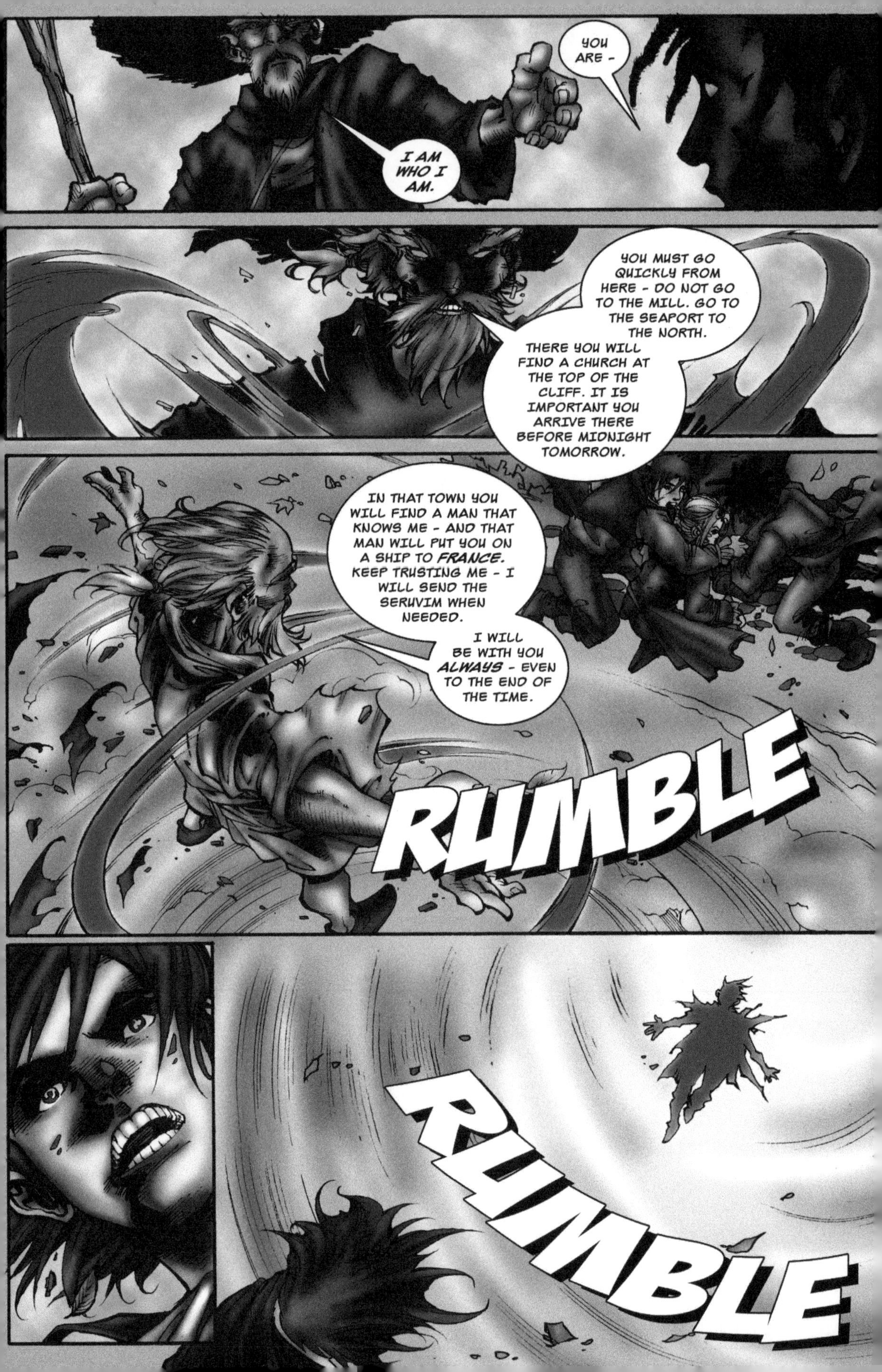
YOU ARE -
I AM WHO I AM.
YOU MUST GO QUICKLY FROM HERE - DO NOT GO TO THE MILL. GO TO THE SEAPORT TO THE NORTH.
THERE YOU WILL FIND A CHURCH AT THE TOP OF THE CLIFF. IT IS IMPORTANT YOU ARRIVE THERE BEFORE MIDNIGHT TOMORROW.
IN THAT TOWN YOU WILL FIND A MAN THAT KNOWS ME - AND THAT MAN WILL PUT YOU ON A SHIP TO FRANCE. KEEP TRUSTING ME - I WILL SEND THE SERUVIM WHEN NEEDED.
I WILL BE WITH YOU ALWAYS - EVEN TO THE END OF THE TIME.
RUMBLE
RUMBLE

IT'S STOPPED!

WAS THAT —

IT WAS *RIATHAMUS* - I JUST KNOW IT WAS.

HOW DO YOU KNOW IT WASN'T THOSE CREATURES IN ANOTHER FORM?

HE COULD HAVE KILLED US WITH THAT STORM! WHERE IS HE NOW, HOW CAN YOU BE SURE IT WAS HIM?

I JUST KNOW, DON'T ASK ME HOW. IT WAS SOMETHING IN HIS EYES, HOW HE KNEW SO MUCH ABOUT US.

THEN WE DO AS HE SAYS. WHITBY IS A GOOD WALK - IT'LL BE DARK WITHIN TWO HOURS AND WE'LL NEVER MAKE IT BEFORE NIGHT-FALL.

WHAT'S INSIDE?

BREAD, FISH, SOME GOLD COINS AND A SMALL SILVER FLASK.

THERE'S SOMETHING ELSE - TWO PIECES OF *STONE* -

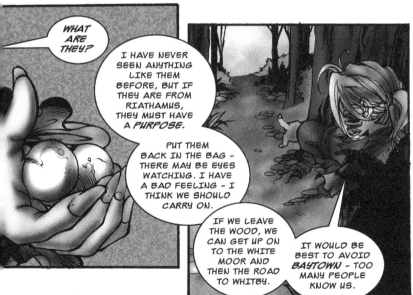

WHAT ARE THEY?

I HAVE NEVER SEEN ANYTHING LIKE THEM BEFORE, BUT IF THEY ARE FROM RIATHAMUS, THEY MUST HAVE A *PURPOSE*.

PUT THEM BACK IN THE BAG - THERE MAY BE EYES WATCHING. I HAVE A BAD FEELING - I THINK WE SHOULD CARRY ON.

IF WE LEAVE THE WOOD, WE CAN GET UP ON TO THE WHITE MOOR AND THEN THE ROAD TO WHITBY.

IT WOULD BE BEST TO AVOID *BAYTOWN* - TOO MANY PEOPLE KNOW US.

WE TAKE THE BAG WITH US. IT HAS EVERYTHING WE NEED FOR THE JOURNEY.

IT HAS BEEN GIVEN TO US FOR A REASON -

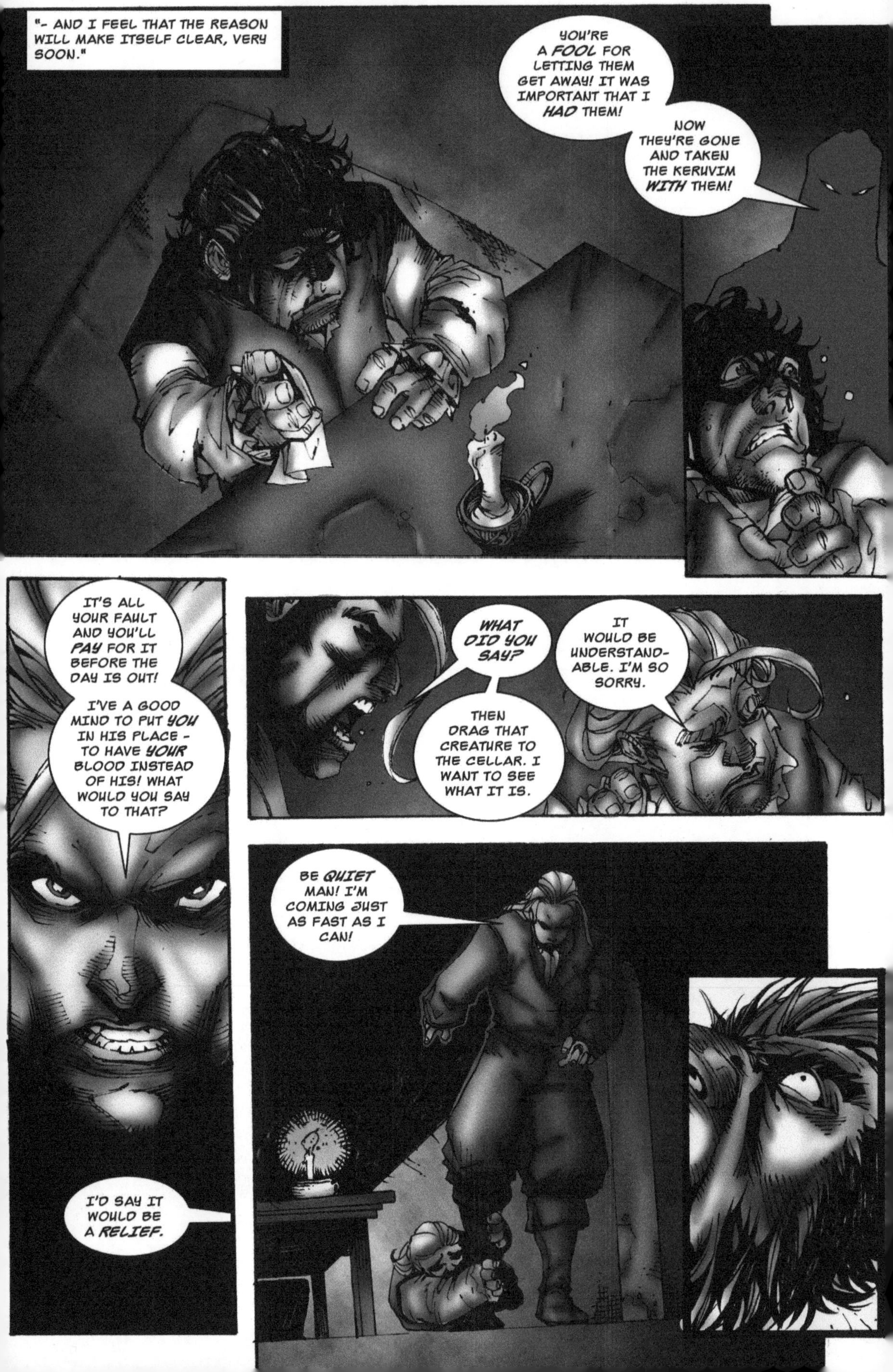
"- AND I FEEL THAT THE REASON WILL MAKE ITSELF CLEAR, VERY SOON."
YOU'RE A FOOL FOR LETTING THEM GET AWAY! IT WAS IMPORTANT THAT I HAD THEM!
NOW THEY'RE GONE AND TAKEN THE KERUVIM WITH THEM!
IT'S ALL YOUR FAULT AND YOU'LL PAY FOR IT BEFORE THE DAY IS OUT!
I'VE A GOOD MIND TO PUT YOU IN HIS PLACE - TO HAVE YOUR BLOOD INSTEAD OF HIS! WHAT WOULD YOU SAY TO THAT?
I'D SAY IT WOULD BE A RELIEF.
WHAT DID YOU SAY?
IT WOULD BE UNDERSTAND-ABLE. I'M SO SORRY.
THEN DRAG THAT CREATURE TO THE CELLAR. I WANT TO SEE WHAT IT IS.
BE QUIET MAN! I'M COMING JUST AS FAST AS I CAN!

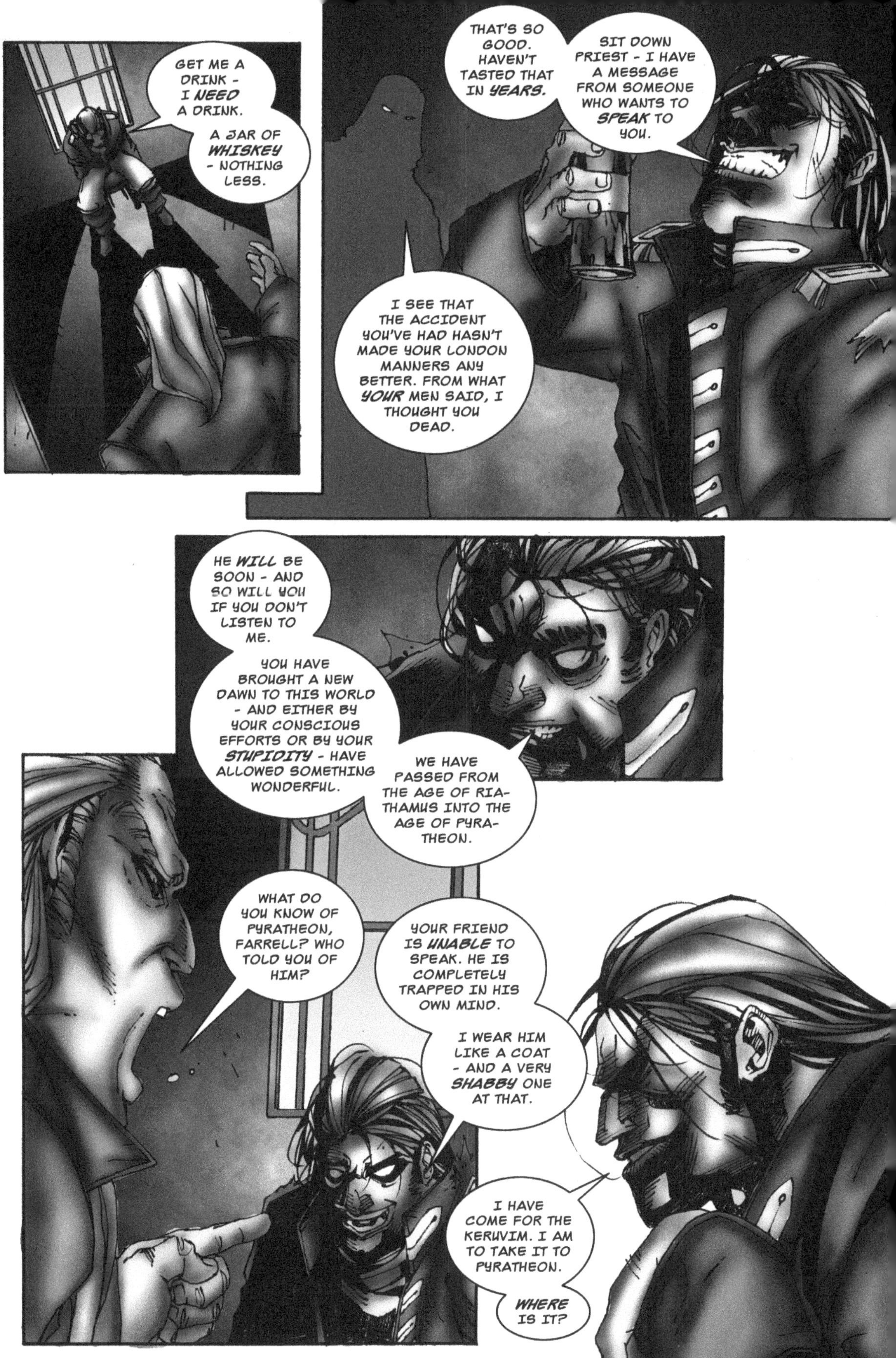
GET ME A DRINK - I NEED A DRINK.
A JAR OF WHISKEY - NOTHING LESS.
THAT'S SO GOOD. HAVEN'T TASTED THAT IN YEARS.
SIT DOWN PRIEST - I HAVE A MESSAGE FROM SOMEONE WHO WANTS TO SPEAK TO YOU.
I SEE THAT THE ACCIDENT YOU'VE HAD HASN'T MADE YOUR LONDON MANNERS ANY BETTER. FROM WHAT YOUR MEN SAID, I THOUGHT YOU DEAD.
HE WILL BE SOON - AND SO WILL YOU IF YOU DON'T LISTEN TO ME.
YOU HAVE BROUGHT A NEW DAWN TO THIS WORLD - AND EITHER BY YOUR CONSCIOUS EFFORTS OR BY YOUR STUPIDITY - HAVE ALLOWED SOMETHING WONDERFUL.
WE HAVE PASSED FROM THE AGE OF RIATHAMUS INTO THE AGE OF PYRATHEON.
WHAT DO YOU KNOW OF PYRATHEON, FARRELL? WHO TOLD YOU OF HIM?
YOUR FRIEND IS UNABLE TO SPEAK. HE IS COMPLETELY TRAPPED IN HIS OWN MIND.
I WEAR HIM LIKE A COAT - AND A VERY SHABBY ONE AT THAT.
I HAVE COME FOR THE KERUVIM. I AM TO TAKE IT TO PYRATHEON.
WHERE IS IT?

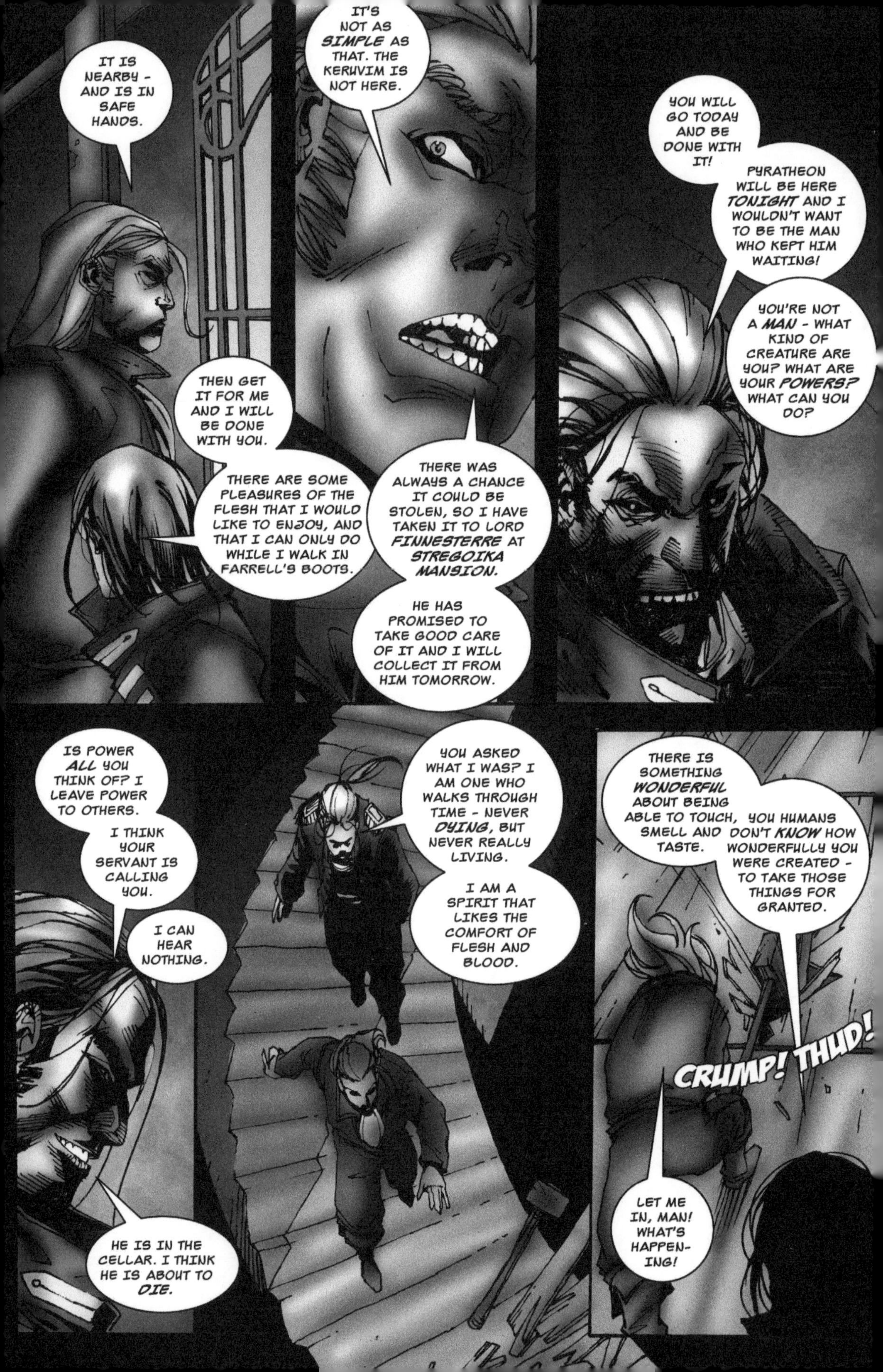

IT IS NEARBY - AND IS IN SAFE HANDS.
IT'S NOT AS SIMPLE AS THAT. THE KERUVIM IS NOT HERE.
YOU WILL GO TODAY AND BE DONE WITH IT!
PYRATHEON WILL BE HERE TONIGHT AND I WOULDN'T WANT TO BE THE MAN WHO KEPT HIM WAITING!
YOU'RE NOT A MAN - WHAT KIND OF CREATURE ARE YOU? WHAT ARE YOUR POWERS? WHAT CAN YOU DO?
THEN GET IT FOR ME AND I WILL BE DONE WITH YOU.
THERE ARE SOME PLEASURES OF THE FLESH THAT I WOULD LIKE TO ENJOY, AND THAT I CAN ONLY DO WHILE I WALK IN FARRELL'S BOOTS.
THERE WAS ALWAYS A CHANCE IT COULD BE STOLEN, SO I HAVE TAKEN IT TO LORD FINNESTERRE AT STREGOIKA MANSION.
HE HAS PROMISED TO TAKE GOOD CARE OF IT AND I WILL COLLECT IT FROM HIM TOMORROW.
IS POWER ALL YOU THINK OF? I LEAVE POWER TO OTHERS.
I THINK YOUR SERVANT IS CALLING YOU.
I CAN HEAR NOTHING.
HE IS IN THE CELLAR. I THINK HE IS ABOUT TO DIE.
YOU ASKED WHAT I WAS? I AM ONE WHO WALKS THROUGH TIME - NEVER DYING, BUT NEVER REALLY LIVING.
I AM A SPIRIT THAT LIKES THE COMFORT OF FLESH AND BLOOD.
THERE IS SOMETHING WONDERFUL ABOUT BEING ABLE TO TOUCH, SMELL AND TASTE.
YOU HUMANS DON'T KNOW HOW WONDERFULLY YOU WERE CREATED - TO TAKE THOSE THINGS FOR GRANTED.
CRUMP! THUD!
LET ME IN, MAN! WHAT'S HAPPEN-ING!

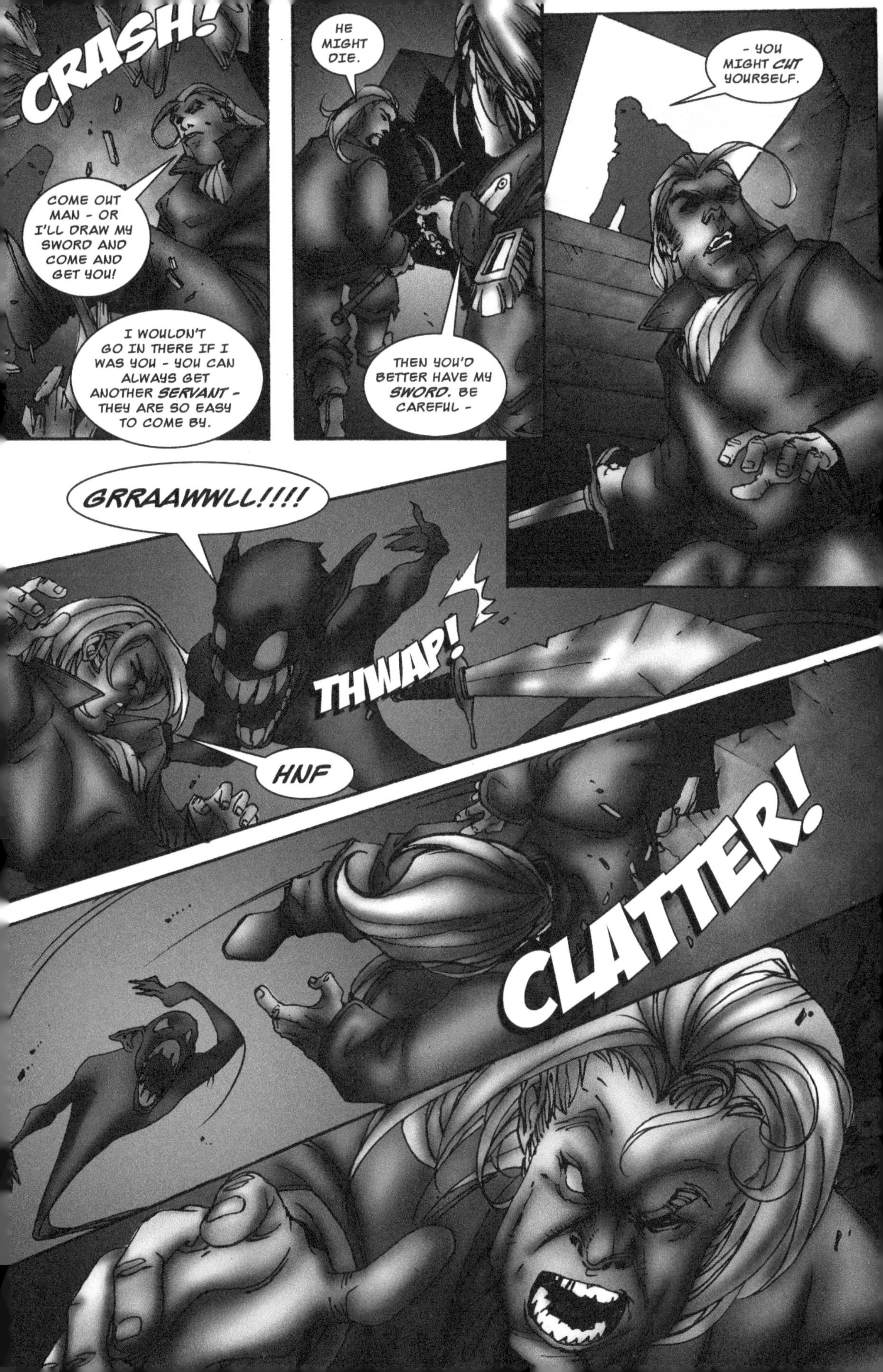
CRASH!
COME OUT MAN - OR I'LL DRAW MY SWORD AND COME AND GET YOU!
I WOULDN'T GO IN THERE IF I WAS YOU - YOU CAN ALWAYS GET ANOTHER SERVANT - THEY ARE SO EASY TO COME BY.
HE MIGHT DIE.
THEN YOU'D BETTER HAVE MY SWORD. BE CAREFUL -
- YOU MIGHT CUT YOURSELF.
GRRAAWWLL!!!!
THWAP!
HNF
CLATTER!

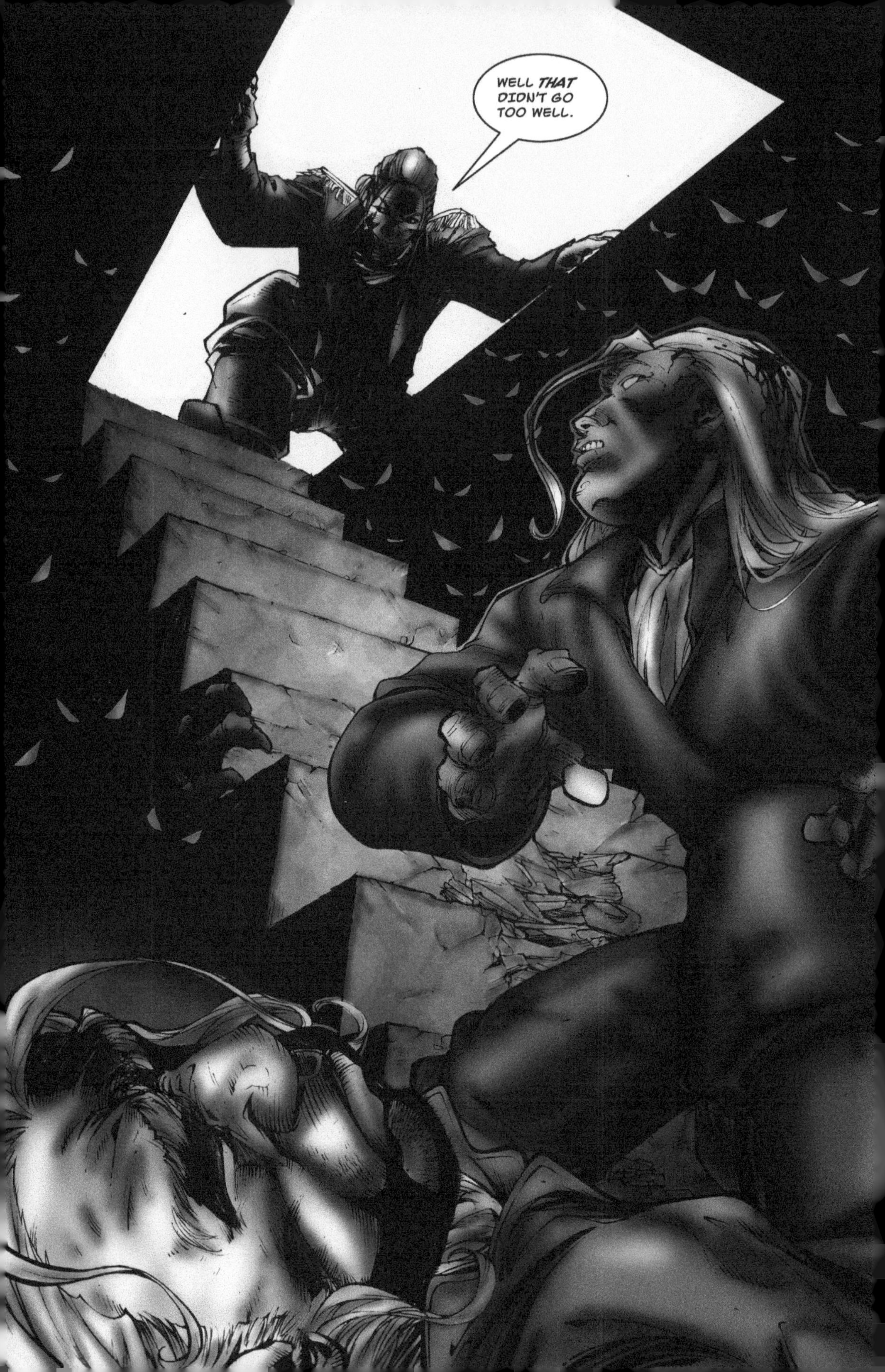
WELL *THAT* DIDN'T GO TOO WELL.

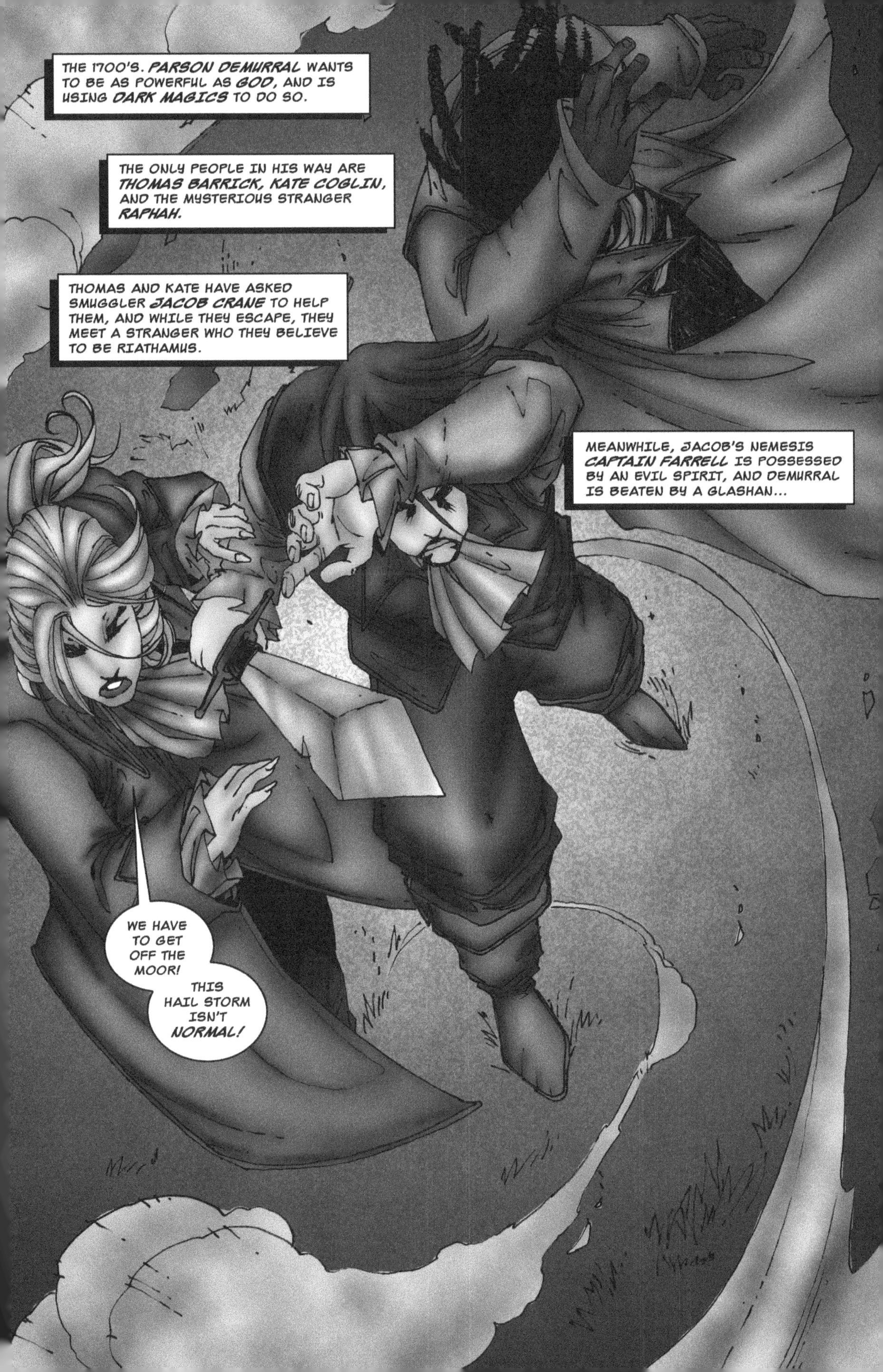
THE 1700'S. PARSON DEMURRAL WANTS TO BE AS POWERFUL AS GOD, AND IS USING DARK MAGICS TO DO SO.
THE ONLY PEOPLE IN HIS WAY ARE THOMAS BARRICK, KATE COGLIN, AND THE MYSTERIOUS STRANGER RAPHAH.
THOMAS AND KATE HAVE ASKED SMUGGLER JACOB CRANE TO HELP THEM, AND WHILE THEY ESCAPE, THEY MEET A STRANGER WHO THEY BELIEVE TO BE RIATHAMUS.
MEANWHILE, JACOB'S NEMESIS CAPTAIN FARRELL IS POSSESSED BY AN EVIL SPIRIT, AND DEMURRAL IS BEATEN BY A GLASHAN...
WE HAVE TO GET OFF THE MOOR!
THIS HAIL STORM ISN'T NORMAL!

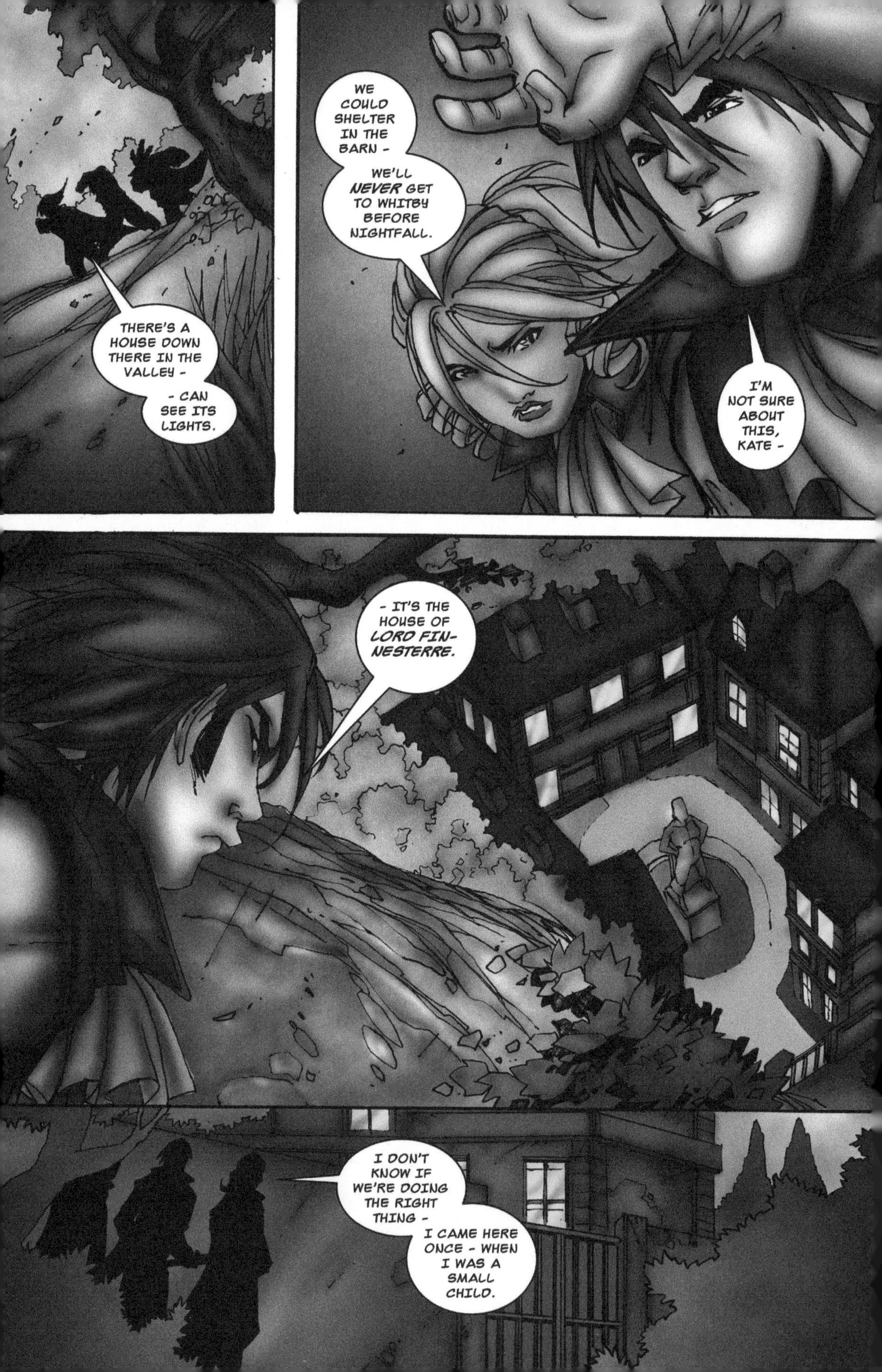
THERE'S A HOUSE DOWN THERE IN THE VALLEY -
- CAN SEE ITS LIGHTS.
WE COULD SHELTER IN THE BARN -
WE'LL NEVER GET TO WHITBY BEFORE NIGHTFALL.
I'M NOT SURE ABOUT THIS, KATE -
- IT'S THE HOUSE OF LORD FINNESTERRE.
I DON'T KNOW IF WE'RE DOING THE RIGHT THING -
I CAME HERE ONCE - WHEN I WAS A SMALL CHILD.

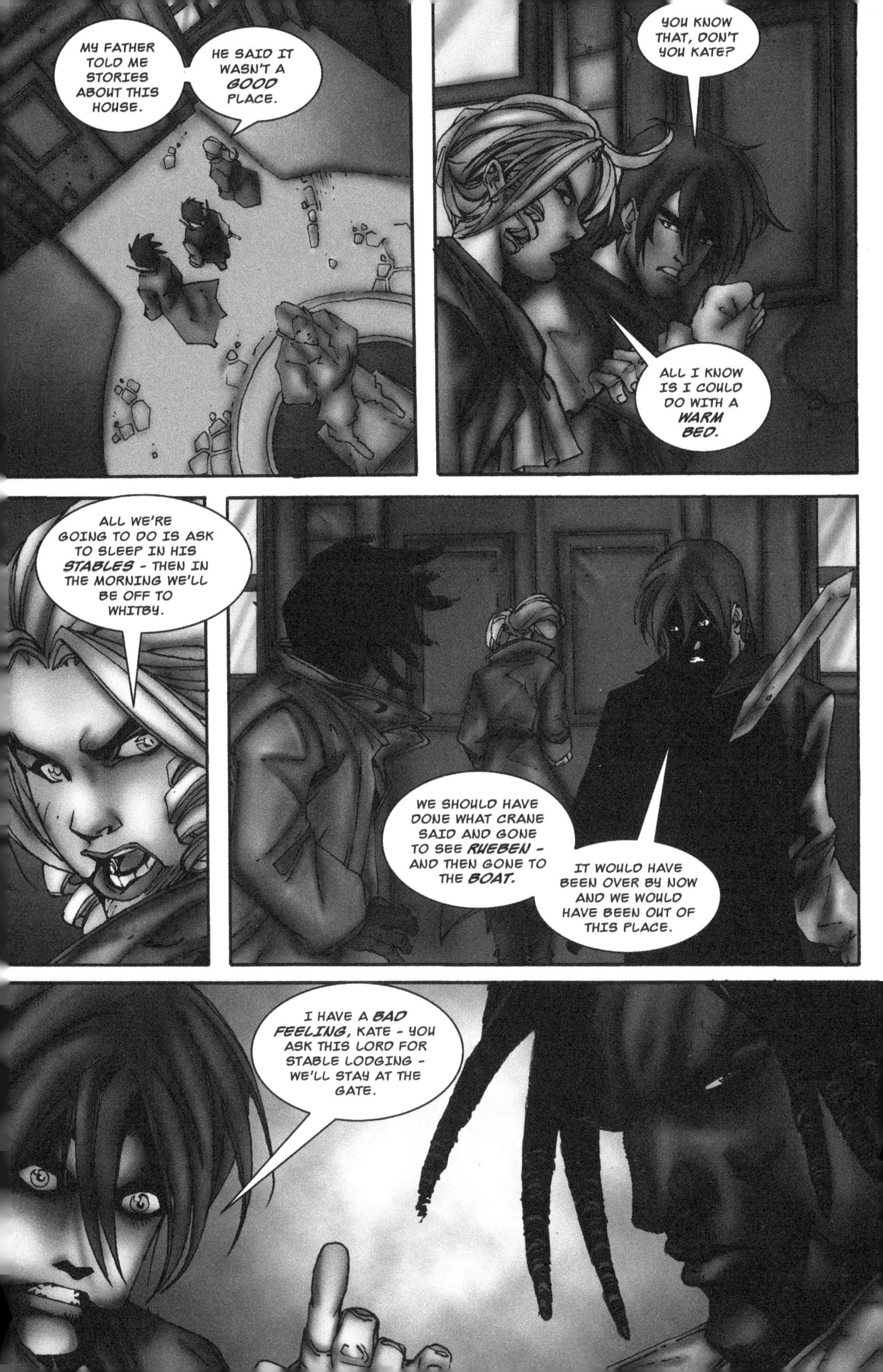
MY FATHER TOLD ME STORIES ABOUT THIS HOUSE.
HE SAID IT WASN'T A GOOD PLACE.
YOU KNOW THAT, DON'T YOU KATE?
ALL I KNOW IS I COULD DO WITH A WARM BED.
ALL WE'RE GOING TO DO IS ASK TO SLEEP IN HIS STABLES - THEN IN THE MORNING WE'LL BE OFF TO WHITBY.
WE SHOULD HAVE DONE WHAT CRANE SAID AND GONE TO SEE RUEBEN - AND THEN GONE TO THE BOAT.
IT WOULD HAVE BEEN OVER BY NOW AND WE WOULD HAVE BEEN OUT OF THIS PLACE.
I HAVE A BAD FEELING, KATE - YOU ASK THIS LORD FOR STABLE LODGING - WE'LL STAY AT THE GATE.

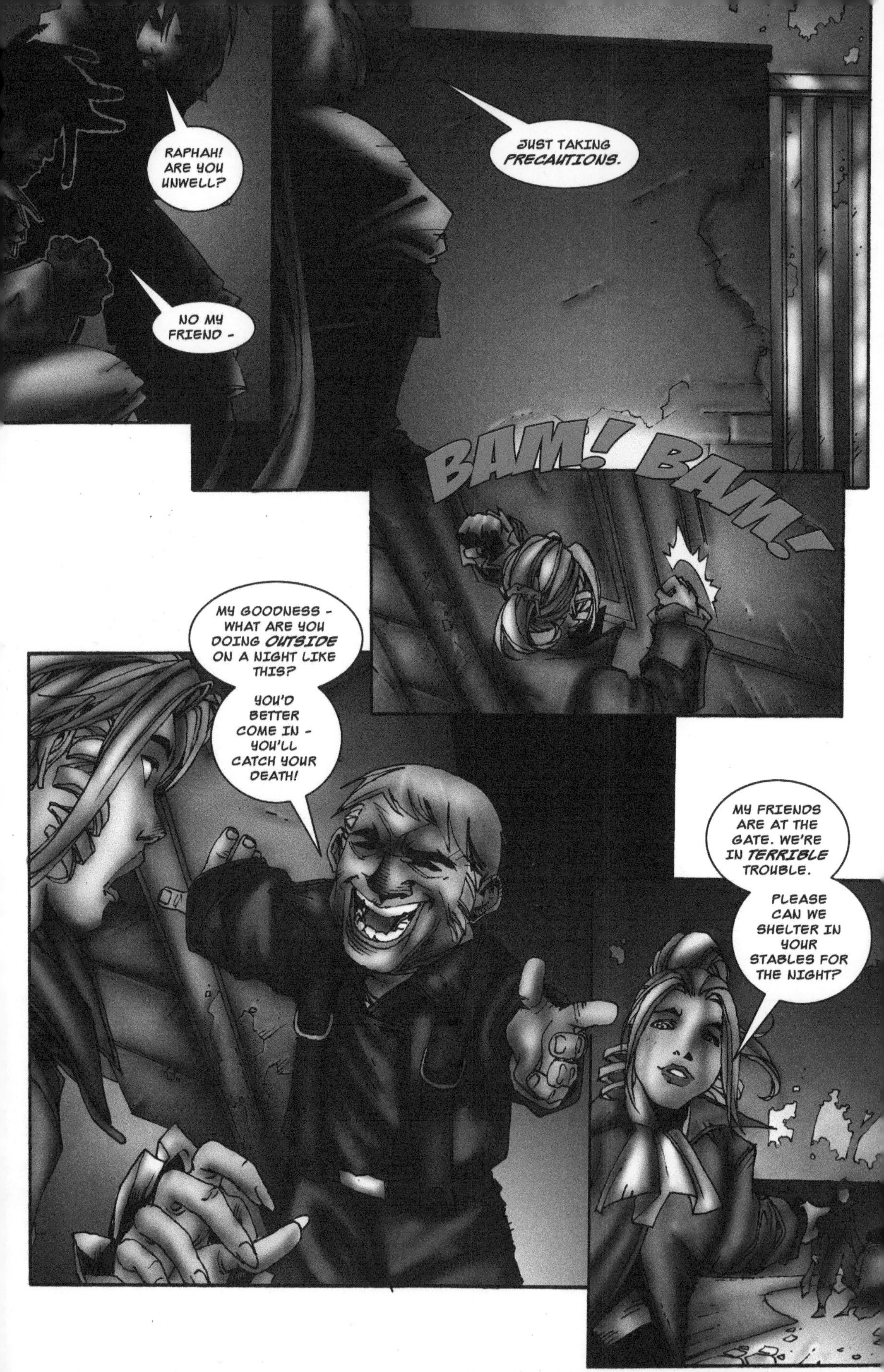
RAPHAH! ARE YOU UNWELL?
NO MY FRIEND -
JUST TAKING *PRECAUTIONS.*
BAM! BAM!
MY GOODNESS - WHAT ARE YOU DOING *OUTSIDE* ON A NIGHT LIKE THIS?
YOU'D BETTER COME IN - YOU'LL CATCH YOUR DEATH!
MY FRIENDS ARE AT THE GATE. WE'RE IN *TERRIBLE* TROUBLE.
PLEASE CAN WE SHELTER IN YOUR STABLES FOR THE NIGHT?

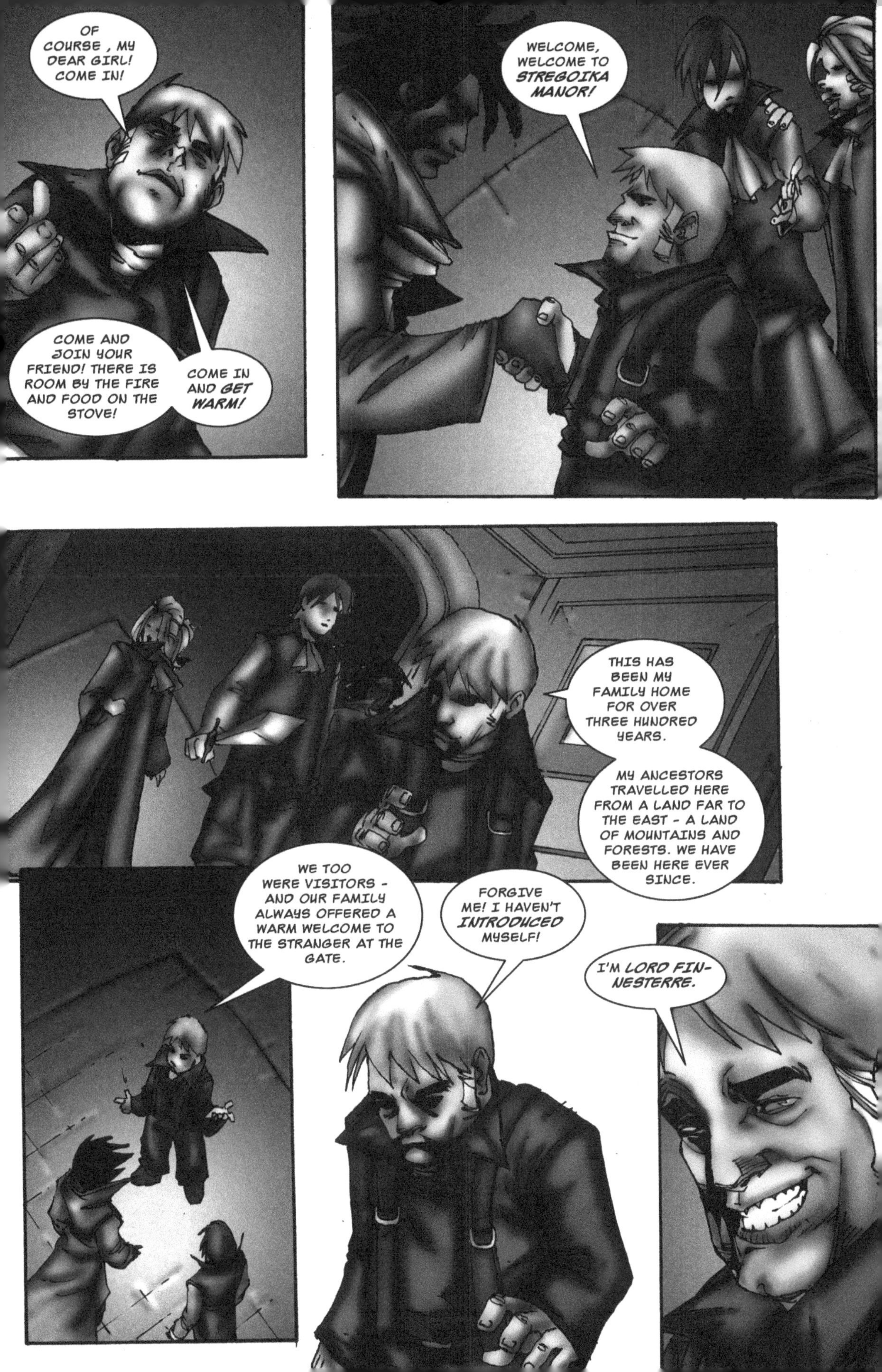
OF COURSE, MY DEAR GIRL! COME IN!
COME AND JOIN YOUR FRIEND! THERE IS ROOM BY THE FIRE AND FOOD ON THE STOVE!
COME IN AND GET WARM!
WELCOME, WELCOME TO STREGOIKA MANOR!
THIS HAS BEEN MY FAMILY HOME FOR OVER THREE HUNDRED YEARS.
MY ANCESTORS TRAVELLED HERE FROM A LAND FAR TO THE EAST - A LAND OF MOUNTAINS AND FORESTS. WE HAVE BEEN HERE EVER SINCE.
WE TOO WERE VISITORS - AND OUR FAMILY ALWAYS OFFERED A WARM WELCOME TO THE STRANGER AT THE GATE.
FORGIVE ME! I HAVEN'T INTRODUCED MYSELF!
I'M LORD FIN-NESTERRE.

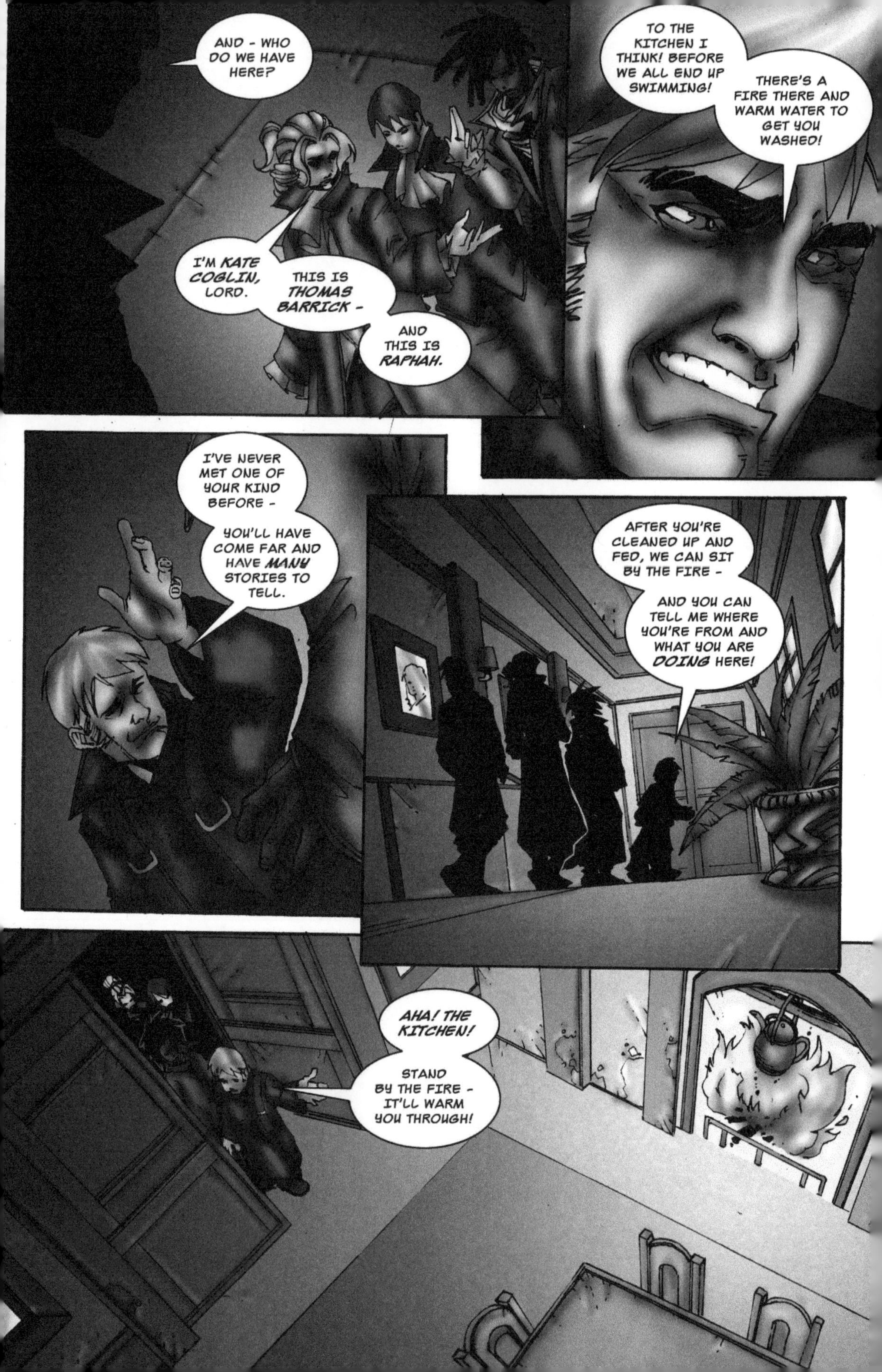
AND - WHO DO WE HAVE HERE?
I'M KATE COGLIN, LORD.
THIS IS THOMAS BARRICK -
AND THIS IS RAPHAH.
TO THE KITCHEN I THINK! BEFORE WE ALL END UP SWIMMING!
THERE'S A FIRE THERE AND WARM WATER TO GET YOU WASHED!
I'VE NEVER MET ONE OF YOUR KIND BEFORE -
YOU'LL HAVE COME FAR AND HAVE MANY STORIES TO TELL.
AFTER YOU'RE CLEANED UP AND FED, WE CAN SIT BY THE FIRE -
AND YOU CAN TELL ME WHERE YOU'RE FROM AND WHAT YOU ARE DOING HERE!
AHA! THE KITCHEN!
STAND BY THE FIRE - IT'LL WARM YOU THROUGH!

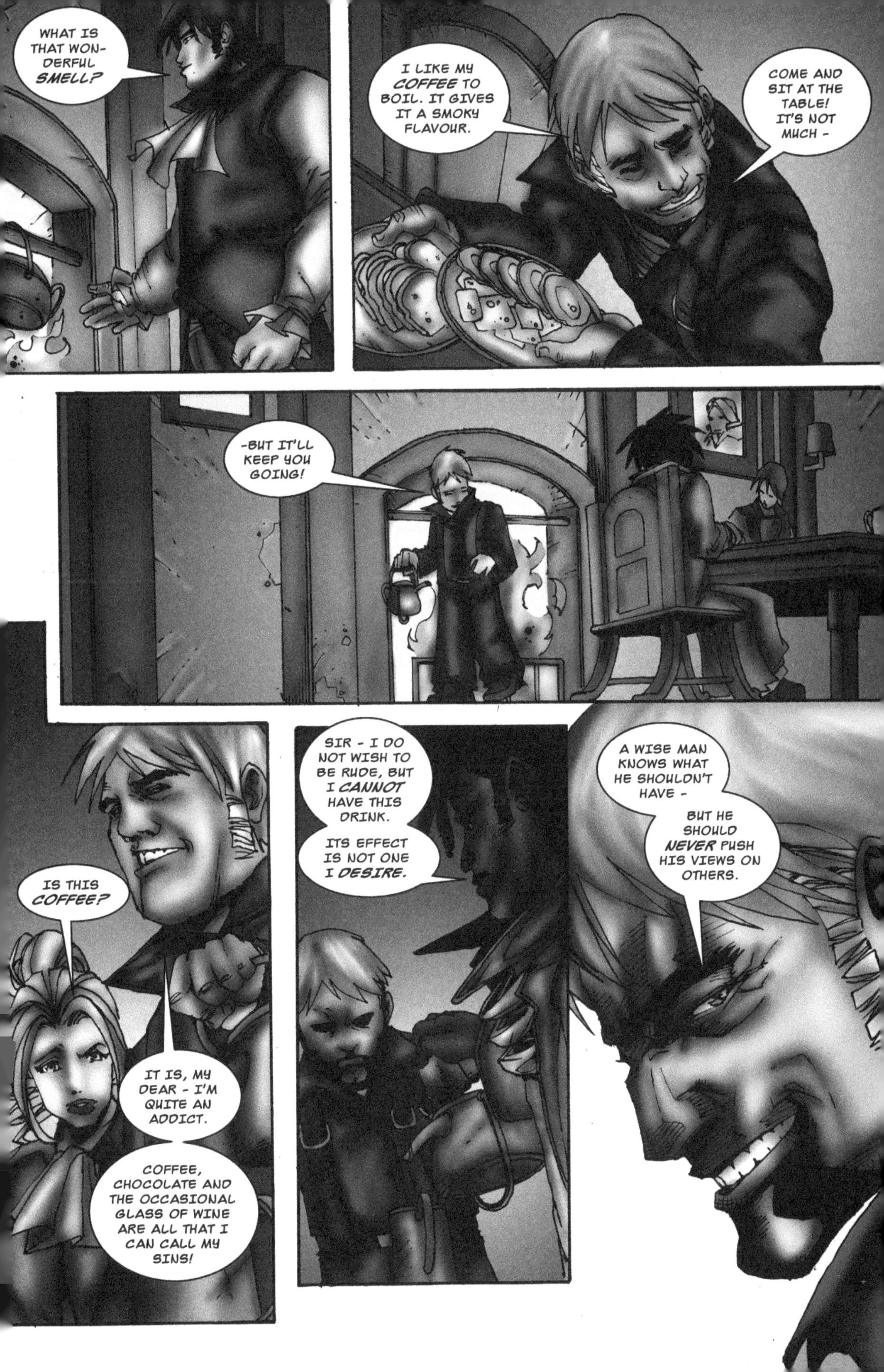

WHAT IS THAT WON-DERFUL SMELL?
I LIKE MY COFFEE TO BOIL. IT GIVES IT A SMOKY FLAVOUR.
COME AND SIT AT THE TABLE! IT'S NOT MUCH -
-BUT IT'LL KEEP YOU GOING!
IS THIS COFFEE?
IT IS, MY DEAR - I'M QUITE AN ADDICT.
COFFEE, CHOCOLATE AND THE OCCASIONAL GLASS OF WINE ARE ALL THAT I CAN CALL MY SINS!
SIR - I DO NOT WISH TO BE RUDE, BUT I CANNOT HAVE THIS DRINK.
ITS EFFECT IS NOT ONE I DESIRE.
A WISE MAN KNOWS WHAT HE SHOULDN'T HAVE -
BUT HE SHOULD NEVER PUSH HIS VIEWS ON OTHERS.

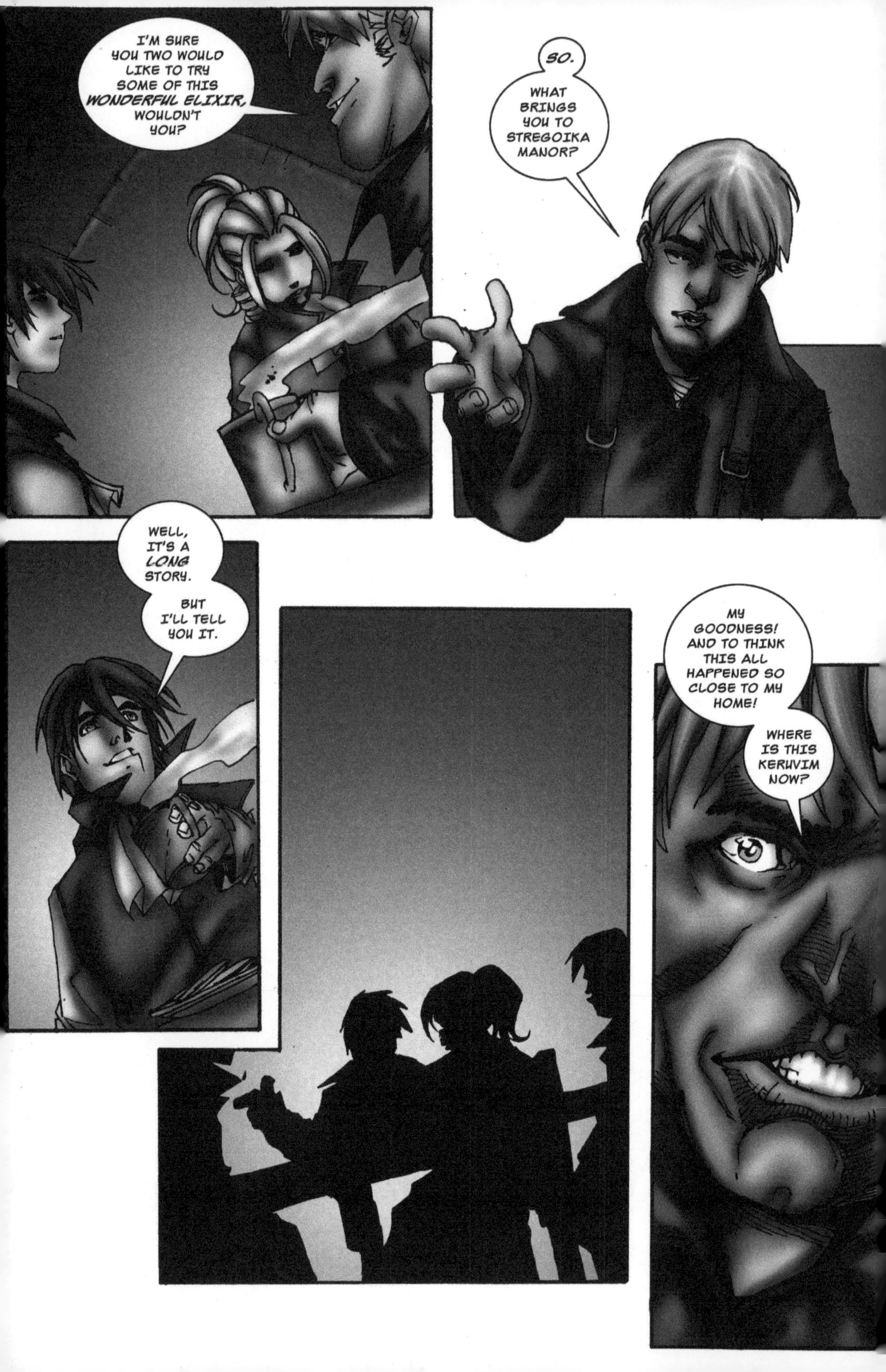
I'M SURE YOU TWO WOULD LIKE TO TRY SOME OF THIS WONDERFUL ELIXIR, WOULDN'T YOU?
SO.
WHAT BRINGS YOU TO STREGOIKA MANOR?
WELL, IT'S A LONG STORY.
BUT I'LL TELL YOU IT.
MY GOODNESS! AND TO THINK THIS ALL HAPPENED SO CLOSE TO MY HOME!
WHERE IS THIS KERUVIM NOW?

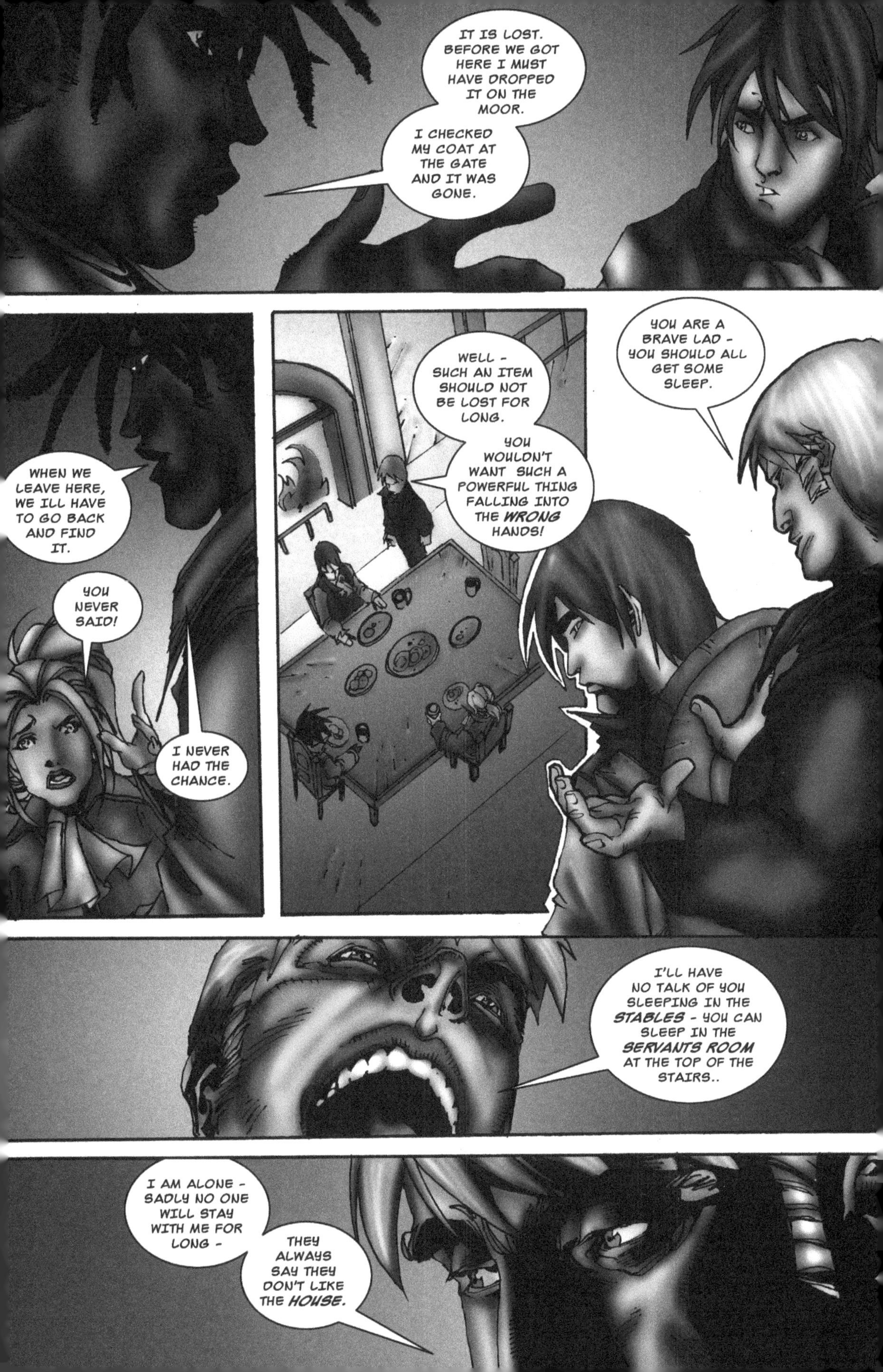
IT IS LOST. BEFORE WE GOT HERE I MUST HAVE DROPPED IT ON THE MOOR.
I CHECKED MY COAT AT THE GATE AND IT WAS GONE.
WHEN WE LEAVE HERE, WE ILL HAVE TO GO BACK AND FIND IT.
YOU NEVER SAID!
I NEVER HAD THE CHANCE.
WELL - SUCH AN ITEM SHOULD NOT BE LOST FOR LONG.
YOU WOULDN'T WANT SUCH A POWERFUL THING FALLING INTO THE WRONG HANDS!
YOU ARE A BRAVE LAD - YOU SHOULD ALL GET SOME SLEEP.
I'LL HAVE NO TALK OF YOU SLEEPING IN THE STABLES - YOU CAN SLEEP IN THE SERVANTS ROOM AT THE TOP OF THE STAIRS..
I AM ALONE - SADLY NO ONE WILL STAY WITH ME FOR LONG -
THEY ALWAYS SAY THEY DON'T LIKE THE HOUSE.

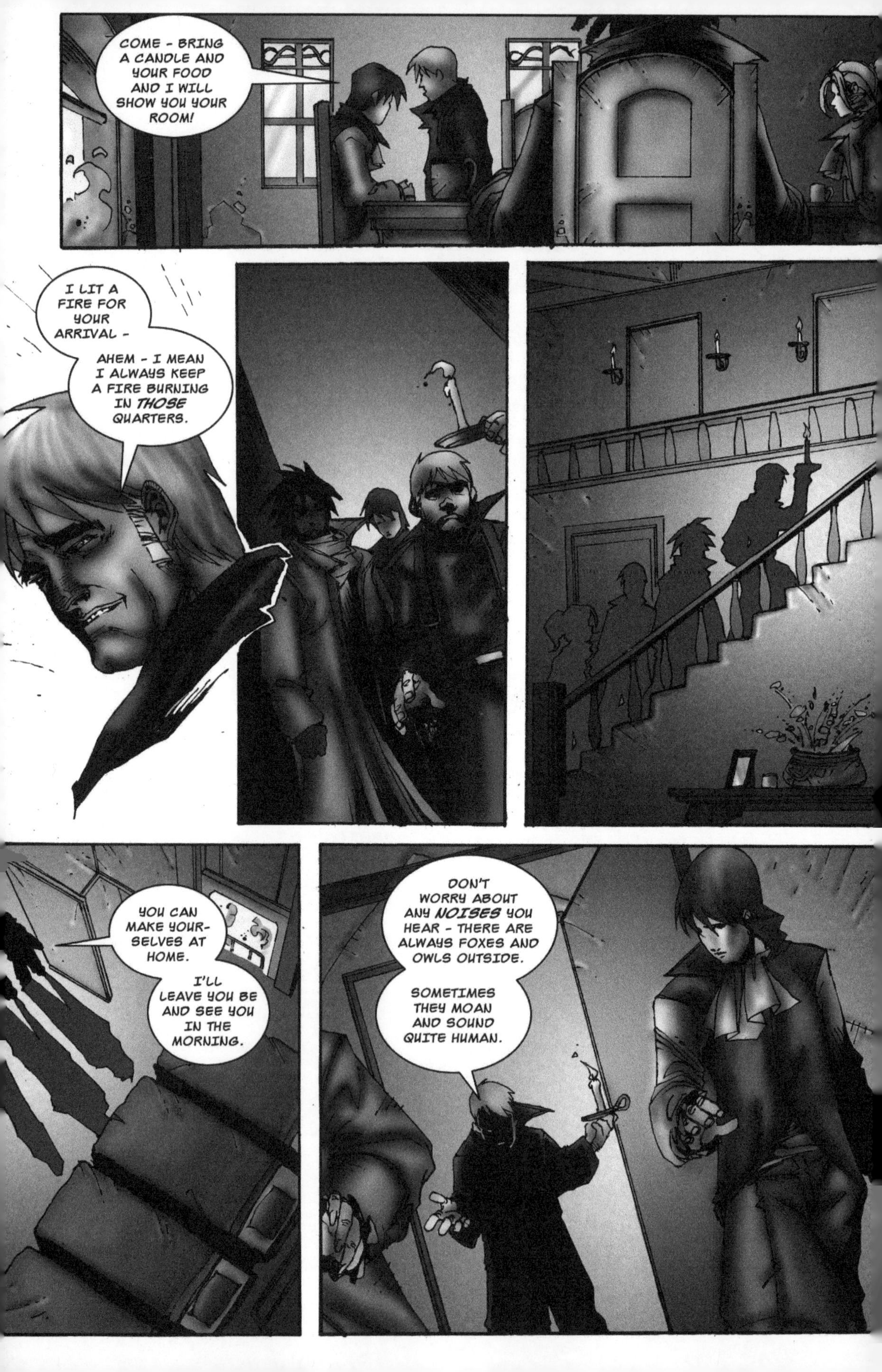

COME - BRING A CANDLE AND YOUR FOOD AND I WILL SHOW YOU YOUR ROOM!
I LIT A FIRE FOR YOUR ARRIVAL -
AHEM - I MEAN I ALWAYS KEEP A FIRE BURNING IN *THOSE* QUARTERS.
YOU CAN MAKE YOURSELVES AT HOME.
I'LL LEAVE YOU BE AND SEE YOU IN THE MORNING.
DON'T WORRY ABOUT ANY *NOISES* YOU HEAR - THERE ARE ALWAYS FOXES AND OWLS OUTSIDE.
SOMETIMES THEY MOAN AND SOUND QUITE HUMAN.

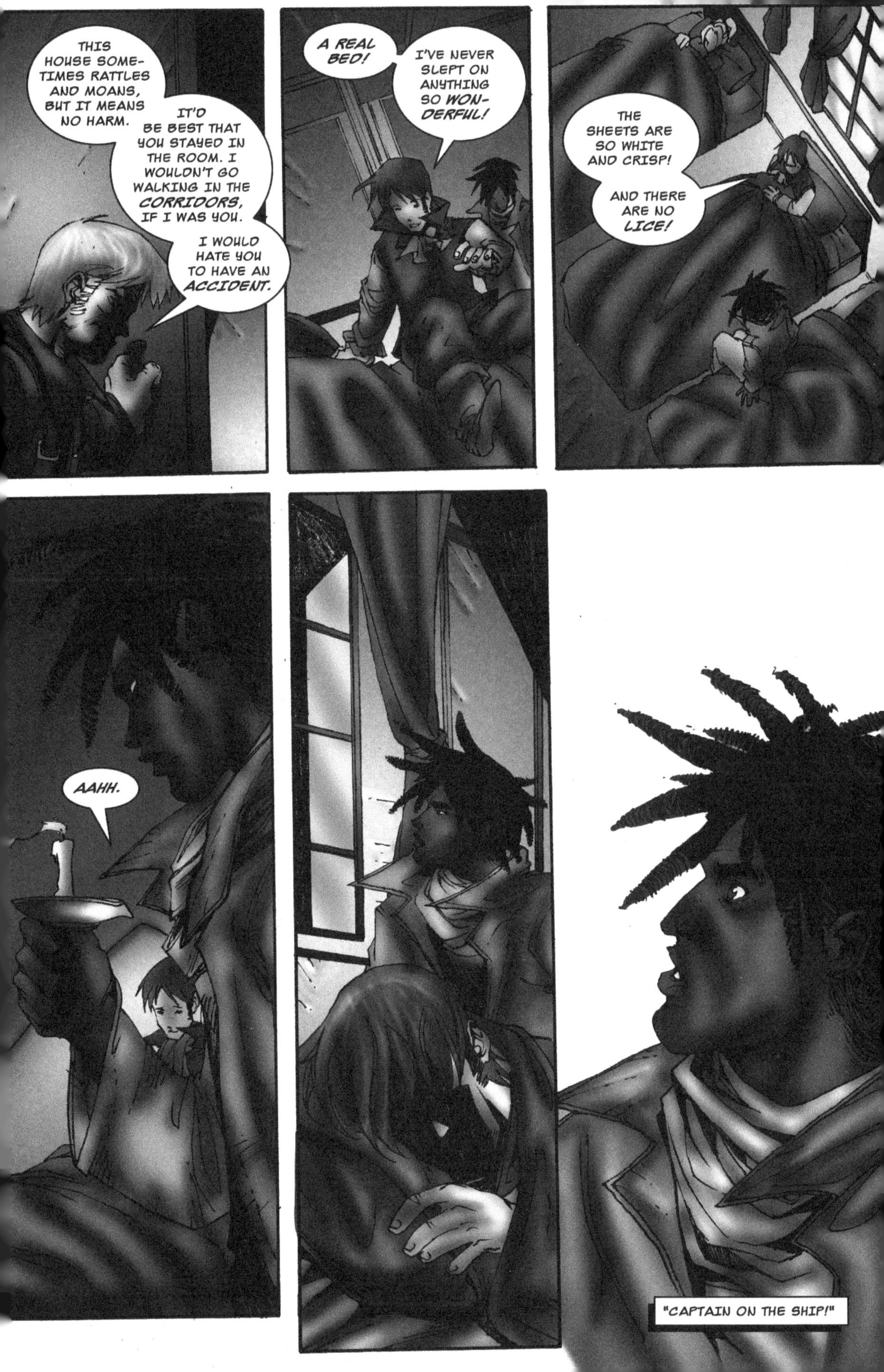
THIS HOUSE SOMETIMES RATTLES AND MOANS, BUT IT MEANS NO HARM.
IT'D BE BEST THAT YOU STAYED IN THE ROOM. I WOULDN'T GO WALKING IN THE CORRIDORS, IF I WAS YOU.
I WOULD HATE YOU TO HAVE AN ACCIDENT.
A REAL BED!
I'VE NEVER SLEPT ON ANYTHING SO WONDERFUL!
THE SHEETS ARE SO WHITE AND CRISP!
AND THERE ARE NO LICE!
AAHH.
"CAPTAIN ON THE SHIP!"

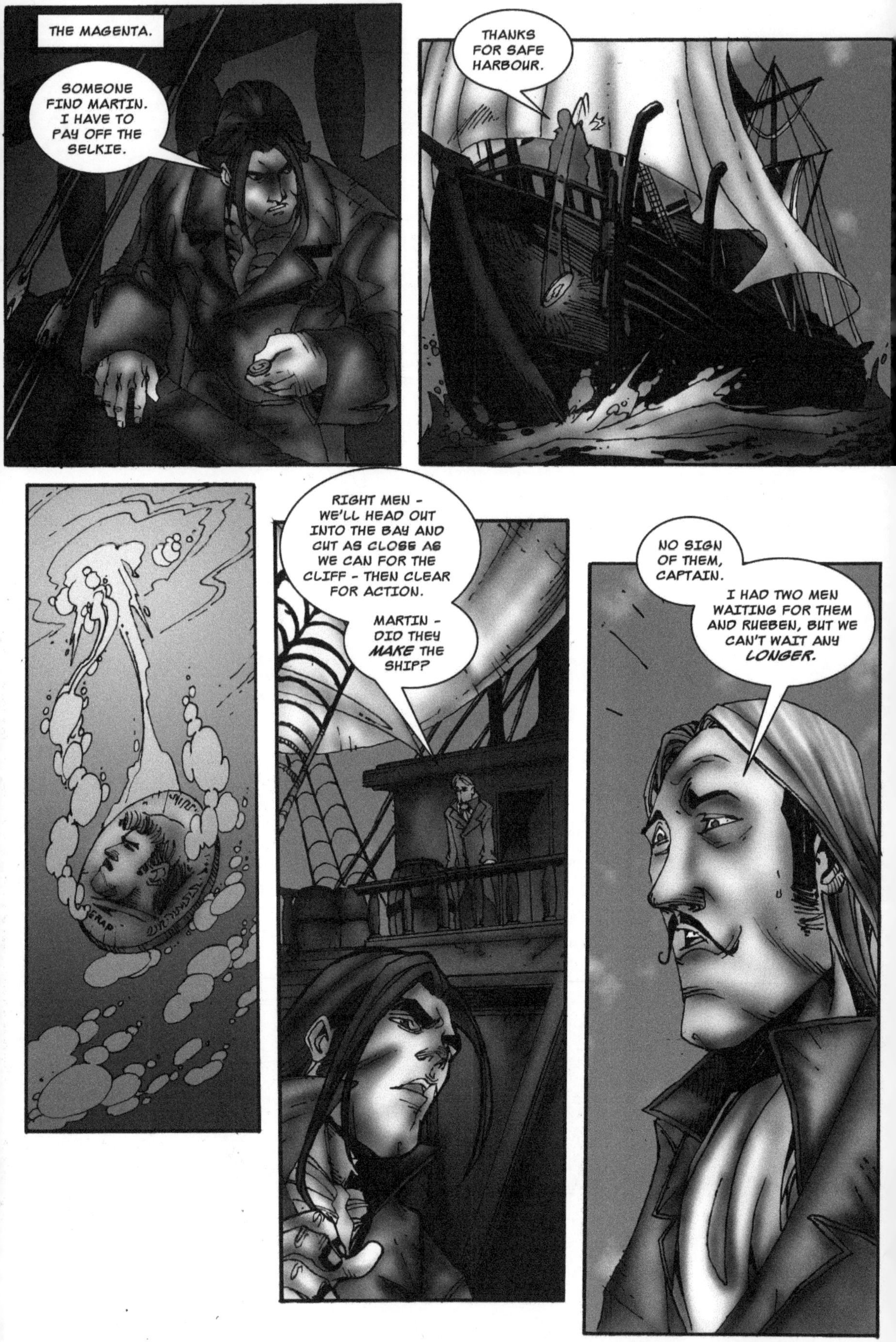
THE MAGENTA.
SOMEONE FIND MARTIN. I HAVE TO PAY OFF THE SELKIE.
THANKS FOR SAFE HARBOUR.
RIGHT MEN - WE'LL HEAD OUT INTO THE BAY AND CUT AS CLOSE AS WE CAN FOR THE CLIFF - THEN CLEAR FOR ACTION.
MARTIN - DID THEY *MAKE* THE SHIP?
NO SIGN OF THEM, CAPTAIN.
I HAD TWO MEN WAITING FOR THEM AND RUEBEN, BUT WE CAN'T WAIT ANY *LONGER.*

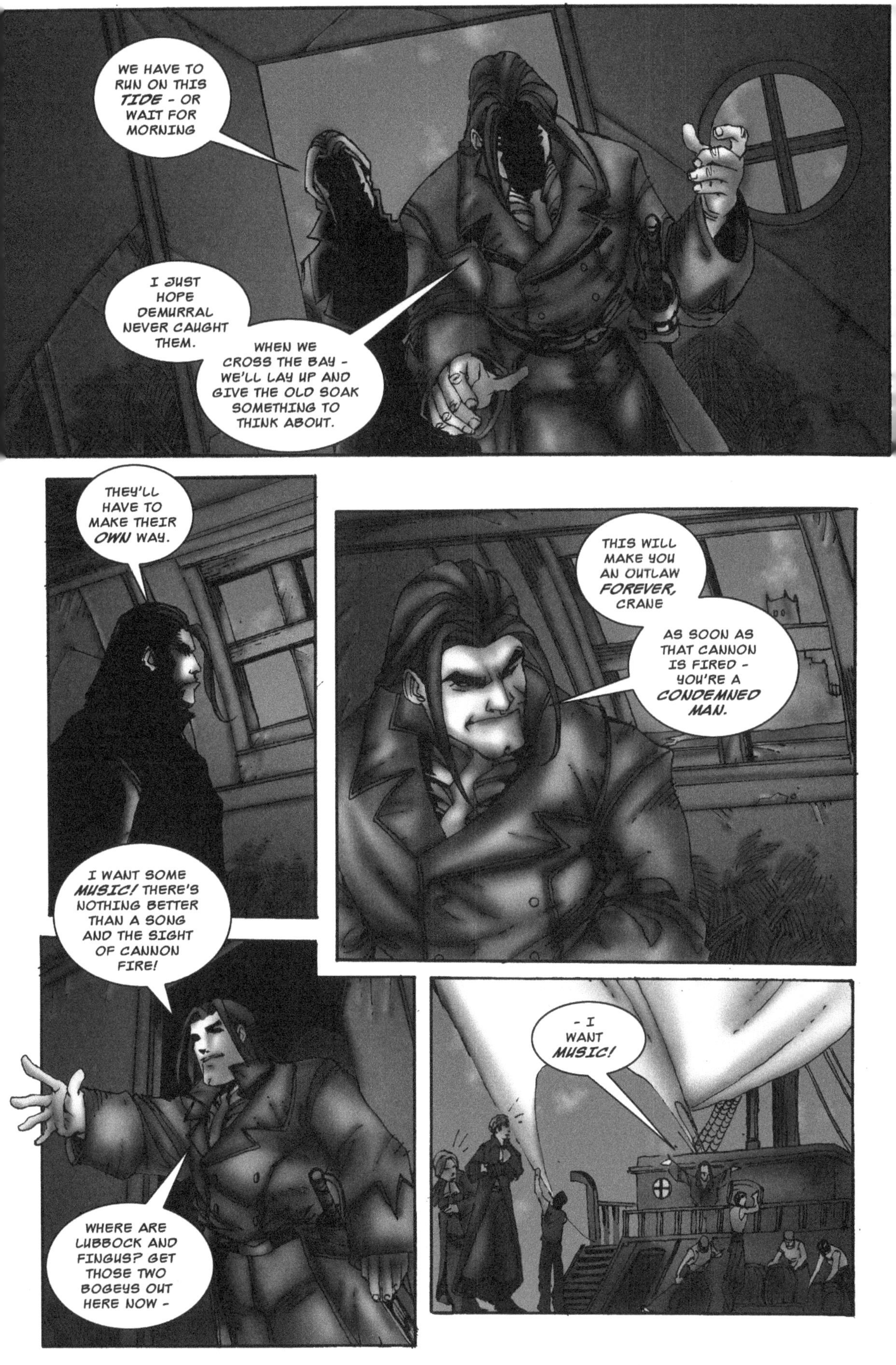
WE HAVE TO RUN ON THIS TIDE - OR WAIT FOR MORNING
I JUST HOPE DEMURRAL NEVER CAUGHT THEM.
WHEN WE CROSS THE BAY - WE'LL LAY UP AND GIVE THE OLD SOAK SOMETHING TO THINK ABOUT.
THEY'LL HAVE TO MAKE THEIR OWN WAY.
THIS WILL MAKE YOU AN OUTLAW FOREVER, CRANE
AS SOON AS THAT CANNON IS FIRED - YOU'RE A CONDEMNED MAN.
I WANT SOME MUSIC! THERE'S NOTHING BETTER THAN A SONG AND THE SIGHT OF CANNON FIRE!
WHERE ARE LUBBOCK AND FINGUS? GET THOSE TWO BOGEYS OUT HERE NOW -
- I WANT MUSIC!

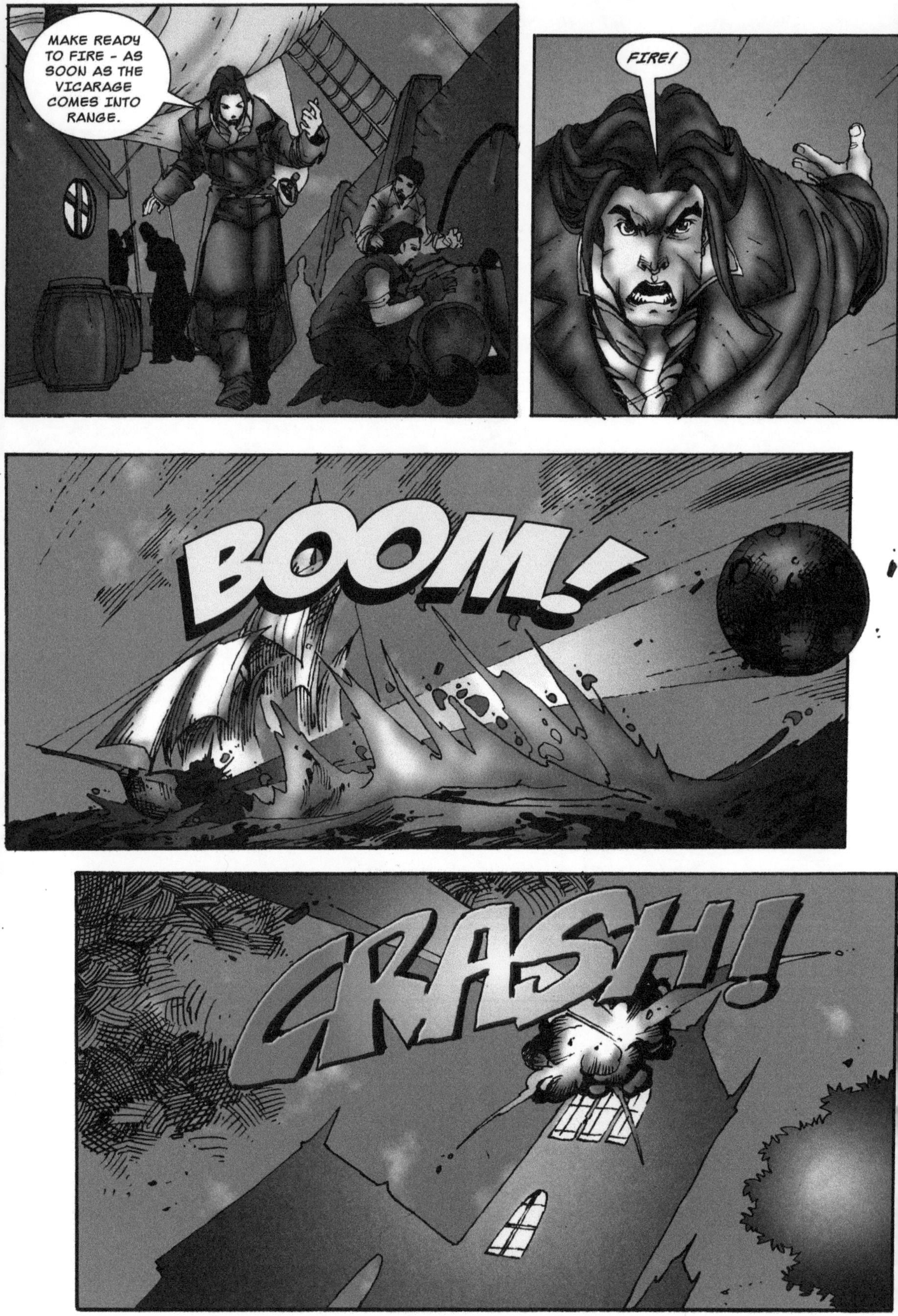
MAKE READY TO FIRE - AS SOON AS THE VICARAGE COMES INTO RANGE.
FIRE!
BOOM!
CRASH!

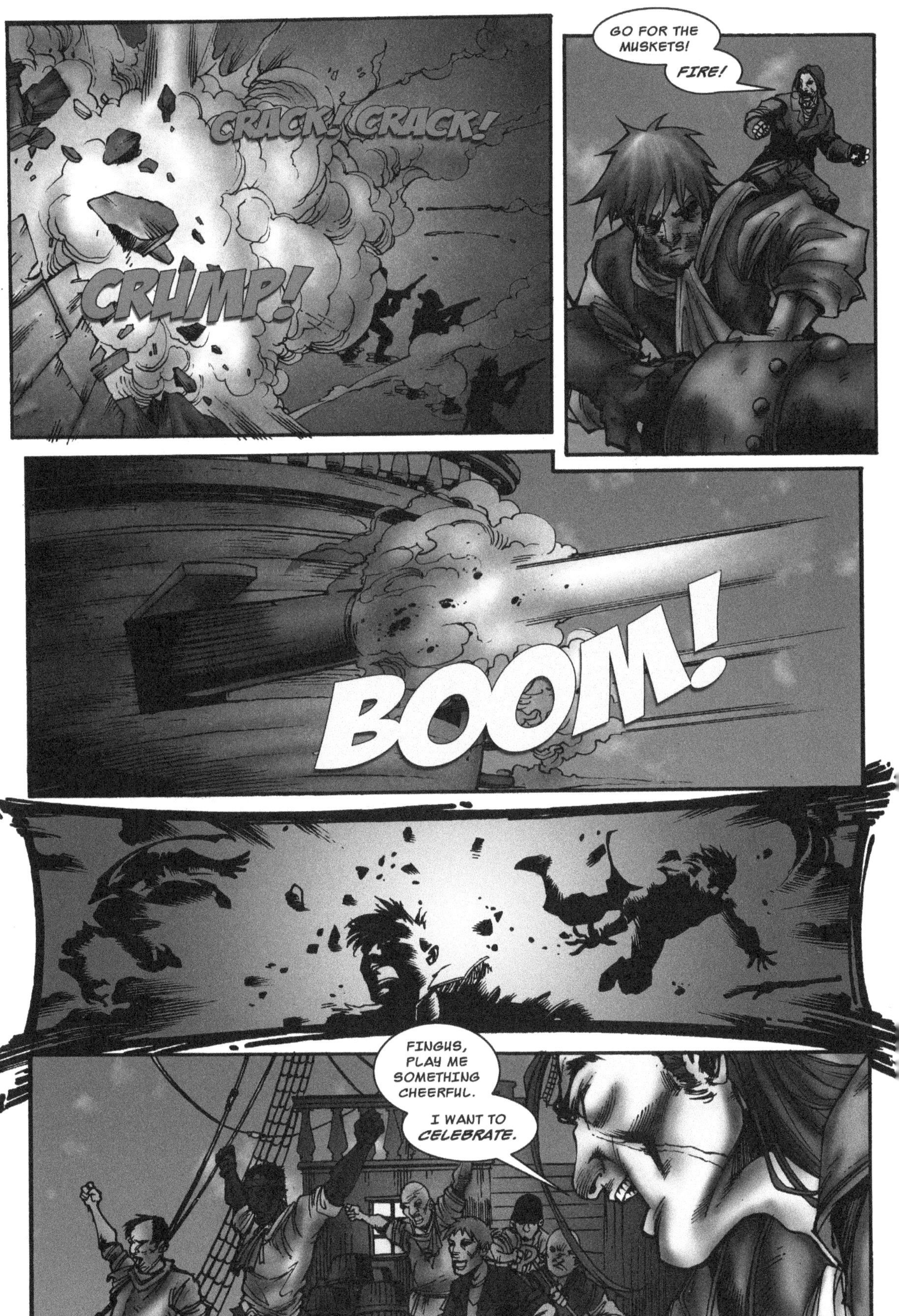
CRACK! CRACK!
CRUMP!
GO FOR THE MUSKETS!
FIRE!
BOOM!
FINGUS, PLAY ME SOMETHING CHEERFUL.
I WANT TO CELEBRATE.

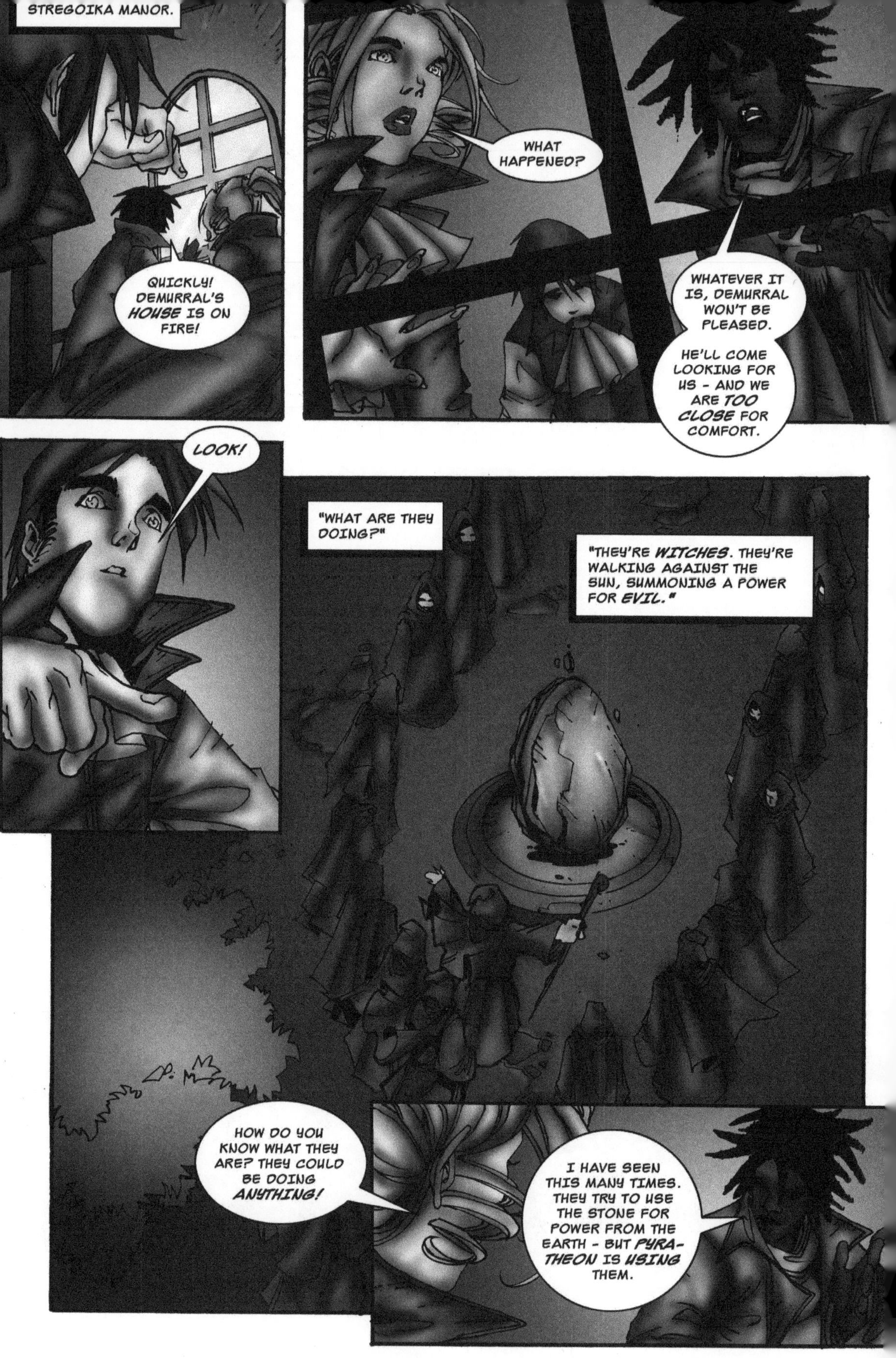
STREGOIKA MANOR.
QUICKLY! DEMURRAL'S HOUSE IS ON FIRE!
WHAT HAPPENED?
WHATEVER IT IS, DEMURRAL WON'T BE PLEASED.
HE'LL COME LOOKING FOR US - AND WE ARE TOO CLOSE FOR COMFORT.
LOOK!
"WHAT ARE THEY DOING?"
"THEY'RE WITCHES. THEY'RE WALKING AGAINST THE SUN, SUMMONING A POWER FOR EVIL."
HOW DO YOU KNOW WHAT THEY ARE? THEY COULD BE DOING ANYTHING!
I HAVE SEEN THIS MANY TIMES. THEY TRY TO USE THE STONE FOR POWER FROM THE EARTH - BUT PYRA-THEON IS USING THEM.

ONE, THE WIND THAT SPRINGS FROM THE WEST –

TWO, THE EARTH THAT BRINGS FORTH LIGHT –

THREE, THE FIRE THAT CONSUMES OUR BREATH –

FOUR, THE WATER THAT BRINGS OUR HEALING –

FIVE, THE MOON THAT LIGHTS OUR PATH –

SIX, THE SUN, THE GREATEST LIGHT –

SEVEN, THE MASTER WE SUMMON THIS NIGHT!

WE MUST LEAVE HERE AS SOON AS WE CAN. THEY MUST *NEVER* GET THE KERUVIM –

AND THEY ARE CLOSER TO IT THAN THEY COULD *EVER* IMAGINE.

"LOOK! IT'S DEMURRAL! AND CAPTAIN FARRELL!"

"THAT IS NOT FARRELL. HE HAS BEEN POSSESSED BY A *DUNAMEZ*."

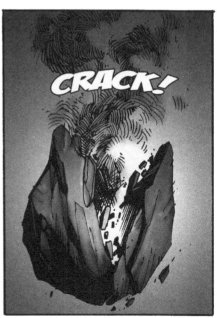

CRACK!

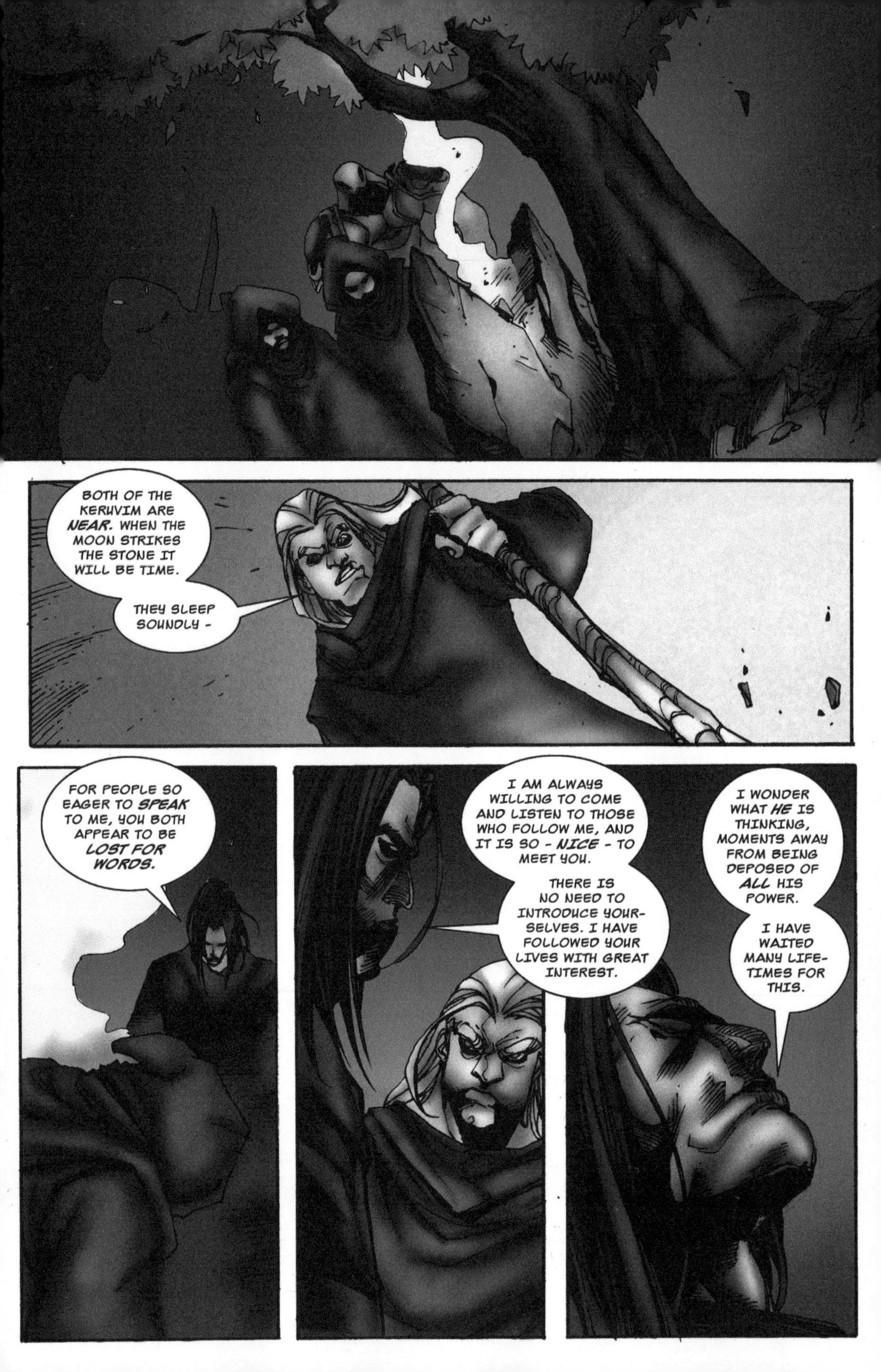
BOTH OF THE KERUVIM ARE NEAR. WHEN THE MOON STRIKES THE STONE IT WILL BE TIME.
THEY SLEEP SOUNDLY -
FOR PEOPLE SO EAGER TO SPEAK TO ME, YOU BOTH APPEAR TO BE LOST FOR WORDS.
I AM ALWAYS WILLING TO COME AND LISTEN TO THOSE WHO FOLLOW ME, AND IT IS SO - NICE - TO MEET YOU.
THERE IS NO NEED TO INTRODUCE YOURSELVES. I HAVE FOLLOWED YOUR LIVES WITH GREAT INTEREST.
I WONDER WHAT HE IS THINKING, MOMENTS AWAY FROM BEING DEPOSED OF ALL HIS POWER.
I HAVE WAITED MANY LIFETIMES FOR THIS.

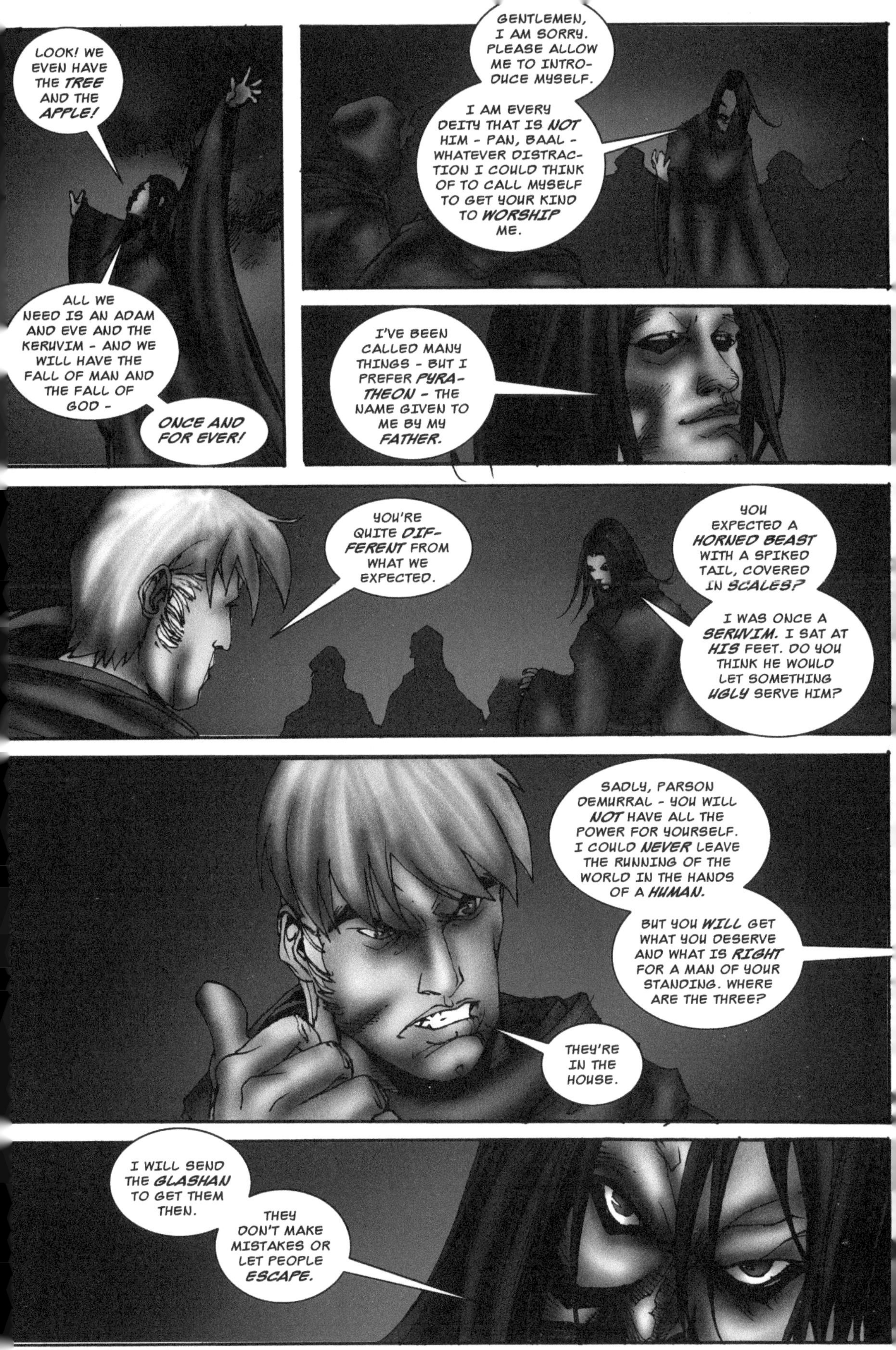

LOOK! WE EVEN HAVE THE TREE AND THE APPLE!
ALL WE NEED IS AN ADAM AND EVE AND THE KERUVIM - AND WE WILL HAVE THE FALL OF MAN AND THE FALL OF GOD -
ONCE AND FOR EVER!
GENTLEMEN, I AM SORRY. PLEASE ALLOW ME TO INTRODUCE MYSELF.
I AM EVERY DEITY THAT IS NOT HIM - PAN, BAAL - WHATEVER DISTRACTION I COULD THINK OF TO CALL MYSELF TO GET YOUR KIND TO WORSHIP ME.
I'VE BEEN CALLED MANY THINGS - BUT I PREFER PYRATHEON - THE NAME GIVEN TO ME BY MY FATHER.
YOU'RE QUITE DIFFERENT FROM WHAT WE EXPECTED.
YOU EXPECTED A HORNED BEAST WITH A SPIKED TAIL, COVERED IN SCALES?
I WAS ONCE A SERUVIM. I SAT AT HIS FEET. DO YOU THINK HE WOULD LET SOMETHING UGLY SERVE HIM?
SADLY, PARSON DEMURRAL - YOU WILL NOT HAVE ALL THE POWER FOR YOURSELF. I COULD NEVER LEAVE THE RUNNING OF THE WORLD IN THE HANDS OF A HUMAN.
BUT YOU WILL GET WHAT YOU DESERVE AND WHAT IS RIGHT FOR A MAN OF YOUR STANDING. WHERE ARE THE THREE?
THEY'RE IN THE HOUSE.
I WILL SEND THE GLASHAN TO GET THEM THEN.
THEY DON'T MAKE MISTAKES OR LET PEOPLE ESCAPE.

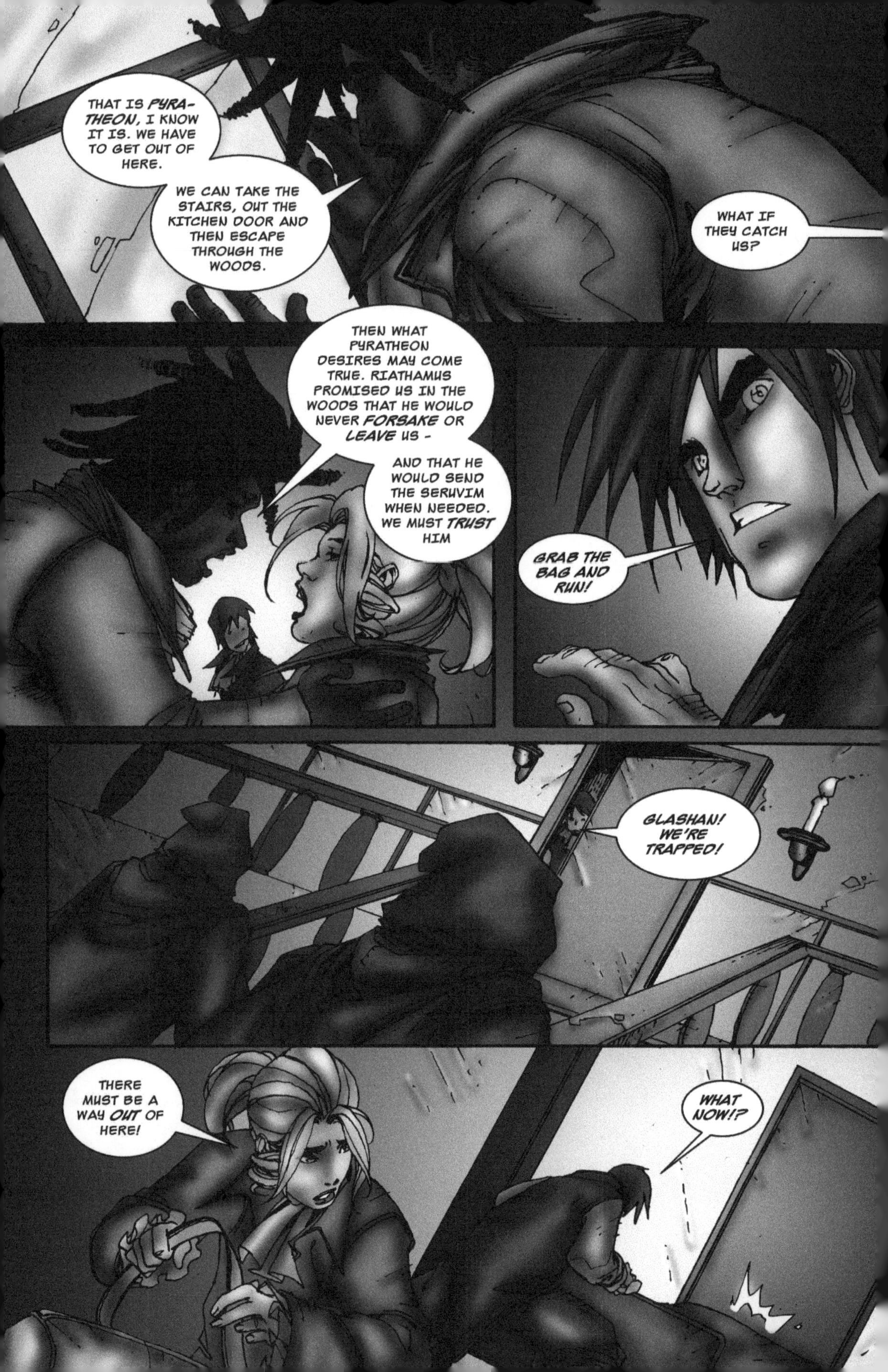
THAT IS PYRATHEON, I KNOW IT IS. WE HAVE TO GET OUT OF HERE.
WE CAN TAKE THE STAIRS, OUT THE KITCHEN DOOR AND THEN ESCAPE THROUGH THE WOODS.
WHAT IF THEY CATCH US?
THEN WHAT PYRATHEON DESIRES MAY COME TRUE. RIATHAMUS PROMISED US IN THE WOODS THAT HE WOULD NEVER FORSAKE OR LEAVE US -
AND THAT HE WOULD SEND THE SERUVIM WHEN NEEDED. WE MUST TRUST HIM
GRAB THE BAG AND RUN!
GLASHAN! WE'RE TRAPPED!
THERE MUST BE A WAY OUT OF HERE!
WHAT NOW!?

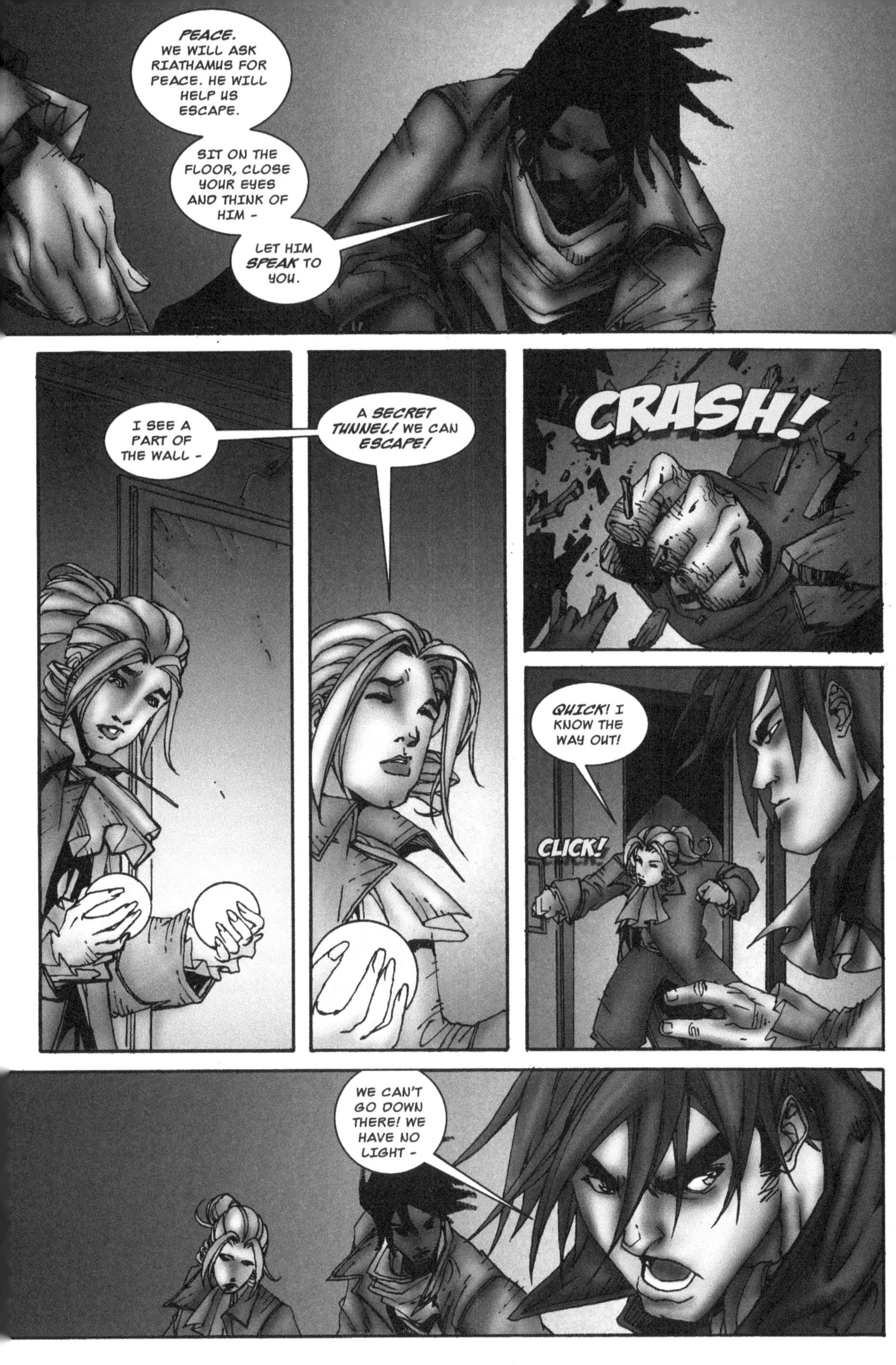
PEACE. WE WILL ASK RIATHAMUS FOR PEACE. HE WILL HELP US ESCAPE.
SIT ON THE FLOOR, CLOSE YOUR EYES AND THINK OF HIM -
LET HIM SPEAK TO YOU.
I SEE A PART OF THE WALL -
A SECRET TUNNEL! WE CAN ESCAPE!
CRASH!
QUICK! I KNOW THE WAY OUT!
CLICK!
WE CAN'T GO DOWN THERE! WE HAVE NO LIGHT -

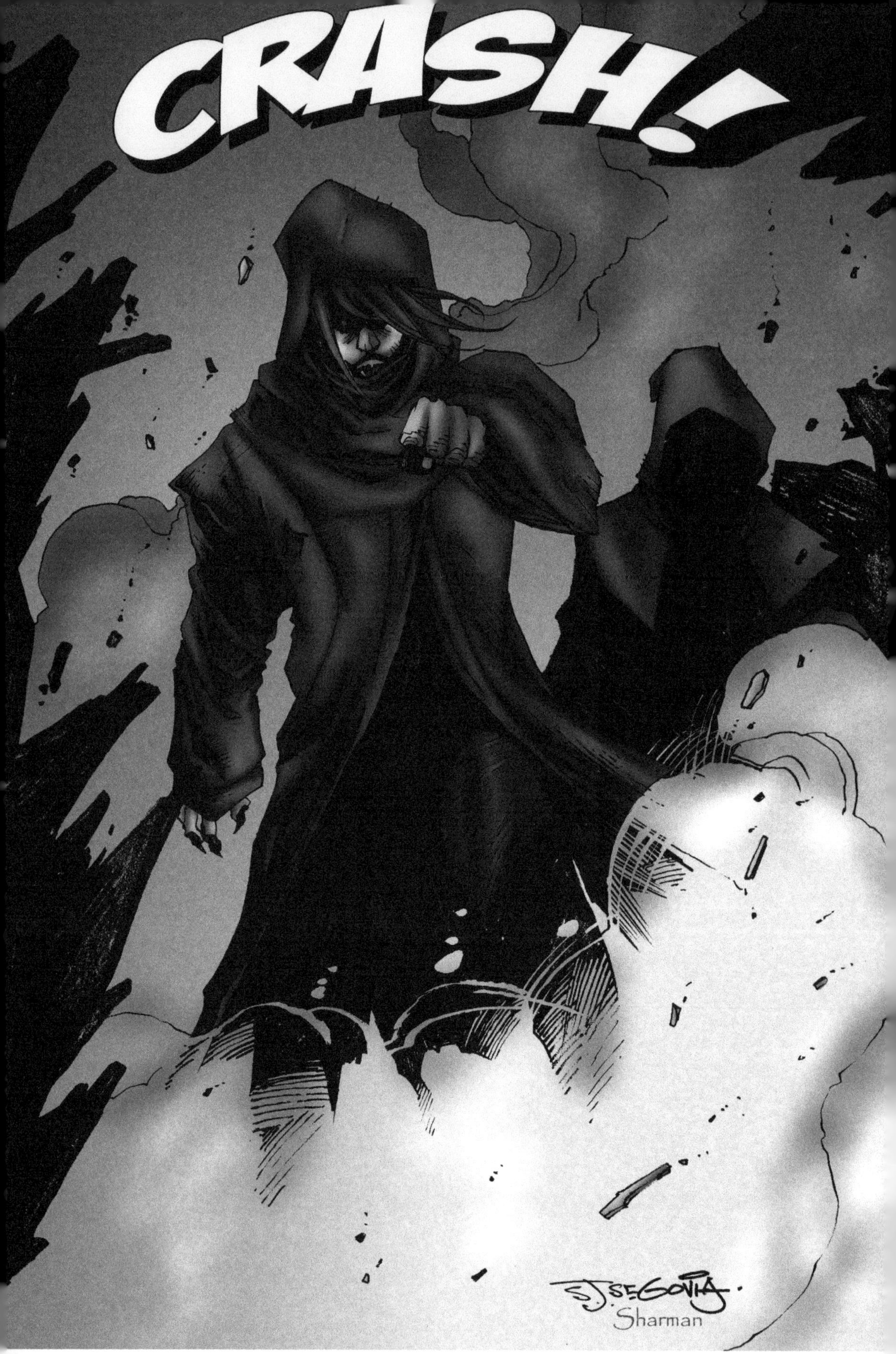
CRASH!
SJ SEGOVIA
Sharman

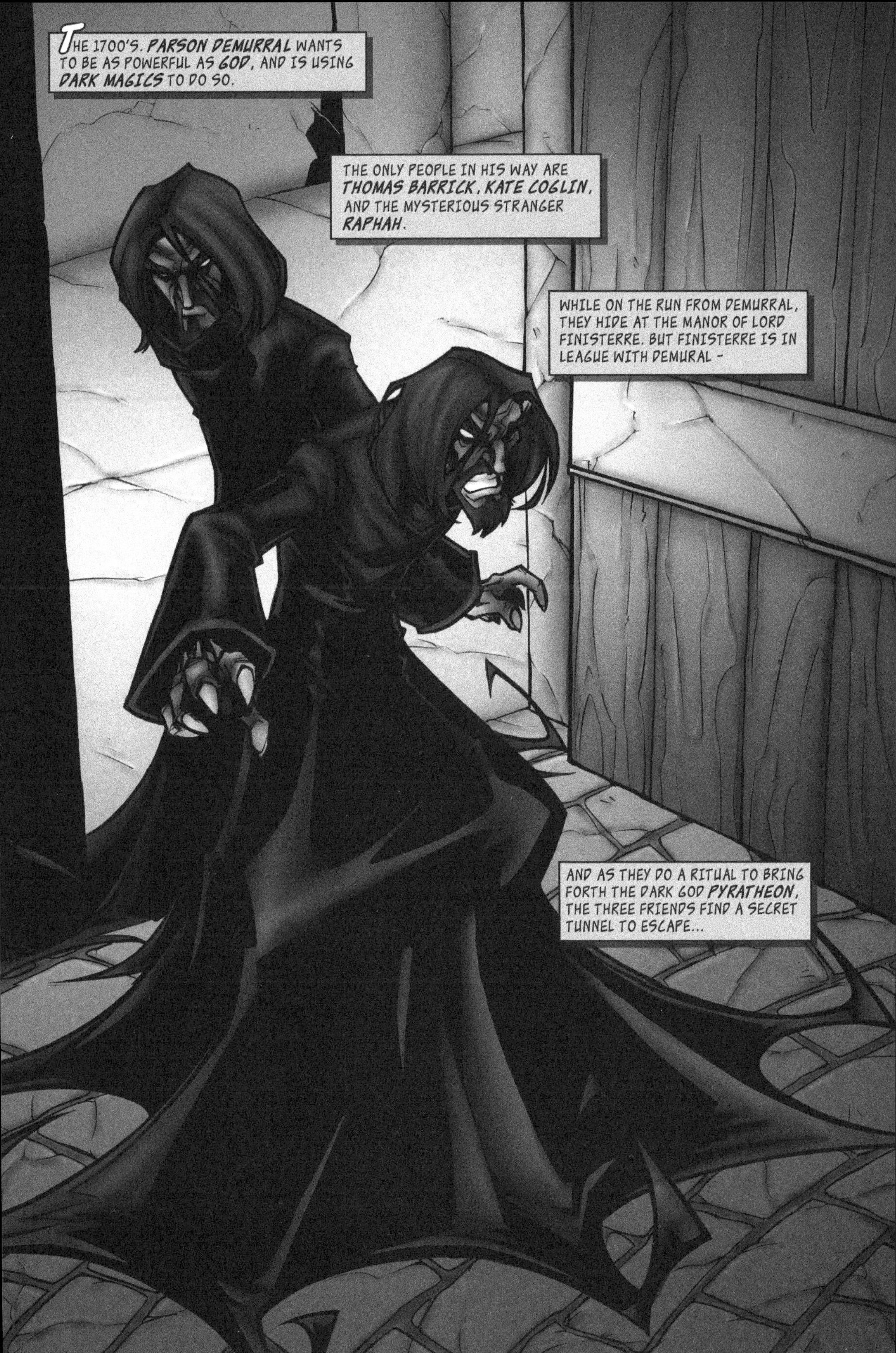
THE 1700'S. PARSON DEMURRAL WANTS TO BE AS POWERFUL AS GOD, AND IS USING DARK MAGICS TO DO SO.
THE ONLY PEOPLE IN HIS WAY ARE THOMAS BARRICK, KATE COGLIN, AND THE MYSTERIOUS STRANGER RAPHAH.
WHILE ON THE RUN FROM DEMURRAL, THEY HIDE AT THE MANOR OF LORD FINISTERRE. BUT FINISTERRE IS IN LEAGUE WITH DEMURAL -
AND AS THEY DO A RITUAL TO BRING FORTH THE DARK GOD PYRATHEON, THE THREE FRIENDS FIND A SECRET TUNNEL TO ESCAPE...

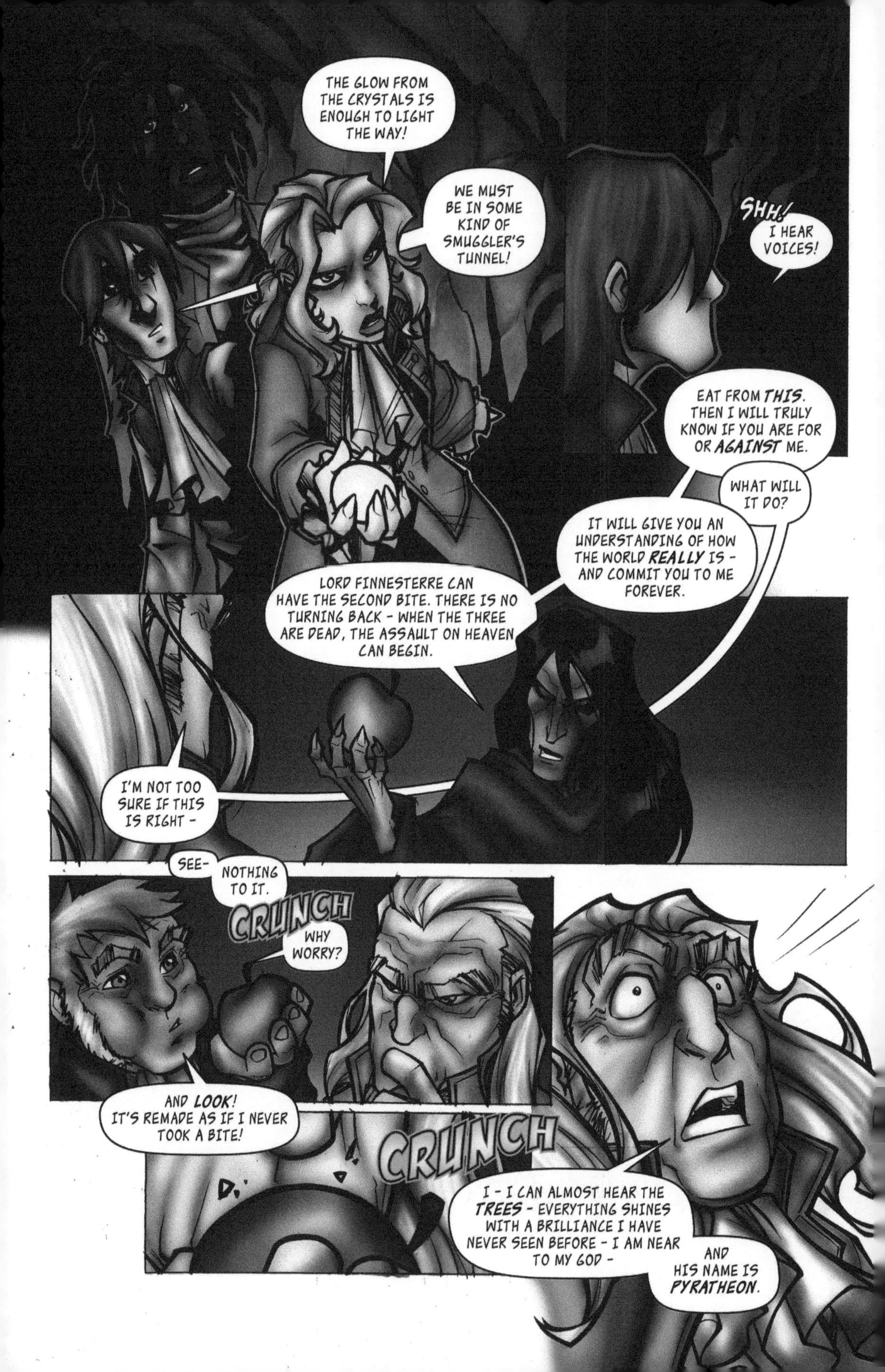
THE GLOW FROM THE CRYSTALS IS ENOUGH TO LIGHT THE WAY!
WE MUST BE IN SOME KIND OF SMUGGLER'S TUNNEL!
SHH!
I HEAR VOICES!
EAT FROM THIS. THEN I WILL TRULY KNOW IF YOU ARE FOR OR AGAINST ME.
WHAT WILL IT DO?
IT WILL GIVE YOU AN UNDERSTANDING OF HOW THE WORLD REALLY IS - AND COMMIT YOU TO ME FOREVER.
LORD FINNESTERRE CAN HAVE THE SECOND BITE. THERE IS NO TURNING BACK - WHEN THE THREE ARE DEAD, THE ASSAULT ON HEAVEN CAN BEGIN.
I'M NOT TOO SURE IF THIS IS RIGHT -
SEE-
NOTHING TO IT.
CRUNCH
WHY WORRY?
AND LOOK! IT'S REMADE AS IF I NEVER TOOK A BITE!
CRUNCH
I - I CAN ALMOST HEAR THE TREES - EVERYTHING SHINES WITH A BRILLIANCE I HAVE NEVER SEEN BEFORE - I AM NEAR TO MY GOD -
AND HIS NAME IS PYRATHEON.

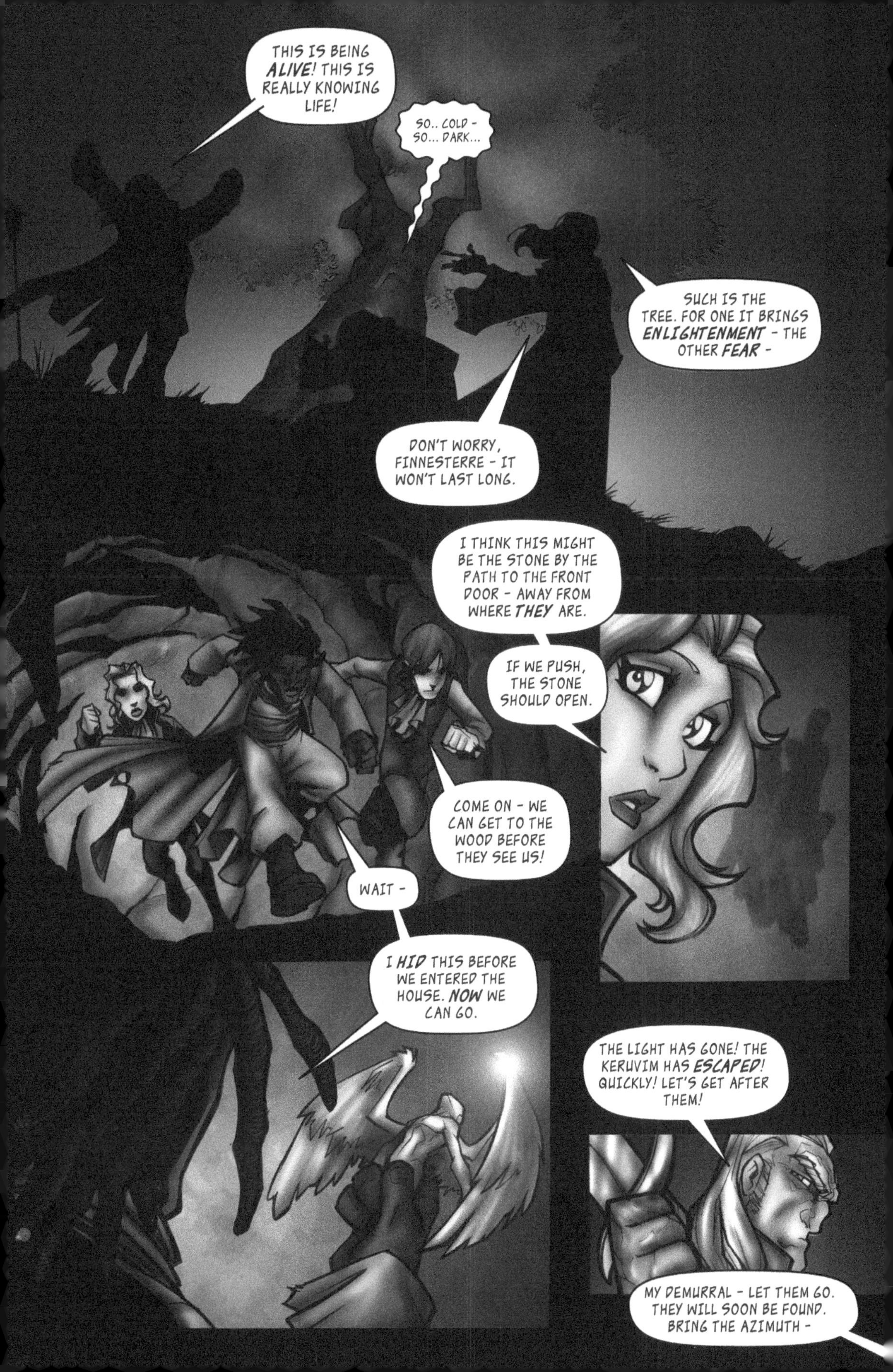
THIS IS BEING ALIVE! THIS IS REALLY KNOWING LIFE!
SO.. COLD - SO... DARK...
SUCH IS THE TREE. FOR ONE IT BRINGS ENLIGHTENMENT - THE OTHER FEAR -
DON'T WORRY, FINNESTERRE - IT WON'T LAST LONG.
I THINK THIS MIGHT BE THE STONE BY THE PATH TO THE FRONT DOOR - AWAY FROM WHERE THEY ARE.
IF WE PUSH, THE STONE SHOULD OPEN.
COME ON - WE CAN GET TO THE WOOD BEFORE THEY SEE US!
WAIT -
I HID THIS BEFORE WE ENTERED THE HOUSE. NOW WE CAN GO.
THE LIGHT HAS GONE! THE KERUVIM HAS ESCAPED! QUICKLY! LET'S GET AFTER THEM!
MY DEMURRAL - LET THEM GO. THEY WILL SOON BE FOUND. BRING THE AZIMUTH -

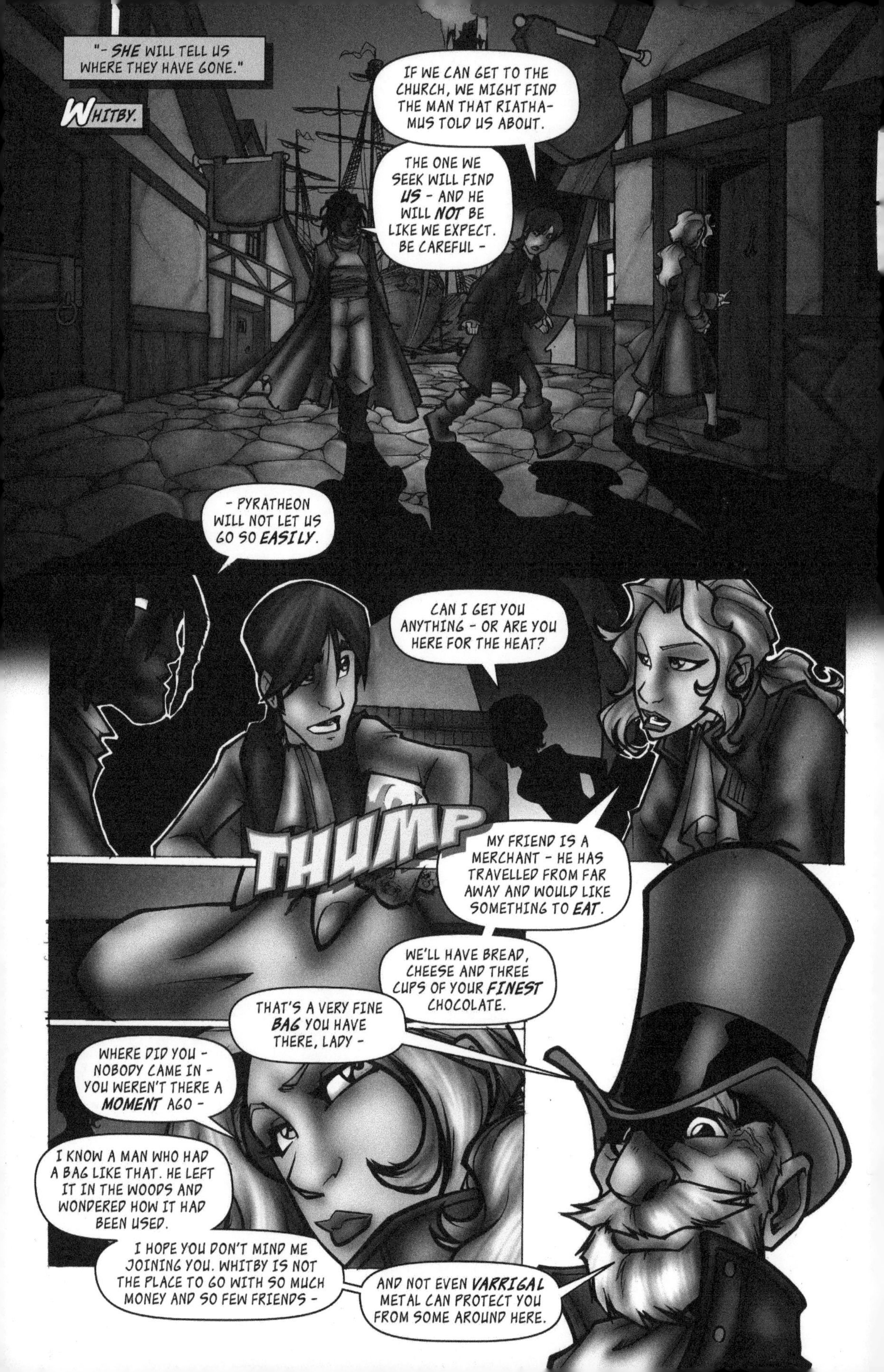
"- SHE WILL TELL US WHERE THEY HAVE GONE."
WHITBY.
IF WE CAN GET TO THE CHURCH, WE MIGHT FIND THE MAN THAT RIATHAMUS TOLD US ABOUT.
THE ONE WE SEEK WILL FIND US - AND HE WILL NOT BE LIKE WE EXPECT. BE CAREFUL -
- PYRATHEON WILL NOT LET US GO SO EASILY.
CAN I GET YOU ANYTHING - OR ARE YOU HERE FOR THE HEAT?
THUMP
MY FRIEND IS A MERCHANT - HE HAS TRAVELLED FROM FAR AWAY AND WOULD LIKE SOMETHING TO EAT.
WE'LL HAVE BREAD, CHEESE AND THREE CUPS OF YOUR FINEST CHOCOLATE.
THAT'S A VERY FINE BAG YOU HAVE THERE, LADY -
WHERE DID YOU - NOBODY CAME IN - YOU WEREN'T THERE A MOMENT AGO -
I KNOW A MAN WHO HAD A BAG LIKE THAT. HE LEFT IT IN THE WOODS AND WONDERED HOW IT HAD BEEN USED.
I HOPE YOU DON'T MIND ME JOINING YOU. WHITBY IS NOT THE PLACE TO GO WITH SO MUCH MONEY AND SO FEW FRIENDS -
AND NOT EVEN VARRIGAL METAL CAN PROTECT YOU FROM SOME AROUND HERE.

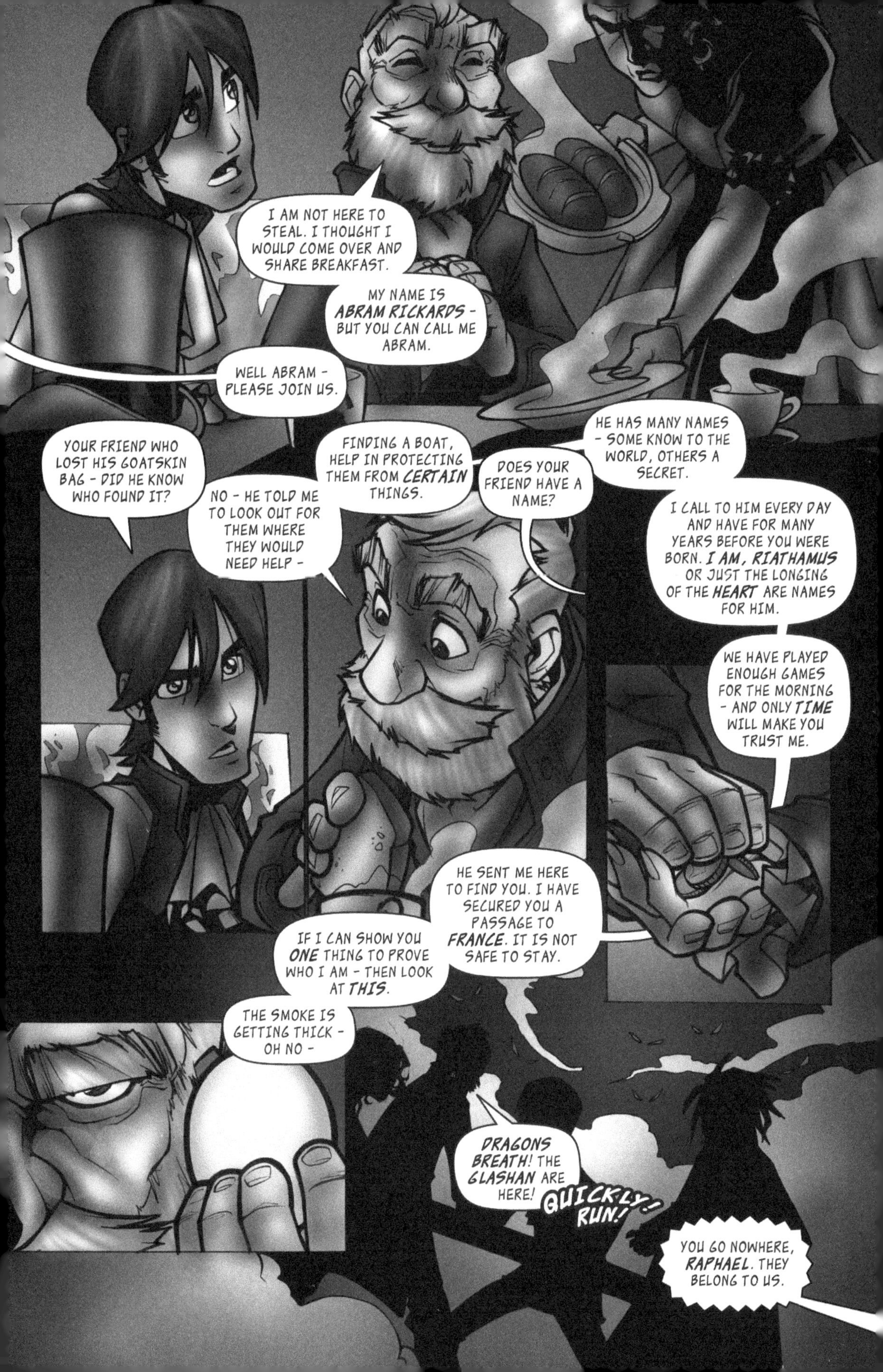
I AM NOT HERE TO STEAL. I THOUGHT I WOULD COME OVER AND SHARE BREAKFAST.
MY NAME IS ABRAM RICKARDS - BUT YOU CAN CALL ME ABRAM.
WELL ABRAM - PLEASE JOIN US.
YOUR FRIEND WHO LOST HIS GOATSKIN BAG - DID HE KNOW WHO FOUND IT?
NO - HE TOLD ME TO LOOK OUT FOR THEM WHERE THEY WOULD NEED HELP -
FINDING A BOAT, HELP IN PROTECTING THEM FROM CERTAIN THINGS.
DOES YOUR FRIEND HAVE A NAME?
HE HAS MANY NAMES - SOME KNOW TO THE WORLD, OTHERS A SECRET.
I CALL TO HIM EVERY DAY AND HAVE FOR MANY YEARS BEFORE YOU WERE BORN. I AM, RIATHAMUS OR JUST THE LONGING OF THE HEART ARE NAMES FOR HIM.
WE HAVE PLAYED ENOUGH GAMES FOR THE MORNING - AND ONLY TIME WILL MAKE YOU TRUST ME.
HE SENT ME HERE TO FIND YOU. I HAVE SECURED YOU A PASSAGE TO FRANCE. IT IS NOT SAFE TO STAY.
IF I CAN SHOW YOU ONE THING TO PROVE WHO I AM - THEN LOOK AT THIS.
THE SMOKE IS GETTING THICK - OH NO -
DRAGONS BREATH! THE GLASHAN ARE HERE!
QUICKLY! RUN!
YOU GO NOWHERE, RAPHAEL. THEY BELONG TO US.

THEY BELONG TO RIATHAMUS!
KEERASH!
THEN LET HIM COME FOR THEM HIMSELF, IF HE DARES-
KATE! THE CRYSTALS! THROW ONE AT THE WALL!
-OR DOES HE STILL SEND YOU TO DO HIS WORK FOR HIM?
PLINK
FOOOOM!
THE GLASHAN - THEY'RE GONE!
IT WORKED WELL, MY GIRL. THE ABARIS CRYSTAL HAS MANY USES. NOW YOU SEE HOW IMPORTANT IT IS TO LEAVE.
HE CALLED YOU RAPHAEL.
I HEARD HIM CALL YOU BY THAT NAME!
WHAT'S IN A NAME? ALL YOU NEED TO KNOW THAT I AM HERE TO HELP YOU. COME NOW - THERE MAY BE OTHERS AFTER YOU -

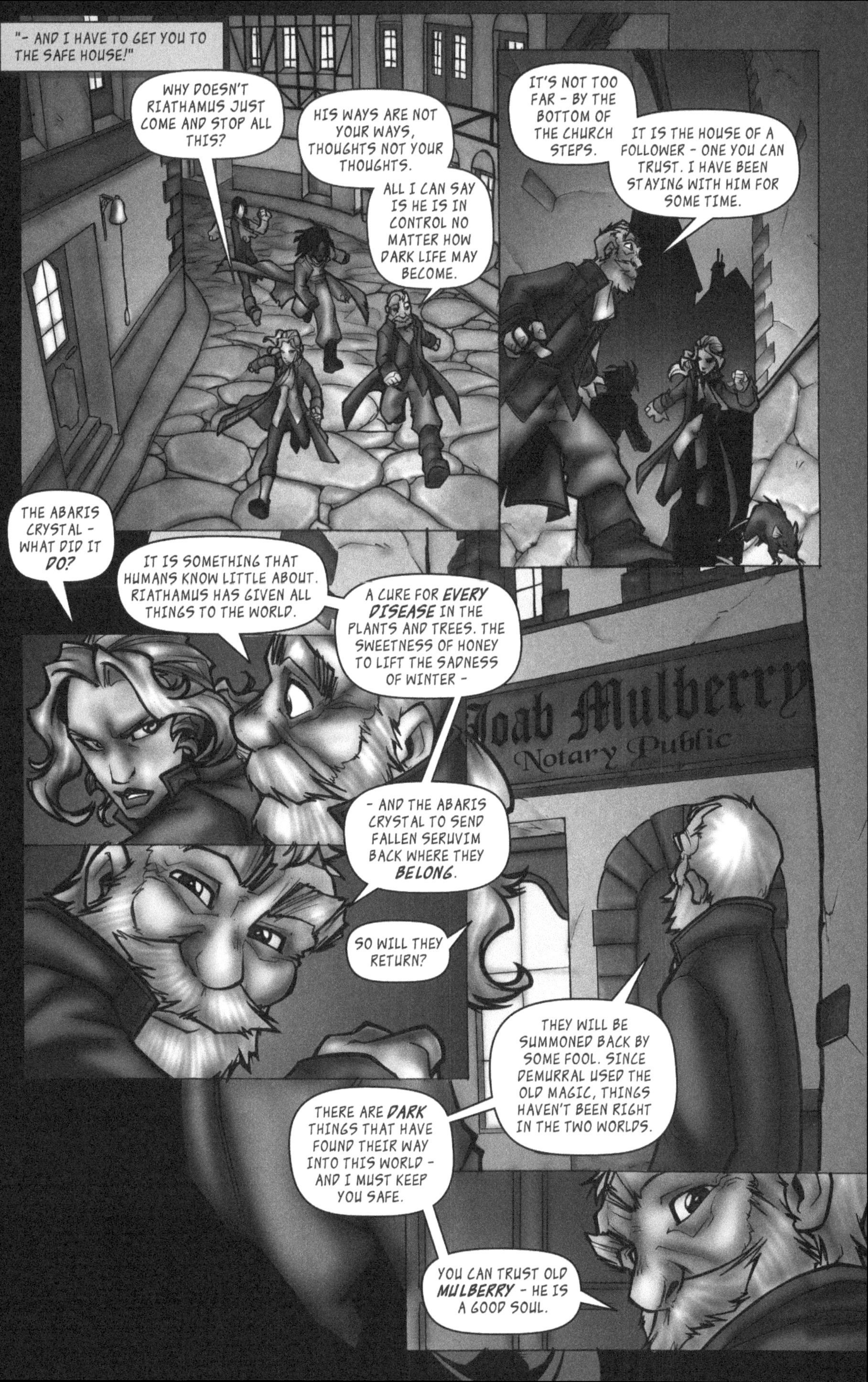
"– AND I HAVE TO GET YOU TO THE SAFE HOUSE!"
WHY DOESN'T RIATHAMUS JUST COME AND STOP ALL THIS?
HIS WAYS ARE NOT YOUR WAYS, THOUGHTS NOT YOUR THOUGHTS.
ALL I CAN SAY IS HE IS IN CONTROL NO MATTER HOW DARK LIFE MAY BECOME.
IT'S NOT TOO FAR – BY THE BOTTOM OF THE CHURCH STEPS.
IT IS THE HOUSE OF A FOLLOWER – ONE YOU CAN TRUST. I HAVE BEEN STAYING WITH HIM FOR SOME TIME.
THE ABARIS CRYSTAL – WHAT DID IT DO?
IT IS SOMETHING THAT HUMANS KNOW LITTLE ABOUT. RIATHAMUS HAS GIVEN ALL THINGS TO THE WORLD.
A CURE FOR EVERY DISEASE IN THE PLANTS AND TREES. THE SWEETNESS OF HONEY TO LIFT THE SADNESS OF WINTER –
Joab Mulberry
Notary Public
– AND THE ABARIS CRYSTAL TO SEND FALLEN SERUVIM BACK WHERE THEY BELONG.
SO WILL THEY RETURN?
THEY WILL BE SUMMONED BACK BY SOME FOOL. SINCE DEMURRAL USED THE OLD MAGIC, THINGS HAVEN'T BEEN RIGHT IN THE TWO WORLDS.
THERE ARE DARK THINGS THAT HAVE FOUND THEIR WAY INTO THIS WORLD – AND I MUST KEEP YOU SAFE.
YOU CAN TRUST OLD MULBERRY – HE IS A GOOD SOUL.

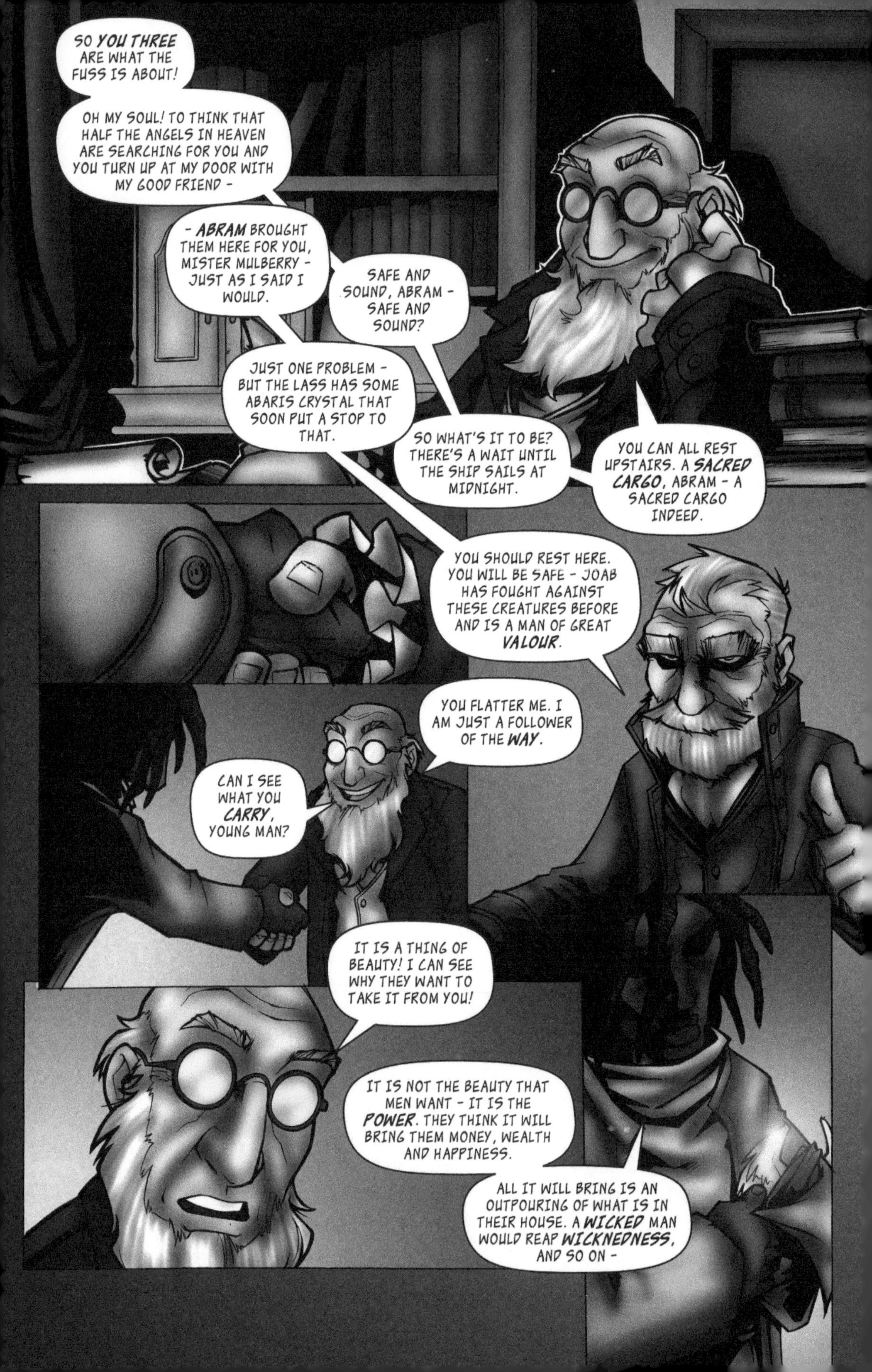

SO YOU THREE ARE WHAT THE FUSS IS ABOUT!
OH MY SOUL! TO THINK THAT HALF THE ANGELS IN HEAVEN ARE SEARCHING FOR YOU AND YOU TURN UP AT MY DOOR WITH MY GOOD FRIEND -
- ABRAM BROUGHT THEM HERE FOR YOU, MISTER MULBERRY - JUST AS I SAID I WOULD.
SAFE AND SOUND, ABRAM - SAFE AND SOUND?
JUST ONE PROBLEM - BUT THE LASS HAS SOME ABARIS CRYSTAL THAT SOON PUT A STOP TO THAT.
SO WHAT'S IT TO BE? THERE'S A WAIT UNTIL THE SHIP SAILS AT MIDNIGHT.
YOU CAN ALL REST UPSTAIRS. A SACRED CARGO, ABRAM - A SACRED CARGO INDEED.
YOU SHOULD REST HERE. YOU WILL BE SAFE - JOAB HAS FOUGHT AGAINST THESE CREATURES BEFORE AND IS A MAN OF GREAT VALOUR.
YOU FLATTER ME. I AM JUST A FOLLOWER OF THE WAY.
CAN I SEE WHAT YOU CARRY, YOUNG MAN?
IT IS A THING OF BEAUTY! I CAN SEE WHY THEY WANT TO TAKE IT FROM YOU!
IT IS NOT THE BEAUTY THAT MEN WANT - IT IS THE POWER. THEY THINK IT WILL BRING THEM MONEY, WEALTH AND HAPPINESS.
ALL IT WILL BRING IS AN OUTPOURING OF WHAT IS IN THEIR HOUSE. A WICKED MAN WOULD REAP WICKNEDNESS, AND SO ON -

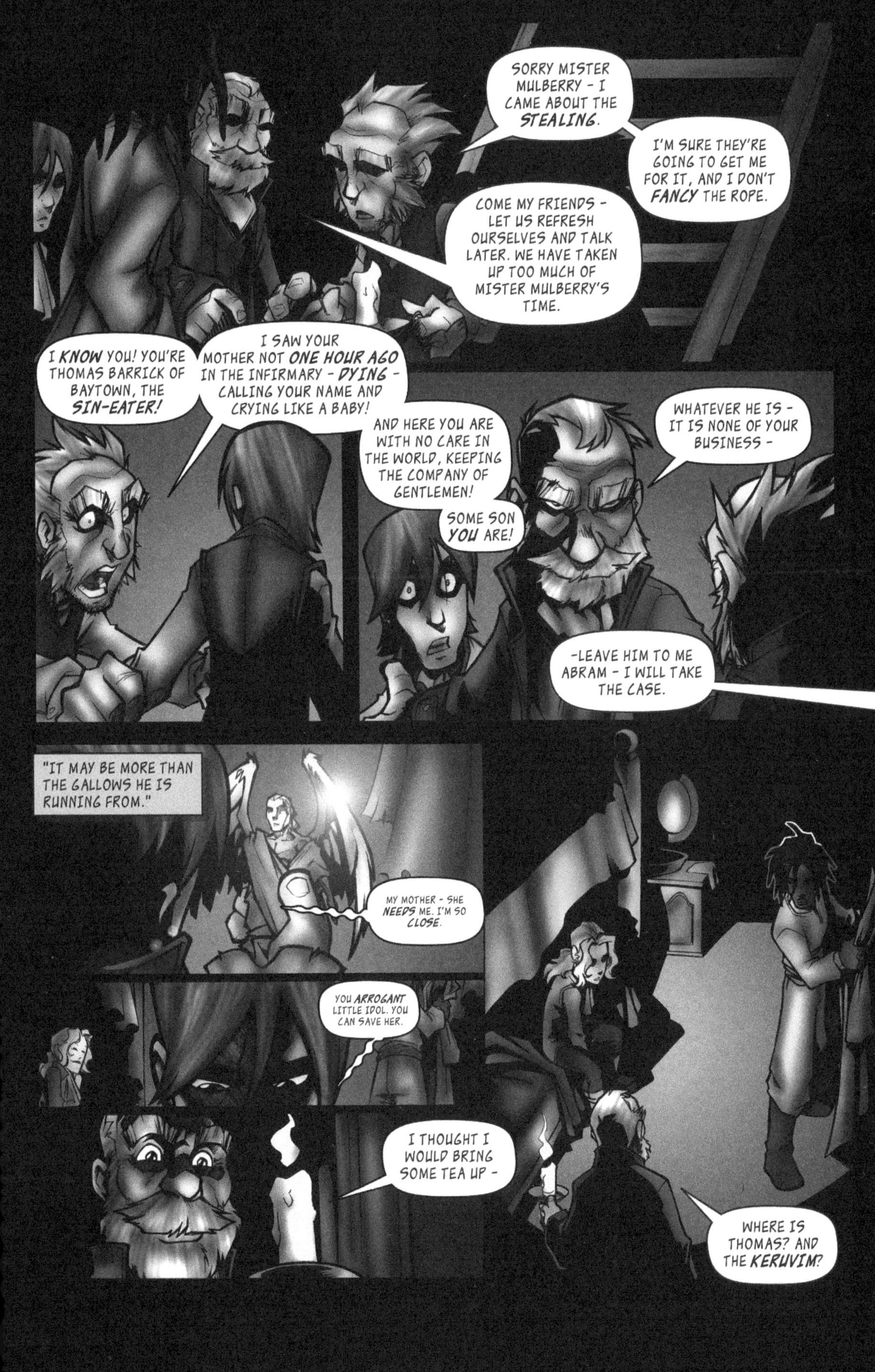
SORRY MISTER MULBERRY - I CAME ABOUT THE STEALING.
I'M SURE THEY'RE GOING TO GET ME FOR IT, AND I DON'T FANCY THE ROPE.
COME MY FRIENDS - LET US REFRESH OURSELVES AND TALK LATER. WE HAVE TAKEN UP TOO MUCH OF MISTER MULBERRY'S TIME.
I KNOW YOU! YOU'RE THOMAS BARRICK OF BAYTOWN, THE SIN-EATER!
I SAW YOUR MOTHER NOT ONE HOUR AGO IN THE INFIRMARY - DYING - CALLING YOUR NAME AND CRYING LIKE A BABY!
AND HERE YOU ARE WITH NO CARE IN THE WORLD, KEEPING THE COMPANY OF GENTLEMEN!
SOME SON YOU ARE!
WHATEVER HE IS - IT IS NONE OF YOUR BUSINESS -
-LEAVE HIM TO ME ABRAM - I WILL TAKE THE CASE.
"IT MAY BE MORE THAN THE GALLOWS HE IS RUNNING FROM."
MY MOTHER - SHE NEEDS ME. I'M SO CLOSE.
YOU ARROGANT LITTLE IDOL. YOU CAN SAVE HER.
I THOUGHT I WOULD BRING SOME TEA UP -
WHERE IS THOMAS? AND THE KERUVIM?

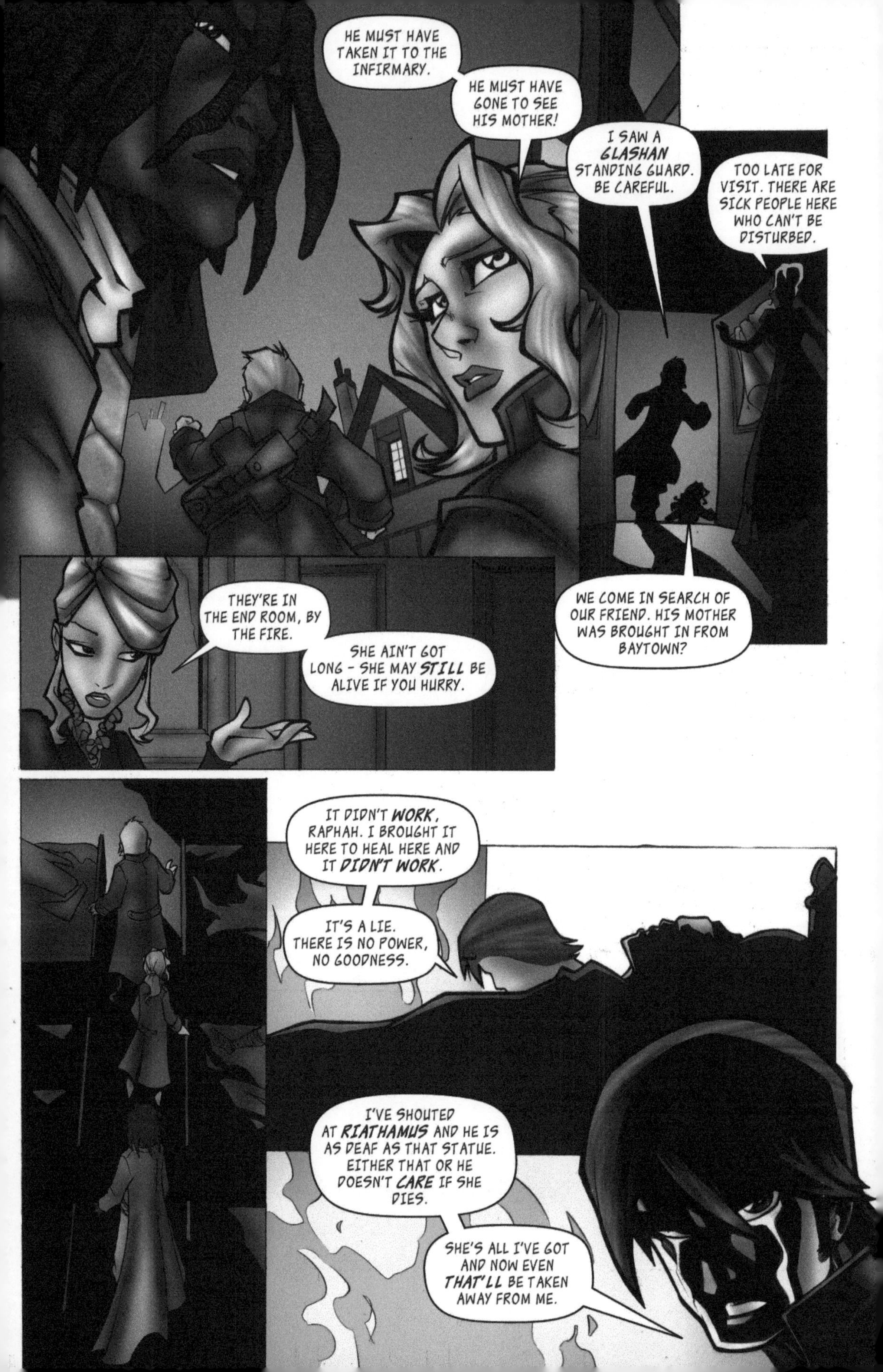
HE MUST HAVE TAKEN IT TO THE INFIRMARY.
HE MUST HAVE GONE TO SEE HIS MOTHER!
I SAW A GLASHAN STANDING GUARD. BE CAREFUL.
TOO LATE FOR VISIT. THERE ARE SICK PEOPLE HERE WHO CAN'T BE DISTURBED.
WE COME IN SEARCH OF OUR FRIEND. HIS MOTHER WAS BROUGHT IN FROM BAYTOWN?
THEY'RE IN THE END ROOM, BY THE FIRE.
SHE AIN'T GOT LONG - SHE MAY STILL BE ALIVE IF YOU HURRY.
IT DIDN'T WORK, RAPHAH. I BROUGHT IT HERE TO HEAL HERE AND IT DIDN'T WORK.
IT'S A LIE. THERE IS NO POWER, NO GOODNESS.
I'VE SHOUTED AT RIATHAMUS AND HE IS AS DEAF AS THAT STATUE. EITHER THAT OR HE DOESN'T CARE IF SHE DIES.
SHE'S ALL I'VE GOT AND NOW EVEN THAT'LL BE TAKEN AWAY FROM ME.

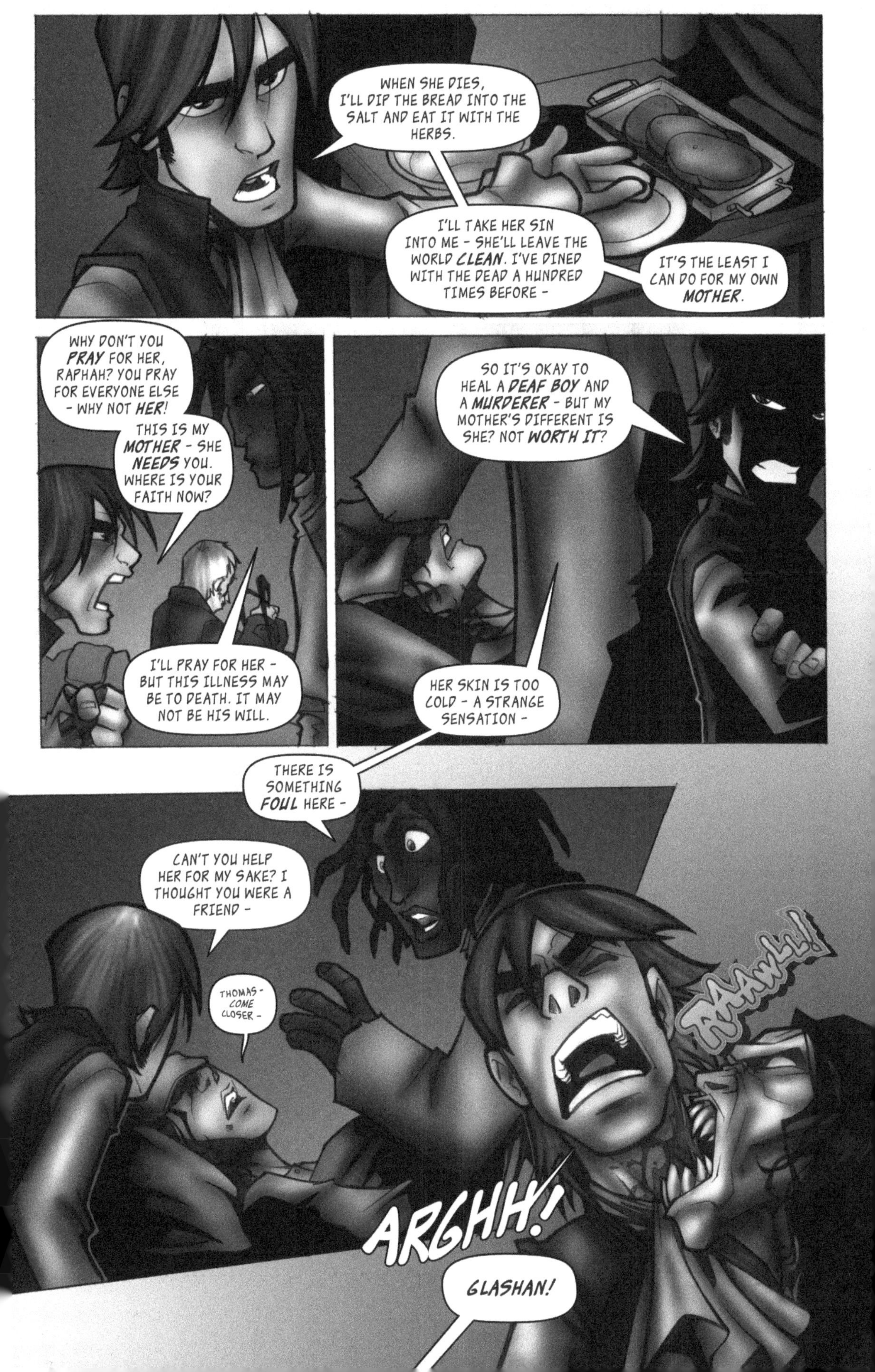
WHEN SHE DIES, I'LL DIP THE BREAD INTO THE SALT AND EAT IT WITH THE HERBS.
I'LL TAKE HER SIN INTO ME - SHE'LL LEAVE THE WORLD CLEAN. I'VE DINED WITH THE DEAD A HUNDRED TIMES BEFORE -
IT'S THE LEAST I CAN DO FOR MY OWN MOTHER.
WHY DON'T YOU PRAY FOR HER, RAPHAH? YOU PRAY FOR EVERYONE ELSE - WHY NOT HER!
THIS IS MY MOTHER - SHE NEEDS YOU. WHERE IS YOUR FAITH NOW?
I'LL PRAY FOR HER - BUT THIS ILLNESS MAY BE TO DEATH. IT MAY NOT BE HIS WILL.
SO IT'S OKAY TO HEAL A DEAF BOY AND A MURDERER - BUT MY MOTHER'S DIFFERENT IS SHE? NOT WORTH IT?
HER SKIN IS TOO COLD - A STRANGE SENSATION -
THERE IS SOMETHING FOUL HERE -
CAN'T YOU HELP HER FOR MY SAKE? I THOUGHT YOU WERE A FRIEND -
THOMAS - COME CLOSER -
RAAWLL!
ARGHH!
GLASHAN!

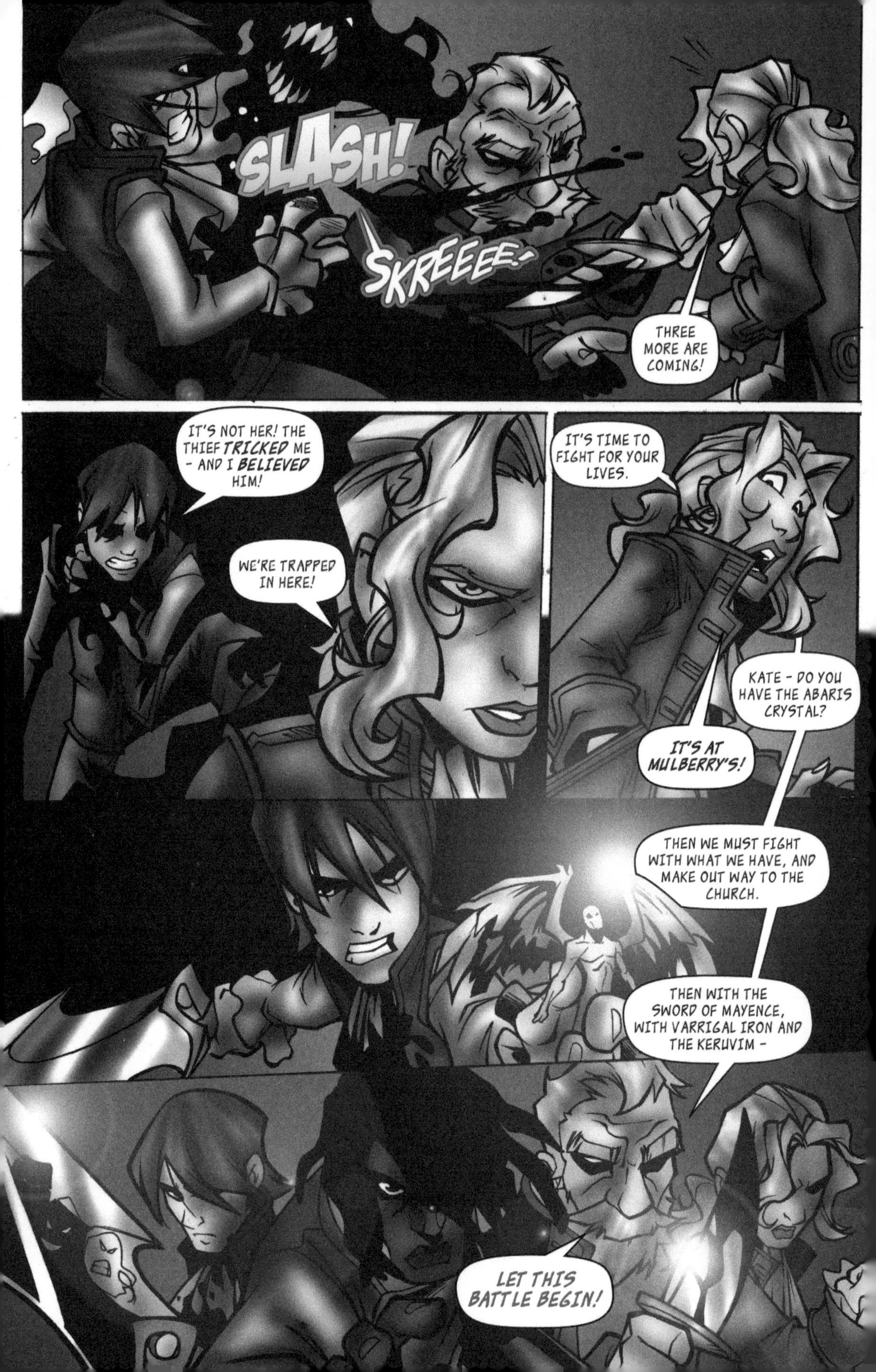
SLASH!
SKREEEEE-
THREE MORE ARE COMING!
IT'S NOT HER! THE THIEF TRICKED ME - AND I BELIEVED HIM!
WE'RE TRAPPED IN HERE!
IT'S TIME TO FIGHT FOR YOUR LIVES.
KATE - DO YOU HAVE THE ABARIS CRYSTAL?
IT'S AT MULBERRY'S!
THEN WE MUST FIGHT WITH WHAT WE HAVE, AND MAKE OUT WAY TO THE CHURCH.
THEN WITH THE SWORD OF MAYENCE, WITH VARRIGAL IRON AND THE KERUVIM -
LET THIS BATTLE BEGIN!

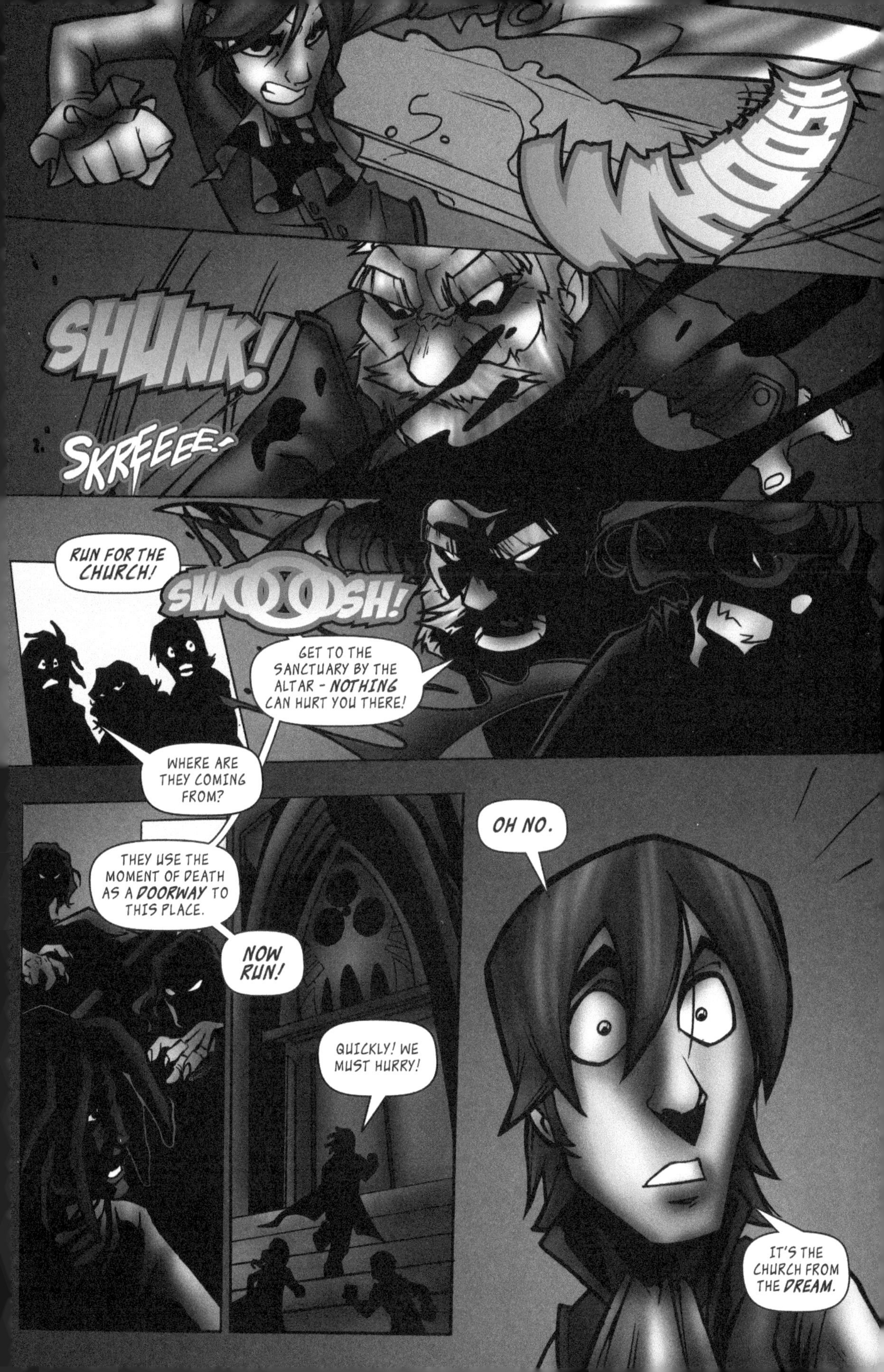
WHOOSH
SHUNK!
SKRFEEE!
RUN FOR THE CHURCH!
SWOOOSH!
GET TO THE SANCTUARY BY THE ALTAR - NOTHING CAN HURT YOU THERE!
WHERE ARE THEY COMING FROM?
THEY USE THE MOMENT OF DEATH AS A DOORWAY TO THIS PLACE.
NOW RUN!
QUICKLY! WE MUST HURRY!
OH NO.
IT'S THE CHURCH FROM THE DREAM.

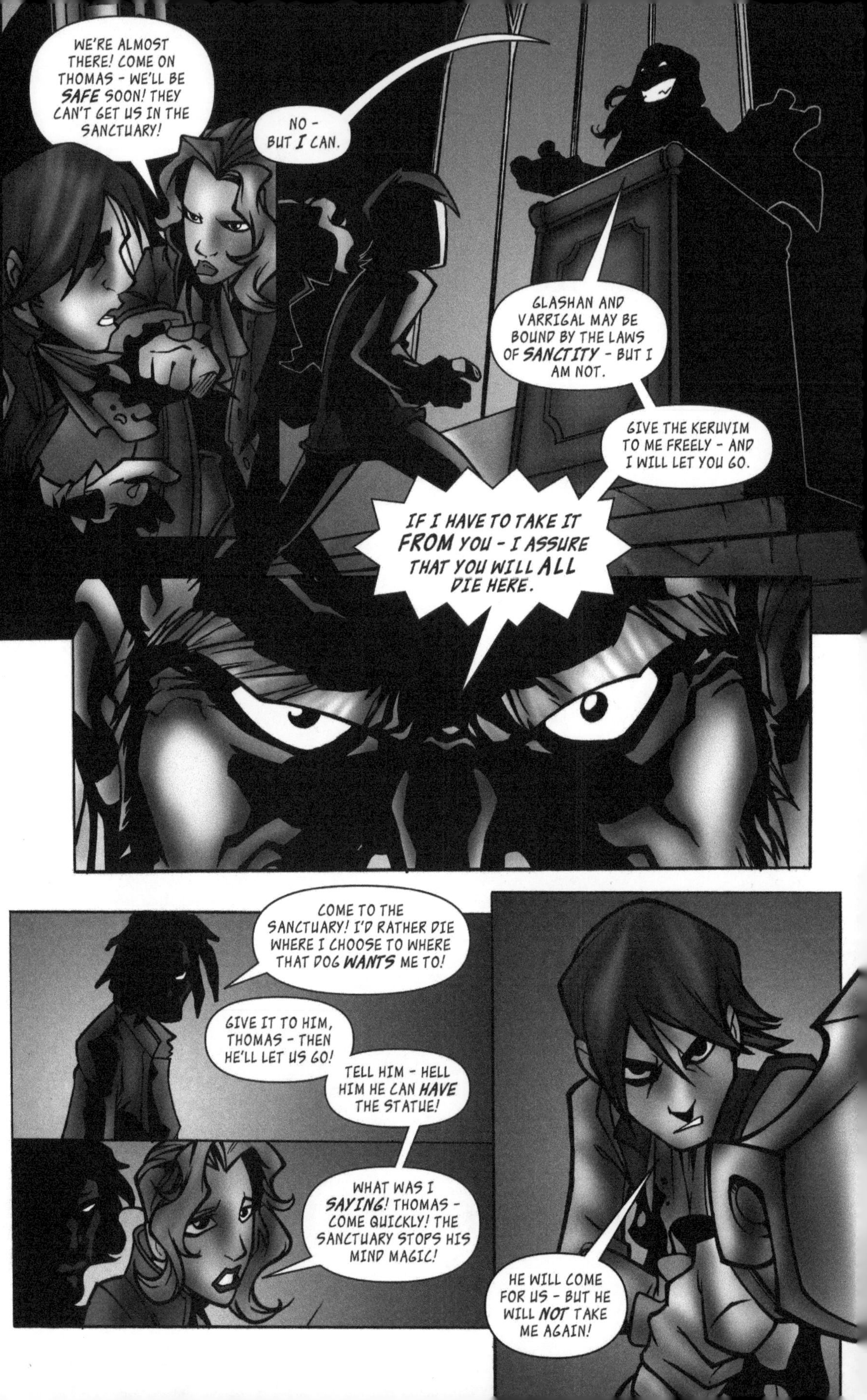
WE'RE ALMOST THERE! COME ON THOMAS - WE'LL BE SAFE SOON! THEY CAN'T GET US IN THE SANCTUARY!
NO - BUT I CAN.
GLASHAN AND VARRIGAL MAY BE BOUND BY THE LAWS OF SANCTITY - BUT I AM NOT.
GIVE THE KERUVIM TO ME FREELY - AND I WILL LET YOU GO.
IF I HAVE TO TAKE IT FROM YOU - I ASSURE THAT YOU WILL ALL DIE HERE.
COME TO THE SANCTUARY! I'D RATHER DIE WHERE I CHOOSE TO WHERE THAT DOG WANTS ME TO!
GIVE IT TO HIM, THOMAS - THEN HE'LL LET US GO!
TELL HIM - HELL HIM HE CAN HAVE THE STATUE!
WHAT WAS I SAYING! THOMAS - COME QUICKLY! THE SANCTUARY STOPS HIS MIND MAGIC!
HE WILL COME FOR US - BUT HE WILL NOT TAKE ME AGAIN!

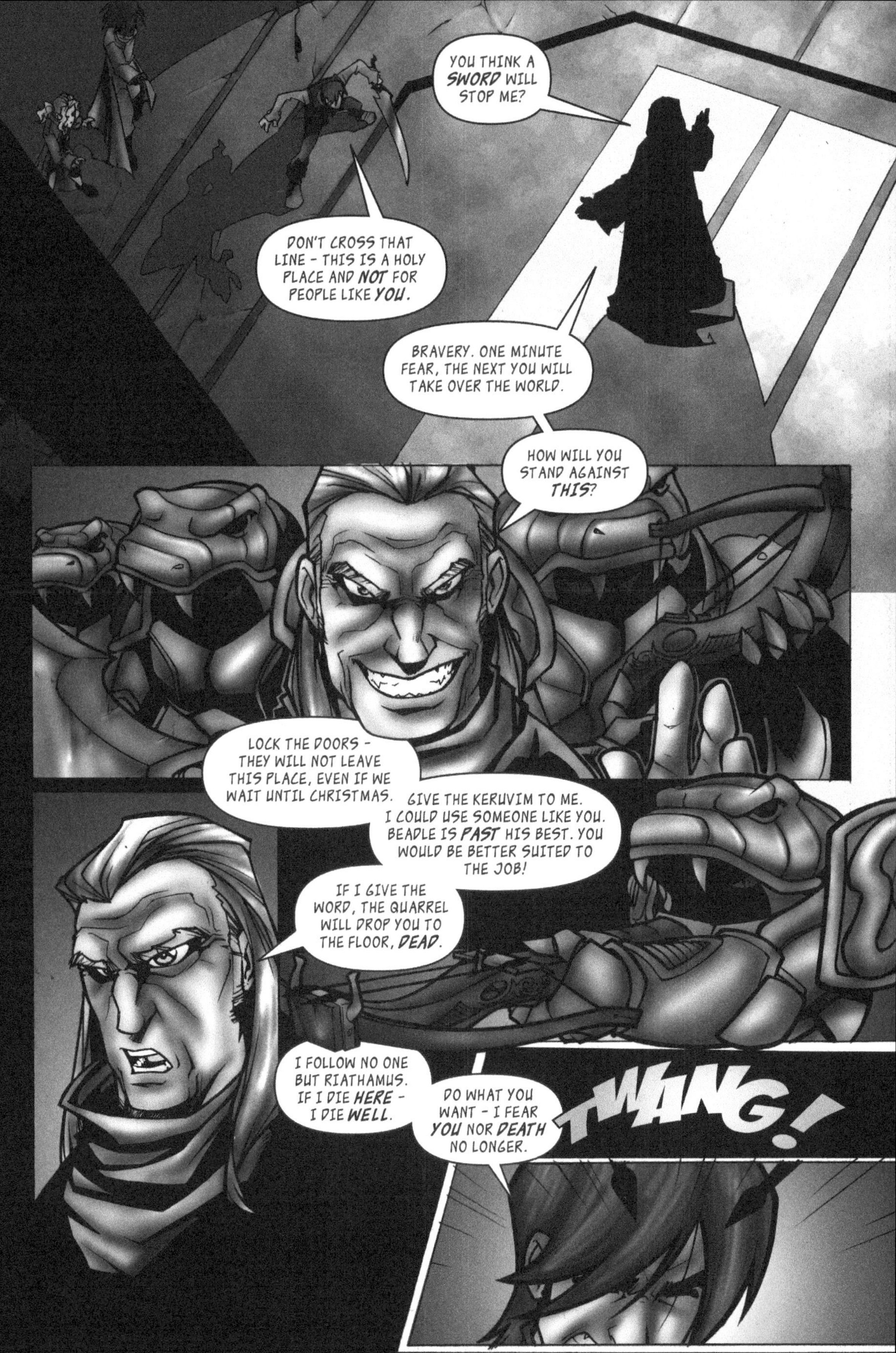
YOU THINK A SWORD WILL STOP ME?
DON'T CROSS THAT LINE - THIS IS A HOLY PLACE AND NOT FOR PEOPLE LIKE YOU.
BRAVERY. ONE MINUTE FEAR, THE NEXT YOU WILL TAKE OVER THE WORLD.
HOW WILL YOU STAND AGAINST THIS?
LOCK THE DOORS - THEY WILL NOT LEAVE THIS PLACE, EVEN IF WE WAIT UNTIL CHRISTMAS.
GIVE THE KERUVIM TO ME. I COULD USE SOMEONE LIKE YOU. BEADLE IS PAST HIS BEST. YOU WOULD BE BETTER SUITED TO THE JOB!
IF I GIVE THE WORD, THE QUARREL WILL DROP YOU TO THE FLOOR, DEAD.
I FOLLOW NO ONE BUT RIATHAMUS. IF I DIE HERE - I DIE WELL.
DO WHAT YOU WANT - I FEAR YOU NOR DEATH NO LONGER.
TWANG!

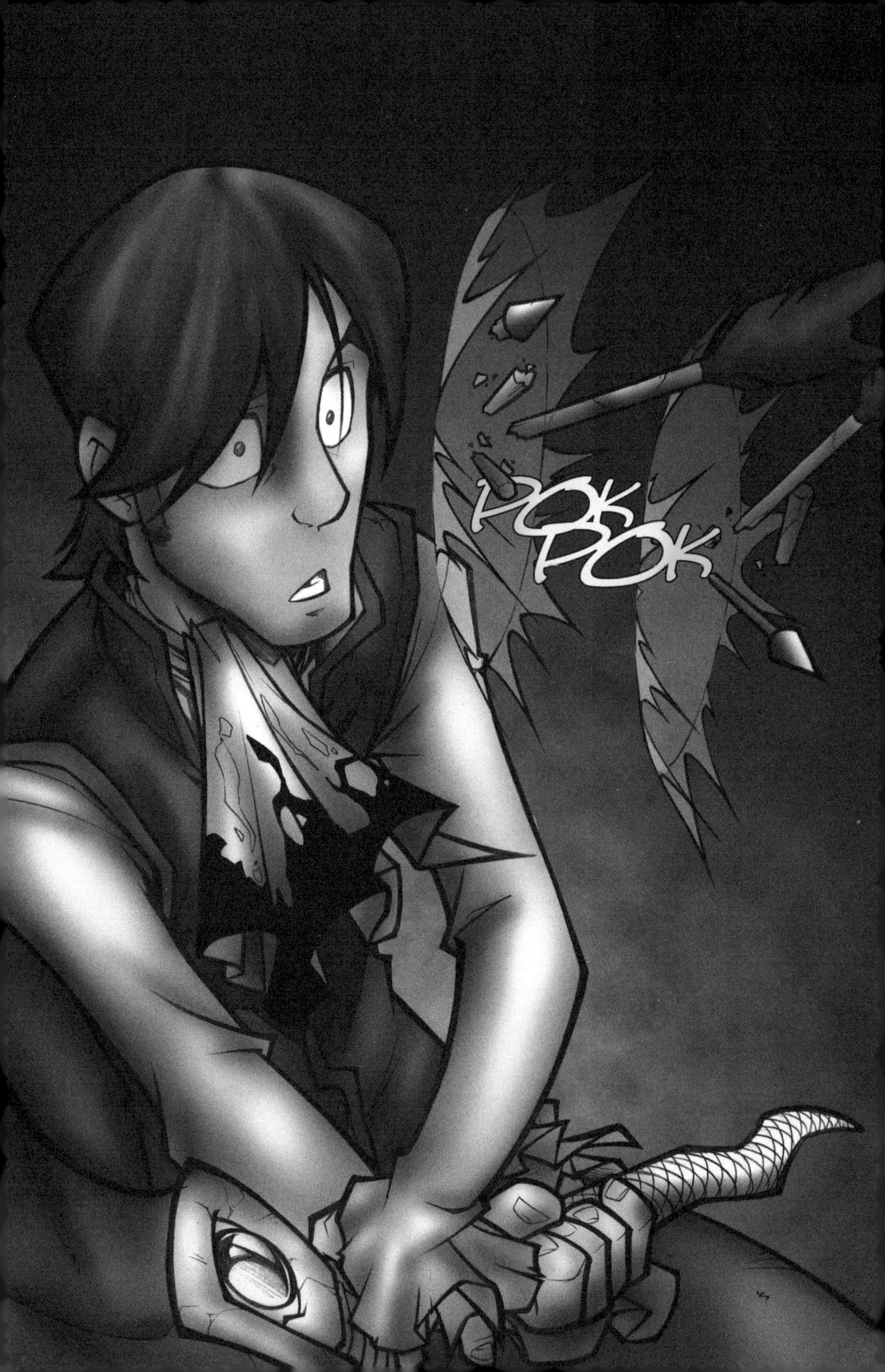
POK
POK

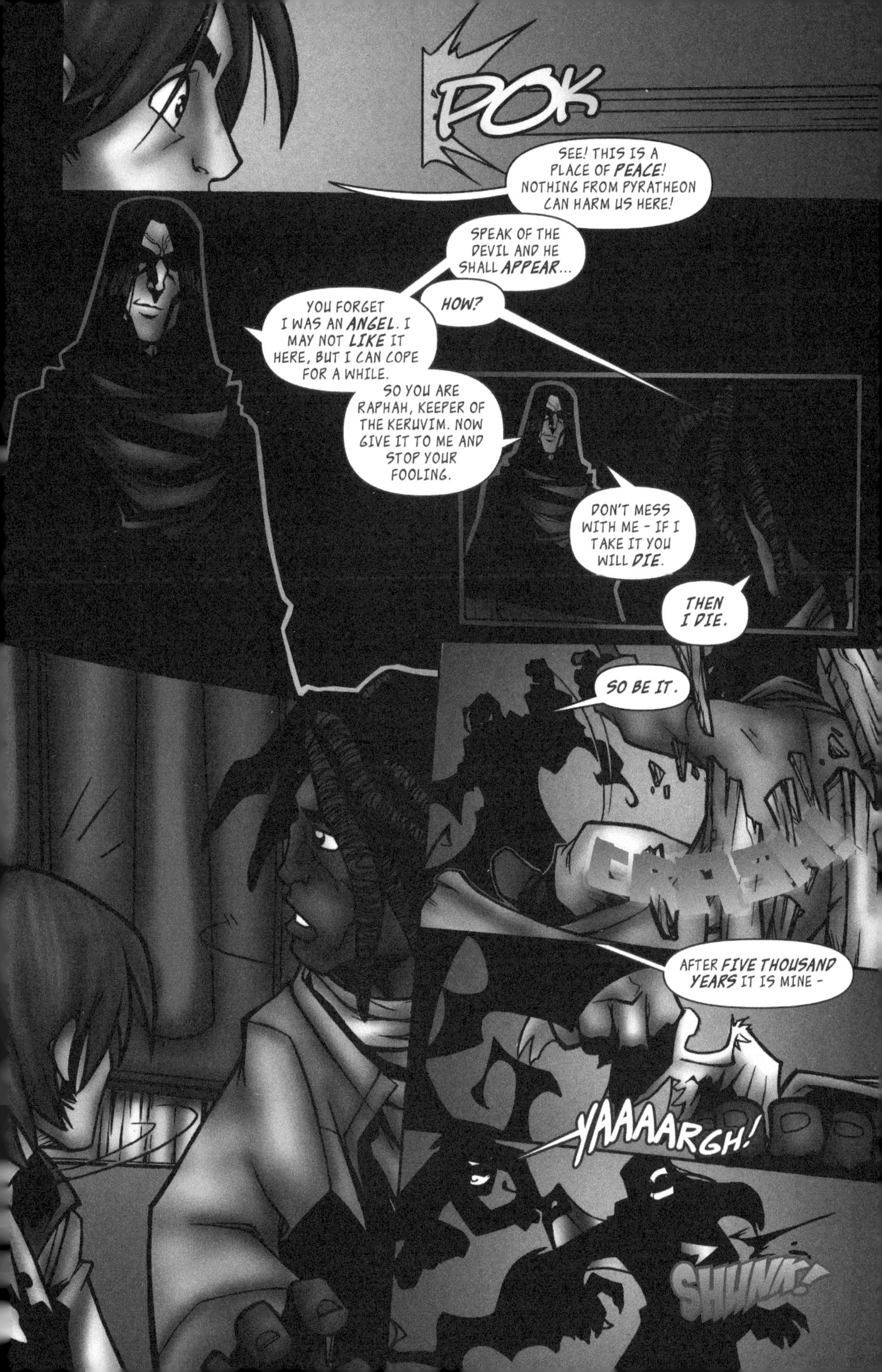
POK
SEE! THIS IS A PLACE OF PEACE! NOTHING FROM PYRATHEON CAN HARM US HERE!
SPEAK OF THE DEVIL AND HE SHALL APPEAR...
HOW?
YOU FORGET I WAS AN ANGEL. I MAY NOT LIKE IT HERE, BUT I CAN COPE FOR A WHILE.
SO YOU ARE RAPHAH, KEEPER OF THE KERUVIM. NOW GIVE IT TO ME AND STOP YOUR FOOLING.
DON'T MESS WITH ME - IF I TAKE IT YOU WILL DIE.
THEN I DIE.
SO BE IT.
AFTER FIVE THOUSAND YEARS IT IS MINE -
YAAAARGH!
SHUNK!

TAKE THE BOY - HE WILL COME IN USEFUL.
GIVE THE GIRL TO THE GLASHAN.
FOOOOM!
CRASH!
DAMN.
MISSED YOU, DEMURRAL.
LET THEM GO!
WHO IS THIS MAN?
A SMUGGLER - A PIRATE - AN IRRITAT-ING CARBUNCLE.
DONG! DONG! DONG! DONG!
YOU HAVE UNTIL THE LAST BELL HAS SOUNDED AND THEN I'LL BLOW YOUR HEAD FROM YOUR SHOULDERS.

EVERYTHING HAS CHANGED. YOU CAN KILL HIM IF YOU WANT. HE IS EXPENDABLE.
DONG! DONG! DONG! DONG!
DONG! DONG! DONG! DONG!
IT IS FINISHED! I AM!
I AM! RIATHAMUS IS DEAD!
CLATTER!
IT'S NOT OVER - LISTEN TO ME, IT'S NOT OVER.
THE CRYING OF A CHILD.
HOW TOUCHING THAT THE FIRST THING I SHOULD HEAR IN MY NEW WORLD IS THE CRYING OF A CHILD.
YOU KEPT THIS IN LIFE - NOW KEEP THIS IN DEATH.
CRASH!
RAPHAEL! YOU ARE -
STILL ALIVE. THE GLASHAN TOOK LONGER THAN I EXPECTED.
YOUR MEDDLING HAS GONE TOO FAR THIS TIME, SEIRIZZIM. RIATHAMUS WILL NOT BE PLEASED.
RIATHAMUS IS DEAD! HE IS GONE! THE BRIGHT MORNING STAR HAS FLICKERED AND SHIMMERED IT'S LAST ON THIS WORLD!
SO GO DOWN ON ONE KNEE.

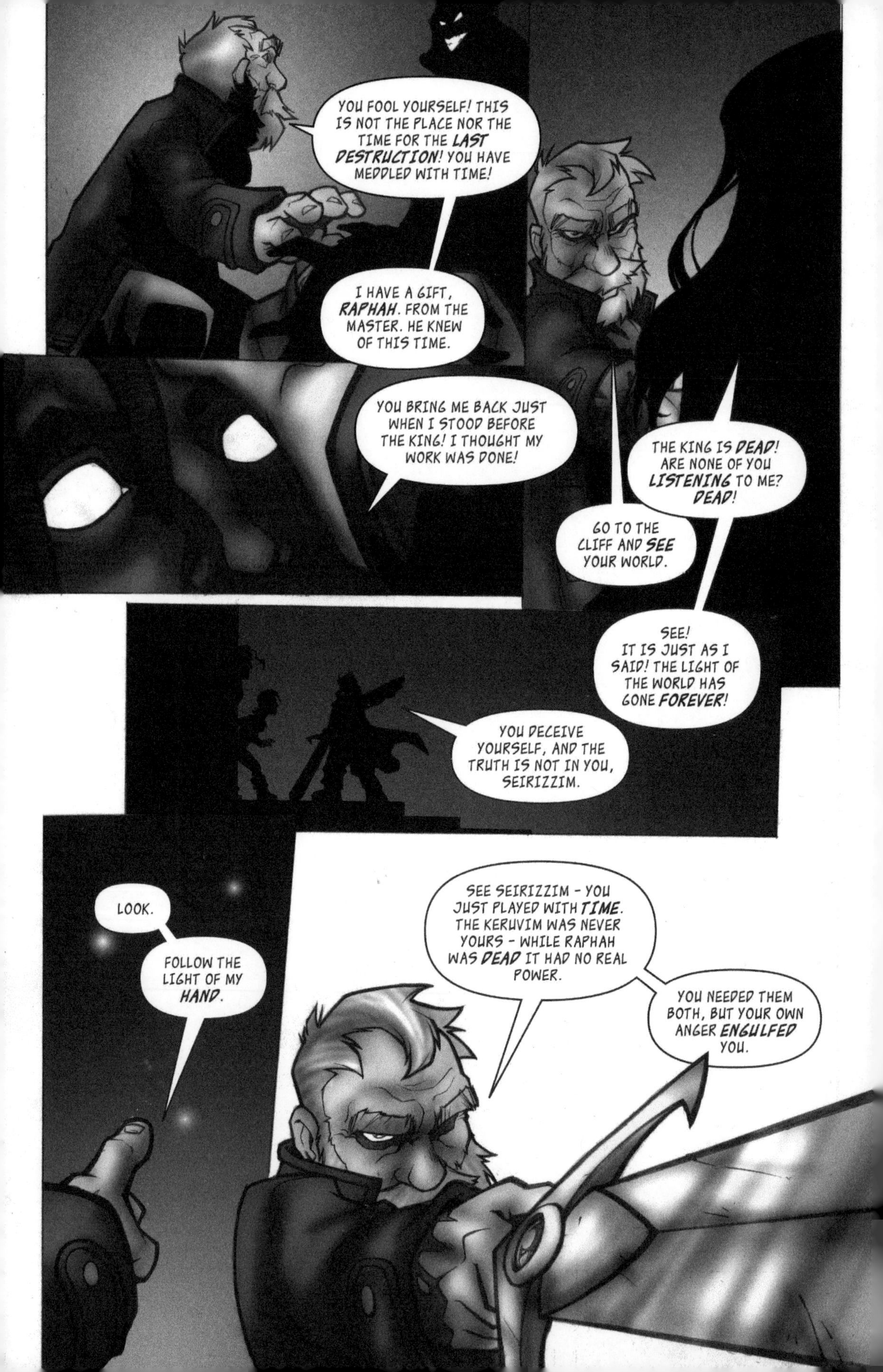
YOU FOOL YOURSELF! THIS IS NOT THE PLACE NOR THE TIME FOR THE LAST DESTRUCTION! YOU HAVE MEDDLED WITH TIME!
I HAVE A GIFT, RAPHAH. FROM THE MASTER. HE KNEW OF THIS TIME.
YOU BRING ME BACK JUST WHEN I STOOD BEFORE THE KING! I THOUGHT MY WORK WAS DONE!
THE KING IS DEAD! ARE NONE OF YOU LISTENING TO ME? DEAD!
GO TO THE CLIFF AND SEE YOUR WORLD.
SEE! IT IS JUST AS I SAID! THE LIGHT OF THE WORLD HAS GONE FOREVER!
YOU DECEIVE YOURSELF, AND THE TRUTH IS NOT IN YOU, SEIRIZZIM.
LOOK.
FOLLOW THE LIGHT OF MY HAND.
SEE SEIRIZZIM - YOU JUST PLAYED WITH TIME. THE KERUVIM WAS NEVER YOURS - WHILE RAPHAH WAS DEAD IT HAD NO REAL POWER.
YOU NEEDED THEM BOTH, BUT YOUR OWN ANGER ENGULFED YOU.

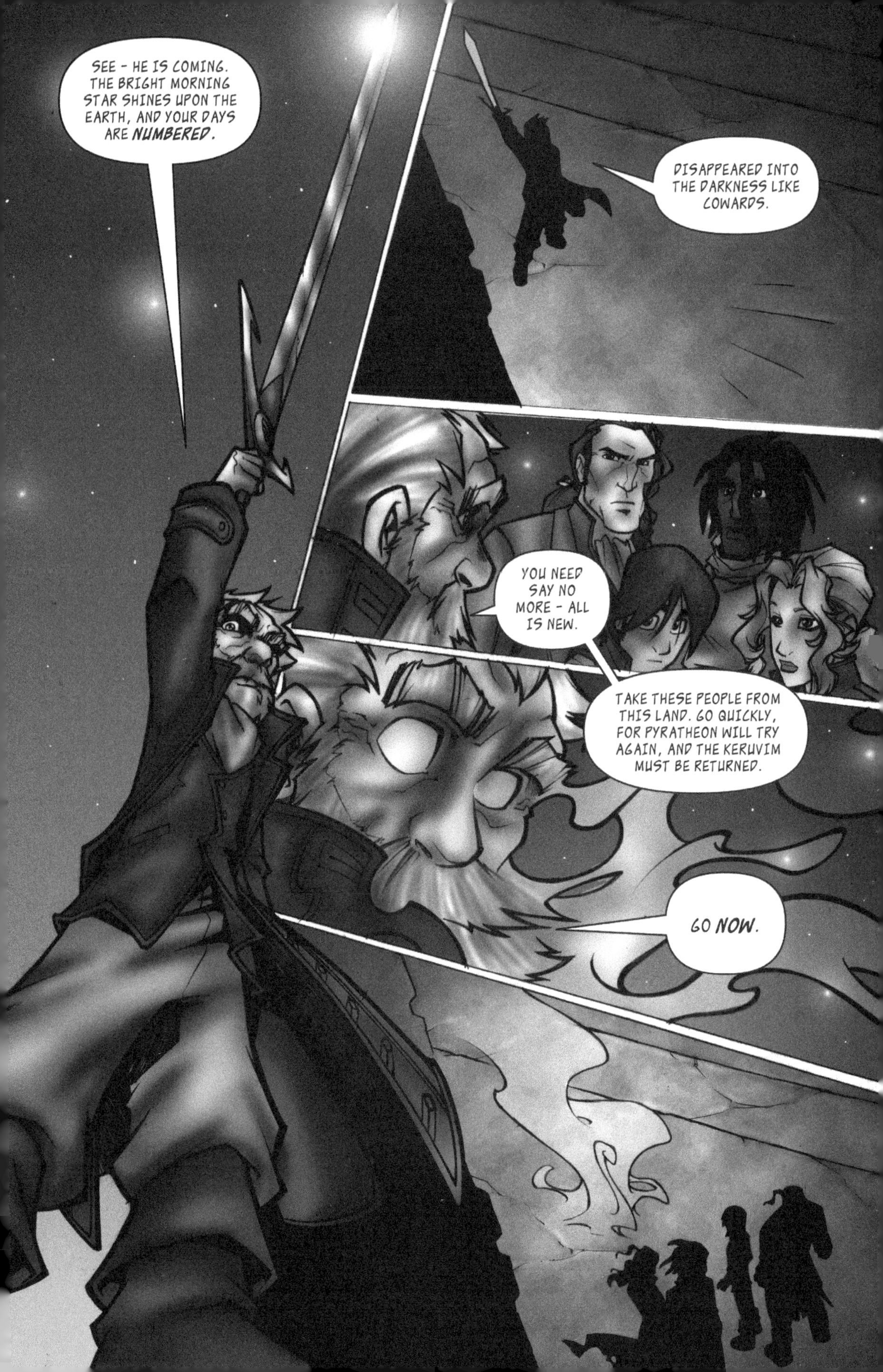
SEE - HE IS COMING. THE BRIGHT MORNING STAR SHINES UPON THE EARTH, AND YOUR DAYS ARE NUMBERED.
DISAPPEARED INTO THE DARKNESS LIKE COWARDS.
YOU NEED SAY NO MORE - ALL IS NEW.
TAKE THESE PEOPLE FROM THIS LAND. GO QUICKLY, FOR PYRATHEON WILL TRY AGAIN, AND THE KERUVIM MUST BE RETURNED.
GO NOW.

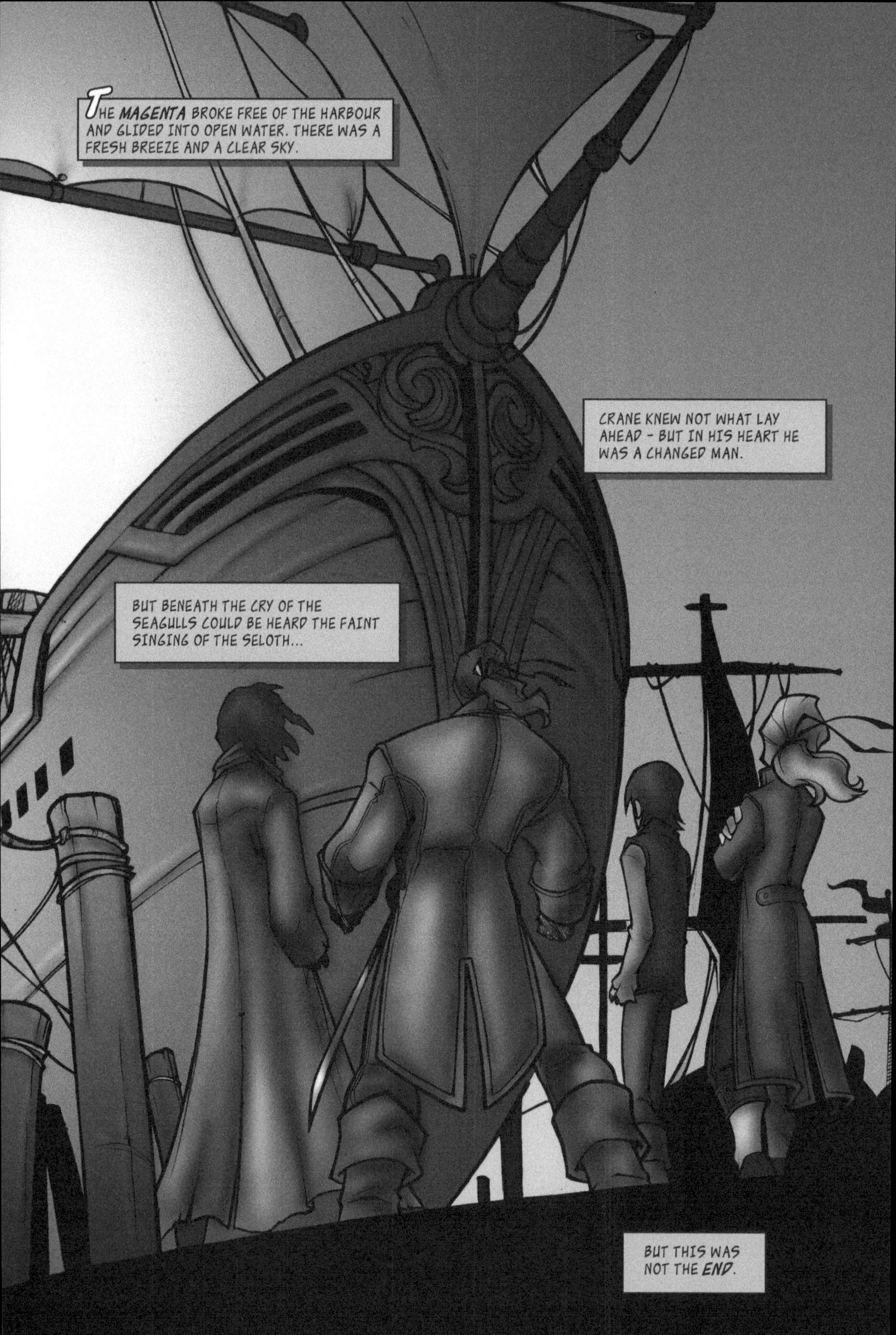
THE MAGENTA BROKE FREE OF THE HARBOUR AND GLIDED INTO OPEN WATER. THERE WAS A FRESH BREEZE AND A CLEAR SKY.
CRANE KNEW NOT WHAT LAY AHEAD - BUT IN HIS HEART HE WAS A CHANGED MAN.
BUT BENEATH THE CRY OF THE SEAGULLS COULD BE HEARD THE FAINT SINGING OF THE SELOTH...
BUT THIS WAS NOT THE END.

WHEN G.P. TAYLOR FIRST FINISHED
SHADOWMANCER, HE WAS UNABLE
TO FINISH THE BOOK WITH THE
ENDING HE TRULY WANTED.

WHEN HE RELEASED THE HARDBACK
SPECIAL EDITION LATER THAT YEAR,
HE RE-INSERTED THE ORIGINAL, AND
DARKER ENDING.

THE FOLLOWING PAGES ARE WHAT
REALLY HAPPENED IN THOSE FINAL
MOMENTS – FROM THE MOMENT THEY
LEFT THE CHURCH AND MADE THEIR
WAY TO THE BOAT – THEY SHOW A
SURPRISE ENDING FOR A CHARACTER,
AND LEAD INTO G.P. TAYLOR'S SOON
TO BE RELEASED SEQUEL TO
SHADOWMANCER...

READ ON AT YOUR PERIL.

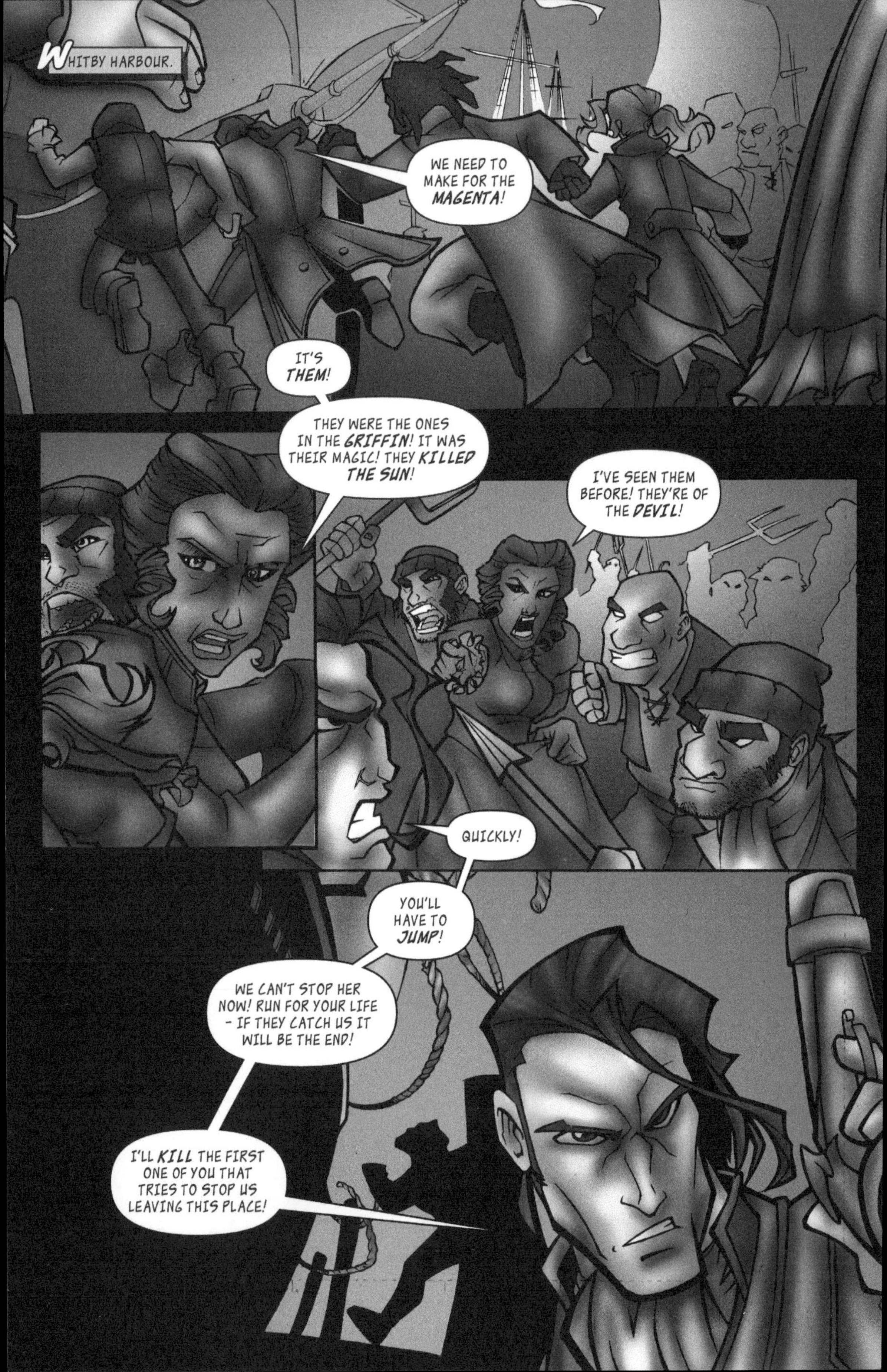
WHITBY HARBOUR.
WE NEED TO MAKE FOR THE MAGENTA!
IT'S THEM!
THEY WERE THE ONES IN THE GRIFFIN! IT WAS THEIR MAGIC! THEY KILLED THE SUN!
I'VE SEEN THEM BEFORE! THEY'RE OF THE DEVIL!
QUICKLY!
YOU'LL HAVE TO JUMP!
WE CAN'T STOP HER NOW! RUN FOR YOUR LIFE - IF THEY CATCH US IT WILL BE THE END!
I'LL KILL THE FIRST ONE OF YOU THAT TRIES TO STOP US LEAVING THIS PLACE!

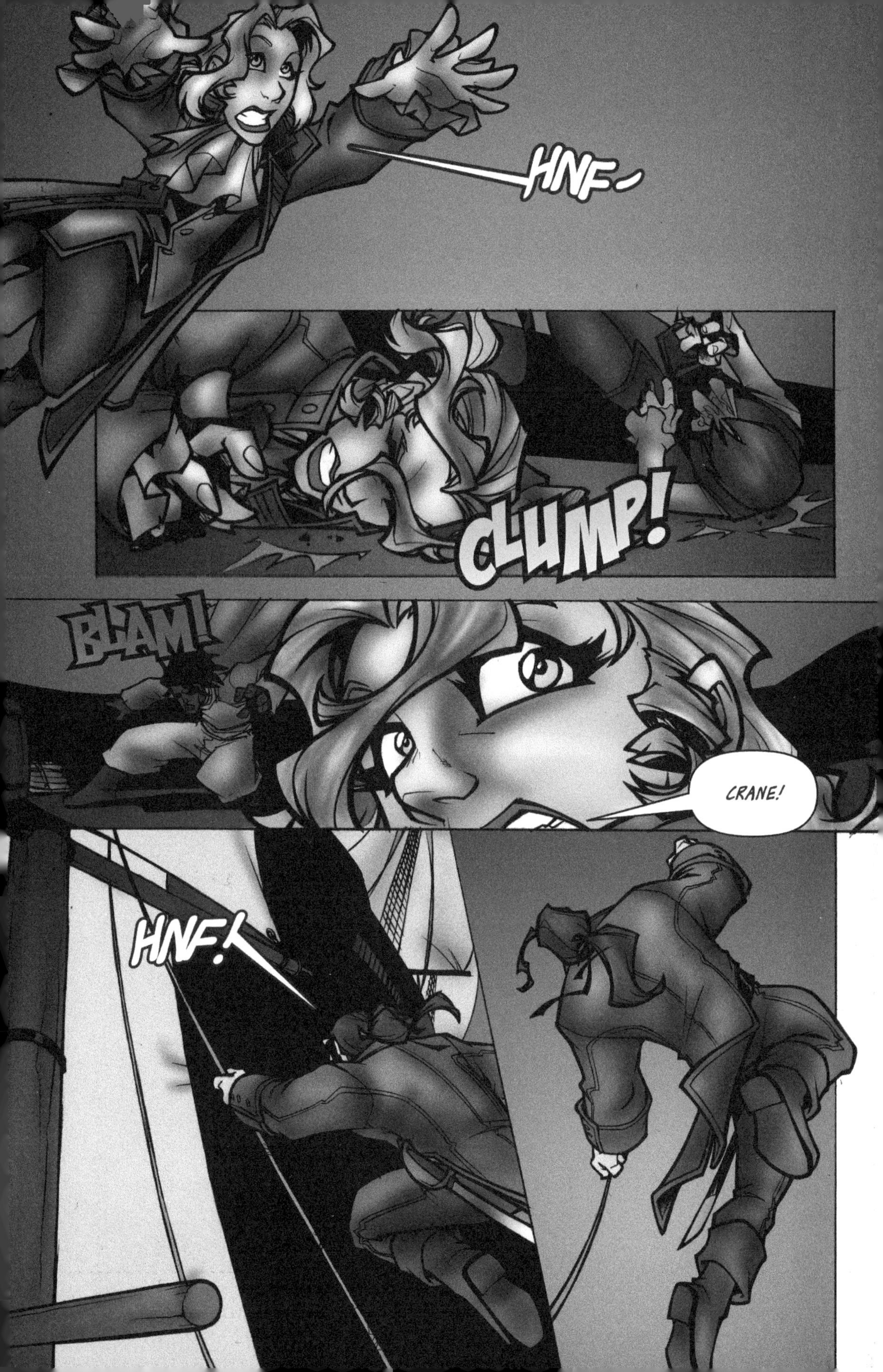
HNF-
CLUMP!
BLAM!
CRANE!
HNF!

THUMP!

I **CURSE** YOU FOR THIS! YOU'VE **KILLED** HER!

MAY YOU BURN IN **HELL** CRANE –

YOUR MAGIC WILL **NEVER** SAVE YA!

I WONDER WHAT DID HAPPEN TO DEMURRAL?

CRANE – THERE IS A BROWN FOG MOVING CLOSER. IS THIS NORMAL?

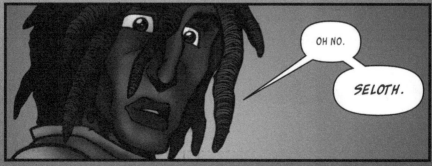

OH NO.

SELOTH.

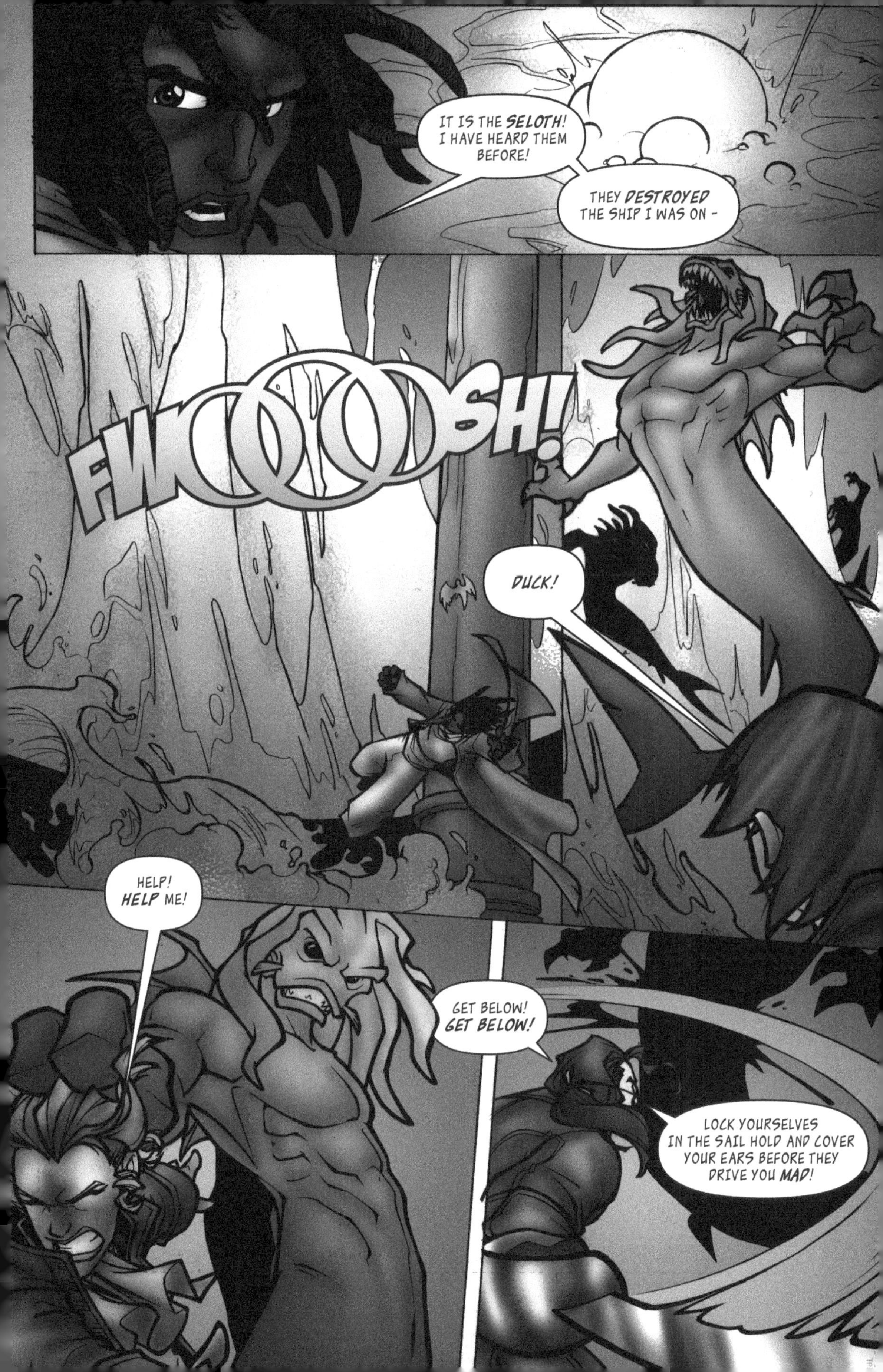
IT IS THE SELOTH! I HAVE HEARD THEM BEFORE!
THEY DESTROYED THE SHIP I WAS ON -
FWOOOSH!
DUCK!
HELP! HELP ME!
GET BELOW! GET BELOW!
LOCK YOURSELVES IN THE SAIL HOLD AND COVER YOUR EARS BEFORE THEY DRIVE YOU MAD!

LET HER GO! **LET - HER - GO!**
SHE BELONGS TO **ME** - YOU CAN'T TAKE HER!
RAPHAH - **DO** SOMETHING!
SLASH!
CAN'T... FOCUS... DIZZY -
ARGH!

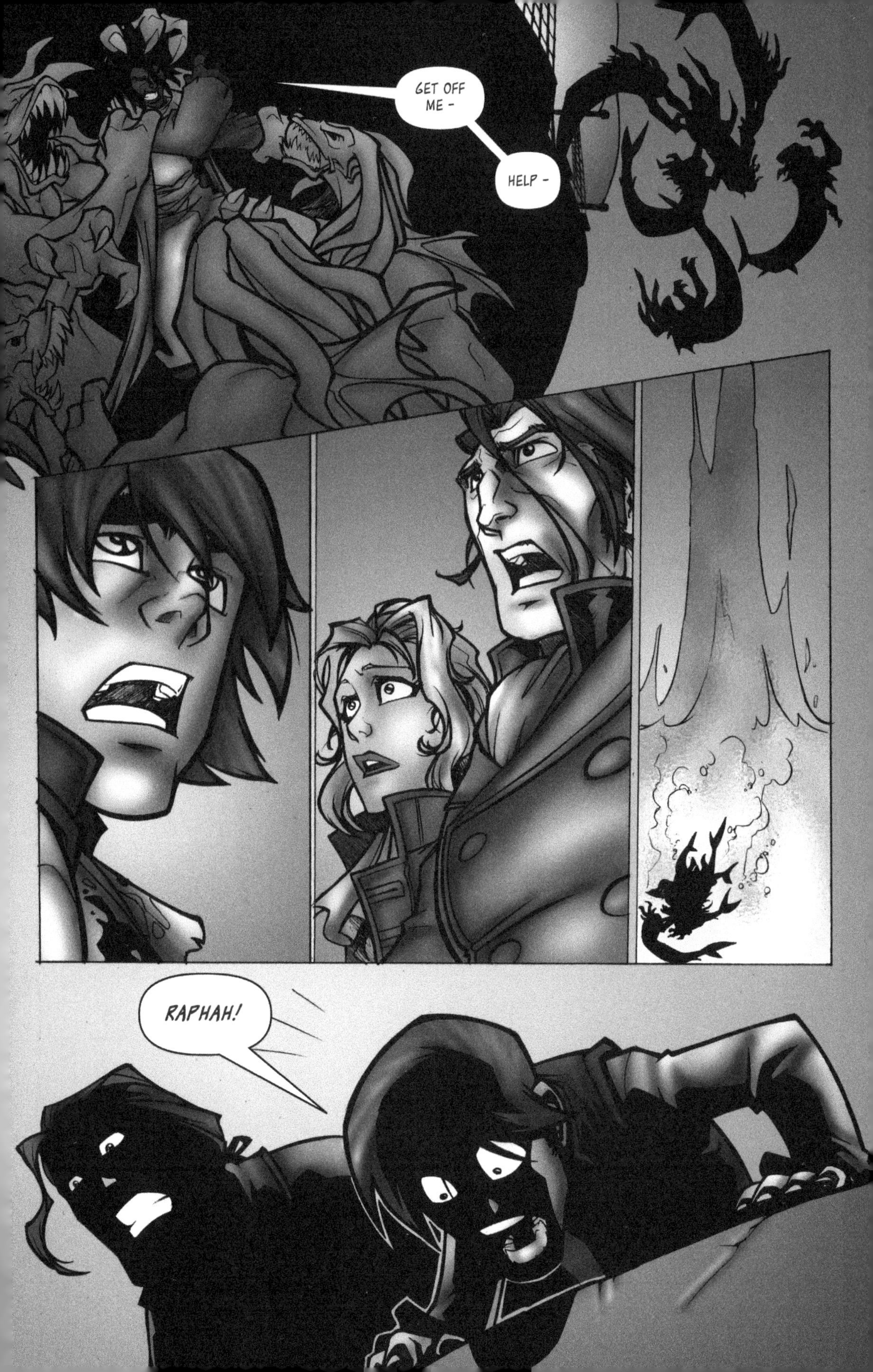
GET OFF ME -
HELP -
RAPHAH!

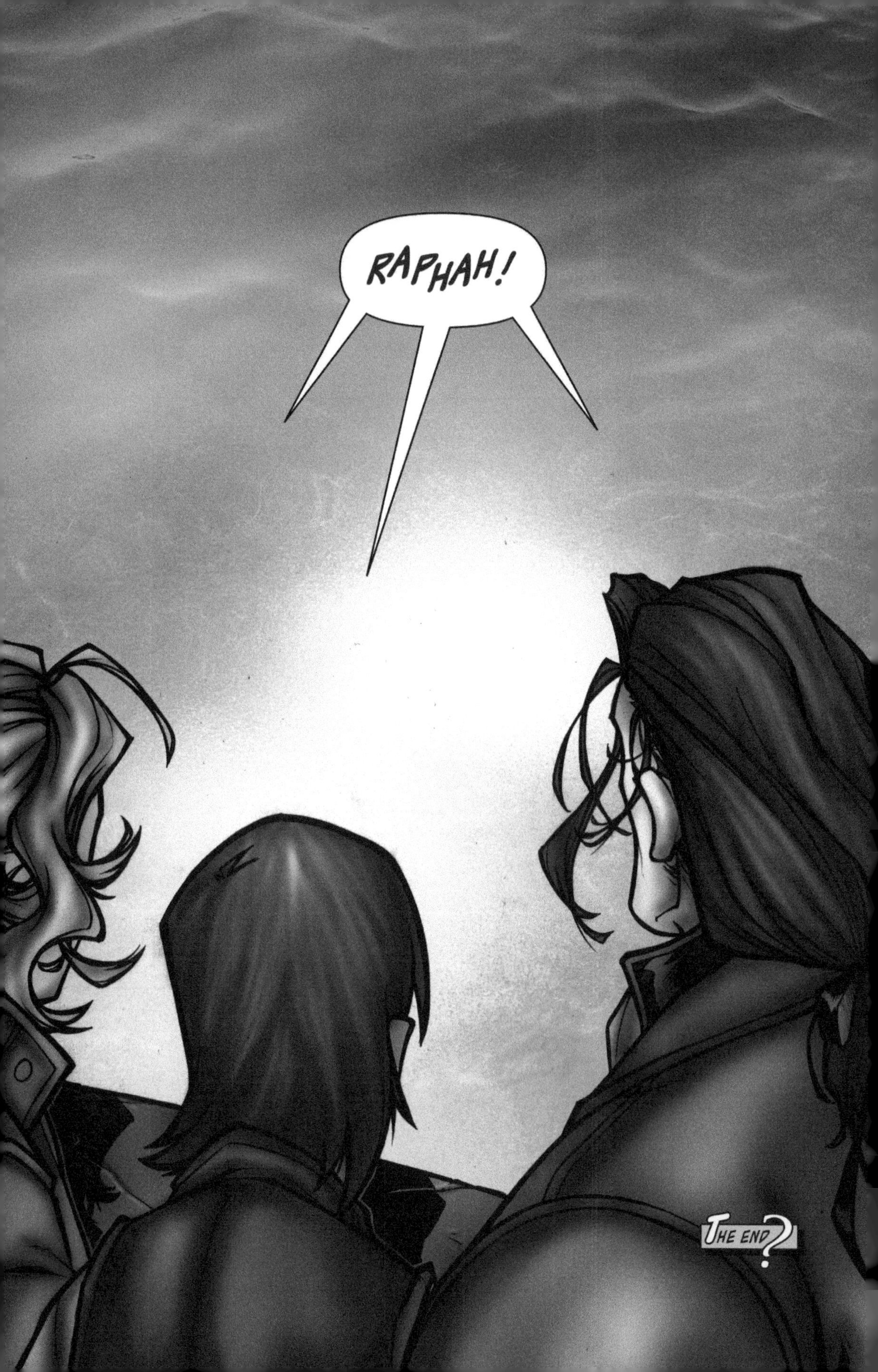
RAPHAH!
THE END?

NOTE FROM THE AUTHOR

"It was a still October night..."

On the evening of 21 March 2002 I turned over the idea in my head that maybe I could write a book – but what would I write about? I was driving home over the Yorkshire moors under an increasingly dark and foreboding sky. As I headed due north the rain started to pelt down in unrelenting sheets, thunder roared as lightning forked across the horizon. My old car was no match for the ferocious battering. I could barely see the road ahead as I pressed on into the unremitting gloom. The Yorkshire moors are a vast sprawling expanse of natural moorland, which can be a wild and lonely place but tonight I gave no thought to anything other than the possibility that I could, maybe, write a book.

The lighthouse at Flamborough appeared on the horizon about twenty miles off, sending beacons of warning light. The darkness and gloom of the night seemed to enfold me. Suddenly an idea for a story came into my mind. It was like I had been hooked up to some kind of weird database and I was downloading the story. And that is how it all began. As the idea took shape I began seeing smugglers out on the beach on a stormy night, a figure dressed in black, a wizard's staff in his hands whipping up the storm. A ship battling the raging sea, a stranger to these parts on board, a boy from Africa, who was filled with the supernatural, divine powers of God. Alongside him an angel like one of those from the Ark of the Covenant in the Old Testament. And so the download continued.

The next morning I wrote those first six words which would become the opening to the novel, Shadowmancer – "It was a still October night..."

Twenty years have gone by since that early beginning. The book you have in your hands has been read by literally millions of people, in many and various languages around the world. This is way beyond even my wildest hopes and dreams. After witnessing many people viewing God as some kind of wimp and loser I wanted to show the God of the Bible. God who is the creator of the universe, not somebody to be blasphemed against or treated lightly. The angels of the Bible are not pushovers. They are powerfully made, over 8 feet tall, courageous and fearless as they wield their swords against the demons and evil of this world. Yes, the kind of hero to grab anyone's attention.

The whole epic story has now been bought into the graphic dimension by a gifted and talented team. I am enormously proud to see the story and characters come graphically to life in this edition.

Head over to the Shadowmancerbooks. com website to find out more about the characters, the story, the events that take place, plus additional graphic content. Join the Shadowmancer conversation today – be great to hear from you.

G.P. Taylor

Lightning Source UK Ltd.
Milton Keynes UK
UKHW051321161222
413993UK00004B/25